Introduction to Psychology Version 1.0

By
Charles Stangor

D0781627

Introduction to Psychology Version 1.0

Charles Stangor

Published by:

Flat World Knowledge, Inc.
1133 15th Street. NW, 12th Floor
Washington, DC 20005-2710

© 2013 by Flat World Knowledge, Inc. All rights reserved. Your use of this work is subject to the License Agreement available here http://www.flatworldknowledge.com/legal.

No part of this work may be used, modified, or reproduced in any form or by any means except as expressly permitted under the License Agreement.

Brief Contents

Contents

About the Author

Charles Stangor is professor and associate chair of psychology within the Social, Decisional, and Organizational Sciences Specialty Area at the University of Maryland. He has also taught at the New School for Social Research, Michigan State University, and at the University of Tübingen in Germany. He received his BA from Beloit College in 1973 and his PhD from New York University in 1986. Dr. Stangor is the recipient of research grants from the National Institute of Mental Health and from the National Science Foundation. He has published seven books and over 70 research articles and book chapters and has served as an associate editor of the *European Journal of Social Psychology*. He is a charter fellow of the American Psychological Society. He has served as the chair of the executive committee and is currently executive officer for the Society for Experimental Social Psychology. Dr. Stangor's research interests concern the development of stereotypes and prejudice and their influences upon individuals who are potential victims of discrimination. Dr. Stangor regularly teaches Social Psychology, Research Methods, and at the graduate level, Fundamentals of Social Psychology and Group Processes. Dr. Stangor is chair of the undergraduate committee in the psychology department and has won the distinguished teaching award from the University of Maryland. Dr. Stangor also serves as the chair of the department's human subjects committee.

Acknowledgments

The development of *Introduction to Psychology* was made possible through the combined efforts of many people, each of whom brought special skills to the project.

One important resource was an advisory board of instructors from across the country. Their thoughtful and insightful feedback throughout development was invaluable in creating this first edition. I am deeply grateful to the following people for their time and effort:

- M. Janelle Cambron-Mellott, University of Alabama; Birmingham Southern College
- Celeste Doerr, Florida State University
- Jerry Green, Tarrant County College–NW Campus
- Richard Hass, University of Delaware
- Adam Hutcheson, University of South Carolina
- Matthew I. Isaak, University of Louisiana at Lafayette
- Kerry Jordan, Utah State University
- Jerwen Jou, University of Texas–Pan American
- Peggy Norwood, Community College of Aurora
- Karen Rhines, Northampton Community College
- Eva Szeli, Arizona State University
- Anton Villado, Rice University

Introduction to Psychology also benefited from reviews at various stages of the book's development. Many thanks to the following reviewers for their contributions:

- Eileen J. Achorn, The University of Texas at San Antonio
- Mara Aruguete, Lincoln University
- David Carlston, Midwestern State University
- Jenel T. Cavazos, Cameron University
- Stephanie B. Ding, Del Mar College
- Gaithri A. Fernando, California State University, Los Angeles
- William Goggin, University of Southern Mississippi
- Karla A. Lassonde, Minnesota State University, Mankato
- Greg Loviscky, Pennsylvania State University
- Michael A. Mangan, University of New Hampshire, Durham
- Anne Moyer, SUNY at Stony Brook
- Todd Nelson, California State University, Stanislaus
- Bridgette J. Peteet, University of Cincinnati
- Brad Pinter, Pennsylvania State University, Altoona
- Steven V. Rouse, Pepperdine University
- Glenda S. Williams, Lone Star College, North Harris

Thanks also to Maren Voss, Hagerstown (MD) Community College, for her research and writing assistance; to Matthew I. Isaak, University of Louisiana at Lafayette, for his work on the accompanying Test Item File and PowerPoint slides; and to Chrissy Chimi and Stacy Claxton of Scribe, Inc., who expertly handled the many details of the production process.

And special thanks to the team at Flat World Knowledge. Completion of the book and supplements required the attention of many people, including Michael Boezi, who signed the book and supported my efforts from beginning to end; Pam Hersperger, who managed the book through development; and Gina Huck Siegert, who worked closely with me on all aspects of the project.

Dedication

To Leslie

Preface

When I first started teaching Introduction to Psychology, I found it difficult—much harder than teaching classes in statistics or research methods. I was able to give a lecture on the sympathetic nervous system, a lecture on Piaget, and a lecture on social cognition, but how could I link these topics together for the student? I felt a bit like I was presenting a laundry list of research findings rather than an integrated set of principles and knowledge. Of course, what was difficult for me was harder still for my students. How could they be expected to remember and understand all the many phenomena of psychology? How could they tell what was most important? And why, given the abundance of information that was freely available to them on the web, should they care about my approach? My pedagogy needed something to structure, integrate, and motivate their learning.

Eventually, I found some techniques to help my students understand and appreciate what I found to be important. First, I realized that psychology actually did matter to my students, but that I needed to make it clear to them why it did. I therefore created a more consistent focus on the theme of *behavior*. One of the most fundamental integrating principles of the discipline of psychology is its focus on behavior, and yet that is often not made clear to students. Affect, cognition, and motivation are critical and essential, and yet are frequently best understood and made relevant through their links with behavior. Once I figured this out, I began tying all the material to this concept: The sympathetic nervous system matters *because it has specific and predictable influences on our behavior*. Piaget's findings matter *because they help us understand the child's behavior* (not just his or her thinking). And social cognition matters *because our social thinking helps us better relate to the other people in our everyday social lives*. This integrating theme allows me to organize my lectures, my writing assignments, and my testing.

Second was the issue of empiricism: I emphasized that what seems true might not be true, and we need to try to determine whether it is. The idea of empirical research testing falsifiable hypotheses and explaining much (but never all) behavior—the idea of *psychology as a science*—was critical, and it helped me differentiate psychology from other disciplines. Another reason for emphasizing empiricism is that the Introduction to Psychology course represents many students' best opportunity to learn about the fundamentals of scientific research.

The length of existing textbooks was creating a real and unnecessary impediment to student learning. I was condensing and abridging my coverage, but often without a clear rationale for choosing to cover one topic and omit another. My focus on behavior, coupled with a consistent focus on empiricism, helped in this regard—focusing on these themes helped me identify the underlying principles of psychology and separate more essential topics from less essential ones.

APPROACH AND PEDAGOGY

I wrote this book to help students organize their thinking about psychology at a conceptual level. Five or ten years from now, I do not expect my students to remember the details of most of what I teach them. However, I do hope that they will remember that psychology matters because it helps us understand behavior and that our knowledge of psychology is based on empirical study.

This book is designed to facilitate these learning outcomes. I have used three techniques to help focus students on behavior:

1. **Chapter openers.** I begin my focus on behavior by opening each chapter with a chapter opener showcasing an interesting real-world example of people who are dealing with behavioral questions and who can use psychology to help them answer those questions. The opener is designed to draw the student into the chapter and create an interest in learning about the topic.

2. **Psychology in everyday life.** Each chapter contains one or two features designed to link the principles from the chapter to real-world applications in business, environment, health, law, learning, and other relevant domains. For instance, the application in Chapter 6—"What Makes a Good Parent?"—applies the concepts of parenting styles in a minihandbook about parenting, and the application in Chapter 3 is about the difficulties that left-handed people face performing everyday tasks in a right-handed world.

3. **Research focus.** I have also emphasized empiricism throughout, but without making it a distraction from the main story line. Each chapter presents two close-ups on research—well-articulated and specific examples of research within the content area, each including a summary of the hypotheses, methods, results, and interpretations. This feature provides a continuous thread that reminds students of the importance of empirical research. The research foci also emphasize the fact that findings are not always predictable ahead of time (dispelling the myth of hindsight bias) and help students understand how research really works.

My focus on behavior and empiricism has produced a text that is better organized, has fewer chapters, and is somewhat shorter than many of the leading books.

Finally, as with all Flat World Knowledge texts, this textbook also includes learning objectives, key takeaways, exercises and critical thinking activities, and a marginal glossary of key terms.

In short, I think that this book will provide a useful and productive synthesis between your goals and the goals of your students. I have tried to focus on the forest rather than the trees and to bring psychology to life—in ways that really matter—for the students.

At the same time, the book maintains content and conceptual rigor, with a strong focus on the fundamental principles of empiricism and the scientific method.

CHAPTER 1
Introducing Psychology

Psychology is the *scientific study of mind and behavior*. The word "psychology" comes from the Greek words "psyche," meaning *life*, and "logos," meaning *explanation*. Psychology is a popular major for students, a popular topic in the public media, and a part of our everyday lives. Television shows such as *Dr. Phil* feature psychologists who provide personal advice to those with personal or family difficulties. Crime dramas such as *CSI, Lie to Me*, and others feature the work of forensic psychologists who use psychological principles to help solve crimes. And many people have direct knowledge about psychology because they have visited psychologists, for instance, school counselors, family therapists, and religious, marriage, or bereavement counselors.

Because we are frequently exposed to the work of psychologists in our everyday lives, we all have an idea about what psychology is and what psychologists do. In many ways I am sure that your conceptions are correct. Psychologists do work in forensic fields, and they do provide counseling and therapy for people in distress. But there are hundreds of thousands of psychologists in the world, and most of them work in other places, doing work that you are probably not aware of.

Most psychologists work in research laboratories, hospitals, and other field settings where they study the behavior of humans and animals. For instance, my colleagues in the Psychology Department at the University of Maryland study such diverse topics as anxiety in children, the interpretation of dreams, the effects of caffeine on thinking, how birds recognize each other, how praying mantises hear, how people from different cultures react differently in negotiation, and the factors that lead people to engage in terrorism. Other psychologists study such topics as alcohol and drug addiction, memory, emotion, hypnosis, love, what makes people aggressive or helpful, and the psychologies of politics, prejudice, culture, and religion. Psychologists also work in schools and businesses, and they use a variety of methods, including observation, questionnaires, interviews, and laboratory studies, to help them understand behavior.

This chapter provides an introduction to the broad field of psychology and the many approaches that psychologists take to understanding human behavior. We will consider how psychologists conduct scientific research, with an overview of some of the most important approaches used and topics studied by psychologists, and also consider the variety of fields in which psychologists work and the careers that are available to people with psychology degrees. I expect that you may find that at least some of your preconceptions about psychology will be challenged and changed, and you will learn that psychology is a field that will provide you with new ways of thinking about your own thoughts, feelings, and actions.

psychology

The scientific study of mind and behavior.

FIGURE 1.1

Psychology is in part the study of behavior. Why do you think these people are behaving the way they are?

*Sources: "The Robot: It's not a dance, it's a lifestyle!" photo courtesy of Alla, http://www.flickr.com/photos/alla2/2481846545/. Other photos ©
Thinkstock.*

1. PSYCHOLOGY AS A SCIENCE

LEARNING OBJECTIVES

1. Explain why using our intuition about everyday behavior is insufficient for a complete understanding of the causes of behavior.
2. Describe the difference between values and facts and explain how the scientific method is used
   to differentiate between the two.

Despite the differences in their interests, areas of study, and approaches, all psychologists have one
thing in common: They rely on scientific methods. *Research psychologists* use scientific methods to create new knowledge about the causes of behavior, whereas *psychologist-practitioners*, such as clinical,
counseling, industrial-organizational, and school psychologists, use existing research to enhance the
everyday life of others. The science of psychology is important for both researchers and practitioners.

> **data**
>
> Any information collected
> through formal observation
> or measurement.

In a sense all humans are scientists. We all have an interest in asking and answering questions
about our world. We want to know why things happen, when and if they are likely to happen again,
and how to reproduce or change them. Such knowledge enables us to predict our own behavior and
that of others. We may even collect **data** (i.e., *any information collected through formal observation or
measurement*) to aid us in this undertaking. It has been argued that people are "everyday scientists"
who conduct research projects to answer questions about behavior (Nisbett & Ross, 1980).[1] When we
perform poorly on an important test, we try to understand what caused our failure to remember or understand the material and what might help us do better the next time. When our good friends Monisha
and Charlie break up, despite the fact that they appeared to have a relationship made in heaven, we try
to determine what happened. When we contemplate the rise of terrorist acts around the world, we try
to investigate the causes of this problem by looking at the terrorists themselves, the situation around
them, and others' responses to them.

1.1 The Problem of Intuition

The results of these "everyday" research projects can teach us many principles of human behavior. We
learn through experience that if we give someone bad news, he or she may blame us even though the
news was not our fault. We learn that people may become depressed after they fail at an important task.
We see that aggressive behavior occurs frequently in our society, and we develop theories to explain

why this is so. These insights are part of everyday social life. In fact, much research in psychology involves the scientific study of everyday behavior (Heider, 1958; Kelley, 1967).[2]

The problem, however, with the way people collect and interpret data in their everyday lives is that they are not always particularly thorough. Often, when one explanation for an event seems "right," we adopt that explanation as the truth even when other explanations are possible and potentially more accurate. For example, eyewitnesses to violent crimes are often extremely confident in their identifications of the perpetrators of these crimes. But research finds that eyewitnesses are no less confident in their identifications when they are incorrect than when they are correct (Cutler & Wells, 2009; Wells & Hasel, 2008).[3] People may also become convinced of the existence of extrasensory perception (ESP), or the predictive value of astrology, when there is no evidence for either (Gilovich, 1993).[4] Furthermore, psychologists have also found that there are a variety of cognitive and motivational biases that frequently influence our perceptions and lead us to draw erroneous conclusions (Fiske & Taylor, 2007; Hsee & Hastie, 2006).[5] In summary, accepting explanations for events without testing them thoroughly may lead us to think that we know the causes of things when we really do not.

Research Focus: Unconscious Preferences for the Letters of Our Own Name

A study reported in the *Journal of Consumer Research* (Brendl, Chattopadhyay, Pelham, & Carvallo, 2005)[6] demonstrates the extent to which people can be unaware of the causes of their own behavior. The research demonstrated that, at least under certain conditions (and although they do not know it), people frequently prefer brand names that contain the letters of their own name to brand names that do not contain the letters of their own name.

The research participants were recruited in pairs and were told that the research was a taste test of different types of tea. For each pair of participants, the experimenter created two teas and named them by adding the word stem "oki" to the first three letters of each participant's first name. For example, for Jonathan and Elisabeth, the names of the teas would have been Jonoki and Elioki.

The participants were then shown 20 packets of tea that were supposedly being tested. Eighteen packets were labeled with made-up Japanese names (e.g., "Mataku" or "Somuta"), and two were labeled with the brand names constructed from the participants' names. The experimenter explained that each participant would taste only two teas and would be allowed to choose one packet of these two to take home.

One of the two participants was asked to draw slips of paper to select the two brands that would be tasted at this session. However, the drawing was rigged so that the two brands containing the participants' name stems were always chosen for tasting. Then, while the teas were being brewed, the participants completed a task designed to heighten their needs for self-esteem, and that was expected to increase their desire to choose a brand that had the letters of their own name. Specifically, the participants all wrote about an aspect of themselves that they would like to change.

After the teas were ready, the participants tasted them and then chose to take a packet of one of the teas home with them. After they made their choice, the participants were asked why they chose the tea they had chosen, and then the true purpose of the study was explained to them.

The results of this study found that participants chose the tea that included the first three letters of their own name significantly more frequently (64% of the time) than they chose the tea that included the first three letters of their partner's name (only 36% of the time). Furthermore, the decisions were made unconsciously; the participants did not know why they chose the tea they chose. When they were asked, more than 90% of the participants thought that they had chosen on the basis of taste, whereas only 5% of them mentioned the real cause—that the brand name contained the letters of their name.

Once we learn about the outcome of a given event (e.g., when we read about the results of a research project), we frequently believe that we would have been able to predict the outcome ahead of time. For instance, if half of a class of students is told that research concerning attraction between people has demonstrated that "opposites attract" and the other half is told that research has demonstrated that "birds of a feather flock together," most of the students will report believing that the outcome that they just read about is true, and that they would have predicted the outcome before they had read about it. Of course, both of these contradictory outcomes cannot be true. (In fact, psychological research finds that "birds of a feather flock together" is generally the case.) The problem is that just reading a description of research findings leads us to think of the many cases we know that support the findings, and thus makes them seem believable. *The tendency to think that we could have predicted something that has already occurred that we probably would not have been able to predict* is called the **hindsight bias**.

hindsight bias

The tendency to think that we could have predicted something that has already occurred that we probably would not have been able to predict.

1.2   Why Psychologists Rely on Empirical Methods

scientific method

The set of assumptions, rules, and procedures that scientists use to conduct empirical research.

All scientists, whether they are physicists, chemists, biologists, sociologists, or psychologists, use *empirical methods* to study the topics that interest them. Empirical methods include the processes of collecting and organizing data and drawing conclusions about those data. The empirical methods used by scientists have developed over many years and provide a basis for collecting, analyzing, and interpreting data within a common framework in which information can be shared. We can label the **scientific method** as *the set of assumptions, rules, and procedures that scientists use to conduct empirical research.*

FIGURE 1.2

Psychologists use a variety of techniques to measure and understand human behavior.

Sources: Poster photo courtesy of Wesleyan University, http://newsletter.blogs.wesleyan.edu/files/2009/04/psychposter11.jpg. Language lab photo courtesy of Evansville University, http://psychology.evansville.edu/langlab.jpg. Other photo © Thinkstock.

Although scientific research is an important method of studying human behavior, not all questions can be answered using scientific approaches. Statements that cannot be objectively measured or objectively determined to be true or false are not within the domain of scientific inquiry. Scientists therefore draw a distinction between values and facts. *Values* are personal statements such as "Abortion should not be permitted in this country," "I will go to heaven when I die," or "It is important to study psychology." *Facts* are objective statements determined to be accurate through empirical study. Examples are "There were more than 21,000 homicides in the United States in 2009," or "Research demonstrates that individuals who are exposed to highly stressful situations over long periods of time develop more health problems than those who are not."

Because values cannot be considered to be either true or false, science cannot prove or disprove them. Nevertheless, as shown in Table 1.1, research can sometimes provide facts that can help people develop their values. For instance, science may be able to objectively measure the impact of unwanted children on a society or the psychological trauma suffered by women who have abortions. The effect of capital punishment on the crime rate in the United States may also be determinable. This factual information can and should be made available to help people formulate their values about abortion and capital punishment, as well as to enable governments to articulate appropriate policies. Values also frequently come into play in determining what research is appropriate or important to conduct. For instance, the U.S. government has recently supported and provided funding for research on HIV, AIDS, and terrorism, while denying funding for research using human stem cells.

TABLE 1.1   Examples of Values and Facts in Scientific Research

Personal value	Scientific fact
Welfare payments should be reduced for unmarried parents.	The U.S. government paid more than $21 billion in unemployment insurance in 2010.
Handguns should be outlawed.	There were more than 30,000 deaths caused by handguns in the United States in 2009.
Blue is my favorite color.	More than 35% of college students indicate that blue is their favorite color.
It is important to quit smoking.	Smoking increases the incidence of cancer and heart disease.

Source: Stangor, C. (2011). Research methods for the behavioral sciences (4th ed.). Mountain View, CA: Cengage.

Although scientists use research to help establish facts, the distinction between values and facts is not always clear-cut. Sometimes statements that scientists consider to be factual later, on the basis of further research, turn out to be partially or even entirely incorrect. Although scientific procedures do not necessarily guarantee that the answers to questions will be objective and unbiased, science is still the best method for drawing objective conclusions about the world around us. When old facts are discarded, they are replaced with new facts based on newer and more correct data. Although science is not perfect, the requirements of empiricism and objectivity result in a much greater chance of producing an accurate understanding of human behavior than is available through other approaches.

1.3 Levels of Explanation in Psychology

The study of psychology spans many different topics at many different **levels of explanation**, which are *the perspectives that are used to understand behavior.* Lower levels of explanation are more closely tied to biological influences, such as genes, neurons, neurotransmitters, and hormones, whereas the middle levels of explanation refer to the abilities and characteristics of individual people, and the highest levels of explanation relate to social groups, organizations, and cultures (Cacioppo, Berntson, Sheridan, & McClintock, 2000).[7]

> **levels of explanation**
>
> The perspectives that are used to understand behavior.

The same topic can be studied within psychology at different levels of explanation, as shown in Figure 1.3. For instance, the psychological disorder known as *depression* affects millions of people worldwide and is known to be caused by biological, social, and cultural factors. Studying and helping alleviate depression can be accomplished at low levels of explanation by investigating how chemicals in the brain influence the experience of depression. This approach has allowed psychologists to develop and prescribe drugs, such as Prozac, which may decrease depression in many individuals (Williams, Simpson, Simpson, & Nahas, 2009).[8] At the middle levels of explanation, psychological therapy is directed at helping individuals cope with negative life experiences that may cause depression. And at the highest level, psychologists study differences in the prevalence of depression between men and women and across cultures. The occurrence of psychological disorders, including depression, is substantially higher for women than for men, and it is also higher in Western cultures, such as in the United States, Canada, and Europe, than in Eastern cultures, such as in India, China, and Japan (Chen, Wang, Poland, & Lin, 2009; Seedat et al., 2009).[9] These sex and cultural differences provide insight into the factors that cause depression. The study of depression in psychology helps remind us that no one level of explanation can explain everything. All levels of explanation, from biological to personal to cultural, are essential for a better understanding of human behavior.

FIGURE 1.3 Levels of Explanation

Level of explanation	Underlying process	Examples
Lower	Biological	Depression is in part genetically influenced. Depression is influenced by the action of neurotransmitters in the brain.
Middle	Interpersonal	People who are depressed may interpret the events that occur to them too negatively. Psychotherapy can be used to help people talk about and combat depression.
Higher	Cultural and social	Women experience more depression than do men. The prevalence of depression varies across cultures and historical time periods.

1.4 The Challenges of Studying Psychology

Understanding and attempting to alleviate the costs of psychological disorders such as depression is not easy, because psychological experiences are extremely complex. The questions psychologists pose are as difficult as those posed by doctors, biologists, chemists, physicists, and other scientists, if not more so (Wilson, 1998).[10]

individual differences

The variations among people on physical or psychological dimensions.

A major goal of psychology is to predict behavior by understanding its causes. Making predictions is difficult in part because people vary and respond differently in different situations. **Individual differences** are *the variations among people on physical or psychological dimensions*. For instance, although many people experience at least some symptoms of depression at some times in their lives, the experience varies dramatically among people. Some people experience major negative events, such as severe physical injuries or the loss of significant others, without experiencing much depression, whereas other people experience severe depression for no apparent reason. Other important individual differences that we will discuss in the chapters to come include differences in extraversion, intelligence, self-esteem, anxiety, aggression, and conformity.

Because of the many individual difference variables that influence behavior, we cannot always predict who will become aggressive or who will perform best in graduate school or on the job. The predictions made by psychologists (and most other scientists) are only probabilistic. We can say, for instance, that people who score higher on an intelligence test will, on average, do better than people who score lower on the same test, but we cannot make very accurate predictions about exactly how any one person will perform.

Another reason that it is difficult to predict behavior is that almost all behavior is *multiply determined*, or produced by many factors. And these factors occur at different levels of explanation. We have seen, for instance, that depression is caused by lower-level genetic factors, by medium-level personal factors, and by higher-level social and cultural factors. You should always be skeptical about people who attempt to explain important human behaviors, such as violence, child abuse, poverty, anxiety, or depression, in terms of a single cause.

Furthermore, these multiple causes are not independent of one another; they are associated such that when one cause is present other causes tend to be present as well. This overlap makes it difficult to pinpoint which cause or causes are operating. For instance, some people may be depressed because of biological imbalances in neurotransmitters in their brain. The resulting depression may lead them to act more negatively toward other people around them, which then leads those other people to respond more negatively to them, which then increases their depression. As a result, the biological determinants of depression become intertwined with the social responses of other people, making it difficult to disentangle the effects of each cause.

Another difficulty in studying psychology is that much human behavior is caused by factors that are outside our conscious awareness, making it impossible for us, as individuals, to really understand them. The role of unconscious processes was emphasized in the theorizing of the Austrian neurologist Sigmund Freud (1856–1939), who argued that many psychological disorders were caused by memories that we have *repressed* and thus remain outside our consciousness. Unconscious processes will be an important part of our study of psychology, and we will see that current research has supported many of Freud's ideas about the importance of the unconscious in guiding behavior.

KEY TAKEAWAYS

- Psychology is the scientific study of mind and behavior.
- Though it is easy to think that everyday situations have commonsense answers, scientific studies have found that people are not always as good at predicting outcomes as they think they are.
- The hindsight bias leads us to think that we could have predicted events that we actually could not have predicted.
- People are frequently unaware of the causes of their own behaviors.
- Psychologists use the scientific method to collect, analyze, and interpret evidence.
- Employing the scientific method allows the scientist to collect empirical data objectively, which adds to the accumulation of scientific knowledge.
- Psychological phenomena are complex, and making predictions about them is difficult because of individual differences and because they are multiply determined at different levels of explanation.

EXERCISES AND CRITICAL THINKING

1. Can you think of a time when you used your intuition to analyze an outcome, only to be surprised later to find that your explanation was completely incorrect? Did this surprise help you understand how intuition may sometimes lead us astray?

2. Describe the scientific method in a way that someone who knows nothing about science could understand it.

3. Consider a behavior that you find to be important and think about its potential causes at different levels of explanation. How do you think psychologists would study this behavior?

2. THE EVOLUTION OF PSYCHOLOGY: HISTORY, APPROACHES, AND QUESTIONS

LEARNING OBJECTIVES

1. Explain how psychology changed from a philosophical to a scientific discipline.
2. List some of the most important questions that concern psychologists.
3. Outline the basic schools of psychology and how each school has contributed to psychology.

In this section we will review the history of psychology with a focus on the important questions that psychologists ask and the major approaches (or schools) of psychological inquiry. The schools of psychology that we will review are summarized in Table 1.2, and Figure 1.5 presents a timeline of some of the most important psychologists, beginning with the early Greek philosophers and extending to the present day. Table 1.2 and Figure 1.5 both represent a selection of the most important schools and people; to mention all the approaches and all the psychologists who have contributed to the field is not possible in one chapter.

The approaches that psychologists have used to assess the issues that interest them have changed dramatically over the history of psychology. Perhaps most importantly, the field has moved steadily from speculation about behavior toward a more objective and scientific approach as the technology available to study human behavior has improved (Benjamin & Baker, 2004).[11] There has also been an increasing influx of women into the field. Although most early psychologists were men, now most psychologists, including the presidents of the most important psychological organizations, are women.

TABLE 1.2 The Most Important Approaches (Schools) of Psychology

School of psychology	Description	Important contributors
Structuralism	Uses the method of introspection to identify the basic elements or "structures" of psychological experience	Wilhelm Wundt, Edward B. Titchener
Functionalism	Attempts to understand why animals and humans have developed the particular psychological aspects that they currently possess	William James
Psychodynamic	Focuses on the role of our unconscious thoughts, feelings, and memories and our early childhood experiences in determining behavior	Sigmund Freud, Carl Jung, Alfred Adler, Erik Erickson
Behaviorism	Based on the premise that it is not possible to objectively study the mind, and therefore that psychologists should limit their attention to the study of behavior itself	John B. Watson, B. F. Skinner
Cognitive	The study of mental processes, including perception, thinking, memory, and judgments	Hermann Ebbinghaus, Sir Frederic Bartlett, Jean Piaget
Social-cultural	The study of how the social situations and the cultures in which people find themselves influence thinking and behavior	Fritz Heider, Leon Festinger, Stanley Schachter

FIGURE 1.4 Female Psychologists

Although most of the earliest psychologists were men, women are increasingly contributing to psychology. The first female president of the American Psychological Association was Mary Whiton Calkins (1861–1930; lower right). Calkins made significant contributions to the study of memory and the self-concept. Mahzarin Banaji (upper left), Marilynn Brewer (upper right), and Linda Bartoshuk (lower left) all have been recent presidents of the American Psychological Society.

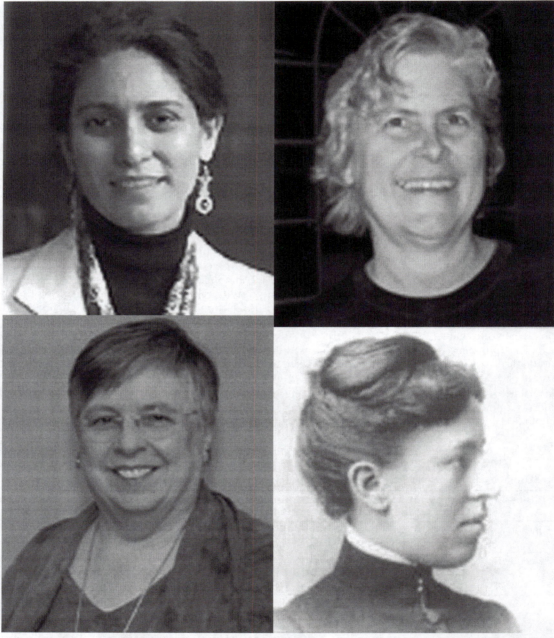

Sources: Bartoshuk photo courtesy of Linda Bartoshuk, http://www.psychologicalscience.org/?s=bartoshuk. Banaji photo courtesy of Mahzarin Rustum Banaji, http://banaji.socialpsychology.org. Brewer photo courtesy of Marilynn Brewer, http://brewer.socialpsychology.org. Calkins photo courtesy of Vlad Sfichi, http://www.flickr.com/photos/24110800@N08/2779490726.

FIGURE 1.5 Timeline Showing Some of the Most Important Psychologists

Although it cannot capture every important psychologist, this timeline shows some of the most important contributors to the history of psychology.

Date	Psychologist(s)	Description
428–347 BC	Plato	Greek philosopher who argued for the role of nature in psychological development.
384–322 BC	Aristotle	Greek philosopher who argued for the role of nurture in psychological development.
1588–1679	Thomas Hobbes	English philosopher.
1596–1650	René Descartes	French philosopher.
1632–1704	John Locke	English philosopher.
1712–1778	Jean-Jacques Rousseau	French philosopher.
1801–1887	Gustav Fechner	German experimental psychologist who developed the idea of the just noticeable difference (JND), which is considered to be the first empirical psychological measurement.
1809–1882	Charles Darwin	British naturalist whose theory of natural selection influenced the functionalist school and the field of evolutionary psychology.
1832–1920	Wilhelm Wundt	German psychologist who opened one of the first psychology laboratories and helped develop the field of structuralism.
1842–1910	William James	American psychologist who opened one of the first psychology laboratories and helped develop the field of functionalism.
1849–1936	Ivan Pavlov	Russian physiologist whose experiments on learning led to the principles of classical conditioning.
1850–1909	Hermann Ebbinghaus	German psychologist who studied the ability of people to remember lists of nonsense syllables under different conditions.
1856–1939	Sigmund Freud	Austrian psychologist who founded the field of psychodynamic psychology.
1867–1927	Edward Bradford Titchener	American psychologist who contributed to the field of structuralism.
1878–1958	John B. Watson	American psychologist who contributed to the field of behaviorism.
1886–1969	Sir Frederic Bartlett	British psychologist who studied the cognitive and social processes of remembering.
1896–1980	Jean Piaget	Swiss psychologist who developed an important theory of cognitive development in children.
1904–1990	B. F. Skinner	American psychologist who contributed to the school of behaviorism.
1926–1993	Donald Broadbent	British cognitive psychologist who was a pioneer in the study of attention.
20th and 21st centuries	Linda Bartoshuk; Daniel Kahneman; Elizabeth Loftus; George Miller	American psychologists who contributed to the cognitive school of psychology by studying learning, memory, and judgment. An important contribution is the advancement of the field of neuroscience. Daniel Kahneman won the Nobel Prize in Economics for his work on psychological decision making.
20th and 21st centuries	Mahzarin Banaji; Marilynn Brewer; Susan Fiske; Fritz Heider; Kurt Lewin; Stanley Schachter; Claude Steele; Harry Triandis	American psychologists who contributed to the social-cultural school of psychology. Their contributions have included an understanding of how people develop and are influenced by social norms.

Although psychology has changed dramatically over its history, the most important questions that psychologists address have remained constant. Some of these questions follow, and we will discuss them both in this chapter and in the chapters to come:

- *Nature versus nurture.* Are genes or environment most influential in determining the behavior of individuals and in accounting for differences among people? Most scientists now agree that both genes and environment play crucial roles in most human behaviors, and yet we still have much to learn about how nature (our biological makeup) and nurture (the experiences that we have during our lives) work together (Harris, 1998; Pinker, 2002).[12] *The proportion of the observed differences on characteristics among people (e.g., in terms of their height, intelligence, or optimism) that is due to genetics* is known as the **heritability** of the characteristic, and we will make much use of this term in the chapters to come. We will see, for example, that the heritability of intelligence is very high (about .85 out of 1.0) and that the heritability of extraversion is about .50.

heritability

The proportion of the observed differences on characteristics among people (e.g., in terms of their height, intelligence, or optimism) that is due to genetics.

But we will also see that nature and nurture interact in complex ways, making the question of "Is it nature or is it nurture?" very difficult to answer.

- *Free will versus determinism.* This question concerns the extent to which people have control over their own actions. Are we the products of our environment, guided by forces out of our control, or are we able to choose the behaviors we engage in? Most of us like to believe in free will, that we are able to do what we want—for instance, that we could get up right now and go fishing. And our legal system is premised on the concept of free will; we punish criminals because we believe that they have choice over their behaviors and freely choose to disobey the law. But as we will discuss later in the research focus in this section, recent research has suggested that we may have less control over our own behavior than we think we do (Wegner, 2002).[13]

- *Accuracy versus inaccuracy.* To what extent are humans good information processors? Although it appears that people are "good enough" to make sense of the world around them and to make decent decisions (Fiske, 2003),[14] they are far from perfect. Human judgment is sometimes compromised by inaccuracies in our thinking styles and by our motivations and emotions. For instance, our judgment may be affected by our desires to gain material wealth and to see ourselves positively and by emotional responses to the events that happen to us.

FIGURE 1.6

President Barack Obama and Vice President Joe Biden (left photo) meet with BP executives to discuss the disastrous oil spill in the Gulf of Mexico (right photo). Psychologists study the causes of poor judgments such as those made by these executives.

Sources: Obama-Hayward photo courtesy of Pete Souza, http://commons.wikimedia.org/wiki/File:Obama-hayward.jpg. Pelican photo courtesy of the International Bird Rescue Research Center, http://commons.wikimedia.org/wiki/File:Pelican_wash_from_oil_spill_Louisiana_13_Dawn_IBRRC_2010.05.04_B6X2141.jpg.

- *Conscious versus unconscious processing.* To what extent are we conscious of our own actions and the causes of them, and to what extent are our behaviors caused by influences that we are not aware of? Many of the major theories of psychology, ranging from the Freudian psychodynamic theories to contemporary work in cognitive psychology, argue that much of our behavior is determined by variables that we are not aware of.

- *Differences versus similarities.* To what extent are we all similar, and to what extent are we different? For instance, are there basic psychological and personality differences between men and women, or are men and women by and large similar? And what about people from different ethnicities and cultures? Are people around the world generally the same, or are they influenced by their backgrounds and environments in different ways? Personality, social, and cross-cultural psychologists attempt to answer these classic questions.

2.1 Early Psychologists

The earliest psychologists that we know about are the Greek philosophers Plato (428–347 BC) and Aristotle (384–322 BC). These philosophers asked many of the same questions that today's psychologists ask; for instance, they questioned the distinction between nature and nurture and the existence of free will. In terms of the former, Plato argued on the nature side, believing that certain kinds of knowledge are innate or inborn, whereas Aristotle was more on the nurture side, believing that each child is born as an "empty slate" (in Latin a *tabula rasa*) and that knowledge is primarily acquired through learning and experience.

European philosophers continued to ask these fundamental questions during the Renaissance. For instance, the French philosopher René Descartes (1596–1650) also considered the issue of free will, arguing in its favor and believing that the mind controls the body through the pineal gland in the brain (an idea that made some sense at the time but was later proved incorrect). Descartes also believed in the existence of innate natural abilities. A scientist as well as a philosopher, Descartes dissected animals and was among the first to understand that the nerves controlled the muscles. He also addressed the relationship between mind (the mental aspects of life) and body (the physical aspects of life). Descartes believed in the principle of *dualism*: that the mind is fundamentally different from the mechanical body. Other European philosophers, including Thomas Hobbes (1588–1679), John Locke (1632–1704), and Jean-Jacques Rousseau (1712–1778), also weighed in on these issues.

The fundamental problem that these philosophers faced was that they had few methods for settling their claims. Most philosophers didn't conduct any research on these questions, in part because they didn't yet know how to do it, and in part because they weren't sure it was even possible to objectively study human experience. But dramatic changes came during the 1800s with the help of the first two research psychologists: the German psychologist Wilhelm Wundt (1832–1920), who developed a psychology laboratory in Leipzig, Germany, and the American psychologist William James (1842–1910), who founded a psychology laboratory at Harvard University.

2.2 Structuralism: Introspection and the Awareness of Subjective Experience

Wundt's research in his laboratory in Liepzig focused on the nature of consciousness itself. Wundt and his students believed that it was possible to analyze the basic elements of the mind and to classify our conscious experiences scientifically. Wundt began the field known as **structuralism**, *a school of psychology whose goal was to identify the basic elements or "structures" of psychological experience.* Its goal was to create a "periodic table" of the "elements of sensations," similar to the periodic table of elements that had recently been created in chemistry.

Structuralists used the method of *introspection* to attempt to create a map of the elements of consciousness. **Introspection** involves *asking research participants to describe exactly what they experience as they work on mental tasks,* such as viewing colors, reading a page in a book, or performing a math problem. A participant who is reading a book might report, for instance, that he saw some black and colored straight and curved marks on a white background. In other studies the structuralists used newly invented reaction time instruments to systematically assess not only what the participants were thinking but how long it took them to do so. Wundt discovered that it took people longer to report what sound they had just heard than to simply respond that they had heard the sound. These studies marked the first time researchers realized that there is a difference between the *sensation* of a stimulus and the *perception* of that stimulus, and the idea of using reaction times to study mental events has now become a mainstay of cognitive psychology.

Perhaps the best known of the structuralists was Edward Bradford Titchener (1867–1927). Titchener was a student of Wundt who came to the United States in the late 1800s and founded a laboratory at Cornell University. In his research using introspection, Titchener and his students claimed to have identified more than 40,000 sensations, including those relating to vision, hearing, and taste.

An important aspect of the structuralist approach was that it was rigorous and scientific. The research marked the beginning of psychology as a science, because it demonstrated that mental events could be quantified. But the structuralists also discovered the limitations of introspection. Even highly trained research participants were often unable to report on their subjective experiences. When the participants were asked to do simple math problems, they could easily do them, but they could not easily answer *how* they did them. Thus the structuralists were the first to realize the importance of unconscious processes—that many important aspects of human psychology occur outside our conscious awareness, and that psychologists cannot expect research participants to be able to accurately report on all of their experiences.

FIGURE 1.7

The earliest psychologists were the Greek philosophers Plato (left) and Aristotle. Plato believed that much knowledge was innate, whereas Aristotle thought that each child was born as an "empty slate" and that knowledge was primarily acquired through learning and experience.

Sources: Plato photo courtesy of http://commons.wikimedia.org/wiki/File:Platon2.jpg. Aristotle photo courtesy of Giovanni Dall'Orto, http://commons.wikimedia.org/wiki/File:Busto_di_Aristotele_conservato_a_Palazzo_Altaemps,_Roma._Foto_di_Giovanni_Dall%27Orto.jpg.

structuralism

A school of psychology whose goal was to identify the basic elements (or "structures") of psychological experience.

introspection

A method of learning about psychological processes in which research participants are asked to describe exactly what they experience as they work on mental tasks.

FIGURE 1.8

Wilhelm Wundt (seated at left) and Edward Titchener (right) helped create the structuralist school of psychology. Their goal was to classify the elements of sensation through introspection.

Sources: Wundt photo courtesy of Kenosis, http://commons.wikimedia.org/wiki/File:Wundt-research-group.jpg. Titchener photo courtesy of Amaro Studios, http://www.flickr.com/photos/39584782@N08/4197763373.

2.3 Functionalism and Evolutionary Psychology

functionalism

A school of psychology whose goal was to understand why animals and humans have developed the particular psychological aspects that they currently possess.

In contrast to Wundt, who attempted to understand the nature of consciousness, the goal of William James and the other members of the school of **functionalism** was *to understand why animals and humans have developed the particular psychological aspects that they currently possess* (Hunt, 1993).[15] For James, one's thinking was relevant only to one's behavior. As he put it in his psychology textbook, "My thinking is first and last and always for the sake of my doing" (James, 1890).[16]

James and the other members of the functionalist school were influenced by Charles Darwin's (1809–1882) *theory of natural selection*, which proposed that the physical characteristics of animals and humans evolved because they were useful, or functional. The functionalists believed that Darwin's theory applied to psychological characteristics too. Just as some animals have developed strong muscles to allow them to run fast, the human brain, so functionalists thought, must have adapted to serve a particular function in human experience.

FIGURE 1.9

The functionalist school of psychology, founded by the American psychologist William James (left), was influenced by the work of Charles Darwin.

Although functionalism no longer exists as a school of psychology, its basic principles have been absorbed into psychology and continue to influence it in many ways. The work of the functionalists has developed into the field of **evolutionary psychology**, *a branch of psychology that applies the Darwinian theory of natural selection to human and animal behavior* (Dennett, 1995; Tooby & Cosmides, 1992).[17] Evolutionary psychology accepts the functionalists' basic assumption, namely that many human psychological systems, including memory, emotion, and personality, serve key adaptive functions. As we will see in the chapters to come, evolutionary psychologists use evolutionary theory to understand many different behaviors including romantic attraction, stereotypes and prejudice, and even the causes of many psychological disorders.

Source: James photo courtesy of
http://commons.wikimedia.org/wiki/
File:William_James,_philosopher.jpg. Darwin portrait
courtesy of George Richmond,
http://commons.wikimedia.org/wiki/
File:Charles_Darwin_by_G._Richmond.jpg.

A key component of the ideas of evolutionary psychology is *fitness*. **Fitness** refers to *the extent to which having a given characteristic helps the individual organism survive and reproduce at a higher rate than do other members of the species who do not have the characteristic.* Fitter organisms pass on their genes more successfully to later generations, making the characteristics that produce fitness more likely to become part of the organism's nature than characteristics that do not produce fitness. For example, it has been argued that the emotion of jealousy has survived over time in men because men who experience jealousy are more fit than men who do not. According to this idea, the experience of jealously leads men to be more likely to protect their mates and guard against rivals, which increases their reproductive success (Buss, 2000).[18]

Despite its importance in psychological theorizing, evolutionary psychology also has some limitations. One problem is that many of its predictions are extremely difficult to test. Unlike the fossils that are used to learn about the physical evolution of species, we cannot know which psychological characteristics our ancestors possessed or did not possess; we can only make guesses about this. Because it is difficult to directly test evolutionary theories, it is always possible that the explanations we apply are made up after the fact to account for observed data (Gould & Lewontin, 1979).[19] Nevertheless, the evolutionary approach is important to psychology because it provides logical explanations for why we have many psychological characteristics.

evolutionary psychology

A branch of psychology that applies the Darwinian theory of natural selection to human and animal behavior.

fitness

The extent to which having a given genetic characteristic helps an individual organism survive and reproduce at a higher rate than do other members of the species who do not have the characteristic.

psychodynamic psychology

An approach to understanding human behavior that focuses on the role of unconscious thoughts, feelings, and memories.

2.4 Psychodynamic Psychology

Perhaps the school of psychology that is most familiar to the general public is the *psychodynamic approach* to understanding behavior, which was championed by Sigmund Freud (1856–1939) and his followers. **Psychodynamic psychology** is an *approach to understanding human behavior that focuses on the role of unconscious thoughts, feelings, and memories.* Freud developed his theories about behavior through extensive analysis of the patients that he treated in his private clinical practice. Freud believed that many of the problems that his patients experienced, including anxiety, depression, and sexual dysfunction, were the result of the effects of painful childhood experiences that the person could no longer remember.

Freud's ideas were extended by other psychologists whom he influenced, including Carl Jung (1875–1961), Alfred Adler (1870–1937), Karen Horney (1855–1952), and Erik Erikson (1902–1994). These and others who follow the psychodynamic approach believe that it is possible to help the patient if the unconscious drives can be remembered, particularly through a deep and thorough exploration of the person's early sexual experiences and current sexual desires. These explorations are revealed through talk therapy and dream analysis, in a process called *psychoanalysis*.

The founders of the school of psychodynamics were primarily practitioners who worked with individuals to help them understand and confront their psychological symptoms. Although they did not conduct much research on their ideas, and although later, more sophisticated tests of their theories have not always supported their proposals, psychodynamics has nevertheless had substantial impact on the field of psychology, and indeed on thinking about human behavior more generally (Moore & Fine, 1995).[20] The importance of the unconscious in human behavior, the idea that early childhood experiences are critical, and the concept of therapy as a way of improving human lives are all ideas that are derived from the psychodynamic approach and that remain central to psychology.

2.5 Behaviorism and the Question of Free Will

Although they differed in approach, both structuralism and functionalism were essentially studies of the mind. The psychologists associated with the school of *behaviorism*, on the other hand, were reacting in part to the difficulties psychologists encountered when they tried to use introspection to understand behavior. **Behaviorism** is *a school of psychology that is based on the premise that it is not possible to objectively study the mind, and therefore that psychologists should limit their attention to the study of behavior itself.* Behaviorists believe that the human mind is a "black box" into which stimuli are sent and from which responses are received. They argue that there is no point in trying to determine what happens in the box because we can successfully predict behavior without knowing what happens inside the mind. Furthermore, behaviorists believe that it is possible to develop laws of learning that can explain all behaviors.

The first behaviorist was the American psychologist John B. Watson (1878–1958). Watson was influenced in large part by the work of the Russian physiologist Ivan Pavlov (1849–1936), who had discovered that dogs would salivate at the sound of a tone that had previously been associated with the presentation of food. Watson and the other behaviorists began to use these ideas to explain how events that people and other organisms experienced in their environment (*stimuli*) could produce specific behaviors (*responses*). For instance, in Pavlov's research the *stimulus* (either the food or, after learning, the tone) would produce the *response* of salivation in the dogs.

In his research Watson found that systematically exposing a child to fearful stimuli in the presence of objects that did not themselves elicit fear could lead the child to respond with a fearful behavior to the presence of the stimulus (Watson & Rayner, 1920; Beck, Levinson, & Irons, 2009).[21] In the best known of his studies, an 8-month-old boy named Little Albert was used as the subject. Here is a summary of the findings:

> The boy was placed in the middle of a room; a white laboratory rat was placed near him and he was allowed to play with it. The child showed no fear of the rat. In later trials, the researchers made a loud sound behind Albert's back by striking a steel bar with a hammer whenever the baby touched the rat. The child cried when he heard the noise. After several such pairings of the two stimuli, the child was again shown the rat. Now, however, he cried and tried to move away from the rat.

In line with the behaviorist approach, the boy had learned to associate the white rat with the loud noise, resulting in crying.

FIGURE 1.10

Sigmund Freud and the other psychodynamic psychologists believed that many of our thoughts and emotions are unconscious. Psychotherapy was designed to help patients recover and confront their "lost" memories.

Source: Photo courtesy of Max Halberstadt,
http://commons.wikimedia.org/wiki/
File:Sigmund_Freud_LIFE.jpg.

behaviorism

A school of psychology that is based on the premise that it is not possible to objectively study the mind, and therefore that psychologists should limit their attention to the study of behavior itself.

FIGURE 1.11

B. F. Skinner was a member of the behaviorist school of psychology. He argued that free will is an illusion and that all behavior is determined by environmental factors.

Source: Photo courtesy of http://commons.wikimedia.org/wiki/ File:B.F._Skinner_at_Harvard_circa _1950.jpg.

The most famous behaviorist was Burrhus Frederick (B. F.) Skinner (1904–1990), who expanded the principles of behaviorism and also brought them to the attention of the public at large. Skinner used the ideas of stimulus and response, along with the application of rewards or *reinforcements*, to train pigeons and other animals. And he used the general principles of behaviorism to develop theories about how best to teach children and how to create societies that were peaceful and productive. Skinner even developed a method for studying thoughts and feelings using the behaviorist approach (Skinner, 1957, 1968, 1972).[22]

Research Focus: Do We Have Free Will?

The behaviorist research program had important implications for the fundamental questions about nature and nurture and about free will. In terms of the nature-nurture debate, the behaviorists agreed with the nurture approach, believing that we are shaped exclusively by our environments. They also argued that there is no free will, but rather that our behaviors are determined by the events that we have experienced in our past. In short, this approach argues that organisms, including humans, are a lot like puppets in a show who don't realize that other people are controlling them. Furthermore, although we do not cause our own actions, we nevertheless believe that we do because we don't realize all the influences acting on our behavior.

Recent research in psychology has suggested that Skinner and the behaviorists might well have been right, at least in the sense that we overestimate our own free will in responding to the events around us (Libet, 1985; Matsuhashi & Hallett, 2008; Wegner, 2002).[23] In one demonstration of the misperception of our own free will, neuroscientists Soon, Brass, Heinze, and Haynes (2008)[24] placed their research participants in a *functional magnetic resonance imaging (fMRI)* brain scanner while they presented them with a series of letters on a computer screen. The letter on the screen changed every one-half second. The participants were asked, whenever they decided to, to press either of two buttons. Then they were asked to indicate which letter was showing on the screen when they decided to press the button. The researchers analyzed the brain images to see if they could predict which of the two buttons the participant was going to press, even before the letter at which he or she had indicated the decision to press a button. Suggesting that the intention to act occurred in the brain before the research participants became aware of it, the researchers found that the prefrontal cortex region of the brain showed activation that could be used to predict the button press as long as 10 seconds before the participants said that they decided which button to press.

Research has found that we are more likely to think that we control our behavior when the desire to act occurs immediately prior to the outcome, when the thought is consistent with the outcome, and when there are no other apparent causes for the behavior. Aarts, Custers, and Wegner (2005)[25] asked their research participants to control a rapidly moving square along with a computer that was also controlling the square independently. The participants pressed a button to stop the movement. When participants were exposed to words related to the location of the square just before they stopped its movement, they became more likely to think that they controlled the motion, even when it was actually the computer that stopped it. And Dijksterhuis, Preston, Wegner, and Aarts (2008)[26] found that participants who had just been exposed to first-person singular pronouns, such as "I" and "me," were more likely to believe that they controlled their actions than were people who had seen the words "computer" or "God."

The idea that we are more likely to take ownership for our actions in some cases than in others is also seen in our attributions for success and failure. Because we normally expect that our behaviors will be met with success, when we are successful we easily believe that the success is the result of our own free will. When an action is met with failure, on the other hand, we are less likely to perceive this outcome as the result of our free will, and we are more likely to blame the outcome on luck or our teacher (Wegner, 2003).[27]

The behaviorists made substantial contributions to psychology by identifying the principles of *learning*. Although the behaviorists were incorrect in their beliefs that it was not possible to measure thoughts and feelings, their ideas provided new ideas that helped further our understanding regarding the nature-nurture debate as well as the question of free will. The ideas of behaviorism are fundamental to psychology and have been developed to help us better understand the role of prior experiences in a variety of areas of psychology.

2.6 The Cognitive Approach and Cognitive Neuroscience

Science is always influenced by the technology that surrounds it, and psychology is no exception. Thus it is no surprise that beginning in the 1960s, growing numbers of psychologists began to think about the brain and about human behavior in terms of the computer, which was being developed and becoming publicly available at that time. The analogy between the brain and the computer, although by no means perfect, provided part of the impetus for a new school of psychology called *cognitive psychology*. **Cognitive psychology** is *a field of psychology that studies mental processes, including perception, thinking, memory, and judgment*. These actions correspond well to the processes that computers perform.

Although cognitive psychology began in earnest in the 1960s, earlier psychologists had also taken a cognitive orientation. Some of the important contributors to cognitive psychology include the German psychologist Hermann Ebbinghaus (1850–1909), who studied the ability of people to remember lists of words under different conditions, and the English psychologist Sir Frederic Bartlett (1886–1969), who studied the cognitive and social processes of remembering. Bartlett created short stories that were in some ways logical but also contained some very unusual and unexpected events. Bartlett discovered that people found it very difficult to recall the stories exactly, even after being allowed to study them repeatedly, and he hypothesized that the stories were difficult to remember because they did not fit the participants' expectations about how stories should go. The idea that our memory is influenced by what we already know was also a major idea behind the cognitive-developmental stage model of Swiss psychologist Jean Piaget (1896–1980). Other important cognitive psychologists include Donald E. Broadbent (1926–1993), Daniel Kahneman (1934–), George Miller (1920–), Eleanor Rosch (1938–), and Amos Tversky (1937–1996).

> ### cognitive psychology
> A field of psychology that studies mental processes, including perception, thinking, memory, and judgment.

The War of the Ghosts

The War of the Ghosts was a story used by Sir Frederic Bartlett to test the influence of prior expectations on memory. Bartlett found that even when his British research participants were allowed to read the story many times they still could not remember it well, and he believed this was because it did not fit with their prior knowledge.

One night two young men from Egulac went down to the river to hunt seals and while they were there it became foggy and calm. Then they heard war-cries, and they thought: "Maybe this is a war-party." They escaped to the shore, and hid behind a log. Now canoes came up, and they heard the noise of paddles, and saw one canoe coming up to them. There were five men in the canoe, and they said:

"What do you think? We wish to take you along. We are going up the river to make war on the people."

One of the young men said, "I have no arrows."

"Arrows are in the canoe," they said.

"I will not go along. I might be killed. My relatives do not know where I have gone. But you," he said, turning to the other, "may go with them."

So one of the young men went, but the other returned home.

And the warriors went on up the river to a town on the other side of Kalama. The people came down to the water and they began to fight, and many were killed. But presently the young man heard one of the warriors say, "Quick, let us go home: that Indian has been hit." Now he thought: "Oh, they are ghosts." He did not feel sick, but they said he had been shot.

So the canoes went back to Egulac and the young man went ashore to his house and made a fire. And he told everybody and said: "Behold I accompanied the ghosts, and we went to fight. Many of our fellows were killed, and many of those who attacked us were killed. They said I was hit, and I did not feel sick."

He told it all, and then he became quiet. When the sun rose he fell down. Something black came out of his mouth. His face became contorted. The people jumped up and cried.

He was dead. (Bartlett, 1932)[28]

FIGURE 1.12

Cognitive psychologists, such as (from left to right) Jean Piaget, George Miller, and Eleanor Rosch work to understand how people learn, remember, and make judgments about the world around them.

Sources: Piaget photo courtesy of David Kauppi, http://www.flickr.com/photos/vansterpsykologerna/3407151541/in/photostream. Miller photo courtesy of Association for Psychological Science http://www.psychologicalscience.org/anniversary/timeline.cfm. Rosch photo courtesy of the University of Pittsburgh, http://www.sis.pitt.edu/~mbsclass/hall_of_fame/rosch.html.

In its argument that our thinking has a powerful influence on behavior, the cognitive approach provided a distinct alternative to behaviorism. According to cognitive psychologists, ignoring the mind itself will never be sufficient because people interpret the stimuli that they experience. For instance, when a boy turns to a girl on a date and says, "You are so beautiful," a behaviorist would probably see that as a reinforcing (positive) stimulus. And yet the girl might not be so easily fooled. She might try to understand why the boy is making this particular statement at this particular time and wonder if he might be attempting to influence her through the comment. Cognitive psychologists maintain that when we take into consideration how stimuli are evaluated and interpreted, we understand behavior more deeply.

neuroimaging

The use of various techniques to provide pictures of the structure and function of the living brain.

Cognitive psychology remains enormously influential today, and it has guided research in such varied fields as language, problem solving, memory, intelligence, education, human development, social psychology, and psychotherapy. The cognitive revolution has been given even more life over the past decade as the result of recent advances in our ability to see the brain in action using *neuroimaging* techniques. **Neuroimaging** is *the use of various techniques to provide pictures of the structure and function of the living brain* (Ilardi & Feldman, 2001).[29] These images are used to diagnose brain disease and injury, but they also allow researchers to view information processing as it occurs in the brain, because the processing causes the involved area of the brain to increase metabolism and show up on the scan. We have already discussed the use of one neuroimaging technique, functional magnetic resonance imaging (fMRI), in the research focus earlier in this section, and we will discuss the use of neuroimaging techniques in many areas of psychology in the chapters to follow.

2.7 Social-Cultural Psychology

social-cultural psychology

A field of psychology that focuses on how the social situations and the cultures in which people find themselves influence thinking and behavior.

A final school, which takes a higher level of analysis and which has had substantial impact on psychology, can be broadly referred to as the *social-cultural approach*. The field of **social-cultural psychology** is *the study of how the social situations and the cultures in which people find themselves influence thinking and behavior*. Social-cultural psychologists are particularly concerned with how people perceive themselves and others, and how people influence each other's behavior. For instance, social psychologists have found that we are attracted to others who are similar to us in terms of attitudes and interests (Byrne, 1969),[30] that we develop our own beliefs and attitudes by comparing our opinions to those of others (Festinger, 1954),[31] and that we frequently change our beliefs and behaviors to be similar to those of the people we care about—a process known as *conformity*.

An important aspect of social-cultural psychology are **social norms**—*the ways of thinking, feeling, or behaving that are shared by group members and perceived by them as appropriate* (Asch, 1952; Cialdini, 1993).[32] Norms include customs, traditions, standards, and rules, as well as the general values of the group. Many of the most important social norms are determined by the *culture* in which we live, and these cultures are studied by *cross-cultural psychologists*. A **culture** represents *the common set of social norms, including religious and family values and other moral beliefs, shared by the people who live in a geographical region* (Fiske, Kitayama, Markus, & Nisbett, 1998; Markus, Kitayama, & Heiman, 1996; Matsumoto, 2001).[33] Cultures influence every aspect of our lives, and it is not inappropriate to say that our culture defines our lives just as much as does our evolutionary experience (Mesoudi, 2009).[34]

Psychologists have found that there is a fundamental difference in social norms between Western cultures (including those in the United States, Canada, Western Europe, Australia, and New Zealand) and East Asian cultures (including those in China, Japan, Taiwan, Korea, India, and Southeast Asia). Norms in Western cultures are primarily oriented toward *individualism*, which is about valuing the self and one's independence from others. Children in Western cultures are taught to develop and to value a sense of their personal self, and to see themselves in large part as separate from the other people around them. Children in Western cultures feel special about themselves; they enjoy getting gold stars on their projects and the best grade in the class. Adults in Western cultures are oriented toward promoting their own individual success, frequently in comparison to (or even at the expense of) others.

Norms in the East Asian culture, on the other hand, are oriented toward interdependence or *collectivism*. In these cultures children are taught to focus on developing harmonious social relationships with others. The predominant norms relate to group togetherness and connectedness, and duty and responsibility to one's family and other groups. When asked to describe themselves, the members of East Asian cultures are more likely than those from Western cultures to indicate that they are particularly concerned about the interests of others, including their close friends and their colleagues.

Another important cultural difference is the extent to which people in different cultures are bound by social norms and customs, rather than being free to express their own individuality without considering social norms (Chan, Gelfand, Triandis, & Tzeng, 1996).[35] Cultures also differ in terms of personal space, such as how closely individuals stand to each other when talking, as well as the communication styles they employ.

It is important to be aware of cultures and cultural differences because people with different cultural backgrounds increasingly come into contact with each other as a result of increased travel and immigration and the development of the Internet and other forms of communication. In the United States, for instance, there are many different ethnic groups, and the proportion of the population that comes from minority (non-White) groups is increasing from year to year. The social-cultural approach to understanding behavior reminds us again of the difficulty of making broad generalizations about human nature. Different people experience things differently, and they experience them differently in different cultures.

social norms

The ways of thinking, feeling, or behaving that are shared by group members and are perceived by them as appropriate.

culture

A common set of social norms, including religious and family values and other moral beliefs, shared by the people who live in a geographical region.

FIGURE 1.13

In Western cultures social norms promote a focus on the self (*individualism*), whereas in Eastern cultures the focus is more on families and social groups (*collectivism*).

© *Thinkstock*

2.8 The Many Disciplines of Psychology

Psychology is not one discipline but rather a collection of many subdisciplines that all share at least some common approaches and that work together and exchange knowledge to form a coherent discipline (Yang & Chiu, 2009).[36] Because the field of psychology is so broad, students may wonder which areas are most suitable for their interests and which types of careers might be available to them. Table 1.3 will help you consider the answers to these questions. You can learn more about these different fields of psychology and the careers associated with them at http://www.apa.org/careers/psyccareers/.

TABLE 1.3 Some Career Paths in Psychology

Psychology field	Description	Career opportunities
Biopsychology and neuroscience	This field examines the physiological bases of behavior in animals and humans by studying the functioning of different brain areas and the effects of hormones and neurotransmitters on behavior.	Most biopsychologists work in research settings—for instance, at universities, for the federal government, and in private research labs.
Clinical and counseling psychology	These are the largest fields of psychology. The focus is on the assessment, diagnosis, causes, and treatment of mental disorders.	Clinical and counseling psychologists provide therapy to patients with the goal of improving their life experiences. They work in hospitals, schools, social agencies, and in private practice. Because the demand for this career is high, entry to academic programs is highly competitive.
Cognitive psychology	This field uses sophisticated research methods, including reaction time and brain imaging to study memory, language, and thinking of humans.	Cognitive psychologists work primarily in research settings, although some (such as those who specialize in human-computer interactions) consult for businesses.
Developmental psychology	These psychologists conduct research on the cognitive, emotional, and social changes that occur across the lifespan.	Many work in research settings, although others work in schools and community agencies to help improve and evaluate the effectiveness of intervention programs such as Head Start.
Forensic psychology	Forensic psychologists apply psychological principles to understand the behavior of judges, attorneys, courtroom juries, and others in the criminal justice system.	Forensic psychologists work in the criminal justice system. They may testify in court and may provide information about the reliability of eyewitness testimony and jury selection.
Health psychology	Health psychologists are concerned with understanding how biology, behavior, and the social situation influence health and illness.	Health psychologists work with medical professionals in clinical settings to promote better health, conduct research, and teach at universities.
Industrial-organizational and environmental psychology	Industrial-organizational psychology applies psychology to the workplace with the goal of improving the performance and well-being of employees.	There are a wide variety of career opportunities in these fields, generally working in businesses. These psychologists help select employees, evaluate employee performance, and examine the effects of different working conditions on behavior. They may also work to design equipment and environments that improve employee performance and reduce accidents.
Personality psychology	These psychologists study people and the differences among them. The goal is to develop theories that explain the psychological processes of individuals, and to focus on individual differences.	Most work in academic settings, but the skills of personality psychologists are also in demand in business—for instance, in advertising and marketing. PhD programs in personality psychology are often connected with programs in social psychology.
School and educational psychology	This field studies how people learn in school, the effectiveness of school programs, and the psychology of teaching.	School psychologists work in elementary and secondary schools or school district offices with students, teachers, parents, and administrators. They may assess children's psychological and learning problems and develop programs to minimize the impact of these problems.
Social and cross-cultural psychology	This field examines people's interactions with other people. Topics of study include conformity, group behavior, leadership, attitudes, and person perception.	Many social psychologists work in marketing, advertising, organizational, systems design, and other applied psychology fields.
Sports psychology	This field studies the psychological aspects of sports behavior. The goal is to understand the psychological factors that influence performance in sports, including the role of exercise and team interactions.	Sports psychologists work in gyms, schools, professional sports teams, and other areas where sports are practiced.

Psychology in Everyday Life: How to Effectively Learn and Remember

One way that the findings of psychological research may be particularly helpful to you is in terms of improving your learning and study skills. Psychological research has provided a substantial amount of knowledge about the principles of learning and memory. This information can help you do better in this and other courses, and can also help you better learn new concepts and techniques in other areas of your life.

The most important thing you can learn in college is how to better study, learn, and remember. These skills will help you throughout your life, as you learn new jobs and take on other responsibilities. There are substantial individual differences in learning and memory, such that some people learn faster than others. But even if it takes you longer to learn than you think it should, the extra time you put into studying is well worth the effort. And you can learn to learn—learning to effectively study and to remember information is just like learning any other skill, such as playing a sport or a video game.

To learn well, you need to be ready to learn. You cannot learn well when you are tired, when you are under stress, or if you are abusing alcohol or drugs. Try to keep a consistent routine of sleeping and eating. Eat moderately and nutritiously, and avoid drugs that can impair memory, particularly alcohol. There is no evidence that stimulants such as caffeine, amphetamines, or any of the many "memory enhancing drugs" on the market will help you learn (Gold, Cahill, & Wenk, 2002; McDaniel, Maier, & Einstein, 2002).[37] Memory supplements are usually no more effective than drinking a can of sugared soda, which also releases glucose and thus improves memory slightly.

Psychologists have studied the ways that best allow people to acquire new information, to retain it over time, and to retrieve information that has been stored in our memories. One important finding is that learning is an active process. To acquire information most effectively, we must actively manipulate it. One active approach is rehearsal—repeating the information that is to be learned over and over again. Although simple repetition does help us learn, psychological research has found that we acquire information most effectively when we actively think about or elaborate on its meaning and relate the material to something else.

When you study, try to elaborate by connecting the information to other things that you already know. If you want to remember the different schools of psychology, for instance, try to think about how each of the approaches is different from the others. As you make the comparisons among the approaches, determine what is most important about each one and then relate it to the features of the other approaches. In an important study showing the effectiveness of elaborative encoding, Rogers, Kuiper, and Kirker (1977)[38] found that students learned information best when they related it to aspects of themselves (a phenomenon known as the *self-reference effect*). This research suggests that imagining how the material relates to your own interests and goals will help you learn it.

An approach known as the *method of loci* involves linking each of the pieces of information that you need to remember to places that you are familiar with. You might think about the house that you grew up in and the rooms in it. Then you could put the behaviorists in the bedroom, the structuralists in the living room, and the functionalists in the kitchen. Then when you need to remember the information, you retrieve the mental image of your house and should be able to "see" each of the people in each of the areas.

One of the most fundamental principles of learning is known as the *spacing effect*. Both humans and animals more easily remember or learn material when they study the material in several shorter study periods over a longer period of time, rather than studying it just once for a long period of time. Cramming for an exam is a particularly ineffective way to learn.

Psychologists have also found that performance is improved when people set difficult yet realistic goals for themselves (Locke & Latham, 2006).[39] You can use this knowledge to help you learn. Set realistic goals for the time you are going to spend studying and what you are going to learn, and try to stick to those goals. Do a small amount every day, and by the end of the week you will have accomplished a lot.

Our ability to adequately assess our own knowledge is known as *metacognition*. Research suggests that our metacognition may make us overconfident, leading us to believe that we have learned material even when we have not. To counteract this problem, don't just go over your notes again and again. Instead, make a list of questions and then see if you can answer them. Study the information again and then test yourself again after a few minutes. If you made any mistakes, study again. Then wait for a half hour and test yourself again. Then test again after 1 day and after 2 days. Testing yourself by attempting to retrieve information in an active manner is better than simply studying the material because it will help you determine if you really know it.

In summary, everyone can learn to learn better. Learning is an important skill, and following the previously mentioned guidelines will likely help you learn better.

KEY TAKEAWAYS

- The first psychologists were philosophers, but the field became more empirical and objective as more sophisticated scientific approaches were developed and employed.
- Some basic questions asked by psychologists include those about nature versus nurture, free will versus determinism, accuracy versus inaccuracy, and conscious versus unconscious processing.
- The structuralists attempted to analyze the nature of consciousness using introspection.
- The functionalists based their ideas on the work of Darwin, and their approaches led to the field of evolutionary psychology.
- The behaviorists explained behavior in terms of stimulus, response, and reinforcement, while denying the presence of free will.
- Cognitive psychologists study how people perceive, process, and remember information.
- Psychodynamic psychology focuses on unconscious drives and the potential to improve lives through psychoanalysis and psychotherapy.
- The social-cultural approach focuses on the social situation, including how cultures and social norms influence our behavior.

EXERCISES AND CRITICAL THINKING

1. What type of questions can psychologists answer that philosophers might not be able to answer as completely or as accurately? Explain why you think psychologists can answer these questions better than philosophers can.
2. Choose one of the major questions of psychology and provide some evidence from your own experience that supports one side or the other.
3. Choose two of the fields of psychology discussed in this section and explain how they differ in their approaches to understanding behavior and the level of explanation at which they are focused.

3. CHAPTER SUMMARY

Psychology is the scientific study of mind and behavior. Most psychologists work in research laboratories, hospitals, and other field settings where they study the behavior of humans and animals. Some psychologists are researchers and others are practitioners, but all psychologists use scientific methods to inform their work.

Although it is easy to think that everyday situations have commonsense answers, scientific studies have found that people are not always as good at predicting outcomes as they often think they are. The hindsight bias leads us to think that we could have predicted events that we could not actually have predicted.

Employing the scientific method allows psychologists to objectively and systematically understand human behavior.

Psychologists study behavior at different levels of explanation, ranging from lower biological levels to higher social and cultural levels. The same behaviors can be studied and explained within psychology at different levels of explanation.

The first psychologists were philosophers, but the field became more objective as more sophisticated scientific approaches were developed and employed. Some of the most important historical schools of psychology include structuralism, functionalism, behaviorism, and psychodynamic psychology. Cognitive psychology, evolutionary psychology, and social-cultural psychology are some important contemporary approaches.

Some of the basic questions asked by psychologists, both historically and currently, include those about the relative roles of nature versus nurture in behavior, free will versus determinism, accuracy versus inaccuracy, and conscious versus unconscious processing.

Psychological phenomena are complex, and making predictions about them is difficult because they are multiply determined at different levels of explanation. Research has found that people are frequently unaware of the causes of their own behaviors.

There are a variety of available career choices within psychology that provide employment in many different areas of interest.

ENDNOTES

1. Nisbett, R. E., & Ross, L. (1980). *Human inference: Strategies and shortcomings of social judgment.* Englewood Cliffs, NJ: Prentice Hall.

2. Heider, F. (1958). *The psychology of interpersonal relations.* Hillsdale, NJ: Erlbaum; Kelley, H. H. (1967). Attribution theory in social psychology. In D. Levine (Ed.), *Nebraska symposium on motivation* (Vol. 15, pp. 192–240). Lincoln: University of Nebraska Press.

3. Cutler, B. L., & Wells, G. L. (2009). Expert testimony regarding eyewitness identification. In J. L. Skeem, S. O. Lilienfeld, & K. S. Douglas (Eds.), *Psychological science in the courtroom: Consensus and controversy* (pp. 100–123). New York, NY: Guilford Press; Wells, G. L., & Hasel, L. E. (2008). Eyewitness identification: Issues in common knowledge and generalization. In E. Borgida & S. T. Fiske (Eds.), *Beyond common sense: Psychological science in the courtroom* (pp. 159–176). Malden, NJ: Blackwell.

4. Gilovich, T. (1993). *How we know what isn't so: The fallibility of human reason in everyday life.* New York, NY: Free Press.

5. Fiske, S. T., & Taylor, S. E. (2007). *Social cognition: From brains to culture.* New York, NY: McGraw-Hill.; Hsee, C. K., & Hastie, R. (2006). Decision and experience: Why don't we choose what makes us happy? *Trends in Cognitive Sciences, 10*(1), 31–37.

6. Brendl, C. M., Chattopadhyay, A., Pelham, B. W., & Carvallo, M. (2005). Name letter branding: Valence transfers when product specific needs are active. *Journal of Consumer Research, 32*(3), 405–415.

7. Cacioppo, J. T., Berntson, G. G., Sheridan, J. F., & McClintock, M. K. (2000). Multilevel integrative analyses of human behavior: Social neuroscience and the complementing nature of social and biological approaches. *Psychological Bulletin, 126*(6), 829–843.

8. Williams, N., Simpson, A. N., Simpson, K., & Nahas, Z. (2009). Relapse rates with long-term antidepressant drug therapy: A meta-analysis. *Human Psychopharmacology: Clinical and Experimental, 24*(5), 401–408.

9. Chen, P.-Y., Wang, S.-C., Poland, R. E., & Lin, K.-M. (2009). Biological variations in depression and anxiety between East and West. *CNS Neuroscience & Therapeutics, 15*(3), 283–294; Seedat, S., Scott, K. M., Angermeyer, M. C., Berglund, P., Bromet, E. J., Brugha, T. S.,…Kessler, R. C. (2009). Cross-national associations between gender and mental disorders in the World Health Organization World Mental Health Surveys. *Archives of General Psychiatry, 66*(7), 785–795.

10. Wilson, E. O. (1998). *Consilience: The unity of knowledge.* New York, NY: Vintage Books.

11. Benjamin, L. T., Jr., & Baker, D. B. (2004). *From seance to science: A history of the profession of psychology in America.* Belmont, CA: Wadsworth/Thomson.

12. Harris, J. (1998). *The nurture assumption: Why children turn out the way they do.* New York, NY: Touchstone Books; Pinker, S. (2002). *The blank slate: The modern denial of human nature.* New York, NY: Penguin Putnam.

13. Wegner, D. M. (2002). *The illusion of conscious will.* Cambridge, MA: MIT Press.

14. Fiske, S. T. (2003). *Social beings.* Hoboken, NJ: John Wiley & Sons.

15. Hunt, M. (1993). *The story of psychology.* New York, NY: Anchor Books.

16. James, W. (1890). *The principles of psychology.* New York, NY: Dover.

17. Dennett, D. (1995). *Darwin's dangerous idea: Evolution and the meanings of life.* New York, NY: Simon and Schuster; Tooby, J., & Cosmides, L. (1992). The psychological foundations of culture. In J. H. Barkow & L. Cosmides (Eds.), *The adapted mind: Evolutionary psychology and the generation of culture* (p. 666). New York, NY: Oxford University Press.

18. Buss, D. M. (2000). *The dangerous passion: Why jealousy is as necessary as love and sex.* New York, NY: Free Press.

19. Gould, S. J., & Lewontin, R. C. (1979). The spandrels of San Marco and the Panglossian paradigm: A critique of the adaptationist programme. In *Proceedings of the Royal Society of London* (Series B, Vol. 205, pp. 581–598).

20. Moore, B. E., & Fine, B. D. (1995). *Psychoanalysis: The major concepts.* New Haven, CT: Yale University Press.

21. Watson, J. B., Rayner, R. (1920). Conditioned emotional reactions. *Journal of Experimental Psychology, 3*(1), 1–14; Beck, H. P., Levinson, S., & Irons, G. (2009). Finding Little Albert: A journey to John B. Watson's infant laboratory. *American Psychologist, 64*(7), 605–614.

22. Skinner, B. (1957). *Verbal behavior.* Acton, MA: Copley; Skinner, B. (1968). *The technology of teaching.* New York, NY: Appleton-Century-Crofts; Skinner, B. (1972). *Beyond freedom and dignity.* New York, NY: Vintage Books.

23. Libet, B. (1985). Unconscious cerebral initiative and the role of conscious will in voluntary action. *Behavioral and Brain Sciences, 8*(4), 529–566; Matsuhashi, M., & Hallett, M. (2008). The timing of the conscious intention to move. *European Journal of Neuroscience, 28*(11), 2344–2351; Wegner, D. M. (2002). *The illusion of conscious will.* Cambridge, MA: MIT Press.

24. Soon, C. S., Brass, M., Heinze, H.-J., & Haynes, J.-D. (2008). Unconscious determinants of free decisions in the human brain. *Nature Neuroscience, 11*(5), 543–545.

25. Aarts, H., Custers, R., & Wegner, D. M. (2005). On the inference of personal authorship: Enhancing experienced agency by priming effect information. *Consciousness and Cognition: An International Journal, 14*(3), 439–458.

26. Dijksterhuis, A., Preston, J., Wegner, D. M., & Aarts, H. (2008). Effects of subliminal priming of self and God on self-attribution of authorship for events. *Journal of Experimental Social Psychology, 44*(1), 2–9.

27. Wegner, D. M. (2003). The mind's best trick: How we experience conscious will. *Trends in Cognitive Sciences, 7*(2), 65–69.

28. Bartlett, F. C. (1932). *Remembering.* Cambridge: Cambridge University Press.

29. Ilardi, S. S., & Feldman, D. (2001). The cognitive neuroscience paradigm: A unifying metatheoretical framework for the science and practice of clinical psychology. *Journal of Clinical Psychology, 57*(9), 1067–1088.

30. Byrne, D. (1969). Attitudes and attraction. In L. Berkowitz (Ed.), *Advances in experimental social psychology* (Vol. 4, pp. 35–89). New York, NY: Academic Press.

31. Festinger, L. (1954). A theory of social comparison processes. *Human Relations, 7,* 117–140.

32. Asch, S. E. (1952). *Social psychology.* Englewood Cliffs, NJ: Prentice Hall; Cialdini, R. B. (1993). *Influence: Science and practice* (3rd ed.). New York, NY: Harper Collins College.

33. Fiske, A., Kitayama, S., Markus, H., & Nisbett, R. (1998). The cultural matrix of social psychology. In D. Gilbert, S. Fiske, & G. Lindzey (Eds.), *The handbook of social psychology* (4th ed., pp. 915–981). New York, NY: McGraw-Hill; Markus, H. R., Kitayama, S., & Heiman, R. J. (1996). Culture and "basic" psychological principles. In E. T. Higgins & A. W. Kruglanski (Eds.), *Social psychology: Handbook of basic principles* (pp. 857–913). New York, NY: Guilford Press; Matsumoto, D. (Ed.). (2001). *The handbook of culture and psychology.* New York, NY: Oxford University Press.

34. Mesoudi, A. (2009). How cultural evolutionary theory can inform social psychology and vice versa. *Psychological Review, 116*(4), 929–952.

35. Chan, D. K. S., Gelfand, M. J., Triandis, H. C., & Tzeng, O. (1996). Tightness-looseness revisited: Some preliminary analyses in Japan and the United States. *International Journal of Psychology, 31,* 1–12.

36. Yang, Y.-J., & Chiu, C.-Y. (2009). Mapping the structure and dynamics of psychological knowledge: Forty years of APA journal citations (1970–2009). *Review of General Psychology, 13*(4), 349–356.

37. Gold, P. E., Cahill, L., & Wenk, G. L. (2002). Ginkgo biloba: A cognitive enhancer? *Psychological Science in the Public Interest, 3*(1), 2–11; McDaniel, M. A., Maier, S. F., & Einstein, G. O. (2002). "Brain-specific" nutrients: A memory cure? *Psychological Science in the Public Interest, 3*(1), 12–38.

38. Rogers, T. B., Kuiper, N. A., & Kirker, W. S. (1977). Self-reference and the encoding of personal information. *Journal of Personality & Social Psychology, 35*(9), 677–688.

39. Locke, E. A., & Latham, G. P. (2006). New directions in goal-setting theory. *Current Directions in Psychological Science, 15*(5), 265–268

CHAPTER 2
Psychological Science

Psychologists study the behavior of both humans and animals, and the main purpose of this research is to help us understand people and to improve the quality of human lives. The results of psychological research are relevant to problems such as learning and memory, homelessness, psychological disorders, family instability, and aggressive behavior and violence. Psychological research is used in a range of important areas, from public policy to driver safety. It guides court rulings with respect to racism and sexism (Brown v. Board of Education, 1954; Fiske, Bersoff, Borgida, Deaux, & Heilman, 1991),[1] as well as court procedure, in the use of lie detectors during criminal trials, for example (Saxe, Dougherty, & Cross, 1985).[2] Psychological research helps us understand how driver behavior affects safety (Fajen & Warren, 2003),[3] which methods of educating children are most effective (Alexander & Winne, 2006; Woolfolk-Hoy, 2005),[4] how to best detect deception (DePaulo et al., 2003),[5] and the causes of terrorism (Borum, 2004).[6]

Some psychological research is basic research. **Basic research** is *research that answers fundamental questions about behavior*. For instance, biopsychologists study how nerves conduct impulses from the receptors in the skin to the brain, and cognitive psychologists investigate how different types of studying influence memory for pictures and words. There is no particular reason to examine such things except to acquire a better knowledge of how these processes occur. **Applied research** is *research that investigates issues that have implications for everyday life and provides solutions to everyday problems*. Applied research has been conducted to study, among many other things, the most effective methods for reducing depression, the types of advertising campaigns that serve to reduce drug and alcohol abuse, the key predictors of managerial success in business, and the indicators of effective government programs, such as Head Start.

Basic research and applied research inform each other, and advances in science occur more rapidly when each type of research is conducted (Lewin, 1999).[7] For instance, although research concerning the role of practice on memory for lists of words is basic in orientation, the results could potentially be applied to help children learn to read. Correspondingly, psychologist-practitioners who wish to reduce the spread of AIDS or to promote volunteering frequently base their programs on the results of basic research. This basic AIDS or volunteering research is then applied to help change people's attitudes and behaviors.

The results of psychological research are reported primarily in research articles published in scientific journals, and your instructor may require you to read some of these. The research reported in scientific journals has been evaluated, critiqued, and improved by scientists in the field through the process of *peer review*. In this book there are many citations to original research articles, and I encourage you to read those reports when you find a topic interesting. Most of these papers are readily available online through your college or university library. It is only by reading the original reports that you will really see how the research process works. Some of the most important journals in psychology are provided here for your information.

basic research

Research that answers fundamental questions about behavior.

applied research

Research that investigates issues that have implications for everyday life and provides solutions to everyday problems.

Psychological Journals

The following is a list of some of the most important journals in various subdisciplines of psychology. The research articles in these journals are likely to be available in your college library. You should try to read the primary source material in these journals when you can.

General Psychology

- *American Journal of Psychology*
- *American Psychologist*
- *Behavioral and Brain Sciences*
- *Psychological Bulletin*
- *Psychological Methods*
- *Psychological Review*
- *Psychological Science*

Biopsychology and Neuroscience

- *Behavioral Neuroscience*
- *Journal of Comparative Psychology*
- *Psychophysiology*

Clinical and Counseling Psychology

- *Journal of Abnormal Psychology*
- *Journal of Consulting and Clinical Psychology*
- *Journal of Counseling Psychology*

Cognitive Psychology

- *Cognition*
- *Cognitive Psychology*
- *Journal of Experimental Psychology*
- *Journal of Memory and Language*
- *Perception & Psychophysics*

Cross-Cultural, Personality, and Social Psychology

- *Journal of Cross-Cultural Psychology*
- *Journal of Experimental Social Psychology*
- *Journal of Personality*
- *Journal of Personality and Social Psychology*
- *Personality and Social Psychology Bulletin*

Developmental Psychology

- *Child Development*
- *Developmental Psychology*

Educational and School Psychology

- *Educational Psychologist*
- *Journal of Educational Psychology*
- *Review of Educational Research*

Environmental, Industrial, and Organizational Psychology

- *Journal of Applied Psychology*
- *Organizational Behavior and Human Decision Processes*
- *Organizational Psychology*
- *Organizational Research Methods*
- *Personnel Psychology*

In this chapter you will learn how psychologists develop and test their research ideas; how they measure the thoughts, feelings, and behavior of individuals; and how they analyze and interpret the data they collect. To really understand psychology, you must also understand how and why the research you are reading about was conducted and what the collected data mean. Learning about the principles and practices of psychological research will allow you to critically read, interpret, and evaluate research.

In addition to helping you learn the material in this course, the ability to interpret and conduct research is also useful in many of the careers that you might choose. For instance, advertising and marketing researchers study how to make advertising more effective, health and medical researchers study the impact of behaviors such as drug use and smoking on illness, and computer scientists study how people interact with computers. Furthermore, even if you are not planning a career as a researcher, jobs in almost any area of social, medical, or mental health science require that a worker be informed about psychological research.

1.   PSYCHOLOGISTS USE THE SCIENTIFIC METHOD TO GUIDE THEIR RESEARCH

LEARNING OBJECTIVES

1. Describe the principles of the scientific method and explain its importance in conducting and interpreting research.
2. Differentiate laws from theories and explain how research hypotheses are developed and tested.
3. Discuss the procedures that researchers use to ensure that their research with humans and with animals is ethical.

Psychologists aren't the only people who seek to understand human behavior and solve social problems. Philosophers, religious leaders, and politicians, among others, also strive to provide explanations for human behavior. But psychologists believe that research is the best tool for understanding human beings and their relationships with others. Rather than accepting the claim of a philosopher that people do (or do not) have free will, a psychologist would collect data to empirically test whether or not people are able to actively control their own behavior. Rather than accepting a politician's contention that creating (or abandoning) a new center for mental health will improve the lives of individuals in the inner city, a psychologist would empirically assess the effects of receiving mental health treatment on the quality of life of the recipients. The statements made by psychologists are **empirical**, which means they are *based on systematic collection and analysis of data.*

empirical

Based on systematic collection and analysis of data.

1.1   The Scientific Method

All scientists (whether they are physicists, chemists, biologists, sociologists, or psychologists) are engaged in the basic processes of collecting data and drawing conclusions about those data. The methods used by scientists have developed over many years and provide a common framework for developing, organizing, and sharing information. The **scientific method** is *the set of assumptions, rules, and procedures scientists use to conduct research.*

In addition to requiring that science be empirical, the scientific method demands that the procedures used be **objective**, or *free from the personal bias or emotions of the scientist.* The scientific method proscribes how scientists collect and analyze data, how they draw conclusions from data, and how they share data with others. These rules increase objectivity by placing data under the scrutiny of other scientists and even the public at large. Because data are reported objectively, other scientists know exactly how the scientist collected and analyzed the data. This means that they do not have to rely only on the scientist's own interpretation of the data; they may draw their own, potentially different, conclusions.

Most new research is designed to *replicate*—that is, to repeat, add to, or modify—previous research findings. The scientific method therefore results in an accumulation of scientific knowledge through

scientific method

The set of assumptions, rules, and procedures scientists use to conduct research.

objective

Free from the personal bias or emotions of the scientist.

the reporting of research and the addition to and modifications of these reported findings by other scientists.

1.2   Laws and Theories as Organizing Principles

laws

Principles that are so general as to apply to all situations in a given domain of inquiry.

One goal of research is to organize information into meaningful statements that can be applied in many situations. *Principles that are so general as to apply to all situations in a given domain of inquiry* are known as **laws**. There are well-known laws in the physical sciences, such as the law of gravity and the laws of thermodynamics, and there are some universally accepted laws in psychology, such as the law of effect and Weber's law. But because laws are very general principles and their validity has already been well established, they are themselves rarely directly subjected to scientific test.

theory

An integrated set of principles that explains and predicts many, but not all, observed relationships within a given domain of inquiry.

The next step down from laws in the hierarchy of organizing principles is theory. A **theory** is *an integrated set of principles that explains and predicts many, but not all, observed relationships within a given domain of inquiry*. One example of an important theory in psychology is the stage theory of cognitive development proposed by the Swiss psychologist Jean Piaget. The theory states that children pass through a series of cognitive stages as they grow, each of which must be mastered in succession before movement to the next cognitive stage can occur. This is an extremely useful theory in human development because it can be applied to many different content areas and can be tested in many different ways.

Good theories have four important characteristics. First, good theories are *general*, meaning they summarize many different outcomes. Second, they are *parsimonious*, meaning they provide the simplest possible account of those outcomes. The stage theory of cognitive development meets both of these requirements. It can account for developmental changes in behavior across a wide variety of domains, and yet it does so parsimoniously—by hypothesizing a simple set of cognitive stages. Third, good theories *provide ideas for future research*. The stage theory of cognitive development has been applied not only to learning about cognitive skills, but also to the study of children's moral (Kohlberg, 1966)[8] and gender (Ruble & Martin, 1998)[9] development.

falsifiable

A characteristic of a theory or research hypothesis in which the variables of interest can be adequately measured and the predicted relationships among the variables can be shown through research to be incorrect.

Finally, good theories are **falsifiable** (Popper, 1959),[10] which means *the variables of interest can be adequately measured and the relationships between the variables that are predicted by the theory can be shown through research to be incorrect*. The stage theory of cognitive development is falsifiable because the stages of cognitive reasoning can be measured and because if research discovers, for instance, that children learn new tasks before they have reached the cognitive stage hypothesized to be required for that task, then the theory will be shown to be incorrect.

No single theory is able to account for all behavior in all cases. Rather, theories are each limited in that they make accurate predictions in some situations or for some people but not in other situations or for other people. As a result, there is a constant exchange between theory and data: Existing theories are modified on the basis of collected data, and the new modified theories then make new predictions that are tested by new data, and so forth. When a better theory is found, it will replace the old one. This is part of the accumulation of scientific knowledge.

1.3   The Research Hypothesis

research hypothesis

A specific and falsifiable prediction about the relationship between or among two or more variables.

Theories are usually framed too broadly to be tested in a single experiment. Therefore, scientists use a more precise statement of the presumed relationship among specific parts of a theory—a research hypothesis—as the basis for their research. A **research hypothesis** is *a specific and falsifiable prediction about the relationship between or among two or more variables*, where a **variable** is *any attribute that can assume different values among different people or across different times or places*. The research hypothesis states the existence of a relationship between the variables of interest and the specific direction of that relationship. For instance, the research hypothesis "Using marijuana will reduce learning" predicts that there is a relationship between a variable "using marijuana" and another variable called "learning." Similarly, in the research hypothesis "Participating in psychotherapy will reduce anxiety," the variables that are expected to be related are "participating in psychotherapy" and "level of anxiety."

variable

Any attribute that can assume different values among different people or across different times or places.

When stated in an abstract manner, the ideas that form the basis of a research hypothesis are known as conceptual variables. **Conceptual variables** are *abstract ideas that form the basis of research hypotheses*. Sometimes the conceptual variables are rather simple—for instance, "age," "gender," or "weight." In other cases the conceptual variables represent more complex ideas, such as "anxiety," "cognitive development," "learning," self-esteem," or "sexism."

conceptual variables

Abstract ideas that form the basis of research hypotheses.

The first step in testing a research hypothesis involves turning the conceptual variables into **measured variables**, which are *variables consisting of numbers that represent the conceptual variables.* For instance, the conceptual variable "participating in psychotherapy" could be represented as the measured variable "number of psychotherapy hours the patient has accrued" and the conceptual variable "using marijuana" could be assessed by having the research participants rate, on a scale from 1 to 10, how often they use marijuana or by administering a blood test that measures the presence of the chemicals in marijuana.

Psychologists use the term **operational definition** to refer to *a precise statement of how a conceptual variable is turned into a measured variable.* The relationship between conceptual and measured variables in a research hypothesis is diagrammed in Figure 2.1. The conceptual variables are represented within circles at the top of the figure, and the measured variables are represented within squares at the bottom. The two vertical arrows, which lead from the conceptual variables to the measured variables, represent the operational definitions of the two variables. The arrows indicate the expectation that changes in the conceptual variables (psychotherapy and anxiety in this example) will cause changes in the corresponding measured variables. The measured variables are then used to draw inferences about the conceptual variables.

FIGURE 2.1   Diagram of a Research Hypothesis

In this research hypothesis, the conceptual variable of attending psychotherapy is operationalized using the number of hours of psychotherapy the client has completed, and the conceptual variable of anxiety is operationalized using self-reported levels of anxiety. The research hypothesis is that more psychotherapy will be related to less reported anxiety.

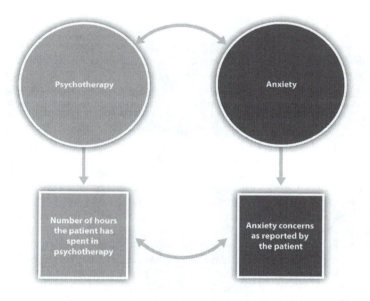

Table 2.1 lists some potential operational definitions of conceptual variables that have been used in psychological research. As you read through this list, note that in contrast to the abstract conceptual variables, the measured variables are very specific. This specificity is important for two reasons. First, more specific definitions mean that there is less danger that the collected data will be misunderstood by others. Second, specific definitions will enable future researchers to replicate the research.

measured variables

Variables consisting of numbers that represent the conceptual variables.

operational definition

A precise statement of how a conceptual variable is turned into a measured variable.

TABLE 2.1 Examples of the Operational Definitions of Conceptual Variables That Have Been Used in Psychological Research

Conceptual variable	Operational definitions
Aggression	■ Number of presses of a button that administers shock to another student ■ Number of seconds taken to honk the horn at the car ahead after a stoplight turns green
Interpersonal attraction	■ Number of inches that an individual places his or her chair away from another person ■ Number of millimeters of pupil dilation when one person looks at another
Employee satisfaction	■ Number of days per month an employee shows up to work on time ■ Rating of job satisfaction from 1 (*not at all satisfied*) to 9 (*extremely satisfied*)
Decision-making skills	■ Number of groups able to correctly solve a group performance task ■ Number of seconds in which a person solves a problem
Depression	■ Number of negative words used in a creative story ■ Number of appointments made with a psychotherapist

1.4   Conducting Ethical Research

One of the questions that all scientists must address concerns the ethics of their research. Physicists are concerned about the potentially harmful outcomes of their experiments with nuclear materials. Biologists worry about the potential outcomes of creating genetically engineered human babies. Medical researchers agonize over the ethics of withholding potentially beneficial drugs from control groups in clinical trials. Likewise, psychologists are continually considering the ethics of their research.

Research in psychology may cause some stress, harm, or inconvenience for the people who participate in that research. For instance, researchers may require introductory psychology students to participate in research projects and then deceive these students, at least temporarily, about the nature of the research. Psychologists may induce stress, anxiety, or negative moods in their participants, expose them to weak electrical shocks, or convince them to behave in ways that violate their moral standards. And researchers may sometimes use animals in their research, potentially harming them in the process.

Decisions about whether research is ethical are made using established ethical codes developed by scientific organizations, such as the American Psychological Association, and federal governments. In the United States, the Department of Health and Human Services provides the guidelines for ethical standards in research. Some research, such as the research conducted by the Nazis on prisoners during World War II, is perceived as immoral by almost everyone. Other procedures, such as the use of animals in research testing the effectiveness of drugs, are more controversial.

Scientific research has provided information that has improved the lives of many people. Therefore, it is unreasonable to argue that because scientific research has costs, no research should be conducted. This argument fails to consider the fact that there are significant costs to *not* doing research and that these costs may be greater than the potential costs of conducting the research (Rosenthal, 1994).[11] In each case, before beginning to conduct the research, scientists have attempted to determine the potential risks and benefits of the research and have come to the conclusion that the potential benefits of conducting the research outweigh the potential costs to the research participants.

Characteristics of an Ethical Research Project Using Human Participants

- Trust and positive rapport are created between the researcher and the participant.
- The rights of both the experimenter and participant are considered, and the relationship between them is mutually beneficial.
- The experimenter treats the participant with concern and respect and attempts to make the research experience a pleasant and informative one.
- Before the research begins, the participant is given all information relevant to his or her decision to participate, including any possibilities of physical danger or psychological stress.
- The participant is given a chance to have questions about the procedure answered, thus guaranteeing his or her free choice about participating.

- After the experiment is over, any deception that has been used is made public, and the necessity for it is explained.
- The experimenter carefully debriefs the participant, explaining the underlying research hypothesis and the purpose of the experimental procedure in detail and answering any questions.
- The experimenter provides information about how he or she can be contacted and offers to provide information about the results of the research if the participant is interested in receiving it. (Stangor, 2011)[12]

This list presents some of the most important factors that psychologists take into consideration when designing their research. The most direct ethical concern of the scientist is to *prevent harm* to the research participants. One example is the well-known research of Stanley Milgram (1974)[13] investigating obedience to authority. In these studies, participants were induced by an experimenter to administer electric shocks to another person so that Milgram could study the extent to which they would obey the demands of an authority figure. Most participants evidenced high levels of stress resulting from the psychological conflict they experienced between engaging in aggressive and dangerous behavior and following the instructions of the experimenter. Studies such as those by Milgram are no longer conducted because the scientific community is now much more sensitized to the potential of such procedures to create emotional discomfort or harm.

Another goal of ethical research is to guarantee that participants have *free choice* regarding whether they wish to participate in research. Students in psychology classes may be allowed, or even required, to participate in research, but they are also always given an option to choose a different study to be in, or to perform other activities instead. And once an experiment begins, the research participant is always free to leave the experiment if he or she wishes to. Concerns with free choice also occur in institutional settings, such as in schools, hospitals, corporations, and prisons, when individuals are required by the institutions to take certain tests, or when employees are told or asked to participate in research.

Researchers must also protect the *privacy* of the research participants. In some cases data can be kept anonymous by not having the respondents put any identifying information on their questionnaires. In other cases the data cannot be anonymous because the researcher needs to keep track of which respondent contributed the data. In this case one technique is to have each participant use a unique code number to identify his or her data, such as the last four digits of the student ID number. In this way the researcher can keep track of which person completed which questionnaire, but no one will be able to connect the data with the individual who contributed them.

Perhaps the most widespread ethical concern to the participants in behavioral research is the extent to which researchers employ deception. **Deception** *occurs whenever research participants are not completely and fully informed about the nature of the research project before participating in it.* Deception may occur in an active way, such as when the researcher tells the participants that he or she is studying learning when in fact the experiment really concerns obedience to authority. In other cases the deception is more passive, such as when participants are not told about the hypothesis being studied or the potential use of the data being collected.

Some researchers have argued that no deception should ever be used in any research (Baumrind, 1985).[14] They argue that participants should always be told the complete truth about the nature of the research they are in, and that when participants are deceived there will be negative consequences, such as the possibility that participants may arrive at other studies already expecting to be deceived. Other psychologists defend the use of deception on the grounds that it is needed to get participants to act naturally and to enable the study of psychological phenomena that might not otherwise get investigated. They argue that it would be impossible to study topics such as altruism, aggression, obedience, and stereotyping without using deception because if participants were informed ahead of time what the study involved, this knowledge would certainly change their behavior. The codes of ethics of the American Psychological Association and other organizations allow researchers to use deception, but these codes also require them to explicitly consider how their research might be conducted without the use of deception.

deception

A situation that occurs whenever research participants are not completely and fully informed about the nature of the research project before participating in it.

1.5 Ensuring That Research Is Ethical

Making decisions about the ethics of research involves weighing the costs and benefits of conducting versus not conducting a given research project. The costs involve potential harm to the research participants and to the field, whereas the benefits include the potential for advancing knowledge about human behavior and offering various advantages, some educational, to the individual participants. Most generally, the ethics of a given research project are determined through a *cost-benefit analysis*, in which the costs are compared to the benefits. If the potential costs of the research appear to outweigh any potential benefits that might come from it, then the research should not proceed.

Institutional Review Board (IRB)

A committee of at least five members whose goal it is to determine cost-benefit ratio of research conducted within an institution.

informed consent

A procedure, conducted before a participant begins a research session, designed to explain the research procedures and inform the participant of his or her rights during the investigation.

Arriving at a cost-benefit ratio is not simple. For one thing, there is no way to know ahead of time what the effects of a given procedure will be on every person or animal who participates or what benefit to society the research is likely to produce. In addition, what is ethical is defined by the current state of thinking within society, and thus perceived costs and benefits change over time. The U.S. Department of Health and Human Services regulations require that all universities receiving funds from the department set up an *Institutional Review Board (IRB)* to determine whether proposed research meets department regulations. The **Institutional Review Board (IRB)** is *a committee of at least five members whose goal it is to determine the cost-benefit ratio of research conducted within an institution.* The IRB approves the procedures of all the research conducted at the institution before the research can begin. The board may suggest modifications to the procedures, or (in rare cases) it may inform the scientist that the research violates Department of Health and Human Services guidelines and thus cannot be conducted at all.

One important tool for ensuring that research is ethical is the use of *informed consent.* A sample informed consent form is shown in Figure 2.2. **Informed consent,** *conducted before a participant begins a research session, is designed to explain the research procedures and inform the participant of his or her rights during the investigation.* The informed consent explains as much as possible about the true nature of the study, particularly everything that might be expected to influence willingness to participate, but it may in some cases withhold some information that allows the study to work.

FIGURE 2.2 Sample Consent Form

The informed consent form explains the research procedures and informs the participant of his or her rights during the investigation.

Consent Form: Interactions

I state that I am 18 years of age or older and wish to participate in a program of research being conducted by Dr. Charles Stangor at the University of Maryland, College Park, Department of Psychology.

The purpose of the research is to study how individuals get to know each other. In the remainder of the study I will be having a short conversation with another person. This interaction will be videotaped. At the end of the interaction, I will be asked to complete some questionnaires about how I felt during and what I remember about the interaction. The entire experiment will take about 45 minutes.

I furthermore consent to allow the videotape that has been made of me and my partner to be used in the research. I understand that the videotape will be used for research purposes only, and no one else except the present experimenter and one other person who will help code the tape will ever view it.

I understand that code numbers will be used to identify the videotapes and that all written material that I contribute will be kept separate from the videos. As a result, it will not be possible to connect my name to my videotape.

I understand that both my partner and I have the right to withdraw the tape from the study at any point.

I understand that the experiment is not designed to help me personally but that the researchers hope to learn more about interpersonal interactions.

I understand that I am free to ask questions or to withdraw from participation at any time without penalty.

Dr. Charles Stangor
Department of Psychology
Room 3123
555-5921

Signature of participant

_____

Date

_____

Source: Adapted from Stangor, C. (2011). Research methods for the behavioral sciences (4th ed.). Mountain View, CA: Cengage.

debriefing

A procedure designed to fully
explain the purposes and
procedures of the research
and remove any harmful
aftereffects of participation.

Because participating in research has the potential for producing long-term changes in the research participants, all participants should be fully debriefed immediately after their participation. The **debriefing** is *a procedure designed to fully explain the purposes and procedures of the research and remove any harmful aftereffects of participation.*

1.6 Research With Animals

Because animals make up an important part of the natural world, and because some research cannot be conducted using humans, animals are also participants in psychological research. Most psychological research using animals is now conducted with rats, mice, and birds, and the use of other animals in research is declining (Thomas & Blackman, 1992).[15] As with ethical decisions involving human participants, a set of basic principles has been developed that helps researchers make informed decisions about such research; a summary is shown below.

APA Guidelines on Humane Care and Use of Animals in Research

The following are some of the most important ethical principles from the American Psychological Association's guidelines on research with animals.

- Psychologists acquire, care for, use, and dispose of animals in compliance with current federal, state, and local laws and regulations, and with professional standards.
- Psychologists trained in research methods and experienced in the care of laboratory animals supervise all procedures involving animals and are responsible for ensuring appropriate consideration of their comfort, health, and humane treatment.
- Psychologists ensure that all individuals under their supervision who are using animals have received instruction in research methods and in the care, maintenance, and handling of the species being used, to the extent appropriate to their role.
- Psychologists make reasonable efforts to minimize the discomfort, infection, illness, and pain of animal subjects.
- Psychologists use a procedure subjecting animals to pain, stress, or privation only when an alternative procedure is unavailable and the goal is justified by its prospective scientific, educational, or applied value.
- Psychologists perform surgical procedures under appropriate anesthesia and follow techniques to avoid infection and minimize pain during and after surgery.
- When it is appropriate that an animal's life be terminated, psychologists proceed rapidly, with an effort to minimize pain and in accordance with accepted procedures. (American Psychological Association, 2002)[16]

FIGURE 2.3

Psychologists may use animals in their research, but they make reasonable efforts to minimize the discomfort the animals experience.

© Thinkstock

Because the use of animals in research involves a personal value, people naturally disagree about this practice. Although many people accept the value of such research (Plous, 1996),[17] a minority of people, including animal-rights activists, believes that it is ethically wrong to conduct research on animals. This argument is based on the assumption that because animals are living creatures just as humans are, no harm should ever be done to them.

Most scientists, however, reject this view. They argue that such beliefs ignore the potential benefits that have and continue to come from research with animals. For instance, drugs that can reduce the incidence of cancer or AIDS may first be tested on animals, and surgery that can save human lives may first be practiced on animals. Research on animals has also led to a better understanding of the physiological causes of depression, phobias, and stress, among other illnesses. In contrast to animal-rights activists, then, scientists believe that because there are many benefits that accrue from animal research, such research can and should continue as long as the humane treatment of the animals used in the research is guaranteed.

KEY TAKEAWAYS

- Psychologists use the scientific method to generate, accumulate, and report scientific knowledge.
- Basic research, which answers questions about behavior, and applied research, which finds solutions to everyday problems, inform each other and work together to advance science.
- Research reports describing scientific studies are published in scientific journals so that other scientists and laypersons may review the empirical findings.
- Organizing principles, including laws, theories and research hypotheses, give structure and uniformity to scientific methods.
- Concerns for conducting ethical research are paramount. Researchers assure that participants are given free choice to participate and that their privacy is protected. Informed consent and debriefing help provide humane treatment of participants.
- A cost-benefit analysis is used to determine what research should and should not be allowed to proceed.

EXERCISES AND CRITICAL THINKING

1. Give an example from personal experience of how you or someone you know have benefited from the results of scientific research.
2. Find and discuss a research project that in your opinion has ethical concerns. Explain why you find these concerns to be troubling.
3. Indicate your personal feelings about the use of animals in research. When should and should not animals be used? What principles have you used to come to these conclusions?

2. PSYCHOLOGISTS USE DESCRIPTIVE, CORRELATIONAL, AND EXPERIMENTAL RESEARCH DESIGNS TO UNDERSTAND BEHAVIOR

LEARNING OBJECTIVES

1. Differentiate the goals of descriptive, correlational, and experimental research designs and explain the advantages and disadvantages of each.
2. Explain the goals of descriptive research and the statistical techniques used to interpret it.
3. Summarize the uses of correlational research and describe why correlational research cannot be used to infer causality.
4. Review the procedures of experimental research and explain how it can be used to draw causal inferences.

research design

An approach used to collect, analyze, and interpret data.

descriptive research

Research designed to provide a snapshot of the current state of affairs.

correlational research

Research designed to discover relationships among variables and to allow the prediction of future events from present knowledge.

experimental research

Research in which initial equivalence among research participants in more than one group is created, followed by a manipulation of a given experience for these groups and a measurement of the influence of the manipulation.

Psychologists agree that if their ideas and theories about human behavior are to be taken seriously, they must be backed up by data. However, the research of different psychologists is designed with different goals in mind, and the different goals require different approaches. These varying approaches, summarized in Table 2.2, are known as *research designs*. A **research design** is *the specific method a researcher uses to collect, analyze, and interpret data*. Psychologists use three major types of research designs in their research, and each provides an essential avenue for scientific investigation. **Descriptive research** is *research designed to provide a snapshot of the current state of affairs*. **Correlational research** is *research designed to discover relationships among variables and to allow the prediction of future events from present knowledge*. **Experimental research** is *research in which initial equivalence among research participants in more than one group is created, followed by a manipulation of a given experience for these groups and a measurement of the influence of the manipulation*. Each of the three research designs varies according to its strengths and limitations, and it is important to understand how each differs.

TABLE 2.2 Characteristics of the Three Research Designs

Research design	Goal	Advantages	Disadvantages
Descriptive	To create a snapshot of the current state of affairs	Provides a relatively complete picture of what is occurring at a given time. Allows the development of questions for further study.	Does not assess relationships among variables. May be unethical if participants do not know they are being observed.
Correlational	To assess the relationships between and among two or more variables	Allows testing of expected relationships between and among variables and the making of predictions. Can assess these relationships in everyday life events.	Cannot be used to draw inferences about the causal relationships between and among the variables.
Experimental	To assess the causal impact of one or more experimental manipulations on a dependent variable	Allows drawing of conclusions about the causal relationships among variables.	Cannot experimentally manipulate many important variables. May be expensive and time consuming.

There are three major research designs used by psychologists, and each has its own advantages and disadvantages.

Source: Stangor, C. (2011). Research methods for the behavioral sciences (4th ed.). Mountain View, CA: Cengage.

2.1 Descriptive Research: Assessing the Current State of Affairs

Descriptive research is designed to create a snapshot of the current thoughts, feelings, or behavior of individuals. This section reviews three types of descriptive research: *case studies*, *surveys*, and *naturalistic observation*.

Sometimes the data in a descriptive research project are based on only a small set of individuals, often only one person or a single small group. These research designs are known as **case studies**—*descriptive records of one or more individual's experiences and behavior.* Sometimes case studies involve ordinary individuals, as when developmental psychologist Jean Piaget used his observation of his own children to develop his stage theory of cognitive development. More frequently, case studies are conducted on individuals who have unusual or abnormal experiences or characteristics or who find themselves in particularly difficult or stressful situations. The assumption is that by carefully studying individuals who are socially marginal, who are experiencing unusual situations, or who are going through a difficult phase in their lives, we can learn something about human nature.

Sigmund Freud was a master of using the psychological difficulties of individuals to draw conclusions about basic psychological processes. Freud wrote case studies of some of his most interesting patients and used these careful examinations to develop his important theories of personality. One classic example is Freud's description of "Little Hans," a child whose fear of horses the psychoanalyst interpreted in terms of repressed sexual impulses and the Oedipus complex (Freud (1909/1964).[18]

Another well-known case study is Phineas Gage, a man whose thoughts and emotions were extensively studied by cognitive psychologists after a railroad spike was blasted through his skull in an accident. Although there is question about the interpretation of this case study (Kotowicz, 2007),[19] it did provide early evidence that the brain's frontal lobe is involved in emotion and morality (Damasio et al., 2005).[20] An interesting example of a case study in clinical psychology is described by Rokeach (1964),[21] who investigated in detail the beliefs and interactions among three patients with schizophrenia, all of whom were convinced they were Jesus Christ.

In other cases the data from descriptive research projects come in the form of a **survey**—*a measure administered through either an interview or a written questionnaire to get a picture of the beliefs or behaviors of a sample of people of interest.* The people *chosen to participate in the research* (known as the **sample**) are selected to be representative of *all the people that the researcher wishes to know about* (the **population**). In election polls, for instance, a sample is taken from the population of all "likely voters" in the upcoming elections.

The results of surveys may sometimes be rather mundane, such as "Nine out of ten doctors prefer Tymenocin," or "The median income in Montgomery County is $36,712." Yet other times (particularly in discussions of social behavior), the results can be shocking: "More than 40,000 people are killed by gunfire in the United States every year," or "More than 60% of women between the ages of 50 and 60 suffer from depression." Descriptive research is frequently used by psychologists to get an estimate of the prevalence (or *incidence*) of psychological disorders.

A final type of descriptive research—known as **naturalistic observation**—is *research based on the observation of everyday events.* For instance, a developmental psychologist who watches children on a playground and describes what they say to each other while they play is conducting descriptive research, as is a biopsychologist who observes animals in their natural habitats. One example of observational research involves a systematic procedure known as the *strange situation*, used to get a picture of how adults and young children interact. The data that are collected in the strange situation are systematically coded in a coding sheet such as that shown in Table 2.3.

case study

A descriptive record of one or more individual's experiences and behavior.

FIGURE 2.4

Political polls reported in newspapers and on the Internet are descriptive research designs that provide snapshots of the likely voting behavior of a population.

© *Thinkstock*

survey

A measure administered either through interviews or written questionnaires to get a picture of the beliefs or behaviors of a sample of people of interest.

sample

The people chosen to participate in a research project.

population

In a descriptive research design, the people that the researcher wishes to know about.

naturalistic observation

Research based on the observation of everyday events.

TABLE 2.3 Sample Coding Form Used to Assess Child's and Mother's Behavior in the Strange Situation

Coder name: *Olive*				
	Coding categories			
Episode	**Proximity**	**Contact**	**Resistance**	**Avoidance**
Mother and baby play alone	*1*	*1*	*1*	*1*
Mother puts baby down	*4*	*1*	*1*	*1*
Stranger enters room	*1*	*2*	*3*	*1*
Mother leaves room; stranger plays with baby	*1*	*3*	*1*	*1*
Mother reenters, greets and may comfort baby, then leaves again	*4*	*2*	*1*	*2*
Stranger tries to play with baby	*1*	*3*	*1*	*1*
Mother reenters and picks up baby	*6*	*6*	*1*	*2*
Coding categories explained				
Proximity	The baby moves toward, grasps, or climbs on the adult.			
Maintaining contact	The baby resists being put down by the adult by crying or trying to climb back up.			
Resistance	The baby pushes, hits, or squirms to be put down from the adult's arms.			
Avoidance	The baby turns away or moves away from the adult.			
This table represents a sample coding sheet from an episode of the "strange situation," in which an infant (usually about 1 year old) is observed playing in a room with two adults—the child's mother and a stranger. Each of the four coding categories is scored by the coder from 1 (the baby makes no effort to engage in the behavior) to 7 (the baby makes a significant effort to engage in the behavior). More information about the meaning of the coding can be found in Ainsworth, Blehar, Waters, and Wall (1978).[22]				

Source: Stangor, C. (2011). Research methods for the behavioral sciences (4th ed.). Mountain View, CA: Cengage.

descriptive statistics

Numbers that summarize the distribution of scores on a measured variable.

normal distribution

A data distribution that is shaped like a bell.

The results of descriptive research projects are analyzed using **descriptive statistics**—*numbers that summarize the distribution of scores on a measured variable.* Most variables have distributions similar to that shown in Figure 2.5, where most of the scores are located near the center of the distribution, and the distribution is symmetrical and bell-shaped. *A data distribution that is shaped like a bell* is known as a **normal distribution**.

TABLE 2.4 Height and Family Income for 25 Students

Student name	Height in inches	Family income in dollars
Lauren	62	48,000
Courtnie	62	57,000
Leslie	63	93,000
Renee	64	107,000
Katherine	64	110,000
Jordan	65	93,000
Rabiah	66	46,000
Alina	66	84,000
Young Su	67	68,000
Martin	67	49,000
Hanzhu	67	73,000
Caitlin	67	3,800,000
Steven	67	107,000
Emily	67	64,000
Amy	68	67,000
Jonathan	68	51,000
Julian	68	48,000
Alissa	68	93,000
Christine	69	93,000
Candace	69	111,000
Xiaohua	69	56,000
Charlie	70	94,000
Timothy	71	73,000
Ariane	72	70,000
Logan	72	44,000

FIGURE 2.5 Height Distribution

The distribution of the heights of the students in a class will form a normal distribution. In this sample the mean (M) = 67.12 and the standard deviation (s) = 2.74.

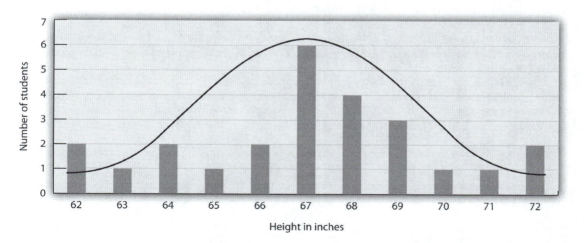

A distribution can be described in terms of its *central tendency*—that is, the point in the distribution around which the data are centered—and its *dispersion*, or spread. The arithmetic average, or **arithmetic mean**, is *the most commonly used measure of central tendency*. It is computed by calculating the sum of all the scores of the variable and dividing this sum by the number of participants in the

arithmetic mean

Symbolized by the letter *M*, the most commonly used measure of central tendency.

distribution (denoted by the letter *N*). In the data presented in Figure 2.5, the mean height of the students is 67.12 inches. The sample mean is usually indicated by the letter *M*.

In some cases, however, the data distribution is not symmetrical. This occurs when there are one or more extreme scores (known as *outliers*) at one end of the distribution. Consider, for instance, the variable of family income (see Figure 2.6), which includes an outlier (a value of $3,800,000). In this case the mean is not a good measure of central tendency. Although it appears from Figure 2.6 that the central tendency of the family income variable should be around $70,000, the mean family income is actually $223,960. The single very extreme income has a disproportionate impact on the mean, resulting in a value that does not well represent the central tendency.

The *median* is used as an alternative measure of central tendency when distributions are not symmetrical. The median is *the score in the center of the distribution, meaning that 50% of the scores are greater than the median and 50% of the scores are less than the median.* In our case, the median household income ($73,000) is a much better indication of central tendency than is the mean household income ($223,960).

median

The score in the center of the distribution, meaning that 50% of the scores are greater than the median and 50% of the scores are less than the median.

FIGURE 2.6 Family Income Distribution

The distribution of family incomes is likely to be nonsymmetrical because some incomes can be very large in comparison to most incomes. In this case the median or the mode is a better indicator of central tendency than is the mean.

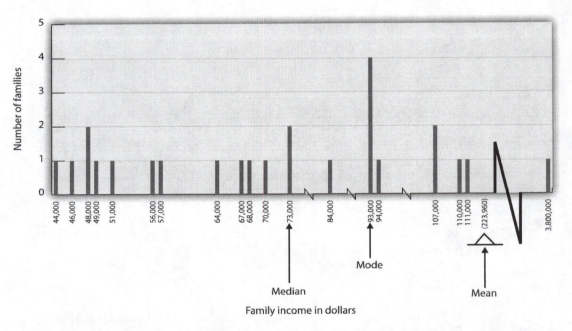

A final measure of central tendency, known as the **mode**, represents *the value that occurs most frequently in the distribution.* You can see from Figure 2.6 that the mode for the family income variable is $93,000 (it occurs four times).

In addition to summarizing the central tendency of a distribution, descriptive statistics convey information about how the scores of the variable are spread around the central tendency. *Dispersion* refers to the extent to which the scores are all tightly clustered around the central tendency, like this:

mode

The value or values that occur most frequently in a variable's distribution.

FIGURE 2.7

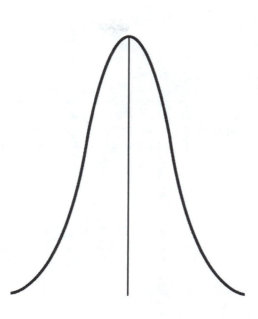

Or they may be more spread out away from it, like this:

FIGURE 2.8

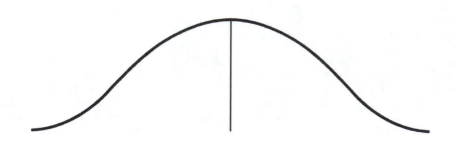

One simple measure of dispersion is to find the largest (the *maximum*) and the smallest (the *minimum*) observed values of the variable and to compute the *range* of the variable as the maximum observed score minus the minimum observed score. You can check that the range of the height variable in Figure 2.5 is 72 – 62 = 10. The **standard deviation**, symbolized as *s*, is *the most commonly used measure of dispersion*. Distributions with a larger standard deviation have more spread. The standard deviation of the height variable is *s* = 2.74, and the standard deviation of the family income variable is *s* = $745,337.

An advantage of descriptive research is that it attempts to capture the complexity of everyday behavior. Case studies provide detailed information about a single person or a small group of people, surveys capture the thoughts or reported behaviors of a large population of people, and naturalistic observation objectively records the behavior of people or animals as it occurs naturally. Thus descriptive research is used to provide a relatively complete understanding of what is currently happening.

Despite these advantages, descriptive research has a distinct disadvantage in that, although it allows us to get an idea of what is currently happening, it is usually limited to static pictures. Although descriptions of particular experiences may be interesting, they are not always transferable to other individuals in other situations, nor do they tell us exactly why specific behaviors or events occurred. For instance, descriptions of individuals who have suffered a stressful event, such as a war or an earthquake, can be used to understand the individuals' reactions to the event but cannot tell us anything about the long-term effects of the stress. And because there is no comparison group that did not experience the stressful situation, we cannot know what these individuals would be like if they hadn't had the stressful experience.

standard deviation

Symbolized by the letter *s*, the most commonly used measure of the dispersion of a variable's distribution.

2.2   Correlational Research: Seeking Relationships Among Variables

In contrast to descriptive research, which is designed primarily to provide static pictures, correlational research involves the measurement of two or more relevant variables and an assessment of the relationship between or among those variables. For instance, the variables of height and weight are systematically related (correlated) because taller people generally weigh more than shorter people. In the same way, study time and memory errors are also related, because the more time a person is given to study a list of words, the fewer errors he or she will make. When there are two variables in the research design, one of them is called the *predictor variable* and the other the *outcome variable*. The research design can be visualized like this, where the curved arrow represents the expected correlation between the two variables:

FIGURE 2.9

scatter plot

A visual image of the relationship between two variables.

One way of organizing the data from a correlational study with two variables is to graph the values of each of the measured variables using a *scatter plot*. As you can see in Figure 2.10, a scatter plot is *a visual image of the relationship between two variables*. A point is plotted for each individual at the intersection of his or her scores for the two variables. When the association between the variables on the scatter plot can be easily approximated with a straight line, as in parts (a) and (b) of Figure 2.10, the variables are said to have a *linear relationship*.

When the straight line indicates that individuals who have above-average values for one variable also tend to have above-average values for the other variable, as in part (a), the relationship is said to be *positive linear*. Examples of positive linear relationships include those between height and weight, between education and income, and between age and mathematical abilities in children. In each case people who score higher on one of the variables also tend to score higher on the other variable. *Negative linear relationships*, in contrast, as shown in part (b), occur when above-average values for one variable tend to be associated with below-average values for the other variable. Examples of negative linear relationships include those between the age of a child and the number of diapers the child uses, and between practice on and errors made on a learning task. In these cases people who score higher on one of the variables tend to score lower on the other variable.

Relationships between variables that cannot be described with a straight line are known as *nonlinear relationships*. Part (c) of Figure 2.10 shows a common pattern in which the distribution of the points is essentially random. In this case there is no relationship at all between the two variables, and they are said to be *independent*. Parts (d) and (e) of Figure 2.10 show patterns of association in which, although there is an association, the points are not well described by a single straight line. For instance, part (d) shows the type of relationship that frequently occurs between anxiety and performance. Increases in anxiety from low to moderate levels are associated with performance increases, whereas increases in anxiety from moderate to high levels are associated with decreases in performance. Relationships that change in direction and thus are not described by a single straight line are called *curvilinear relationships*.

FIGURE 2.10   Examples of Scatter Plots

Some examples of relationships between two variables as shown in scatter plots. Note that the Pearson correlation coefficient (*r*) between variables that have curvilinear relationships will likely be close to zero.

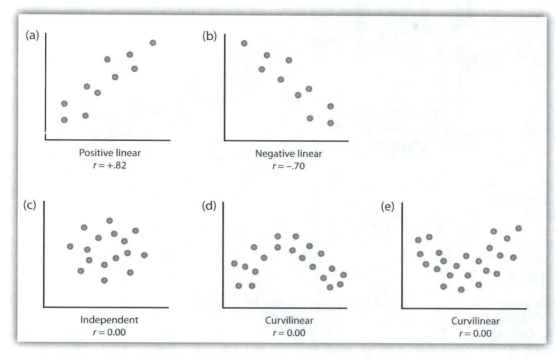

Source: *Adapted from Stangor, C. (2011). Research methods for the behavioral sciences (4th ed.). Mountain View, CA: Cengage.*

The most common statistical measure of the strength of linear relationships among variables is the **Pearson correlation coefficient**, which is symbolized by the letter *r*. The value of the correlation coefficient ranges from *r* = −1.00 to *r* = +1.00. The direction of the linear relationship is indicated by the sign of the correlation coefficient. Positive values of *r* (such as *r* = .54 or *r* = .67) indicate that the relationship is positive linear (i.e., the pattern of the dots on the scatter plot runs from the lower left to the upper right), whereas negative values of *r* (such as *r* = −.30 or *r* = −.72) indicate negative linear relationships (i.e., the dots run from the upper left to the lower right). The strength of the linear relationship is indexed by the distance of the correlation coefficient from zero (its absolute value). For instance, *r* = −.54 is a stronger relationship than *r* = .30, and *r* = .72 is a stronger relationship than *r* = −.57. Because the Pearson correlation coefficient only measures linear relationships, variables that have curvilinear relationships are not well described by *r*, and the observed correlation will be close to zero.

It is also possible to study relationships among more than two measures at the same time. A research design in which more than one predictor variable is used to predict a single outcome variable is analyzed through *multiple regression* (Aiken & West, 1991).[23] **Multiple regression** is *a statistical technique, based on correlation coefficients among variables, that allows predicting a single outcome variable from more than one predictor variable.* For instance, Figure 2.11 shows a multiple regression analysis in which three predictor variables are used to predict a single outcome. The use of multiple regression analysis shows an important advantage of correlational research designs—they can be used to make predictions about a person's likely score on an outcome variable (e.g., job performance) based on knowledge of other variables.

Pearson correlation coefficient

Symbolized by the letter *r*, a statistic indicating the strength and direction of a linear relationship. The value of the correlation coefficient ranges from *r* = −1.00 to *r* = +1.00.

multiple regression

A statistical technique, based on correlation coefficients among variables, that allows predicting a single outcome variable from more than one predictor variable.

FIGURE 2.11 **Prediction of Job Performance From Three Predictor Variables**

Multiple regression allows scientists to predict the scores on a single outcome variable using more than one predictor variable.

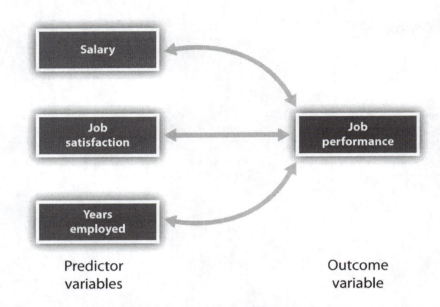

Predictor
variables

Outcome
variable

An important limitation of correlational research designs is that they cannot be used to draw conclusions about the causal relationships among the measured variables. Consider, for instance, a researcher who has hypothesized that viewing violent behavior will cause increased aggressive play in children. He has collected, from a sample of fourth-grade children, a measure of how many violent television shows each child views during the week, as well as a measure of how aggressively each child plays on the school playground. From his collected data, the researcher discovers a positive correlation between the two measured variables.

Although this positive correlation appears to support the researcher's hypothesis, it cannot be taken to indicate that viewing violent television causes aggressive behavior. Although the researcher is tempted to assume that viewing violent television causes aggressive play,

FIGURE 2.12

Viewing violent TV ⟶ Aggressive play

there are other possibilities. One alternate possibility is that the causal direction is exactly opposite from what has been hypothesized. Perhaps children who have behaved aggressively at school develop residual excitement that leads them to want to watch violent television shows at home:

FIGURE 2.13

Viewing violent TV ⟵ Aggressive play

Although this possibility may seem less likely, there is no way to rule out the possibility of such reverse causation on the basis of this observed correlation. It is also possible that both causal directions are operating and that the two variables cause each other:

FIGURE 2.14

Viewing violent TV ← → Aggressive play

Still another possible explanation for the observed correlation is that it has been produced by the presence of a *common-causal variable* (also known as a *third variable*). A **common-causal variable** is *a variable that is not part of the research hypothesis but that causes both the predictor and the outcome variable and thus produces the observed correlation between them.* In our example a potential common-causal variable is the discipline style of the children's parents. Parents who use a harsh and punitive discipline style may produce children who both like to watch violent television and who behave aggressively in comparison to children whose parents use less harsh discipline:

common-causal variable

A variable that is not part of the research hypothesis but that causes both the predictor and the outcome variable and thus produces the observed correlation between them.

FIGURE 2.15

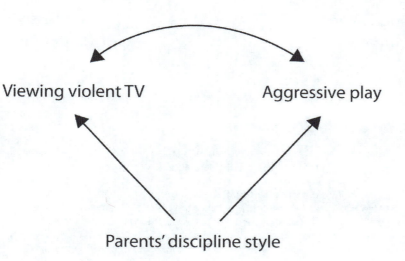

Viewing violent TV   Aggressive play

Parents' discipline style

In this case, television viewing and aggressive play would be positively correlated (as indicated by the curved arrow between them), even though neither one caused the other but they were both caused by the discipline style of the parents (the straight arrows). When the predictor and outcome variables are both caused by a common-causal variable, the observed relationship between them is said to be *spurious*. A **spurious relationship** is *a relationship between two variables in which a common-causal variable produces and "explains away" the relationship.* If effects of the common-causal variable were taken away, or controlled for, the relationship between the predictor and outcome variables would disappear. In the example the relationship between aggression and television viewing might be spurious because by controlling for the effect of the parents' disciplining style, the relationship between television viewing and aggressive behavior might go away.

Common-causal variables in correlational research designs can be thought of as "mystery" variables because, as they have not been measured, their presence and identity are usually unknown to the researcher. Since it is not possible to measure every variable that could cause both the predictor and outcome variables, the existence of an unknown common-causal variable is always a possibility. For this reason, we are left with the basic limitation of correlational research: Correlation does not demonstrate causation. It is important that when you read about correlational research projects, you keep in mind the possibility of spurious relationships, and be sure to interpret the findings appropriately. Although correlational research is sometimes reported as demonstrating causality without any mention being made of the possibility of reverse causation or common-causal variables, informed consumers of research, like you, are aware of these interpretational problems.

In sum, correlational research designs have both strengths and limitations. One strength is that they can be used when experimental research is not possible because the predictor variables cannot be manipulated. Correlational designs also have the advantage of allowing the researcher to study behavior as it occurs in everyday life. And we can also use correlational designs to make predictions—for instance, to predict from the scores on their battery of tests the success of job trainees during a training

spurious relationship

A relationship between two variables in which a common-causal variable produces and "explains away" the relationship.

session. But we cannot use such correlational information to determine whether the training caused better job performance. For that, researchers rely on experiments.

2.3 Experimental Research: Understanding the Causes of Behavior

The goal of experimental research design is to provide more definitive conclusions about the causal relationships among the variables in the research hypothesis than is available from correlational designs. In an experimental research design, the variables of interest are called the *independent variable* (or *variables*) and the *dependent variable*. The **independent variable** in an experiment is *the causing variable that is created (manipulated) by the experimenter*. The **dependent variable** in an experiment is *a measured variable that is expected to be influenced by the experimental manipulation*. The research hypothesis suggests that the manipulated independent variable or variables will cause changes in the measured dependent variables. We can diagram the research hypothesis by using an arrow that points in one direction. This demonstrates the expected direction of causality:

independent variable

In and experiment, the causing variable that is created (manipulated) by the experimenter.

dependent variable

In an experiment, the measured variable that is expected to be influenced by the experimental manipulation.

FIGURE 2.16

Viewing violence
(independent variable) ⟶ Aggressive behavior
(dependent variable)

random assignment to conditions

A procedure used in experimental research designs in which the condition that each participant is assigned to is determined through a random process.

Research Focus: Video Games and Aggression

Consider an experiment conducted by Anderson and Dill (2000).[24] The study was designed to test the hypothesis that viewing violent video games would increase aggressive behavior. In this research, male and female undergraduates from Iowa State University were given a chance to play with either a violent video game (Wolfenstein 3D) or a nonviolent video game (Myst). During the experimental session, the participants played their assigned video games for 15 minutes. Then, after the play, each participant played a competitive game with an opponent in which the participant could deliver blasts of white noise through the earphones of the opponent. The operational definition of the dependent variable (aggressive behavior) was the level and duration of noise delivered to the opponent. The design of the experiment is shown in Figure 2.17.

An Experimental Research Design

Two advantages of the experimental research design are (1) the assurance that the independent variable (also known as the experimental manipulation) occurs prior to the measured dependent variable, and (2) the creation of initial equivalence between the conditions of the experiment (in this case by using random assignment to conditions).

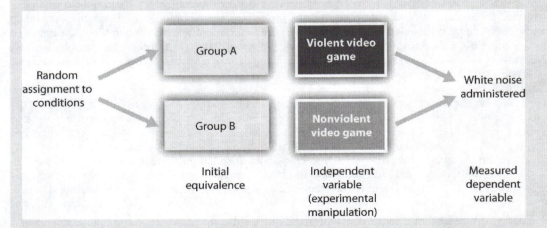

Experimental designs have two very nice features. For one, they guarantee that the independent variable occurs prior to the measurement of the dependent variable. This eliminates the possibility of reverse causation. Second, the influence of common-causal variables is controlled, and thus eliminated, by creating *initial equivalence* among the participants in each of the experimental conditions before the manipulation occurs.

The most common method of creating equivalence among the experimental conditions is through **random assignment to conditions**, *a procedure in which the condition that each participant is assigned to is determined through a random process, such as drawing numbers out of an envelope or using a random number table.* Anderson and Dill first randomly assigned about 100 participants to each of their two groups (Group A and Group B). Because they used random assignment to conditions, they could be confident that, before the experimental manipulation occurred, the students in Group A were, on average, equivalent to the students in Group B on every possible variable, including variables that are likely to be related to aggression, such as parental discipline style, peer relationships, hormone levels, diet—and in fact everything else.

Then, after they had created initial equivalence, Anderson and Dill created the experimental manipulation—they had the participants in Group A play the violent game and the participants in Group B play the nonviolent game. Then they compared the dependent variable (the white noise blasts) between the two groups, finding that the students who had viewed the violent video game gave significantly longer noise blasts than did the students who had played the nonviolent game.

Anderson and Dill had from the outset created initial equivalence between the groups. This initial equivalence allowed them to observe differences in the white noise levels between the two groups after the experimental manipulation, leading to the conclusion that it was the independent variable (and not some other variable) that caused these differences. The idea is that the only thing that was different between the students in the two groups was the video game they had played.

Despite the advantage of determining causation, experiments do have limitations. One is that they are often conducted in laboratory situations rather than in the everyday lives of people. Therefore, we do not know whether results that we find in a laboratory setting will necessarily hold up in everyday life. Second, and more important, is that some of the most interesting and key social variables cannot be experimentally manipulated. If we want to study the influence of the size of a mob on the destructiveness of its behavior, or to compare the personality characteristics of people who join suicide cults with those of people who do not join such cults, these relationships must be assessed using correlational designs, because it is simply not possible to experimentally manipulate these variables.

KEY TAKEAWAYS

- Descriptive, correlational, and experimental research designs are used to collect and analyze data.
- Descriptive designs include case studies, surveys, and naturalistic observation. The goal of these designs is to get a picture of the current thoughts, feelings, or behaviors in a given group of people. Descriptive research is summarized using descriptive statistics.
- Correlational research designs measure two or more relevant variables and assess a relationship between or among them. The variables may be presented on a scatter plot to visually show the relationships. The Pearson Correlation Coefficient (r) is a measure of the strength of linear relationship between two variables.
- Common-causal variables may cause both the predictor and outcome variable in a correlational design, producing a spurious relationship. The possibility of common-causal variables makes it impossible to draw causal conclusions from correlational research designs.
- Experimental research involves the manipulation of an independent variable and the measurement of a dependent variable. Random assignment to conditions is normally used to create initial equivalence between the groups, allowing researchers to draw causal conclusions.

EXERCISES AND CRITICAL THINKING

1. There is a negative correlation between the row that a student sits in in a large class (when the rows are numbered from front to back) and his or her final grade in the class. Do you think this represents a causal relationship or a spurious relationship, and why?
2. Think of two variables (other than those mentioned in this book) that are likely to be correlated, but in which the correlation is probably spurious. What is the likely common-causal variable that is producing the relationship?
3. Imagine a researcher wants to test the hypothesis that participating in psychotherapy will cause a decrease in reported anxiety. Describe the type of research design the investigator might use to draw this conclusion. What would be the independent and dependent variables in the research?

3. YOU CAN BE AN INFORMED CONSUMER OF PSYCHOLOGICAL RESEARCH

LEARNING OBJECTIVES

1. Outline the four potential threats to the validity of research and discuss how they may make it difficult to accurately interpret research findings.
2. Describe how confounding may reduce the internal validity of an experiment.
3. Explain how generalization, replication, and meta-analyses are used to assess the external validity of research findings.

Good research is *valid* research. When research is valid, the conclusions drawn by the researcher are legitimate. For instance, if a researcher concludes that participating in psychotherapy reduces anxiety, or that taller people are smarter than shorter people, the research is valid only if the therapy really works or if taller people really are smarter. Unfortunately, there are many threats to the validity of research, and these threats may sometimes lead to unwarranted conclusions. Often, and despite researchers' best intentions, some of the research reported on websites as well as in newspapers, magazines, and even scientific journals is invalid. Validity is not an all-or-nothing proposition, which means that some research is more valid than other research. Only by understanding the potential threats to validity will you be able to make knowledgeable decisions about the conclusions that can or cannot be drawn from a research project. There are four major types of threats to the validity of research, and informed consumers of research are aware of each type.

Threats to the Validity of Research

1. *Threats to construct validity.* Although it is claimed that the measured variables measure the conceptual variables of interest, they actually may not.
2. *Threats to statistical conclusion validity.* Conclusions regarding the research may be incorrect because no statistical tests were made or because the statistical tests were incorrectly interpreted.
3. *Threats to internal validity.* Although it is claimed that the independent variable caused the dependent variable, the dependent variable actually may have been caused by a confounding variable.
4. *Threats to external validity.* Although it is claimed that the results are more general, the observed effects may actually only be found under limited conditions or for specific groups of people. (Stangor, 2011)[25]

construct validity

The extent to which the variables used in the research adequately assess the conceptual variables they were designed to measure.

reliability

The consistency of a measured variable.

One threat to valid research occurs when there is a threat to *construct validity*. **Construct validity** refers to *the extent to which the variables used in the research adequately assess the conceptual variables they were designed to measure*. One requirement for construct validity is that the measure be *reliable*, where **reliability** refers to *the consistency of a measured variable*. A bathroom scale is usually reliable, because if we step on and off it a couple of times the scale will consistently measure the same weight every time. Other measures, including some psychological tests, may be less reliable, and thus less useful.

Normally, we can assume that the researchers have done their best to assure the construct validity of their measures, but it is not inappropriate for you, as an informed consumer of research, to question this. It is always important to remember that the ability to learn about the relationship between the conceptual variables in a research hypothesis is dependent on the operational definitions of the measured variables. If the measures do not really measure the conceptual variables that they are designed to assess (e.g., if a supposed IQ test does not really measure intelligence), then they cannot be used to draw inferences about the relationship between the conceptual variables (Nunnally, 1978).[26]

statistical significance

The confidence with which we can conclude that data are not due to chance or random error.

The statistical methods that scientists use to test their research hypotheses are based on probability estimates. You will see statements in research reports indicating that the results were "statistically significant" or "not statistically significant." These statements will be accompanied by statistical tests, often including statements such as "$p < 0.05$" or about confidence intervals. These statements describe the *statistical significance* of the data that have been collected. **Statistical significance** refers to *the confidence with which a scientist can conclude that data are not due to chance or random error*. When a researcher concludes that a result is statistically significant, he or she has determined that the observed data was very unlikely to have been caused by chance factors alone. Hence, there is likely a real relationship between or among the variables in the research design. Otherwise, the researcher concludes that the results were not statistically significant.

Statistical conclusion validity refers to *the extent to which we can be certain that the researcher has drawn accurate conclusions about the statistical significance of the research*. Research will be invalid if the conclusions made about the research hypothesis are incorrect because statistical inferences about the collected data are in error. These errors can occur either because the scientist inappropriately infers that the data do support the research hypothesis when in fact they are due to chance, or when the researcher mistakenly fails to find support for the research hypothesis. Normally, we can assume that the researchers have done their best to ensure the statistical conclusion validity of a research design, but we must always keep in mind that inferences about data are probabilistic and never certain—this is why research never "proves" a theory.

Internal validity refers to *the extent to which we can trust the conclusions that have been drawn about the causal relationship between the independent and dependent variables* (Campbell & Stanley, 1963).[27] Internal validity applies primarily to experimental research designs, in which the researcher hopes to conclude that the independent variable has caused the dependent variable. Internal validity is maximized when the research is free from the presence of **confounding variables**—*variables other than the independent variable on which the participants in one experimental condition differ systematically from those in other conditions.*

Consider an experiment in which a researcher tested the hypothesis that drinking alcohol makes members of the opposite sex look more attractive. Participants older than 21 years of age were randomly assigned either to drink orange juice mixed with vodka or to drink orange juice alone. To eliminate the need for deception, the participants were told whether or not their drinks contained vodka. After enough time had passed for the alcohol to take effect, the participants were asked to rate the attractiveness of pictures of members of the opposite sex. The results of the experiment showed that, as predicted, the participants who drank the vodka rated the photos as significantly more attractive.

If you think about this experiment for a minute, it may occur to you that although the researcher wanted to draw the conclusion that the alcohol caused the differences in perceived attractiveness, the expectation of having consumed alcohol is confounded with the presence of alcohol. That is, the people who drank alcohol also knew they drank alcohol, and those who did not drink alcohol knew they did not. It is possible that simply knowing that they were drinking alcohol, rather than the effect of the alcohol itself, may have caused the differences (see Figure 2.18). One solution to the problem of potential *expectancy effects* is to tell both groups that they are drinking orange juice and vodka but really give alcohol to only half of the participants (it is possible to do this because vodka has very little smell or taste). If differences in perceived attractiveness are found, the experimenter could then confidently attribute them to the alcohol rather than to the expectancies about having consumed alcohol.

statistical conclusion validity

The extent to which we can be certain that the researcher has drawn accurate conclusions about the statistical significance of the research.

internal validity

The extent to which we can trust the conclusions that have been drawn about the causal relationship between the independent and dependent variables.

confounding variable

A variable other than the independent variable on which the participants in one experimental condition differ systematically from those in other conditions.

FIGURE 2.18 An Example of Confounding

Confounding occurs when a variable that is not part of the research hypothesis is "mixed up," or confounded with, the variable in the research hypothesis. In the bottom panel alcohol consumed and alcohol expectancy are confounded, but in the top panel they are separate (independent). Confounding makes it impossible to be sure that the independent variable (rather than the confounding variable) caused the dependent variable.

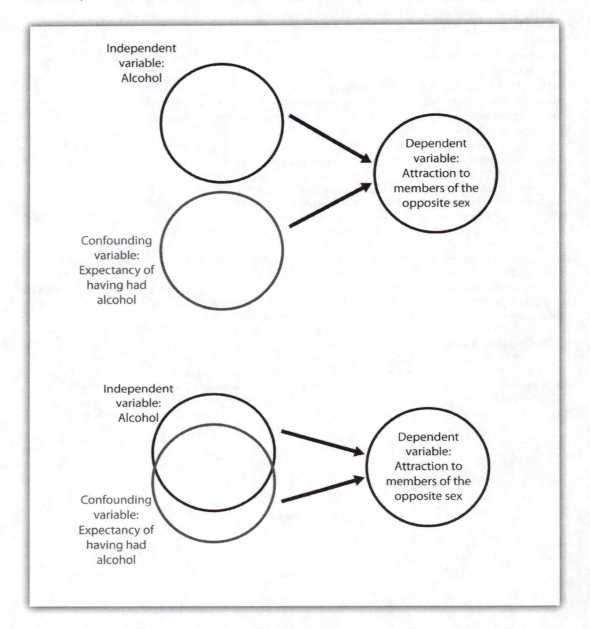

experimenter bias

A situation in which the experimenter subtly treats the research participants in the various experimental conditions differently, resulting in an invalid confirmation of the research hypothesis.

Another threat to internal validity can occur when the experimenter knows the research hypothesis and also knows which experimental condition the participants are in. The outcome is the potential for **experimenter bias,** *a situation in which the experimenter subtly treats the research participants in the various experimental conditions differently, resulting in an invalid confirmation of the research hypothesis.* In one study demonstrating experimenter bias, Rosenthal and Fode (1963)[28] sent twelve students to test a research hypothesis concerning maze learning in rats. Although it was not initially revealed to the students, they were actually the participants in an experiment. Six of the students were randomly told that the rats they would be testing had been bred to be highly intelligent, whereas the other six students were led to believe that the rats had been bred to be unintelligent. In reality there were no differences among the rats given to the two groups of students. When the students returned with their data, a startling result emerged. The rats run by students who expected them to be intelligent showed significantly better maze learning than the rats run by students who expected them to be unintelligent. Somehow the students' expectations influenced their data. They evidently did something different when they tested the rats, perhaps subtly changing how they timed the maze running or how they treated the rats. And this experimenter bias probably occurred entirely out of their awareness.

To avoid experimenter bias, researchers frequently run experiments in which the researchers are *blind to condition*. This means that although the experimenters know the research hypotheses, they do not know which conditions the participants are assigned to. Experimenter bias cannot occur if the researcher is blind to condition. In a **double-blind experiment**, *both the researcher and the research participants are blind to condition.* For instance, in a double-blind trial of a drug, the researcher does not know whether the drug being given is the real drug or the ineffective placebo, and the patients also do not know which they are getting. Double-blind experiments eliminate the potential for experimenter effects and at the same time eliminate participant expectancy effects.

While internal validity refers to conclusions drawn about events that occurred within the experiment, **external validity** refers to *the extent to which the results of a research design can be generalized beyond the specific way the original experiment was conducted.* **Generalization** refers to *the extent to which relationships among conceptual variables can be demonstrated in a wide variety of people and a wide variety of manipulated or measured variables.*

Psychologists who use college students as participants in their research may be concerned about generalization, wondering if their research will generalize to people who are not college students. And researchers who study the behaviors of employees in one company may wonder whether the same findings would translate to other companies. Whenever there is reason to suspect that a result found for one sample of participants would not hold up for another sample, then research may be conducted with these other populations to test for generalization.

Recently, many psychologists have been interested in testing hypotheses about the extent to which a result will replicate across people from different cultures (Heine, 2010).[29] For instance, a researcher might test whether the effects on aggression of viewing violent video games are the same for Japanese children as they are for American children by showing violent and nonviolent films to a sample of both Japanese and American schoolchildren. If the results are the same in both cultures, then we say that the results have generalized, but if they are different, then we have learned a *limiting condition* of the effect (see Figure 2.19).

FIGURE 2.19 A Cross-Cultural Replication

In a cross-cultural replication, external validity is observed if the same effects that have been found in one culture are replicated in another culture. If they are not replicated in the new culture, then a limiting condition of the original results is found.

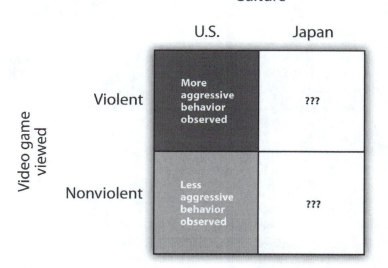

Unless the researcher has a specific reason to believe that generalization will not hold, it is appropriate to assume that a result found in one population (even if that population is college students) will generalize to other populations. Because the investigator can never demonstrate that the research results generalize to all populations, it is not expected that the researcher will attempt to do so. Rather, the burden of proof rests on those who claim that a result will not generalize.

double-blind experiment

An experimental design in which both the researcher and the research participants are blind to condition.

external validity

The extent to which the results of a research design can be generalized beyond the specific way the original experiment was conducted.

generalization

The tendency to respond to stimuli that resemble the original conditioned stimulus.

replication

The process of repeating previous research.

meta-analysis

A statistical technique that uses the results of existing studies to integrate and draw conclusions about those studies.

Because any single test of a research hypothesis will always be limited in terms of what it can show, important advances in science are never the result of a single research project. Advances occur through the accumulation of knowledge that comes from many different tests of the same theory or research hypothesis. These tests are conducted by different researchers using different research designs, participants, and operationalizations of the independent and dependent variables. *The process of repeating previous research, which forms the basis of all scientific inquiry,* is known as **replication**.

Scientists often use a procedure known as *meta-analysis* to summarize replications of research findings. A **meta-analysis** is *a statistical technique that uses the results of existing studies to integrate and draw conclusions about those studies.* Because meta-analyses provide so much information, they are very popular and useful ways of summarizing research literature.

A meta-analysis provides a relatively objective method of reviewing research findings because it (1) specifies inclusion criteria that indicate exactly which studies will or will not be included in the analysis, (2) systematically searches for all studies that meet the inclusion criteria, and (3) provides an objective measure of the strength of observed relationships. Frequently, the researchers also include—if they can find them—studies that have not been published in journals.

Psychology in Everyday Life: Critically Evaluating the Validity of Websites

The validity of research reports published in scientific journals is likely to be high because the hypotheses, methods, results, and conclusions of the research have been rigorously evaluated by other scientists, through peer review, before the research was published. For this reason, you will want to use peer-reviewed journal articles as your major source of information about psychological research.

Although research articles are the gold standard for validity, you may also need and desire to get at least some information from other sources. The Internet is a vast source of information from which you can learn about almost anything, including psychology. Search engines—such as Google or Yahoo!—bring hundreds or thousands of hits on a topic, and online encyclopedias, such as Wikipedia, provide articles about relevant topics.

Although you will naturally use the web to help you find information about fields such as psychology, you must also realize that it is important to carefully evaluate the validity of the information you get from the web. You must try to distinguish information that is based on empirical research from information that is based on opinion, and between valid and invalid data. The following material may be helpful to you in learning to make these distinctions.

The techniques for evaluating the validity of websites are similar to those that are applied to evaluating any other source of information. Ask first about the source of the information. Is the domain a ".com" (business), ".gov" (government), or ".org" (nonprofit) entity? This information can help you determine the author's (or organization's) purpose in publishing the website. Try to determine where the information is coming from. Is the data being summarized from objective sources, such as journal articles or academic or government agencies? Does it seem that the author is interpreting the information as objectively as possible, or is the data being interpreted to support a particular point of view? Consider what groups, individuals, and political or commercial interests stand to gain from the site. Is the website potentially part of an advocacy group whose web pages reflect the particular positions of the group? Material from any group's site may be useful, but try to be aware of the group's purposes and potential biases.

Also, ask whether or not the authors themselves appear to be a trustworthy source of information. Do they hold positions in an academic institution? Do they have peer-reviewed publications in scientific journals? Many useful web pages appear as part of organizational sites and reflect the work of that organization. You can be more certain of the validity of the information if it is sponsored by a professional organization, such as the American Psychological Association or the American Psychological Society.

Try to check on the accuracy of the material and discern whether the sources of information seem current. Is the information cited such that you can read it in its original form? Reputable websites will probably link to other reputable sources, such as journal articles and scholarly books. Try to check the accuracy of the information by reading at least some of these sources yourself.

It is fair to say that all authors, researchers, and organizations have at least some bias and that the information from any site can be invalid. But good material attempts to be fair by acknowledging other possible positions, interpretations, or conclusions. A critical examination of the nature of the websites you browse for information will help you determine if the information is valid and will give you more confidence in the information you take from it.

KEY TAKEAWAYS

- Research is said to be valid when the conclusions drawn by the researcher are legitimate. Because all research has the potential to be invalid, no research ever "proves" a theory or research hypothesis.
- Construct validity, statistical conclusion validity, internal validity, and external validity are all types of validity that people who read and interpret research need to be aware of.
- Construct validity refers to the assurance that the measured variables adequately measure the conceptual variables
- Statistical conclusion validity refers to the assurance that inferences about statistical significance are appropriate.
- Internal validity refers to the assurance that the independent variable has caused the dependent variable. Internal validity is greater when confounding variables are reduced or eliminated.
- External validity is greater when effects can be replicated across different manipulations, measures, and populations. Scientists use meta-analyses to better understand the external validity of research.

EXERCISES AND CRITICAL THINKING

1. The Pepsi Cola Corporation, now PepsiCo Inc., conducted the "Pepsi Challenge" by randomly assigning individuals to taste either a Pepsi or a Coke. The researchers labeled the glasses with only an "M" (for Pepsi) or a "Q" (for Coke) and asked the participants to rate how much they liked the beverage. The research showed that subjects overwhelmingly preferred glass "M" over glass "Q," and the researchers concluded that Pepsi was preferred to Coke. Can you tell what confounding variable is present in this research design? How would you redesign the research to eliminate the confound?
2. Locate a research report of a meta-analysis. Determine the criteria that were used to select the studies and report on the findings of the research.

4. CHAPTER SUMMARY

Psychologists study the behavior of both humans and animals in order to understand and improve the quality of human lives.

Psychological research may be either basic or applied in orientation. Basic research and applied research inform each other, and advances in science occur more rapidly when both types of research are conducted.

The results of psychological research are reported primarily in research reports in scientific journals. These research reports have been evaluated, critiqued, and improved by other scientists through the process of peer review.

The methods used by scientists have developed over many years and provide a common framework through which information can be collected, organized, and shared.

The scientific method is the set of assumptions, rules, and procedures that scientists use to conduct research. In addition to requiring that science be empirical, the scientific method demands that the procedures used be objective, or free from personal bias.

Scientific findings are organized by theories, which are used to summarize and make new predictions, but theories are usually framed too broadly to be tested in a single experiment. Therefore, scientists normally use the research hypothesis as a basis for their research.

Scientists use operational definitions to turn the ideas of interest—conceptual variables—into measured variables.

Decisions about whether psychological research using human and animals is ethical are made using established ethical codes developed by scientific organizations and on the basis of judgments made by the local Institutional Review Board. These decisions are made through a cost-benefit analysis, in which the costs are compared to the benefits. If the potential costs of the research appear to outweigh any potential benefits that might come from it, then the research should not proceed.

Descriptive research is designed to provide a snapshot of the current state of affairs. Descriptive research allows the development of questions for further study but does not assess relationships among variables. The results of descriptive research projects are analyzed using descriptive statistics.

Correlational research assesses the relationships between and among two or more variables. It allows making predictions but cannot be used to draw inferences about the causal relationships between and among the variables. Linear relationships between variables are normally analyzed using the Pearson correlation coefficient.

The goal of experimental research is to assess the causal impact of one or more experimental manipulations on a dependent variable. Because experimental research creates initial equivalence among the participants in the different experimental conditions, it allows drawing conclusions about the causal relationships among variables. Experimental designs are not always possible because many important variables cannot be experimentally manipulated.

Because all research has the potential for invalidity, research never "proves" a theory or hypothesis.

Threats to construct validity involve potential inaccuracies in the measurement of the conceptual variables.

Threats to statistical conclusion validity involve potential inaccuracies in the statistical testing of the relationships among variables.

Threats to internal validity involve potential inaccuracies in assumptions about the causal role of the independent variable on the dependent variable.

Threats to external validity involve potential inaccuracy regarding the generality of observed findings.

Informed consumers of research are aware of the strengths of research but are also aware of its potential limitations.

ENDNOTES

1. Brown v. Board of Education, 347 U.S. 483 (1954); Fiske, S. T., Bersoff, D. N., Borgida, E., Deaux, K., & Heilman, M. E. (1991). Social science research on trial: Use of sex stereotyping research in Price Waterhouse v. Hopkins. *American Psychologist, 46*(10), 1049–1060.

2. Saxe, L., Dougherty, D., & Cross, T. (1985). The validity of polygraph testing: Scientific analysis and public controversy. *American Psychologist, 40*, 355–366.

3. Fajen, B. R., & Warren, W. H. (2003). Behavioral dynamics of steering, obstacle avoidance, and route selection. *Journal of Experimental Psychology: Human Perception and Performance, 29*(2), 343–362.

4. Alexander, P. A., & Winne, P. H. (Eds.). (2006). *Handbook of educational psychology* (2nd ed.). Mahwah, NJ: Lawrence Erlbaum Associates; Woolfolk-Hoy, A. E. (2005). *Educational psychology* (9th ed.). Boston, MA: Allyn & Bacon.

5. DePaulo, B. M., Lindsay, J. J., Malone, B. E., Muhlenbruck, L., Charlton, K., & Cooper, H. (2003). Cues to deception. *Psychological Bulletin, 129*(1), 74–118.

6. Borum, R. (2004). *Psychology of terrorism.* Tampa: University of South Florida.

7. Lewin, K. (1999). *The complete social scientist: A Kurt Lewin reader* (M. Gold, Ed.). Washington, DC: American Psychological Association.

8. Kohlberg, L. (1966). A cognitive-developmental analysis of children's sex-role concepts and attitudes. In E. E. Maccoby (Ed.), *The development of sex differences.* Stanford, CA: Stanford University Press.

9. Ruble, D., & Martin, C. (1998). Gender development. In W. Damon (Ed.), *Handbook of child psychology* (5th ed., pp. 933–1016). New York, NY: John Wiley & Sons.

10. Popper, K. R. (1959). *The logic of scientific discovery.* New York, NY: Basic Books.

11. Rosenthal, R. (1994). Science and ethics in conducting, analyzing, and reporting psychological research. *Psychological Science, 5*, 127–134.

12. Stangor, C. (2011). *Research methods for the behavioral sciences* (4th ed.). Mountain View, CA: Cengage.

13. Milgram, S. (1974). *Obedience to authority: An experimental view.* New York, NY: Harper and Row.

14. Baumrind, D. (1985). Research using intentional deception: Ethical issues revisited. *American Psychologist, 40*, 165–174.

15. Thomas, G., & Blackman, D. (1992). The future of animal studies in psychology. *American Psychologist, 47*, 1678.

16. American Psychological Association. (2002). Ethical principles of psychologists. *American Psychologist, 57*, 1060–1073.

17. Plous, S. (1996). Attitudes toward the use of animals in psychological research and education. *Psychological Science, 7*, 352–358.

18. Freud, S. (1964). Analysis of phobia in a five-year-old boy. In E. A. Southwell & M. Merbaum (Eds.), *Personality: Readings in theory and research* (pp. 3–32). Belmont, CA: Wadsworth. (Original work published 1909)

19. Kotowicz, Z. (2007). The strange case of Phineas Gage. *History of the Human Sciences, 20*(1), 115–131.

20. Damasio, H., Grabowski, T., Frank, R., Galaburda, A. M., Damasio, A. R., Cacioppo, J. T., & Berntson, G. G. (2005). The return of Phineas Gage: Clues about the brain from the skull of a famous patient. In *Social neuroscience: Key readings.* (pp. 21–28). New York, NY: Psychology Press.

21. Rokeach, M. (1964). *The three Christs of Ypsilanti: A psychological study.* New York, NY: Knopf.

22. Ainsworth, M. S., Blehar, M. C., Waters, E., & Wall, S. (1978). *Patterns of attachment: A psychological study of the strange situation.* Hillsdale, NJ: Lawrence Erlbaum Associates.

23. Aiken, L., & West, S. (1991). *Multiple regression: Testing and interpreting interactions.* Newbury Park, CA: Sage.

24. Anderson, C. A., & Dill, K. E. (2000). Video games and aggressive thoughts, feelings, and behavior in the laboratory and in life. *Journal of Personality and Social Psychology, 78*(4), 772–790.

25. Stangor, C. (2011). *Research methods for the behavioral sciences* (4th ed.). Mountain View, CA: Cengage.

26. Nunnally, J. C. (1978). *Pyschometric theory.* New York, NY: McGraw-Hill.

27. Campbell, D. T., & Stanley, J. C. (1963). *Experimental and quasi-experimental designs for research.* Chicago: Rand McNally.

28. Rosenthal, R., & Fode, K. L. (1963). The effect of experimenter bias on the performance of the albino rat. *Behavioral Science, 8*, 183–189.

29. Heine, S. J. (2010). Cultural psychology. In S. T. Fiske, D. T. Gilbert, & G. Lindzey (Eds.), *Handbook of social psychology* (5th ed., Vol. 2, pp. 1423–1464). Hoboken, NJ: John Wiley & Sons.

CHAPTER 3
Brains, Bodies, and Behavior

Did a Neurological Disorder Cause a Musician to Compose *Boléro* and an Artist to Paint It 66 Years Later?

In 1986 Anne Adams was working as a cell biologist at the University of Toronto in Ontario, Canada. She took a leave of absence from her work to care for a sick child, and while she was away, she completely changed her interests, dropping biology entirely and turning her attention to art. In 1994 she completed her painting *Unravelling Boléro*, a translation of Maurice Ravel's famous orchestral piece onto canvas. As you can see in Figure 3.1, this artwork is a filled with themes of repetition. Each bar of music is represented by a lacy vertical figure, with the height representing volume, the shape representing note quality, and the color representing the music's pitch. Like Ravel's music (see the video below), which is a hypnotic melody consisting of two melodial themes repeated eight times over 340 musical bars, the theme in the painting repeats and builds, leading to a dramatic change in color from blue to orange and pink, a representation of *Boléro*'s sudden and dramatic climax.

Unravelling Boléro
Adams's depiction of Ravel's orchestral piece *Boléro* was painted during the very early phase of her illness in 1994.

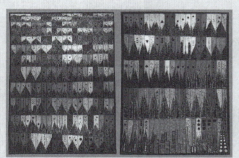

Source: Photo courtesy of New Scientist, http://www.newscientist.com/data/images/ns/cms/dn13599/dn13599-1_567.jpg.

Maurice Ravel's Composition *Boléro* (1928)
This is a video clip of Maurice Ravel's *Boléro*, composed in 1928 during the early phases of his illness.

View the video online at: http://www.youtube.com/embed/3-4J5j74VPw

Shortly after finishing the painting, Adams began to experience behavioral problems, including increased difficulty speaking. Neuroimages of Adams's brain taken during this time show that regions in the front part of her brain, which are normally associated with language processing, had begun to deteriorate, while at the same time, regions of the brain responsible for the integration of information from the five senses were unusually well developed (Seeley et al., 2008).[1] The deterioration of the frontal cortex is a symptom of *frontotemporal dementia*, a disease that is associated with changes in artistic and musical tastes and skills (Miller, Boone, Cummings, Read, & Mishkin, 2000),[2] as well as with an increase in repetitive behaviors (Aldhous, 2008).[3]

What Adams did not know at the time was that her brain may have been undergoing the same changes that Ravel's had undergone 66 years earlier. In fact, it appears that Ravel may have suffered from the same neurological disorder. Ravel composed *Boléro* at age 53, when he himself was beginning to show behavioral symptoms that were interfering with his ability to move and speak. Scientists have concluded, based on an analysis of his written notes and letters, that Ravel was also experiencing the effects of frontotemporal dementia (Amaducci, Grassi, & Boller, 2002).[4] If Adams and Ravel were both affected by the same disease, this could explain why they both became fascinated with the repetitive aspects of their arts, and it would present a remarkable example of the influence of our brains on behavior.

Every behavior begins with biology. Our behaviors, as well as our thoughts and feelings, are produced by the actions of our brains, nerves, muscles, and glands. In this chapter we will begin our journey into the world of psychology by considering the biological makeup of the human being, including the most remarkable of human organs—the brain. We'll consider the structure of the brain and also the methods that psychologists use to study the brain and to understand how it works.

We will see that the body is controlled by an information highway known as the **nervous system**, *a collection of hundreds of billions of specialized and interconnected cells through which messages are sent between the brain and the rest of the body*. The nervous system consists of the **central nervous system (CNS)**, *made up of the brain and the spinal cord*, and the **peripheral nervous system (PNS)**, *the neurons that link the CNS to our skin, muscles, and glands*. And we will see that our behavior is also influenced in large part by the **endocrine system**, *the chemical regulator of the body that consists of glands that secrete hormones*.

Although this chapter begins at a very low level of explanation, and although the topic of study may seem at first to be far from the everyday behaviors that we all engage in, a full understanding of the biology underlying psychological processes is an important cornerstone of your new understanding of psychology. We will consider throughout the chapter how our biology influences important human behaviors, including our mental and physical health, our reactions to drugs, as well as our aggressive responses and our perceptions of other people. This chapter is particularly important for contemporary psychology because the ability to measure biological aspects of behavior, including the structure and function of the human brain, is progressing rapidly, and understanding the biological foundations of behavior is an increasingly important line of psychological study.

nervous system

A collection of hundreds of billions of specialized cells that transmit information between different parts of the body.

central nervous system (CNS)

The brain and the spinal cord.

peripheral nervous system (PNS)

The nerves that link the CNS to the skin, muscles, and glands.

endocrine system

The chemical regulator of the body, composed of the glands that secrete hormones.

1. THE NEURON IS THE BUILDING BLOCK OF THE NERVOUS SYSTEM

LEARNING OBJECTIVES

1. Describe the structure and functions of the neuron.
2. Draw a diagram of the pathways of communication within and between neurons.
3. List three of the major neurotransmitters and describe their functions.

The nervous system is composed of more than 100 billion cells known as *neurons*. A **neuron** is *a cell in the nervous system whose function it is to receive and transmit information*. As you can see in Figure 3.2, neurons are made up of three major parts: a cell body, or **soma**, which *contains the nucleus of the cell and keeps the cell alive*; a branching treelike fiber known as the **dendrite**, which *collects information from other cells and sends the information to the soma*; and a long, segmented fiber known as the **axon**, which *transmits information away from the cell body toward other neurons or to the muscles and glands*.

FIGURE 3.2 Components of the Neuron

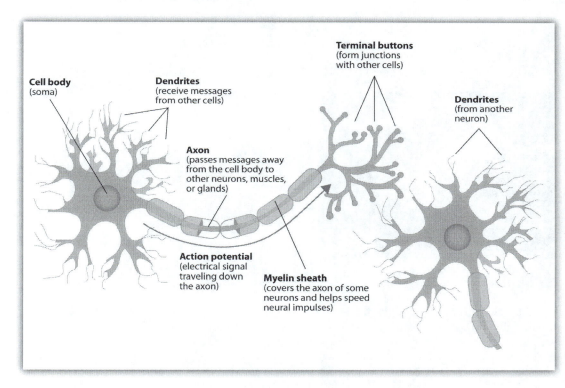

neuron

One of the more than 100 billion cells in the nervous system.

soma

The part of the neuron that contains the nucleus of the cell and that keeps the cell alive.

dendrite

The part of the neuron that collects information from other cells and sends the information to the soma.

axon

The part of the neuron that transmits information away from the cell body toward other neurons.

FIGURE 3.3

The nervous system, including the brain, is made up of billions of interlinked neurons. This vast interconnected web is responsible for all human thinking, feeling, and behavior.

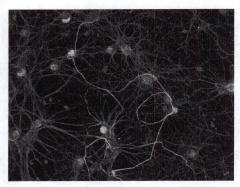

Source: Photo courtesy of GE Healthcare,
http://www.flickr.com/photos/gehealthcare/4253587827/.

Some neurons have hundreds or even thousands of dendrites, and these dendrites may themselves be branched to allow the cell to receive information from thousands of other cells. The axons are also specialized, and some, such as those that send messages from the spinal cord to the muscles in the hands or feet, may be very long—even up to several feet in length. To improve the speed of their communication, and to keep their electrical charges from shorting out with other neurons, axons are often surrounded by a *myelin sheath*. The **myelin sheath** is *a layer of fatty tissue surrounding the axon of a neuron that both acts as an insulator and allows faster transmission of the electrical signal*. Axons branch out toward their ends, and at the tip of each branch is a *terminal button*.

1.1   Neurons Communicate Using Electricity and Chemicals

The nervous system operates using an *electrochemical* process (see "Video Clip: The Electrochemical Action of the Neuron"). An electrical charge moves through the neuron itself and chemicals are used to transmit information between neurons. Within the neuron, when a signal is received by the dendrites, is it transmitted to the soma in the form of an electrical signal, and, if the signal is strong enough, it may then be passed on to the axon and then to the terminal buttons. If the signal reaches the terminal buttons, they are signaled to emit chemicals known as *neurotransmitters*, which communicate with other neurons across the spaces between the cells, known as *synapses*.

myelin sheath

A layer of fatty tissue surrounding the axon of a neuron that acts as an insulator and allows faster transmission of the electrical signal.

Video Clip: The Electrochemical Action of the Neuron

This video clip shows a model of the electrochemical action of the neuron and neurotransmitters.

View the video online at: http://www.youtube.com/embed/TKG0MtH5crc

resting potential

A state in which the interior of the neuron contains a greater number of negatively charged ions than does the area outside the cell.

action potential

A change in electrical charge that occurs in a neuron when a nerve impulse is transmitted.

node of Ranvier

The break in the myelin sheath of a nerve fiber.

The electrical signal moves through the neuron as a result of changes in the electrical charge of the axon. Normally, the axon remains in the **resting potential**, *a state in which the interior of the neuron contains a greater number of negatively charged ions than does the area outside the cell*. When the segment of the axon that is closest to the cell body is stimulated by an electrical signal from the dendrites, and if this electrical signal is strong enough that it passes a certain level or *threshold*, the cell membrane in this first segment opens its gates, allowing positively charged sodium ions that were previously kept out to enter. This *change in electrical charge that occurs in a neuron when a nerve impulse is transmitted* is known as the **action potential**. Once the action potential occurs, the number of positive ions exceeds the number of negative ions in this segment, and the segment temporarily becomes positively charged.

As you can see in Figure 3.4, the axon is segmented by a series of *breaks between the sausage-like segments of the myelin sheath*. Each of these gaps is a **node of Ranvier**. The electrical charge moves down the axon from segment to segment, in a set of small jumps, moving from node to node. When the action potential occurs in the first segment of the axon, it quickly creates a similar change in the next segment, which then stimulates the next segment, and so forth as the positive electrical impulse continues all the way down to the end of the axon. As each new segment becomes positive, the membrane in the prior segment closes up again, and the segment returns to its negative resting potential. In this way the action potential is transmitted along the axon, toward the terminal buttons. The entire response along the length of the axon is very fast—it can happen up to 1,000 times each second.

FIGURE 3.4 The Myelin Sheath and the Nodes of Ranvier

The myelin sheath wraps around the axon but also leaves small gaps called the nodes of Ranvier. The action potential jumps from node to node as it travels down the axon.

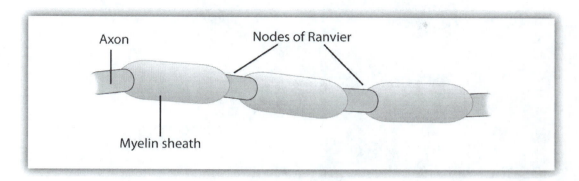

An important aspect of the action potential is that it operates in an *all or nothing* manner. What this means is that the neuron either fires completely, such that the action potential moves all the way down the axon, or it does not fire at all. Thus neurons can provide more energy to the neurons down the line by firing faster but not by firing more strongly. Furthermore, the neuron is prevented from repeated firing by the presence of a *refractory period*—a brief time after the firing of the axon in which the axon cannot fire again because the neuron has not yet returned to its resting potential.

1.2   Neurotransmitters: The Body's Chemical Messengers

Not only do the neural signals travel via electrical charges *within* the neuron, but they also travel via chemical transmission *between* the neurons. Neurons are separated by junction areas known as **syn-apses**, *areas where the terminal buttons at the end of the axon of one neuron nearly, but don't quite, touch the dendrites of another*. The synapses provide a remarkable function because they allow each axon to communicate with many dendrites in neighboring cells. Because a neuron may have synaptic connections with thousands of other neurons, the communication links among the neurons in the nervous system allow for a highly sophisticated communication system.

When the electrical impulse from the action potential reaches the end of the axon, it signals the terminal buttons to release neurotransmitters into the synapse. A **neurotransmitter** is *a chemical that relays signals across the synapses between neurons*. Neurotransmitters travel across the synaptic space between the terminal button of one neuron and the dendrites of other neurons, where they bind to the dendrites in the neighboring neurons. Furthermore, different terminal buttons release different neuro-transmitters, and different dendrites are particularly sensitive to different neurotransmitters. The dend-rites will admit the neurotransmitters only if they are the right shape to fit in the receptor sites on the receiving neuron. For this reason, the receptor sites and neurotransmitters are often compared to a lock and key (Figure 3.5).

synapse

The small gap between neurons across which nerve impulses are transmitted.

neurotransmitter

A chemical that relays signals across the synapses between neurons.

FIGURE 3.5 The Synapse

When the nerve impulse reaches the terminal button, it triggers the release of neurotransmitters into the synapse. The neurotransmitters fit into receptors on the receiving dendrites in the manner of a lock and key.

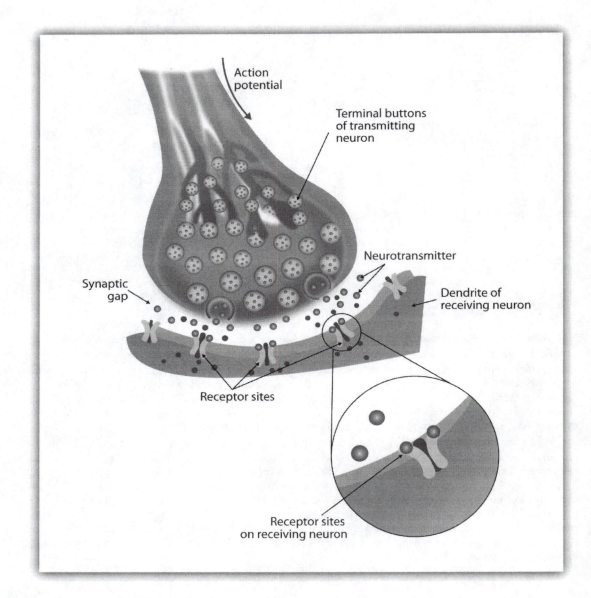

When neurotransmitters are accepted by the receptors on the receiving neurons their effect may be either *excitatory* (i.e., they make the cell more likely to fire) or *inhibitory* (i.e., they make the cell less likely to fire). Furthermore, if the receiving neuron is able to accept more than one neurotransmitter, then it will be influenced by the excitatory and inhibitory processes of each. If the excitatory effects of the neurotransmitters are greater than the inhibitory influences of the neurotransmitters, the neuron moves closer to its firing threshold, and if it reaches the threshold, the action potential and the process of transferring information through the neuron begins.

Neurotransmitters that are not accepted by the receptor sites must be removed from the synapse in order for the next potential stimulation of the neuron to happen. This process occurs in part through the breaking down of the neurotransmitters by enzymes, and in part through **reuptake**, *a process in which neurotransmitters that are in the synapse are reabsorbed into the transmitting terminal buttons, ready to again be released after the neuron fires.*

More than 100 chemical substances produced in the body have been identified as neurotransmitters, and these substances have a wide and profound effect on emotion, cognition, and behavior. Neurotransmitters regulate our appetite, our memory, our emotions, as well as our muscle action and movement. And as you can see in Table 3.1, some neurotransmitters are also associated with psychological and physical diseases.

---

reuptake

The process in which the neurotransmitters in the synapse are reabsorbed into the transmitting terminal buttons.

Drugs that we might ingest—either for medical reasons or recreationally—can act like neurotransmitters to influence our thoughts, feelings, and behavior. An **agonist** is *a drug that has chemical properties similar to a particular neurotransmitter and thus mimics the effects of the neurotransmitter*. When an agonist is ingested, it binds to the receptor sites in the dendrites to excite the neuron, acting as if more of the neurotransmitter had been present. As an example, cocaine is an agonist for the neurotransmitter dopamine. Because dopamine produces feelings of pleasure when it is released by neurons, cocaine creates similar feelings when it is ingested. An **antagonist** is *a drug that reduces or stops the normal effects of a neurotransmitter*. When an antagonist is ingested, it binds to the receptor sites in the dendrite, thereby blocking the neurotransmitter. As an example, the poison curare is an antagonist for the neurotransmitter acetylcholine. When the poison enters the brain, it binds to the dendrites, stops communication among the neurons, and usually causes death. Still other drugs work by blocking the reuptake of the neurotransmitter itself—when reuptake is reduced by the drug, more neurotransmitter remains in the synapse, increasing its action.

agonist

A drug that has chemical properties similar to a particular neurotransmitter and thus mimics the effects of the neurotransmitter.

antagonist

A drug that reduces or stops the normal effects of a neurotransmitter.

TABLE 3.1   The Major Neurotransmitters and Their Functions

Neurotransmitter	Description and function	Notes
Acetylcholine (ACh)	A common neurotransmitter used in the spinal cord and motor neurons to stimulate muscle contractions. It's also used in the brain to regulate memory, sleeping, and dreaming.	Alzheimer's disease is associated with an undersupply of acetylcholine. Nicotine is an agonist that acts like acetylcholine.
Dopamine	Involved in movement, motivation, and emotion, Dopamine produces feelings of pleasure when released by the brain's reward system, and it's also involved in learning.	Schizophrenia is linked to increases in dopamine, whereas Parkinson's disease is linked to reductions in dopamine (and dopamine agonists may be used to treat it).
Endorphins	Released in response to behaviors such as vigorous exercise, orgasm, and eating spicy foods.	Endorphins are natural pain relievers. They are related to the compounds found in drugs such as opium, morphine, and heroin. The release of endorphins creates the runner's high that is experienced after intense physical exertion.
GABA (gamma-aminobutyric acid)	The major inhibitory neurotransmitter in the brain.	A lack of GABA can lead to involuntary motor actions, including tremors and seizures. Alcohol stimulates the release of GABA, which inhibits the nervous system and makes us feel drunk. Low levels of GABA can produce anxiety, and GABA agonists (tranquilizers) are used to reduce anxiety.
Glutamate	The most common neurotransmitter, it's released in more than 90% of the brain's synapses. Glutamate is found in the food additive MSG (monosodium glutamate).	Excess glutamate can cause overstimulation, migraines and seizures.
Serotonin	Involved in many functions, including mood, appetite, sleep, and aggression.	Low levels of serotonin are associated with depression, and some drugs designed to treat depression (known as selective serotonin reuptake inhibitors, or SSRIs) serve to prevent their reuptake.

KEY TAKEAWAYS

- The central nervous system (CNS) is the collection of neurons that make up the brain and the spinal cord.
- The peripheral nervous system (PNS) is the collection of neurons that link the CNS to our skin, muscles, and glands.
- Neurons are specialized cells, found in the nervous system, which transmit information. Neurons contain a dendrite, a soma, and an axon.
- Some axons are covered with a fatty substance known as the myelin sheath, which surrounds the axon, acting as an insulator and allowing faster transmission of the electrical signal
- The dendrite is a treelike extension that receives information from other neurons and transmits electrical stimulation to the soma.
- The axon is an elongated fiber that transfers information from the soma to the terminal buttons.
- Neurotransmitters relay information chemically from the terminal buttons and across the synapses to the receiving dendrites using a type of lock and key system.
- The many different neurotransmitters work together to influence cognition, memory, and behavior.
- Agonists are drugs that mimic the actions of neurotransmitters, whereas antagonists are drugs that block the action of neurotransmitters.

EXERCISES AND CRITICAL THINKING

1. Draw a picture of a neuron and label its main parts.
2. Imagine an action that you engage in every day and explain how neurons and neurotransmitters might work together to help you engage in that action.

2. OUR BRAINS CONTROL OUR THOUGHTS, FEELINGS, AND BEHAVIOR

LEARNING OBJECTIVES

1. Describe the structures and function of the "old brain" and its influence on behavior.
2. Explain the structure of the cerebral cortex (its hemispheres and lobes) and the function of each area of the cortex.
3. Define the concepts of brain plasticity, neurogenesis, and brain lateralization.

If you were someone who understood brain anatomy and were to look at the brain of an animal that you had never seen before, you would nevertheless be able to deduce the likely capacities of the animal. This is because the brains of all animals are very similar in overall form. In each animal the brain is layered, and the basic structures of the brain are similar (see Figure 3.6). The innermost structures of the brain—the parts nearest the spinal cord—are the oldest part of the brain, and these areas carry out the same the functions they did for our distant ancestors. The "old brain" regulates basic survival functions, such as breathing, moving, resting, and feeding, and creates our experiences of emotion. Mammals, including humans, have developed further brain layers that provide more advanced functions—for instance, better memory, more sophisticated social interactions, and the ability to experience emotions. Humans have a very large and highly developed outer layer known as the *cerebral cortex* (see Figure 3.7), which makes us particularly adept at these processes.

FIGURE 3.6 The Major Structures in the Human Brain

The major brain parts are colored and labeled.

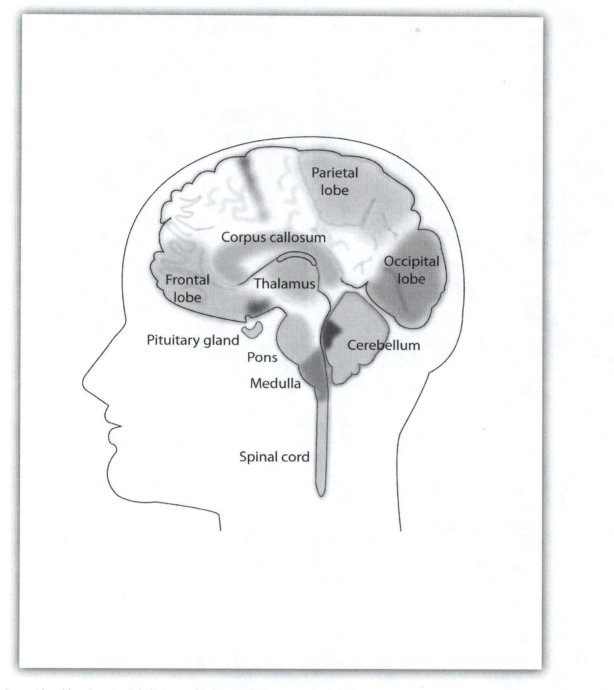

Source: Adapted from Camazine, S. (n.d.). Images of the brain. Medical, science, and nature things: Photography and digital imagery by Scott Camazine. Retrieved from http://www.scottcamazine.com/photos/brain/pages/09MRIBrain_jpg.htm.

FIGURE 3.7 Cerebral Cortex

Humans have a very large and highly developed outer brain layer known as the *cerebral cortex*. The cortex provides humans with excellent memory, outstanding cognitive skills, and the ability to experience complex emotions.

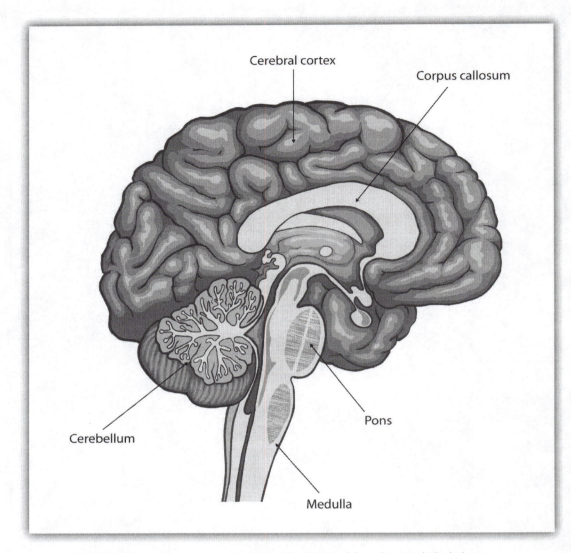

Source: Adapted from Wikia Education. (n.d.). Cerebral cortex. Retrieved from http://psychology.wikia.com/wiki/Cerebral_cortex.

2.1 The Old Brain: Wired for Survival

The **brain stem** is *the oldest and innermost region of the brain*. It's designed to control the most basic functions of life, including breathing, attention, and motor responses (Figure 3.8). The brain stem begins where the spinal cord enters the skull and forms the **medulla**, *the area of the brain stem that controls heart rate and breathing*. In many cases the medulla alone is sufficient to maintain life—animals that have the remainder of their brains above the medulla severed are still able to eat, breathe, and even move. The spherical shape above the medulla is the **pons**, *a structure in the brain stem that helps control the movements of the body, playing a particularly important role in balance and walking*.

Running through the medulla and the pons is a long, narrow network of neurons known as the **reticular formation**. The job of the reticular formation is to filter out some of the stimuli that are coming into the brain from the spinal cord and to relay the remainder of the signals to other areas of the brain. The reticular formation also plays important roles in walking, eating, sexual activity, and sleeping. When electrical stimulation is applied to the reticular formation of an animal, it immediately becomes fully awake, and when the reticular formation is severed from the higher brain regions, the animal falls into a deep coma.

FIGURE 3.8 The Brain Stem and the Thalamus

The brain stem is an extension of the spinal cord, including the medulla, the pons, the thalamus, and the reticular formation.

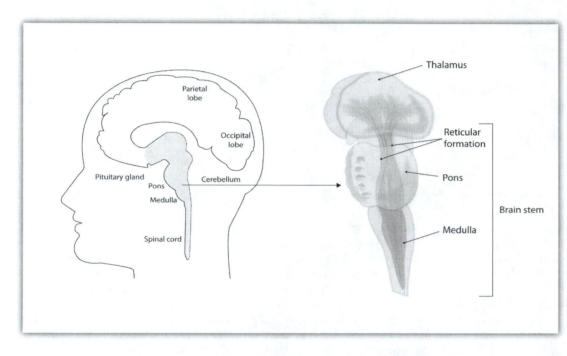

Above the brain stem are other parts of the old brain that also are involved in the processing of behavior and emotions (see Figure 3.9). The **thalamus** is *the egg-shaped structure above the brain stem that applies still more filtering to the sensory information that is coming up from the spinal cord and through the reticular formation, and it relays some of these remaining signals to the higher brain levels* (Guillery & Sherman, 2002).[5] The thalamus also receives some of the higher brain's replies, forwarding them to the medulla and the cerebellum. The thalamus is also important in sleep because it shuts off incoming signals from the senses, allowing us to rest.

brain stem

The oldest and innermost region of the brain, it serves to control the most basic functions of life, including breathing, attention, and motor responses.

medulla

The area of the brain stem that controls heart rate and breathing.

pons

A structure in the brain stem that helps control the movements of the body, playing a particularly important role in balance and walking.

reticular formation

A long, narrow network of neurons that runs through the medulla and the pons.

thalamus

The egg-shaped structure above the brain stem that filters sensory information coming up from the spinal cord and relays signals to the higher brain levels.

FIGURE 3.9 The Limbic System

This diagram shows the major parts of the limbic system, as well as the pituitary gland, which is controlled by it.

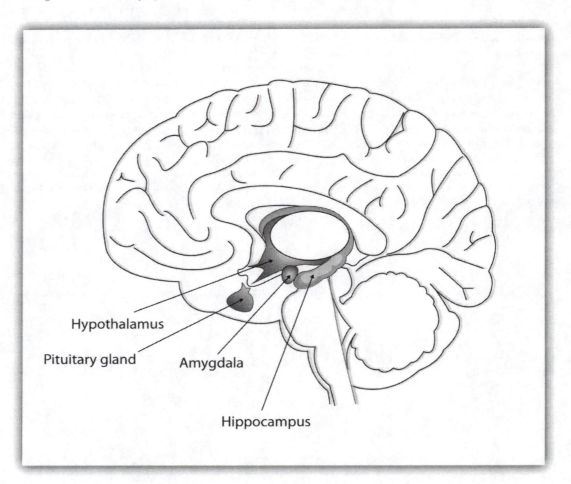

The **cerebellum** (literally, "little brain") *consists of two wrinkled ovals behind the brain stem. It functions to coordinate voluntary movement.* People who have damage to the cerebellum have difficulty walking, keeping their balance, and holding their hands steady. Consuming alcohol influences the cerebellum, which is why people who are drunk have more difficulty walking in a straight line. Also, the cerebellum contributes to emotional responses, helps us discriminate between different sounds and textures, and is important in learning (Bower & Parsons, 2003).[6]

Whereas the primary function of the brain stem is to regulate the most basic aspects of life, including motor functions, the *limbic system* is largely responsible for memory and emotions, including our responses to reward and punishment. The **limbic system** is *a brain area, located between the brain stem and the two cerebral hemispheres, that governs emotion and memory. It includes the amygdala, the hypothalamus, and the hippocampus.*

The **amygdala** *consists of two "almond-shaped" clusters (amygdala comes from the Latin word for "almond") and is primarily responsible for regulating our perceptions of, and reactions to, aggression and fear.* The amygdala has connections to other bodily systems related to fear, including the sympathetic nervous system (which we will see later is important in fear responses), facial responses (which perceive and express emotions), the processing of smells, and the release of neurotransmitters related to stress and aggression (Best, 2009).[7] In one early study, Klüver and Bucy (1939)[8] damaged the amygdala of an aggressive rhesus monkey. They found that the once angry animal immediately became passive and no longer responded to fearful situations with aggressive behavior. Electrical stimulation of the amygdala in other animals also influences aggression. In addition to helping us experience fear, the amygdala also helps us learn from situations that create fear. When we experience events that are dangerous, the amygdala stimulates the brain to remember the details of the situation so that we learn to avoid it in the future (Sigurdsson, Doyère, Cain, & LeDoux, 2007).[9]

---

cerebellum

Two wrinkled ovals located behind the brain stem that function to coordinate voluntary movement.

limbic system

A brain area located between the brain stem and the two cerebral hemispheres that governs emotion and memory.

amygdala

A region of the old brain primarily responsible for regulating our perceptions of, and reactions to, aggression and fear.

Located just under the thalamus (hence its name) the **hypothalamus** is *a brain structure that contains a number of small areas that perform a variety of functions, including the important role of linking the nervous system to the endocrine system via the pituitary gland.* Through its many interactions with other parts of the brain, the hypothalamus helps regulate body temperature, hunger, thirst, and sex, and responds to the satisfaction of these needs by creating feelings of pleasure. Olds and Milner (1954)[10] discovered these reward centers accidentally after they had momentarily stimulated the hypothalamus of a rat. The researchers noticed that after being stimulated, the rat continued to move to the exact spot in its cage where the stimulation had occurred, as if it were trying to re-create the circumstances surrounding its original experience. Upon further research into these reward centers, Olds (1958)[11] discovered that animals would do almost anything to re-create enjoyable stimulation, including crossing a painful electrified grid to receive it. In one experiment a rat was given the opportunity to electrically stimulate its own hypothalamus by pressing a pedal. The rat enjoyed the experience so much that it pressed the pedal more than 7,000 times per hour until it collapsed from sheer exhaustion.

The **hippocampus** *consists of two "horns" that curve back from the amygdala.* The hippocampus is important in storing information in long-term memory. If the hippocampus is damaged, a person cannot build new memories, living instead in a strange world where everything he or she experiences just fades away, even while older memories from the time before the damage are untouched.

2.2 The Cerebral Cortex Creates Consciousness and Thinking

All animals have adapted to their environments by developing abilities that help them survive. Some animals have hard shells, others run extremely fast, and some have acute hearing. Human beings do not have any of these particular characteristics, but we do have one big advantage over other animals—we are very, very smart.

You might think that we should be able to determine the intelligence of an animal by looking at the ratio of the animal's brain weight to the weight of its entire body. But this does not really work. The elephant's brain is one thousandth of its weight, but the whale's brain is only one ten-thousandth of its body weight. On the other hand, although the human brain is one 60th of its body weight, the mouse's brain represents one fortieth of its body weight. Despite these comparisons, elephants do not seem 10 times smarter than whales, and humans definitely seem smarter than mice.

The key to the advanced intelligence of humans is not found in the size of our brains. What sets humans apart from other animals is our larger **cerebral cortex**—*the outer bark-like layer of our brain that allows us to so successfully use language, acquire complex skills, create tools, and live in social groups* (Gibson, 2002).[12] In humans, the cerebral cortex is wrinkled and folded, rather than smooth as it is in most other animals. This creates a much greater surface area and size, and allows increased capacities for learning, remembering, and thinking. The folding of the cerebral cortex is referred to as *corticalization.*

Although the cortex is only about one tenth of an inch thick, it makes up more than 80% of the brain's weight. The cortex contains about 20 billion nerve cells and 300 trillion synaptic connections (de Courten-Myers, 1999).[13] Supporting all these neurons are billions more **glial cells (glia)**, *cells that surround and link to the neurons, protecting them, providing them with nutrients, and absorbing unused neurotransmitters.* The glia come in different forms and have different functions. For instance, the myelin sheath surrounding the axon of many neurons is a type of glial cell. The glia are essential partners of neurons, without which the neurons could not survive or function (Miller, 2005).[14]

hypothalamus

A brain structure that performs a variety of functions, including the regulation of hunger and sexual behavior, as well as linking the nervous system to the endocrine system via the pituitary gland.

hippocampus

A limbic system brain structure important in storing information in long-term memory.

cerebral cortex

The outer bark-like layer of the brain that allows us to so successfully use language, acquire complex skills, create tools, and live in social groups.

glial cells (glia)

Cells that surround and link to the neurons, protecting them, providing them with nutrients, and absorbing unused neurotransmitters.

frontal lobe

One of the four brain lobes, responsible primarily for thinking, planning, memory, and judgment.

parietal lobe

One of the four brain lobes, responsible primarily for processing information about touch.

occipital lobe

One of the four brain lobes, responsible primarily for processing visual information.

temporal lobe

One of the four brain lobes, responsible primarily for hearing and language.

The cerebral cortex is divided into two *hemispheres*, and each hemisphere is divided into four *lobes*, each separated by folds known as *fissures*. If we look at the cortex starting at the front of the brain and moving over the top (see Figure 3.10), we see first the **frontal lobe** (behind the forehead), *which is responsible primarily for thinking, planning, memory, and judgment.* Following the frontal lobe is the **parietal lobe**, *which extends from the middle to the back of the skull and which is responsible primarily for processing information about touch.* Then comes the **occipital lobe**, *at the very back of the skull, which processes visual information.* Finally, in front of the occipital lobe (pretty much between the ears) is the **temporal lobe**, *responsible primarily for hearing and language.*

FIGURE 3.10 The Two Hemispheres

The brain is divided into two hemispheres (left and right), each of which has four lobes (temporal, frontal, occipital, and parietal). Furthermore, there are specific cortical areas that control different processes.

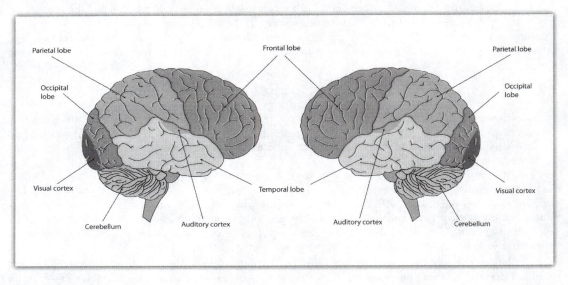

Functions of the Cortex

When the German physicists Gustav Fritsch and Eduard Hitzig (1870/2009)[15] applied mild electric stimulation to different parts of a dog's cortex, they discovered that they could make different parts of the dog's body move. Furthermore, they discovered an important and unexpected principle of brain activity. They found that stimulating the right side of the brain produced movement in the left side of the dog's body, and vice versa. This finding follows from a general principle about how the brain is structured, called *contralateral control*. The brain is wired such that in most cases the left hemisphere receives sensations from and controls the right side of the body, and vice versa.

motor cortex

The part of the cortex that controls and executes movements of the body by sending signals to the cerebellum and the spinal cord.

Fritsch and Hitzig also found that the movement that followed the brain stimulation only occurred when they stimulated a specific arch-shaped region that runs across the top of the brain from ear to ear, just at the front of the parietal lobe (see Figure 3.11). Fritsch and Hitzig had discovered the **motor cortex**, *the part of the cortex that controls and executes movements of the body by sending signals to the cerebellum and the spinal cord.* More recent research has mapped the motor cortex even more fully, by providing mild electronic stimulation to different areas of the motor cortex in fully conscious patients while observing their bodily responses (because the brain has no sensory receptors, these patients feel no pain). As you can see in Figure 3.11, this research has revealed that the motor cortex is specialized for providing control over the body, in the sense that the parts of the body that require more precise and finer movements, such as the face and the hands, also are allotted the greatest amount of cortical space.

FIGURE 3.11   The Sensory Cortex and the Motor Cortex

The portion of the sensory and motor cortex devoted to receiving messages that control specific regions of the body is determined by the amount of fine movement that area is capable of performing. Thus the hand and fingers have as much area in the cerebral cortex as does the entire trunk of the body.

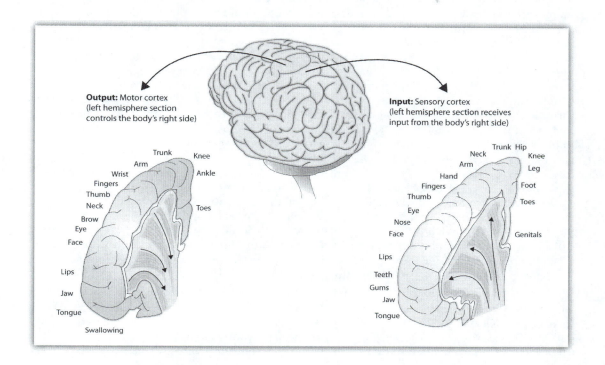

Just as the motor cortex sends out messages to the specific parts of the body, the **somatosensory cortex**, *an area just behind and parallel to the motor cortex at the back of the frontal lobe, receives information from the skin's sensory receptors and the movements of different body parts*. Again, the more sensitive the body region, the more area is dedicated to it in the sensory cortex. Our sensitive lips, for example, occupy a large area in the sensory cortex, as do our fingers and genitals.

Other areas of the cortex process other types of sensory information. The **visual cortex** is *the area located in the occipital lobe (at the very back of the brain) that processes visual information*. If you were stimulated in the visual cortex, you would see flashes of light or color, and perhaps you remember having had the experience of "seeing stars" when you were hit in, or fell on, the back of your head. The temporal lobe, located on the lower side of each hemisphere, contains the **auditory cortex**, *which is responsible for hearing and language*. The temporal lobe also processes some visual information, providing us with the ability to name the objects around us (Martin, 2007).[16]

As you can see in Figure 3.11, the motor and sensory areas of the cortex account for a relatively small part of the total cortex. The remainder of the cortex is made up of **association areas** *in which sensory and motor information is combined and associated with our stored knowledge*. These association areas are the places in the brain that are responsible for most of the things that make human beings seem human. The association areas are involved in higher mental functions, such as learning, thinking, planning, judging, moral reflecting, figuring, and spatial reasoning.

somatosensory cortex

An area just behind and parallel to the motor cortex at the back of the frontal lobe that receives information from the skin's sensory receptors and the movements of different body parts.

visual cortex

The area located in the occipital lobe that processes visual information.

auditory cortex

The area located in the temporal lobe that is responsible for hearing and language.

association areas

Brain regions in which sensory and motor information is combined and associated with stored knowledge.

The Brain Is Flexible: Neuroplasticity

neuroplasticity

The brain's ability to change its structure and function in response to experience or damage.

The control of some specific bodily functions, such as movement, vision, and hearing, is performed in specified areas of the cortex, and if these areas are damaged, the individual will likely lose the ability to perform the corresponding function. For instance, if an infant suffers damage to facial recognition areas in the temporal lobe, it is likely that he or she will never be able to recognize faces (Farah, Rabinowitz, Quinn, & Liu, 2000).[17] On the other hand, the brain is not divided up in an entirely rigid way. The brain's neurons have a remarkable capacity to reorganize and extend themselves to carry out particular functions in response to the needs of the organism, and to repair damage. As a result, the brain constantly creates new neural communication routes and rewires existing ones. Neuroplasticity refers to *the brain's ability to change its structure and function in response to experience or damage*. Neuroplasticity enables us to learn and remember new things and adjust to new experiences.

Our brains are the most "plastic" when we are young children, as it is during this time that we learn the most about our environment. On the other hand, neuroplasticity continues to be observed even in adults (Kolb & Fantie, 1989).[18] The principles of neuroplasticity help us understand how our brains develop to reflect our experiences. For instance, accomplished musicians have a larger auditory cortex compared with the general population (Bengtsson et al., 2005)[19] and also require less neural activity to move their fingers over the keys than do novices (Münte, Altenmüller, & Jäncke, 2002).[20] These observations reflect the changes in the brain that follow our experiences.

Plasticity is also observed when there is damage to the brain or to parts of the body that are represented in the motor and sensory cortexes. When a tumor in the left hemisphere of the brain impairs language, the right hemisphere will begin to compensate to help the person recover the ability to speak (Thiel et al., 2006).[21] And if a person loses a finger, the area of the sensory cortex that previously received information from the missing finger will begin to receive input from adjacent fingers, causing the remaining digits to become more sensitive to touch (Fox, 1984).[22]

neurogenesis

The forming of new neurons

Although neurons cannot repair or regenerate themselves as skin or blood vessels can, new evidence suggests that the brain can engage in **neurogenesis**, *the forming of new neurons* (Van Praag, Zhao, Gage, & Gazzaniga, 2004).[23] These new neurons originate deep in the brain and may then migrate to other brain areas where they form new connections with other neurons (Gould, 2007).[24] This leaves open the possibility that someday scientists might be able to "rebuild" damaged brains by creating drugs that help grow neurons.

brain lateralization

The idea that the left and the right hemispheres of the brain are specialized to perform different functions.

corpus callosum

The region that connects the two halves of the brain and supports communication between the hemispheres.

Research Focus: Identifying the Unique Functions of the Left and Right Hemispheres Using Split-Brain Patients

We have seen that the left hemisphere of the brain primarily senses and controls the motor movements on the right side of the body, and vice versa. This fact provides an interesting way to study **brain lateralization**—*the idea that the left and the right hemispheres of the brain are specialized to perform different functions*. Gazzaniga, Bogen, and Sperry (1965)[25] studied a patient, known as W. J., who had undergone an operation to relieve severe seizures. In this surgery *the region that normally connects the two halves of the brain and supports communication between the hemispheres*, known as the **corpus callosum**, is severed. As a result, the patient essentially becomes a person with two separate brains. Because the left and right hemispheres are separated, each hemisphere develops a mind of its own, with its own sensations, concepts, and motivations (Gazzaniga, 2005).[26]

In their research, Gazzaniga and his colleagues tested the ability of W. J. to recognize and respond to objects and written passages that were presented to only the left or to only the right brain hemispheres (see Figure 3.12). The researchers had W. J. look straight ahead and then flashed, for a fraction of a second, a picture of a geometrical shape to the left of where he was looking. By doing so, they assured that—because the two hemispheres had been separated—the image of the shape was experienced only in the right brain hemisphere (remember that sensory input from the left side of the body is sent to the right side of the brain). Gazzaniga and his colleagues found that W. J. was able to identify what he had been shown when he was asked to pick the object from a series of shapes, using his left hand, but that he could not do this when the object was shown in the right visual field. On the other hand, W. J. could easily read written material presented in the right visual field (and thus experienced in the left hemisphere) but not when it was presented in the left visual field.

Visual and Verbal Processing in the Split-Brain Patient

The information that is presented on the left side of our field of vision is transmitted to the right brain hemisphere, and vice versa. In split-brain patients, the severed corpus callosum does not permit information to be transferred between hemispheres, which allows researchers to learn about the functions of each hemisphere. In the sample on the left, the split-brain patient could not choose which image had been presented because the left hemisphere cannot process visual information. In the sample on the right the patient could not read the passage because the right brain hemisphere cannot process language.

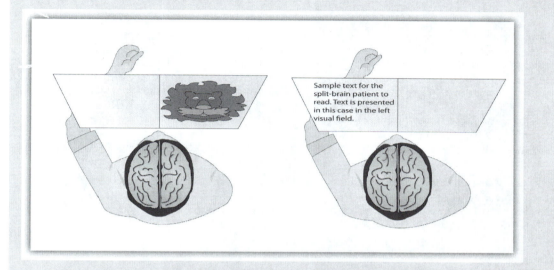

This research, and many other studies following it, has demonstrated that the two brain hemispheres specialize in different abilities. In most people the ability to speak, write, and understand language is located in the left hemisphere. This is why W. J. could read passages that were presented on the right side and thus transmitted to the left hemisphere, but could not read passages that were only experienced in the right brain hemisphere. The left hemisphere is also better at math and at judging time and rhythm. It is also superior in coordinating the order of complex movements—for example, lip movements needed for speech. The right hemisphere, on the other hand, has only very limited verbal abilities, and yet it excels in perceptual skills. The right hemisphere is able to recognize objects, including faces, patterns, and melodies, and it can put a puzzle together or draw a picture. This is why W. J. could pick out the image when he saw it on the left, but not the right, visual field.

Although Gazzaniga's research demonstrated that the brain is in fact lateralized, such that the two hemispheres specialize in different activities, this does not mean that when people behave in a certain way or perform a certain activity they are only using one hemisphere of their brains at a time. That would be drastically oversimplifying the concept of brain differences. We normally use both hemispheres at the same time, and the difference between the abilities of the two hemispheres is not absolute (Soroker et al., 2005).[27]

Psychology in Everyday Life: Why Are Some People Left-Handed?

Across cultures and ethnic groups, about 90% of people are mainly right-handed, whereas only 10% are primarily left-handed (Peters, Reimers, & Manning, 2006).[28] This fact is puzzling, in part because the number of left-handers is so low, and in part because other animals, including our closest primate relatives, do not show any type of handedness. The existence of right-handers and left-handers provides an interesting example of the relationship among evolution, biology, and social factors and how the same phenomenon can be understood at different levels of analysis (Harris, 1990; McManus, 2002).[29]

At least some handedness is determined by genetics. Ultrasound scans show that 9 out of 10 fetuses suck the thumb of their right hand, suggesting that the preference is determined before birth (Hepper, Wells, & Lynch, 2005),[30] and the mechanism of transmission has been linked to a gene on the X chromosome (Jones & Martin, 2000).[31] It has also been observed that left-handed people are likely to have fewer children, and this may be in part because the mothers of left-handers are more prone to miscarriages and other prenatal problems (McKeever, Cerone, Suter, & Wu, 2000).[32]

But culture also plays a role. In the past, left-handed children were forced to write with their right hands in many countries, and this practice continues, particularly in collectivistic cultures, such as India and Japan, where left-handedness is viewed negatively as compared with individualistic societies, such as the United States. For example, India has about half as many left-handers as the United States (Ida & Mandal, 2003).[33]

There are both advantages and disadvantages to being left-handed in a world where most people are right-handed. One problem for lefties is that the world is designed for right-handers. Automatic teller machines (ATMs), classroom desks, scissors, microscopes, drill presses, and table saws are just some examples of every-day machinery that is designed with the most important controls on the right side. This may explain in part why left-handers suffer somewhat more accidents than do right-handers (Dutta & Mandal, 2006).[34]

Despite the potential difficulty living and working in a world designed for right-handers, there seem to be some advantages to being left-handed. Throughout history, a number of prominent artists have been left-handed, including Leonardo da Vinci, Michelangelo, Pablo Picasso, and Max Escher. Because the right hemisphere is superior in imaging and visual abilities, there may be some advantage to using the left hand for drawing or painting (Springer & Deutsch, 1998).[35] Left-handed people are also better at envisioning three-dimensional objects, which may explain why there is such a high number of left-handed architects, artists, and chess players in proportion to their numbers (Coren, 1992).[36] However, there are also more left-handers among those with reading disabilities, allergies, and migraine headaches (Geschwind & Behan, 2007),[37] perhaps due to the fact that a small minority of left-handers owe their handedness to a birth trauma, such as being born prematurely (Betancur, Vélez, Cabanieu, & le Moal, 1990).[38]

In sports in which handedness may matter, such as tennis, boxing, fencing, or judo, left-handers may have an advantage. They play many games against right-handers and learn how to best handle their styles. Right-handers, however, play very few games against left-handers, which may make them more vulnerable. This explains why a disproportionately high number of left-handers are found in sports where direct one-on-one action predominates. In other sports, such as golf, there are fewer left-handed players because the handedness of one player has no effect on the competition.

The fact that left-handers excel in some sports suggests the possibility that they may have also had an evolutionary advantage because their ancestors may have been more successful in important skills such as hand-to-hand combat (Bodmer & McKie, 1994).[39] At this point, however, this idea remains only a hypothesis, and determinants of human handedness are yet to be fully understood.

KEY TAKEAWAYS

- The old brain—including the brain stem, medulla, pons, reticular formation, thalamus, cerebellum, amygdala, hypothalamus, and hippocampus—regulates basic survival functions, such as breathing, moving, resting, feeding, emotions, and memory.

- The cerebral cortex, made up of billions of neurons and glial cells, is divided into the right and left hemispheres and into four lobes.

- The frontal lobe is primarily responsible for thinking, planning, memory, and judgment. The parietal lobe is primarily responsible for bodily sensations and touch. The temporal lobe is primarily responsible for hearing and language. The occipital lobe is primarily responsible for vision. Other areas of the cortex act as association areas, responsible for integrating information.

- The brain changes as a function of experience and potential damage in a process known as plasticity. The brain can generate new neurons through neurogenesis.

- The motor cortex controls voluntary movements. Body parts requiring the most control and dexterity take up the most space in the motor cortex.

- The sensory cortex receives and processes bodily sensations. Body parts that are the most sensitive occupy the greatest amount of space in the sensory cortex.

- The left cerebral hemisphere is primarily responsible for language and speech in most people, whereas the right hemisphere specializes in spatial and perceptual skills, visualization, and the recognition of patterns, faces, and melodies.

- The severing of the corpus callosum, which connects the two hemispheres, creates a "split-brain patient," with the effect of creating two separate minds operating in one person.

- Studies with split-brain patients as research participants have been used to study brain lateralization.

- Neuroplasticity allows the brain to adapt and change as a function of experience or damage.

EXERCISES AND CRITICAL THINKING

1. Do you think that animals experience emotion? What aspects of brain structure might lead you to believe that they do or do not?

2. Consider your own experiences and speculate on which parts of your brain might be particularly well developed as a result of these experiences.

3. Which brain hemisphere are you likely to be using when you search for a fork in the silverware drawer? Which brain hemisphere are you most likely to be using when you struggle to remember the name of an old friend?

4. Do you think that encouraging left-handed children to use their right hands is a good idea? Why or why not?

3. PSYCHOLOGISTS STUDY THE BRAIN USING MANY DIFFERENT METHODS

LEARNING OBJECTIVE

1. **Compare and contrast the techniques that scientists use to view and understand brain structures and functions.**

One problem in understanding the brain is that it is difficult to get a good picture of what is going on inside it. But there are a variety of empirical methods that allow scientists to look at brains in action, and the number of possibilities has increased dramatically in recent years with the introduction of new *neuroimaging* techniques. In this section we will consider the various techniques that psychologists use to learn about the brain. Each of the different techniques has some advantages, and when we put them together, we begin to get a relatively good picture of how the brain functions and which brain structures control which activities.

Perhaps the most immediate approach to visualizing and understanding the structure of the brain is to directly analyze the brains of human cadavers. When Albert Einstein died in 1955, his brain was removed and stored for later analysis. Researcher Marian Diamond (1999)[40] later analyzed a section of the Einstein's cortex to investigate its characteristics. Diamond was interested in the role of glia, and she hypothesized that the ratio of glial cells to neurons was an important determinant of intelligence. To test this hypothesis, she compared the ratio of glia to neurons in Einstein's brain with the ratio in the preserved brains of 11 other more "ordinary" men. However, Diamond was able to find support for only part of her research hypothesis. Although she found that Einstein's brain had relatively more glia in all the areas that she studied than did the control group, the difference was only statistically significant in one of the areas she tested. Diamond admits a limitation in her study is that she had only one Einstein to compare with 11 ordinary men.

3.1 Lesions Provide a Picture of What Is Missing

An advantage of the cadaver approach is that the brains can be fully studied, but an obvious disadvantage is that the brains are no longer active. In other cases, however, we can study living brains. The brains of living human beings may be damaged, for instance, as a result of strokes, falls, automobile accidents, gunshots, or tumors. These damages are called *lesions*. In rare occasions, brain lesions may be created intentionally through surgery, such as that designed to remove brain tumors or (as in split-brain patients) to reduce the effects of epilepsy. Psychologists also sometimes intentionally create lesions in animals to study the effects on their behavior. In so doing, they hope to be able to draw inferences about the likely functions of human brains from the effects of the lesions in animals.

Lesions allow the scientist to observe any loss of brain function that may occur. For instance, when an individual suffers a stroke, a blood clot deprives part of the brain of oxygen, killing the neurons in the area and rendering that area unable to process information. In some cases, the result of the stroke is a specific lack of ability. For instance, if the stroke influences the occipital lobe, then vision may suffer, and if the stroke influences the areas associated with language or speech, these functions will suffer. In fact, our earliest understanding of the specific areas involved in speech and language were gained by studying patients who had experienced strokes.

FIGURE 3.13

Areas in the frontal lobe of Phineas Gage were damaged when a metal rod blasted through it. Although Gage lived through the accident, his personality, emotions, and moral reasoning were influenced. The accident helped scientists understand the role of the frontal lobe in these processes.

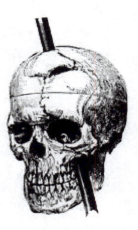

Source: Photo courtesy of John M. Harlow,
http://en.wikipedia.org/wiki/
File:Phineas_gage_-_1868_skull_diagram.jpg.

It is now known that a good part of our moral reasoning abilities are located in the frontal lobe, and at least some of this understanding comes from lesion studies. For instance, consider the well-known case of Phineas Gage, a 25-year-old railroad worker who, as a result of an explosion, had an iron rod driven into his cheek and out through the top of his skull, causing major damage to his frontal lobe (Macmillan, 2000).[41] Although remarkably Gage was able to return to work after the wounds healed, he no longer seemed to be the same person to those who knew him. The amiable, soft-spoken Gage had become irritable, rude, irresponsible, and dishonest. Although there are questions about the interpretation of this case study (Kotowicz, 2007),[42] it did provide early evidence that the frontal lobe is involved in emotion and morality (Damasio et al., 2005).[43]

More recent and more controlled research has also used patients with lesions to investigate the source of moral reasoning. Michael Koenigs and his colleagues (Koenigs et al., 2007)[44] asked groups of normal persons, individuals with lesions in the frontal lobes, and individuals with lesions in other places in the brain to respond to scenarios that involved doing harm to a person, even though the harm ultimately saved the lives of other people (Miller, 2008).[45]

In one of the scenarios the participants were asked if they would be willing to kill one person in order to prevent five other people from being killed. As you can see in Figure 3.14, they found that the individuals with lesions in the frontal lobe were significantly more likely to agree to do the harm than were individuals from the two other groups.

FIGURE 3.14 The Frontal Lobe and Moral Judgment

Koenigs and his colleagues (2007)[46] found that the frontal lobe is important in moral judgment. Persons with lesions in the frontal lobe were more likely to be willing to harm one person in order to save the lives of five others than were control participants or those with lesions in other parts of the brain.

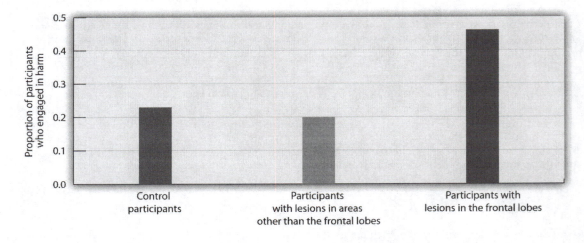

3.2 Recording Electrical Activity in the Brain

In addition to lesion approaches, it is also possible to learn about the brain by studying the electrical activity created by the firing of its neurons. One approach, primarily used with animals, is to place detectors in the brain to study the responses of specific neurons. Research using these techniques has found, for instance, that there are specific neurons, known as *feature detectors*, in the visual cortex that detect movement, lines and edges, and even faces (Kanwisher, 2000).[47]

FIGURE 3.15

A participant in an EEG study has a number of electrodes placed around the head, which allows the researcher to study the activity of the person's brain. The patterns of electrical activity vary depending on the participant's current state (e.g., whether he or she is sleeping or awake) and on the tasks the person is engaging in.

Source: Photo courtesy of the University of Oregon Child and Family Center, http://www.uoregon.edu/~cfc/projects-bbl.htm.

A less invasive approach, and one that can be used on living humans, is **electroencephalography (EEG)**. The EEG is *a technique that records the electrical activity produced by the brain's neurons through the use of electrodes that are placed around the research participant's head.* An EEG can show if a person is asleep, awake, or anesthetized because the brain wave patterns are known to differ during each state. EEGs can also track the waves that are produced when a person is reading, writing, and speaking, and are useful for understanding brain abnormalities, such as epilepsy. A particular advantage of EEG is that the participant can move around while the recordings are being taken, which is useful when measuring brain activity in children who often have difficulty keeping still. Furthermore, by following electrical impulses across the surface of the brain, researchers can observe changes over very fast time periods.

electroencephalography (EEG)

A technique that records the electrical activity produced by the brain's neurons through the use of electrodes placed around the research participant's head.

3.3   Peeking Inside the Brain: Neuroimaging

Although the EEG can provide information about the general patterns of electrical activity within the brain, and although the EEG allows the researcher to see these changes quickly as they occur in real time, the electrodes must be placed on the surface of the skull and each electrode measures brain waves from large areas of the brain. As a result, EEGs do not provide a very clear picture of the structure of the brain.

But techniques exist to provide more specific brain images. **Functional magnetic resonance imaging (fMRI)** is *a type of brain scan that uses a magnetic field to create images of brain activity in each brain area.* The patient lies on a bed within a large cylindrical structure containing a very strong magnet. Neurons that are firing use more oxygen, and the need for oxygen increases blood flow to the area. The fMRI detects the amount of blood flow in each brain region, and thus is an indicator of neural activity.

Very clear and detailed pictures of brain structures (see, e.g., Figure 3.16) can be produced via fMRI. Often, the images take the form of cross-sectional "slices" that are obtained as the magnetic field is passed across the brain. The images of these slices are taken repeatedly and are superimposed on images of the brain structure itself to show how activity changes in different brain structures over time. When the research participant is asked to engage in tasks while in the scanner (e.g., by playing a game with another person), the images can show which parts of the brain are associated with which types of tasks. Another advantage of the fMRI is that is it noninvasive. The research participant simply enters the machine and the scans begin.

Although the scanners themselves are expensive, the advantages of fMRIs are substantial, and they are now available in many university and hospital settings. fMRI is now the most commonly used method of learning about brain structure.

functional magnetic resonance imaging (fMRI)

A neuroimaging technique that uses a magnetic field to create images of brain structure and function.

FIGURE 3.16   fMRI Image

The fMRI creates brain images of brain structure and activity. In this image the red and yellow areas represent increased blood flow and thus increased activity. From your knowledge of brain structure, can you guess what this person is doing?

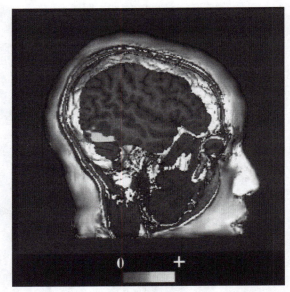

Source: Photo courtesy of the National Institutes of Health, http://commons.wikimedia.org/wiki/File:Face_recognition.jpg.

transcranial magnetic stimulation (TMS)

A procedure in which magnetic pulses are applied to the brain of living persons with the goal of temporarily and safely deactivating a small brain region.

There is still one more approach that is being more frequently implemented to understand brain function, and although it is new, it may turn out to be the most useful of all. **Transcranial magnetic stimulation (TMS)** is *a procedure in which magnetic pulses are applied to the brain of living persons with the goal of temporarily and safely deactivating a small brain region.* In TMS studies the research participant is first scanned in an fMRI machine to determine the exact location of the brain area to be tested. Then the electrical stimulation is provided to the brain before or while the participant is working on a cognitive task, and the effects of the stimulation on performance are assessed. If the participant's ability to perform the task is influenced by the presence of the stimulation, then the researchers can conclude that this particular area of the brain is important to carrying out the task.

The primary advantage of TMS is that it allows the researcher to draw causal conclusions about the influence of brain structures on thoughts, feelings, and behaviors. When the TMS pulses are applied, the brain region becomes less active, and this deactivation is expected to influence the research participant's responses. Current research has used TMS to study the brain areas responsible for emotion and cognition and their roles in how people perceive intention and approach moral reasoning (Kalbe et al., 2010; Van den Eynde et al., 2010; Young, Camprodon, Hauser, Pascual-Leone, & Saxe, 2010).[48] TMS is also used as a treatment for a variety of psychological conditions, including migraine, Parkinson's disease, and major depressive disorder.

Research Focus: Cyberostracism

Neuroimaging techniques have important implications for understanding our behavior, including our responses to those around us. Naomi Eisenberger and her colleagues (2003)[49] tested the hypothesis that people who were excluded by others would report emotional distress and that images of their brains would show that they experienced pain in the same part of the brain where physical pain is normally experienced. In the experiment, 13 participants were each placed into an fMRI brain-imaging machine. The participants were told that they would be playing a computer "Cyberball" game with two other players who were also in fMRI machines (the two opponents did not actually exist, and their responses were controlled by the computer).

Each of the participants was measured under three different conditions. In the first part of the experiment, the participants were told that as a result of technical difficulties, the link to the other two scanners could not yet be made, and thus at first they could not engage in, but only watch, the game play. This allowed the researchers to take a baseline fMRI reading. Then, during a second inclusion scan, the participants played the game, supposedly with the two other players. During this time, the other players threw the ball to the participants. In the third, exclusion, scan, however, the participants initially received seven throws from the other two players but were then excluded from the game because the two players stopped throwing the ball to the participants for the remainder of the scan (45 throws).

The results of the analyses showed that activity in two areas of the frontal lobe was significantly greater during the exclusion scan than during the inclusion scan. Because these brain regions are known from prior research to be active for individuals who are experiencing physical pain, the authors concluded that these results show that the physiological brain responses associated with being socially excluded by others are similar to brain responses experienced upon physical injury.

Further research (Chen, Williams, Fitness, & Newton, 2008; Wesselmann, Bagg, & Williams, 2009)[50] has documented that people react to being excluded in a variety of situations with a variety of emotions and behaviors. People who feel that they are excluded, or even those who observe other people being excluded, not only experience pain, but feel worse about themselves and their relationships with people more generally, and they may work harder to try to restore their connections with others.

KEY TAKEAWAYS

- Studying the brains of cadavers can lead to discoveries about brain structure, but these studies are limited due to the fact that the brain is no longer active.
- Lesion studies are informative about the effects of lesions on different brain regions.
- Electrophysiological recording may be used in animals to directly measure brain activity.
- Measures of electrical activity in the brain, such as electroencephalography (EEG), are used to assess brain-wave patterns and activity.
- Functional magnetic resonance imaging (fMRI) measures blood flow in the brain during different activities, providing information about the activity of neurons and thus the functions of brain regions.
- Transcranial magnetic stimulation (TMS) is used to temporarily and safely deactivate a small brain region, with the goal of testing the causal effects of the deactivation on behavior.

EXERCISE AND CRITICAL THINKING

1. Consider the different ways that psychologists study the brain, and think of a psychological characteristic or behavior that could be studied using each of the different techniques.

4. PUTTING IT ALL TOGETHER: THE NERVOUS SYSTEM AND THE ENDOCRINE SYSTEM

LEARNING OBJECTIVES

1. Summarize the primary functions of the CNS and of the subsystems of the PNS.
2. Explain how the electrical components of the nervous system and the chemical components of the endocrine system work together to influence behavior.

Now that we have considered how individual neurons operate and the roles of the different brain areas, it is time to ask how the body manages to "put it all together." How do the complex activities in the various parts of the brain, the simple all-or-nothing firings of billions of interconnected neurons, and the various chemical systems within the body, work together to allow the body to respond to the social environment and engage in everyday behaviors? In this section we will see that the complexities of human behavior are accomplished through the joint actions of electrical and chemical processes in the nervous system and the endocrine system.

4.1   Electrical Control of Behavior: The Nervous System

The nervous system (see Figure 3.17), the electrical information highway of the body, is made up of **nerves**—*bundles of interconnected neurons that fire in synchrony to carry messages.* The *central nervous system (CNS)*, made up of the brain and spinal cord, is the major controller of the body's functions, charged with interpreting sensory information and responding to it with its own directives. The CNS interprets information coming in from the senses, formulates an appropriate reaction, and sends responses to the appropriate system to respond accordingly. Everything that we see, hear, smell, touch, and taste is conveyed to us from our sensory organs as neural impulses, and each of the commands that the brain sends to the body, both consciously and unconsciously, travels through this system as well.

FIGURE 3.17   The Functional Divisions of the Nervous System

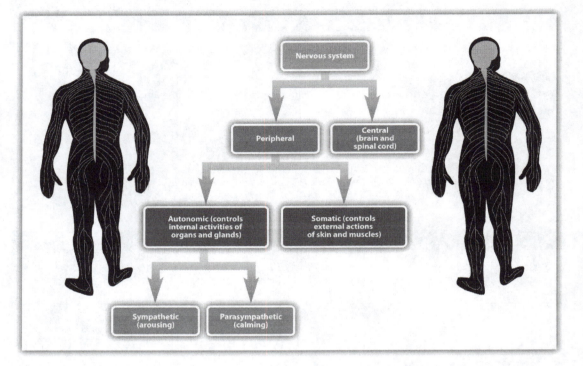

Nerves are differentiated according to their function. A **sensory (or afferent) neuron** *carries information from the sensory receptors,* whereas a **motor (or efferent) neuron** *transmits information to the muscles and glands.* An **interneuron**, which is by far the most common type of neuron, is located primarily within the CNS and is *responsible for communicating among the neurons.* Interneurons allow the brain to combine the multiple sources of available information to create a coherent picture of the sensory information being conveyed.

nerve

A bundle of interconnected neurons that fires in synchrony to carry messages.

sensory (or afferent) neuron

A neuron that carries information from the sensory receptors.

motor (or efferent) neuron

A neuron that transmits information to the muscles and glands.

interneuron

The most common type of neuron, responsible for communicating among neurons.

The **spinal cord** is *the long, thin, tubular bundle of nerves and supporting cells that extends down from the brain.* It is the central throughway of information for the body. Within the spinal cord, ascending tracts of sensory neurons relay sensory information from the sense organs to the brain while descending tracts of motor neurons relay motor commands back to the body. When a quicker-than-usual response is required, the spinal cord can do its own processing, bypassing the brain altogether. A **reflex** is *an involuntary and nearly instantaneous movement in response to a stimulus.* Reflexes are triggered when sensory information is powerful enough to reach a given threshold and the interneurons in the spinal cord act to send a message back through the motor neurons without relaying the information to the brain (see Figure 3.18). When you touch a hot stove and immediately pull your hand back, or when you fumble your cell phone and instinctively reach to catch it before it falls, reflexes in your spinal cord order the appropriate responses before your brain even knows what is happening.

FIGURE 3.18 The Reflex

The central nervous system can interpret signals from sensory neurons and respond to them extremely quickly via the motor neurons without any need for the brain to be involved. These quick responses, known as reflexes, can reduce the damage that we might experience as a result of, for instance, touching a hot stove.

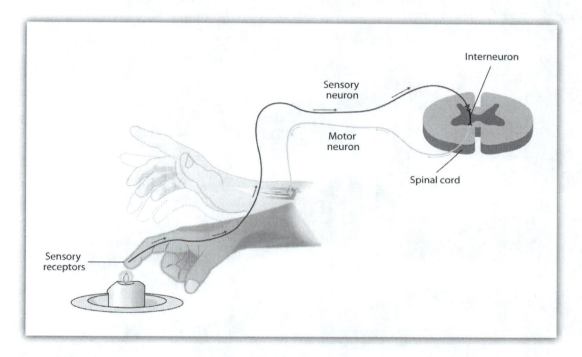

If the central nervous system is the command center of the body, the *peripheral nervous system (PNS)* represents the front line. The PNS links the CNS to the body's sense receptors, muscles, and glands. As you can see in Figure 3.19, the peripheral nervous system is itself divided into two subsystems, one controlling internal responses and one controlling external responses.

The **autonomic nervous system (ANS)** is *the division of the PNS that governs the internal activities of the human body, including heart rate, breathing, digestion, salivation, perspiration, urination, and sexual arousal.* Many of the actions of the ANS, such as heart rate and digestion, are automatic and out of our conscious control, but others, such as breathing and sexual activity, can be controlled and influenced by conscious processes.

The **somatic nervous system (SNS)** is *the division of the PNS that controls the external aspects of the body,* including the skeletal muscles, skin, and sense organs. The somatic nervous system consists primarily of motor nerves responsible for sending brain signals for muscle contraction.

---

spinal cord

The long, thin, tubular bundle of nerves and supporting cells that extends down from the brain.

reflex

An involuntary and nearly instantaneous movement in response to a stimulus.

autonomic nervous system (ANS)

The division of the PNS that governs the internal activities of the human body, including heart rate, breathing, digestion, salivation, perspiration, urination, and sexual arousal.

somatic nervous system (SNS)

The division of the PNS that controls the external aspects of the body, including the skeletal muscles, skin, and sense organs.

sympathetic division of the ANS

Involved in preparing the body for behavior, particularly in response to stress, by activating the organs and the glands in the endocrine system.

parasympathetic division of the ANS

Tends to calm the body by slowing the heart and breathing and by allowing the body to recover from the activities that the sympathetic system causes.

The autonomic nervous system itself can be further subdivided into the *sympathetic* and *parasympathetic* systems (see Figure 3.19). The **sympathetic division of the ANS** is *involved in preparing the body for behavior, particularly in response to stress, by activating the organs and the glands in the endocrine system.* The **parasympathetic division of the ANS** *tends to calm the body by slowing the heart and breathing and by allowing the body to recover from the activities that the sympathetic system causes.* The sympathetic and the parasympathetic divisions normally function in opposition to each other, such that the sympathetic division acts a bit like the accelerator pedal on a car and the parasympathetic division acts like the brake.

FIGURE 3.19 The Autonomic Nervous System

The autonomic nervous system has two divisions: The sympathetic division acts to energize the body, preparing it for action. The parasympathetic division acts to calm the body, allowing it to rest.

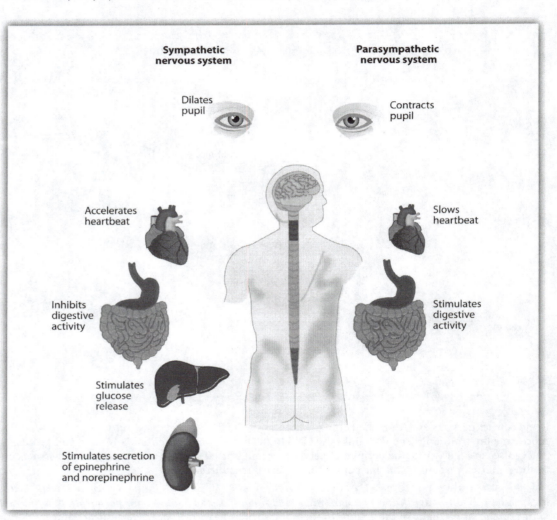

homeostasis

The natural balance in the body's systems.

Our everyday activities are controlled by the interaction between the sympathetic and parasympathetic nervous systems. For example, when we get out of bed in the morning, we would experience a sharp drop in blood pressure if it were not for the action of the sympathetic system, which automatically increases blood flow through the body. Similarly, after we eat a big meal, the parasympathetic system automatically sends more blood to the stomach and intestines, allowing us to efficiently digest the food. And perhaps you've had the experience of not being at all hungry before a stressful event, such as a sports game or an exam (when the sympathetic division was primarily in action), but suddenly finding yourself starved afterward, as the parasympathetic takes over. The two systems work together to maintain vital bodily functions, resulting in **homeostasis**, *the natural balance in the body's systems.*

4.2   The Body's Chemicals Help Control Behavior: The Endocrine System

The nervous system is designed to protect us from danger through its interpretation of and reactions to stimuli. But a primary function of the sympathetic and parasympathetic nervous systems is to interact with the *endocrine system* to elicit chemicals that provide another system for influencing our feelings and behaviors.

A **gland** in the endocrine system is made up of *groups of cells that function to secrete hormones.* A **hormone** is *a chemical that moves throughout the body to help regulate emotions and behaviors.* When the hormones released by one gland arrive at receptor tissues or other glands, these receiving receptors may trigger the release of other hormones, resulting in a series of complex chemical chain reactions. The endocrine system works together with the nervous system to influence many aspects of human behavior, including growth, reproduction, and metabolism. And the endocrine system plays a vital role in emotions. Because the glands in men and women differ, hormones also help explain some of the observed behavioral differences between men and women. The major glands in the endocrine system are shown in Figure 3.20.

gland

A groups of cells that functions to secrete hormones.

hormone

A chemical that moves throughout the body to help regulate emotions and behaviors.

FIGURE 3.20 **The Major Glands of the Endocrine System**

The male is shown on the left and the female on the right.

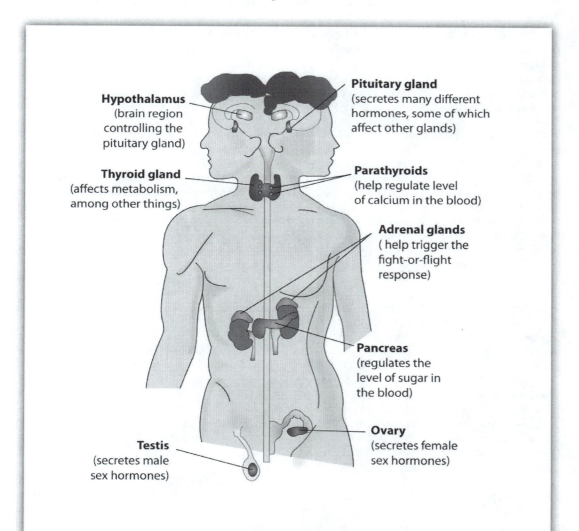

pituitary gland

A small pea-sized gland located near the center of the brain that is responsible for controlling the body's growth.

The **pituitary gland**, *a small pea-sized gland located near the center of the brain, is responsible for controlling the body's growth*, but it also has many other influences that make it of primary importance to regulating behavior. The pituitary secretes hormones that influence our responses to pain as well as hormones that signal the ovaries and testes to make sex hormones. The pituitary gland also controls ovulation and the menstrual cycle in women. Because the pituitary has such an important influence on other glands, it is sometimes known as the "master gland."

Other glands in the endocrine system include the *pancreas*, which secretes hormones designed to keep the body supplied with fuel to produce and maintain stores of energy; the *pineal gland*, located in the middle of the brain, which secretes melatonin, a hormone that helps regulate the wake-sleep cycle; and the *thyroid* and *parathyroid glands*, which are responsible for determining how quickly the body uses energy and hormones, and controlling the amount of calcium in the blood and bones.

adrenal glands

Produce hormones that regulate salt and water balance in the body, and are involved in metabolism, the immune system, and sexual development and function.

The body has two triangular *adrenal glands*, one atop each kidney. The **adrenal glands** *produce hormones that regulate salt and water balance in the body, and they are involved in metabolism, the immune system, and sexual development and function.* The most important function of the adrenal glands is to secrete the hormones *epinephrine* (also known as *adrenaline*) and *norepinephrine* (also known as *noradrenaline*) when we are excited, threatened, or stressed. Epinephrine and norepinephrine stimulate the sympathetic division of the ANS, causing increased heart and lung activity, dilation of the pupils, and increases in blood sugar, which give the body a surge of energy to respond to a threat. The activity and role of the adrenal glands in response to stress provides an excellent example of the close relationship and interdependency of the nervous and endocrine systems. A quick-acting nervous system is essential for immediate activation of the adrenal glands, while the endocrine system mobilizes the body for action.

testes

The male sex glands.

testosterone

The male sex hormone.

ovaries

The female sex glands.

The male sex glands, known as the **testes**, secrete a number of hormones, the most important of which is **testosterone**, *the male sex hormone*. Testosterone regulates body changes associated with sexual development, including enlargement of the penis, deepening of the voice, growth of facial and pubic hair, and the increase in muscle growth and strength. The **ovaries**, *the female sex glands*, are located in the pelvis. They produce eggs and secrete the female hormones *estrogen* and *progesterone*. Estrogen is involved in the development of female sexual features, including breast growth, the accumulation of body fat around the hips and thighs, and the growth spurt that occurs during puberty. Both estrogen and progesterone are also involved in pregnancy and the regulation of the menstrual cycle.

Recent research has pinpointed some of the important roles of the sex hormones in social behavior. Dabbs, Hargrove, and Heusel (1996)[51] measured the testosterone levels of 240 men who were members of 12 fraternities at two universities. They also obtained descriptions of the fraternities from university officials, fraternity officers, yearbook and chapter house photographs, and researcher field notes. The researchers correlated the testosterone levels and the descriptions of each fraternity. They found that the fraternities with the highest average testosterone levels were also more wild and unruly, and one of these fraternities was known across campus for the crudeness of its behavior. On the other hand, the fraternities with the lowest average testosterone levels were more well behaved, friendly and pleasant, academically successful, and socially responsible. Banks and Dabbs (1996)[52] found that juvenile delinquents and prisoners who had high levels of testosterone also acted more violently, and Tremblay et al. (1998) [53] found that testosterone was related to toughness and leadership behaviors in adolescent boys. Although testosterone levels are higher in men than in women, the relationship between testosterone and aggression is not limited to males. Studies have also shown a positive relationship between testosterone and aggression and related behaviors (such as competitiveness) in women (Cashdan, 2003).[54]

It must be kept in mind that the observed relationships between testosterone levels and aggressive behavior that have been found in these studies do not prove that testosterone causes aggression—the relationships are only correlational. In fact, there is evidence that the relationship between violence and testosterone also goes in the other direction: Playing an aggressive game, such as tennis or even chess, increases the testosterone levels of the winners and decreases the testosterone levels of losers (Gladue, Boechler, & McCaul, 1989; Mazur, Booth, & Dabbs, 1992),[55] and perhaps this is why excited soccer fans sometimes riot when their team wins.

Recent research has also begun to document the role that female sex hormones may play in reactions to others. A study about hormonal influences on social-cognitive functioning (Macrae, Alnwick, Milne, & Schloerscheidt, 2002)[56] found that women were more easily able to perceive and categorize male faces during the more fertile phases of their menstrual cycles. Although researchers did not directly measure the presence of hormones, it is likely that phase-specific hormonal differences influenced the women's perceptions.

At this point you can begin to see the important role the hormones play in behavior. But the hormones we have reviewed in this section represent only a subset of the many influences that hormones have on our behaviors. In the chapters to come we will consider the important roles that hormones play in many other behaviors, including sleeping, sexual activity, and helping and harming others.

KEY TAKEAWAYS

- The body uses both electrical and chemical systems to create homeostasis.
- The CNS is made up of bundles of nerves that carry messages to and from the PNS
- The peripheral nervous system is composed of the autonomic nervous system (ANS) and the peripheral nervous system (PNS). The ANS is further divided into the sympathetic (activating) and parasympathetic (calming) nervous systems. These divisions are activated by glands and organs in the endocrine system.
- Specific nerves, including sensory neurons, motor neurons, and interneurons, each have specific functions.
- The spinal cord may bypass the brain by responding rapidly using reflexes.
- The pituitary gland is a master gland, affecting many other glands.
- Hormones produced by the pituitary and adrenal glands regulate growth, stress, sexual functions, and chemical balance in the body.
- The adrenal glands produce epinephrine and norepinephrine, the hormones responsible for our reactions to stress.
- The sex hormones, testosterone, estrogen, and progesterone, play an important role in sex differences.

EXERCISES AND CRITICAL THINKING

1. Recall a time when you were threatened or stressed. What physiological reactions did you experience in the situation, and what aspects of the endocrine system do you think created those reactions?
2. Consider the emotions that you have experienced over the past several weeks. What hormones do you think might have been involved in creating those emotions?

5.   CHAPTER SUMMARY

All human behavior, thoughts, and feelings are produced by the actions of our brains, nerves, muscles, and glands.

The body is controlled by the nervous system, consisting of the central nervous system (CNS) and the peripheral nervous system (PNS) and the endocrine system, which is made up of glands that create and control hormones.

Neurons are the cells in the nervous system. Neurons are composed of a soma that contains the nucleus of the cell; a dendrite that collects information from other cells and sends the information to the soma; and a long segmented fiber, known as the axon, which transmits information away from the cell body toward other neurons and to the muscles and glands.

The nervous system operates using an electrochemical process. An electrical charge moves through the neuron itself, and chemicals are used to transmit information between neurons. Within the neuron, the electrical charge occurs in the form of an action potential. The action potential operates in an all-or-nothing manner.

Neurons are separated by junction areas known as synapses. Neurotransmitters travel across the synaptic space between the terminal button of one neuron and the dendrites of other neurons, where they bind to the dendrites in the neighboring neurons. More than 100 chemical substances produced in the body have been identified as neurotransmitters, and these substances have a wide and profound effect on emotion, cognition, and behavior.

Drugs that we may ingest may either mimic (agonists) or block (antagonists) the operations of neurotransmitters.

The brains of all animals are layered, and generally quite similar in overall form.

The brain stem is the oldest and innermost region of the brain. It controls the most basic functions of life, including breathing, attention, and motor responses. The brain stem includes the medulla, the pons, and the reticular formation.

Above the brain stem are other parts of the old brain involved in the processing of behavior and emotions, including the thalamus, the cerebellum, and the limbic system. The limbic system includes the amygdala, the hypothalamus, and the hippocampus.

The cerebral cortex contains about 20 billion nerve cells and 300 trillion synaptic connections, and it's supported by billions more glial cells that surround and link to the neurons. The cerebral cortex is divided into two hemispheres, and each hemisphere is divided into four lobes, each separated by folds known as fissures.

The frontal lobe is primarily responsible for thinking, planning, memory, and judgment. The parietal lobe is responsible for processing information about touch. The occipital lobe processes visual information, and the temporal lobe is responsible for hearing and language. The cortex also includes the motor cortex, the somatosensory cortex, the visual cortex, the auditory cortex, and the association areas.

The brain can develop new neurons, a process known as neurogenesis, as well as new routes for neural communications (neuroplasticity).

Psychologists study the brain using cadaver and lesion approaches, as well as through neuroimaging techniques that include electroencephalography (EEG), functional magnetic resonance imaging (fMRI), and transcranial magnetic stimulation (TMS).

Sensory (afferent) neurons carry information from the sensory receptors, whereas motor (efferent) neurons transmit information to the muscles and glands. Interneurons, by far the most common of neurons, are located primarily within the CNS and responsible for communicating among the neurons.

The peripheral nervous system is itself divided into two subsystems, one controlling internal responses (the autonomic nervous system, ANS) and one controlling external responses (the somatic nervous system). The sympathetic division of the ANS is involved in preparing the body for behavior by activating the organs and the glands in the endocrine system. The parasympathetic division of the ANS tends to calm the body by slowing the heart and breathing and by allowing the body to recover from the activities that the sympathetic system causes.

Glands in the endocrine system include the pituitary gland, the pancreas, the adrenal glands, and the male and female sex glands. The male sex hormone testosterone and the female sex hormones estrogen and progesterone play important roles in behavior and contribute to gender differences.

ENDNOTES

1. Seeley, W. W., Matthews, B. R., Crawford, R. K., Gorno-Tempini, M. L., Foti, D., Mackenzie, I. R., & Miller, B. L. (2008). "Unravelling Boléro": Progressive aphasia, transmodal creativity, and the right posterior neocortex. *Brain, 131*(1), 39–49.

2. Miller, B. L., Boone, K., Cummings, J. L., Read, S. L., & Mishkin, F. (2000). Functional correlates of musical and visual ability in frontotemporal dementia. *British Journal of Psychiatry, 176*, 458–463.

3. Aldhous, P. (2008, April 7). "Boléro": Beautiful symptom of a terrible disease. *New Scientist*. Retrieved from http://www.newscientist.com/article/dn13599-bolero-beautiful-symptom-of-a-terrible-disease.html

4. Amaducci, L., Grassi, E., & Boller, F. (2002). Maurice Ravel and right-hemisphere musical creativity: Influence of disease on his last musical works? *European Journal of Neurology, 9*(1), 75–82.

5. Sherman, S. M., & Guillery, R. W. (2006). *Exploring the thalamus and its role in cortical function* (2nd ed.). Cambridge, MA: MIT Press.

6. Bower, J. M., & Parsons, J. M. (2003). Rethinking the lesser brain. *Scientific American, 289*, 50–57.

7. Best, B. (2009). The amygdala and the emotions. In *Anatomy of the mind* (chap. 9). Retrieved from Welcome to the World of Ben Best website: http://www.benbest.com/science/anatmind/anatmd9.html

8. Klüver, H., & Bucy, P. C. (1939). Preliminary analysis of functions of the temporal lobes in monkeys. *Archives of Neurology & Psychiatry (Chicago), 42*, 979–1000.

9. Sigurdsson, T., Doyère, V., Cain, C. K., & LeDoux, J. E. (2007). Long-term potentiation in the amygdala: A cellular mechanism of fear learning and memory. *Neuropharmacology, 52*(1), 215–227.

10. Olds, J., & Milner, P. (1954). Positive reinforcement produced by electrical stimulation of septal area and other regions of rat brain. *Journal of Comparative and Physiological Psychology, 47*, 419–427.

11. Olds, J. (1958). Self-stimulation of the brain: Its use to study local effects of hunger, sex, and drugs. *Science, 127*, 315–324.

12. Gibson, K. R. (2002). Evolution of human intelligence: The roles of brain size and mental construction. *Brain Behavior and Evolution 59*, 10–20.

13. de Courten-Myers, G. M. (1999). The human cerebral cortex: Gender differences in structure and function. *Journal of Neuropathology and Experimental Neurology, 58*, 217–226.

14. Miller, G. (2005). Neuroscience: The dark side of glia. *Science, 308*(5723), 778–781.

15. Fritsch, G., & Hitzig, E. (2009). Electric excitability of the cerebrum (Über die Elektrische erregbarkeit des Grosshirns). *Epilepsy & Behavior, 15*(2), 123–130. (Original work published 1870)

16. Martin, A. (2007). The representation of object concepts in the brain. *Annual Review of Psychology, 58*, 25–45.

17. Farah, M. J., Rabinowitz, C., Quinn, G. E., & Liu, G. T. (2000). Early commitment of neural substrates for face recognition. *Cognitive Neuropsychology, 17*(1–3), 117–123.

18. Kolb, B., & Fantie, B. (1989). Development of the child's brain and behavior. In C. R. Reynolds & E. Fletcher-Janzen (Eds.), *Handbook of clinical child neuropsychology* (pp. 17–39). New York, NY: Plenum Press.

19. Bengtsson, S. L., Nagy, Z., Skare, S., Forsman, L., Forssberg, H., & Ullén, F. (2005). Extensive piano practicing has regionally specific effects on white matter development. *Nature Neuroscience, 8*(9), 1148–1150.

20. Münte, T. F., Altenmüller, E., & Jäncke, L. (2002). The musician's brain as a model of neuroplasticity. *Nature Reviews Neuroscience, 3*(6), 473–478.

21. Thiel, A., Habedank, B., Herholz, K., Kessler, J., Winhuisen, L., Haupt, W. F., & Heiss, W. D. (2006). From the left to the right: How the brain compensates progressive loss of language function. *Brain and Language, 98*(1), 57–65.

22. Fox, J. L. (1984). The brain's dynamic way of keeping in touch. *Science, 225*(4664), 820–821.

23. Van Praag, H., Zhao, X., Gage, F. H., & Gazzaniga, M. S. (2004). Neurogenesis in the adult mammalian brain. In *The cognitive neurosciences* (3rd ed., pp. 127–137). Cambridge, MA: MIT Press.

24. Gould, E. (2007). How widespread is adult neurogenesis in mammals? *Nature Reviews Neuroscience 8*, 481–488. doi:10.1038/nrn2147

25. Gazzaniga, M. S., Bogen, J. E., & Sperry, R. W. (1965). Observations on visual perception after disconnexion of the cerebral hemispheres in man. *Brain, 88*(2), 221–236.

26. Gazzaniga, M. S. (2005). Forty-five years of split-brain research and still going strong. *Nature Reviews Neuroscience, 6*(8), 653–659.

27. Soroker, N., Kasher, A., Giora, R., Batori, G., Corn, C., Gil, M., & Zaidel, E. (2005). Processing of basic speech acts following localized brain damage: A new light on the neuroanatomy of language. *Brain and Cognition, 57*(2), 214–217.

28. Peters, M., Reimers, S., & Manning, J. T. (2006). Hand preference for writing and associations with selected demographic and behavioral variables in 255,100 subjects: The BBC Internet study. *Brain and Cognition, 62*(2), 177–189.

29. Harris, L. J. (1990). Cultural influences on handedness: Historical and contemporary theory and evidence. In S. Coren (Ed.), *Left-handedness: Behavioral implications and anomalies*. New York, NY: Elsevier; McManus, I. C. (2002). *Right hand, left hand: The origins of asymmetry in brains, bodies, atoms, and cultures*. Cambridge, MA: Harvard University Press.

30. Hepper, P. G., Wells, D. L., & Lynch, C. (2005). Prenatal thumb sucking is related to postnatal handedness. *Neuropsychologia, 43*, 313–315.

31. Jones, G. V., & Martin, M. (2000). A note on Corballis (1997) and the genetics and evolution of handedness: Developing a unified distributional model from the sex-chromosomes gene hypothesis. *Psychological Review, 107*(1), 213–218.

32. McKeever, W. F., Cerone, L. J., Suter, P. J., & Wu, S. M. (2000). Family size, miscarriage-proneness, and handedness: Tests of hypotheses of the developmental instability theory of handedness. *Laterality: Asymmetries of Body, Brain, and Cognition, 5*(2), 111–120.

33. Ida, Y., & Mandal, M. K. (2003). Cultural differences in side bias: Evidence from Japan and India. *Laterality: Asymmetries of Body, Brain, and Cognition, 8*(2), 121–133.

34. Dutta, T., & Mandal, M. K. (2006). Hand preference and accidents in India. *Laterality: Asymmetries of Body, Brain, and Cognition, 11*, 368–372.

35. Springer, S. P., & Deutsch, G. (1998). *Left brain, right brain: Perspectives from cognitive neuroscience* (5th ed.). A series of books in psychology. New York, NY: W. H. Freeman/Times Books/Henry Holt & Co.

36. Coren, S. (1992). *The left-hander syndrome: The causes and consequences of left-handedness*. New York, NY: Free Press.

37. Geschwind, N., & Behan, P. (2007). *Left-handedness: Association with immune disease, migraine, and developmental learning disorder*. Cambridge, MA: MIT Press.

38. Betancur, C., Vélez, A., Cabanieu, G., & le Moal, M. (1990). Association between left-handedness and allergy: A reappraisal. *Neuropsychologia, 28*(2), 223–227.

39. Bodmer, W., & McKie, R. (1994). *The book of man: The quest to discover our genetic heritage*. London, England: Little, Brown and Company.

40. Diamond, M. C. (1999). Why Einstein's brain? *New Horizons for Learning*. Retrieved from http://www.newhorizons.org/neuro/diamond_einstein.htm

41. Macmillan, M. (2000). *An odd kind of fame: Stories of Phineas Gage*. Cambridge, MA: MIT Press.

42. Kotowicz, Z. (2007). The strange case of Phineas Gage. *History of the Human Sciences, 20*(1), 115–131.

43. Damasio, H., Grabowski, T., Frank, R., Galaburda, A. M., Damasio, A. R., Cacioppo, J. T., & Berntson, G. G. (2005). The return of Phineas Gage: Clues about the brain from the skull of a famous patient. In *Social neuroscience: Key readings* (pp. 21–28). New York, NY: Psychology Press.

44. Koenigs, M., Young, L., Adolphs, R., Tranel, D., Cushman, F., Hauser, M., & Damasio, A. (2007). Damage to the prefontal cortex increases utilitarian moral judgments. *Nature, 446*(7138), 908–911.

45. Miller, G. (2008). The roots of morality. *Science, 320*, 734–737.

46. Koenigs, M., Young, L., Adolphs, R., Tranel, D., Cushman, F., Hauser, M., & Damasio, A. (2007). Damage to the prefontal cortex increases utilitarian moral judgments. *Nature, 446*(7138), 908–911.

47. Kanwisher, N. (2000). Domain specificity in face perception. *Nature Neuroscience, 3*(8), 759–763.

48. Kalbe, E., Schlegel, M., Sack, A. T., Nowak, D. A., Dafotakis, M., Bangard, C.,…Kessler, J. (2010). Dissociating cognitive from affective theory of mind: A TMS study. *Cortex: A Journal Devoted to the Study of the Nervous System and Behavior, 46*(6), 769–780; Van den Eynde, F., Claudino, A. M., Mogg, A., Horrell, L., Stahl, D.,…Schmidt, U. (2010). Repetitive transcranial magnetic stimulation reduces cue-induced food craving in bulimic disorders. *Biological Psychiatry, 67*(8), 793–795; Young, L., Camprodon, J. A., Hauser, M., Pascual-Leone, A., & Saxe, R. (2010). Disruption of the right temporoparietal junction with transcranial magnetic stimulation reduces the role of beliefs in moral judgments. *PNAS Proceedings of the National Academy of Sciences of the United States of America, 107*(15), 6753–6758.

49. Eisenberger, N. I., Lieberman, M. D., & Williams, K. D. (2003). Does rejection hurt? An fMRI study of social exclusion. *Science, 302*(5643), 290–292.

50. Chen, Z., Williams, K. D., Fitness, J., & Newton, N. C. (2008). When hurt will not heal: Exploring the capacity to relive social and physical pain. *Psychological Science, 19*(8), 789–795; Wesselmann, E. D., Bagg, D., & Williams, K. D. (2009). "I feel your pain": The effects of observing ostracism on the ostracism detection system. *Journal of Experimental Social Psychology, 45*(6), 1308–1311.

51. Dabbs, J. M., Jr., Hargrove, M. F., & Heusel, C. (1996). Testosterone differences among college fraternities: Well-behaved vs. rambunctious. *Personality and Individual Differences, 20*(2), 157–161.

52. Banks, T., & Dabbs, J. M., Jr. (1996). Salivary testosterone and cortisol in delinquent and violent urban subculture. *Journal of Social Psychology, 136*(1), 49–56.

53. Tremblay, R. E., Schaal, B., Boulerice, B., Arseneault, L., Soussignan, R. G., Paquette, D., & Laurent, D. (1998). Testosterone, physical aggression, dominance, and physical development in early adolescence. *International Journal of Behavioral Development, 22*(4), 753–777.

54. Cashdan, E. (2003). Hormones and competitive aggression in women. *Aggressive Behavior, 29*(2), 107–115.

55. Gladue, B. A., Boechler, M., & McCaul, K. D. (1989). Hormonal response to competition in human males. *Aggressive Behavior, 15*(6), 409–422; Mazur, A., Booth, A., & Dabbs, J. M. (1992). Testosterone and chess competition. *Social Psychology Quarterly, 55*(1), 70–77.

56. Macrae, C. N., Alnwick, K. A., Milne, A. B., & Schloerscheidt, A. M. (2002). Person perception across the menstrual cycle: Hormonal influences on social-cognitive functioning. *Psychological Science, 13*(6), 532–536.

Sensing and Perceiving

Misperception by Those Trained to Accurately Perceive a Threat

On September 6, 2007, the Asia-Pacific Economic Cooperation (APEC) leaders' summit was being held in downtown Sydney, Australia. World leaders, including the then-current U.S. president, George W. Bush, were attending the summit. Many roads in the area were closed for security reasons, and police presence was high.

As a prank, eight members of the Australian television satire *The Chaser's War on Everything* assembled a false motorcade made up of two black four-wheel-drive vehicles, a black sedan, two motorcycles, body guards, and chauffeurs (see the video below). Group member Chas Licciardello was in one of the cars disguised as Osama bin Laden. The motorcade drove through Sydney's central business district and entered the security zone of the meeting. The motorcade was waved on by police, through two checkpoints, until the Chaser group decided it had taken the gag far enough and stopped outside the InterContinental Hotel where former President Bush was staying. Licciardello stepped out onto the street and complained, in character as bin Laden, about not being invited to the APEC Summit. Only at this time did the police belatedly check the identity of the group members, finally arresting them.

Chaser APEC Motorcade Stunt
Motorcade Stunt performed by the Chaser pranksters in 2007.

View the video online at: http://www.youtube.com/embed/TdnAaQ0n5-8

Afterward, the group testified that it had made little effort to disguise its attempt as anything more than a prank. The group's only realistic attempt to fool police was its Canadian-flag marked vehicles. Other than that, the group used obviously fake credentials, and its security passes were printed with "JOKE," "Insecurity," and "It's pretty obvious this isn't a real pass," all clearly visible to any police officer who might have been troubled to look closely as the motorcade passed. The required APEC 2007 Official Vehicle stickers had the name of the group's show printed on them, and this text: "This dude likes trees and poetry and certain types of carnivorous plants excite him." In addition, a few of the "bodyguards" were carrying camcorders, and one of the motorcyclists was dressed in jeans, both details that should have alerted police that something was amiss.

The Chaser pranksters later explained the primary reason for the stunt. They wanted to make a statement about the fact that bin Laden, a world leader, had not been invited to an APEC Summit where issues of terror were being discussed. The secondary motive was to test the event's security. The show's lawyers approved the stunt, under the assumption that the motorcade would be stopped at the APEC meeting.

The ability to detect and interpret the events that are occurring around us allows us to respond to these stimuli appropriately (Gibson & Pick, 2000).[1] In most cases the system is successful, but as you can see from the above example, it is not perfect. In this chapter we will discuss the strengths and limitations of these capacities, focusing on both **sensation**—*awareness resulting from the stimulation of a sense organ*, and **perception**—*the organization and interpretation of sensations*. Sensation and perception work seamlessly together to allow us to experience the

sensation
Awareness resulting from the stimulation of a sense organ.

perception
The organization and interpretation of sensations.

world through our eyes, ears, nose, tongue, and skin, but also to combine what we are currently learning from the environment with what we already know about it to make judgments and to choose appropriate behaviors.

The study of sensation and perception is exceedingly important for our everyday lives because the knowledge generated by psychologists is used in so many ways to help so many people. Psychologists work closely with mechanical and electrical engineers, with experts in defense and military contractors, and with clinical, health, and sports psychologists to help them apply this knowledge to their everyday practices. The research is used to help us understand and better prepare people to cope with such diverse events as driving cars, flying planes, creating robots, and managing pain (Fajen & Warren, 2003).[2]

FIGURE 4.1

Mechanical engineers, industrial psychologists, sports psychologists, and video game designers use knowledge about sensation and perception to create and improve everyday objects and behaviors.

© Thinkstock

transduction

The conversion of stimuli detected by receptor cells to electrical impulses that are then transported to the brain.

We will begin the chapter with a focus on the six senses of *seeing, hearing, smelling, touching, tasting,* and *monitoring the body's positions (proprioception)*. We will see that sensation is sometimes relatively direct, in the sense that the wide variety of stimuli around us inform and guide our behaviors quickly and accurately, but nevertheless is always the result of at least some interpretation. We do not directly experience stimuli, but rather we experience those stimuli as they are created by our senses. Each sense accomplishes the basic process of **transduction**—*the conversion of stimuli detected by receptor cells to electrical impulses that are then transported to the brain*—in different, but related, ways.

After we have reviewed the basic processes of sensation, we will turn to the topic of perception, focusing on how the brain's processing of sensory experience can not only help us make quick and accurate judgments, but also mislead us into making perceptual and judgmental errors, such as those that allowed the Chaser group to breach security at the APEC meeting.

1.   WE EXPERIENCE OUR WORLD THROUGH SENSATION

L E A R N I N G   O B J E C T I V E S

1. Review and summarize the capacities and limitations of human sensation.
2. Explain the difference between sensation and perception and describe how psychologists measure sensory and difference thresholds.

1.1   Sensory Thresholds: What Can We Experience?

Humans possess powerful sensory capacities that allow us to sense the kaleidoscope of sights, sounds, smells, and tastes that surround us. Our eyes detect light energy and our ears pick up sound waves. Our skin senses touch, pressure, hot, and cold. Our tongues react to the molecules of the foods we eat, and our noses detect scents in the air. The human perceptual system is wired for accuracy, and people are exceedingly good at making use of the wide variety of information available to them (Stoffregen & Bardy, 2001).[3]

In many ways our senses are quite remarkable. The human eye can detect the equivalent of a single candle flame burning 30 miles away and can distinguish among more than 300,000 different colors. The human ear can detect sounds as low as 20 *hertz* (vibrations per second) and as high as 20,000 hertz, and it can hear the tick of a clock about 20 feet away in a quiet room. We can taste a teaspoon of sugar dissolved in 2 gallons of water, and we are able to smell one drop of perfume diffused in a three-room apartment. We can feel the wing of a bee on our cheek dropped from 1 centimeter above (Galanter, 1962).[4]

Link

To get an idea of the range of sounds that the human ear can sense, try testing your hearing here:

http://test-my-hearing.com

Although there is much that we do sense, there is even more that we do not. Dogs, bats, whales, and some rodents all have much better hearing than we do, and many animals have a far richer sense of smell. Birds are able to see the ultraviolet light that we cannot (see Figure 4.3) and can also sense the pull of the earth's magnetic field. Cats have an extremely sensitive and sophisticated sense of touch, and they are able to navigate in complete darkness using their whiskers. The fact that different organisms have different sensations is part of their evolutionary adaptation. Each species is adapted to sensing the things that are most important to them, while being blissfully unaware of the things that don't matter.

FIGURE 4.2

The dog's highly sensitive sense of smell comes in useful in searches for missing persons, explosives, foods, and drugs.

Source: Photo courtesy of Harald Dettenborn,

http://commons.wikimedia.org/wiki/ File:Msc2010_dett_0036.jpg.

FIGURE 4.3   Ultraviolet Light and Bird Vision

Because birds can see ultraviolet light but humans cannot, what looks to us like a plain black bird looks much different to a bird.

Source: Adapted from Fatal Light Awareness Program. (2008). Our research program. Retrieved from http://www.flap.org/research.htm.

1.2 Measuring Sensation

psychophysics

Is the branch of psychology that studies the effects of physical stimuli on sensory perceptions and mental states.

Psychophysics is *the branch of psychology that studies the effects of physical stimuli on sensory perceptions and mental states*. The field of psychophysics was founded by the German psychologist Gustav Fechner (1801–1887), who was the first to study the relationship between the strength of a stimulus and a person's ability to detect the stimulus.

The measurement techniques developed by Fechner and his colleagues are designed in part to help determine the limits of human sensation. One important criterion is the ability to detect very faint stimuli. The **absolute threshold** of a sensation is defined as *the intensity of a stimulus that allows an organism to just barely detect it.*

absolute threshold

The intensity of a stimulus that allows an organism to just barely detect it.

In a typical psychophysics experiment, an individual is presented with a series of trials in which a signal is sometimes presented and sometimes not, or in which two stimuli are presented that are either the same or different. Imagine, for instance, that you were asked to take a hearing test. On each of the trials your task is to indicate either "yes" if you heard a sound or "no" if you did not. The signals are purposefully made to be very faint, making accurate judgments difficult.

The problem for you is that the very faint signals create uncertainty. Because our ears are constantly sending background information to the brain, you will sometimes think that you heard a sound when none was there, and you will sometimes fail to detect a sound that is there. Your task is to determine whether the neural activity that you are experiencing is due to the background noise alone or is a result of a signal within the noise.

signal detection analysis

A technique used to determine the ability of the perceiver to separate true signals from background noise.

The responses that you give on the hearing test can be analyzed using *signal detection analysis*. **Signal detection analysis** is *a technique used to determine the ability of the perceiver to separate true signals from background noise* (Macmillan & Creelman, 2005; Wickens, 2002).[5] As you can see in Figure 4.4, each judgment trial creates four possible outcomes: A *hit* occurs when you, as the listener, correctly say "yes" when there was a sound. A *false alarm* occurs when you respond "yes" to no signal. In the other two cases you respond "no"—either a *miss* (saying "no" when there was a signal) or a *correct rejection* (saying "no" when there was in fact no signal).

FIGURE 4.4 Outcomes of a Signal Detection Analysis

Our ability to accurately detect stimuli is measured using a signal detection analysis. Two of the possible decisions (hits and correct rejections) are accurate; the other two (misses and false alarms) are errors.

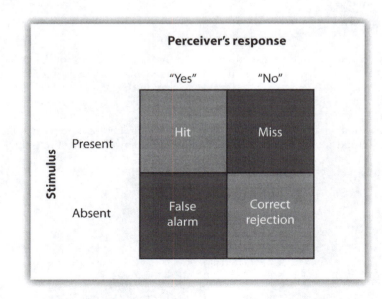

The analysis of the data from a psychophysics experiment creates two measures. One measure, known as *sensitivity*, refers to the true ability of the individual to detect the presence or absence of signals. People who have better hearing will have higher sensitivity than will those with poorer hearing. The other measure, *response bias*, refers to a behavioral tendency to respond "yes" to the trials, which is independent of sensitivity.

Imagine for instance that rather than taking a hearing test, you are a soldier on guard duty, and your job is to detect the very faint sound of the breaking of a branch that indicates that an enemy is nearby. You can see that in this case making a false alarm by alerting the other soldiers to the sound might not be as costly as a miss (a failure to report the sound), which could be deadly. Therefore, you might well adopt a very lenient response bias in which whenever you are at all unsure, you send a warning signal. In this case your responses may not be very accurate (your sensitivity may be low because you are making a lot of false alarms) and yet the extreme response bias can save lives.

Another application of signal detection occurs when medical technicians study body images for the presence of cancerous tumors. Again, a miss (in which the technician incorrectly determines that there is no tumor) can be very costly, but false alarms (referring patients who do not have tumors to further testing) also have costs. The ultimate decisions that the technicians make are based on the quality of the signal (clarity of the image), their experience and training (the ability to recognize certain shapes and textures of tumors), and their best guesses about the relative costs of misses versus false alarms.

Although we have focused to this point on the absolute threshold, a second important criterion concerns the ability to assess differences between stimuli. The **difference threshold (or just noticeable difference [JND])**, refers to *the change in a stimulus that can just barely be detected by the organism*. The German physiologist Ernst Weber (1795–1878) made an important discovery about the JND—namely, that the ability to detect differences depends not so much on the size of the difference but on the size of the difference in relationship to the absolute size of the stimulus. **Weber's law** maintains that the *just noticeable difference of a stimulus is a constant proportion of the original intensity of the stimulus*. As an example, if you have a cup of coffee that has only a very little bit of sugar in it (say 1 teaspoon), adding another teaspoon of sugar will make a big difference in taste. But if you added that same teaspoon to a cup of coffee that already had 5 teaspoons of sugar in it, then you probably wouldn't taste the difference as much (in fact, according to Weber's law, you would have to add 5 more teaspoons to make the same difference in taste).

One interesting application of Weber's law is in our everyday shopping behavior. Our tendency to perceive cost differences between products is dependent not only on the amount of money we will spend or save, but also on the amount of money saved relative to the price of the purchase. I would venture to say that if you were about to buy a soda or candy bar in a convenience store and the price of the items ranged from $1 to $3, you would think that the $3 item cost "a lot more" than the $1 item. But now imagine that you were comparing between two music systems, one that cost $397 and one that cost $399. Probably you would think that the cost of the two systems was "about the same," even though buying the cheaper one would still save you $2.

Research Focus: Influence without Awareness

If you study Figure 4.5, you will see that the absolute threshold is the point where we become aware of a faint stimulus. After that point, we say that the stimulus is *conscious* because we can accurately report on its existence (or its nonexistence) better than 50% of the time. But can **subliminal stimuli** (*events that occur below the absolute threshold and of which we are not conscious*) have an influence on our behavior?

Absolute Threshold

As the intensity of a stimulus increases, we are more likely to perceive it. Stimuli below the absolute threshold can still have at least some influence on us, even though we cannot consciously detect them.

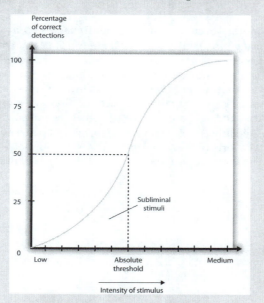

difference threshold (or just noticeable difference [JND])

The change in a stimulus that can just barely be detected by the organism.

Weber's law

Just noticeable difference of a stimulus is a constant proportion of the original intensity of the stimulus.

subliminal stimuli

Stimuli that are below the absolute threshold and of which we are not conscious.

A variety of research programs have found that subliminal stimuli can influence our judgments and behavior, at least in the short term (Dijksterhuis, 2010).[6] But whether the presentation of subliminal stimuli can influence the products that we buy has been a more controversial topic in psychology. In one relevant experiment, Karremans, Stroebe, and Claus (2006)[7] had Dutch college students view a series of computer trials in which a string of letters such as *BBBBBBBBB* or *BBBbBBBBB* were presented on the screen. To be sure they paid attention to the display, the students were asked to note whether the strings contained a small *b*. However, immediately before each of the letter strings, the researchers presented either the name of a drink that is popular in Holland (Lipton Ice) or a control string containing the same letters as Lipton Ice (NpeicTol). These words were presented so quickly (for only about one fiftieth of a second) that the participants could not see them.

Then the students were asked to indicate their intention to drink Lipton Ice by answering questions such as "If you would sit on a terrace now, how likely is it that you would order Lipton Ice," and also to indicate how thirsty they were at the time. The researchers found that the students who had been exposed to the "Lipton Ice" words (and particularly those who indicated that they were already thirsty) were significantly more likely to say that they would drink Lipton Ice than were those who had been exposed to the control words.

If it were effective, procedures such as this (we can call the technique "subliminal advertising" because it advertises a product outside awareness) would have some major advantages for advertisers, because it would allow them to promote their products without directly interrupting the consumers' activity and without the consumers' knowing they are being persuaded. People cannot counterargue with, or attempt to avoid being influenced by, messages received outside awareness. Due to fears that people may be influenced without their knowing, subliminal advertising has been legally banned in many countries, including Australia, Great Britain, and the United States.

Although it has been proven to work in some research, subliminal advertising's effectiveness is still uncertain. Charles Trappey (1996)[8] conducted a meta-analysis in which he combined 23 leading research studies that had tested the influence of subliminal advertising on consumer choice. The results of his meta-analysis showed that subliminal advertising had a negligible effect on consumer choice. And Saegert (1987, p. 107)[9] concluded that "marketing should quit giving subliminal advertising the benefit of the doubt," arguing that the influences of subliminal stimuli are usually so weak that they are normally overshadowed by the person's own decision making about the behavior.

Taken together then, the evidence for the effectiveness of subliminal advertising is weak, and its effects may be limited to only some people and in only some conditions. You probably don't have to worry too much about being subliminally persuaded in your everyday life, even if subliminal ads are allowed in your country. But even if subliminal advertising is not all that effective itself, there are plenty of other indirect advertising techniques that are used and that do work. For instance, many ads for automobiles and alcoholic beverages are subtly sexualized, which encourages the consumer to indirectly (even if not subliminally) associate these products with sexuality. And there is the ever more frequent "product placement" techniques, where images of brands (cars, sodas, electronics, and so forth) are placed on websites and in popular television shows and movies. Harris, Bargh, & Brownell (2009)[10] found that being exposed to food advertising on television significantly increased child and adult snacking behaviors, again suggesting that the effects of perceived images, even if presented above the absolute threshold, may nevertheless be very subtle.

blindsight

A condition brought on by damage to the visual cortex, in which people are unable to consciously report on visual stimuli but nevertheless are able to accurately answer questions about what they are seeing.

Another example of processing that occurs outside our awareness is seen when certain areas of the visual cortex are damaged, causing **blindsight**, *a condition in which people are unable to consciously report on visual stimuli but nevertheless are able to accurately answer questions about what they are seeing.* When people with blindsight are asked directly what stimuli look like, or to determine whether these stimuli are present at all, they cannot do so at better than chance levels. They report that they cannot see anything. However, when they are asked more indirect questions, they are able to give correct answers. For example, people with blindsight are able to correctly determine an object's location and direction of movement, as well as identify simple geometrical forms and patterns (Weiskrantz, 1997).[11] It seems that although conscious reports of the visual experiences are not possible, there is still a parallel and implicit process at work, enabling people to perceive certain aspects of the stimuli.

KEY TAKEAWAYS

- Sensation is the process of receiving information from the environment through our sensory organs. Perception is the process of interpreting and organizing the incoming information in order that we can understand it and react accordingly.
- Transduction is the conversion of stimuli detected by receptor cells to electrical impulses that are transported to the brain.
- Although our experiences of the world are rich and complex, humans—like all species—have their own adapted sensory strengths and sensory limitations.
- Sensation and perception work together in a fluid, continuous process.
- Our judgments in detection tasks are influenced by both the absolute threshold of the signal as well as our current motivations and experiences. Signal detection analysis is used to differentiate sensitivity from response biases.
- The difference threshold, or just noticeable difference, is the ability to detect the smallest change in a stimulus about 50% of the time. According to Weber's law, the just noticeable difference increases in proportion to the total intensity of the stimulus.
- Research has found that stimuli can influence behavior even when they are presented below the absolute threshold (i.e., subliminally). The effectiveness of subliminal advertising, however, has not been shown to be of large magnitude.

EXERCISES AND CRITICAL THINKING

1. The accidental shooting of one's own soldiers (friendly fire) frequently occurs in wars. Based on what you have learned about sensation, perception, and psychophysics, why do you think soldiers might mistakenly fire on their own soldiers?
2. If we pick up two letters, one that weighs 1 ounce and one that weighs 2 ounces, we can notice the difference. But if we pick up two packages, one that weighs 3 pounds 1 ounce and one that weighs 3 pounds 2 ounces, we can't tell the difference. Why?
3. Take a moment and lie down quietly in your bedroom. Notice the variety and levels of what you can see, hear, and feel. Does this experience help you understand the idea of the absolute threshold?

2. SEEING

LEARNING OBJECTIVES

1. Identify the key structures of the eye and the role they play in vision.
2. Summarize how the eye and the visual cortex work together to sense and perceive the visual stimuli in the environment, including processing colors, shape, depth, and motion.

Whereas other animals rely primarily on hearing, smell, or touch to understand the world around them, human beings rely in large part on vision. A large part of our cerebral cortex is devoted to seeing, and we have substantial visual skills. Seeing begins when light falls on the eyes, initiating the process of transduction. Once this visual information reaches the visual cortex, it is processed by a variety of neurons that detect colors, shapes, and motion, and that create meaningful perceptions out of the incoming stimuli.

The air around us is filled with a sea of *electromagnetic energy*; pulses of energy waves that can carry information from place to place. As you can see in Figure 4.6, electromagnetic waves vary in their **wavelength**—*the distance between one wave peak and the next wave peak*, with the shortest gamma waves being only a fraction of a millimeter in length and the longest radio waves being hundreds of kilometers long. Humans are blind to almost all of this energy—our eyes detect only the range from about 400 to 700 billionths of a meter, the part of the electromagnetic spectrum known as the *visible spectrum*.

wavelength

The distance between one wave peak and the next wave peak.

FIGURE 4.6 The Electromagnetic Spectrum

Only a small fraction of the electromagnetic energy that surrounds us (the visible spectrum) is detectable by the human eye.

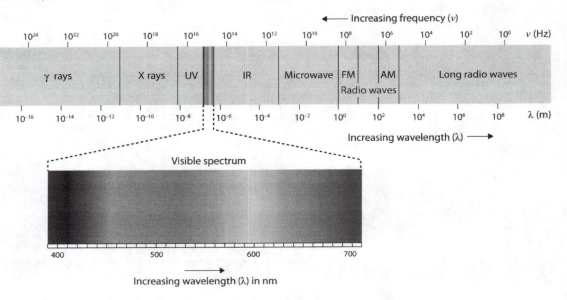

2.1   The Sensing Eye and the Perceiving Visual Cortex

cornea

A clear covering that protects the eye and begins to focus the incoming light.

pupil

The small opening in the center of the eye that allows light to enter.

iris

The colored part of the eye that controls the size of the pupil by constricting or dilating in response to light intensity.

lens

A structure that focuses the incoming light on the retina.

retina

The layer of tissue at the back of the eye that contains photoreceptor cells.

visual accommodation

The process of changing the curvature of the lens to keep the light entering the eye focused on the retina.

As you can see in Figure 4.7, light enters the eye through the **cornea**, *a clear covering that protects the eye and begins to focus the incoming light.* The light then passes through the **pupil**, *a small opening in the center of the eye.* The pupil is surrounded by the **iris**, *the colored part of the eye that controls the size of the pupil by constricting or dilating in response to light intensity.* When we enter a dark movie theater on a sunny day, for instance, muscles in the iris open the pupil and allow more light to enter. Complete adaptation to the dark may take up to 20 minutes.

Behind the pupil is the **lens**, *a structure that focuses the incoming light on the* **retina**, *the layer of tissue at the back of the eye that contains photoreceptor cells.* As our eyes move from near objects to distant objects, a process known as *visual accommodation* occurs. **Visual accommodation** is *the process of changing the curvature of the lens to keep the light entering the eye focused on the retina.* Rays from the top of the image strike the bottom of the retina and vice versa, and rays from the left side of the image strike the right part of the retina and vice versa, causing the image on the retina to be upside down and backward. Furthermore, the image projected on the retina is flat, and yet our final perception of the image will be three dimensional.

FIGURE 4.7   Anatomy of the Human Eye

Light enters the eye through the transparent cornea, passing through the pupil at the center of the iris. The lens adjusts to focus the light on the retina, where it appears upside down and backward. Receptor cells on the retina send information via the optic nerve to the visual cortex.

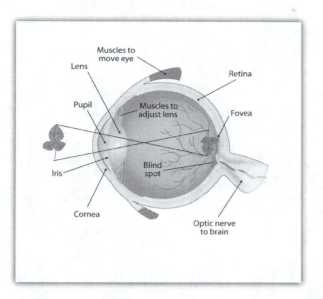

Accommodation is not always perfect, and in some cases the light that is hitting the retina is a bit out of focus. As you can see in Figure 4.8, if the focus is in front of the retina, we say that the person is *nearsighted*, and when the focus is behind the retina we say that the person is *farsighted*. Eyeglasses and contact lenses correct this problem by adding another lens in front of the eye, and laser eye surgery corrects the problem by reshaping the eye's own lens.

FIGURE 4.8   Normal, Nearsighted, and Farsighted Eyes

For people with normal vision (left), the lens properly focuses incoming light on the retina. For people who are nearsighted (center), images from far objects focus too far in front of the retina, whereas for people who are farsighted (right), images from near objects focus too far behind the retina. Eyeglasses solve the problem by adding a secondary, corrective, lens.

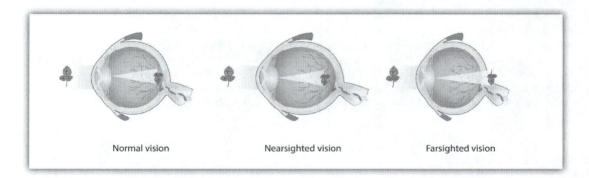

The retina contains layers of neurons specialized to respond to light (see Figure 4.9). As light falls on the retina, it first activates receptor cells known as *rods* and *cones*. The activation of these cells then spreads to the *bipolar cells* and then to the *ganglion cells*, which gather together and converge, like the strands of a rope, forming the *optic nerve*. The **optic nerve** is *a collection of millions of ganglion neurons that sends vast amounts of visual information, via the thalamus, to the brain*. Because the retina and the optic nerve are active processors and analyzers of visual information, it is not inappropriate to think of these structures as an extension of the brain itself.

optic nerve

A collection of millions of ganglion neurons that sends vast amounts of visual information, via the thalamus, to the brain.

FIGURE 4.9 The Retina With Its Specialized Cells

When light falls on the retina, it creates a photochemical reaction in the rods and cones at the back of the retina. The reactions then continue to the bipolar cells, the ganglion cells, and eventually to the optic nerve.

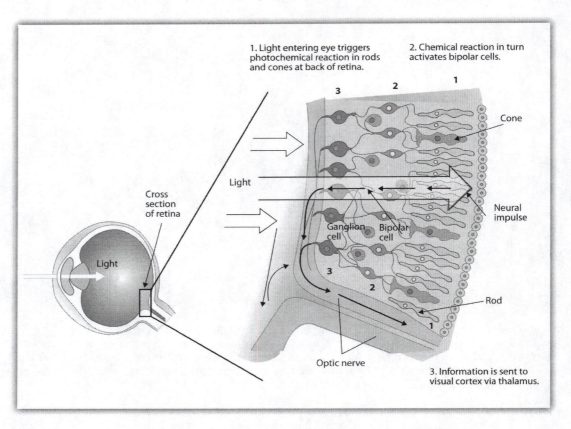

rods

Visual neurons that specialize in detecting black, white, and gray colors.

cones

Visual neurons that are specialized in detecting fine detail and colors.

fovea

The central point of the retina.

Rods are *visual neurons that specialize in detecting black, white, and gray colors*. There are about 120 million rods in each eye. The rods do not provide a lot of detail about the images we see, but because they are highly sensitive to shorter-waved (darker) and weak light, they help us see in dim light, for instance, at night. Because the rods are located primarily around the edges of the retina, they are particularly active in peripheral vision (when you need to see something at night, try looking away from what you want to see). **Cones** are *visual neurons that are specialized in detecting fine detail and colors*. The 5 million or so cones in each eye enable us to see in color, but they operate best in bright light. The cones are located primarily in and around the fovea, which is *the central point of the retina*.

To demonstrate the difference between rods and cones in attention to detail, choose a word in this text and focus on it. Do you notice that the words a few inches to the side seem more blurred? This is because the word you are focusing on strikes the detail-oriented cones, while the words surrounding it strike the less-detail-oriented rods, which are located on the periphery.

FIGURE 4.10 Mona Lisa's Smile

Margaret Livingstone (2002)[12] found an interesting effect that demonstrates the different processing capacities of the eye's rods and cones—namely, that the Mona Lisa's smile, which is widely referred to as "elusive," is perceived differently depending on how one looks at the painting. Because Leonardo da Vinci painted the smile in low-detail brush strokes, these details are better perceived by our peripheral vision (the rods) than by the cones. Livingstone found that people rated the Mona Lisa as more cheerful when they were instructed to focus on her eyes than they did when they were asked to look directly at her mouth. As Livingstone put it, "She smiles until you look at her mouth, and then it fades, like a dim star that disappears when you look directly at it."

Source: Photo courtesy of the Louvre Museum, http://commons.wikimedia.org/wiki/File:Mona_Lisa_detail_face.jpg.

As you can see in Figure 4.11, the sensory information received by the retina is relayed through the thalamus to corresponding areas in the visual cortex, which is located in the occipital lobe at the back of the brain. Although the principle of contralateral control might lead you to expect that the left eye would send information to the right brain hemisphere and vice versa, nature is smarter than that. In fact, the left and right eyes each send information to both the left and the right hemisphere, and the visual cortex processes each of the cues separately and in parallel. This is an adaptational advantage to an organism that loses sight in one eye, because even if only one eye is functional, both hemispheres will still receive input from it.

FIGURE 4.11 Pathway of Visual Images Through the Thalamus and Into the Visual Cortex

The left and right eyes each send information to both the left and the right brain hemisphere.

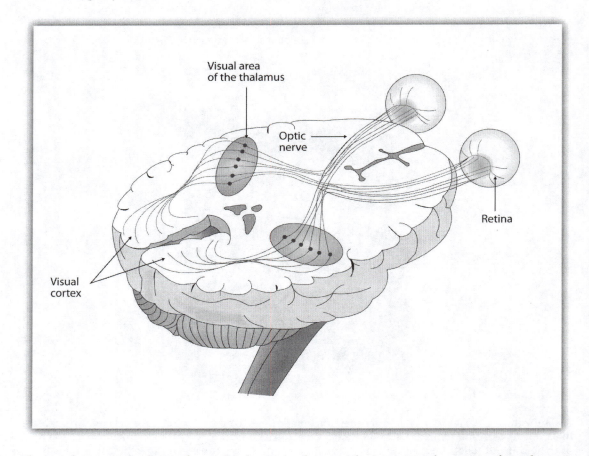

The visual cortex is made up of specialized neurons that turn the sensations they receive from the optic nerve into meaningful images. Because there are no photoreceptor cells at the place where the optic nerve leaves the retina, a hole or *blind spot* in our vision is created (see Figure 4.12). When both of our eyes are open, we don't experience a problem because our eyes are constantly moving, and one eye makes up for what the other eye misses. But the visual system is also designed to deal with this problem if only one eye is open—the visual cortex simply fills in the small hole in our vision with similar patterns from the surrounding areas, and we never notice the difference. The ability of the visual system to cope with the blind spot is another example of how sensation and perception work together to create meaningful experience.

FIGURE 4.12 Blind Spot Demonstration

You can get an idea of the extent of your blind spot (the place where the optic nerve leaves the retina) by trying this demonstration. Close your left eye and stare with your right eye at the cross in the diagram. You should be able to see the elephant image to the right (don't look at it, just notice that it is there). If you can't see the elephant, move closer or farther away until you can. Now slowly move so that you are closer to the image while you keep looking at the cross. At one distance (probably a foot or so), the elephant will completely disappear from view because its image has fallen on the blind spot.

Perception is created in part through the simultaneous action of thousands of **feature detector neurons**—*specialized neurons, located in the visual cortex, that respond to the strength, angles, shapes, edges, and movements of a visual stimulus* (Kelsey, 1997; Livingstone & Hubel, 1988).[13] The feature detectors work in parallel, each performing a specialized function. When faced with a red square, for instance, the parallel line feature detectors, the horizontal line feature detectors, and the red color feature detectors all become activated. This activation is then passed on to other parts of the visual cortex where other neurons compare the information supplied by the feature detectors with images stored in memory. Suddenly, in a flash of recognition, the many neurons fire together, creating the single image of the red square that we experience (Rodriguez et al., 1999).[14]

> **feature detector neurons**
>
> Specialized neurons, located in the visual cortex, that respond to the strength, angles, shapes, edges, and movements of a visual stimulus.

FIGURE 4.13 The Necker Cube

The Necker cube is an example of how the visual system creates perceptions out of sensations. We do not see a series of lines, but rather a cube. Which cube we see varies depending on the momentary outcome of perceptual processes in the visual cortex.

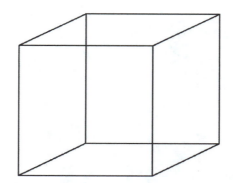

Some feature detectors are tuned to selectively respond to particularly important objects, for instance, faces, smiles, and other parts of the body (Downing, Jiang, Shuman, & Kanwisher, 2001; Haxby et al., 2001).[15] When researchers disrupted face recognition areas of the cortex using the magnetic pulses of transcranial magnetic stimulation (TMS), people were temporarily unable to recognize faces, and yet they were still able to recognize houses (McKone, Kanwisher, & Duchaine, 2007; Pitcher, Walsh, Yovel, & Duchaine, 2007).[16]

2.2 Perceiving Color

hue

Color conveyed by the wavelength of the light that enters the eye.

It has been estimated that the human visual system can detect and discriminate among 7 million color variations (Geldard, 1972),[17] but these variations are all created by the combinations of the three primary colors: red, green, and blue. *The shade of a color*, known as **hue**, is conveyed by the wavelength of the light that enters the eye (we see shorter wavelengths as more blue and longer wavelengths as more red), and we detect brightness from the *intensity* or height of the wave (bigger or more intense waves are perceived as brighter).

FIGURE 4.14 Low- and High-Frequency Sine Waves and Low- and High-Intensity Sine Waves and Their Corresponding Colors

Light waves with shorter frequencies are perceived as more blue than red; light waves with higher intensity are seen as brighter.

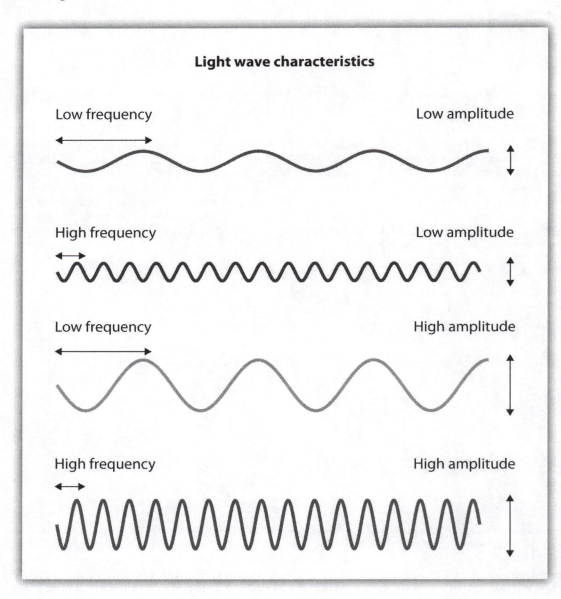

In his important research on color vision, Hermann von Helmholtz (1821–1894) theorized that color is perceived because the cones in the retina come in three types. One type of cone reacts primarily to blue light (short wavelengths), another reacts primarily to green light (medium wavelengths), and a third reacts primarily to red light (long wavelengths). The visual cortex then detects and compares the strength of the signals from each of the three types of cones, creating the experience of color. According to this **Young-Helmholtz trichromatic color theory**, *what color we see depends on the mix of the signals from the three types of cones*. If the brain is receiving primarily red and blue signals, for instance, it will perceive purple; if it is receiving primarily red and green signals it will perceive yellow; and if it is receiving messages from all three types of cones it will perceive white.

The different functions of the three types of cones are apparent in people who experience **color blindness**—*the inability to detect either green and/or red colors*. About 1 in 50 people, mostly men, lack functioning in the red- or green-sensitive cones, leaving them only able to experience either one or two colors (Figure 4.15).

FIGURE 4.15

People with normal color vision can see the number 42 in the first image and the number 12 in the second (they are vague but apparent). However, people who are color blind cannot see the numbers at all.

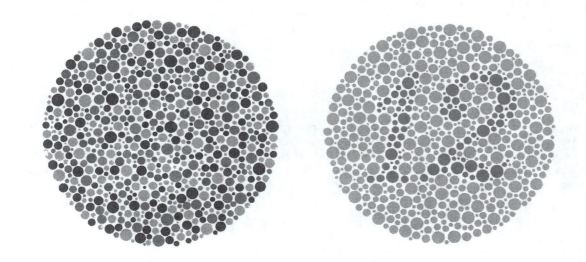

Source: Courtesy of http://commons.wikimedia.org/wiki/File:Ishihara_11.PNG and http://commons.wikimedia.org/wiki/File:Ishihara_23.PNG.

The trichromatic color theory cannot explain all of human vision, however. For one, although the color purple does appear to us as a mixing of red and blue, yellow does not appear to be a mix of red and green. And people with color blindness, who cannot see either green or red, nevertheless can still see yellow. An alternative approach to the Young-Helmholtz theory, known as the **opponent-process color theory**, *proposes that we analyze sensory information not in terms of three colors but rather in three sets of "opponent colors": red-green, yellow-blue, and white-black*. Evidence for the opponent-process theory comes from the fact that some neurons in the retina and in the visual cortex are excited by one color (e.g., red) but inhibited by another color (e.g., green).

One example of opponent processing occurs in the experience of an afterimage. If you stare at the flag on the left side of Figure 4.16 for about 30 seconds (the longer you look, the better the effect), and then move your eyes to the blank area to the right of it, you will see the afterimage. When we stare at the green stripes, our green receptors habituate and begin to process less strongly, whereas the red receptors remain at full strength. When we switch our gaze, we see primarily the red part of the opponent process. Similar processes create blue after yellow and white after black.

Young-Helmholtz trichromatic color theory

The theory of color perception that proposes that what color we see depends on the mix of the signals from the three types of cones.

color blindness

The inability to detect either green and/or red colors.

opponent-process color theory

The theory of color perception that proposes that we analyze sensory information in three sets of "opponent colors": red-green, yellow-blue, and white-black.

FIGURE 4.16 U.S. Flag

The presence of an afterimage is best explained by the opponent-process theory of color perception. Stare at the flag for a few seconds, and then move your gaze to the blank space next to it. Do you see the afterimage?

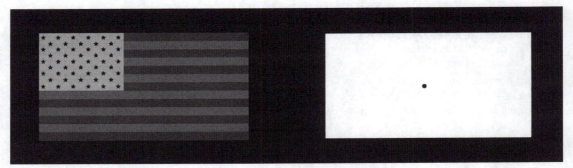

Source: Photo courtesy of Mike Swanson, http://en.wikipedia.org/wiki/File:US_flag(inverted).svg.

The tricolor and the opponent-process mechanisms work together to produce color vision. When light rays enter the eye, the red, blue, and green cones on the retina respond in different degrees, and send different strength signals of red, blue, and green through the optic nerve. The color signals are then processed both by the ganglion cells and by the neurons in the visual cortex (Gegenfurtner & Kiper, 2003).[18]

2.3 Perceiving Form

gestalt

A meaningful organized whole.

One of the important processes required in vision is the perception of form. German psychologists in the 1930s and 1940s, including Max Wertheimer (1880–1943), Kurt Koffka (1886–1941), and Wolfgang Köhler (1887–1967), argued that we create forms out of their component sensations based on the idea of the **gestalt**, *a meaningfully organized whole*. The idea of the gestalt is that the "whole is more than the sum of its parts." Some examples of how gestalt principles lead us to see more than what is actually there are summarized in Table 4.1.

TABLE 4.1 Summary of Gestalt Principles of Form Perception

Principle	Description	Example	Image
Figure and ground	We structure input such that we always see a figure (image) against a ground (background).	At right, you may see a vase or you may see two faces, but in either case, you will organize the image as a figure against a ground.	**FIGURE 4.17** 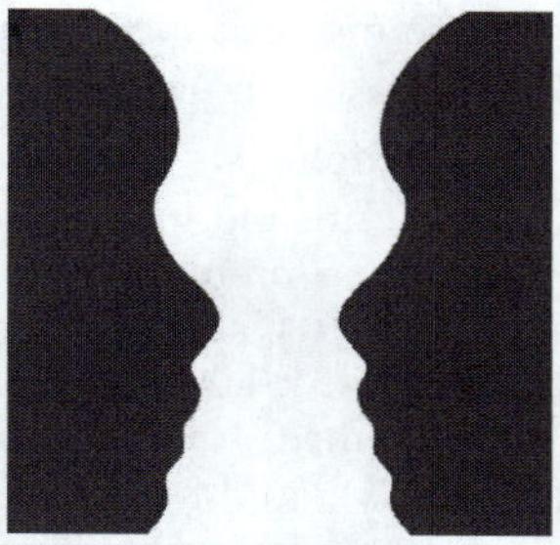
Similarity	Stimuli that are similar to each other tend to be grouped together.	You are more likely to see three similar columns among the *XYX* characters at right than you are to see four rows.	**FIGURE 4.18** 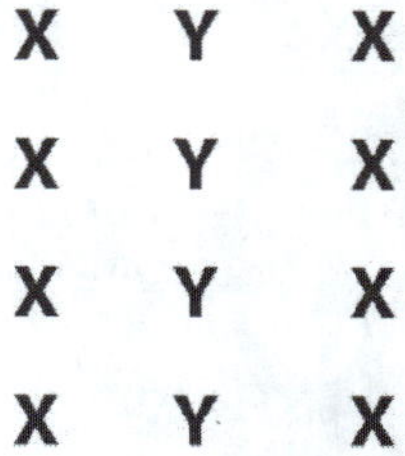
Proximity	We tend to group nearby figures together.	Do you see four or eight images at right? Principles of proximity suggest that you might see only four.	**FIGURE 4.19** 
Continuity	We tend to perceive stimuli in smooth, continuous ways rather than in more discontinuous ways.	At right, most people see a line of dots that moves from the lower left to the upper right, rather than a line that moves from the left and then suddenly turns down. The principle of continuity leads us to see most lines as following the smoothest possible path.	**FIGURE 4.20** 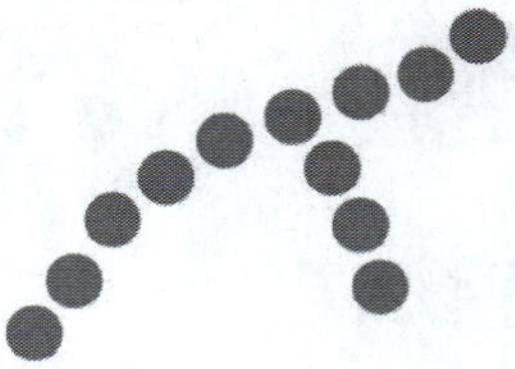
Closure	We tend to fill in gaps in an incomplete image to create a complete, whole object.	Closure leads us to see a single spherical object at right rather than a set of unrelated cones.	**FIGURE 4.21** 

2.4 Perceiving Depth

depth perception

The ability to perceive three-dimensional space and to accurately judge distance.

visual cliff

A mechanism that gives the perception of a dangerous drop-off, in which infants can be safely tested for their perception of depth.

Depth perception is *the ability to perceive three-dimensional space and to accurately judge distance*. Without depth perception, we would be unable to drive a car, thread a needle, or simply navigate our way around the supermarket (Howard & Rogers, 2001).[19] Research has found that depth perception is in part based on innate capacities and in part learned through experience (Witherington, 2005).[20]

Psychologists Eleanor Gibson and Richard Walk (1960)[21] tested the ability to perceive depth in 6- to 14-month-old infants by placing them on a **visual cliff,** *a mechanism that gives the perception of a dangerous drop-off, in which infants can be safely tested for their perception of depth* (Figure 4.22). The infants were placed on one side of the "cliff," while their mothers called to them from the other side. Gibson and Walk found that most infants either crawled away from the cliff or remained on the board and cried because they wanted to go to their mothers, but the infants perceived a chasm that they instinctively could not cross. Further research has found that even very young children who cannot yet crawl are fearful of heights (Campos, Langer, & Krowitz, 1970).[22] On the other hand, studies have also found that infants improve their hand-eye coordination as they learn to better grasp objects and as they gain more experience in crawling, indicating that depth perception is also learned (Adolph, 2000).[23]

FIGURE 4.22 Visual Cliff

Babies appear to have the innate ability to perceive depth, as seen by this baby's reluctance to cross the "visual cliff."

Depth perception is the result of our use of **depth cues,** *messages from our bodies and the external environment that supply us with information about space and distance*. **Binocular depth cues** are *depth cues that are created by retinal image disparity—that is, the space between our eyes, and thus which require the coordination of both eyes*. One outcome of retinal disparity is that the images projected on each eye are slightly different from each other. The visual cortex automatically merges the two images into one, enabling us to perceive depth. Three-dimensional movies make use of retinal disparity by using 3-D glasses that the viewer wears to create a different image on each eye. The perceptual system quickly, easily, and unconsciously turns the disparity into 3-D.

An important binocular depth cue is **convergence,** *the inward turning of our eyes that is required to focus on objects that are less than about 50 feet away from us*. The visual cortex uses the size of the convergence angle between the eyes to judge the object's distance. You will be able to feel your eyes converging if you slowly bring a finger closer to your nose while continuing to focus on it. When you close one eye, you no longer feel the tension—convergence is a binocular depth cue that requires both eyes to work.

depth cues

Messages from our bodies and the external environment that supply us with information about space and distance.

The visual system also uses *accommodation* to help determine depth. As the lens changes its curvature to focus on distant or close objects, information relayed from the muscles attached to the lens helps us determine an object's distance. Accommodation is only effective at short viewing distances, however, so while it comes in handy when threading a needle or tying shoelaces, it is far less effective when driving or playing sports.

Although the best cues to depth occur when both eyes work together, we are able to see depth even with one eye closed. **Monocular depth cues** are *depth cues that help us perceive depth using only one eye* (Sekuler & Blake, 2006).[24] Some of the most important are summarized in Table 4.2.

binocular depth cues

Depth cues that are created by retinal disparity—that is, the space between our eyes, and thus require the coordination of both eyes.

convergence

The inward turning of our eyes that is required to focus on objects that are less than about 50 feet away from us.

monocular depth cues

Depth cues that help us perceive depth using only one eye.

TABLE 4.2 Monocular Depth Cues That Help Us Judge Depth at a Distance

Name	Description	Example	Image
Position	We tend to see objects higher up in our field of vision as farther away.	The fence posts at right appear farther away not only because they become smaller but also because they appear higher up in the picture.	**FIGURE 4.23** 
Relative size	Assuming that the objects in a scene are the same size, smaller objects are perceived as farther away.	At right, the cars in the distance appear smaller than those nearer to us.	**FIGURE 4.24** 
Linear perspective	Parallel lines appear to converge at a distance.	We know that the tracks at right are parallel. When they appear closer together, we determine they are farther away.	**FIGURE 4.25** 
Light and shadow	The eye receives more reflected light from objects that are closer to us. Normally, light comes from above, so darker images are in shadow.	We see the images at right as extending and indented according to their shadowing. If we invert the picture, the images will reverse.	**FIGURE 4.26** 
Interposition	When one object overlaps another object, we view it as closer.	At right, because the blue star covers the pink bar, it is seen as closer than the yellow moon.	**FIGURE 4.27** 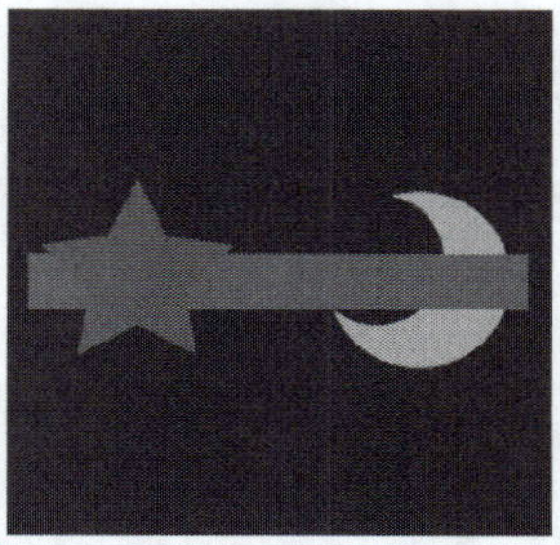
Aerial perspective	Objects that appear hazy, or that are covered with smog or dust, appear farther away.	The artist who painted the picture on the right used aerial perspective to make the clouds more hazy and thus appear farther away.	**FIGURE 4.28** 

Photo sources: TBD

2.5 Perceiving Motion

Many animals, including human beings, have very sophisticated perceptual skills that allow them to co-ordinate their own motion with the motion of moving objects in order to create a collision with that object. Bats and birds use this mechanism to catch up with prey, dogs use it to catch a Frisbee, and humans use it to catch a moving football. The brain detects motion partly from the changing size of an image on the retina (objects that look bigger are usually closer to us) and in part from the relative brightness of objects.

We also experience motion when objects near each other change their appearance. The **beta effect** refers to *the perception of motion that occurs when different images are presented next to each other in succession* (see "Beta Effect and Phi Phenomenon"). The visual cortex fills in the missing part of the motion and we see the object moving. The beta effect is used in movies to create the experience of motion. A related effect is the **phi phenomenon**, in which *we perceive a sensation of motion caused by the appearance and disappearance of objects that are near each other*. The phi phenomenon looks like a moving zone or cloud of background color surrounding the flashing objects. The beta effect and the phi phenomenon are other examples of the importance of the gestalt—our tendency to "see more than the sum of the parts."

beta effect

The perception of motion that occurs when different images are presented next to each other in succession.

phi phenomenon

The perception of motion caused by the appearance and disappearance of objects that are near each other.

Beta Effect and Phi Phenomenon

In the beta effect, our eyes detect motion from a series of still images, each with the object in a different place. This is the fundamental mechanism of motion pictures (movies). In the phi phenomenon, the perception of motion is based on the momentary hiding of an image.

Phi phenomenon: http://upload.wikimedia.org/wikipedia/commons/6/6e/Lilac-Chaser.gif

Beta effect: http://upload.wikimedia.org/wikipedia/commons/0/09/Phi_phenomenom_no_watermark.gif

KEY TAKEAWAYS

- Vision is the process of detecting the electromagnetic energy that surrounds us. Only a small fraction of the electromagnetic spectrum is visible to humans.
- The visual receptor cells on the retina detect shape, color, motion, and depth.
- Light enters the eye through the transparent cornea and passes through the pupil at the center of the iris. The lens adjusts to focus the light on the retina, where it appears upside down and backward. Receptor cells on the retina are excited or inhibited by the light and send information to the visual cortex through the optic nerve.
- The retina has two types of photoreceptor cells: rods, which detect brightness and respond to black and white, and cones, which respond to red, green, and blue. Color blindness occurs when people lack function in the red- or green-sensitive cones.
- Feature detector neurons in the visual cortex help us recognize objects, and some neurons respond selectively to faces and other body parts.
- The Young-Helmholtz trichromatic color theory proposes that color perception is the result of the signals sent by the three types of cones, whereas the opponent-process color theory proposes that we perceive color as three sets of opponent colors: red-green, yellow-blue, and white-black.
- The ability to perceive depth occurs through the result of binocular and monocular depth cues.
- Motion is perceived as a function of the size and brightness of objects. The beta effect and the phi phenomenon are examples of perceived motion.

EXERCISES AND CRITICAL THINKING

1. Consider some ways that the processes of visual perception help you engage in an everyday activity, such as driving a car or riding a bicycle.
2. Imagine for a moment what your life would be like if you couldn't see. Do you think you would be able to compensate for your loss of sight by using other senses?

3. HEARING

LEARNING OBJECTIVES

1. Draw a picture of the ear and label its key structures and functions, and describe the role they play in hearing.
2. Describe the process of transduction in hearing.

Like vision and all the other senses, hearing begins with transduction. Sound waves that are collected by our ears are converted into neural impulses, which are sent to the brain where they are integrated with past experience and interpreted as the sounds we experience. The human ear is sensitive to a wide range of sounds, ranging from the faint tick of a clock in a nearby room to the roar of a rock band at a nightclub, and we have the ability to detect very small variations in sound. But the ear is particularly sensitive to sounds in the same frequency as the human voice. A mother can pick out her child's voice from a host of others, and when we pick up the phone we quickly recognize a familiar voice. In a fraction of a second, our auditory system receives the sound waves, transmits them to the auditory cortex, compares them to stored knowledge of other voices, and identifies the identity of the caller.

3.1 The Ear

Just as the eye detects light waves, the ear detects sound waves. Vibrating objects (such as the human vocal chords or guitar strings) cause air molecules to bump into each other and produce sound waves, which travel from their source as peaks and valleys much like the ripples that expand outward when a stone is tossed into a pond. Unlike light waves, which can travel in a vacuum, sound waves are carried within mediums such as air, water, or metal, and it is the changes in pressure associated with these mediums that the ear detects.

As with light waves, we detect both the wavelength and the *amplitude* of sound waves. The *wavelength of the sound wave* (known as **frequency**) is measured in terms of the number of waves that arrive per second and determines our perception of **pitch**, *the perceived frequency of a sound*. Longer sound waves have lower frequency and produce a lower pitch, whereas shorter waves have higher frequency and a higher pitch.

The **amplitude**, or *height of the sound wave*, determines how much energy it contains and is perceived as **loudness** (*the degree of sound volume*). Larger waves are perceived as louder. Loudness is measured using *the unit of relative loudness* known as the **decibel**. Zero decibels represent the absolute threshold for human hearing, below which we cannot hear a sound. Each increase in 10 decibels represents a tenfold increase in the loudness of the sound (see Figure 4.29). The sound of a typical conversation (about 60 decibels) is 1,000 times louder than the sound of a faint whisper (30 decibels), whereas the sound of a jackhammer (130 decibels) is 10 billion times louder than the whisper.

frequency

The wavelength of a sound wave.

pitch

The perceived frequency of a sound.

amplitude

The height of a sound wave.

loudness

The degree of sound volume.

decibel

The unit of relative loudness.

FIGURE 4.29 Sounds in Everyday Life

The human ear can comfortably hear sounds up to 80 decibels. Prolonged exposure to sounds above 80 decibels can cause hearing loss.

Levels of Noise in decibels (dB)

Category	Warning	dB / Source
Painful and dangerous		
	Use hearing protection or avoid	140 Fireworks Gunshots Custom car stereos (at full volume)
		130 Jackhammers Ambulances
Uncomfortable		
	Dangerous over 30 seconds	120 Jet planes (during takeoff)
Very loud		
	Dangerous over 30 minutes	110 Concerts (any genre of music) Car horns Sporting events
		100 Snowmobiles MP3 players (at full volume)
		90 Lawnmowers Power tools Blenders Hair dryers
Over 85 dB for extended periods can cause permanent hearing loss.		
Loud		
		80 Alarm clocks
		70 Traffic Vacuum cleaners
Moderate		
		60 Normal conversation Dishwashers
		50 Moderate rainfall
Soft		
		40 Quiet library
Faint		
		20 Leaves rustling

Audition begins in the **pinna**, *the external and visible part of the ear*, which is shaped like a funnel to draw in sound waves and guide them into the auditory canal. At the end of the canal, the sound waves strike the *tightly stretched, highly sensitive membrane* known as the **tympanic membrane (or eardrum)**, which vibrates with the waves. The resulting vibrations are relayed into the middle ear through three tiny bones, known as the **ossicles**—the hammer (or malleus), anvil (or incus), and stirrup (or stapes)—to the **cochlea**, *a snail-shaped liquid-filled tube in the inner ear*. The vibrations cause the **oval window**, *the membrane covering the opening of the cochlea*, to vibrate, disturbing the fluid inside the cochlea.

The movements of the fluid in the cochlea bend the hair cells of the inner ear, much in the same way that a gust of wind bends over wheat stalks in a field. The movements of the hair cells trigger nerve impulses in the attached neurons, which are sent to the auditory nerve and then to the auditory cortex in the brain. The cochlea contains about 16,000 hair cells, each of which holds a bundle of fibers known as *cilia* on its tip. The cilia are so sensitive that they can detect a movement that pushes them the width of a single atom. To put things in perspective, cilia swaying at the width of an atom is equivalent to the tip of the Eiffel Tower swaying by half an inch (Corey et al., 2004).[25]

FIGURE 4.30 The Human Ear

Sound waves enter the outer ear and are transmitted through the auditory canal to the eardrum. The resulting vibrations are moved by the three small ossicles into the cochlea, where they are detected by hair cells and sent to the auditory nerve.

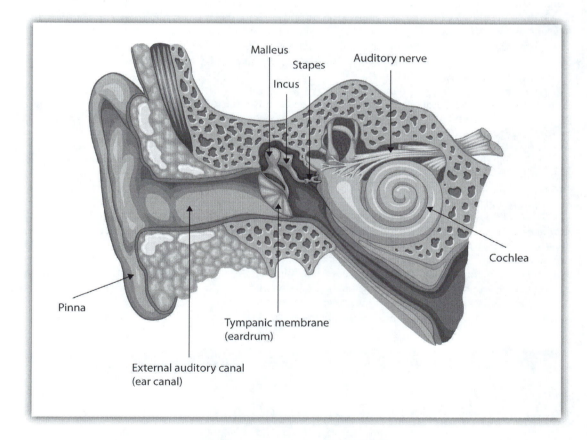

Although loudness is directly determined by the number of hair cells that are vibrating, two different mechanisms are used to detect pitch. The **frequency theory of hearing** proposes that *whatever the pitch of a sound wave, nerve impulses of a corresponding frequency will be sent to the auditory nerve*. For example, a tone measuring 600 hertz will be transduced into 600 nerve impulses a second. This theory has a problem with high-pitched sounds, however, because the neurons cannot fire fast enough. To reach the necessary speed, the neurons work together in a sort of volley system in which different neurons fire in sequence, allowing us to detect sounds up to about 4,000 hertz.

pinna

The external and visible part of the ear.

tympanic membrane (eardrum)

The membrane at the end of the ear canal that relays vibrations into the middle ear.

ossicles

The three tiny bones in the ear (hammer, anvil, and stirrup) that relay sound from the eardrum to the cochlea.

cochlea

A snail-shaped liquid-filled tube in the inner ear that contains the cilia.

oval window

The membrane covering the opening of the cochlea.

frequency theory of hearing

A theory of pitch perception that proposes that nerve impulses corresponding to the pitch of a sound are sent to the auditory nerve.

place theory of hearing

A theory of pitch perception that proposes that different areas of the cochlea respond to different sound frequencies.

Not only is frequency important, but location is critical as well. The cochlea relays information about the specific area, or place, in the cochlea that is most activated by the incoming sound. The **place theory of hearing** proposes that *different areas of the cochlea respond to different frequencies*. Higher tones excite areas closest to the opening of the cochlea (near the oval window). Lower tones excite areas near the narrow tip of the cochlea, at the opposite end. Pitch is therefore determined in part by the area of the cochlea firing the most frequently.

Just as having two eyes in slightly different positions allows us to perceive depth, so the fact that the ears are placed on either side of the head enables us to benefit from stereophonic, or three-dimensional, hearing. If a sound occurs on your left side, the left ear will receive the sound slightly sooner than the right ear, and the sound it receives will be more intense, allowing you to quickly determine the location of the sound. Although the distance between our two ears is only about 6 inches, and sound waves travel at 750 miles an hour, the time and intensity differences are easily detected (Middlebrooks & Green, 1991).[26] When a sound is equidistant from both ears, such as when it is directly in front, behind, beneath or overhead, we have more difficulty pinpointing its location. It is for this reason that dogs (and people, too) tend to cock their heads when trying to pinpoint a sound, so that the ears receive slightly different signals.

3.2 Hearing Loss

More than 31 million Americans suffer from some kind of hearing impairment (Kochkin, 2005).[27] *Conductive hearing loss* is caused by physical damage to the ear (such as to the eardrums or ossicles) that reduce the ability of the ear to transfer vibrations from the outer ear to the inner ear. *Sensorineural hearing loss*, which is caused by damage to the cilia or to the auditory nerve, is less common overall but frequently occurs with age (Tennesen, 2007).[28] The cilia are extremely fragile, and by the time we are 65 years old, we will have lost 40% of them, particularly those that respond to high-pitched sounds (Chisolm, Willott, & Lister, 2003).[29]

Prolonged exposure to loud sounds will eventually create sensorineural hearing loss as the cilia are damaged by the noise. People who constantly operate noisy machinery without using appropriate ear protection are at high risk of hearing loss, as are people who listen to loud music on their headphones or who engage in noisy hobbies, such as hunting or motorcycling. Sounds that are 85 decibels or more can cause damage to your hearing, particularly if you are exposed to them repeatedly. Sounds of more than 130 decibels are dangerous even if you are exposed to them infrequently. People who experience *tinnitus* (a ringing or a buzzing sensation) after being exposed to loud sounds have very likely experienced some damage to their cilia. Taking precautions when being exposed to loud sound is important, as cilia do not grow back.

While conductive hearing loss can often be improved through hearing aids that amplify the sound, they are of little help to sensorineural hearing loss. But if the auditory nerve is still intact, a *cochlear implant* may be used. A cochlear implant is a device made up of a series of electrodes that are placed inside the cochlea. The device serves to bypass the hair cells by stimulating the auditory nerve cells directly. The latest implants utilize place theory, enabling different spots on the implant to respond to different levels of pitch. The cochlear implant can help children hear who would normally be deaf, and if the device is implanted early enough, these children can frequently learn to speak, often as well as normal children do (Dettman, Pinder, Briggs, Dowell, & Leigh, 2007; Dorman & Wilson, 2004).[30]

KEY TAKEAWAYS

- Sound waves vibrating through mediums such as air, water, or metal are the stimulus energy that is sensed by the ear.
- The hearing system is designed to assess frequency (pitch) and amplitude (loudness).
- Sound waves enter the outer ear (the pinna) and are sent to the eardrum via the auditory canal. The resulting vibrations are relayed by the three ossicles, causing the oval window covering the cochlea to vibrate. The vibrations are detected by the cilia (hair cells) and sent via the auditory nerve to the auditory cortex.
- There are two theories as to how we perceive pitch: The frequency theory of hearing suggests that as a sound wave's pitch changes, nerve impulses of a corresponding frequency enter the auditory nerve. The place theory of hearing suggests that we hear different pitches because different areas of the cochlea respond to higher and lower pitches.
- Conductive hearing loss is caused by physical damage to the ear or eardrum and may be improved by hearing aids or cochlear implants. Sensorineural hearing loss, caused by damage to the hair cells or auditory nerves in the inner ear, may be produced by prolonged exposure to sounds of more than 85 decibels.

EXERCISE AND CRITICAL THINKING

1. Given what you have learned about hearing in this chapter, are you engaging in any activities that might cause long-term hearing loss? If so, how might you change your behavior to reduce the likelihood of suffering damage?

4. TASTING, SMELLING, AND TOUCHING

LEARNING OBJECTIVES

1. Summarize how the senses of taste and olfaction transduce stimuli into perceptions.
2. Describe the process of transduction in the senses of touch and proprioception.
3. Outline the gate control theory of pain. Explain why pain matters and how it may be controlled.

Although vision and hearing are by far the most important, human sensation is rounded out by four other senses, each of which provides an essential avenue to a better understanding of and response to the world around us. These other senses are *touch, taste, smell,* and our *sense of body position and movement (proprioception).*

4.1 Tasting

Taste is important not only because it allows us to enjoy the food we eat, but even more crucial, because it leads us toward foods that provide energy (sugar, for instance) and away from foods that could be harmful. Many children are picky eaters for a reason—they are biologically predisposed to be very careful about what they eat. Together with the sense of smell, taste helps us maintain appetite, assess potential dangers (such as the odor of a gas leak or a burning house), and avoid eating poisonous or spoiled food.

Our ability to taste begins at the taste receptors on the tongue. The tongue detects six different taste sensations, known respectively as *sweet, salty, sour, bitter, piquancy (spicy),* and *umami (savory).* Umami is a meaty taste associated with meats, cheeses, soy, seaweed, and mushrooms, and particularly found in monosodium glutamate (MSG), a popular flavor enhancer (Ikeda, 1909/2002; Sugimoto & Ninomiya, 2005).[31]

Our tongues are covered with *taste buds,* which are designed to sense chemicals in the mouth. Most taste buds are located in the top outer edges of the tongue, but there are also receptors at the back of the tongue as well as on the walls of the mouth and at the back of the throat. As we chew food, it dissolves and enters the taste buds, triggering nerve impulses that are transmitted to the brain (Northcutt, 2004).[32] Human tongues are covered with 2,000 to 10,000 taste buds, and each bud contains between 50 and 100 taste receptor cells. Taste buds are activated very quickly; a salty or sweet taste that touches a taste bud for even one tenth of a second will trigger a neural impulse (Kelling & Halpern, 1983).[33] On average, taste buds live for about 5 days, after which new taste buds are created to replace them. As we get older, however, the rate of creation decreases making us less sensitive to taste. This change helps explain why some foods that seem so unpleasant in childhood are more enjoyable in adulthood.

The area of the sensory cortex that responds to taste is in a very similar location to the area that responds to smell, a fact that helps explain why the sense of smell also contributes to our experience of the things we eat. You may remember having had difficulty tasting food when you had a bad cold, and if you block your nose and taste slices of raw potato, apple, and parsnip, you will not be able to taste the differences between them. Our experience of texture in a food (the way we feel it on our tongues) also influences how we taste it.

4.2 Smelling

As we breathe in air through our nostrils, we inhale airborne chemical molecules, which are detected by the 10 million to 20 million receptor cells embedded in the *olfactory membrane* of the upper nasal passage. The *olfactory receptor cells* are topped with tentacle-like protrusions that contain receptor proteins. When an odor receptor is stimulated, the membrane sends neural messages up the olfactory nerve to the brain (see Figure 4.31).

FIGURE 4.31 Smell Receptors

There are more than 1,000 types of odor receptor cells in the olfactory membrane.

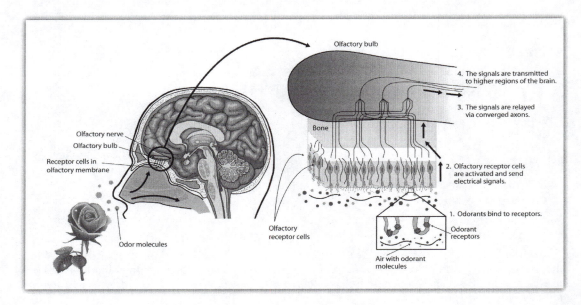

We have approximately 1,000 types of odor receptor cells (Bensafi et al., 2004),[34] and it is estimated that we can detect 10,000 different odors (Malnic, Hirono, Sato, & Buck, 1999).[35] The receptors come in many different shapes and respond selectively to different smells. Like a lock and key, different chemical molecules "fit" into different receptor cells, and odors are detected according to their influence on a combination of receptor cells. Just as the 10 digits from *0* to *9* can combine in many different ways to produce an endless array of phone numbers, odor molecules bind to different combinations of receptors, and these combinations are decoded in the olfactory cortex. As you can see in Figure 4.32, women tend to have a more acute sense of smell than men. The sense of smell peaks in early adulthood and then begins a slow decline. By ages 60 to 70, the sense of smell has become sharply diminished.

FIGURE 4.32 Age Differences in Smell

The ability to identify common odorants declines markedly between 20 and 70 years of age.

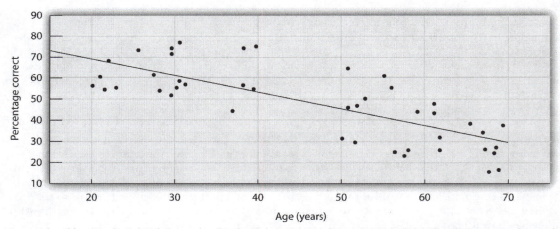

Source: Adapted from Murphy, C. (1986). Taste and smell in the elderly. In H. L. Meiselman & R. S. Rivlin (Eds.), Clinical measurement of taste and smell (Vol. 1, pp. 343–371). New York, NY: Macmillan.

4.3 Touching

The sense of touch is essential to human development. Infants thrive when they are cuddled and attended to, but not if they are deprived of human contact (Baysinger, Plubell, & Harlow, 1973; Feldman, 2007; Haradon, Bascom, Dragomir, & Scripcaru, 1994).[36] Touch communicates warmth, caring, and support, and is an essential part of the enjoyment we gain from our social interactions with close others (Field et al., 1997; Kelter, 2009).[37]

The skin, the largest organ in the body, is the sensory organ for touch. The skin contains a variety of nerve endings, combinations of which respond to particular types of pressures and temperatures. When you touch different parts of the body, you will find that some areas are more ticklish, whereas other areas respond more to pain, cold, or heat.

The thousands of nerve endings in the skin respond to four basic sensations: *Pressure, hot, cold*, and *pain*, but only the sensation of pressure has its own specialized receptors. Other sensations are created by a combination of the other four. For instance:

- The experience of a tickle is caused by the stimulation of neighboring pressure receptors.
- The experience of heat is caused by the stimulation of hot and cold receptors.
- The experience of itching is caused by repeated stimulation of pain receptors.
- The experience of wetness is caused by repeated stimulation of cold and pressure receptors.

The skin is important not only in providing information about touch and temperature but also in **proprioception**—*the ability to sense the position and movement of our body parts*. Proprioception is accomplished by specialized neurons located in the skin, joints, bones, ears, and tendons, which send messages about the compression and the contraction of muscles throughout the body. Without this feedback from our bones and muscles, we would be unable to play sports, walk, or even stand upright.

The ability to keep track of where the body is moving is also provided by the **vestibular system**, *a set of liquid-filled areas in the inner ear that monitors the head's position and movement, maintaining the body's balance*. As you can see in Figure 4.33, the vestibular system includes the *semicircular canals* and the *vestibular sacs*. These sacs connect the canals with the cochlea. The semicircular canals sense the rotational movements of the body and the vestibular sacs sense linear accelerations. The vestibular system sends signals to the neural structures that control eye movement and to the muscles that keep the body upright.

proprioception

The ability to sense the position and movement of our body parts.

vestibular system

A set of liquid-filled areas in the inner ear that monitors the head's position and movement, maintaing the body's balance.

FIGURE 4.33 The Vestibular System

The vestibular system includes the semicircular canals (brown) that transduce the rotational movements of the body and the vestibular sacs (blue) that sense linear accelerations.

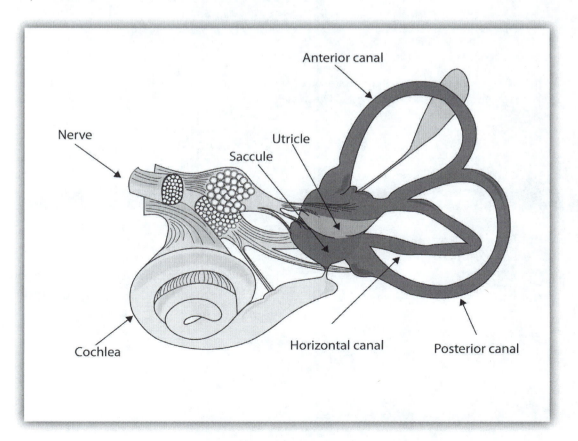

4.4 Experiencing Pain

We do not enjoy it, but the experience of pain is how the body informs us that we are in danger. The burn when we touch a hot radiator and the sharp stab when we step on a nail lead us to change our behavior, preventing further damage to our bodies. People who cannot experience pain are in serious danger of damage from wounds that others with pain would quickly notice and attend to.

gate control theory of pain

A theory of pain proposing that pain is determined by the operation of two types of nerve fibers in the spinal cord.

The **gate control theory of pain** *proposes that pain is determined by the operation of two types of nerve fibers in the spinal cord.* One set of smaller nerve fibers carries pain from the body to the brain, whereas a second set of larger fibers is designed to stop or start (as a gate would) the flow of pain (Melzack & Wall, 1996).[38] It is for this reason that massaging an area where you feel pain may help alleviate it—the massage activates the large nerve fibers that block the pain signals of the small nerve fibers (Wall, 2000).[39]

Experiencing pain is a lot more complicated than simply responding to neural messages, however. It is also a matter of perception. We feel pain less when we are busy focusing on a challenging activity (Bantick, Wise, Ploghaus, Clare, Smith, & Tracey, 2002),[40] which can help explain why sports players may feel their injuries only after the game. We also feel less pain when we are distracted by humor (Zweyer, Velker, & Ruch, 2004).[41] And pain is soothed by the brain's release of endorphins, natural hormonal pain killers. The release of endorphins can explain the euphoria experienced in the running of a marathon (Sternberg, Bailin, Grant, & Gracely, 1998).[42]

KEY TAKEAWAYS

- The ability to taste, smell, and touch are important because they help us avoid harm from environmental toxins.
- The many taste buds on our tongues and inside our mouths allow us to detect six basic taste sensations: sweet, salty, sour, bitter, piquancy, and umami.
- In olfaction, transduction occurs as airborne chemicals that are inhaled through the nostrils are detected by receptors in the olfactory membrane. Different chemical molecules fit into different receptor cells, creating different smells.
- On average, women have a better sense of smell than men, and the ability to smell diminishes with age.
- We have a range of different nerve endings embedded in the skin, combinations of which respond to the four basic sensations of pressure, hot, cold, and pain. But only the sensation of pressure has its own specialized receptors.
- Proprioception is our ability to sense the positions and movements of our body parts. Postural and movement information is detected by special neurons located in the skin, joints, bones, ears, and tendons, which pick up messages from the compression and the contraction of muscles throughout the body.
- The vestibular system, composed of structures in the inner ear, monitors the head's position and movement, maintaining the body's balance.
- Gate control theory explains how large and small neurons work together to transmit and regulate the flow of pain to the brain.

EXERCISES AND CRITICAL THINKING

1. Think of the foods that you like to eat the most. Which of the six taste sensations do these foods have, and why do you think that you like these particular flavors?
2. Why do you think that women might have a better developed sense of smell than do men?
3. Why is experiencing pain a benefit for human beings?

5.   ACCURACY AND INACCURACY IN PERCEPTION

LEARNING OBJECTIVES

1. Describe how sensation and perception work together through sensory interaction, selective attention, sensory adaptation, and perceptual constancy.
2. Give examples of how our expectations may influence our perception, resulting in illusions and potentially inaccurate judgments.

The eyes, ears, nose, tongue, and skin sense the world around us, and in some cases perform preliminary information processing on the incoming data. But by and large, we do not experience sensation—we experience the outcome of perception—the total package that the brain puts together from the pieces it receives through our senses and that the brain creates for us to experience. When we look out the window at a view of the countryside, or when we look at the face of a good friend, we don't just see a jumble of colors and shapes—we see, instead, an image of a countryside or an image of a friend (Goodale & Milner, 2006).[43]

5.1   How the Perceptual System Interprets the Environment

This meaning-making involves the automatic operation of a variety of essential perceptual processes. One of these is **sensory interaction**—*the working together of different senses to create experience.* Sensory interaction is involved when taste, smell, and texture combine to create the flavor we experience in food. It is also involved when we enjoy a movie because of the way the images and the music work together.

Although you might think that we understand speech only through our sense of hearing, it turns out that the visual aspect of speech is also important. One example of sensory interaction is shown in the *McGurk effect*—an error in perception that occurs when we misperceive sounds because the audio and visual parts of the speech are mismatched. You can witness the effect yourself by viewing "Video Clip: The McGurk Effect".

sensory interaction

The working together of different senses to create experience.

Video Clip: The McGurk Effect

The McGurk effect is an error in sound perception that occurs when there is a mismatch between the senses of hearing and seeing. You can experience it here.

Keep your eyes closed.

View the video online at: http://www.youtube.com/embed/jtsfidRq2tw

Other examples of sensory interaction include the experience of nausea that can occur when the sensory information being received from the eyes and the body does not match information from the vestibular system (Flanagan, May, & Dobie, 2004)[44] and *synesthesia*—an experience in which one sensation (e.g., hearing a sound) creates experiences in another (e.g., vision). Most people do not experience synesthesia, but those who do link their perceptions in unusual ways, for instance, by experiencing color when they taste a particular food or by hearing sounds when they see certain objects (Ramachandran, Hubbard, Robertson, & Sagiv, 2005).[45]

selective attention

The ability to focus on some sensory inputs while tuning out others.

Another important perceptual process is **selective attention**—*the ability to focus on some sensory inputs while tuning out others.* View "Video Clip: Selective Attention" and count the number of times the people playing with the ball pass it to each other. You may find that, like many other people who view it for the first time, you miss something important because you selectively attend to only one aspect of the video (Simons & Chabris, 1999).[46] Perhaps the process of selective attention can help you see why the security guards completely missed the fact that the Chaser group's motorcade was a fake—they focused on some aspects of the situation, such as the color of the cars and the fact that they were there at all, and completely ignored others (the details of the security information).

 Video Clip: Selective Attention

Watch this video and carefully count how many times the people pass the ball to each other.

copyright (c) 1999 Daniel J. Simons. All rights

View the video online at: http://www.youtube.com/embed/vJG698U2Mvo

Selective attention also allows us to focus on a single talker at a party while ignoring other conversations that are occurring around us (Broadbent, 1958; Cherry, 1953).[47] Without this automatic selective attention, we'd be unable to focus on the single conversation we want to hear. But selective attention is not complete; we also at the same time monitor what's happening in the channels we are not focusing on. Perhaps you have had the experience of being at a party and talking to someone in one part of the room, when suddenly you hear your name being mentioned by someone in another part of the room. This *cocktail party phenomenon* shows us that although selective attention is limiting what we processes, we are nevertheless at the same time doing a lot of unconscious monitoring of the world around us—you didn't know you were attending to the background sounds of the party, but evidently you were.

sensory adaptation

A decreased sensitivity to a stimulus after prolonged and constant exposure.

A second fundamental process of perception is **sensory adaptation**—*a decreased sensitivity to a stimulus after prolonged and constant exposure.* When you step into a swimming pool, the water initially feels cold, but after a while you stop noticing it. After prolonged exposure to the same stimulus, our sensitivity toward it diminishes and we no longer perceive it. The ability to adapt to the things that don't change around us is essential to our survival, as it leaves our sensory receptors free to detect the important and informative changes in our environment and to respond accordingly. We ignore the sounds that our car makes every day, which leaves us free to pay attention to the sounds that are different from normal, and thus likely to need our attention. Our sensory receptors are alert to novelty and are fatigued after constant exposure to the same stimulus.

If sensory adaptation occurs with all senses, why doesn't an image fade away after we stare at it for a period of time? The answer is that, although we are not aware of it, our eyes are constantly flitting from one angle to the next, making thousands of tiny movements (called *saccades*) every minute. This constant eye movement guarantees that the image we are viewing always falls on fresh receptor cells. What would happen if we could stop the movement of our eyes? Psychologists have devised a way of testing the sensory adaptation of the eye by attaching an instrument that ensures a constant image is maintained on the eye's inner surface. Participants are fitted with a contact lens that has miniature slide projector attached to it. Because the projector follows the exact movements of the eye, the same image is always projected, stimulating the same spot, on the retina. Within a few seconds, interesting things begin to happen. The image will begin to vanish, then reappear, only to disappear again, either in pieces or as a whole. Even the eye experiences sensory adaptation (Yarbus, 1967).[48]

One of the major problems in perception is to ensure that we always perceive the same object in the same way, despite the fact that the sensations that it creates on our receptors changes dramatically. *The ability to perceive a stimulus as constant despite changes in sensation* is known as **perceptual constancy**. Consider our image of a door as it swings. When it is closed, we see it as rectangular, but when it is open, we see only its edge and it appears as a line. But we never perceive the door as changing shape as it swings—perceptual mechanisms take care of the problem for us by allowing us to see a constant shape.

The visual system also corrects for color constancy. Imagine that you are wearing blue jeans and a bright white t-shirt. When you are outdoors, both colors will be at their brightest, but you will still perceive the white t-shirt as bright and the blue jeans as darker. When you go indoors, the light shining on the clothes will be significantly dimmer, but you will still perceive the t-shirt as bright. This is because we put colors in context and see that, compared to its surroundings, the white t-shirt reflects the most light (McCann, 1992).[49] In the same way, a green leaf on a cloudy day may reflect the same wavelength of light as a brown tree branch does on a sunny day. Nevertheless, we still perceive the leaf as green and the branch as brown.

perceptual constancy

The ability to perceive a stimulus as constant despite changes in sensation.

5.2 Illusions

Although our perception is very accurate, it is not perfect. **Illusions** *occur when the perceptual processes that normally help us correctly perceive the world around us are fooled by a particular situation so that we see something that does not exist or that is incorrect.* Figure 4.34 presents two situations in which our normally accurate perceptions of visual constancy have been fooled.

illusion

When the perceptual processes that normally help us correctly perceive the world around us are fooled by a particular situation so that we see something that does not exist or that is incorrect.

FIGURE 4.34 Optical Illusions as a Result of Brightness Constancy (Left) and Color Constancy (Right)

Look carefully at the snakelike pattern on the left. Are the green strips really brighter than the background? Cover the white curves and you'll see they are not. Square A in the right-hand image looks very different from square B, even though they are exactly the same.

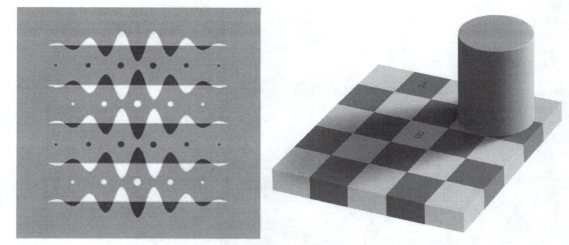

Source: Right image courtesy of Edward H. Adelson, http://commons.wikimedia.org/wiki/File:Grey_square_optical_illusion.PNG.

Another well-known illusion is the *Mueller-Lyer illusion* (see Figure 4.35). The line segment in the bottom arrow looks longer to us than the one on the top, even though they are both actually the same length. It is likely that the illusion is, in part, the result of the failure of monocular depth cues—the bottom line looks like an edge that is normally farther away from us, whereas the top one looks like an edge that is normally closer.

FIGURE 4.35 The Mueller-Lyre Illusion

The Mueller-Lyre illusion makes the line segment at the top of the left picture appear shorter than the one at the bottom. The illusion is caused, in part, by the monocular distance cue of depth—the bottom line looks like an edge that is normally farther away from us, whereas the top one looks like an edge that is normally closer.

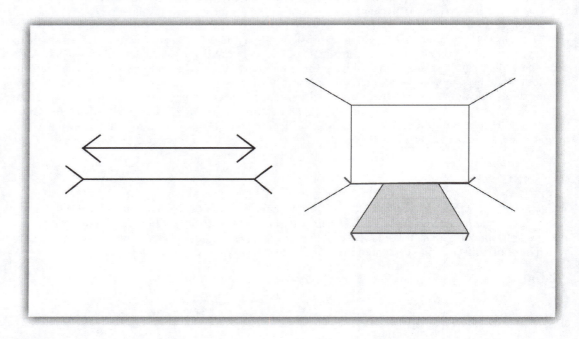

The *moon illusion* refers to the fact that the moon is perceived to be about 50% larger when it is near the horizon than when it is seen overhead, despite the fact that both moons are the same size and cast the same size retinal image. The monocular depth cues of position and aerial perspective (see Figure 4.36) create the illusion that things that are lower and more hazy are farther away. The skyline of the horizon (trees, clouds, outlines of buildings) also gives a cue that the moon is far away, compared to a moon at its zenith. If we look at a horizon moon through a tube of rolled up paper, taking away the surrounding horizon cues, the moon will immediately appear smaller.

FIGURE 4.36 The Moon Illusion

The moon always looks larger on the horizon than when it is high above. But if we take away the surrounding distance cues of the horizon, the illusion disappears.

© *Thinkstock*

The *Ponzo illusion* operates on the same principle. As you can see in Figure 4.37, the top yellow bar seems longer than the bottom one, but if you measure them you'll see that they are exactly the same length. The monocular depth cue of linear perspective leads us to believe that, given two similar objects, the distant one can only cast the same size retinal image as the closer object if it is larger. The topmost bar therefore appears longer.

FIGURE 4.37 The Ponzo Illusion

The Ponzo illusion is caused by a failure of the monocular depth cue of linear perspective: Both bars are the same size even though the top one looks larger.

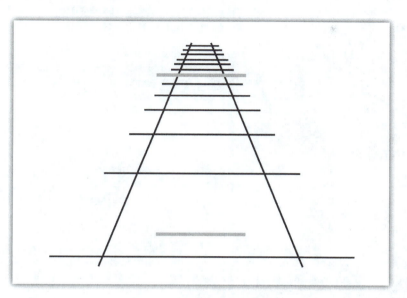

Illusions demonstrate that our perception of the world around us may be influenced by our prior knowledge. But the fact that some illusions exist in some cases does not mean that the perceptual system is generally inaccurate—in fact, humans normally become so closely in touch with their environment that that the physical body and the particular environment that we sense and perceive becomes *embodied*—that is, built into and linked with—our cognition, such that the worlds around us become part of our brain (Calvo & Gamila, 2008).[50] The close relationship between people and their environments means that, although illusions can be created in the lab and under some unique situations, they may be less common with active observers in the real world (Runeson, 1988).[51]

5.3   The Important Role of Expectations in Perception

Our emotions, mind-set, expectations, and the contexts in which our sensations occur all have a profound influence on perception. People who are warned that they are about to taste something bad rate what they do taste more negatively than people who are told that the taste won't be so bad (Nitschke et al., 2006),[52] and people perceive a child and adult pair as looking more alike when they are told that they are parent and child (Bressan & Dal Martello, 2002).[53] Similarly, participants who see images of the same baby rate it as stronger and bigger when they are told it is a boy as opposed to when they are told it is a girl (Stern & Karraker, 1989),[54] and research participants who learn that a child is from a lower-class background perceive the child's scores on an intelligence test as lower than people who see the same test taken by a child they are told is from an upper-class background (Darley & Gross, 1983).[55] Plassmann, O'Doherty, Shiv, and Rangel (2008)[56] found that wines were rated more positively and caused greater brain activity in brain areas associated with pleasure when they were said to cost more than when they were said to cost less. And even experts can be fooled: Professional referees tended to assign more penalty cards to soccer teams for videotaped fouls when they were told that the team had a history of aggressive behavior than when they had no such expectation (Jones, Paull, & Erskine, 2002).[57]

Our perceptions are also influenced by our desires and motivations. When we are hungry, food-related words tend to grab our attention more than non-food-related words (Mogg, Bradley, Hyare, & Lee, 1998),[58] we perceive objects that we can reach as bigger than those that we cannot reach (Witt & Proffitt, 2005),[59] and people who favor a political candidate's policies view the candidate's skin color more positively than do those who oppose the candidate's policies (Caruso, Mead, & Balcetis, 2009).[60] Even our culture influences perception. Chua, Boland, and Nisbett (2005)[61] showed American and Asian graduate students different images, such as an airplane, an animal, or a train, against complex backgrounds. They found that (consistent with their overall individualistic orientation) the American students tended to focus more on the foreground image, while Asian students (consistent with their interdependent orientation) paid more attention to the image's context. Furthermore, Asian-American students focused more or less on the context depending on whether their Asian or their American identity had been activated.

Psychology in Everyday Life: How Understanding Sensation and Perception Can Save Lives

Human factors is the field of psychology that uses psychological knowledge, including the principles of sensation and perception, to improve the development of technology. Human factors has worked on a variety of projects, ranging from nuclear reactor control centers and airplane cockpits to cell phones and websites (Proctor & Van Zandt, 2008).[62] For instance, modern televisions and computer monitors were developed on the basis of the trichromatic color theory, using three color elements placed close enough together so that the colors are blended by the eye. Knowledge of the visual system also helped engineers create new kinds of displays, such as those used on notebook computers and music players, and better understand how using cell phones while driving may contribute to automobile accidents (Lee & Strayer, 2004).[63]

Human factors also has made substantial contributions to airline safety. About two thirds of accidents on commercial airplane flights are caused by human error (Nickerson, 1998).[64] During takeoff, travel, and landing, the pilot simultaneously communicates with ground control, maneuvers the plane, scans the horizon for other aircraft, and operates controls. The need for a useable interface that works easily and naturally with the pilot's visual perception is essential.

Psychologist Conrad Kraft (1978)[65] hypothesized that as planes land, with no other distance cues visible, pilots may be subjected to a type of moon illusion, in which the city lights beyond the runway appear much larger on the retina than they really are, deceiving the pilot into landing too early. Kraft's findings caused airlines to institute new flight safety measures, where copilots must call out the altitude progressively during the descent, which has probably decreased the number of landing accidents.

Figure 4.38 presents the design of an airplane instrument panel before and after it was redesigned by human factors psychologists. On the left is the initial design in which the controls were crowded and cluttered, in no logical sequence, each control performing one task. The controls were more or less the same in color, and the gauges were not easy to read. The redesigned digital cockpit (right on Figure 4.38) shows a marked improvement in usability. More of the controls are color-coded and multifunctional so that there is less clutter on the dashboard. Screens make use of LCD and 3-D graphics. Text sizes are changeable—increasing readability—and many of the functions have become automated, freeing up the pilots concentration for more important activities.

Initial design of the airplane cockpit (left); the digital design of the airplane cockpit (right), which has taken human factors into account.

Source: TBD.

One important aspect of the redesign was based on the principles of sensory adaptation. Displays that are easy to see in darker conditions quickly become unreadable when the sun shines directly on them. It takes the pilot a relatively long time to adapt to the suddenly much brighter display. Furthermore, perceptual contrast is important. The display cannot be so bright at night that the pilot is unable to see targets in the sky or on the land. Human factors psychologists used these principles to determine the appropriate stimulus intensity needed on these displays so that pilots would be able to read them accurately and quickly under a wide range of conditions. The psychologists accomplished this by developing an automatic control mechanism that senses the ambient light visible through the front cockpit windows and that detects the light falling on the display surface, and then automatically adjusts the intensity of the display for the pilot (Silverstein, Krantz, Gomer, Yeh, & Monty, 1990; Silverstein & Merrifield, 1985).[66]

KEY TAKEAWAYS

- Sensory interaction occurs when different senses work together, for instance, when taste, smell, and touch together produce the flavor of food.
- Selective attention allows us to focus on some sensory experiences while tuning out others.
- Sensory adaptation occurs when we become less sensitive to some aspects of our environment, freeing us to focus on more important changes.
- Perceptual constancy allows us to perceive an object as the same, despite changes in sensation.
- Cognitive illusions are examples of how our expectations can influence our perceptions.
- Our emotions, motivations, desires, and even our culture can influence our perceptions.

EXERCISES AND CRITICAL THINKING

1. Consider the role of the security personnel at the APEC meeting who let the Chaser group's car enter the security area. List some perceptual processes that might have been at play.
2. Consider some cases where your expectations about what you think you might be going to experience have influenced your perceptions of what you actually experienced.

6.   CHAPTER SUMMARY

Sensation and perception work seamlessly together to allow us to detect both the presence of, and changes in, the stimuli around us.

The study of sensation and perception is exceedingly important for our everyday lives because the knowledge generated by psychologists is used in so many ways to help so many people.

Each sense accomplishes the basic process of transduction—the conversion of stimuli detected by receptor cells into electrical impulses that are then transported to the brain—in different, but related, ways.

Psychophysics is the branch of psychology that studies the effects of physical stimuli on sensory perceptions. Psychophysicists study the absolute threshold of sensation as well as the difference threshold, or just noticeable difference (JND). Weber's law maintains that the JND of a stimulus is a constant proportion of the original intensity of the stimulus.

Most of our cerebral cortex is devoted to seeing, and we have substantial visual skills. The eye is a specialized system that includes the cornea, pupil, iris, lens, and retina. Neurons, including rods and cones, react to light landing on the retina and send it to the visual cortex via the optic nerve.

Images are perceived, in part, through the action of feature detector neurons.

The shade of a color, known as hue, is conveyed by the wavelength of the light that enters the eye. The Young-Helmholtz trichromatic color theory and the opponent-process color theory are theories of how the brain perceives color.

Depth is perceived using both binocular and monocular depth cues. Monocular depth cues are based on gestalt principles. The beta effect and the phi phenomenon are important in detecting motion.

The ear detects both the amplitude (loudness) and frequency (pitch) of sound waves.

Important structures of the ear include the pinna, eardrum, ossicles, cochlea, and the oval window.

The frequency theory of hearing proposes that as the pitch of a sound wave increases, nerve impulses of a corresponding frequency are sent to the auditory nerve. The place theory of hearing proposes that different areas of the cochlea respond to different frequencies.

Sounds that are 85 decibels or more can cause damage to your hearing, particularly if you are exposed to them repeatedly. Sounds that exceed 130 decibels are dangerous, even if you are exposed to them infrequently.

The tongue detects six different taste sensations, known respectively as sweet, salty, sour, bitter, piquancy (spicy), and umami (savory).

We have approximately 1,000 types of odor receptor cells and it is estimated that we can detect 10,000 different odors.

Thousands of nerve endings in the skin respond to four basic sensations: Pressure, hot, cold, and pain, but only the sensation of pressure has its own specialized receptors. The ability to keep track of where the body is moving is provided by the vestibular system.

Perception involves the processes of sensory interaction, selective attention, sensory adaptation, and perceptual constancy.

Although our perception is very accurate, it is not perfect. Our expectations and emotions color our perceptions and may result in illusions.

ENDNOTES

1. Gibson, E. J., & Pick, A. D. (2000). *An ecological approach to perceptual learning and development*. New York, NY: Oxford University Press.

2. Fajen, B. R., & Warren, W. H. (2003). Behavioral dynamics of steering, obstacle avoidance, and route selection. *Journal of Experimental Psychology: Human Perception and Performance, 29*(2), 343–362.

3. Stoffregen, T. A., & Bardy, B. G. (2001). On specification and the senses. *Behavioral and Brain Sciences, 24*(2), 195–261.

4. Galanter, E. (1962). *Contemporary Psychophysics*. In R. Brown, E. Galanter, E. H. Hess, & G. Mandler (Eds.), *New directions in psychology*. New York, NY: Holt, Rinehart and Winston.

5. Macmillan, N. A., & Creelman, C. D. (2005). *Detection theory: A user's guide* (2nd ed). Mahwah, NJ: Lawrence Erlbaum Associates; Wickens, T. D. (2002). *Elementary signal detection theory*. New York, NY: Oxford University Press.

6. Dijksterhuis, A. (2010). Automaticity and the unconscious. In S. T. Fiske, D. T. Gilbert, & G. Lindzey (Eds.), *Handbook of social psychology* (5th ed., Vol. 1, pp. 228–267). Hoboken, NJ: John Wiley & Sons.

7. Karremans, J. C., Stroebe, W., & Claus, J. (2006). Beyond Vicary's fantasies: The impact of subliminal priming and brand choice. *Journal of Experimental Social Psychology, 42*(6), 792–798.

8. Trappey, C. (1996). A meta-analysis of consumer choice and subliminal advertising. *Psychology and Marketing, 13*, 517–530.

9. Saegert, J. (1987). Why marketing should quit giving subliminal advertising the benefit of the doubt. *Psychology and Marketing, 4*(2), 107–120.

10. Harris, J. L., Bargh, J. A., & Brownell, K. D. (2009). Priming effects of television food advertising on eating behavior. *Health Psychology, 28*(4), 404–413.

11. Weiskrantz, L. (1997). *Consciousness lost and found: A neuropsychological exploration*. New York, NY: Oxford University Press.

12. Livingstone M. S. (2000). Is it warm? Is it real? Or just low spatial frequency? *Science, 290*, 1299.

13. Kelsey, C.A. (1997). Detection of visual information. In W. R. Hendee & P. N. T. Wells (Eds.), *The perception of visual information* (2nd ed.). New York, NY: Springer Verlag; Livingstone, M., & Hubel, D. (1998). Segregation of form, color, movement, and depth: Anatomy, physiology, and perception. *Science, 240*, 740–749.

14. Rodriguez, E., George, N., Lachaux, J.-P., Martinerie, J., Renault, B., & Varela, F. J. (1999). Perception's shadow: Long-distance synchronization of human brain activity. *Nature, 397*(6718), 430–433.

15. Downing, P. E., Jiang, Y., Shuman, M., & Kanwisher, N. (2001). A cortical area selective for visual processing of the human body. *Science, 293*(5539), 2470–2473; Haxby, J. V., Gobbini, M. I., Furey, M. L., Ishai, A., Schouten, J. L., & Pietrini, P. (2001). Distributed and overlapping representations of faces and objects in ventral temporal cortex. *Science, 293*(5539), 2425–2430.

16. McKone, E., Kanwisher, N., & Duchaine, B. C. (2007). Can generic expertise explain special processing for faces? *Trends in Cognitive Sciences, 11*, 8–15; Pitcher, D., Walsh, V., Yovel, G., & Duchaine, B. (2007). TMS evidence for the involvement of the right occipital face area in early face processing. *Current Biology, 17*, 1568–1573.

17. Geldard, F. A. (1972). *The human senses* (2nd ed.). New York, NY: John Wiley & Sons.

18. Gegenfurtner, K. R., & Kiper, D. C. (2003). Color vision. *Annual Review of Neuroscience, 26*, 181–206.

19. Howard, I. P., & Rogers, B. J. (2001). *Seeing in depth: Basic mechanisms* (Vol. 1). Toronto, Ontario, Canada: Porteous.

20. Witherington, D. C. (2005). The development of prospective grasping control between 5 and 7 months: A longitudinal study. *Infancy, 7*(2), 143–161.

21. Gibson, E. J., & Walk, R. D. (1960). The "visual cliff." *Scientific American, 202*(4), 64–71.

22. Campos, J. J., Langer, A., & Krowitz, A. (1970). Cardiac responses on the visual cliff in prelocomotor human infants. *Science, 170*(3954), 196–197.

23. Adolph, K. E. (2000). Specificity of learning: Why infants fall over a veritable cliff. *Psychological Science, 11*(4), 290–295.

24. Sekuler, R., & Blake, R., (2006). *Perception* (5th ed.). New York, NY: McGraw-Hill.

25. Corey, D. P., García-Añoveros, J., Holt, J. R., Kwan, K. Y., Lin, S.-Y., Vollrath, M. A., Amalfitano, A.,…Zhang, D.-S. (2004). TRPA1 is a candidate for the mechano-sensitive transduction channel of vertebrate hair cells. *Nature, 432*, 723–730. Retrieved from http://www.nature.com/nature/journal/v432/n7018/full/nature03066.html

26. Middlebrooks, J. C., & Green, D. M. (1991). Sound localization by human listeners. *Annual Review of Psychology, 42*, 135–159.

27. Kochkin, S. (2005). MarkeTrak VII: Hearing loss population tops 31 million people. *Hearing Review, 12*(7) 16–29.

28. Tennesen, M. (2007, March 10). Gone today, hear tomorrow. *New Scientist, 2594*, 42–45.

29. Chisolm, T. H., Willott, J. F., & Lister, J. J. (2003). The aging auditory system: Anatomic and physiologic changes and implications for rehabilitation. *International Journal of Audiology, 42*(Suppl. 2), 2S3–2S10.

30. Dettman, S. J., Pinder, D., Briggs, R. J. S., Dowell, R. C., & Leigh, J. R. (2007). Communication development in children who receive the cochlear implant younger than 12 months: Risk versus benefits. *Ear and Hearing, 28*(2, Suppl.), 11S–18S; Dorman, M. F., &

Wilson, B. S. (2004). The design and function of cochlear implants. *American Scientist, 92*, 436–445.

31. Ikeda, K. (2002). [New seasonings]. *Chemical Senses, 27*(9), 847–849. Translated and shortened to 75% by Y. Ogiwara & Y. Ninomiya from the *Journal of the Chemical Society of Tokyo, 30*, 820–836. (Original work published 1909); Sugimoto, K., & Ninomiya, Y. (2005). Introductory remarks on umami research: Candidate receptors and signal transduction mechanisms on umami. *Chemical Senses, 30*(Suppl. 1), Pi21–i22.

32. Northcutt, R. G. (2004). Taste buds: Development and evolution. *Brain, Behavior and Evolution, 64*(3), 198–206.

33. Kelling, S. T., & Halpern, B. P. (1983). Taste flashes: Reaction times, intensity, and quality. *Science, 219*, 412–414.

34. Bensafi, M., Zelano, C., Johnson, B., Mainland, J., Kahn, R., & Sobel, N. (2004). Olfaction: From sniff to percept. In M. S. Gazzaniga (Ed.), *The cognitive neurosciences* (3rd ed.). Cambridge, MA: MIT Press.

35. Malnic, B., Hirono, J., Sato, T., & Buck, L. B. (1999). Combinatorial receptor codes for odors. *Cell, 96*, 713–723.

36. Baysinger, C. M., Plubell, P. E., & Harlow, H. F. (1973). A variable-temperature surrogate mother for studying attachment in infant monkeys. *Behavior Research Methods & Instrumentation, 5*(3), 269–272; Feldman, R. (2007). Maternal-infant contact and child development: Insights from the kangaroo intervention. In L. L'Abate (Ed.), *Low-cost approaches to promote physical and mental health: Theory, research, and practice* (pp. 323–351). New York, NY: Springer Science + Business Media; Haradon, G., Bascom, B., Dragomir, C., & Scripcaru, V. (1994). Sensory functions of institutionalized Romanian infants: A pilot study. *Occupational Therapy International, 1*(4), 250–260.

37. Field, T., Lasko, D., Mundy, P., Henteleff, T., Kabat, S., Talpins, S., & Dowling, M. (1997). Brief report: Autistic children's attentiveness and responsivity improve after touch therapy. *Journal of Autism and Developmental Disorders, 27*(3), 333–338; Keltner, D. (2009). *Born to be good: The science of a meaningful life*. New York, NY: Norton.

38. Melzack, R., & Wall, P. (1996). *The challenge of pain*. London, England: Penguin.

39. Wall, P. (2000). *Pain: The science of suffering*. New York, NY: Columbia University Press.

40. Bantick, S. J., Wise, R. G., Ploghaus, A., Clare, S., Smith, S. M., & Tracey, I. (2002). Imaging how attention modulates pain in humans using functional MRI. *Brain: A Journal of Neurology, 125*(2), 310–319.

41. Zweyer, K., Velker, B., & Ruch, W. (2004). Do cheerfulness, exhilaration, and humor production moderate pain tolerance? A FACS study. *Humor: International Journal of Humor Research, 17*(1-2), 85–119.

42. Sternberg, W. F., Bailin, D., Grant, M., & Gracely, R. H. (1998). Competition alters the perception of noxious stimuli in male and female athletes. *Pain, 76*(1–2), 231–238.

43. Goodale, M., & Milner, D. (2006). One brain—Two visual systems. *Psychologist, 19*(11), 660–663.

44. Flanagan, M. B., May, J. G., & Dobie, T. G. (2004). The role of vection, eye movements, and postural instability in the etiology of motion sickness. *Journal of Vestibular Research: Equilibrium and Orientation, 14*(4), 335–346.

45. Ramachandran, V. S., Hubbard, E. M., Robertson, L. C., & Sagiv, N. (2005). The emergence of the human mind: Some clues from synesthesia. In *Synesthesia: Perspectives From Cognitive Neuroscience* (pp. 147–190). New York, NY: Oxford University Press.

46. Simons, D. J., & Chabris, C. F. (1999). Gorillas in our midst: Sustained inattentional blindness for dynamic events. *Perception, 28*(9), 1059–1074.

47. Broadbent, D. E. (1958). *Perception and communication*. New York, NY: Pergamon; Cherry, E. C. (1953). Some experiments on the recognition of speech, with one and with two ears. *Journal of the Acoustical Society of America, 25*, 975–979.

48. Yarbus, A. L. (1967). *Eye movements and vision*. New York, NY: Plenum Press.

49. McCann, J. J. (1992). Rules for color constancy. *Ophthalmic and Physiologic Optics, 12*(2), 175–177.

50. Calvo, P., & Gomila, T. (Eds.). (2008). *Handbook of cognitive science: An embodied approach*. San Diego, CA: Elsevier.

51. Runeson, S. (1988). The distorted room illusion, equivalent configurations, and the specificity of static optic arrays. *Journal of Experimental Psychology: Human Perception and Performance, 14*(2), 295–304.

52. Nitschke, J. B., Dixon, G. E., Sarinopoulos, I., Short, S. J., Cohen, J. D., Smith, E. E.,…Davidson, R. J. (2006). Altering expectancy dampens neural response to aversive taste in primary taste cortex. *Nature Neuroscience 9*, 435–442.

53. Bressan, P., & Dal Martello, M. F. (2002). Talis pater, talis filius: Perceived resemblance and the belief in genetic relatedness. *Psychological Science, 13*, 213–218.

54. Stern, M., & Karraker, K. H. (1989). Sex stereotyping of infants: A review of gender labeling studies. *Sex Roles, 20*(9–10), 501–522.

55. Darley, J. M., & Gross, P. H. (1983). A hypothesis-confirming bias in labeling effects. *Journal of Personality and Social Psychology, 44*, 20–33.

56. Plassmann, H., O'Doherty, J., Shiv, B., & Rangel, A. (2008). Marketing actions can moderate neural representations of experienced pleasantness. *Proceedings of the National Academy of Sciences, 105*(3), 1050–1054.

57. Jones, M. V., Paull, G. C., & Erskine, J. (2002). The impact of a team's aggressive reputation on the decisions of association football referees. *Journal of Sports Sciences, 20*, 991–1000.

58. Mogg, K., Bradley, B. P., Hyare, H., & Lee, S. (1998). Selective attention to food related stimuli in hunger. *Behaviour Research & Therapy, 36*(2), 227–237.

59. Witt, J. K., & Proffitt, D. R. (2005). See the ball, hit the ball: Apparent ball size is correlated with batting average. *Psychological Science, 16*(12), 937–938.

60. Caruso, E. M., Mead, N. L., & Balcetis, E. (2009). Political partisanship influences perception of biracial candidates' skin tone. *PNAS Proceedings of the National Academy of Sciences of the United States of America, 106*(48), 20168–20173.

61. Chua, H. F., Boland, J. E., & Nisbett, R. E. (2005). Cultural variation in eye movements during scene perception. *Proceedings of the National Academy of Sciences, 102,* 12629–12633.

62. Proctor, R. W., & Van Zandt, T. (2008). Human factors in simple and complex systems (2nd ed.). Boca Raton, FL: CRC Press.

63. Lee, J., & Strayer, D. (2004). Preface to the special section on driver distraction. *Human Factors, 46*(4), 583.

64. Nickerson, R. S. (1998). Applied experimental psychology. *Applied Psychology: An International Review, 47,* 155–173.

65. Kraft, C. (1978). A psychophysical approach to air safety: Simulator studies of visual illusions in night approaches. In H. L. Pick, H. W. Leibowitz, J. E. Singer, A. Steinschneider, & H. W. Steenson (Eds.), *Psychology: From research to practice.* New York, NY: Plenum Press.

66. Silverstein, L. D., Krantz, J. H., Gomer, F. E., Yeh, Y., & Monty, R. W. (1990). The effects of spatial sampling and luminance quantization on the image quality of color matrix displays. *Journal of the Optical Society of America, Part A, 7,* 1955–1968; Silverstein, L. D., & Merrifield, R. M. (1985). *The development and evaluation of color systems for airborne applications: Phase I Fundamental visual, perceptual, and display systems considerations* (Tech. Report DOT/FAA/PM085019). Washington, DC: Federal Aviation Administration.

CHAPTER 5
States of Consciousness

An Unconscious Killing

During the night of May 23, 1987, Kenneth Parks, a 23-year old Canadian with a wife, a baby daughter, and heavy gambling debts, got out of his bed, climbed into his car, and drove 15 miles to the home of his wife's parents in the suburbs of Toronto. There, he attacked them with a knife, killing his mother-in-law and severely injuring his father-in-law. Parks then drove to a police station and stumbled into the building, holding up his bloody hands and saying, "I think I killed some people…my hands." The police arrested him and took him to a hospital, where surgeons repaired several deep cuts on his hands. Only then did police discover that he had indeed assaulted his in-laws.

Parks claimed that he could not remember anything about the crime. He said that he remembered going to sleep in his bed, then awakening in the police station with bloody hands, but nothing in between. His defense was that he had been asleep during the entire incident and was not aware of his actions (Martin, 2009).[1]

Not surprisingly, no one believed this explanation at first. However, further investigation established that he did have a long history of sleepwalking, he had no motive for the crime, and despite repeated attempts to trip him up in numerous interviews, he was completely consistent in his story, which also fit the timeline of events. Parks was examined by a team of sleep specialists, who found that the pattern of brain waves that occurred while he slept was very abnormal (Broughton, Billings, Cartwright, & Doucette, 1994).[2] The specialists eventually concluded that sleepwalking, probably precipitated by stress and anxiety over his financial troubles, was the most likely explanation of his aberrant behavior. They also agreed that such a combination of stressors was unlikely to happen again, so he was not likely to undergo another such violent episode and was probably not a hazard to others. Given this combination of evidence, the jury acquitted Parks of murder and assault charges. He walked out of the courtroom a free man (Wilson, 1998).[3]

Consciousness is defined as *our subjective awareness of ourselves and our environment* (Koch, 2004).[4] The experience of consciousness is fundamental to human nature. We all know what it means to be conscious, and we assume (although we can never be sure) that other human beings experience their consciousness similarly to how we experience ours.

The study of consciousness has long been important to psychologists and plays a role in many important psychological theories. For instance, Sigmund Freud's personality theories differentiated between the unconscious and the conscious aspects of behavior, and present-day psychologists distinguish between *automatic* (unconscious) and *controlled* (conscious) behaviors and between *implicit* (unconscious) and *explicit* (conscious) memory (Petty, Wegener, Chaiken, & Trope, 1999; Shanks, 2005).[5]

Some philosophers and religious practices argue that the mind (or soul) and the body are separate entities. For instance, the French philosopher René Descartes (1596–1650) was a proponent of *dualism*, the idea that the mind, a nonmaterial entity, is separate from (although connected to) the physical body. In contrast to the dualists, psychologists believe that consciousness (and thus the mind) exists in the brain, not separate from it. In fact, psychologists believe that consciousness is the result of the activity of the many neural connections in the brain, and that we experience different states of consciousness depending on what our brain is currently doing (Dennett, 1991; Koch & Greenfield, 2007).[6]

consciousness

The subjective awareness of ourselves and our environment.

FIGURE 5.1

The French philosopher René Descartes (1596–1650) was a proponent of *dualism*, the theory that the mind and body are two separate entities. Psychologists reject this idea, however, believing that consciousness is a result of activity in the brain, not separate from it.

Source: Photo courtesy of André Hatala, http://commons.wikimedia.org/wiki/ File:Frans_Hals_-_Portret_van_René_Descartes.jpg.

The study of consciousness is also important to the fundamental psychological question regarding the presence of free will. Although we may understand and believe that some of our behaviors are caused by forces that are outside our awareness (i.e., unconscious), we nevertheless believe that we have control over, and are aware that we are engaging in, most of our behaviors. To discover that we, or even someone else, has engaged in a complex behavior, such as driving in a car and causing severe harm to others, without being at all conscious of one's actions, is so unusual as to be shocking. And yet psychologists are increasingly certain that a great deal of our behavior is caused by processes of which we are unaware and over which we have little or no control (Libet, 1999; Wegner, 2003).[7]

Our experience of consciousness is functional because we use it to guide and control our behavior, and to think logically about problems (DeWall, Baumeister, & Masicampo, 2008).[8] Consciousness allows us to plan activities and to monitor our progress toward the goals we set for ourselves. And consciousness is fundamental to our sense of morality—we believe that we have the free will to perform moral actions while avoiding immoral behaviors.

But in some cases consciousness may become aversive, for instance when we become aware that we are not living up to our own goals or expectations, or when we believe that other people perceive us negatively. In these cases we may engage in behaviors that help us escape from consciousness, for example through the use of alcohol or other psychoactive drugs (Baumeister, 1998).[9]

Because the brain varies in its current level and type of activity, consciousness is transitory. If we drink too much coffee or beer, the caffeine or alcohol influences the activity in our brain, and our consciousness may change. When we are anesthetized before an operation or experience a concussion after a knock on the head, we may lose consciousness entirely as a result of changes in brain activity. We also lose consciousness when we sleep, and it is with this altered state of consciousness that we begin our chapter.

1.   SLEEPING AND DREAMING REVITALIZE US FOR ACTION

LEARNING OBJECTIVES

1. Draw a graphic showing the usual phases of sleep during a normal night and notate the characteristics of each phase.
2. Review the disorders that affect sleep and the costs of sleep deprivation.
3. Outline and explain the similarities and differences among the different theories of dreaming.

The lives of all organisms, including humans, are influenced by *regularly occurring cycles of behaviors* known as **biological rhythms**. One important biological rhythm is the annual cycle that guides the migration of birds and the hibernation of bears. Women also experience a 28-day cycle that guides their fertility and menstruation. But perhaps the strongest and most important biorhythm is the daily **circadian rhythm** (from the Latin *circa*, meaning "about" or "approximately," and *dian*, meaning "daily") *that guides the daily waking and sleeping cycle in many animals.*

Many biological rhythms are coordinated by changes in the level and duration of ambient light, for instance, as winter turns into summer and as night turns into day. In some animals, such as birds, the pineal gland in the brain is directly sensitive to light and its activation influences behavior, such as mating and annual migrations. Light also has a profound effect on humans. We are more likely to experience depression during the dark winter months than during the lighter summer months, an experience known as *seasonal affective disorder (SAD)*, and exposure to bright lights can help reduce this depression (McGinnis, 2007).[10]

Sleep is also influenced by ambient light. The ganglion cells in the retina send signals to a brain area above the thalamus called the *suprachiasmatic nucleus*, which is the body's primary circadian "pacemaker." The suprachiasmatic nucleus analyzes the strength and duration of the light stimulus and sends signals to the pineal gland when the ambient light level is low or its duration is short. In response, the pineal gland secretes *melatonin*, a powerful hormone that facilitates the onset of sleep.

biological rhythms

Regularly occurring cycles of behaviors caused by biological factors.

circadian rhythm

The biological cycle that guides the daily waking and sleeping in many animals.

Research Focus: Circadian Rhythms Influence the Use of Stereotypes in Social Judgments

The circadian rhythm influences our energy levels such that we have more energy at some times of day than others. Galen Bodenhausen (1990)[11] argued that people may be more likely to rely on their stereotypes (i.e., their beliefs about the characteristics of social groups) as a shortcut to making social judgments when they are tired than when they have more energy. To test this hypothesis, he asked 189 research participants to consider cases of alleged misbehavior by other college students and to judge the probability of the accused students' guilt. The accused students were identified as members of particular social groups, and they were accused of committing offenses that were consistent with stereotypes of these groups.

One case involved a student athlete accused of cheating on an exam, one case involved a Hispanic student who allegedly physically attacked his roommate, and a third case involved an African American student who had been accused of selling illegal drugs. Each of these offenses had been judged via pretesting in the same student population to be stereotypically (although, of course, unfairly) associated with each social group. The research participants were also provided with some specific evidence about the case that made it ambiguous whether the person had actually committed the crime, and then asked to indicate the likelihood of the student's guilt on an 11-point scale (0 = extremely unlikely to 10 = extremely likely).

Participants also completed a measure designed to assess their circadian rhythms—whether they were more active and alert in the morning (Morning types) or in the evening (Evening types). The participants were then tested at experimental sessions held either in the morning (9 a.m.) or in the evening (8 p.m.). As you can see in Figure 5.2, the participants were more likely to rely on their negative stereotypes of the person they were judging at the time of day in which they reported being less active and alert. Morning people used their stereotypes more when they were tested in the evening, and evening people used their stereotypes more when they were tested in the morning.

Circadian Rhythms and Stereotyping

Students who indicated that they had more energy in the morning relied on their stereotypes more at night, and students who indicated that they had more energy in the night relied on their stereotypes more in the morning.

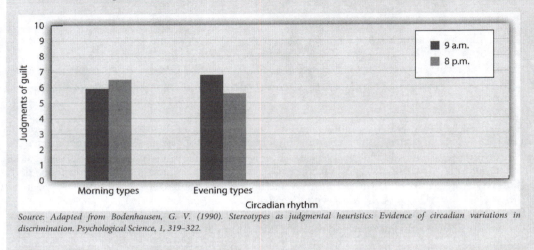

Source: Adapted from Bodenhausen, G. V. (1990). Stereotypes as judgmental heuristics: Evidence of circadian variations in discrimination. Psychological Science, 1, 319–322.

1.1 Sleep Stages: Moving Through the Night

Although we lose consciousness as we sleep, the brain nevertheless remains active. The patterns of sleep have been tracked in thousands of research participants who have spent nights sleeping in research labs while their brain waves were recorded by monitors, such as an *electroencephalogram*, or *EEG* (Figure 5.3).

FIGURE 5.3 Sleep Labs

Sleep researchers measure the activity of the brain, eyes, face, and other parts of the body while the participant sleeps.

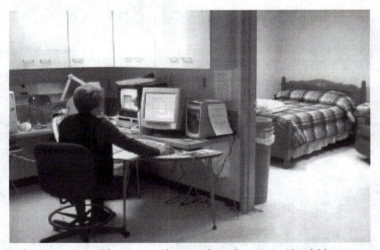

Source: Photo courtesy of Stephens County Hospital, http://www.stephenscountyhospital.com/services/sleep_lab.htm.

Sleep researchers have found that sleeping people undergo a fairly consistent pattern of sleep stages, each lasting about 90 minutes. As you can see in Figure 5.4, these stages are of two major types: **Rapid eye movement (REM) sleep** is *a sleep stage characterized by the presence of quick fast eye movements and dreaming.* REM sleep accounts for about 25% of our total sleep time. During REM sleep, our awareness of external events is dramatically reduced, and consciousness is dominated primarily by internally generated images and a lack of overt thinking (Hobson, 2004).[12] During this sleep stage our muscles shut down, and this is probably a good thing as it protects us from hurting ourselves or trying to act out the scenes that are playing in our dreams. The second major sleep type, **non-rapid eye movement (non-REM) sleep** is *a deep sleep, characterized by very slow brain waves, that is further subdivided into three stages: N1, N2, and N3.* Each of the sleep stages has its own distinct pattern of brain activity (Dement & Kleitman, 1957).[13]

rapid eye movement (REM) sleep

A sleep stage characterized by the presence of fast eye movements and dreaming.

non-rapid eye movement (non-REM) sleep

A deep sleep, characterized by very slow brain waves, which is further subdivided into three substages, labeled as stages N1, N2, and N3.

FIGURE 5.4 Stages of Sleep

During a typical night, our sleep cycles move between REM and non-REM sleep, with each cycle repeating at about 90-minute intervals. The deeper non-REM sleep stages usually occur earlier in the night.

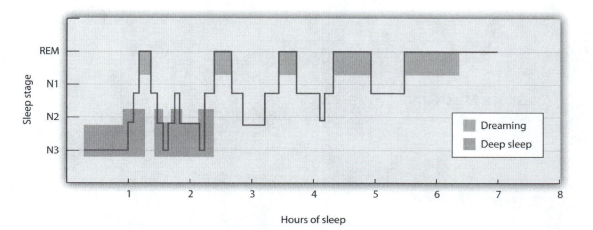

As you can see in Figure 5.5, the brain waves that are recorded by an EEG as we sleep show that the brain's activity changes during each stage of sleeping. When we are awake, our brain activity is characterized by the presence of very fast *beta waves*. When we first begin to fall asleep, the waves get longer (*alpha waves*), and as we move into stage N1 sleep, which is characterized by the experience of drowsiness, the brain begins to produce even slower *theta waves*. During stage N1 sleep, some muscle tone is lost, as well as most awareness of the environment. Some people may experience sudden jerks or twitches and even vivid hallucinations during this initial stage of sleep.

FIGURE 5.5 EEG Recordings of Brain Patterns During Sleep

Each stage of sleep has its own distinct pattern of brain activity.

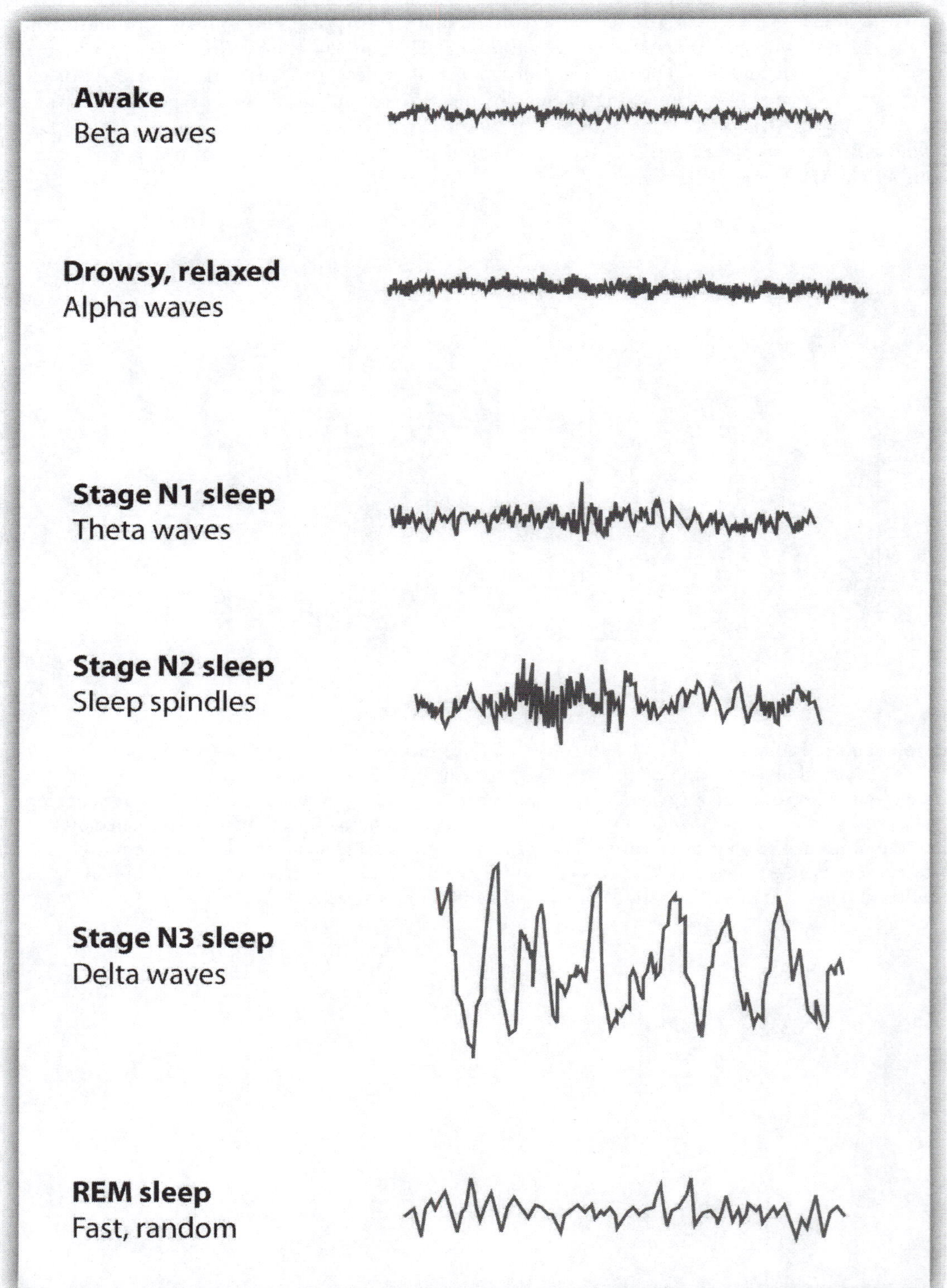

Normally, if we are allowed to keep sleeping, we will move from stage N1 to stage N2 sleep. During stage N2, muscular activity is further decreased and conscious awareness of the environment is lost. This stage typically represents about half of the total sleep time in normal adults. Stage N2 sleep is characterized by theta waves interspersed with bursts of rapid brain activity known as *sleep spindles*.

Stage N3, also known as *slow wave sleep*, is the deepest level of sleep, characterized by an increased proportion of very slow *delta waves*. This is the stage in which most sleep abnormalities, such as sleepwalking, sleeptalking, nightmares, and bed-wetting occur. The sleepwalking murders committed by Mr. Parks would have occurred in this stage. Some skeletal muscle tone remains, making it possible for affected individuals to rise from their beds and engage in sometimes very complex behaviors, but consciousness is distant. Even in the deepest sleep, however, we are still aware of the external world. If smoke enters the room or if we hear the cry of a baby we are likely to react, even though we are sound asleep. These occurrences again demonstrate the extent to which we process information outside consciousness.

After falling initially into a very deep sleep, the brain begins to become more active again, and we normally move into the first period of REM sleep about 90 minutes after falling asleep. REM sleep is accompanied by an increase in heart rate, facial twitches, and the repeated rapid eye movements that give this stage its name. People who are awakened during REM sleep almost always report that they were dreaming, while those awakened in other stages of sleep report dreams much less often. REM sleep is also emotional sleep. Activity in the limbic system, including the amygdala, is increased during REM sleep, and the genitals become aroused, even if the content of the dreams we are having is not sexual. A typical 25-year-old man may have an erection nearly half of the night, and the common "morning erection" is left over from the last REM period before waking.

Normally we will go through several cycles of REM and non-REM sleep each night (Figure 5.5). The length of the REM portion of the cycle tends to increase through the night, from about 5 to 10 minutes early in the night to 15 to 20 minutes shortly before awakening in the morning. Dreams also tend to become more elaborate and vivid as the night goes on. Eventually, as the sleep cycle finishes, the brain resumes its faster alpha and beta waves and we awake, normally refreshed.

1.2 Sleep Disorders: Problems in Sleeping

According to a recent poll (National Sleep Foundation, 2009),[14] about one-fourth of American adults say they get a good night's sleep only a few nights a month or less. These people are suffering from a sleep disorder known as **insomnia**, defined as *persistent difficulty falling or staying asleep*. Most cases of insomnia are temporary, lasting from a few days to several weeks, but in some cases insomnia can last for years.

Insomnia can result from physical disorders such as pain due to injury or illness, or from psychological problems such as stress, financial worries, or relationship difficulties. Changes in sleep patterns, such as jet lag, changes in work shift, or even the movement to or from daylight savings time can produce insomnia. Sometimes the sleep that the insomniac does get is disturbed and nonrestorative, and the lack of quality sleep produces impairment of functioning during the day. Ironically, the problem may be compounded by people's anxiety over insomnia itself: Their fear of being unable to sleep may wind up keeping them awake. Some people may also develop a conditioned anxiety to the bedroom or the bed.

People who have difficulty sleeping may turn to drugs to help them sleep. Barbiturates, benzodiazepines, and other sedatives are frequently marketed and prescribed as sleep aids, but they may interrupt the natural stages of the sleep cycle, and in the end are likely to do more harm than good. In some cases they may also promote dependence. Most practitioners of sleep medicine today recommend making environmental and scheduling changes first, followed by therapy for underlying problems, with pharmacological remedies used only as a last resort.

insomnia

A sleep disorder that involves persistent difficulty falling or staying asleep.

FIGURE 5.6

Taking pills to sleep is not recommended unless all other methods of improving sleep have been tried.

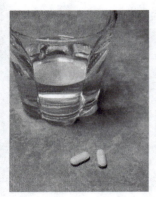

© Thinkstock

sleep apnea

A sleep disorder characterized by pauses in breathing that last at least 10 seconds during sleep.

narcolepsy

A disorder characterized by extreme daytime sleepiness with frequent episodes of "nodding off."

According to the National Sleep Foundation, some steps that can be used to combat insomnia include the following:

- Use the bed and bedroom for sleep and sex only. Do not spend time in bed during the day.
- Establish a regular bedtime routine and a regular sleep-wake schedule.
- Think positively about your sleeping—try not to get anxious just because you are losing a little sleep.
- Do not eat or drink too much close to bedtime.
- Create a sleep-promoting environment that is dark, cool, and comfortable.
- Avoid disturbing noises—consider a bedside fan or white-noise machine to block out disturbing sounds.
- Consume less or no caffeine, particularly late in the day.
- Avoid alcohol and nicotine, especially close to bedtime.
- Exercise, but not within 3 hours before bedtime.
- Avoid naps, particularly in the late afternoon or evening.
- Keep a sleep diary to identify your sleep habits and patterns that you can share with your doctor.

Another common sleep problem is **sleep apnea**, *a sleep disorder characterized by pauses in breathing that last at least 10 seconds during sleep* (Morgenthaler, Kagramanov, Hanak, & Decker, 2006).[15] In addition to preventing restorative sleep, sleep apnea can also cause high blood pressure and may raise the risk of stroke and heart attack (Yaggi et al., 2005).[16]

Most sleep apnea is caused by an obstruction of the walls of the throat that occurs when we fall asleep. It is most common in obese or older individuals who have lost muscle tone and is particularly common in men. Sleep apnea caused by obstructions is usually treated with an air machine that uses a mask to create a continuous pressure that prevents the airway from collapsing, or with mouthpieces that keep the airway open. If all other treatments have failed, sleep apnea may be treated with surgery to open the airway.

Narcolepsy is *a disorder characterized by extreme daytime sleepiness with frequent episodes of "nodding off."* The syndrome may also be accompanied by attacks of *cataplexy*, in which the individual loses muscle tone, resulting in a partial or complete collapse. It is estimated that at least 200,000 Americans suffer from narcolepsy, although only about a quarter of these people have been diagnosed (National Heart, Lung, and Blood Institute, 2008).[17]

Narcolepsy is in part the result of genetics—people who suffer from the disease lack neurotransmitters that are important in keeping us alert (Taheri, Zeitzer, & Mignot, 2002)[18]—and is also the result of a lack of deep sleep. While most people descend through the sequence of sleep stages, then move back up to REM sleep soon after falling asleep, narcolepsy sufferers move directly into REM and undergo numerous awakenings during the night, often preventing them from getting good sleep.

Narcolepsy can be treated with stimulants, such as amphetamines, to counteract the daytime sleepiness, or with antidepressants to treat a presumed underlying depression. However, since these drugs further disrupt already-abnormal sleep cycles, these approaches may, in the long run, make the problem worse. Many sufferers find relief by taking a number of planned short naps during the day, and some individuals may find it easier to work in jobs that allow them to sleep during the day and work at night.

Other sleep disorders occur when cognitive or motor processes that should be turned off or reduced in magnitude during sleep operate at higher than normal levels (Mahowald & Schenck, 2000).[19] One example is *somnamulism* (sleepwalking), in which the person leaves the bed and moves around while still asleep. Sleepwalking is more common in childhood, with the most frequent occurrences around the age of 12 years. About 4% of adults experience somnambulism (Mahowald & Schenck, 2000).[20]

Sleep terrors is a disruptive sleep disorder, most frequently experienced in childhood, that may involve loud screams and intense panic. The sufferer cannot wake from sleep even though he or she is trying to. In extreme cases, sleep terrors may result in bodily harm or property damage as the sufferer moves about abruptly. Up to 3% of adults suffer from sleep terrors, which typically occur in sleep stage N3 (Mahowald & Schenck, 2000).[21]

Other sleep disorders include *bruxism*, in which the sufferer grinds his teeth during sleep; *restless legs syndrome*, in which the sufferer reports an itching, burning, or otherwise uncomfortable feeling in his legs, usually exacerbated when resting or asleep; and *periodic limb movement disorder*, which involves sudden involuntary movement of limbs. The latter can cause sleep disruption and injury for both the sufferer and bed partner.

Although many sleep disorders occur during non-REM sleep, *REM sleep behavior disorder* (Mahowald & Schenck, 2005)[22] is a condition in which people (usually middle-aged or older men) engage in vigorous and bizarre physical activities during REM sleep in response to intense, violent dreams. As their actions may injure themselves or their sleeping partners, this disorder, thought to be neurological in nature, is normally treated with hypnosis and medications.

1.3 The Heavy Costs of Not Sleeping

Our preferred sleep times and our sleep requirements vary throughout our life cycle. Newborns tend to sleep between 16 and 18 hours per day, preschoolers tend to sleep between 10 and 12 hours per day, school-aged children and teenagers usually prefer at least 9 hours of sleep per night, and most adults say that they require 7 to 8 hours per night (Mercer, Merritt, & Cowell, 1998; National Sleep Foundation, 2008).[23] There are also individual differences in need for sleep. Some people do quite well with fewer than 6 hours of sleep per night, whereas others need 9 hours or more. The most recent study by the National Sleep Foundation suggests that adults should get between 7 and 9 hours of sleep per night (Figure 5.8), and yet Americans now average fewer than 7 hours.

FIGURE 5.8 Average Hours of Required Sleep per Night

The average U.S. adult reported getting only 6.7 hours of sleep per night, which is less than the recommended range propose by the National Sleep Foundation.

FIGURE 5.7

Are you getting enough sleep to maintain your health and abilities to concentrate? This student doesn't seem to be.

© Thinkstock

How much sleep do you really need?	
Age	**Sleep needs**
Newborns (0–2 months)	12 to 18 hours
Infants (3–11 months)	14 to 15 hours
Toddlers (1–3 years)	12 to 14 hours
Preschoolers (3–5 years)	11 to 13 hours
School-age children (5–10 years)	10 to 11 hours
Teens (10–17 years)	8.5 to 9.25 hours
Adults	7 to 9 hours

Source: Adapted from National Sleep Foundation. (2008). Sleep in America Poll. Washington, DC: Author. Retrieved from
http://www.sleepfoundation.org/sites/default/files/2008%20POLL%20SOF.PDF.

Getting needed rest is difficult in part because school and work schedules still follow the early-to-rise timetable that was set years ago. We tend to stay up late to enjoy activities in the evening but then are forced to get up early to go to work or school. The situation is particularly bad for college students, who are likely to combine a heavy academic schedule with an active social life and who may, in some cases, also work. Getting enough sleep is a luxury that many of us seem to be unable or unwilling to afford, and yet sleeping is one of the most important things we can do for ourselves. Continued over time, a nightly deficit of even only 1 or 2 hours can have a substantial impact on mood and performance.

Sleep has a vital restorative function, and a prolonged lack of sleep results in increased anxiety, diminished performance, and, if severe and extended, may even result in death. Many road accidents involve sleep deprivation, and people who are sleep deprived show decrements in driving performance similar to those who have ingested alcohol (Hack, Choi, Vijayapalan, Davies, & Stradling, 2001; Williamson & Feyer, 2000).[24] Poor treatment by doctors (Smith-Coggins, Rosekind, Hurd, & Buccino,

1994)[25] and a variety of industrial accidents have also been traced in part to the effects of sleep deprivation.

Good sleep is also important to our health and longevity. It is no surprise that we sleep more when we are sick, because sleep works to fight infection. Sleep deprivation suppresses immune responses that fight off infection, and can lead to obesity, hypertension, and memory impairment (Ferrie et al., 2007; Kushida, 2005).[26] Sleeping well can even save our lives. Dew et al. (2003)[27] found that older adults who had better sleep patterns also lived longer.

FIGURE 5.9 The Effects of Sleep Deprivation

In 1964, 17-year-old high school student Randy Gardner remained awake for 264 hours (11 days) in order to set a new Guinness World Record. At the request of his worried parents, he was monitored by a U.S. Navy psychiatrist, Lt. Cmdr. John J. Ross. This chart maps the progression of his behavioral changes over the 11 days.

Day 1
- Difficulty focusing eyes

Day 2
- Moodiness
- Difficulty focusing eyes

Day 3
- Irritability
- Memory lapses
- First hallucination

Day 4
- Hallucinations, with recognition that they were not real

Day 5 and onward
- Paranoia

Source: Adapted from Ross, J. J. (1965). Neurological findings after prolonged sleep deprivation. Archives of Neurology, 12, 399–403.

dreams

The succession of images, thoughts, sounds, and emotions that passes through our minds while sleeping.

1.4 Dreams and Dreaming

Dreams are *the succession of images, thoughts, sounds, and emotions that passes through our minds while sleeping*. When people are awakened from REM sleep, they normally report that they have been dreaming, suggesting that people normally dream several times a night but that most dreams are forgotten on awakening (Dement, 1997).[28] The content of our dreams generally relates to our everyday experiences and concerns, and frequently our fears and failures (Cartwright, Agargun, Kirkby, & Friedman, 2006; Domhoff, Meyer-Gomes, & Schredl, 2005).[29]

Many cultures regard dreams as having great significance for the dreamer, either by revealing something important about the dreamer's present circumstances or predicting his future. The Austrian psychologist Sigmund Freud (1913/1988) [30] analyzed the dreams of his patients to help him understand their unconscious needs and desires, and psychotherapists still make use of this technique today. Freud believed that the primary function of dreams was *wish fulfillment*, or the idea that dreaming allows us to act out the desires that we must repress during the day. He differentiated between the *manifest content* of the dream (i.e., its literal actions) and its *latent content* (i.e., the hidden psychological meaning of the dream). Freud believed that the real meaning of dreams is often suppressed by the unconscious mind in order to protect the individual from thoughts and feelings that are hard to cope with. By uncovering the real meaning of dreams through *psychoanalysis*, Freud believed that people could better understand their problems and resolve the issues that create difficulties in their lives.

Although Freud and others have focused on the meaning of dreams, other theories about the causes of dreams are less concerned with their content. One possibility is that we dream primarily to help with consolidation, or the moving of information into long-term memory (Alvarenga et al., 2008; Zhang (2004).[31] Rauchs, Desgranges, Foret, and Eustache (2005)[32] found that rats that had been deprived of REM sleep after learning a new task were less able to perform the task again later than were rats that had been allowed to dream, and these differences were greater on tasks that involved learning unusual information or developing new behaviors. Payne and Nadel (2004) [33] argued that the content of dreams is the result of consolidation—we dream about the things that are being moved into long-term memory. Thus dreaming may be an important part of the learning that we do while sleeping (Hobson, Pace-Schott, and Stickgold, 2000).[34]

The *activation-synthesis theory* of dreaming (Hobson & McCarley, 1977; Hobson, 2004)[35] proposes still another explanation for dreaming—namely, that dreams are our brain's interpretation of the random firing of neurons in the brain stem. According to this approach, the signals from the brain stem are sent to the cortex, just as they are when we are awake, but because the pathways from the cortex to skeletal muscles are disconnected during REM sleep, the cortex does not know how to interpret the signals. As a result, the cortex strings the messages together into the coherent stories we experience as dreams.

Although researchers are still trying to determine the exact causes of dreaming, one thing remains clear—we need to dream. If we are deprived of REM sleep, we quickly become less able to engage in the important tasks of everyday life, until we are finally able to dream again.

KEY TAKEAWAYS

- Consciousness, our subjective awareness of ourselves and our environment, is functional because it allows us to plan activities and monitor our goals.
- Psychologists believe the consciousness is the result of neural activity in the brain.
- Human and animal behavior is influenced by biological rhythms, including annual, monthly, and circadian rhythms.
- Sleep consists of two major stages: REM and non-REM sleep. Non-REM sleep has three substages, known as stage N1, N2, and N3.
- Each sleep stage is marked by a specific pattern of biological responses and brain wave patterns.
- Sleep is essential for adequate functioning during the day. Sleep disorders, including insomnia, sleep apnea, and narcolepsy, may make it hard for us to sleep well.
- Dreams occur primarily during REM sleep. Some theories of dreaming, such Freud's, are based on the content of the dreams. Other theories of dreaming propose that dreaming is related to memory consolidation. The activation-synthesis theory of dreaming is based only on neural activity.

EXERCISES AND CRITICAL THINKING

1. If you happen to be home alone one night, try this exercise: At nightfall, leave the lights and any other powered equipment off. Does this influence what time you go to sleep as opposed to your normal sleep time?
2. Review your own sleep patterns. Are you getting enough sleep? What makes you think so?
3. Review some of the dreams that you have had recently. Consider how each of the theories of dreaming we have discussed would explain your dreams.

2. ALTERING CONSCIOUSNESS WITH PSYCHOACTIVE DRUGS

LEARNING OBJECTIVES

1. **Summarize the major psychoactive drugs and their influences on consciousness and behavior.**
2. **Review the evidence regarding the dangers of recreational drugs.**

A **psychoactive drug** is *a chemical that changes our states of consciousness, and particularly our perceptions and moods.* These drugs are commonly found in everyday foods and beverages, including chocolate, coffee, and soft drinks, as well as in alcohol and in over-the-counter drugs, such as aspirin, Tylenol, and cold and cough medication. Psychoactive drugs are also frequently prescribed as sleeping pills, tranquilizers, and antianxiety medications, and they may be taken, illegally, for recreational purposes. As you can see in Table 5.1, the four primary classes of psychoactive drugs are *stimulants*, *depressants*, *opioids*, and *hallucinogens*.

Psychoactive drugs affect consciousness by influencing how neurotransmitters operate at the synapses of the central nervous system (CNS). Some psychoactive drugs are agonists, which mimic the operation of a neurotransmitter; some are antagonists, which block the action of a neurotransmitter; and some work by blocking the reuptake of neurotransmitters at the synapse.

psychoactive drug

A chemical that changes our states of consciousness, and particularly our perceptions and moods.

TABLE 5.1 Psychoactive Drugs by Class

Mechanism	Symptoms	Drug	Dangers and side effects	Psychological dependence	Physical dependence	Addiction potential	Addicti... potentia
Stimulants							
Stimulants block the reuptake of dopamine, norepinephrine, and serotonin in the synapses of the CNS.	Enhanced mood and increased energy	Caffeine	May create dependence	Low	Low	Low	
		Nicotine	Has major negative health effects if smoked or chewed	High	High	High	
		Cocaine	Decreased appetite, headache	Low	Low	Moderate	
		Amphetamines	Possible dependence, accompanied by severe "crash" with depression as drug effects wear off, particularly if smoked or injected	Moderate	Low	Moderate to high	
Depressants							
Depressants change consciousness by increasing the production of the neurotransmitter GABA and decreasing the production of the neurotransmitter acetylcholine, usually at the level of the thalamus and the reticular formation.	Calming effects, sleep, pain relief, slowed heart rate and respiration	Alcohol	Impaired judgment, loss of coordination, dizziness, nausea, and eventually a loss of consciousness	Moderate	Moderate	Moderate	
		Barbiturates and benzodiazepines	Sluggishness, slowed speech, drowsiness, in severe cases, coma or death	Moderate	Moderate	Moderate	
		Toxic inhalants	Brain damage and death	High	High	High	
Opioids							
The chemical makeup of opioids is similar to the endorphins, the neurotransmitters that serve as the body's "natural pain reducers."	Slowing of many body functions, constipation, respiratory and cardiac depression, and the rapid development of tolerance	Opium	Side effects include nausea, vomiting, tolerance, and addiction.	Moderate	Moderate	Moderate	
		Morphine	Restlessness, irritability, headache and body aches, tremors, nausea, vomiting, and severe abdominal pain	High	Moderate	Moderate	
		Heroin	All side effects of morphine but about twice as addictive as morphine	High	Moderate	High	

Mechanism	Symptoms	Drug	Dangers and side effects	Psychological dependence	Physical dependence	Addiction potential	Addiction potential
Hallucinogens							
The chemical compositions of the hallucinogens are similar to the neurotransmitters serotonin and epinephrine, and they act primarily by mimicking them.	Altered consciousness; hallucinations	Marijuana	Mild intoxication; enhanced perception	Low	Low	Low	
		LSD, mescaline, PCP, and peyote	Hallucinations; enhanced perception	Low	Low	Low	

In some cases the effects of psychoactive drugs mimic other naturally occurring states of consciousness. For instance, sleeping pills are prescribed to create drowsiness, and benzodiazepines are prescribed to create a state of relaxation. In other cases psychoactive drugs are taken for recreational purposes with the goal of creating states of consciousness that are pleasurable or that help us escape our normal consciousness.

The use of psychoactive drugs, and especially those that are used illegally, has the potential to create very negative side effects (Table 5.1). This does not mean that all drugs are dangerous, but rather that all drugs can be dangerous, particularly if they are used regularly over long periods of time. Psychoactive drugs create negative effects not so much through their initial use but through the continued use, accompanied by increasing doses, that ultimately may lead to drug abuse.

The problem is that many drugs create **tolerance**: *an increase in the dose required to produce the same effect*, which makes it necessary for the user to increase the dosage or the number of times per day that the drug is taken. As the use of the drug increases, the user may develop a **dependence**, defined as a *need to use a drug or other substance regularly*. Dependence can be psychological, in which the drug is desired and has become part of the everyday life of the user, but no serious physical effects result if the drug is not obtained; or physical, in which serious physical and mental effects appear when the drug is withdrawn. Cigarette smokers who try to quit, for example, experience physical withdrawal symptoms, such as becoming tired and irritable, as well as extreme psychological cravings to enjoy a cigarette in particular situations, such as after a meal or when they are with friends.

Users may wish to stop using the drug, but when they reduce their dosage they experience **withdrawal**—*negative experiences that accompany reducing or stopping drug use, including physical pain and other symptoms. When the user powerfully craves the drug and is driven to seek it out, over and over again, no matter what the physical, social, financial, and legal cost*, we say that he or she has developed an **addiction** to the drug.

It is a common belief that addiction is an overwhelming, irresistibly powerful force, and that withdrawal from drugs is always an unbearably painful experience. But the reality is more complicated and in many cases less extreme. For one, even drugs that we do not generally think of as being addictive, such as caffeine, nicotine, and alcohol, can be very difficult to quit using, at least for some people. On the other hand, drugs that are normally associated with addiction, including amphetamines, cocaine, and heroin, do not immediately create addiction in their users. Even for a highly addictive drug like cocaine, only about 15% of users become addicted (Robinson & Berridge, 2003; Wagner & Anthony, 2002).[36] Furthermore, the rate of addiction is lower for those who are taking drugs for medical reasons than for those who are using drugs recreationally. Patients who have become physically dependent on morphine administered during the course of medical treatment for a painful injury or disease are able to be rapidly weaned off the drug afterward, without becoming addicts. Robins, Davis, and Goodwin (1974)[37] found that the majority of soldiers who had become addicted to morphine while overseas were quickly able to stop using after returning home.

This does not mean that using recreational drugs is not dangerous. For people who do become addicted to drugs, the success rate of recovery is low. These drugs are generally illegal and carry with them potential criminal consequences if one is caught and arrested. Drugs that are smoked may produce throat and lung cancers and other problems. Snorting ("sniffing") drugs can lead to a loss of the sense of smell, nosebleeds, difficulty in swallowing, hoarseness, and chronic runny nose. Injecting drugs intravenously carries with it the risk of contracting infections such as hepatitis and HIV. Furthermore, the quality and contents of illegal drugs are generally unknown, and the doses can vary substantially from purchase to purchase. The drugs may also contain toxic chemicals.

Another problem is the unintended consequences of combining drugs, which can produce serious side effects. Combining drugs is dangerous because their combined effects on the CNS can increase dramatically and can lead to accidental or even deliberate overdoses. For instance, ingesting alcohol or

tolerance

An increase in the dose of a drug required to produce the same effect.

dependence

The need to use a drug or other substance regularly.

withdrawal

Negative experiences that accompany reducing or stopping drug use, including physical pain and other symptoms.

addiction

When the user powerfully craves the drug and is driven to seek it out, over and over again, no matter what the physical, social, financial, and legal cost.

benzodiazepines along with the usual dose of heroin is a frequent cause of overdose deaths in opiate addicts, and combining alcohol and cocaine can have a dangerous impact on the cardiovascular system (McCance-Katz, Kosten, & Jatlow, 1998).[38]

Although all recreational drugs are dangerous, some can be more deadly than others. One way to determine how dangerous recreational drugs are is to calculate a *safety ratio*, based on the dose that is likely to be fatal divided by the normal dose needed to feel the effects of the drug. Drugs with lower ratios are more dangerous because the difference between the normal and the lethal dose is small. For instance, heroin has a safety ratio of 6 because the average fatal dose is only 6 times greater than the average effective dose. On the other hand, marijuana has a safety ratio of 1,000. This is not to say that smoking marijuana cannot be deadly, but it is much less likely to be deadly than is heroin. The safety ratios of common recreational drugs are shown in Table 5.2.

TABLE 5.2 Popular Recreational Drugs and Their Safety Ratios

Drug	Description	Street or brand names	Safety ratio
Heroin	Strong depressant	Smack, junk, H	6
GHB (Gamma hydroxy butyrate)	"Rave" drug (not Ecstacy), also used as a "date rape" drug.	Georgia home boy, liquid ecstasy, liquid X, liquid G, fantasy	8
Isobutyl nitrite	Depressant and toxic inhalant	Poppers, rush, locker room	8
Alcohol	Active compound is ethanol		10
DXM (Dextromethorphan)	Active ingredient in over-the-counter cold and cough medicines		10
Methamphetamine	May be injected or smoked	Meth, crank	10
Cocaine	May be inhaled or smoked	Crack, coke, rock, blue	15
MDMA (methylene-dioxymetham-phetamine)	Very powerful stimulant	Ecstasy	16
Codeine	Depressant		20
Methadone	Opioid		20
Mescaline	Hallucinogen		24
Benzodiazepine	Prescription tranquilizer	Centrax, Dalmane, Doral, Halcion, Librium, ProSom, Restoril, Xanax, Valium	30
Ketamine	Prescription anesthetic	Ketanest, Ketaset, Ketalar	40
DMT (Dimethyl-tryptamine)	Hallucinogen		50
Phenobarbital	Usually prescribed as a sleeping pill	Luminal (Phenobarbital), Mebaraland, Nembutal, Seconal, Sombulex	50
Prozac	Antidepressant		100
Nitrous oxide	Often inhaled from whipped cream dispensers	Laughing gas	150
Lysergic acid diethylamide (LSD)		Acid	1,000
Marijuana (Cannabis)	Active ingredient is THC	Pot, spliff, weed	1,000
Drugs with lower safety ratios have a greater risk of brain damage and death.			

Source: Gable, R. (2004). Comparison of acute lethal toxicity of commonly abused psychoactive substances. Addiction, 99(6), 686–696.

2.1 Speeding Up the Brain With Stimulants: Caffeine, Nicotine, Cocaine, and Amphetamines

stimulant

A class of psychoactive drugs that operate by blocking the reuptake of dopamine, norepinephrine, and serotonin in the synapses of the central nervous system.

A **stimulant** is *a psychoactive drug that operates by blocking the reuptake of dopamine, norepinephrine, and serotonin in the synapses of the CNS.* Because more of these neurotransmitters remain active in the brain, the result is an increase in the activity of the sympathetic division of the autonomic nervous system (ANS). Effects of stimulants include increased heart and breathing rates, pupil dilation, and increases in blood sugar accompanied by decreases in appetite. For these reasons, stimulants are frequently used to help people stay awake and to control weight.

Used in moderation, some stimulants may increase alertness, but used in an irresponsible fashion they can quickly create dependency. A major problem is the "crash" that results when the drug loses its effectiveness and the activity of the neurotransmitters returns to normal. The withdrawal from stimulants can create profound depression and lead to an intense desire to repeat the high.

Caffeine is *a bitter psychoactive drug found in the beans, leaves, and fruits of plants*, where it acts as a natural pesticide. It is found in a wide variety of products, including coffee, tea, soft drinks, candy, and desserts. In North America, more than 80% of adults consume caffeine daily (Lovett, 2005).[39] Caffeine acts as a mood enhancer and provides energy. Although the U.S. Food and Drug Administration lists caffeine as a safe food substance, it has at least some characteristics of dependence. People who reduce their caffeine intake often report being irritable, restless, and drowsy, as well as experiencing strong headaches, and these withdrawal symptoms may last up to a week. Most experts feel that using small amounts of caffeine during pregnancy is safe, but larger amounts of caffeine can be harmful to the fetus (U.S. Food and Drug Administration, 2007).[40]

Nicotine is *a psychoactive drug found in the nightshade family of plants, where it acts as a natural pesticide*. Nicotine is the main cause for the dependence-forming properties of tobacco use, and tobacco use is a major health threat. Nicotine creates both psychological and physical addiction, and it is one of the hardest addictions to break. Nicotine content in cigarettes has slowly increased over the years, making quitting smoking more and more difficult. Nicotine is also found in smokeless (chewing) tobacco.

People who want to quit smoking sometimes use other drugs to help them. For instance, the prescription drug Chantix acts as an antagonist, binding to nicotine receptors in the synapse, which prevents users from receiving the normal stimulant effect when they smoke. At the same time, the drug also releases dopamine, the reward neurotransmitter. In this way Chantix dampens nicotine withdrawal symptoms and cravings. In many cases people are able to get past the physical dependence, allowing them to quit smoking at least temporarily. In the long run, however, the psychological enjoyment of smoking may lead to relapse.

Cocaine is *an addictive drug obtained from the leaves of the coca plant*. In the late 19th and early 20th centuries, it was a primary constituent in many popular tonics and elixirs and, although it was removed in 1905, was one of the original ingredients in Coca-Cola. Today cocaine is taken illegally as recreational drug.

Cocaine has a variety of adverse effects on the body. It constricts blood vessels, dilates pupils, and increases body temperature, heart rate, and blood pressure. It can cause headaches, abdominal pain, and nausea. Since cocaine also tends to decrease appetite, chronic users may also become malnourished. The intensity and duration of cocaine's effects, which include increased energy and reduced fatigue, depend on how the drug is taken. The faster the drug is absorbed into the bloodstream and delivered to the brain, the more intense the high. Injecting or smoking cocaine produces a faster, stronger high than snorting it. However, the faster the drug is absorbed, the faster the effects subside. The high from snorting cocaine may last 30 minutes, whereas the high from smoking "crack" cocaine may last only 10 minutes. In order to sustain the high, the user must administer the drug again, which may lead to frequent use, often in higher doses, over a short period of time (National Institute on Drug Abuse, 2009).[41] Cocaine has a safety ratio of 15, making it a very dangerous recreational drug.

Amphetamine is *a stimulant that produces increased wakefulness and focus, along with decreased fatigue and appetite*. Amphetamine is used in prescription medications to treat attention deficit disorder (ADD) and narcolepsy, and to control appetite. Some brand names of amphetamines are Adderall, Benzedrine, Dexedrine, and Vyvanse. But amphetamine ("speed") is also used illegally as a recreational drug. The methylated version of amphetamine, *methamphetamine* ("meth" or "crank"), is currently favored by users, partly because it is available in ampoules ready for use by injection (Csaky & Barnes, 1984).[42] Meth is a highly dangerous drug with a safety ratio of only 10.

Amphetamines may produce a very high level of tolerance, leading users to increase their intake, often in "jolts" taken every half hour or so. Although the level of physical dependency is small, amphetamines may produce very strong psychological dependence, effectively amounting to addiction. Continued use of stimulants may result in severe psychological depression. The effects of the stimulant methylenedioxymethamphetamine (MDMA), also known as "Ecstasy," provide a good example. MDMA is a very strong stimulant that very successfully prevents the reuptake of serotonin, dopamine, and norepinephrine. It is so effective that when used repeatedly it can seriously deplete the amount of neurotransmitters available in the brain, producing a catastrophic mental and physical "crash" resulting in serious, long-lasting depression. MDMA also affects the temperature-regulating mechanisms of the brain, so in high doses, and especially when combined with vigorous physical activity like dancing, it can cause the body to become so drastically overheated that users can literally "burn up" and die from hyperthermia and dehydration.

caffeine

A bitter psychoactive drug found in the beans, leaves, and fruits of plants.

nicotine

A psychoactive drug found in tobacco products.

cocaine

An addictive drug obtained from the leaves of the coca plant.

FIGURE 5.10

Snorting cocaine tends to cause a high that averages about 15 to 30 minutes.

© *Thinkstock*

amphetamine

A stimulant that produces increased wakefulness and focus, along with decreased fatigue and appetite.

2.2 Slowing Down the Brain With Depressants: Alcohol, Barbiturates and Benzodiazepines, and Toxic Inhalants

depressant

A class of psychoactive drugs that reduce the activity of the CNS.

In contrast to stimulants, which work to increase neural activity, a *depressant* acts to slow down consciousness. A **depressant** is *a psychoactive drug that reduces the activity of the CNS.* Depressants are widely used as prescription medicines to relieve pain, to lower heart rate and respiration, and as anticonvulsants. Depressants change consciousness by increasing the production of the neurotransmitter GABA and decreasing the production of the neurotransmitter acetylcholine, usually at the level of the thalamus and the reticular formation. The outcome of depressant use (similar to the effects of sleep) is a reduction in the transmission of impulses from the lower brain to the cortex (Csaky & Barnes, 1984).[43]

alcohol

A colorless liquid, produced by the fermentation of sugar or starch, that is the intoxicating agent in fermented drinks.

The most commonly used of the depressants is **alcohol**, *a colorless liquid, produced by the fermentation of sugar or starch, that is the intoxicating agent in fermented drinks.* Alcohol is the oldest and most widely used drug of abuse in the world. In low to moderate doses, alcohol first acts to remove social inhibitions by slowing activity in the sympathetic nervous system. In higher doses, alcohol acts on the cerebellum to interfere with coordination and balance, producing the staggering gait of drunkenness. At high blood levels, further CNS depression leads to dizziness, nausea, and eventually a loss of consciousness. High enough blood levels such as those produced by "guzzling" large amounts of hard liquor at parties can be fatal. Alcohol is not a "safe" drug by any means—its safety ratio is only 10.

Alcohol use is highly costly to societies because so many people abuse alcohol and because judgment after drinking can be substantially impaired. It is estimated that almost half of automobile fatalities are caused by alcohol use, and excessive alcohol consumption is involved in a majority of violent crimes, including rape and murder (Abbey, Ross, McDuffie, & McAuslan, 1996).[44] Alcohol increases the likelihood that people will respond aggressively to provocations (Bushman, 1993, 1997; Graham, Osgood, Wells, & Stockwell, 2006).[45] Even people who are not normally aggressive may react with aggression when they are intoxicated. Alcohol use also leads to rioting, unprotected sex, and other negative outcomes.

FIGURE 5.11

Alcohol is the most widely used drug of abuse in the world. Alcohol acts as a general depressant in the central nervous system, where its actions are similar to those of general anesthetics.

Source: Photo courtesy of theskywatcher,
http://www.flickr.com/photos/theskywatcher/2466121364.

Alcohol increases aggression in part because it reduces the ability of the person who has consumed it to inhibit his or her aggression (Steele & Southwick, 1985).[46] When people are intoxicated, they become more self-focused and less aware of the social situation. As a result, they become less likely to notice the social constraints that normally prevent them from engaging aggressively, and are less likely to use those social constraints to guide them. For instance, we might normally notice the presence of a police officer or other people around us, which would remind us that being aggressive is not appropriate. But when we are drunk, we are less likely to be so aware. The narrowing of attention that occurs when we are intoxicated also prevents us from being cognizant of the negative outcomes of our aggression. When we are sober, we realize that being aggressive may produce retaliation, as well as cause a host of other problems, but we are less likely to realize these potential consequences when we have been drinking (Bushman & Cooper, 1990).[47] Alcohol also influences aggression through expectations. If we expect that alcohol will make us more aggressive, then we tend to become more aggressive when we drink.

Barbiturates are *depressants that are commonly prescribed as sleeping pills and painkillers.* Brand names include Luminal (Phenobarbital), Mebaraland, Nembutal, Seconal, and Sombulex. In small to moderate doses, barbiturates produce relaxation and sleepiness, but in higher doses symptoms may include sluggishness, difficulty in thinking, slowness of speech, drowsiness, faulty judgment, and eventually coma or even death (Medline Plus, 2008).[48]

barbiturates

A family of depressants that are commonly prescribed as sleeping pills and painkillers.

Related to barbiturates, **benzodiazepines** are *a family of depressants used to treat anxiety, insomnia, seizures, and muscle spasms.* In low doses, they produce mild sedation and relieve anxiety; in high doses, they induce sleep. In the United States, benzodiazepines are among the most widely prescribed medications that affect the CNS. Brand names include Centrax, Dalmane, Doral, Halcion, Librium, ProSom, Restoril, Xanax, and Valium.

benzodiazepines

A family of depressants used to treat anxiety, insomnia, seizures, and muscle spasms.

Toxic inhalants are also frequently abused as depressants. These drugs are easily accessible as the vapors of glue, gasoline, propane, hair spray, and spray paint, and are inhaled to create a change in consciousness. Related drugs are the nitrites (amyl and butyl nitrite; "poppers," "rush," "locker room") and anesthetics such as nitrous oxide (laughing gas) and ether. Inhalants are some of the most dangerous recreational drugs, with a safety index below 10, and their continued use may lead to permanent brain damage.

2.3 Opioids: Opium, Morphine, Heroin, and Codeine

Opioids are *chemicals that increase activity in opioid receptor neurons in the brain and in the digestive system, producing euphoria, analgesia, slower breathing, and constipation.* Their chemical makeup is similar to the endorphins, the neurotransmitters that serve as the body's "natural pain reducers." Natural opioids are derived from the opium poppy, which is widespread in Eurasia, but they can also be created synthetically.

Opium is *the dried juice of the unripe seed capsule of the opium poppy.* It may be the oldest drug on record, known to the Sumerians before 4000 BC. **Morphine** and **heroin** are *stronger, more addictive drugs derived from opium,* while **codeine** is a *weaker analgesic and less addictive member of the opiate family.* When morphine was first refined from opium in the early 19th century, it was touted as a cure for opium addiction, but it didn't take long to discover that it was actually more addicting than raw opium. When heroin was produced a few decades later, it was also initially thought to be a more potent, less addictive painkiller but was soon found to be much more addictive than morphine. Heroin is about twice as addictive as morphine, and creates severe tolerance, moderate physical dependence, and severe psychological dependence. The danger of heroin is demonstrated in the fact that it has the lowest safety ratio (6) of all the drugs listed in Table 5.1.

The opioids activate the sympathetic division of the ANS, causing blood pressure and heart rate to increase, often to dangerous levels that can lead to heart attack or stroke. At the same time the drugs also influence the parasympathetic division, leading to constipation and other negative side effects. Symptoms of opioid withdrawal include diarrhea, insomnia, restlessness, irritability, and vomiting, all accompanied by a strong craving for the drug. The powerful psychological dependence of the opioids and the severe effects of withdrawal make it very difficult for morphine and heroin abusers to quit using. In addition, because many users take these drugs intravenously and share contaminated needles, they run a very high risk of being infected with diseases. Opioid addicts suffer a high rate of infections such as HIV, pericarditis (an infection of the membrane around the heart), and hepatitis B, any of which can be fatal.

opioids

A family of chemicals that increase activity in opioid receptor neurons in the brain and in the digestive system, producing euphoria, analgesia, slower breathing, and constipation.

opium

The dried juice of the unripe seed capsule of the opium poppy.

morphine

A powerful and addictive drug derived from opium.

heroin

A powerful and addictive drug derived from opium.

codeine

A powerful and addictive drug derived from opium.

2.4 Hallucinogens: Cannabis, Mescaline, and LSD

The drugs that produce the most extreme alteration of consciousness are the **hallucinogens**, *psychoactive drugs that alter sensation and perception and that may create hallucinations.* The hallucinogens are frequently known as "psychedelics." Drugs in this class include lysergic acid diethylamide (LSD, or "Acid"), mescaline, and phencyclidine (PCP), as well as a number of natural plants including cannabis (marijuana), peyote, and psilocybin. The chemical compositions of the hallucinogens are similar to the neurotransmitters serotonin and epinephrine, and they act primarily as agonists by mimicking the action of serotonin at the synapses. The hallucinogens may produce striking changes in perception through one or more of the senses. The precise effects a user experiences are a function not only of the drug itself, but also of the user's preexisting mental state and expectations of the drug experience. In large part, the user tends to get out of the experience what he or she brings to it. The hallucinations that may be experienced when taking these drugs are strikingly different from everyday experience and frequently are more similar to dreams than to everyday consciousness.

Cannabis (marijuana) is the most widely used hallucinogen. Until it was banned in the United States under the Marijuana Tax Act of 1938, it was widely used for medical purposes. In recent years, cannabis has again been frequently prescribed for the treatment of pain and nausea, particularly in cancer sufferers, as well as for a wide variety of other physical and psychological disorders (Ben Amar, 2006).[49] While medical marijuana is now legal in several American states, it is still banned under federal law, putting those states in conflict with the federal government. Marijuana also acts as a stimulant, producing giggling, laughing, and mild intoxication. It acts to enhance perception of sights, sounds, and smells, and may produce a sensation of time slowing down. It is much less likely to lead to antisocial acts than that other popular intoxicant, alcohol, and it is also the one psychedelic drug whose use has not declined in recent years (National Institute on Drug Abuse, 2009).[50]

Although the hallucinogens are powerful drugs that produce striking "mind-altering" effects, they do not produce physiological or psychological tolerance or dependence. While they are not addictive and pose little physical threat to the body, their use is not advisable in any situation in which the user needs to be alert and attentive, exercise focused awareness or good judgment, or demonstrate normal mental functioning, such as driving a car, studying, or operating machinery.

FIGURE 5.12

Intravenous injection of heroin typically causes a rush within 7 to 8 seconds. This method of drug use provides the highest intensity and quickest onset of the initial rush but is also the most dangerous.

Source: Photo courtesy of BBC News, http://news.bbc.co.uk/olmedia/855000/images/_855018_inject300.jpg.

hallucinogens

A family of psychoactive drugs that alter sensation and perception.

2.5 Why We Use Psychoactive Drugs

People have used, and often abused, psychoactive drugs for thousands of years. Perhaps this should not be suprising, because many people find using drugs to be fun and enjoyable. Even when we know the potential costs of using drugs, we may engage in them anyway because the pleasures of using the drugs are occurring right now, whereas the potential costs are abstract and occur in the future.

Research Focus: Risk Tolerance Predicts Cigarette Use

Because drug and alcohol abuse is a behavior that has such important negative consequences for so many people, researchers have tried to understand what leads people to use drugs. Carl Lejuez and his colleagues (Lejuez, Aklin, Bornovalova, & Moolchan, 2005)[51] tested the hypothesis that cigarette smoking was related to a desire to take risks. In their research they compared risk-taking behavior in adolescents who reported having tried a cigarette at least once with those who reported that they had never tried smoking.

Participants in the research were 125 5th- through 12th-graders attending after-school programs throughout inner-city neighborhoods in the Washington, DC, metropolitan area. Eighty percent of the adolescents indicated that they had never tried even a puff of a cigarette, and 20% indicated that they had had at least one puff of a cigarette.

The participants were tested in a laboratory where they completed the Balloon Analogue Risk Task (BART), a measure of risk taking (Lejuez et al., 2002).[52] The BART is a computer task in which the participant pumps up a series of simulated balloons by pressing on a computer key. With each pump the balloon appears bigger on the screen, and more money accumulates in a temporary "bank account." However, when a balloon is pumped up too far, the computer generates a popping sound, the balloon disappears from the screen, and all the money in the temporary bank is lost. At any point during each balloon trial, the participant can stop pumping up the balloon, click on a button, transfer all money from the temporary bank to the permanent bank, and begin with a new balloon.

Because the participants do not have precise information about the probability of each balloon exploding, and because each balloon is programmed to explode after a different number of pumps, the participants have to determine how much to pump up the balloon. The number of pumps that participants take is used as a measure of their tolerance for risk. Low-tolerance people tend to make a few pumps and then collect the money, whereas more risky people pump more times into each balloon.

Supporting the hypothesis that risk tolerance is related to smoking, Lejuez et al. found that the tendency to take risks was indeed correlated with cigarette use: The participants who indicated that they had puffed on a cigarette had significantly higher risk-taking scores on the BART than did those who had never tried smoking.

Individual ambitions, expectations, and values also influence drug use. Vaughan, Corbin, and Fromme (2009)[53] found that college students who expressed positive academic values and strong ambitions had less alcohol consumption and alcohol-related problems, and cigarette smoking has declined more among youth from wealthier and more educated homes than among those from lower socioeconomic backgrounds (Johnston, O'Malley, Bachman, & Schulenberg, 2004).[54]

Drug use is in part the result of socialization. Children try drugs when their friends convince them to do it, and these decisions are based on social norms about the risks and benefits of various drugs. In the period 1991 to 1997, the percentage of 12th-graders who responded that they perceived "great harm in regular marijuana use" declined from 79% to 58%, while annual use of marijuana in this group rose from 24% to 39% (Johnston et al., 2004).[55] And students binge drink in part when they see that many other people around them are also binging (Clapp, Reed, Holmes, Lange, & Voas, 2006).[56]

FIGURE 5.13 Use of Various Drugs by 12th-Graders in 2005

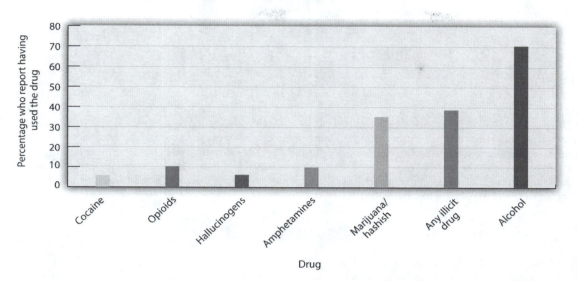

Despite the fact that young people have experimented with cigarettes, alcohol, and other dangerous drugs for many generations, it would be better if they did not. All recreational drug use is associated with at least some risks, and those who begin using drugs earlier are also more likely to use more dangerous drugs later (Lynskey et al., 2003).[57] Furthermore, as we will see in the next section, there are many other enjoyable ways to alter consciousness that are safer.

KEY TAKEAWAYS

- Psychoactive drugs are chemicals that change our state of consciousness. They work by influencing neurotransmitters in the CNS.
- Using psychoactive drugs may create tolerance and, when they are no longer used, withdrawal. Addiction may result from tolerance and the difficulty of withdrawal.
- Stimulants, including caffeine, nicotine, and amphetamine, increase neural activity by blocking the reuptake of dopamine, norepinephrine, and serotonin in the CNS.
- Depressants, including, alcohol, barbiturates, and benzodiazepines, decrease consciousness by increasing the production of the neurotransmitter GABA and decreasing the production of the neurotransmitter acetylcholine.
- Opioids, including codeine, opium, morphine and heroin, produce euphoria and analgesia by increasing activity in opioid receptor neurons.
- Hallucinogens, including cannabis, mescaline, and LSD, create an extreme alteration of consciousness as well as the possibility of hallucinations.
- Recreational drug use is influenced by social norms as well as by individual differences. People who are more likely to take risks are also more likely to use drugs.

EXERCISES AND CRITICAL THINKING

1. Do people you know use psychoactive drugs? Which ones? Based on what you have learned in this section, why do you think that they are used, and do you think that their side effects are harmful?
2. Consider the research reported in the research focus on risk and cigarette smoking. What are the potential implications of the research for drug use? Can you see any weaknesses in the study caused by the fact that the results are based on correlational analyses?

3.   ALTERING CONSCIOUSNESS WITHOUT DRUGS

LEARNING OBJECTIVE

1. Review the ways that people may alter consciousness without using drugs.

Although the use of psychoactive drugs can easily and profoundly change our experience of consciousness, we can also—and often more safely—alter our consciousness without drugs. These altered states of consciousness are sometimes the result of simple and safe activities, such as sleeping, watching television, exercising, or working on a task that intrigues us. In this section we consider the changes in consciousness that occur through *hypnosis*, *sensory deprivation*, and *meditation*, as well as through other non-drug-induced mechanisms.

3.1   Changing Behavior Through Suggestion: The Power of Hypnosis

Franz Anton Mesmer (1734–1815) was an Austrian doctor who believed that all living bodies were filled with magnetic energy. In his practice, Mesmer passed magnets over the bodies of his patients while telling them their physical and psychological problems would disappear. The patients frequently lapsed into a trancelike state (they were said to be "mesmerized") and reported feeling better when they awoke (Hammond, 2008).[58]

FIGURE 5.14 Franz Anton Mesmer passed magnets over the bodies of his patients to put them in a trancelike state; the patients were "mesmerized."

A. MESMER

Source: Courtesy of http://commons.wikimedia.org/wiki/File:Franz_Anton_Mesmer.jpg.

Although subsequent research testing the effectiveness of Mesmer's techniques did not find any long-lasting improvements in his patients, the idea that people's experiences and behaviors could be changed through the power of suggestion has remained important in psychology. James Braid, a Scottish physician, coined the term *hypnosis* in 1843, basing it on the Greek word for *sleep* (Callahan, 1997).[59]

Hypnosis is *a trance-like state of consciousness, usually induced by a procedure known as hypnotic induction, which consists of heightened suggestibility, deep relaxation, and intense focus* (Nash & Barnier, 2008).[60] Hypnosis became famous in part through its use by Sigmund Freud in an attempt to make unconscious desires and emotions conscious and thus able to be considered and confronted (Baker & Nash, 2008).[61]

Because hypnosis is based on the power of suggestion, and because some people are more suggestible than others, these people are more easily hypnotized. Hilgard (1965)[62] found that about 20% of the participants he tested were entirely unsusceptible to hypnosis, whereas about 15% were highly responsive to it. The best participants for hypnosis are people who are willing or eager to be hypnotized, who are able to focus their attention and block out peripheral awareness, who are open to new experiences, and who are capable of fantasy (Spiegel, Greenleaf, & Spiegel, 2005).[63]

People who want to become hypnotized are motivated to be good subjects, to be open to suggestions by the hypnotist, and to fulfill the role of a hypnotized person as they perceive it (Spanos, 1991).[64] The hypnotized state results from a combination of conformity, relaxation, obedience, and suggestion (Fassler, Lynn, & Knox, 2008).[65] This does not necessarily indicate that hypnotized people are "faking" or lying about being hypnotized. Kinnunen, Zamansky, and Block (1994)[66] used measures of skin conductance (which indicates emotional response by measuring perspiration, and therefore renders it a reliable indicator of deception) to test whether hypnotized people were lying about having been hypnotized. Their results suggested that almost 90% of their supposedly hypnotized subjects truly believed that they had been hypnotized.

One common misconception about hypnosis is that the hypnotist is able to "take control" of hypnotized patients and thus can command them to engage in behaviors against their will. Although hypnotized people are suggestible (Jamieson & Hasegawa, 2007),[67] they nevertheless retain awareness and control of their behavior and are able to refuse to comply with the hypnotist's suggestions if they so choose (Kirsch & Braffman, 2001).[68] In fact, people who have not been hypnotized are often just as suggestible as those who have been (Orne & Evans, 1965).[69]

Another common belief is that hypnotists can lead people to forget the things that happened to them while they were hypnotized. Hilgard and Cooper (1965)[70] investigated this question and found that they could lead people who were very highly susceptible through hypnosis to show at least some signs of posthypnotic amnesia (e.g., forgetting where they had learned information that had been told to them while they were under hypnosis), but that this effect was not strong or common.

hypnosis

A trance-like state of consciousness, usually induced by a procedure known as hypnotic induction, which consists of heightened suggestibility, deep relaxation, and intense focus.

Some hypnotists have tried to use hypnosis to help people remember events, such as childhood experiences or details of crime scenes, that they have forgotten or repressed. The idea is that some memories have been stored but can no longer be retrieved, and that hypnosis can aid in the retrieval process. But research finds that this is not successful: People who are hypnotized and then asked to relive their childhood act like children, but they do not accurately recall the things that occurred to them in their own childhood (Silverman & Retzlaff, 1986).[71] Furthermore, the suggestibility produced through hypnosis may lead people to erroneously recall experiences that they did not have (Newman & Baumeister, 1996).[72] Many states and jurisdictions have therefore banned the use of hypnosis in criminal trials because the "evidence" recovered through hypnosis is likely to be fabricated and inaccurate.

Hypnosis is also frequently used to attempt to change unwanted behaviors, such as to reduce smoking, overeating, and alcohol abuse. The effectiveness of hypnosis in these areas is controversial, although at least some successes have been reported. Kirsch, Montgomery, and Sapirstein (1995)[73] found that that adding hypnosis to other forms of therapies increased the effectiveness of the treatment, and Elkins and Perfect (2008)[74] reported that hypnosis was useful in helping people stop smoking. Hypnosis is also effective in improving the experiences of patients who are experiencing anxiety disorders, such as PTSD (Cardena, 2000; Montgomery, David, Winkel, Silverstein, & Bovbjerg, 2002),[75] and for reducing pain (Montgomery, DuHamel, & Redd, 2000; Paterson & Jensen, 2003).[76]

3.2 Reducing Sensation to Alter Consciousness: Sensory Deprivation

Sensory deprivation is the *intentional reduction of stimuli affecting one or more of the five senses, with the possibility of resulting changes in consciousness.* Sensory deprivation is used for relaxation or meditation purposes, and in physical and mental health-care programs to produce enjoyable changes in consciousness. But when deprivation is prolonged, it is unpleasant and can be used as a means of torture.

Although the simplest forms of sensory deprivation require nothing more than a blindfold to block the person's sense of sight or earmuffs to block the sense of sound, more complex devices have also been devised to temporarily cut off the senses of smell, taste, touch, heat, and gravity. In 1954 John Lilly, a neurophysiologist at the National Institute of Mental Health, developed the sensory deprivation tank. The tank is filled with water that is the same temperature as the human body, and salts are added to the water so that the body floats, thus reducing the sense of gravity. The tank is dark and soundproof, and the person's sense of smell is blocked by the use of chemicals in the water, such as chlorine.

The sensory deprivation tank has been used for therapy and relaxation. In a typical session for alternative healing and meditative purposes, a person may rest in an isolation tank for up to an hour. Treatment in isolation tanks has been shown to help with a variety of medical issues, including insomnia and muscle pain (Suedfeld, 1990b; Bood, Sundequist, Kjellgren, Nordström, & Norlander, 2007; Kjellgren, Sundequist, Norlander, & Archer, 2001),[77] headaches (Wallbaum, Rzewnicki, Steele, & Suedfeld, 1991),[78] and addictive behaviors such as smoking, alcoholism, and obesity (Suedfeld, 1990a).[79]

Although relatively short sessions of sensory deprivation can be relaxing and both mentally and physically beneficial, prolonged sensory deprivation can lead to disorders of perception, including confusion and hallucinations (Yuksel, Kisa, Avdemin, & Goka, 2004).[80] It is for this reason that sensory deprivation is sometimes used as an instrument of torture (Benjamin, 2006).[81]

sensory deprivation

Intentional reduction of stimuli affecting one or more of the five senses, with the possibility of resulting changes in consciousness.

FIGURE 5.15

Treatment in sensory deprivation tanks has been shown to help with a variety of psychological and medical issues.

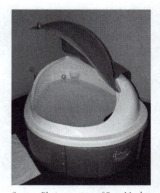

Source: Photo courtesy of SeanMack, http://commons.wikimedia.org/wiki/File:Flotation_tank_SMC.jpg.

3.3 Meditation

meditation

To techniques in which the individual focuses on something specific, such as an object, a word, or one's breathing, with the goal of ignoring external distractions, focusing on one's internal state, and achieving a state of relaxation and well-being.

Meditation refers to *techniques in which the individual focuses on something specific, such as an object, a word, or one's breathing, with the goal of ignoring external distractions, focusing on one's internal state, and achieving a state of relaxation and well-being.* Followers of various Eastern religions (Hinduism, Buddhism, and Taoism) use meditation to achieve a higher spiritual state, and popular forms of meditation in the West, such as yoga, Zen, and Transcendental Meditation, have originated from these practices. Many meditative techniques are very simple. You simply need to sit in a comfortable position with your eyes closed and practice deep breathing. You might want to try it out for yourself ("Video Clip: Try Meditation").

Video Clip: Try Meditation

Here is a simple meditation exercise you can do in your own home.

Chakra-Balance.com

View the video online at: http://www.youtube.com/embed/qs_DuZigRzY

Brain imaging studies have indicated that meditation is not only relaxing but can also induce an altered state of consciousness. Cahn and Polich (2006)[82] found that experienced meditators in a meditative state had more prominent alpha and theta waves, and other studies have shown declines in heart rate, skin conductance, oxygen consumption, and carbon dioxide elimination during meditation (Dillbeck, Glenn, & Orme-Johnson, 1987; Fenwick, 1987).[83] These studies suggest that the action of the sympathetic division of the autonomic nervous system (ANS) is suppressed during meditation, creating a more relaxed physiological state as the meditator moves into deeper states of relaxation and consciousness.

FIGURE 5.16

Research has found that regular meditation has positive physiological and psychological effects.

© *Thinkstock*

Research has found that regular meditation can mediate the effects of stress and depression, and promote well-being (Grossman, Niemann, Schmidt, & Walach, 2004; Reibel, Greeson, Brainard, & Rosenzweig, 2001; Salmon et al., 2004).[84] Meditation has also been shown to assist in controlling blood pressure (Barnes, Treiber, & Davis, 2001; Walton et al., 2004).[85] A study by Lyubimov (1992)[86] showed that during meditation, a larger area of the brain was responsive to sensory stimuli, suggesting that there is greater coordination between the two brain hemispheres as a result of meditation. Lutz and others (2004)[87] demonstrated that those who meditate regularly (as opposed to those who do not) tend to utilize a greater part of their brain and that their gamma waves are faster and more powerful. And a study of Tibetan Buddhist monks who meditate daily found that several areas of the brain can be permanently altered by the long-term practice of meditation (Lutz, Greischar, Rawlings, Ricard, & Davidson, 2004).[88]

It is possible that the positive effects of meditation could also be found by using other methods of relaxation. Although advocates of meditation claim that meditation enables people to attain a higher and purer consciousness, perhaps any kind of activity that calms and relaxes the mind, such as working on crossword puzzles, watching television or movies, or engaging in other enjoyed behaviors, might be equally effective in creating positive outcomes. Regardless of the debate, the fact remains that meditation is, at the very least, a worthwhile relaxation strategy.

Psychology in Everyday Life: The Need to Escape Everyday Consciousness

We may use recreational drugs, drink alcohol, overeat, have sex, and gamble for fun, but in some cases these normally pleasurable behaviors are abused, leading to exceedingly negative consequences for us. We frequently refer to the abuse of any type of pleasurable behavior as an "addiction," just as we refer to drug or alcohol addiction.

Roy Baumeister and his colleagues (Baumeister, 1991)[89] have argued that the desire to avoid thinking about the self (what they call the "escape from consciousness") is an essential component of a variety of self-defeating behaviors. Their approach is based on the idea that consciousness involves *self-awareness*, the process of thinking about and examining the self. Normally we enjoy being self-aware, as we reflect on our relationships with others, our goals, and our achievements. But if we have a setback or a problem, or if we behave in a way that we determine is inappropriate or immoral, we may feel stupid, embarrassed, or unlovable. In these cases self-awareness may become burdensome. And even if nothing particularly bad is happening at the moment, self-awareness may still feel unpleasant because we have fears about what might happen to us or about mistakes that we might make in the future.

Baumeister argues that when self-awareness becomes unpleasant, the need to forget about the negative aspects of the self may become so strong that we turn to altered states of consciousness. Baumeister believes that in these cases we escape the self by narrowing our focus of attention to a particular action or activity, which prevents us from having to think about ourselves and the implications of various events for our self-concept.

Baumeister has analyzed a variety of self-defeating behaviors in terms of the desire to escape consciousness. Perhaps most obvious is suicide—the ultimate self-defeating behavior and the ultimate solution for escaping the negative aspects of self-consciousness. People who commit suicide are normally depressed and isolated. They feel bad about themselves, and suicide is a relief from the negative aspects of self-reflection. Suicidal behavior is often preceded by a period of narrow and rigid cognitive functioning that serves as an escape from the very negative view of the self brought on by recent setbacks or traumas (Baumeister, 1990).[90]

Alcohol abuse may also accomplish an escape from self-awareness by physically interfering with cognitive functioning, making it more difficult to recall the aspects of our self-consciousness (Steele & Josephs, 1990).[91] And cigarette smoking may appeal to people as a low-level distractor that helps them to escape self-awareness. Heatherton and Baumeister (1991)[92] argued that binge eating is another way of escaping from consciousness. Binge eaters, including those who suffer from bulimia nervosa, have unusually high standards for the self, including success, achievement, popularity, and body thinness. As a result they find it difficult to live up to these standards. Because these individuals evaluate themselves according to demanding criteria, they will tend to fall short periodically. Becoming focused on eating, according to Heatherton and Baumeister, is a way to focus only on one particular activity and to forget the broader, negative aspects of the self.

The removal of self-awareness has also been depicted as the essential part of the appeal of masochism, in which people engage in bondage and other aspects of submission. Masochists are frequently tied up using ropes, scarves, neckties, stockings, handcuffs, and gags, and the outcome is that they no longer feel that they are in control of themselves, which relieves them from the burdens of the self (Baumeister, 1991).[93]

Newman and Baumeister (1996)[94] have argued that even the belief that one has been abducted by aliens may be driven by the need to escape everyday consciousness. Every day at least several hundred (and more likely several thousand) Americans claim that they are abducted by these aliens, although most of these stories occur after the individuals have consulted with a psychotherapist or someone else who believes in alien abduction. Again, Baumeister and his colleagues have found a number of indications that people who believe that they have been abducted may be using the belief as a way of escaping self-consciousness.

KEY TAKEAWAYS

- Hypnosis is a trance-like state of conscious consisting of heightened susceptibility, deep relaxation, and intense focus.
- Hypnosis is not useful for helping people remember past events, but it can be used to alleviate anxiety and pain.
- Sensory deprivation is the intentional reduction of stimulation to one or more of the senses. It can be used therapeutically to treat insomnia, muscle tension, and pain.
- Meditation refers to a range of techniques that can create relaxation and well-being.

EXERCISES AND CRITICAL THINKING

1. Do you think that you would be a good candidate for hypnosis? Why or why not?
2. Try the meditation exercise in this section for three consecutive days. Do you feel any different when or after you meditate?

4. CHAPTER SUMMARY

Consciousness is our subjective awareness of ourselves and our environment.

Consciousness is functional because we use it to reason logically, to plan activities, and to monitor our progress toward the goals we set for ourselves.

Consciousness has been central to many theories of psychology. Freud's personality theories differentiated between the unconscious and the conscious aspects of behavior, and present-day psychologists distinguish between automatic (unconscious) and controlled (conscious) behaviors and between implicit (unconscious) and explicit (conscious) cognitive processes.

The French philosopher René Descartes (1596–1650) was a proponent of dualism, the idea that the mind, a nonmaterial entity, is separate from (although connected to) the physical body. In contrast to the dualists, psychologists believe the consciousness (and thus the mind) exists in the brain, not separate from it.

The behavior of organisms is influenced by biological rhythms, including the daily circadian rhythms that guide the waking and sleeping cycle in many animals.

Sleep researchers have found that sleeping people undergo a fairly consistent pattern of sleep stages, each lasting about 90 minutes. Each of the sleep stages has its own distinct pattern of brain activity. Rapid eye movement (REM) accounts for about 25% of our total sleep time, during which we dream. Non-rapid eye movement (non-REM) sleep is a deep sleep characterized by very slow brain waves, and is further subdivided into three stages: stages N1, N2, and N3.

Sleep has a vital restorative function, and a prolonged lack of sleep results in increased anxiety, diminished performance, and if severe and extended, even death. Sleep deprivation suppresses immune responses that fight off infection, and can lead to obesity, hypertension, and memory impairment.

Some people suffer from sleep disorders, including insomnia, sleep apnea, narcolepsy, sleepwalking, and REM sleep behavior disorder.

Freud believed that the primary function of dreams was wish fulfillment, and he differentiated between the manifest and latent content of dreams. Other theories of dreaming propose that we dream primarily to help with consolidation—the moving of information into long-term memory. The activation-synthesis theory of dreaming proposes that dreams are simply our brain's interpretation of the random firing of neurons in the brain stem.

Psychoactive drugs are chemicals that change our states of consciousness, and particularly our perceptions and moods. The use (especially in combination) of psychoactive drugs has the potential to create very negative side effects, including tolerance, dependence, withdrawal symptoms, and addiction.

Stimulants, including caffeine, nicotine, cocaine, and amphetamine, are psychoactive drugs that operate by blocking the reuptake of dopamine, norepinephrine, and serotonin in the synapses of the central nervous system (CNS). Some amphetamines, such as Ecstasy, have very low safety ratios and thus are highly dangerous.

Depressants, including alcohol, barbiturates, benzodiazepines, and toxic inhalants, reduce the activity of the CNS. They are widely used as prescription medicines to relieve pain, to lower heart rate and respiration, and as anticonvulsants. Toxic inhalants are some of the most dangerous recreational drugs, with a safety index below 10, and their continued use may lead to permanent brain damage.

Opioids, including opium, morphine, heroin, and codeine, are chemicals that increase activity in opioid receptor neurons in the brain and in the digestive system, producing euphoria, analgesia, slower breathing, and constipation.

Hallucinogens, including cannabis, mescaline, and LSD, are psychoactive drugs that alter sensation and perception and which may create hallucinations.

Even when we know the potential costs of using drugs, we may engage in using them anyway because the rewards from using the drugs are occurring right now, whereas the potential costs are abstract and only in the future. And drugs are not the only things we enjoy or can abuse. It is normal to refer to the abuse of other behaviors, such as gambling, sex, overeating, and even overworking as "addictions" to describe the overuse of pleasant stimuli.

Hypnosis is a trance-like state of consciousness, usually induced by a procedure known as hypnotic induction, which consists of heightened suggestibility, deep relaxation, and intense focus. Hypnosis also is frequently used to attempt to change unwanted behaviors, such as to reduce smoking, eating, and alcohol abuse.

Sensory deprivation is the intentional reduction of stimuli affecting one or more of the five senses, with the possibility of resulting changes in consciousness. Although sensory deprivation is used for relaxation or meditation purposes and to produce enjoyable changes in consciousness, when deprivation is prolonged, it is unpleasant and can be used as a means of torture.

Meditation refers to techniques in which the individual focuses on something specific, such as an object, a word, or one's breathing, with the goal of ignoring external distractions. Meditation has a variety of positive health effects.

ENDNOTES

1. Martin, L. (2009). Can sleepwalking be a murder defense? *Sleep Disorders: For Patients and Their Families*. Retrieved from http://www.lakesidepress.com/pulmonary/Sleep/sleep-murder.htm

2. Broughton, R. J., Billings, R., Cartwright, R., & Doucette, D. (1994). Homicidal somnambulism: A case report. *Sleep: Journal of Sleep Research & Sleep Medicine, 17*(3), 253–264.

3. Wilson, C. (1998). *The mammoth book of true crime*. New York, NY: Robinson Publishing.

4. Koch, C. (2004). *The quest for consciousness: A neurobiological approach*. Englewood, CO: Roberts & Co.

5. Petty, R., Wegener, D., Chaiken, S., & Trope, Y. (1999). Dual-process theories in social psychology. New York, NY: Guilford Press; Shanks, D. (2005). Implicit learning. In K. Lamberts (Ed.), *Handbook of cognition* (pp. 202–220). London, England: Sage.

6. Dennett, D. C. (1991). *Consciousness explained*. Boston, MA: Little, Brown and Company; Koch, C., & Greenfield, S. (2007). How does consciousness happen? *Scientific American*, 76–83.

7. Libet, B. (1999). Do we have free will? *Journal of Consciousness Studies, 6, 8*(9), 47–57; Wegner, D. M. (2003). The mind's best trick: How we experience conscious will. *Trends in Cognitive Sciences, 7*(2), 65–69.

8. DeWall, C., Baumeister, R., & Masicampo, E. (2008). Evidence that logical reasoning depends on conscious processing. *Consciousness and Cognition, 17*(3), 628.

9. Baumeister, R. (1998). The self. In *The handbook of social psychology* (4th ed., Vol. 2, pp. 680–740). New York, NY: McGraw-Hill.

10. McGinniss, P. (2007). Seasonal affective disorder (SAD)—Treatment and drugs. Mayo Clinic. Retrieved from http://www.mayoclinic.com/health/seasonal-affective-disorder/DS00195/DSECTION=treatments%2Dand%2Ddrugs

11. Bodenhausen, G. V. (1990). Stereotypes as judgmental heuristics: Evidence of circadian variations in discrimination. *Psychological Science, 1*, 319–322.

12. Hobson, A. (2004). A model for madness? Dream consciousness: Our understanding of the neurobiology of sleep offers insight into abnormalities in the waking brain. *Nature, 430*, 69–95.

13. Dement, W., & Kleitman, N. (1957). Cyclic variations in EEG during sleep. *Electroencephalography & Clinical Neurophysiology, 9*, 673–690.

14. National Sleep Foundation. (2009). *Sleep in America Poll*. Washington, DC: Author. Retrieved from http://www.sleepfoundation.org/sites/default/files/2009%20Sleep%20in%20America%2SOF%20EMBARGOED.pdf

15. Morgenthaler, T. I., Kagramanov, V., Hanak, V., & Decker, P. A. (2006). Complex sleep apnea syndrome: Is it a unique clinical syndrome? *Sleep, 29*(9), 1203–1209. Retrieved from http://www.journalsleep.org/ViewAbstract.aspx?pid=26630

16. Yaggi, H. K., Concato, J., Kernan, W. N., Lichtman, J. H., Brass, L. M., & Mohsenin, V. (2005). Obstructive sleep apnea as a risk factor for stroke and death. *The New England Journal of Medicine, 353*(19), 2034–2041. doi:10.1056/NEJMoa043104

17. National Heart, Lung, and Blood Institute. (2008). Who is at risk for narcolepsy? Retrieved from http://www.nhlbi.nih.gov/health/dci/Diseases/nar/nar_who.html

18. Taheri, S., Zeitzer, J. M., & Mignot, E. (2002). The role of hypocretins (Orexins) in sleep regulation and narcolepsy. *Annual Review of Neuroscience, 25*, 283–313.

19. Mahowald, M., & Schenck, C. (2000). REM sleep parasomnias. *Principles and Practice of Sleep Medicine*, 724–741.

20. Mahowald, M., & Schenck, C. (2000). REM sleep parasomnias. *Principles and Practice of Sleep Medicine*, 724–741.

21. Mahowald, M., & Schenck, C. (2000). REM sleep parasomnias. *Principles and Practice of Sleep Medicine*, 724–741.

22. Mahowald, M., & Schenck, C. (2005). REM sleep behavior disorder. *Handbook of Clinical Neurophysiology, 6*, 245–253.

23. Mercer, P., Merritt, S., & Cowell, J. (1998). Differences in reported sleep need among adolescents. *Journal of Adolescent Health, 23*(5), 259–263; National Sleep Foundation. (2008). *Sleep in America Poll*. Washington, DC: Author. Retrieved from http://www.sleepfoundation.org/sites/default/files/2008%20POLL%20SOF.PDF

24. Hack, M. A., Choi, S. J., Vijayapalan, P., Davies, R. J. O., & Stradling, J. R. S. (2001). Comparison of the effects of sleep deprivation, alcohol and obstructive sleep apnoea (OSA) on simulated steering performance. *Respiratory medicine, 95*(7), 594–601; Williamson, A., & Feyer, A. (2000). Moderate sleep deprivation produces impairments in cognitive and motor performance equivalent to legally prescribed levels of alcohol intoxication. *Occupational and Environmental Medicine, 57*(10), 649.

25. Smith-Coggins, R., Rosekind, M. R., Hurd, S., & Buccino, K. R. (1994). Relationship of day versus night sleep to physician performance and mood. *Annals of Emergency Medicine, 24*(5), 928–934.

26. Ferrie, J. E., Shipley, M. J., Cappuccio, F. P., Brunner, E., Miller, M. A., Kumari, M., & Marmot, M. G. (2007). A prospective study of change in sleep duration: Associations with mortality in the Whitehall II cohort. *Sleep, 30*(12), 1659; Kushida, C. (2005). *Sleep deprivation: basic science, physiology, and behavior*. London, England: Informa Healthcare.

27. Dew, M. A., Hoch, C. C., Buysse, D. J., Monk, T. H., Begley, A. E., Houck, P. R.,...Reynolds, C. F., III. (2003). Healthy older adults' sleep predicts all-cause mortality at 4 to 19 years of follow-up. *Psychosomatic Medicine, 65*(1), 63–73.

28. Dement, W. (1997) What all undergraduates should know about how their sleeping lives affect their waking lives. *Sleepless at Stanford*. Retrieved from http://www.Stanford.edu/~dement/sleepless.html

29. Cartwright, R., Agargun, M., Kirkby, J., & Friedman, J. (2006). Relation of dreams to waking concerns. *Psychiatry Research, 141*(3), 261–270; Domhoff, G. W., Meyer-Gomes, K., & Schredl, M. (2005). Dreams as the expression of conceptions and concerns: A comparison of German and American college students. *Imagination, Cognition and Personality, 25*(3), 269–282.

30. Freud, S., & Classics of Medicine Library. (1988). *The interpretation of dreams* (Special ed.). Birmingham, AL: The Classics of Medicine Library. (Original work published 1913)

31. Alvarenga, T. A., Patti, C. L., Andersen, M. L., Silva, R. H., Calzavara, M. B., Lopez, G.B.,...Tufik, S. (2008). Paradoxical sleep deprivation impairs acquisition, consolidation and retrieval of a discriminative avoidance task in rats. *Neurobiology of Learning and Memory, 90*, 624–632; Zhang, J. (2004). Memory process and the function of sleep. *Journal of Theoretics, 6*(6), 1–7.

32. Rauchs, G., Desgranges, B., Foret, J., & Eustache, F. (2005). The relationships between memory systems and sleep stages. *Journal of Sleep Research, 14*, 123–140.

33. Payne, J., & Nadel, L. (2004). Sleep, dreams, and memory consolidation: The role of the stress hormone cortisol. *Learning & Memory, 11*(6), 671.

34. Hobson, J. A., Pace-Schott, E. F., & Stickgold, R. (2000). Dreaming and the brain: Toward a cognitive neuroscience of conscious states. *Behavioral and Brain Sciences, 23*(6), 793–842, 904–1018, 1083–1121.

35. Hobson, J. A., & McCarley, R. (1977). The brain as a dream state generator: An activation-synthesis hypothesis of the dream process. *American Journal of Psychiatry, 134*, 1335–1348; Hobson, J. A. (2004). *Dreams Freud never had: A new mind science*. New York, NY: Pi Press.

36. Robinson, T. E., & Berridge, K. C. (2003). Addiction. *Annual Review of Psychology, 54*, 25–53; Wagner, F. A., & Anthony, J. C. (2002). From first drug use to drug dependence: Developmental periods of risk for dependence upon marijuana, cocaine, and alcohol. *Neuropsychopharmacology, 26*(4), 479–488.

37. Robins, L. N., Davis, D. H., & Goodwin, D. W. (1974). Drug use by U.S. Army enlisted men in Vietnam: A follow-up on their return home. *American Journal of Epidemiology, 99*, 235–249.

38. McCance-Katz, E., Kosten, T., & Jatlow, P. (1998). Concurrent use of cocaine and alcohol is more potent and potentially more toxic than use of either alone—A multiple-dose study 1. *Biological Psychiatry, 44*(4), 250–259.

39. Lovett, R. (2005, September 24). Coffee: The demon drink? *New Scientist, 2518*. Retrieved from http://www.newscientist.com/article.ns?id=mg18725181.700

40. U.S. Food and Drug Administration. (2007). Medicines in my home: Caffeine and your body. Retrieved from http://www.fda.gov/downloads/Drugs/ResourcesForYou/Consumers/BuyingUsingMedicineSafely/UnderstandingOver-the-CounterMedicines/UCM205286.pdf

41. National Institute on Drug Abuse. (2009). *Cocaine abuse and addiction*. Retrieved from http://www.nida.nih.gov/researchreports/cocaine/cocaine.html

42. Csaky, T. Z., & Barnes, B. A. (1984). *Cutting's handbook of pharmacology* (7th ed.). East Norwalk, CT: Appleton-Century-Crofts.

43. Csaky, T. Z., & Barnes, B. A. (1984). *Cutting's handbook of pharmacology* (7th ed.). East Norwalk, CT: Appleton-Century-Crofts.

44. Abbey, A., Ross, L. T., McDuffie, D., & McAuslan, P. (1996). Alcohol and dating risk factors for sexual assault among college women. *Psychology of Women Quarterly, 20*(1), 147–169.

45. Bushman, B. J. (1993). Human aggression while under the influence of alcohol and other drugs: An integrative research review. *Current Directions in Psychological Science, 2*(5), 148–152; Bushman, B. J. (Ed.). (1997). *Effects of alcohol on human aggression: Validity of proposed explanations*. New York, NY: Plenum Press; Graham, K., Osgood, D. W., Wells, S., & Stockwell, T. (2006). To what extent is intoxication associated with aggression in bars? A multilevel analysis. *Journal of Studies on Alcohol, 67*(3), 382–390.

46. Steele, C. M., & Southwick, L. (1985). Alcohol and social behavior: I. The psychology of drunken excess. *Journal of Personality and Social Psychology, 48*(1), 18–34.

47. Bushman, B. J., & Cooper, H. M. (1990). Effects of alcohol on human aggression: An integrative research review. *Psychological Bulletin, 107*(3), 341–354.

48. Medline Plus. (2008). *Barbiturate intoxication and overdose*. Retrieved from http://www.nlm.nih.gov/medlineplus/ency/article/000951.htm

49. Ben Amar, M. (2006). Cannabinoids in medicine: A review of their therapeutic potential. *Journal of Ethnopharmacology, 105*, 1–25.

50. National Institute on Drug Abuse. (2009). NIDA InfoFacts: High School and Youth Trends. Retrieved from http://www.drugabuse.gov/infofacts/HSYouthTrends.html

51. Lejuez, C. W., Aklin, W. M., Bornovalova, M. A., & Moolchan, E. T. (2005). Differences in risk-taking propensity across inner-city adolescent ever- and never-smokers. *Nicotine & Tobacco Research, 7*(1), 71–79.

52. Lejuez, C. W., Read, J. P., Kahler, C. W., Richards, J. B., Ramsey, S. E., Stuart, G. L.,...Brown, R. A. (2002). Evaluation of a behavioral measure of risk taking: The Balloon Analogue Risk Task (BART). *Journal of Experimental Psychology: Applied, 8*(2), 75–85.

53. Vaughan, E. L., Corbin, W. R., & Fromme, K. (2009). Academic and social motives and drinking behavior. *Psychology of Addictive Behaviors. 23*(4), 564–576.

54. Johnston, L. D., O'Malley, P. M., Bachman, J. G., & Schulenberg, J. E. (2004). *Monitoring the future: National results on adolescent drug use*. Ann Arbor, MI: Institute for Social Research, University of Michigan (conducted for the National Institute on Drug Abuse, National Institute of Health).

55. Johnston, L. D., O'Malley, P. M., Bachman, J. G., & Schulenberg, J. E. (2004). *Monitoring the future: National results on adolescent drug use*. Ann Arbor, MI: Institute for Social

Research, University of Michigan (conducted for the National Institute on Drug Abuse, National Institute of Health).

56. Clapp, J., Reed, M., Holmes, M., Lange, J., & Voas, R. (2006). Drunk in public, drunk in private: The relationship between college students, drinking environments and alcohol consumption. *The American Journal of Drug and Alcohol Abuse, 32*(2), 275–285.

57. Lynskey, M. T., Heath, A. C., Bucholz, K. K., Slutske, W. S., Madden, P. A. F., Nelson, E. C.,…Martin, N. G. (2003). Escalation of drug use in early-onset cannabis users vs co-twin controls. *Journal of the American Medical Association, 289*(4), 427–433.

58. Hammond, D. C. (2008). Hypnosis as sole anesthesia for major surgeries: Historical & contemporary perspectives. *American Journal of Clinical Hypnosis, 51*(2), 101–121.

59. Callahan, J. (1997). Hypnosis: Trick or treatment? You'd be amazed at what modern doctors are tackling with an 18th century gimmick. *Health, 11,* 52–55.

60. Nash, M., & Barnier, A. (2008). *The Oxford handbook of hypnosis: Theory, research and practice*: New York, NY: Oxford University Press.

61. Baker, E. L., & Nash, M. R. (2008). Psychoanalytic approaches to clinical hypnosis. In M. R. Nash & A. J. Barnier (Eds.), *The Oxford handbook of hypnosis: Theory, research, and practice* (pp. 439–456). New York, NY: Oxford University Press.

62. Hilgard, E. R. (1965). *Hypnotic susceptibility*. New York, NY: Harcourt, Brace & World.

63. Spiegel, H., Greenleaf, M., & Spiegel, D. (2005). Hypnosis. In B. J. Sadock & V. A. Sadock (Eds.), *Kaplan & Sadock's comprehensive textbook of psychiatry*. Philadelphia, PA: Lippincott Williams & Wilkins.

64. Spanos, N. P. (1991). A sociocognitive approach to hypnosis. In S. J. Lynn & J. W. Rhue (Eds.), *Theories of hypnosis: Current models and perspectives,* New York, NY: Guilford Press.

65. Fassler, O., Lynn, S. J., Knox, J. (2008). Is hypnotic suggestibility a stable trait? *Consciousness and Cognition: An International Journal. 17*(1), 240–253.

66. Kinnunen, T., Zamansky, H. S., & Block, M. L. (1994). Is the hypnotized subject lying? *Journal of Abnormal Psychology, 103,* 184–191.

67. Jamieson, G. A., & Hasegawa, H. (2007). New paradigms of hypnosis research. Hypnosis and conscious states: The cognitive neuroscience perspective. In G.A. Jamieson (Ed.), *Hypnosis and conscious states: The cognitive neuroscience perspective* (pp. 133–144). New York, NY: Oxford University Press.

68. Kirsch, I., & Braffman, W. (2001). Imaginative suggestibility and hypnotizability. *Current Directions in Psychological Science. 10*(2), 57–61.

69. Orne, M. T., & Evans, F. J. (1965). Social control in the psychological experiment: Antisocial behavior and hypnosis. *Journal of Personality and Social Psychology, 1*(3), 189–200.

70. Hilgard, E. R., & Cooper, L. M. (1965). Spontaneous and suggested posthypnotic amnesia. *International Journal of Clinical and Experimental Hypnosis, 13*(4), 261–273.

71. Silverman, P. S., & Retzlaff, P. D. (1986). Cognitive stage regression through hypnosis: Are earlier cognitive stages retrievable? *International Journal of Clinical and Experimental Hypnosis, 34*(3), 192–204.

72. Newman, L. S., & Baumeister, R. F. (1996). Toward an explanation of the UFO abduction phenomenon: Hypnotic elaboration, extraterrestrial sadomasochism, and spurious memories. *Psychological Inquiry, 7*(2), 99–126.

73. Kirsch, I., Montgomery, G., & Sapirstein, G. (1995). Hypnosis as an adjunct to cognitive-behavioral psychotherapy: A meta-analysis. *Journal of Consulting and Clinical Psychology, 63*(2), 214–220.

74. Elkins, G., & Perfect, M. (2008). Hypnosis for health-compromising behaviors. In M. Nash & A. Barnier (Eds.), *The Oxford handbook of hypnosis: Theory, research and practice* (pp. 569–591). New York, NY: Oxford University Press.

75. Cardena, E. (2000). Hypnosis in the treatment of trauma: A promising, but not fully supported, efficacious intervention. *International Journal of Clinical Experimental Hypnosis, 48,* 225–238; Montgomery, G. H., David, D., Winkel, G., Silverstein, J. H., & Bovbjerg, D. H. (2002). The effectiveness of adjunctive hypnosis with surgical patients: A meta-analysis. *Anesthesia and Analgesia, 94*(6), 1639–1645.

76. Montgomery, G. H., DuHamel, K. N., & Redd, W. H. (2000). A meta-analysis of hypnotically induced analgesia: How effective is hypnosis? *International Journal of Clinical and Experimental Hypnosis, 48*(2), 138–153; Patterson, D. R., & Jensen, M. P. (2003). Hypnosis and clinical pain. *Psychological Bulletin, 129*(4), 495–521.

77. Suedfeld, P. (1990b). Restricted environmental stimulation techniques in health enhancement and disease prevention. In K. D. Craig & S. M. Weiss (Eds.), *Health enhancement, disease prevention, and early intervention: Biobehavioral perspectives* (pp. 206–230). New York, NY: Springer Publishing; Bood, S. Å., Sundequist, U., Kjellgren, A., Nordström, G., & Norlander, T. (2007). Effects of flotation rest (restricted environmental stimulation technique) on stress related muscle pain: Are 33 flotation sessions more effective than 12 sessions? *Social Behavior and Personality, 35*(2), 143–156; Kjellgren, A., Sundequist, U., Norlander, T., & Archer, T. (2001). Effects of flotation-REST on muscle tension pain. *Pain Research & Management, 6*(4), 181–189.

78. Wallbaum, A. B., Rzewnicki, R., Steele, H., & Suedfeld, P. (1991). Progressive muscle relaxation and restricted environmental stimulation therapy for chronic tension headache: A pilot study. *International Journal of Psychosomatics. 38*(1–4), 33–39.

79. Suedfeld, P. (1990a). Restricted environmental stimulation and smoking cessation: A 15-year progress report. *International Journal of the Addictions. 25*(8), 861–888.

80. Yuksel, F. V., Kisa, C, Aydemir, C., & Goka, E. (2004). Sensory deprivation and disorders of perception. *The Canadian Journal of Psychiatry, 49*(12), 867–868.

81. Benjamin, M. (2006). The CIA's favorite form of torture. Retrieved from http://www.salon.com/news/feature/2007/06/07/sensory_deprivation/print.html

82. Cahn, B., & Polich, J. (2006). Meditation states and traits: EEG, ERP, and neuroimaging studies. *Psychological Bulletin, 132,* 180–211.

83. Dillbeck, M. C., Cavanaugh, K. L., Glenn, T., & Orme-Johnson, D. W. (1987). Consciousness as a field: The Transcendental Meditation and TM-Sidhi program and changes in social indicators. *Journal of Mind and Behavior. 8*(1), 67–103; Fenwick, P. (1987). Meditation and the EEG. The psychology of meditation. In M.A. West (Ed.), *The psychology of meditation* (pp. 104–117). New York, NY: Clarendon Press/Oxford University Press.

84. Grossman, P., Niemann, L., Schmidt, S., & Walach, H. (2004). Mindfulness-based stress reduction and health benefits: A meta-analysis. *Journal of Psychosomatic Research. 57*(1), 35–43; Reibel, D. K., Greeson, J. M., Brainard, G. C., & Rosenzweig, S. (2001). Mindfulness-based stress reduction and health-related quality of life in a heterogeneous patient population. *General Hospital Psychiatry, 23*(4), 183–192; Salmon, P., Sephton, S., Weissbecker, I., Hoover, K., Ulmer, C., & Studts, J. L. (2004). Mindfulness mediation in clinical practice. *Cognitive and Behavioral Practice, 11*(4), 434–446.

85. Barnes, V. A., Treiber, F., & Davis, H. (2001). Impact of Transcendental Meditation® on cardiovascular function at rest and during acute stress in adolescents with high normal blood pressure. *Journal of Psychosomatic Research, 51*(4), 597–605; Walton, K. G., Fields, J. Z., Levitsky, D. K., Harris, D. A., Pugh, N. D., & Schneider, R. H. (2004). Lowering cortisol and CVD risk in postmenopausal women: A pilot study using the Transcendental Meditation program. In R. Yehuda & B. McEwen (Eds.), *Biobehavioral stress response: Protective and damaging effects (Annals of the New York Academy of Sciences)* (Vol. 1032, pp. 211–215). New York, NY: New York Academy of Sciences.

86. Lyubimov, N. N. (1992). Electrophysiological characteristics of sensory processing and mobilization of hidden brain reserves. 2nd Russian-Swedish Symposium, New Research in Neurobiology. Moscow, Russia: Russian Academy of Science Institute of Human Brain.

87. Lutz, A., Greischar, L., Rawlings, N., Ricard, M., & Davidson, R. (2004). Long-term meditators self-induce high-amplitude gamma synchrony during mental practice. *Proceedings of the National Academy of Sciences, 101,* 16369–16373.

88. Lutz, A., Greischar, L., Rawlings, N., Ricard, M., & Davidson, R. (2004). Long-term meditators self-induce high-amplitude gamma synchrony during mental practice. *Proceedings of the National Academy of Sciences, 101,* 16369–16373.

89. Baumeister, R. F. (1991). *Escaping the self: Alcoholism, spirituality, masochism, and other flights from the burden of selfhood.* New York, NY: Basic Books.

90. Baumeister, R. (1990). Suicide as escape from self. *Psychological Review, 97*(1), 90–113.

91. Steele, C., & Josephs, R. (1990). Alcohol myopia: Its prized and dangerous effects. *American Psychologist, 45*(8), 921–933.

92. Heatherton, T., & Baumeister, R. (1991). Binge eating as escape from self-awareness. *Psychological Bulletin, 110*(1), 86–108.

93. Baumeister, R. F. (1991). *Escaping the self: Alcoholism, spirituality, masochism, and other flights from the burden of selfhood.* New York, NY: Basic Books.

94. Newman, L. S., & Baumeister, R. F. (1996). Toward an explanation of the UFO abduction phenomenon: Hypnotic elaboration, extraterrestrial sadomasochism, and spurious memories. *Psychological Inquiry, 7*(2), 99–126.

CHAPTER 6
Growing and Developing

The Repository for Germinal Choice

During the 1970s, American millionaire Robert Klark Graham began one of the most controversial and unique sperm banks in the world. He called it the Repository for Germinal Choice. The sperm bank was part of a project that attempted to combat the "genetic decay" Graham saw all around him. He believed human reproduction was experiencing a genetic decline, making for a population of "retrograde humans," and he was convinced that the way to save the human race was to breed the best genes of his generation (Plotz, 2001).[1]

Graham began his project by collecting sperm samples from the most intelligent and highly achieving people he could find, including scientists, entrepreneurs, athletes, and even Nobel Prize winners. Then he advertised for potential mothers, who were required to be married to infertile men, educated, and financially well-off. Graham mailed out catalogs to the potential mothers, describing the donors using code names such as "Mr. Grey-White," who was "ruggedly handsome, outgoing, and positive, a university professor, expert marksman who enjoys the classics," and "Mr. Fuchsia," who was an "Olympic gold medalist, tall, dark, handsome, bright, a successful businessman and author" (Plotz, 2001).[2] When the mother had made her choice, the sperm sample was delivered by courier and insemination was carried out at home. Before it closed following Graham's death in 1999, the repository claimed responsibility for the birth of 228 children.

But did Graham's project actually create superintelligent babies? Although it is difficult to be sure, because very few interviews with the offspring have been permitted, at least some of the repository's progeny are indeed smart. Reporter for *Slate* magazine David Plotz (2001)[3] spoke to nine families who benefited from the repository, and they proudly touted their children's achievements. He found that most of the offspring in the families interviewed seem to resemble their genetic fathers. Three from donor Mr. Fuchsia, the Olympic gold medalist, are reportedly gifted athletes. Several who excel in math and science were fathered by professors of math and science.

And the offspring, by and large, seem to be doing well, often attending excellent schools and maintaining very high grade-point averages. One of the offspring, now 26 years old, is particularly intelligent. In infancy, he could mark the beat of classical music with his hands. In kindergarten, he could read *Hamlet* and was learning algebra, and at age 6, his IQ was already 180. But he refused to apply to prestigious universities, such as Harvard or Yale, opting instead to study at a smaller progressive college and to major in comparative religion, with the aim of becoming an elementary school teacher. He is now an author of children's books.

Although it is difficult to know for sure, it appears that at least some of the children of the repository are indeed outstanding. But can the talents, characteristics, and skills of this small repository sample be attributed to genetics alone? After all, consider the parents of these children: Plotz reported that the parents, particularly the mothers, were highly involved in their children's development and took their parental roles very seriously. Most of the parents studied child care manuals, coached their children's sports teams, practiced reading with their kids, and either home-schooled them or sent them to the best schools in their areas. And the families were financially well-off. Furthermore, the mothers approached the repository at a relatively older child-bearing age, when all other options were exhausted. These children were desperately wanted and very well loved. It is undeniable that, in addition to their genetic backgrounds, all this excellent nurturing played a significant role in the development of the repository children.

Although the existence of the repository provides interesting insight into the potential importance of genetics on child development, the results of Graham's experiment are inconclusive. The offspring interviewed are definitely smart and talented, but only one of them was considered a true genius and child prodigy. And nurture may have played as much a role as nature in their outcomes (Olding, 2006; Plotz, 2001).[4]

development

The physiological, behavioral, cognitive, and social changes that occur throughout human life, which are guided by both genetic predispositions (nature) and by environmental influences (nurture).

infancy

The developmental stage from birth to 1 year of age.

childhood

The developmental period from infancy to the onset of puberty.

adolescence

The years between the onset of puberty and the beginning of adulthood.

adulthood

The stage of life after adolescence, including emerging, early, middle, and older adulthood.

The goal of this chapter is to investigate the fundamental, complex, and essential process of human development. **Development** refers to *the physiological, behavioral, cognitive, and social changes that occur throughout human life, which are guided by both genetic predispositions (nature) and by environmental influences (nurture).* We will begin our study of development at the moment of conception, when the father's sperm unites with the mother's egg, and then consider prenatal development in the womb. Next we will focus on **infancy**, *the developmental stage that begins at birth and continues to one year of age*, and **childhood**, *the period between infancy and the onset of puberty*. Finally, we will consider the developmental changes that occur during **adolescence**—*the years between the onset of puberty and the beginning of adulthood*; the stages of **adulthood** itself, including *emerging, early, middle*, and *older adulthood*; and finally, the preparations for and eventual facing of death.

Each of the stages of development has its unique physical, cognitive, and emotional changes that define the stage and that make each stage unique, one from the other. The psychologist and psychoanalyst Erik Erikson (1963, p. 202)[5] proposed a model of life-span development that provides a useful guideline for thinking about the changes we experience throughout life. As you can see in Table 6.1, Erikson believed that each life stage has a unique challenge that the person who reaches it must face. And according to Erikson, successful development involves dealing with and resolving the goals and demands of each of the life stages in a positive way.

TABLE 6.1 Challenges of Development as Proposed by Erik Erikson

Stage	Age range	Key challenge	Positive resolution of challenge
Oral-sensory	Birth to 12 to 18 months	Trust versus mistrust	The child develops a feeling of trust in his or her caregivers.
Muscular-anal	18 months to 3 years	Autonomy versus shame/doubt	The child learns what he or she can and cannot control and develops a sense of free will.
Locomotor	3 to 6 years	Initiative versus guilt	The child learns to become independent by exploring, manipulating, and taking action.
Latency	6 to 12 years	Industry versus inferiority	The child learns to do things well or correctly according to standards set by others, particularly in school.
Adolescence	12 to 18 years	Identity versus role confusion	The adolescent develops a well-defined and positive sense of self in relationship to others.
Young adulthood	19 to 40 years	Intimacy versus isolation	The person develops the ability to give and receive love and to make long-term commitments.
Middle adulthood	40 to 65 years	Generativity versus stagnation	The person develops an interest in guiding the development of the next generation, often by becoming a parent.
Late adulthood	65 to death	Ego integrity versus despair	The person develops acceptance of his or her life as it was lived.

Source: Adapted from Erikson, E. H. (1963). Childhood and society. New York, NY: Norton (p. 202).

As we progress through this chapter, we will see that Robert Klark Graham was in part right—nature does play a substantial role in development (it has been found, for instance, that identical twins, who share all of their genetic code, usually begin sitting up and walking on the exact same days). But nurture is also important—we begin to be influenced by our environments even while still in the womb, and these influences remain with us throughout our development. Furthermore, we will see that we play an active role in shaping our own lives. Our own behavior influences how and what we learn, how people respond to us, and how we develop as individuals. As you read the chapter, you will no doubt get a broader view of how we each pass through our own lives. You will see how we learn and adapt to life's changes, and this new knowledge may help you better understand and better guide your own personal life journey.

1.   CONCEPTION AND PRENATAL DEVELOPMENT

L E A R N I N G   O B J E C T I V E S

1. **Review the stages of prenatal development.**
2. **Explain how the developing embryo and fetus may be harmed by the presence of teratogens and describe what a mother can do to reduce her risk.**

Conception occurs when an egg from the mother is fertilized by a sperm from the father. In humans, the conception process begins with **ovulation**, *when an ovum, or egg (the largest cell in the human body), which has been stored in one of the mother's two ovaries, matures and is released into the fallopian tube.* Ovulation occurs about halfway through the woman's menstrual cycle and is aided by the release of a complex combination of hormones. In addition to helping the egg mature, the hormones also cause the lining of the uterus to grow thicker and more suitable for implantation of a fertilized egg.

If the woman has had sexual intercourse within 1 or 2 days of the egg's maturation, one of the up to 500 million sperm deposited by the man's ejaculation, which are traveling up the fallopian tube, may fertilize the egg. Although few of the sperm are able to make the long journey, some of the strongest swimmers succeed in meeting the egg. As the sperm reach the egg in the fallopian tube, they release enzymes that attack the outer jellylike protective coating of the egg, each trying to be the first to enter. As soon as one of the millions of sperm enters the egg's coating, the egg immediately responds by both blocking out all other challengers and at the same time pulling in the single successful sperm.

ovulation

The process whereby an egg stored in the woman's ovaries matures and is released into the fallopian tube.

1.1   The Zygote

Within several hours, half of the 23 chromosomes from the egg and half of the 23 chromosomes from the sperm fuse together, creating a **zygote**—*a fertilized ovum.* The zygote continues to travel down the fallopian tube to the uterus. Although the uterus is only about 4 inches away in the woman's body, this is nevertheless a substantial journey for a microscopic organism, and fewer than half of zygotes survive beyond this earliest stage of life. If the zygote is still viable when it completes the journey, it will attach itself to the wall of the uterus, but if it is not, it will be flushed out in the woman's menstrual flow. During this time, the cells in the zygote continue to divide: The original two cells become four, those four become eight, and so on, until there are thousands (and eventually trillions) of cells. Soon the cells begin to *differentiate*, each taking on a separate function. The earliest differentiation is between the cells on the inside of the zygote, which will begin to form the developing human being, and the cells on the outside, which will form the protective environment that will provide support for the new life throughout the pregnancy.

zygote

The product of an egg and sperm that merge together during conception.

1.2   The Embryo

Once the zygote attaches to the wall of the uterus, it is known as the **embryo**. During the embryonic phase, which will last for the next 6 weeks, the major internal and external organs are formed, each beginning at the microscopic level, with only a few cells. The changes in the embryo's appearance will continue rapidly from this point until birth.

embryo

The status of a zygote once it is implanted in the uterine wall.

While the inner layer of embryonic cells is busy forming the embryo itself, the outer layer is forming the surrounding protective environment that will help the embryo survive the pregnancy. This environment consists of three major structures: The **amniotic sac** is *the fluid-filled reservoir in which the embryo (soon to be known as a fetus) will live until birth, and which acts as both a cushion against outside pressure and as a temperature regulator*. The **placenta** is *an organ that allows the exchange of nutrients between the embryo and the mother, while at the same time filtering out harmful material*. The filtering occurs through a thin membrane that separates the mother's blood from the blood of the fetus, allowing them to share only the material that is able to pass through the filter. Finally, the **umbilical cord** *links the embryo directly to the placenta and transfers all material to the fetus*. Thus the placenta and the umbilical cord protect the fetus from many foreign agents in the mother's system that might otherwise pose a threat.

1.3   The Fetus

Beginning in the 9th week after conception, the embryo becomes a **fetus**. The defining characteristic of the fetal stage is growth. All the major aspects of the growing organism have been formed in the embryonic phase, and now the fetus has approximately six months to go from weighing less than an ounce to weighing an average of 6 to 8 pounds. That's quite a growth spurt.

The fetus begins to take on many of the characteristics of a human being, including moving (by the 3rd month the fetus is able to curl and open its fingers, form fists, and wiggle its toes), sleeping, as well as early forms of swallowing and breathing. The fetus begins to develop its senses, becoming able to distinguish tastes and respond to sounds. Research has found that the fetus even develops some initial preferences. A newborn prefers the mother's voice to that of a stranger, the languages heard in the womb over other languages (DeCasper & Fifer, 1980; Moon, Cooper, & Fifer, 1993),[6] and even the kinds of foods that the mother ate during the pregnancy (Mennella, Jagnow, & Beauchamp, 2001).[7] By the end of the 3rd month of pregnancy, the sexual organs are visible.

1.4   How the Environment Can Affect the Vulnerable Fetus

Prenatal development is a complicated process and may not always go as planned. About 45% of pregnancies result in a miscarriage, often without the mother ever being aware it has occurred (Moore & Persaud, 1993).[8] Although the amniotic sac and the placenta are designed to protect the embryo, *substances that can harm the fetus*, known as **teratogens**, may nevertheless cause problems. Teratogens include general environmental factors, such as air pollution and radiation, but also the cigarettes, alcohol, and drugs that the mother may use. Teratogens do not always harm the fetus, but they are more likely to do so when they occur in larger amounts, for longer time periods, and during the more sensitive phases, as when the fetus is growing most rapidly. The most vulnerable period for many of the fetal organs is very early in the pregnancy—before the mother even knows she is pregnant.

Harmful substances that the mother ingests may harm the child. Cigarette smoking, for example, reduces the blood oxygen for both the mother and child and can cause a fetus to be born severely underweight. Another serious threat is **fetal alcohol syndrome (FAS)**, *a condition caused by maternal alcohol drinking that can lead to numerous detrimental developmental effects, including limb and facial abnormalities, genital anomalies, and mental retardation*. One in about every 500 babies in the United States is born with fetal alcohol syndrome, and it is considered one of the leading causes of retardation in the world today (Niccols, 1994).[9] Because there is no known safe level of alcohol consumption for a pregnant woman, the U.S. Centers for Disease Control and Prevention indicates that "a pregnant woman should not drink alcohol" (Centers for Disease Control and Prevention, 2005).[10] Therefore, the best approach for expectant mothers is to avoid alcohol completely. Maternal drug abuse is also of major concern and is considered one of the greatest risk factors facing unborn children.

---

amniotic sac

Acting as a cushion as well as a temperature regulator, it is the fluid-filled reservoir in which the fetus lives until birth.

placenta

The organ that allows the exchange of nutrients between the fetus and the mother, while at the same time filtering out harmful material.

umbilical cord

A cord that links the embryo directly to the placenta and transfers all material to the embryo from the mother.

fetus

The stage of the embryo from 9 weeks after conception to birth. The defining aspect of the fetal stage is growth.

teratogens

Any harmful material that can bypass the filter in the placenta and pass from the mother to the fetus.

fetal alcohol syndrome (FAS)

The detrimental effect of large amounts of maternal alcohol consumption on fetal development.

The environment in which the mother is living also has a major impact on infant development (Duncan & Brooks-Gunn, 2000; Haber & Toro, 2004).[11] Children born into homelessness or poverty are more likely to have mothers who are malnourished, who suffer from domestic violence, stress, and other psychological problems, and who smoke or abuse drugs. And children born into poverty are also more likely to be exposed to teratogens. Poverty's impact may also amplify other issues, creating substantial problems for healthy child development (Evans & English, 2002; Gunnar & Quevedo, 2007).[12]

Mothers normally receive genetic and blood tests during the first months of pregnancy to determine the health of the embryo or fetus. They may undergo sonogram, ultrasound, amniocentesis, or other testing. The screenings detect potential birth defects, including neural tube defects, chromosomal abnormalities (such as Down syndrome), genetic diseases, and other potentially dangerous conditions. Early diagnosis of prenatal problems can allow medical treatment to improve the health of the fetus.

FIGURE 6.1

Prenatal screenings, including a sonogram, help detect potential birth defects and other potentially dangerous conditions.

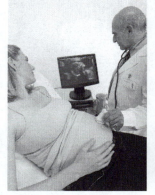

© *Thinkstock*

KEY TAKEAWAYS

- Development begins at the moment of conception, when the sperm from the father merges with the egg from the mother.
- Within a span of 9 months, development progresses from a single cell into a zygote and then into an embryo and fetus.
- The fetus is connected to the mother through the umbilical cord and the placenta, which allow the fetus and mother to exchange nourishment and waste. The fetus is protected by the amniotic sac.
- The embryo and fetus are vulnerable and may be harmed by the presence of teratogens.
- Smoking, alcohol use, and drug use are all likely to be harmful to the developing embryo or fetus, and the mother should entirely refrain from these behaviors during pregnancy or if she expects to become pregnant.
- Environmental factors, especially homelessness and poverty, have a substantial negative effect on healthy child development.

EXERCISES AND CRITICAL THINKING

1. What behaviors must a woman avoid engaging in when she decides to try to become pregnant, or when she finds out she is pregnant? Do you think the ability of a mother to engage in healthy behaviors should influence her choice to have a child?
2. Given the negative effects of poverty on human development, what steps do you think that societies should take to try to reduce poverty?

2. INFANCY AND CHILDHOOD: EXPLORING AND LEARNING

LEARNING OBJECTIVES

1. Describe the abilities that newborn infants possess and how they actively interact with their environments.
2. List the stages in Piaget's model of cognitive development and explain the concepts that are mastered in each stage
3. Critique Piaget's theory of cognitive development and describe other theories that complement and expand on it.
4. Summarize the important processes of social development that occur in infancy and childhood.

If all has gone well, a baby is born sometime around the 38th week of pregnancy. The fetus is responsible, at least in part, for its own birth because chemicals released by the developing fetal brain trigger the muscles in the mother's uterus to start the rhythmic contractions of childbirth. The contractions are initially spaced at about 15-minute intervals but come more rapidly with time. When the contractions reach an interval of 2 to 3 minutes, the mother is requested to assist in the labor and help push the baby out.

2.1 The Newborn Arrives With Many Behaviors Intact

Newborns are already prepared to face the new world they are about to experience. As you can see in Table 6.2, babies are equipped with a variety of reflexes, each providing an ability that will help them survive their first few months of life as they continue to learn new routines to help them survive in and manipulate their environments.

TABLE 6.2 Survival Reflexes in Newborns

Name	Stimulus	Response	Significance
Rooting reflex	The baby's cheek is stroked.	The baby turns its head toward the stroking, opens its mouth, and tries to suck.	Ensures the infant's feeding will be a reflexive habit

View the video online at: http://www.youtube.com/embed/GDQmakJmHfM

Blink reflex	A light is flashed in the baby's eyes.	The baby closes both eyes.	Protects eyes from strong and potentially dangerous stimuli

View the video online at: http://www.youtube.com/embed/glYohCKsBxl

Withdrawal reflex	A soft pinprick is applied to the sole of the baby's foot.	The baby flexes the leg.	Keeps the exploring infant away from painful stimuli

View the video online at: http://www.youtube.com/embed/ZpDUPDU-5jg

Tonic neck reflex	The baby is laid down on its back.	The baby turns its head to one side and extends the arm on the same side.	Helps develop hand-eye coordination

Name	Stimulus	Response	Significance
	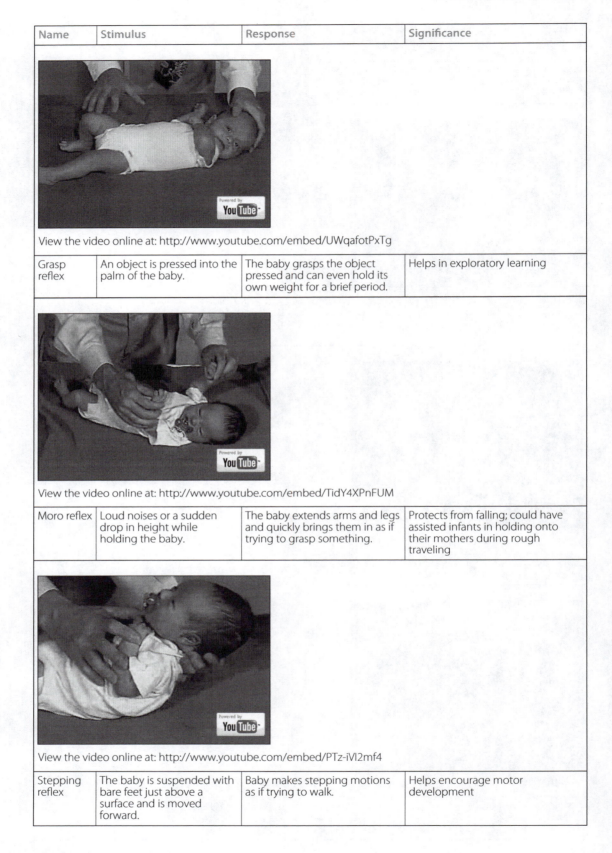 View the video online at: http://www.youtube.com/embed/UWqafotPxTg		
Grasp reflex	An object is pressed into the palm of the baby.	The baby grasps the object pressed and can even hold its own weight for a brief period.	Helps in exploratory learning
	View the video online at: http://www.youtube.com/embed/TidY4XPnFUM		
Moro reflex	Loud noises or a sudden drop in height while holding the baby.	The baby extends arms and legs and quickly brings them in as if trying to grasp something.	Protects from falling; could have assisted infants in holding onto their mothers during rough traveling
	View the video online at: http://www.youtube.com/embed/PTz-iVl2mf4		
Stepping reflex	The baby is suspended with bare feet just above a surface and is moved forward.	Baby makes stepping motions as if trying to walk.	Helps encourage motor development

Name	Stimulus	Response	Significance

View the video online at: http://www.youtube.com/embed/CkGjOwPXsvo

In addition to reflexes, newborns have preferences—they like sweet tasting foods at first, while becoming more open to salty items by 4 months of age (Beauchamp, Cowart, Menellia, & Marsh, 1994; Blass & Smith, 1992).[13] Newborns also prefer the smell of their mothers. An infant only 6 days old is significantly more likely to turn toward its own mother's breast pad than to the breast pad of another baby's mother (Porter, Makin, Davis, & Christensen, 1992),[14] and a newborn also shows a preference for the face of its own mother (Bushnell, Sai, & Mullin, 1989).[15]

Although infants are born ready to engage in some activities, they also contribute to their own development through their own behaviors. The child's knowledge and abilities increase as it babbles, talks, crawls, tastes, grasps, plays, and interacts with the objects in the environment (Gibson, Rosenzweig, & Porter, 1988; Gibson & Pick, 2000; Smith & Thelen, 2003).[16] Parents may help in this process by providing a variety of activities and experiences for the child. Research has found that animals raised in environments with more novel objects and that engage in a variety of stimulating activities have more brain synapses and larger cerebral cortexes, and they perform better on a variety of learning tasks compared with animals raised in more impoverished environments (Juraska, Henderson, & Müller, 1984).[17] Similar effects are likely occurring in children who have opportunities to play, explore, and interact with their environments (Soska, Adolph, & Johnson, 2010).[18]

Research Focus: Using the Habituation Technique to Study What Infants Know

It may seem to you that babies have little ability to view, hear, understand, or remember the world around them. Indeed, the famous psychologist William James presumed that the newborn experiences a "blooming, buzzing confusion" (James, 1890, p. 462).[19] And you may think that, even if babies do know more than James gave them credit for, it might not be possible to find out what they know. After all, infants can't talk or respond to questions, so how would we ever find out? But over the past two decades, developmental psychologists have created new ways to determine what babies know, and they have found that they know much more than you, or William James, might have expected.

One way that we can learn about the cognitive development of babies is by measuring their behavior in response to the stimuli around them. For instance, some researchers have given babies the chance to control which shapes they get to see or which sounds they get to hear according to how hard they suck on a pacifier (Trehub & Rabinovitch, 1972).[20] The sucking behavior is used as a measure of the infants' interest in the stimuli—the sounds or images they suck hardest in response to are the ones we can assume they prefer.

Another approach to understanding cognitive development by observing the behavior of infants is through the use of the habituation technique. **Habituation** refers to *the decreased responsiveness toward a stimulus after it has been presented numerous times in succession.* Organisms, including infants, tend to be more interested in things the first few times they experience them and become less interested in them with more frequent exposure. Developmental psychologists have used this general principle to help them understand what babies remember and understand.

In the **habituation procedure**, a baby is placed in a high chair and presented with visual stimuli while a video camera records the infant's eye and face movements. When the experiment begins, a stimulus (e.g., the face of an adult) appears in the baby's field of view, and the amount of time the baby looks at the face is recorded by the camera. Then the stimulus is removed for a few seconds before it appears again and the gaze is again measured. Over time, the baby starts to habituate to the face, such that each presentation elicits less

habituation

Decreased responsiveness toward a stimulus after it has been presented numerous times in succession.

habituation procedure

A procedure that uses the principles of habituation to allow researchers to infer the cognitive processes of newborns.

gazing at the stimulus. Then, a new stimulus (e.g., the face of a different adult or the same face looking in a different direction) is presented, and the researchers observe whether the gaze time significantly increases. You can see that, if the infant's gaze time increases when a new stimulus is presented, this indicates that the baby can differentiate the two stimuli.

The habituation procedure is used to assess the cognitive abilities of infants.

Source: Photo courtesy of Infant Studies Centre, Department of Psychology, University of British Columbia, http://infantstudies.psych.ubc.ca/research/publications/visual_lang_disc.

Although this procedure is very simple, it allows researchers to create variations that reveal a great deal about a newborn's cognitive ability. The trick is simply to change the stimulus in controlled ways to see if the baby "notices the difference." Research using the habituation procedure has found that babies can notice changes in colors, sounds, and even principles of numbers and physics. For instance, in one experiment reported by Karen Wynn (1995),[21] 6-month-old babies were shown a presentation of a puppet that repeatedly jumped up and down either two or three times, resting for a couple of seconds between sequences (the length of time and the speed of the jumping were controlled). After the infants habituated to this display, the presentation was changed such that the puppet jumped a different number of times. As you can see in Figure 6.3, the infants' gaze time increased when Wynn changed the presentation, suggesting that the infants could tell the difference between the number of jumps.

Can Infants Do Math?

Karen Wynn found that babies that had habituated to a puppet jumping either two or three times significantly increased their gaze when the puppet began to jump a different number of times.

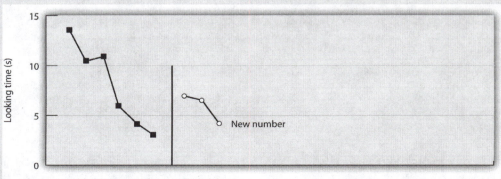

Source: Adapted from Wynn, K. (1995). Infants possess a system of numerical knowledge. Current Directions in Psychological Science, 4, 172–176.

2.2 Cognitive Development During Childhood

Childhood is a time in which changes occur quickly. The child is growing physically, and cognitive abilities are also developing. During this time the child learns to actively manipulate and control the environment, and is first exposed to the requirements of society, particularly the need to control the bladder and bowels. According to Erik Erikson, the challenges that the child must attain in childhood relate to the development of *initiative*, *competence*, and *independence*. Children need to learn to explore the world, to become self-reliant, and to make their own way in the environment.

These skills do not come overnight. Neurological changes during childhood provide children the ability to do some things at certain ages, and yet make it impossible for them to do other things. This fact was made apparent through the groundbreaking work of the Swiss psychologist Jean Piaget. During the 1920s, Piaget was administering intelligence tests to children in an attempt to determine the kinds of logical thinking that children were capable of. In the process of testing the children, Piaget became intrigued, not so much by the answers that the children got right, but more by the answers they got wrong. Piaget believed that the incorrect answers that the children gave were not mere shots in the dark but rather represented specific ways of thinking unique to the children's developmental stage. Just as almost all babies learn to roll over before they learn to sit up by themselves, and learn to crawl before they learn to walk, Piaget believed that children gain their cognitive ability in a developmental order. These insights—that children at different ages think in fundamentally different ways—led to Piaget's *stage model of cognitive development*.

Piaget argued that children do not just passively learn but also actively try to make sense of their worlds. He argued that, as they learn and mature, children develop **schemas**—*patterns of knowledge in long-term memory*—*that help them remember, organize, and respond to information*. Furthermore, Piaget thought that when children experience new things, they attempt to reconcile the new knowledge with existing schemas. Piaget believed that the children use two distinct methods in doing so, methods that he called *assimilation* and *accommodation* (see Figure 6.5).

FIGURE 6.4

Jean Piaget developed his theories of child development by observing the behaviors of children.

Source: Photo courtesy of mirjoran, http://www.flickr.com/photos/mirjoran/455878802.

schema

A pattern of knowledge in long-term memory that helps us organize information.

FIGURE 6.5 Assimilation and Accommodation

assimilation

The use of an already developed schema to understand new information.

accommodation

The change of an existing schema on the basis of new information.

When children employ **assimilation**, they *use already developed schemas to understand new information*. If children have learned a schema for horses, then they may call the striped animal they see at the zoo a horse rather than a zebra. In this case, children fit the existing schema to the new information and label the new information with the existing knowledge. **Accommodation**, on the other hand, involves *learning new information, and thus changing the schema*. When a mother says, "No, honey, that's a zebra, not a horse," the child may adapt the schema to fit the new stimulus, learning that there are different types of four-legged animals, only one of which is a horse.

Piaget's most important contribution to understanding cognitive development, and the fundamental aspect of his theory, was the idea that development occurs in unique and distinct stages, with each stage occurring at a specific time, in a sequential manner, and in a way that allows the child to think about the world using new capacities. Piaget's stages of cognitive development are summarized in Table 6.3.

TABLE 6.3 Piaget's Stages of Cognitive Development

Stage	Approximate age range	Characteristics	Stage attainments
Sensorimotor	Birth to about 2 years	The child experiences the world through the fundamental senses of seeing, hearing, touching, and tasting.	Object permanence
Preoperational	2 to 7 years	Children acquire the ability to internally represent the world through language and mental imagery. They also start to see the world from other people's perspectives.	Theory of mind; rapid increase in language ability
Concrete operational	7 to 11 years	Children become able to think logically. They can increasingly perform operations on objects that are only imagined.	Conservation
Formal operational	11 years to adulthood	Adolescents can think systematically, can reason about abstract concepts, and can understand ethics and scientific reasoning.	Abstract logic

sensorimotor stage

A stage of Piaget's model of cognitive development, lasting from birth to age 2, in which the baby perceives the environment through the senses and motor skills.

object permanence

The ability to be aware of an object's existence even when it is not visible.

The first developmental stage for Piaget was the **sensorimotor stage**, *the cognitive stage that begins at birth and lasts until around the age of 2. It is defined by the direct physical interactions that babies have with the objects around them.* During this stage, babies form their first schemas by using their primary senses—they stare at, listen to, reach for, hold, shake, and taste the things in their environments.

During the sensorimotor stage, babies' use of their senses to perceive the world is so central to their understanding that whenever babies do not directly perceive objects, as far as they are concerned, the objects do not exist. Piaget found, for instance, that if he first interested babies in a toy and then covered the toy with a blanket, children who were younger than 6 months of age would act as if the toy had disappeared completely—they never tried to find it under the blanket but would nevertheless smile and reach for it when the blanket was removed. Piaget found that it was not until about 8 months that the children realized that the object was merely covered and not gone. Piaget used the term **object permanence** to refer to *the child's ability to know that an object exists even when the object cannot be perceived*.

 Video Clip: Object Permanence

Children younger than about 8 months of age do not understand object permanence.

View the video online at: http://www.youtube.com/embed/nwXd7WyWNHY

At about 2 years of age, and until about 7 years of age, children move into the **preoperational stage**. During this stage, *children begin to use language and to think more abstractly about objects, but their understanding is more intuitive and without much ability to deduce or reason.* The thinking is preoperational, meaning that the child lacks the ability to operate on or transform objects mentally. In one study that showed the extent of this inability, Judy DeLoache (1987)[22] showed children a room within a small dollhouse. Inside the room, a small toy was visible behind a small couch. The researchers took the children to another lab room, which was an exact replica of the dollhouse room, but full-sized. When children who were 2.5 years old were asked to find the toy, they did not know where to look—they were simply unable to make the transition across the changes in room size. Three-year-old children, on the other hand, immediately looked for the toy behind the couch, demonstrating that they were improving their operational skills.

The inability of young children to view transitions also leads them to be *egocentric*—unable to readily see and understand other people's viewpoints. Developmental psychologists define the **theory of mind** as *the ability to take another person's viewpoint*, and the ability to do so increases rapidly during the preoperational stage. In one demonstration of the development of theory of mind, a researcher shows a child a video of another child (let's call her Anna) putting a ball in a red box. Then Anna leaves the room, and the video shows that while she is gone, a researcher moves the ball from the red box into a blue box. As the video continues, Anna comes back into the room. The child is then asked to point to the box where Anna will probably look to find her ball. Children who are younger than 4 years of age typically are unable to understand that Anna does not know that the ball has been moved, and they predict that she will look for it in the blue box. After 4 years of age, however, children have developed a theory of mind—they realize that different people can have different viewpoints, and that (although she will be wrong) Anna will nevertheless think that the ball is still in the red box.

After about 7 years of age, the child moves into the **concrete operational stage**, which is *marked by more frequent and more accurate use of transitions, operations, and abstract concepts, including those of time, space, and numbers.* An important milestone during the concrete operational stage is the development of **conservation**—*the understanding that changes in the form of an object do not necessarily mean changes in the quantity of the object.* Children younger than 7 years generally think that a glass of milk that is tall holds more milk than a glass of milk that is shorter and wider, and they continue to believe this even when they see the same milk poured back and forth between the glasses. It appears that these children focus only on one dimension (in this case, the height of the glass) and ignore the other dimension (width). However, when children reach the concrete operational stage, their abilities to understand such transformations make them aware that, although the milk looks different in the different glasses, the amount must be the same.

Video Clip: Conservation

Children younger than about 7 years of age do not understand the principles of conservation.

View the video online at: http://youtu.be/YtLEWVu815o

At about 11 years of age, children enter the **formal operational stage**, which is *marked by the ability to think in abstract terms and to use scientific and philosophical lines of thought.* Children in the formal operational stage are better able to systematically test alternative ideas to determine their influences on outcomes. For instance, rather than haphazardly changing different aspects of a situation that allows no clear conclusions to be drawn, they systematically make changes in one thing at a time and observe what difference that particular change makes. They learn to use deductive reasoning, such as "if this, then that," and they become capable of imagining situations that "might be," rather than just those that actually exist.

preoperational stage

A stage of Piaget's cognitive development model, lasting from 2 to 7 years of age, in which children become capable of forming mental images.

theory of mind

The ability to take another person's viewpoint.

concrete operational stage

A stage of Piaget's cognitive development model, between ages 7 to 11 years, in which children begin to use concepts of time, space, and numbers more accurately, and are able to use deductive or reversible reasoning.

conservation

The understanding that changes in the form of an object do not necessarily mean changes in the quantity of the object.

formal operational stage

A stage of Piaget's cognitive development model, reached by children 11 years and older, in which they begin to think in abstract terms.

Piaget's theories have made a substantial and lasting contribution to developmental psychology. His contributions include the idea that children are not merely passive receptacles of information but rather actively engage in acquiring new knowledge and making sense of the world around them. This general idea has generated many other theories of cognitive development, each designed to help us better understand the development of the child's information-processing skills (Klahr & McWinney, 1998; Shrager & Siegler, 1998).[23] Furthermore, the extensive research that Piaget's theory has stimulated has generally supported his beliefs about the order in which cognition develops. Piaget's work has also been applied in many domains—for instance, many teachers make use of Piaget's stages to develop educational approaches aimed at the level children are developmentally prepared for (Driscoll, 1994; Levin, Siegler, & Druyan, 1990).[24]

Over the years, Piagetian ideas have been refined. For instance, it is now believed that object permanence develops gradually, rather than more immediately, as a true stage model would predict, and that it can sometimes develop much earlier than Piaget expected. Renée Baillargeon and her colleagues (Baillargeon, 2004; Wang, Baillargeon, & Brueckner, 2004)[25] placed babies in a habituation setup, having them watch as an object was placed behind a screen, entirely hidden from view. The researchers then arranged for the object to reappear from behind another screen in a different place. Babies who saw this pattern of events looked longer at the display than did babies who witnessed the same object physically being moved between the screens. These data suggest that the babies were aware that the object still existed even though it was hidden behind the screen, and thus that they were displaying object permanence as early as 3 months of age, rather than the 8 months that Piaget predicted.

Another factor that might have surprised Piaget is the extent to which a child's social surroundings influence learning. In some cases, children progress to new ways of thinking and retreat to old ones depending on the type of task they are performing, the circumstances they find themselves in, and the nature of the language used to instruct them (Courage & Howe, 2002).[26] And children in different cultures show somewhat different patterns of cognitive development. Dasen (1972)[27] found that children in non-Western cultures moved to the next developmental stage about a year later than did children from Western cultures, and that level of schooling also influenced cognitive development. In short, Piaget's theory probably understated the contribution of environmental factors to social development.

More recent theories (Cole, 1996; Rogoff, 1990; Tomasello, 1999),[28] based in large part on the *sociocultural theory* of the Russian scholar Lev Vygotsky (1962, 1978),[29] argue that cognitive development is not isolated entirely within the child but occurs at least in part through social interactions. These scholars argue that children's thinking develops through constant interactions with more competent others, including parents, peers, and teachers.

An extension of Vygotsky's sociocultural theory is the idea of *community learning*, in which children serve as both teachers and learners. This approach is frequently used in classrooms to improve learning as well as to increase responsibility and respect for others. When children work cooperatively together in groups to learn material, they can help and support each other's learning as well as learn about each other as individuals, thereby reducing prejudice (Aronson, Blaney, Stephan, Sikes, & Snapp, 1978; Brown, 1997).[30]

2.3   Social Development During Childhood

It is through the remarkable increases in cognitive ability that children learn to interact with and understand their environments. But these cognitive skills are only part of the changes that are occurring during childhood. Equally crucial is the development of the child's social skills—the ability to understand, predict, and create bonds with the other people in their environments.

Knowing the Self: The Development of the Self-Concept

One of the important milestones in a child's social development is learning about his or her own self-existence. This self-awareness is known as *consciousness*, and the content of consciousness is known as the *self-concept*. The **self-concept** is *a knowledge representation or schema that contains knowledge about us, including our beliefs about our personality traits, physical characteristics, abilities, values, goals, and roles, as well as the knowledge that we exist as individuals* (Kagan, 1991).[31]

self-concept

A schema that contains knowledge about us, including our beliefs about our personality traits, physical characteristics, abilities, values, goals, and roles.

FIGURE 6.6

A simple test of self-awareness is the ability to recognize oneself in a mirror. Humans and chimpanzees can pass the test; dogs never do.

© Thinkstock

Some animals, including chimpanzees, orangutans, and perhaps dolphins, have at least a primitive sense of self (Boysen & Himes, 1999).[32] In one study (Gallup, 1970),[33] researchers painted a red dot on the foreheads of anesthetized chimpanzees and then placed each animal in a cage with a mirror. When the chimps woke up and looked in the mirror, they touched the dot on their faces, not the dot on the faces in the mirror. These actions suggest that the chimps understood that they were looking at themselves and not at other animals, and thus we can assume that they are able to realize that they exist as individuals. On the other hand, most other animals, including, for instance dogs, cats, and monkeys, never realize that it is they themselves in the mirror.

Infants who have a similar red dot painted on their foreheads recognize themselves in a mirror in the same way that the chimps do, and they do this by about 18 months of age (Povinelli, Landau, & Perilloux, 1996).[34] The child's knowledge about the self continues to develop as the child grows. By age 2, the infant becomes aware of his or her sex, as a boy or a girl. By age 4, self-descriptions are likely to be based on physical features, such as hair color and possessions, and by about age 6, the child is able to understand basic emotions and the concepts of traits, being able to make statements such as, "I am a nice person" (Harter, 1998).[35]

Soon after children enter grade school (at about age 5 or 6), they begin to make comparisons with other children, a process known as *social comparison*. For example, a child might describe himself as being faster than one boy but slower than another (Moretti & Higgins, 1990).[36] According to Erikson, the important component of this process is the development of *competence* and *autonomy*—the recognition of one's own abilities relative to other children. And children increasingly show awareness of social situations—they understand that other people are looking at and judging them the same way that they are looking at and judging others (Doherty, 2009).[37]

Successfully Relating to Others: Attachment

One of the most important behaviors a child must learn is how to be accepted by others—the development of close and meaningful social relationships. *The emotional bonds that we develop with those with whom we feel closest, and particularly the bonds that an infant develops with the mother or primary caregiver,* are referred to as **attachment** (Cassidy & Shaver, 1999).[38]

attachment

The strong need of an infant to be close to the primary caregiver.

FIGURE 6.7

Children develop appropriate attachment styles through their interactions with caregivers.

© Thinkstock

As late as the 1930s, psychologists believed that children who were raised in institutions such as orphanages, and who received good physical care and proper nourishment, would develop normally, even if they had little interaction with their caretakers. But studies by the developmental psychologist John Bowlby (1953)[39] and others showed that these children did not develop normally—they were usually sickly, emotionally slow, and generally unmotivated. These observations helped make it clear that normal infant development requires successful attachment with a caretaker.

In one classic study showing the importance of attachment, Wisconsin University psychologists Harry and Margaret Harlow investigated the responses of young monkeys, separated from their biological mothers, to two surrogate mothers introduced to their cages. One—the wire mother—consisted of a round wooden head, a mesh of cold metal wires, and a bottle of milk from which the baby monkey could drink. The second mother was a foam-rubber form wrapped in a heated terry-cloth blanket. The Harlows found that, although the infant monkeys went to the wire mother for food, they overwhelmingly preferred and spent significantly more time with the warm terry-cloth mother that provided no food but did provide comfort (Harlow, 1958).[40]

 Video Clip: The Harlows' Monkeys

The studies by the Harlows showed that young monkeys preferred the warm mother that provided a secure base to the cold mother that provided food.

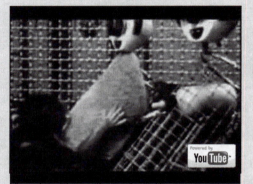

View the video online at: http://www.youtube.com/embed/MmbbfisRiwA

The Harlows' studies confirmed that babies have social as well as physical needs. Both monkeys and human babies need a *secure base* that allows them to feel safe. From this base, they can gain the confidence they need to venture out and explore their worlds. Erikson (Table 6.1) was in agreement on the importance of a secure base, arguing that the most important goal of infancy was the development of a basic sense of trust in one's caregivers.

Developmental psychologist Mary Ainsworth, a student of John Bowlby, was interested in studying the development of attachment in infants. Ainsworth created a laboratory test that measured an infant's attachment to his or her parent. The test is called the **strange situation** because it is *conducted in a context that is unfamiliar to the child and therefore likely to heighten the child's need for his or her parent* (Ainsworth, Blehar, Waters, & Wall, 1978).[41] During the procedure, which lasts about 20 minutes, the parent and the infant are first left alone, while the infant explores the room full of toys. Then a strange adult enters the room and talks for a minute to the parent, after which the parent leaves the room. The stranger stays with the infant for a few minutes, and then the parent again enters and the stranger leaves the room. During the entire session, a video camera records the child's behaviors, which are later coded by trained coders.

strange situation

A measure of attachment in young children in which the child's behaviors are assessed in a situation in which the caregiver and a stranger move in and out of the environment.

Video Clip: The Strange Situation

In the strange situation, children are observed responding to the comings and goings of parents and unfamiliar adults in their environments.

View the video online at: http://www.youtube.com/embed/QTsewNrHUHU

On the basis of their behaviors, the children are categorized into one of four groups, where each group reflects a different kind of attachment relationship with the caregiver. A child with a *secure* attachment style usually explores freely while the mother is present and engages with the stranger. The child may be upset when the mother departs but is also happy to see the mother return. A child with an *ambivalent* (sometimes called *insecure-resistant*) attachment style is wary about the situation in general, particularly the stranger, and stays close or even clings to the mother rather than exploring the toys. When the mother leaves, the child is extremely distressed and is ambivalent when she returns. The child may rush to the mother but then fail to cling to her when she picks up the child. A child with an *avoidant* (sometimes called *insecure-avoidant*) attachment style will avoid or ignore the mother, showing little emotion when the mother departs or returns. The child may run away from the mother when she approaches. The child will not explore very much, regardless of who is there, and the stranger will not be treated much differently from the mother.

Finally, a child with a *disorganized* attachment style seems to have no consistent way of coping with the stress of the strange situation—the child may cry during the separation but avoid the mother when she returns, or the child may approach the mother but then freeze or fall to the floor. Although some cultural differences in attachment styles have been found (Rothbaum, Weisz, Pott, Miyake, & Morelli, 2000),[42] research has also found that the proportion of children who fall into each of the attachment categories is relatively constant across cultures (see Figure 6.8).

FIGURE 6.8 Proportion of Children With Different Attachment Styles

The graph shows the approximate proportion of children who have each of the four attachment styles. These proportions are fairly constant across cultures.

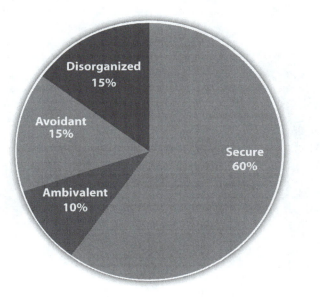

You might wonder whether differences in attachment style are determined more by the child (nature) or more by the parents (nurture). Most developmental psychologists believe that socialization is primary, arguing that a child becomes securely attached when the mother is available and able to meet the needs of the child in a responsive and appropriate manner, but that the insecure styles occur when the mother is insensitive and responds inconsistently to the child's needs. In a direct test of this idea, Dutch researcher Dymphna van den Boom (1994)[43] randomly assigned some babies' mothers to a training session in which they learned to better respond to their children's needs. The research found that these mothers' babies were more likely to show a secure attachment style in comparison to the mothers in a control group that did not receive training.

But the attachment behavior of the child is also likely influenced, at least in part, by **temperament**, *the innate personality characteristics of the infant*. Some children are warm, friendly, and responsive, whereas others tend to be more irritable, less manageable, and difficult to console. These differences may also play a role in attachment (Gillath, Shaver, Baek, & Chun, 2008; Seifer, Schiller, Sameroff, Resnick, & Riordan, 1996).[44] Taken together, it seems safe to say that attachment, like most other developmental processes, is affected by an interplay of genetic and socialization influences.

temperament

The innate personality characteristics of an infant.

longitudinal research design

Research in which individuals are studied over an extended period of time, often over multiple developmental stages.

cross-sectional research design

A research design in which comparisons are made between samples of people at different ages.

cohort effects

Refers to the possibility that differences in cognition or behavior at two points in time may be caused by differences that are unrelated to the changes in age. The differences might instead be due to environmental factors that affect an entire age group.

Research Focus: Using a Longitudinal Research Design to Assess the Stability of Attachment

You might wonder whether the attachment style displayed by infants has much influence later in life. In fact, research has found that the attachment styles of children predict their emotions and their behaviors many years later (Cassidy & Shaver, 1999).[45] Psychologists have studied the persistence of attachment styles over time using **longitudinal research designs**—*research designs in which individuals in the sample are followed and contacted over an extended period of time, often over multiple developmental stages*.

In one such study, Waters, Merrick, Treboux, Crowell, and Albersheim (2000)[46] examined the extent of stability and change in attachment patterns from infancy to early adulthood. In their research, 60 middle-class infants who had been tested in the strange situation at 1 year of age were recontacted 20 years later and interviewed using a measure of adult attachment. Waters and colleagues found that 72% of the infants received the same secure versus insecure attachment classification in early adulthood as they had received as infants. The adults who changed categorization (usually from secure to insecure) were primarily those who had experienced traumatic events, such as the death or divorce of parents, severe illnesses (contracted by the parents or the children themselves), or physical or sexual abuse by a family member.

In addition to finding that people generally display the same attachment style over time, longitudinal studies have also found that the attachment classification received in infancy (as assessed using the strange situation or other measures) predicts many childhood and adult behaviors. Securely attached infants have closer, more harmonious relationship with peers, are less anxious and aggressive, and are better able to understand others' emotions than are those who were categorized as insecure as infants (Lucas-Thompson & Clarke-Stewart, (2007).[47] And securely attached adolescents also have more positive peer and romantic relationships than their less securely attached counterparts (Carlson, Sroufe, & Egeland, 2004).[48]

Conducting longitudinal research is a very difficult task, but one that has substantial rewards. When the sample is large enough and the time frame long enough, the potential findings of such a study can provide rich and important information about how people change over time and the causes of those changes. The drawbacks of longitudinal studies include the cost and the difficulty of finding a large sample that can be tracked accurately over time and the time (many years) that it takes to get the data. In addition, because the results are delayed over an extended period, the research questions posed at the beginning of the study may become less relevant over time as the research continues.

Cross-sectional research designs represent an alternative to longitudinal designs. In a **cross-sectional research design**, *age comparisons are made between samples of different people at different ages at one time*. In one example, Jang, Livesley, and Vernon (1996)[49] studied two groups of identical and nonidentical (fraternal) twins, one group in their 20s and the other group in their 50s, to determine the influence of genetics on personality. They found that genetics played a more significant role in the older group of twins, suggesting that genetics became more significant for personality in later adulthood.

Cross-sectional studies have a major advantage in that the scientist does not have to wait for years to pass to get results. On the other hand, the interpretation of the results in a cross-sectional study is not as clear as those from a longitudinal study, in which the same individuals are studied over time. Most important, the interpretations drawn from cross-sectional studies may be confounded by *cohort effects*. **Cohort effects** refer to *the possibility that differences in cognition or behavior at two points in time may be caused by differences that are unrelated to the changes in age. The differences might instead be due to environmental factors that affect an entire age group*. For instance, in the study by Jang, Livesley, and Vernon (1996)[50] that compared younger and older twins, cohort effects might be a problem. The two groups of adults necessarily grew up in different time periods, and they may have been differentially influenced by societal experiences, such as economic hardship, the presence of wars, or the introduction of new technology. As a result, it is difficult in cross-sectional studies such as this one to determine whether the differences between the groups (e.g., in terms of the relative roles of environment and genetics) are due to age or to other factors.

KEY TAKEAWAYS

- Babies are born with a variety of skills and abilities that contribute to their survival, and they also actively learn by engaging with their environments.
- The habituation technique is used to demonstrate the newborn's ability to remember and learn from experience.
- Children use both assimilation and accommodation to develop functioning schemas of the world.
- Piaget's theory of cognitive development proposes that children develop in a specific series of sequential stages: sensorimotor, preoperational, concrete operational, and formal operational.
- Piaget's theories have had a major impact, but they have also been critiqued and expanded.
- Social development requires the development of a secure base from which children feel free to explore. Attachment styles refer to the security of this base and more generally to the type of relationship that people, and especially children, develop with those who are important to them.
- Longitudinal and cross-sectional studies are each used to test hypotheses about development, and each approach has advantages and disadvantages.

EXERCISES AND CRITICAL THINKING

1. Give an example of a situation in which you or someone else might show cognitive assimilation and cognitive accommodation. In what cases do you think each process is most likely to occur?
2. Consider some examples of how Piaget's and Vygotsky's theories of cognitive development might be used by teachers who are teaching young children.
3. Consider the attachment styles of some of your friends in terms of their relationships with their parents and other friends. Do you think their style is secure?

3. ADOLESCENCE: DEVELOPING INDEPENDENCE AND IDENTITY

LEARNING OBJECTIVES

1. **Summarize the physical and cognitive changes that occur for boys and girls during adolescence.**
2. **Explain how adolescents develop a sense of morality and of self-identity.**

Adolescence is defined as the years between the onset of puberty and the beginning of adulthood. In the past, when people were likely to marry in their early 20s or younger, this period might have lasted only 10 years or less—starting roughly between ages 12 and 13 and ending by age 20, at which time the child got a job or went to work on the family farm, married, and started his or her own family. Today, children mature more slowly, move away from home at later ages, and maintain ties with their parents longer. For instance, children may go away to college but still receive financial support from parents, and they may come home on weekends or even to live for extended time periods. Thus the period between puberty and adulthood may well last into the late 20s, merging into adulthood itself. In fact, it is appropriate now to consider the period of adolescence and that of **emerging adulthood** (*the ages between 18 and the middle or late 20s*) together.

During adolescence, the child continues to grow physically, cognitively, and emotionally, changing from a child into an adult. The body grows rapidly in size and the sexual and reproductive organs become fully functional. At the same time, as adolescents develop more advanced patterns of reasoning and a stronger sense of self, they seek to forge their own identities, developing important attachments

emerging adulthood

The ages between 18 years and the middle or late 20s when the adolescent is first becoming an adult.

with people other than their parents. Particularly in Western societies, where the need to forge a new independence is critical (Baumeister & Tice, 1986; Twenge, 2006),[51] this period can be stressful for many children, as it involves new emotions, the need to develop new social relationships, and an increasing sense of responsibility and independence.

Although adolescence can be a time of stress for many teenagers, most of them weather the trials and tribulations successfully. For example, the majority of adolescents experiment with alcohol sometime before high school graduation. Although many will have been drunk at least once, relatively few teenagers will develop long-lasting drinking problems or permit alcohol to adversely affect their school or personal relationships. Similarly, a great many teenagers break the law during adolescence, but very few young people develop criminal careers (Farrington, 1995).[52] These facts do not, however, mean that using drugs or alcohol is a good idea. The use of recreational drugs can have substantial negative consequences, and the likelihood of these problems (including dependence, addiction, and even brain damage) is significantly greater for young adults who begin using drugs at an early age.

3.1   Physical Changes in Adolescence

puberty

A developmental stage in adolescence in which hormonal changes create rapid physical changes in the body.

primary sex characteristics

The organs concerned with reproduction, including the testicles and the penis in boys and the ovaries, uterus, and vagina in girls.

secondary sex characteristics

Physical features that distinguish the two sexes from each other but that are not involved in reproduction.

Adolescence begins with the onset of **puberty**, *a developmental period in which hormonal changes cause rapid physical alterations in the body, culminating in sexual maturity*. Although the timing varies to some degree across cultures, the average age range for reaching puberty is between 9 and 14 years for girls and between 10 and 17 years for boys (Marshall & Tanner, 1986).[53]

Puberty begins when the pituitary gland begins to stimulate the production of the male sex hormone *testosterone* in boys and the female sex hormones *estrogen* and *progesterone* in girls. The release of these sex hormones triggers the development of the **primary sex characteristics**, *the sex organs concerned with reproduction* (Figure 6.9). These changes include the enlargement of the testicles and the penis in boys and the development of the ovaries, uterus, and vagina in girls. In addition, **secondary sex characteristics** (*features that distinguish the two sexes from each other but are not involved in reproduction*) are also developing, such as an enlarged Adam's apple, a deeper voice, and pubic and underarm hair in boys and enlargement of the breasts, hips, and the appearance of pubic and underarm hair in girls (Figure 6.9). The enlargement of breasts is usually the first sign of puberty in girls and, on average, occurs between ages 10 and 12 (Marshall & Tanner, 1986).[54] Boys typically begin to grow facial hair between ages 14 and 16, and both boys and girls experience a rapid growth spurt during this stage. The growth spurt for girls usually occurs earlier than that for boys, with some boys continuing to grow into their 20s.

FIGURE 6.9 Sex Characteristics

Puberty brings dramatic changes in the body, including the development of primary and secondary sex characteristics.

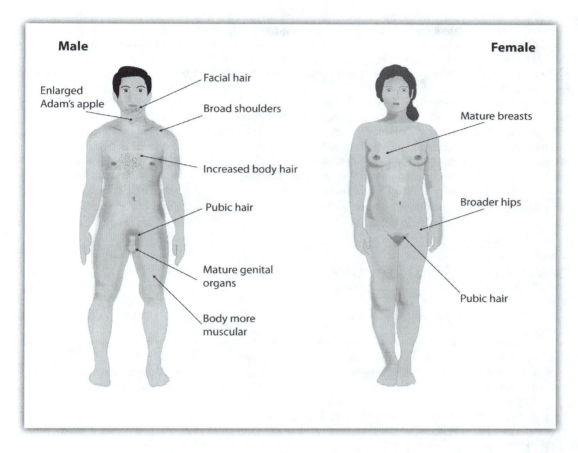

A major milestone in puberty for girls is **menarche**, *the first menstrual period*, typically experienced at around 12 or 13 years of age (Anderson, Dannal, & Must, 2003).[55] The age of menarche varies substantially and is determined by genetics, as well as by diet and lifestyle, since a certain amount of body fat is needed to attain menarche. Girls who are very slim, who engage in strenuous athletic activities, or who are malnourished may begin to menstruate later. Even after menstruation begins, girls whose level of body fat drops below the critical level may stop having their periods. The sequence of events for puberty is more predictable than the age at which they occur. Some girls may begin to grow pubic hair at age 10 but not attain menarche until age 15. In boys, facial hair may not appear until 10 years after the initial onset of puberty.

The timing of puberty in both boys and girls can have significant psychological consequences. Boys who mature earlier attain some social advantages because they are taller and stronger and, therefore, often more popular (Lynne, Graber, Nichols, Brooks-Gunn, & Botvin, 2007).[56] At the same time, however, early-maturing boys are at greater risk for delinquency and are more likely than their peers to engage in antisocial behaviors, including drug and alcohol use, truancy, and precocious sexual activity. Girls who mature early may find their maturity stressful, particularly if they experience teasing or sexual harassment (Mendle, Turkheimer, & Emery, 2007; Pescovitz & Walvoord, 2007).[57] Early-maturing girls are also more likely to have emotional problems, a lower self-image, and higher rates of depression, anxiety, and disordered eating than their peers (Ge, Conger, & Elder, 1996).[58]

menarche

The first menstrual period.

3.2 Cognitive Development in Adolescence

Although the most rapid cognitive changes occur during childhood, the brain continues to develop throughout adolescence, and even into the 20s (Weinberger, Elvevåg, & Giedd, 2005).[59] During adolescence, the brain continues to form new neural connections, but also casts off unused neurons and connections (Blakemore, 2008).[60] As teenagers mature, the prefrontal cortex, the area of the brain responsible for reasoning, planning, and problem solving, also continues to develop (Goldberg, 2001).[61]

And myelin, the fatty tissue that forms around axons and neurons and helps speed transmissions between different regions of the brain, also continues to grow (Rapoport et al., 1999).[62]

Adolescents often seem to act impulsively, rather than thoughtfully, and this may be in part because the development of the prefrontal cortex is, in general, slower than the development of the emotional parts of the brain, including the limbic system (Blakemore, 2008).[63] Furthermore, the hormonal surge that is associated with puberty, which primarily influences emotional responses, may create strong emotions and lead to impulsive behavior. It has been hypothesized that adolescents may engage in risky behavior, such as smoking, drug use, dangerous driving, and unprotected sex in part because they have not yet fully acquired the mental ability to curb impulsive behavior or to make entirely rational judgments (Steinberg, 2007).[64]

The new cognitive abilities that are attained during adolescence may also give rise to new feelings of egocentrism, in which adolescents believe that they can do anything and that they know better than anyone else, including their parents (Elkind, 1978, p. 199).[65] Teenagers are likely to be highly self-conscious, often creating an *imaginary audience* in which they feel that everyone is constantly watching them (Goossens, Beyers, Emmen, & van Aken, 2002).[66] Because teens think so much about themselves, they mistakenly believe that others must be thinking about them, too (Rycek, Stuhr, McDermott, Benker, & Swartz, 1998).[67] It is no wonder that everything a teen's parents do suddenly feels embarrassing to them when they are in public.

3.3 Social Development in Adolescence

Some of the most important changes that occur during adolescence involve the further development of the self-concept and the development of new attachments. Whereas young children are most strongly attached to their parents, the important attachments of adolescents move increasingly away from parents and increasingly toward peers (Harris, 1998).[68] As a result, parents' influence diminishes at this stage.

According to Erikson (Table 6.1), the main social task of the adolescent is the search for a unique identity—the ability to answer the question, "Who am I?" In the search for identity, the adolescent may experience role confusion in which he or she is balancing or choosing among identities, taking on negative or undesirable identities, or temporarily giving up looking for an identity altogether if things are not going well.

One approach to assessing identity development was proposed by James Marcia (1980).[69] In his approach, adolescents are asked questions regarding their exploration of and commitment to issues related to occupation, politics, religion, and sexual behavior. The responses to the questions allow the researchers to classify the adolescent into one of four identity categories (see Table 6.4).

TABLE 6.4 James Marcia's Stages of Identity Development

Identity-diffusion status	The individual does not have firm commitments regarding the issues in question and is not making progress toward them.
Foreclosure status	The individual has not engaged in any identity experimentation and has established an identity based on the choices or values of others.
Moratorium status	The individual is exploring various choices but has not yet made a clear commitment to any of them.
Identity-achievement status	The individual has attained a coherent and committed identity based on personal decisions.

Source: Adapted from Marcia, J. (1980). Identity in adolescence. Handbook of adolescent psychology, 5, 145–160.

FIGURE 6.10

Adolescents search for stable attachments through the development of social identities.

© *Thinkstock*

Studies assessing how teens pass through Marcia's stages show that, although most teens eventually succeed in developing a stable identity, the path to it is not always easy and there are many routes that can be taken. Some teens may simply adopt the beliefs of their parents or the first role that is offered to them, perhaps at the expense of searching for other, more promising possibilities (foreclosure status). Other teens may spend years trying on different possible identities (moratorium status) before finally choosing one.

To help them work through the process of developing an identity, teenagers may well try out different identities in different social situations. They may maintain one identity at home and a different type of persona when they are with their peers. Eventually, most teenagers do integrate the different possibilities into a single self-concept and a comfortable sense of identity (identity-achievement status).

For teenagers, the peer group provides valuable information about the self-concept. For instance, in response to the question "What were you like as a teenager? (e.g., cool, nerdy, awkward?)," posed on the website Answerbag, one teenager replied in this way:

> *I'm still a teenager now, but from 8th–9th grade I didn't really know what I wanted at all. I was smart, so I hung out with the nerdy kids. I still do; my friends mean the world to me. But in the middle of 8th I started hanging out with whom you may call the "cool" kids…and I also hung out with some stoners, just for variety. I pierced various parts of my body and kept my grades up. Now, I'm just trying to find who I am. I'm even doing my sophomore year in China so I can get a better view of what I want. (Answerbag, 2007)[70]*

Responses like this one demonstrate the extent to which adolescents are developing their self-concepts and self-identities and how they rely on peers to help them do that. The writer here is trying out several (perhaps conflicting) identities, and the identities any teen experiments with are defined by the group the person chooses to be a part of. The friendship groups (cliques, crowds, or gangs) that are such an important part of the adolescent experience allow the young adult to try out different identities, and these groups provide a sense of belonging and acceptance (Rubin, Bukowski, & Parker, 2006).[71] A big part of what the adolescent is learning is **social identity**, *the part of the self-concept that is derived from one's group memberships.* Adolescents define their social identities according to how they are similar to and differ from others, finding meaning in the sports, religious, school, gender, and ethnic categories they belong to.

social identity

The part of the self-concept that is derived from one's group memberships.

3.4   Developing Moral Reasoning: Kohlberg's Theory

The independence that comes with adolescence requires independent thinking as well as the development of *morality*—standards of behavior that are generally agreed on within a culture to be right or proper. Just as Piaget believed that children's cognitive development follows specific patterns, Lawrence Kohlberg (1984)[72] argued that children learn their moral values through active thinking and reasoning, and that moral development follows a series of stages. To study moral development, Kohlberg posed moral dilemmas to children, teenagers, and adults, such as the following:

> *A man's wife is dying of cancer and there is only one drug that can save her. The only place to get the drug is at the store of a pharmacist who is known to overcharge people for drugs. The man can only pay $1,000, but the pharmacist wants $2,000, and refuses to sell it to him for less, or to let him pay later. Desperate, the man later breaks into the pharmacy and steals the medicine. Should he have done that? Was it right or wrong? Why? (Kohlberg, 1984)[73]*

Video Clip: People Being Interviewed About Kohlberg's Stages

View the video online at: http://www.youtube.com/embed/zY4etXWYS84

As you can see in Table 6.5, Kohlberg concluded, on the basis of their responses to the moral questions, that, as children develop intellectually, they pass through three stages of moral thinking: the *preconventional level*, the *conventional level*, and the *postconventional level*.

TABLE 6.5 Lawrence Kohlberg's Stages of Moral Reasoning

Age	Moral Stage	Description
Young children	Preconventional morality	Until about the age of 9, children, focus on self-interest. At this stage, punishment is avoided and rewards are sought. A person at this level will argue, "The man shouldn't steal the drug, as he may get caught and go to jail."
Older children, adolescents, most adults	Conventional morality	By early adolescence, the child begins to care about how situational outcomes impact others and wants to please and be accepted. At this developmental phase, people are able to value the good that can be derived from holding to social norms in the form of laws or less formalized rules. For example, a person at this level may say, "He should not steal the drug, as everyone will see him as a thief, and his wife, who needs the drug, wouldn't want to be cured because of thievery," or, "No matter what, he should obey the law because stealing is a crime."
Many adults	Postconventional morality	At this stage, individuals employ abstract reasoning to justify behaviors. Moral behavior is based on self-chosen ethical principles that are generally comprehensive and universal, such as justice, dignity, and equality. Someone with self-chosen principles may say, "The man should steal the drug to cure his wife and then tell the authorities that he has done so. He may have to pay a penalty, but at least he has saved a human life."

Although research has supported Kohlberg's idea that moral reasoning changes from an early emphasis on punishment and social rules and regulations to an emphasis on more general ethical principles, as with Piaget's approach, Kohlberg's stage model is probably too simple. For one, children may use higher levels of reasoning for some types of problems, but revert to lower levels in situations where doing so is more consistent with their goals or beliefs (Rest, 1979).[74] Second, it has been argued that the stage model is particularly appropriate for Western, rather than non-Western, samples in which allegiance to social norms (such as respect for authority) may be particularly important (Haidt, 2001).[75] And there is frequently little correlation between how children score on the moral stages and how they behave in real life.

Perhaps the most important critique of Kohlberg's theory is that it may describe the moral development of boys better than it describes that of girls. Carol Gilligan (1982)[76] has argued that, because of differences in their socialization, males tend to value principles of justice and rights, whereas females value caring for and helping others. Although there is little evidence that boys and girls score differently on Kohlberg's stages of moral development (Turiel, 1998),[77] it is true that girls and women tend to focus more on issues of caring, helping, and connecting with others than do boys and men (Jaffee & Hyde, 2000).[78] If you don't believe this, ask yourself when you last got a thank-you note from a man.

KEY TAKEAWAYS

- Adolescence is the period of time between the onset of puberty and emerging adulthood.
- Emerging adulthood is the period from age 18 years until the mid-20s in which young people begin to form bonds outside the family, attend college, and find work. Even so, they tend not to be fully independent and have not taken on all the responsibilities of adulthood. This stage is most prevalent in Western cultures.
- Puberty is a developmental period in which hormonal changes cause rapid physical alterations in the body.
- The cerebral cortex continues to develop during adolescence and early adulthood, enabling improved reasoning, judgment, impulse control, and long-term planning.
- A defining aspect of adolescence is the development of a consistent and committed self-identity. The process of developing an identity can take time but most adolescents succeed in developing a stable identity.
- Kohlberg's theory proposes that moral reasoning is divided into the following stages: preconventional morality, conventional morality, and postconventional morality.
- Kohlberg's theory of morality has been expanded and challenged, particularly by Gilligan, who has focused on differences in morality between boys and girls.

EXERCISES AND CRITICAL THINKING

1. Based on what you learned in this chapter, do you think that people should be allowed to drive at age 16? Why or why not? At what age do you think they should be allowed to vote and to drink alcohol?
2. Think about your experiences in high school. What sort of cliques or crowds were there? How did people express their identities in these groups? How did you use your groups to define yourself and develop your own identity?

4. EARLY AND MIDDLE ADULTHOOD: BUILDING EFFECTIVE LIVES

LEARNING OBJECTIVE

1. Review the physical and cognitive changes that accompany early and middle adulthood

Until the 1970s, psychologists tended to treat adulthood as a single developmental stage, with few or no distinctions made among the various periods that we pass through between adolescence and death. Present-day psychologists realize, however, that physical, cognitive, and emotional responses continue to develop throughout life, with corresponding changes in our social needs and desires. Thus the three stages of *early adulthood*, *middle adulthood*, and *late adulthood* each has its own physical, cognitive, and social challenges.

In this section, we will consider the development of our cognitive and physical aspects that occur during **early adulthood** and **middle adulthood**—roughly *the ages between 25 and 45 and between 45 and 65, respectively*. These stages represent a long period of time—longer, in fact, than any of the other developmental stages—and the bulk of our lives is spent in them. These are also the periods in which most of us make our most substantial contributions to society, by meeting two of Erik Erikson's life challenges: We learn to give and receive love in a close, long-term relationship, and we develop an interest in guiding the development of the next generation, often by becoming parents.

early adulthood

The ages between 25 and 45.

middle adulthood

The ages between 45 and 65.

parenting style

Parental behaviors that determine the nature of parent-child interactions.

Psychology in Everyday Life: What Makes a Good Parent?

One thing that you may have wondered about as you grew up, and which you may start to think about again if you decide to have children yourself, concerns the skills involved in parenting. Some parents are strict, others are lax; some parents spend a lot of time with their kids, trying to resolve their problems and helping to keep them out of dangerous situations, whereas others leave their children with nannies or in day care. Some parents hug and kiss their kids and say that they love them over and over every day, whereas others never do. Do these behaviors matter? And what makes a "good parent"?

We have already considered two answers to this question, in the form of what all children require: (1) babies need a conscientious mother who does not smoke, drink, or use drugs during her pregnancy, and (2) infants need caretakers who are consistently available, loving, and supportive to help them form a secure base. One case in which these basic goals are less likely to be met is when the mother is an adolescent. Adolescent mothers are more likely to use drugs and alcohol during their pregnancies, to have poor parenting skills in general, and to provide insufficient support for the child (Ekéus, Christensson, & Hjern, 2004).[79] As a result, the babies of adolescent mothers have higher rates of academic failure, delinquency, and incarceration in comparison to children of older mothers (Moore & Brooks-Gunn, 2002).[80]

Normally, it is the mother who provides early attachment, but fathers are not irrelevant. In fact, studies have found that children whose fathers are more involved tend to be more cognitively and socially competent, more empathic, and psychologically better adjusted, compared with children whose fathers are less involved (Rohner & Veneziano, 2001).[81] In fact, Amato (1994)[82] found that, in some cases, the role of the father can be as or even more important than that of the mother in the child's overall psychological health and well-being. Amato concluded, "Regardless of the quality of the mother-child relationship, the closer adult offspring were to their fathers, the happier, more satisfied, and less distressed they reported being" (p. 1039).

As the child grows, parents take on one of four types of **parenting styles**—*parental behaviors that determine the nature of parent-child interactions* and that guide their interaction with the child. These styles depend on whether the parent is more or less *demanding* and more or less *responsive* to the child (see Figure 6.11). *Authoritarian parents* are demanding but not responsive. They impose rules and expect obedience, tending to give orders ("Eat your food!") and enforcing their commands with rewards and punishment, without providing any explanation of where the rules came from, except "Because I said so!" *Permissive parents*, on the other hand, tend to make few demands and give little punishment, but they are responsive in the sense that they generally allow their children to make their own rules. *Authoritative parents* are demanding ("You must be home by curfew"), but they are also responsive to the needs and opinions of the child ("Let's discuss what an appropriate curfew might be"). They set rules and enforce them, but they also explain and discuss the reasons behind the rules. Finally, *rejecting-neglecting parents* are undemanding and unresponsive overall.

Parenting Styles

Parenting styles can be divided into four types, based on the combination of demandingness and responsiveness. The authoritative style, characterized by both responsiveness and also demandingness, is the most effective.

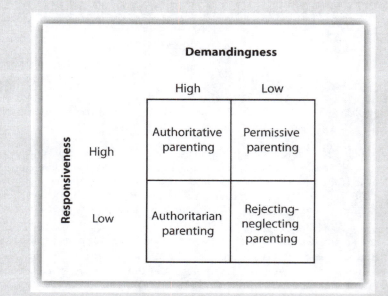

Many studies of children and their parents, using different methods, measures, and samples, have reached the same conclusion—namely, that authoritative parenting, in comparison to the other three styles, is associated with a wide range of psychological and social advantages for children. Parents who use the authoritative style, with its combination of demands on the children as well as responsiveness to the children's needs, have kids who have better psychological adjustment, school performance, and psychosocial maturity, compared with parents who use the other styles (Baumrind, 1996; Grolnick & Ryan, 1989).[83] On the other hand, there are at least some cultural differences in the effectiveness of different parenting styles. Although the reasons for the differences are not completely understood, strict authoritarian parenting styles seem to work better in African American families than in European American families (Tamis-LeMonda, Briggs, McClowry, & Snow, 2008),[84] and better in Chinese families than in American families (Chang, Lansford, Schwartz, & Farver, 2004).[85]

Despite the fact that different parenting styles are differentially effective overall, every child is different and parents must be adaptable. Some children have particularly difficult temperaments, and these children require more parenting. Because these difficult children demand more parenting, the behaviors of the parents matter more for the children's development than they do for other, less demanding children who require less parenting overall (Pleuss & Belsky, 2010).[86] These findings remind us how the behavior of the child can influence the behavior of the people in his or her environment.

Although the focus is on the child, the parents must never forget about each other. Parenting is time consuming and emotionally taxing, and the parents must work together to create a relationship in which both mother and father contribute to the household tasks and support each other. It is also important for the parents to invest time in their own intimacy, as happy parents are more likely to stay together, and divorce has a profoundly negative impact on children, particularly during and immediately after the divorce (Burt, Barnes, McGue, & Iaconon, 2008; Ge, Natsuaki, & Conger, 2006).[87]

4.1 Physical and Cognitive Changes in Early and Middle Adulthood

Compared with the other stages, the physical and cognitive changes that occur in the stages of early and middle adulthood are less dramatic. As individuals pass into their 30s and 40s, their recovery from muscular strain becomes more prolonged, and their sensory abilities may become somewhat diminished, at least when compared with their prime years, during the teens and early 20s (Panno, 2004).[88] Visual acuity diminishes somewhat, and many people in their late 30s and early 40s begin to notice that their eyes are changing and they need eyeglasses. Adults in their 30s and 40s may also begin to suffer some hearing loss because of damage to the hair cells (*cilia*) in the inner ear (Lacher-Fougère & Demany, 2005).[89] And it is during middle adulthood that many people first begin to suffer from ailments such as high cholesterol and high blood pressure as well as low bone density (Shelton, 2006).[90] Corresponding to changes in our physical abilities, our cognitive and sensory abilities also seem to show some, but not dramatic, decline during this stage.

4.2 Menopause

The stages of both early and middle adulthood bring about a gradual decline in fertility, particularly for women. Eventually, women experience **menopause**, *the cessation of the menstrual cycle*, which usually occurs at around age 50. Menopause occurs because of the gradual decrease in the production of the female sex hormones estrogen and progesterone, which slows the production and release of eggs into the uterus. Women whose menstrual cycles have stopped for 12 consecutive months are considered to have entered menopause (Minkin & Wright, 2004).[91]

menopause

The cessation of the menstrual cycle, which usually occurs at around age 50.

Researchers have found that women's responses to menopause are both social as well as physical, and that they vary substantially across both individuals and cultures. Within individuals, some women may react more negatively to menopause, worrying that they have lost their femininity and that their final chance to bear children is over, whereas other women may regard menopause more positively, focusing on the new freedom from menstrual discomfort and unwanted pregnancy. In Western cultures such as in the United States, women are likely to see menopause as a challenging and potentially negative event, whereas in India, where older women enjoy more social privileges than do younger ones, menopause is more positively regarded (Avis & Crawford, 2008).[92]

Menopause may have evolutionary benefits. Infants have better chances of survival when their mothers are younger and have more energy to care for them, and the presence of older women who do not have children of their own to care for (but who can help out with raising grandchildren) can be beneficial to the family group. Also consistent with the idea of an evolutionary benefit of menopause is that the decline in fertility occurs primarily for women, who do most of the child care and who need the energy of youth to accomplish it. If older women were able to have children they might not be as able to effectively care for them. Most men never completely lose their fertility, but they do experience a gradual decrease in testosterone levels, sperm count, and speed of erection and ejaculation.

4.3 Social Changes in Early and Middle Adulthood

Perhaps the major marker of adulthood is the ability to create an effective and independent life. Whereas children and adolescents are generally supported by parents, adults must make their own living and must start their own families. Furthermore, the needs of adults are different from those of younger persons.

Although the timing of the major life events that occur in early and middle adulthood vary substantially across individuals, they nevertheless tend to follow a general sequence, known as a **social clock**. The social clock refers to *the culturally preferred "right time" for major life events, such as moving out of the childhood house, getting married, and having children.* People who do not appear to be following the social clock (e.g., young adults who still live with their parents, individuals who never marry, and couples who choose not to have children) may be seen as unusual or deviant, and they may be stigmatized by others (DePaulo, 2006; Rook, Catalano, & Dooley, 1989).[93]

Although they are doing it later, on average, than they did even 20 or 30 years ago, most people do eventually marry. Marriage is beneficial to the partners, both in terms of mental health and physical health. People who are married report greater life satisfaction than those who are not married and also suffer fewer health problems (Gallagher & Waite, 2001; Liu & Umberson, 2008).[94]

Divorce is more common now than it was 50 years ago. In 2003 almost half of marriages in the United States ended in divorce (Bureau of the Census, 2007),[95] although about three quarters of people who divorce will remarry. Most divorces occur for couples in their 20s, because younger people are frequently not mature enough to make good marriage choices or to make marriages last. Marriages are more successful for older adults and for those with more education (Goodwin, Mosher, & Chandra, 2010).[96]

Parenthood also involves a major and long-lasting commitment, and one that can cause substantial stress on the parents. The time and finances invested in children create stress, which frequently results in decreased marital satisfaction (Twenge, Campbell, & Foster, 2003).[97] This decline is especially true for women, who bear the larger part of the burden of raising the children and taking care of the house, despite the fact they increasingly also work and have careers.

Despite the challenges of early and middle adulthood, the majority of middle-aged adults are not unhappy. These years are often very satisfying, as families have been established, careers have been entered into, and some percentage of life goals has been realized (Eid & Larsen, 2008).[98]

social clock

The culturally preferred "right time" for major life events, such as moving out of the house, getting married, and having children.

KEY TAKEAWAYS

- It is in early and middle adulthood that muscle strength, reaction time, cardiac output, and sensory abilities begin to decline.
- One of the key signs of aging in women is the decline in fertility, culminating in menopause, which is marked by the cessation of the menstrual period.
- The different social stages in adulthood, such as marriage, parenthood, and work, are loosely determined by a social clock, a culturally recognized time for each phase.

EXERCISES AND CRITICAL THINKING

1. Compare your behavior, values, and attitudes regarding marriage and work to the attitudes of your parents and grandparents. In what way are your values similar? In what ways are they different?
2. Draw a timeline of your own planned or preferred social clock. What factors do you think will make it more or less likely that you will be able to follow the timeline?

5. LATE ADULTHOOD: AGING, RETIRING, AND BEREAVEMENT

L E A R N I N G   O B J E C T I V E S

1. Review the physical, cognitive, and social changes that accompany late adulthood.
2. Describe the psychological and physical outcomes of bereavement.

We have seen that, over the course of their lives, most individuals are able to develop secure attachments; reason cognitively, socially and morally; and create families and find appropriate careers. Eventually, however, as people enter into their 60s and beyond, the aging process leads to faster changes in our physical, cognitive, and social capabilities and needs, and life begins to come to its natural conclusion, resulting in *the final life stage, beginning in the 60s*, known as **late adulthood.**

Despite the fact that the body and mind are slowing, most older adults nevertheless maintain an active lifestyle, remain as happy or are happier than when they were younger, and increasingly value their social connections with family and friends (Angner, Ray, Saag, & Allison, 2009).[99] Kennedy, Mather, and Carstensen (2004)[100] found that people's memories of their lives became more positive with age, and Myers and Diener (1996)[101] found that older adults tended to speak more positively about events in their lives, particularly their relationships with friends and family, than did younger adults.

late adulthood

The final stage of life, beginning at about age 65.

5.1   Cognitive Changes During Aging

The changes associated with aging do not affect everyone in the same way, and they do not necessarily interfere with a healthy life. Former Beatles drummer Ringo Starr celebrated his 70th birthday in 2010 by playing at Radio City Music Hall, and Rolling Stones singer Mick Jagger (who once supposedly said, "I'd rather be dead than singing 'Satisfaction' at 45") continues to perform as he pushes 70. The golfer Tom Watson almost won the 2010 British Open golf tournament at the age of 59, playing against competitors in their 20s and 30s. And people such as the financier Warren Buffet, U.S. Senator Frank Lautenberg, and actress Betty White, each in their 80s, all enjoy highly productive and energetic lives.

FIGURE 6.12

Aging does not affect everyone equally. All of these people—in their 60s, 70s, or 80s—still maintain active and productive lives.

Sources: Jagger photo courtesy of Gonzalo Andrés, http://commons.wikimedia.org/wiki/File:Mick_Jagger.jpg. Starr photo courtesy of Tina 63, http://commons.wikimedia.org/wiki/File:Ringo.jpg. Lautenberg-Pascrell photo courtesy of Tony, http://www.flickr.com/photos/tonythemisfit/2551278536. Buffet photo courtesy of Mohammad Bahareth, http://www.flickr.com/photos/mbahareth/3771184817. Watson photo courtesy of Ian Tilbrook, http://commons.wikimedia.org/wiki/File:2008_Open_Championship_-_Tom_Watson.jpg. White photo courtesy of Alan Light, http://www.flickr.com/photos/alan-light/211186811.

Researchers are beginning to better understand the factors that allow some people to age better than others. For one, research has found that the people who are best able to adjust well to changing situations early in life are also able to better adjust later in life (Rubin, 2007; Sroufe, Collins, Egeland, & Carlson, 2009).[102] Perceptions also matter. People who believe that the elderly are sick, vulnerable, and grumpy often act according to such beliefs (Nemmers, 2005),[103] and Levy, Slade, Kunkel, and Kasl (2002)[104] found that the elderly who had more positive perceptions about aging also lived longer.

In one important study concerning the role of expectations on memory, Becca Levy and Ellen Langer (1994)[105] found that, although young American and Chinese students performed equally well on cognitive tasks, older Americans performed significantly more poorly on those tasks than did their Chinese counterparts. Furthermore, this difference was explained by beliefs about aging—in both cultures, the older adults who believed that memory declined with age also showed more actual memory declines than did the older adults who believed that memory did not decline with age. In addition, more older Americans than older Chinese believed that memory declined with age, and as you can see in Figure 6.13, older Americans performed more poorly on the memory tasks.

FIGURE 6.13

Is Memory Influenced by Cultural Stereotypes? Levy and Langer (1994) found that although younger samples did not differ, older Americans performed significantly more poorly on memory tasks than did older Chinese, and that these differences were due to different expectations about memory in the two cultures.

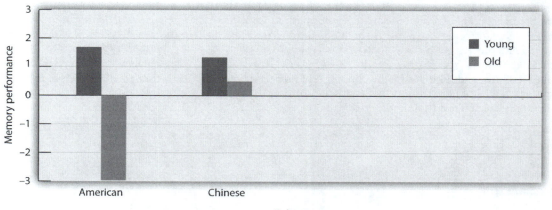

Source: Adapted from Levy, B., & Langer, E. (1994). Aging free from negative stereotypes: Successful memory in China among the American deaf. Journal of Personality and Social Psychology, 66(6), 989–997.

Whereas it was once believed that almost all older adults suffered from a generalized memory loss, research now indicates that healthy older adults actually experience only some particular types of memory deficits, while other types of memory remain relatively intact or may even improve with age. Older adults do seem to process information more slowly—it may take them longer to evaluate information and to understand language, and it takes them longer, on average, than it does younger people, to recall a word that they know, even though they are perfectly able to recognize the word once they see it (Burke, Shafto, Craik, & Salthouse, 2008).[106] Older adults also have more difficulty inhibiting and controlling their attention (Persad, Abeles, Zacks, & Denburg, 2002),[107] making them, for example, more likely to talk about topics that are not relevant to the topic at hand when conversing (Pushkar et al., 2000).[108]

But slower processing and less accurate executive control does not always mean worse memory, or even worse intelligence. Perhaps the elderly are slower in part because they simply have more knowledge. Indeed, older adults have more **crystallized intelligence**—that is, *general knowledge about the world, as reflected in semantic knowledge, vocabulary, and language.* As a result, adults generally outperform younger people on measures of history, geography, and even on crossword puzzles, where this information is useful (Salthouse, 2004).[109] It is this superior knowledge combined with a slower and more complete processing style, along with a more sophisticated understanding of the workings of the world around them, that gives the elderly the advantage of "wisdom" over the advantages of **fluid intelligence**—*the ability to think and acquire information quickly and abstractly*—which favor the young (Baltes, Staudinger, & Lindenberger, 1999; Scheibe, Kunzmann, & Baltes, 2009).[110]

The differential changes in crystallized versus fluid intelligence help explain why the elderly do not necessarily show poorer performance on tasks that also require experience (i.e., crystallized intelligence), although they show poorer memory overall. A young chess player may think more quickly, for instance, but a more experienced chess player has more knowledge to draw on. Older adults are also more effective at understanding the nuances of social interactions than younger adults are, in part because they have more experience in relationships (Blanchard-Fields, Mienaltowski, & Seay, 2007).[111]

crystallized intelligence

A person's accumulated general knowledge about the world, including semantic knowledge, vocabulary, and language.

fluid intelligence

The ability to think and acquire information quickly and abstractly.

5.2 Dementia and Alzheimer's Disease

dementia

A progressive neurological disease that includes loss of cognitive abilities, which affect social and occupational functioning.

Alzheimer's disease

A form of dementia that originates in the cerebral cortex and is ultimately fatal.

Some older adults suffer from biologically based cognitive impairments in which the brain is so adversely affected by aging that it becomes very difficult for the person to continue to function effectively. **Dementia** is defined as *a progressive neurological disease that includes loss of cognitive abilities significant enough to interfere with everyday behaviors*, and **Alzheimer's disease** is *a form of dementia that, over a period of years, leads to a loss of emotions, cognitions, and physical functioning, and which is ultimately fatal*. Dementia and Alzheimer's disease are most likely to be observed in individuals who are 65 and older, and the likelihood of developing Alzheimer's doubles about every 5 years after age 65. After age 85, the risk reaches nearly 8% per year (Hebert et al., 1995).[112] Dementia and Alzheimer's disease both produce a gradual decline in functioning of the brain cells that produce the neurotransmitter acetylcholine. Without this neurotransmitter, the neurons are unable to communicate, leaving the brain less and less functional.

FIGURE 6.14 A Healthy Brain (Left) Versus a Brain With Advanced Alzheimer's Disease (Right)

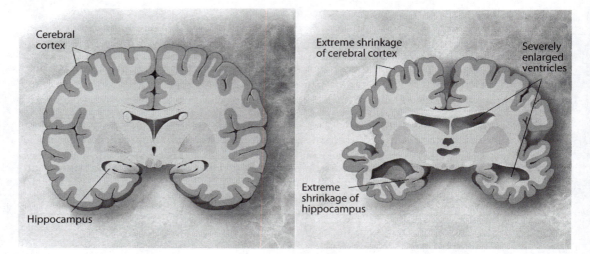

Dementia and Alzheimer's are in part heritable, but there is increasing evidence that the environment also plays a role. And current research is helping us understand the things that older adults can do to help them slow down or prevent the negative cognitive outcomes of aging, including dementia and Alzheimer's (Pushkar, Bukowski, Schwartzman, Stack, & White, 2007).[113] Older adults who continue to keep their minds active by engaging in cognitive activities, such as reading, playing musical instruments, attending lectures, or doing crossword puzzles, who maintain social interactions with others, and who keep themselves physically fit have a greater chance of maintaining their mental acuity than those who do not (Cherkas et al., 2008; Verghese et al., 2003).[114] In short, although physical illnesses may occur to anyone, the more people keep their brains active and the more they maintain a healthy and active lifestyle, the more healthy their brains will remain (Ertel, Glymour, & Berkman, 2008).[115]

5.3 Social Changes During Aging: Retiring Effectively

Because of increased life expectancy in the 21st century, elderly people can expect to spend approximately a quarter of their lives in retirement. Leaving one's career is a major life change and can be a time when people experience anxiety, depression, and other negative changes in the self-concept and in self-identity. On the other hand, retirement may also serve as an opportunity for a positive transition from work and career roles to stronger family and community member roles, and the latter may have a variety of positive outcomes for the individual. Retirement may be a relief for people who have worked in boring or physically demanding jobs, particularly if they have other outlets for stimulation and expressing self-identity.

   Psychologist Mo Wang (2007)[116] observed the well-being of 2,060 people between the ages of 51 and 61 over an 8-year period, and made the following recommendations to make the retirement phase a positive one:

1. Continue to work part time past retirement, in order to ease into retirement status slowly.
2. Plan for retirement—this is a good idea financially, but also making plans to incorporate other kinds of work or hobbies into postemployment life makes sense.

3. Retire with someone—if the retiree is still married, it is a good idea to retire at the same time as a spouse, so that people can continue to work part time and follow a retirement plan together.

4. Have a happy marriage—people with marital problems tend to find retirement more stressful because they do not have a positive home life to return to and can no longer seek refuge in long working hours. Couples that work on their marriages can make their retirements a lot easier.

5. Take care of physical and financial health—a sound financial plan and good physical health can ensure a healthy, peaceful retirement.

6. Retire early from a stressful job—people who stay in stressful jobs for fear that they will lose their pensions or won't be able to find work somewhere else feel trapped. Toxic environments can take a severe emotional toll on an employee. Leaving early from an unsatisfying job may make retirement a relief.

7. Retire "on time"—retiring too early or too late can cause people to feel "out of sync" or to feel they have not achieved their goals.

Whereas these seven tips are helpful for a smooth transition to retirement, Wang also notes that people tend to be adaptable, and that no matter how they do it, retirees will eventually adjust to their new lifestyles.

5.4   Death, Dying, and Bereavement

Living includes dealing with our own and our loved ones' mortality. In her book, *On Death and Dying* (1997),[117] Elizabeth Kübler-Ross describes five phases of grief through which people pass in grappling with the knowledge that they or someone close to them is dying:

1. Denial: "I feel fine." "This can't be happening; not to me."

2. Anger: "Why me? It's not fair!" "How can this happen to me?" "Who is to blame?"

3. Bargaining: "Just let me live to see my children graduate." "I'd do anything for a few more years." "I'd give my life savings if…"

4. Depression: "I'm so sad, why bother with anything?" "I'm going to die. What's the point?" "I miss my loved ones—why go on?"

5. Acceptance: "I know my time has come; it's almost my time."

Despite Ross's popularity, there are a growing number of critics of her theory who argue that her five-stage sequence is too constraining because attitudes toward death and dying have been found to vary greatly across cultures and religions, and these variations make the process of dying different according to culture (Bonanno, 2009).[118] As an example, Japanese Americans restrain their grief (Corr, Nabe, & Corr, 2009)[119] so as not to burden other people with their pain. By contrast, Jews observe a 7-day, publicly announced mourning period. In some cultures the elderly are more likely to be living and coping alone, or perhaps only with their spouse, whereas in other cultures, such as the Hispanic culture, the elderly are more likely to be living with their sons and daughters and other relatives, and this social support may create a better quality of life for them (Diaz-Cabello, 2004).[120]

Margaret Stroebe and her colleagues (2008)[121] found that although most people adjusted to the loss of a loved one without seeking professional treatment, many had an increased risk of mortality, particularly within the early weeks and months after the loss. These researchers also found that people going through the grieving process suffered more physical and psychological symptoms and illnesses and used more medical services.

The health of survivors during the end of life is influenced by factors such as circumstances surrounding the loved one's death, individual personalities, and ways of coping. People serving as caretakers to partners or other family members who are ill frequently experience a great deal of stress themselves, making the dying process even more stressful. Despite the trauma of the loss of a loved one, people do recover and are able to continue with effective lives. Grief intervention programs can go a long way in helping people cope during the bereavement period (Neimeyer, Holland, Currier, & Mehta, 2008).[122]

KEY TAKEAWAYS

- Most older adults maintain an active lifestyle, remain as happy or happier as when they were younger, and increasingly value their social connections with family and friends

- Although older adults have slower cognitive processing overall (fluid intelligence), their experience in the form of crystallized intelligence—or existing knowledge about the world and the ability to use it—is maintained and even strengthened during old age.

- Expectancies about change in aging vary across cultures and may influence how people respond to getting older.

- A portion of the elderly suffer from age-related brain diseases, such as dementia, a progressive neurological disease that includes significant loss of cognitive abilities, and Alzheimer's disease, a fatal form of dementia that is related to changes in the cerebral cortex.

- Two significant social stages in late adulthood are retirement and dealing with grief and bereavement. Studies show that a well-planned retirement can be a pleasant experience.

- A significant number of people going through the grieving process are at increased risk of mortality and physical and mental illness, but grief counseling can be effective in helping these people cope with their loss.

EXERCISES AND CRITICAL THINKING

1. How do the people in your culture view aging? What stereotypes are there about the elderly? Are there other ways that people in your society might learn to think about aging that would be more beneficial?

2. Based on the information you have read in this chapter, what would you tell your parents about how they can best maintain healthy physical and cognitive function into late adulthood?

6. CHAPTER SUMMARY

Development begins at conception when a sperm from the father fertilizes an egg from the mother creating a new life. The resulting zygote grows into an embryo and then a fetus.

Babies are born prepared with reflexes and cognitive skills that contribute to their survival and growth.

Piaget's stage model of cognitive development proposes that children learn through assimilation and accommodation and that cognitive development follows specific sequential stages: sensorimotor, preoperational, concrete operational, and formal operational.

An important part of development is the attainment of social skills, including the formation of the self-concept and attachment.

Adolescence involves rapid physical changes, including puberty, as well as continued cognitive changes. Moral development continues in adolescence. In Western cultures, adolescence blends into emerging adulthood, the period from age 18 until the mid-20s.

Muscle strength, reaction time, cardiac output, and sensory abilities begin to slowly decline in early and middle adulthood. Fertility, particularly for women, also decreases, and women eventually experience menopause.

Most older adults maintain an active lifestyle—remaining as happy or happier than they were when they were younger—and increasingly value their social connections with family and friends.

Although older adults have slower cognitive processing overall (fluid intelligence), their experience in the form of crystallized intelligence, or existing knowledge about the world and the ability to use it, is maintained and even strengthened during aging. A portion of the elderly suffer from age-related brain diseases, such as dementia and Alzheimer's disease.

ENDNOTES

1. Plotz, D. (2001, February 8). The "genius babies," and how they grew. *Slate*. Retrieved from http://www.slate.com/id/100331

2. Plotz, D. (2001, February 8). The "genius babies," and how they grew. *Slate*. Retrieved from http://www.slate.com/id/100331

3. Plotz, D. (2001, February 8). The "genius babies," and how they grew. *Slate*. Retrieved from http://www.slate.com/id/100331

4. Olding, P. (2006, June 15). The genius sperm bank. BBC News. Retrieved from http://www.bbc.co.uk/sn/tvradio/programmes/horizon/broadband/tx/spermbank/doron/index_textonly.shtml; Plotz, D. (2001, February 8). The "genius babies," and how they grew. *Slate*. Retrieved from http://www.slate.com/id/100331

5. Erikson, E. H. (1963). *Childhood and society*. New York, NY: Norton.

6. DeCasper, A. J., & Fifer, W. P. (1980). Of human bonding: Newborns prefer their mothers' voices. *Science, 208*, 1174–1176; Moon, C., Cooper, R. P., & Fifer, W. P. (1993). Two-day-olds prefer their native language. *Infant Behavior & Development, 16*, 495–500.

7. Mennella, J. A., Jagnow, C. P., & Beauchamp, G. K. (2001). Prenatal and postnatal flavor learning by human infants. *Pediatrics, 107*(6), e88.

8. Moore, K., & Persaud, T. (1993). *The developing human: Clinically oriented embryology* (5th ed.). Philadelphia, PA: Saunders.

9. Niccols, G. A. (1994). Fetal alcohol syndrome: Implications for psychologists. *Clinical Psychology Review, 14*, 91–111.

10. Centers for Disease Control and Prevention (2005). *Alcohol use and pregnancy*. Retrieved from http://www.cdc.gov/ncbddd/factsheets/FAS_alcoholuse.pdf

11. Duncan, G., & Brooks-Gunn, J. (2000). Family poverty, welfare reform, and child development. *Child Development, 71*(1), 188–196; Haber, M., & Toro, P. (2004). Homelessness among families, children, and adolescents: An ecological–developmental perspective. *Clinical Child and Family Psychology Review, 7*(3), 123–164.

12. Evans, G. W., & English, K. (2002). The environment of poverty: Multiple stressor exposure, psychophysiological stress, and socio-emotional adjustment. *Child Development, 73*(4), 1238–1248; Gunnar, M., & Quevedo, K. (2007). The neurobiology of stress and development. *Annual Review of Psychology, 58*, 145–173.

13. Beauchamp, D. K., Cowart, B. J., Menellia, J. A., & Marsh, R. R. (1994). Infant salt taste: Developmental, methodological, and contextual factors. *Developmental Psychology, 27*, 353–365; Blass, E. M., & Smith, B. A. (1992). Differential effects of sucrose, fructose, glucose, and lactose on crying in 1- to 3-day-old human infants: Qualitative and quantitative considerations. *Developmental Psychology, 28*, 804–810.

14. Porter, R. H., Makin, J. W., Davis, L. B., & Christensen, K. M. (1992). Breast-fed infants respond to olfactory cues from their own mother and unfamiliar lactating females. *Infant Behavior & Development, 15*(1), 85–93.

15. Bushnell, I. W. R., Sai, F., & Mullin, J. T. (1989). Neonatal recognition of the mother's face. *British Journal of developmental psychology, 7*, 3–15.

16. Gibson, E. J., Rosenzweig, M. R., & Porter, L. W. (1988). Exploratory behavior in the development of perceiving, acting, and the acquiring of knowledge. In *Annual review of psychology* (Vol. 39, pp. 1–41). Palo Alto, CA: Annual Reviews; Gibson, E. J., & Pick, A. D. (2000). *An ecological approach to perceptual learning and development*. New York, NY: Oxford University Press; Smith, L. B., & Thelen, E. (2003). Development as a dynamic system. *Trends in Cognitive Sciences, 7*(8), 343–348.

17. Juraska, J. M., Henderson, C., & Müller, J. (1984). Differential rearing experience, gender, and radial maze performance. *Developmental Psychobiology, 17*(3), 209–215.

18. Soska, K. C., Adolph, K. E., & Johnson, S. P. (2010). Systems in development: Motor skill acquisition facilitates three-dimensional object completion. *Developmental Psychology, 46*(1), 129–138.

19. James, W. (1890). *The principles of psychology*. New York, NY: Dover.

20. Trehub, S., & Rabinovitch, M. (1972). Auditory-linguistic sensitivity in early infancy. *Developmental Psychology, 6*(1), 74–77.

21. Wynn, K. (1995). Infants possess a system of numerical knowledge. *Current Directions in Psychological Science, 4*, 172–176.

22. DeLoache, J. S. (1987). Rapid change in the symbolic functioning of very young children. *Science, 238*(4833), 1556–1556.

23. Klahr, D., & McWhinney, B. (1998). Information Processing. In D. Kuhn & R. S. Siegler (Eds.), *Handbook of child psychology: Cognition, perception, & language* (5th ed., Vol. 2, pp. 631–678). New York, NY: John Wiley & Sons; Shrager, J., & Siegler, R. S. (1998). SCADS: A model of children's strategy choices and strategy discoveries. *Psychological Science, 9*, 405–422.

24. Driscoll, M. P. (1994). *Psychology of learning for instruction*. Boston, MA: Allyn & Bacon; Levin, I., Siegler, S. R., & Druyan, S. (1990). Misconceptions on motion: Development and training effects. *Child Development, 61*, 1544–1556.

25. Baillargeon, R. (2004). Infants' physical world. *Current Directions in Psychological Science, 13*(3), 89–94; Wang, S. H., Baillargeon, R., & Brueckner, L. (2004). Young infants' reasoning about hidden objects: Evidence from violation-of-expectation tasks with test trials only. *Cognition, 93*, 167–198.

26. Courage, M. L., & Howe, M. L. (2002). From infant to child: The dynamics of cognitive change in the second year of life. *Psychological Bulletin, 128*(2), 250–276.

27. Dasen, P. R. (1972). Cross-cultural Piagetian research: A summary. *Journal of Cross-Cultural Psychology, 3*, 23–39.

28. Cole, M. (1996). *Culture in mind*. Cambridge, MA: Harvard University Press; Rogoff, B. (1990). *Apprenticeship in thinking: Cognitive development in social context*. New York,

NY: Oxford University Press; Tomasello, M. (1999). *The cultural origins of human cognition*. Cambridge, MA: Harvard University Press.

29. Vygotsky, L. S. (1962). *Thought and language*. Cambridge, MA: MIT Press; Vygotsky, L. S. (1978). *Mind in society*. Cambridge, MA: Harvard University Press.

30. Aronson, E., Blaney, N., Stephan, C., Sikes, J., & Snapp, M. (1978). *The jigsaw classroom*. Beverly Hills, CA: Sage; Brown, A. L. (1997). Transforming schools into communities of thinking and learning about serious matters. *American Psychologist, 52*(4), 399–413.

31. Kagan, J. (1991). The theoretical utility of constructs of self. *Developmental Review, 11*, 244–250.

32. Boysen, S. T., & Himes, G. T. (1999). Current issues and emerging theories in animal cognition. *Annual Review of Psychology, 50*, 683–705.

33. Gallup, G. G., Jr. (1970). Chimpanzees: Self-recognition. *Science, 167*(3914), 86–87.

34. Povinelli, D. J., Landau, K. R., & Perilloux, H. K. (1996). Self-recognition in young children using delayed versus live feedback: Evidence of a developmental asynchrony. *Child Development, 67*(4), 1540–1554.

35. Harter, S. (1998). The development of self-representations. In W. Damon & N. Eisenberg (Eds.), *Handbook of child psychology: Social, emotional, & personality development* (5th ed., Vol. 3, pp. 553–618). New York, NY: John Wiley & Sons.

36. Moretti, M. M., & Higgins, E. T. (1990). The development of self-esteem vulnerabilities: Social and cognitive factors in developmental psychopathology. In R. J. Sternberg & J. Kolligian, Jr. (Eds.), *Competence considered* (pp. 286–314). New Haven, CT: Yale University Press.

37. Doherty, M. J. (2009). *Theory of mind: How children understand others' thoughts and feelings*. New York, NY: Psychology Press.

38. Cassidy, J. E., & Shaver, P. R. E. (1999). *Handbook of attachment: Theory, research, and clinical applications*. New York, NY: Guilford Press.

39. Bowlby, J. (1953). Some pathological processes set in train by early mother-child separation. *Journal of Mental Science, 99*, 265–272.

40. Harlow, H. (1958). The nature of love. *American Psychologist, 13*, 573–685.

41. Ainsworth, M. S., Blehar, M. C., Waters, E., & Wall, S. (1978). *Patterns of attachment: A psychological study of the strange situation*. Hillsdale, NJ: Lawrence Erlbaum Associates.

42. Rothbaum, F., Weisz, J., Pott, M., Miyake, K., & Morelli, G. (2000). Attachment and culture: Security in the United States and Japan. *American Psychologist, 55*(10), 1093–1104.

43. van den Boom, D. C. (1994). The influence of temperament and mothering on attachment and exploration: An experimental manipulation of sensitive responsiveness among lower-class mothers with irritable infants. *Child Development, 65*(5), 1457–1476.

44. Gillath, O., Shaver, P. R., Baek, J.-M., & Chun, D. S. (2008). Genetic correlates of adult attachment style. *Personality and Social Psychology Bulletin, 34*(10), 1396–1405; Seifer, R., Schiller, M., Sameroff, A. J., Resnick, S., & Riordan, K. (1996). Attachment, maternal sensitivity, and infant temperament during the first year of life. *Developmental Psychology, 32*(1), 12–25.

45. Cassidy, J. E., & Shaver, P. R. E. (1999). *Handbook of attachment: Theory, research, and clinical applications*. New York, NY: Guilford Press.

46. Waters, E., Merrick, S., Treboux, D., Crowell, J., & Albersheim, L. (2000). Attachment security in infancy and early adulthood: A twenty-year longitudinal study. *Child Development, 71*(3), 684–689.

47. Lucas-Thompson, R., & Clarke-Stewart, K. A. (2007). Forecasting friendship: How marital quality, maternal mood, and attachment security are linked to children's peer relationships. *Journal of Applied Developmental Psychology, 28*(5–6), 499–514.

48. Carlson, E. A., Sroufe, L. A., & Egeland, B. (2004). The construction of experience: A longitudinal study of representation and behavior. *Child Development, 75*(1), 66–83.

49. Jang, K. L., Livesley, W. A., & Vernon, P. A. (1996). The genetic basis of personality at different ages: A cross-sectional twin study. *Personality and Individual Differences, 21*, 299–301.

50. Jang, K. L., Livesley, W. A., & Vernon, P. A. (1996). The genetic basis of personality at different ages: A cross-sectional twin study. *Personality and Individual Differences, 21*, 299–301.

51. Baumeister, R. F., & Tice, D. M. (1986). How adolescence became the struggle for self: A historical transformation of psychological development. In J. Suls & A. G. Greenwald (Eds.), *Psychological perspectives on the self* (Vol. 3, pp. 183–201). Hillsdale, NJ: Lawrence Erlbaum Associates; Twenge, J. M. (2006). *Generation me: Why today's young Americans are more confident, assertive, entitled—and more miserable than ever before*. New York, NY: Free Press.

52. Farrington, D. P. (1995). The challenge of teenage antisocial behavior. In M. Rutter & M. E. Rutter (Eds.), *Psychosocial disturbances in young people: Challenges for prevention* (pp. 83–130). New York, NY: Cambridge University Press.

53. Marshall, W. A., & Tanner, J. M. (1986). Puberty. In F. Falkner & J. M. Tanner (Eds.), *Human growth: A comprehensive treatise* (2nd ed., pp. 171–209). New York, NY: Plenum Press.

54. Marshall, W. A., & Tanner, J. M. (1986). Puberty. In F. Falkner & J. M. Tanner (Eds.), *Human growth: A comprehensive treatise* (2nd ed., pp. 171–209). New York, NY: Plenum Press.

55. Anderson, S. E., Dannal, G. E., & Must, A. (2003). Relative weight and race influence average age at menarche: Results from two nationally representative surveys of U.S. girls studied 25 years apart. *Pediatrics, 111*, 844–850.

56. Lynne, S. D., Graber, J. A., Nichols, T. R., Brooks-Gunn, J., & Botvin, G. J. (2007). Links between pubertal timing, peer influences, and externalizing behaviors among urban

students followed through middle school. *Journal of Adolescent Health, 40,* 181.e7–181.e13 (p. 198).

57. Mendle, J., Turkheimer, E., & Emery, R. E. (2007). Detrimental psychological outcomes associated with early pubertal timing in adolescent girls. *Developmental Review, 27,* 151–171; Pescovitz, O. H., & Walvoord, E. C. (2007). *When puberty is precocious: Scientific and clinical aspects.* Totowa, NJ: Humana Press.

58. Ge, X., Conger, R. D., & Elder, G. H., Jr. (1996). Coming of age too early: Pubertal influences on girls' vulnerability to psychological distress. *Child Development, 67*(6), 3386–3400.

59. Weinberger, D. R., Elvevåg, B., & Giedd, J. N. (2005). The adolescent brain: A work in progress. National Campaign to Prevent Teen Pregnancy. Retrieved from http://www.thenationalcampaign.org/resources/pdf/BRAIN.pdf

60. Blakemore, S. J. (2008). Development of the social brain during adolescence. *Quarterly Journal of Experimental Psychology, 61,* 40–49.

61. Goldberg, E. (2001). *The executive brain: Frontal lobes and the civilized mind.* New York, NY: Oxford University Press.

62. Rapoport, J. L., Giedd, J. N., Blumenthal, J., Hamburger, S., Jeffries, N., Fernandez, T.,…Evans, A. (1999). Progressive cortical change during adolescence in childhood-onset schizophrenia: A longitudinal magnetic resonance imaging study. *Archives of General Psychiatry, 56*(7), 649–654.

63. Blakemore, S. J. (2008). Development of the social brain during adolescence. *Quarterly Journal of Experimental Psychology, 61,* 40–49.

64. Steinberg, L. (2007). Risk taking in adolescence: New perspectives from brain and behavioral science. *Current Directions in Psychological Science, 16,* 55–59.

65. Elkind, D. (1978). *The child's reality: Three developmental themes.* Hillsdale, NJ: Lawrence Erlbaum Associates.

66. Goossens, L., Beyers, W., Emmen, M., & van Aken, M. (2002). The imaginary audience and personal fable: Factor analyses and concurrent validity of the "new look" measures. *Journal of Research on Adolescence, 12*(2), 193–215.

67. Rycek, R. F., Stuhr, S. L., Mcdermott, J., Benker, J., & Swartz, M. D. (1998). Adolescent egocentrism and cognitive functioning during late adolescence. *Adolescence, 33,* 746–750.

68. Harris, J. (1998), *The nurture assumption—Why children turn out the way they do.* New York, NY: Free Press.

69. Marcia, J. (1980). Identity in adolescence. *Handbook of Adolescent Psychology, 5,* 145–160.

70. Answerbag. (2007, March 20). What were you like as a teenager? (e.g., cool, nerdy, awkward?). Retrieved from http://www.answerbag.com/q_view/171753

71. Rubin, K. H., Bukowski, W. M., & Parker, J. G. (2006). Peer interactions, relationships, and groups. In N. Eisenberg, W. Damon, & R. M. Lerner (Eds.), *Handbook of child psychology: Social, emotional, and personality development* (6th ed., Vol. 3, pp. 571–645). Hoboken, NJ: John Wiley & Sons.

72. Kohlberg, L. (1984). *The psychology of moral development: Essays on moral development* (Vol. 2, p. 200). San Francisco, CA: Harper & Row.

73. Kohlberg, L. (1984). *The psychology of moral development: Essays on moral development* (Vol. 2, p. 200). San Francisco, CA: Harper & Row.

74. Rest, J. (1979). *Development in judging moral issues.* Minneapolis: University of Minnesota Press.

75. Haidt, J. (2001). The emotional dog and its rational tail: A social intuitionist approach to moral judgment. *Psychological Review, 108*(4), 814–834.

76. Gilligan, C. (1982). *In a different voice: Psychological theory and women's development.* Cambridge, MA: Harvard University Press.

77. Turiel, E. (1998). The development of morality. In W. Damon (Ed.), *Handbook of child psychology: Socialization* (5th ed., Vol. 3, pp. 863–932). New York, NY: John Wiley & Sons.

78. Jaffee, S., & Hyde, J. S. (2000). Gender differences in moral orientation: A meta-analysis. *Psychological Bulletin, 126*(5), 703–726.

79. Ekéus, C., Christensson, K., & Hjern, A. (2004). Unintentional and violent injuries among pre-school children of teenage mothers in Sweden: A national cohort study. *Journal of Epidemiology and Community Health, 58*(8), 680–685.

80. Moore, M. R., & Brooks-Gunn, J. (2002). Adolescent parenthood. In M. H. Bornstein (Ed.), *Handbook of parenting: Being and becoming a parent* (2nd ed., Vol. 3, pp. 173–214). Mahwah, NJ: Lawrence Erlbaum Associates.

81. Rohner, R. P., & Veneziano, R. A. (2001). The importance of father love: History and contemporary evidence. *Review of General Psychology, 5*(4), 382–405.

82. Amato, P. R. (1994). Father-child relations, mother-child relations, and offspring psychological well-being in adulthood. *Journal of Marriage and the Family, 56,* 1031–1042.

83. Baumrind, D. (1996). The discipline controversy revisited. *Family Relations, 45*(4), 405–414; Grolnick, W. S., & Ryan, R. M. (1989). Parent styles associated with children's self-regulation and competence in school. *Journal of Educational Psychology, 81*(2), 143–154.

84. Tamis-LeMonda, C. S., Briggs, R. D., McClowry, S. G., & Snow, D. L. (2008). Challenges to the study of African American parenting: Conceptualization, sampling, research approaches, measurement, and design. *Parenting: Science and Practice, 8*(4), 319–358.

85. Chang, L., Lansford, J. E., Schwartz, D., & Farver, J. M. (2004). Marital quality, maternal depressed affect, harsh parenting, and child externalising in Hong Kong Chinese families. *International Journal of Behavioral Development, 28*(4), 311–318.

86. Pluess, M., & Belsky, J. (2010). Differential susceptibility to parenting and quality child care. *Developmental Psychology, 46*(2), 379–390.

87. Burt, S. A., Barnes, A. R., McGue, M., & Iacono, W. G. (2008). Parental divorce and adolescent delinquency: Ruling out the impact of common genes. *Developmental Psychology, 44*(6), 1668–1677; Ge, X., Natsuaki, M. N., & Conger, R. D. (2006). Trajectories of depressive symptoms and stressful life events among male and female adolescents in divorced and nondivorced families. *Development and Psychopathology, 18*(1), 253–273.

88. Panno, J. (2004). *Aging: Theories and potential therapies.* New York, NY: Facts on File Publishers.

89. Lacher-Fougère, S., & Demany, L. (2005). Consequences of cochlear damage for the detection of inter-aural phase differences. *Journal of the Acoustical Society of America, 118,* 2519–2526.

90. Shelton, H. M. (2006). *High blood pressure.* Whitefish, MT: Kessinger Publishers.

91. Minkin, M. J., & Wright, C. V. (2004). *A woman's guide to menopause and perimenopause.* New Haven, CT: Yale University Press.

92. Avis, N. E., & Crawford, S. (2008). Cultural differences in symptoms and attitudes toward menopause. *Menopause Management, 17*(3), 8–13.

93. DePaulo, B. M. (2006). *Singled out: How singles are stereotyped, stigmatized and ignored, and still live happily ever after.* New York, NY: St. Martin's Press; Rook, K. S., Catalano, R. C., & Dooley, D. (1989). The timing of major life events: Effects of departing from the social clock. *American Journal of Community Psychology, 17,* 223–258.

94. Gallagher, M., & Waite, L. J. (2001). *The case for marriage: Why married people are happier, healthier, and better off financially.* New York, NY: Random House; Liu, H., & Umberson, D. (2008). The times they are a changin': Marital status and health differentials from 1972 to 2003. *Journal of Health and Social Behavior, 49,* 239–253.

95. Bureau of the Census. (2007). Statistical abstract of the United States 2006 (p. 218). Washington, DC: U.S. Government Printing Office.

96. Goodwin, P. Y., Mosher, W. D., Chandra A. (2010, February). Marriage and cohabitation in the United States: A statistical portrait based on Cycle 6 (2002) of the National Survey of Family Growth. *Vital Health Statistics 23*(28), 1–45. Retrieved from National Center for Health Statistics, Centers for Disease Control and Prevention, website: http://www.cdc.gov/nchs/data/series/sr_23/sr23_028.pdf

97. Twenge, J., Campbell, W., & Foster, C. (2003). Parenthood and marital satisfaction: A meta-analytic review. *Journal of Marriage and Family, 65*(3), 574–583.

98. Eid, M., & Larsen, R. J. (Eds.). (2008). *The science of subjective well-being.* New York, NY: Guilford Press.

99. Angner, E., Ray, M. N., Saag, K. G., & Allison, J. J. (2009). Health and happiness among older adults: A community-based study. *Journal of Health Psychology, 14,* 503–512.

100. Kennedy, Q., Mather, M., & Carstensen, L. L. (2004). The role of motivation in the age-related positivity effect in autobiographical memory. *Psychological Science, 15,* 208–214.

101. Myers, D. G., & Diener, E. (1996). The pursuit of happiness. *Scientific American, 274*(5), 70–72.

102. Rubin, L. (2007). *60 on up: The truth about aging in America.* Boston, MA: Beacon Press; Sroufe, L. A., Collins, W. A., Egeland, B., & Carlson, E. A. (2009). *The development of the person: The Minnesota study of risk and adaptation from birth to adulthood.* New York, NY: Guilford Press.

103. Nemmers, T. M. (2005). The influence of ageism and ageist stereotypes on the elderly. *Physical & Occupational Therapy in Geriatrics, 22*(4), 11–20.

104. Levy, B. R., Slade, M. D., Kunkel, S. R., & Kasl, S. V. (2002). Longevity increased by positive self-perceptions of aging. *Journal of Personality and Social Psychology, 83,* 261–270.

105. Levy, B., & Langer, E. (1994). Aging free from negative stereotypes: Successful memory in China among the American deaf. *Journal of Personality and Social Psychology, 66*(6), 989–997.

106. Burke, D. M., Shafto, M. A., Craik, F. I. M., & Salthouse, T. A. (2008). Language and aging. In *The handbook of aging and cognition* (3rd ed., pp. 373–443). New York, NY: Psychology Press.

107. Persad, C. C., Abeles, N., Zacks, R. T., & Denburg, N. L. (2002). Inhibitory changes after age 60 and the relationship to measures of attention and memory. *The Journals of Gerontology: Series B: Psychological Sciences and Social Sciences, 57B*(3), P223–P232.

108. Pushkar, D., Basevitz, P., Arbuckle, T., Nohara-LeClair, M., Lapidus, S., & Peled, M. (2000). Social behavior and off-target verbosity in elderly people. *Psychology and Aging, 15*(2), 361–374.

109. Salthouse, T. A. (2004). What and when of cognitive aging. *Current Directions in Psychological Science, 13*(4), 140–144.

110. Baltes, P. B., Staudinger, U. M., & Lindenberger, U. (1999). Life-span psychology: Theory and application to intellectual functioning. *Annual Review of Psychology, 50,* 471–506; Scheibe, S., Kunzmann, U., & Baltes, P. B. (2009). New territories of positive life-span development: Wisdom and life longings. In S. J. E. Lopez & C. R. E. Snyder (Eds.), *Oxford handbook of positive psychology* (2nd ed., pp. 171–183). New York, NY: Oxford University Press.

111. Blanchard-Fields, F., Mienaltowski, A., & Seay, R. B. (2007). Age differences in everyday problem-solving effectiveness: Older adults select more effective strategies for interpersonal problems. *The Journals of Gerontology: Series B: Psychological Sciences and Social Sciences, 62B*(1), P61–P64.

112. Hebert, L. E., Scherr, P. A., Beckett, L. A., Albert, M. S., Pilgrim, D. M., Chown, M. J.,…Evans, D. A. (1995). Age-specific incidence of Alzheimer's disease in a community population. *Journal of the American Medical Association, 273*(17), 1354–1359.

113. Pushkar, D., Bukowski, W. M., Schwartzman, A. E., Stack, D. M., & White, D. R. (2007). *Responding to the challenges of late life: Strategies for maintaining and enhancing competence.* New York, NY: Springer Publishing.

114. Cherkas, L. F., Hunkin, J. L., Kato, B. S., Richards, J. B., Gardner, J. P., Surdulescu, G. L.,…Aviv, A. (2008). The association between physical activity in leisure time and leukocyte telomere length. *Archives of Internal Medicine, 168*, 154–158; Verghese, J., Lipton, R., Katz, M. J., Hall, C. B., Derby, C. A.,…Buschke, M.D. (2003). Leisure activities and the risk of dementia in the elderly. *New England Journal of Medicine, 348*, 2508–2516.

115. Ertel, K. A., Glymour, M. M., & Berkman, L. F. (2008). Effects of social integration on preserving memory function in a nationally representative U.S. elderly population. *American Journal of Public Health, 98*, 1215–1220.

116. Wang, M. (2007). Profiling retirees in the retirement transition and adjustment process: Examining the longitudinal change patterns of retirees' psychological well-being. *Journal of Applied Psychology, 92*(2), 455–474.

117. Kübler-Ross, E. (1997). *On death and dying.* New York, NY: Scribner.

118. Bonanno, G. (2009). *The other side of sadness: What the new science of bereavement tells us about life after a loss.* New York, NY: Basic Books.

119. Corr, C. A., Nabe, C. M., & Corr, D. M. (2009). *Death and dying: Life and living* (6th ed.). Belmont, CA: Wadsworth.

120. Diaz-Cabello, N. (2004). The Hispanic way of dying: Three families, three perspectives, three cultures. *Illness, Crisis, & Loss, 12*(3), 239–255.

121. Stroebe, M. S., Hansson, R. O., Schut, H., & Stroebe, W. (2008). Bereavement research: Contemporary perspectives. In M. S. Stroebe, R. O. Hansson, H. Schut, & W. Stroebe (Eds.), *Handbook of bereavement research and practice: Advances in theory and intervention* (pp. 3–25). Washington, DC: American Psychological Association.

122. Neimeyer, R. A., Holland, J. M., Currier, J. M., & Mehta, T. (2008). Meaning reconstruction in later life: Toward a cognitive-constructivist approach to grief therapy. In D. Gallagher-Thompson, A. Steffen, & L. Thompson (Eds.), *Handbook of behavioral and cognitive therapies with older adults* (pp. 264–277). New York, NY: Springer Verlag.

CHAPTER 7
Learning

My Story of Posttraumatic Stress Disorder

It is a continuous challenge living with post-traumatic stress disorder (PTSD), and I've suffered from it for most of my life. I can look back now and gently laugh at all the people who thought I had the perfect life. I was young, beautiful, and talented, but unbeknownst to them, I was terrorized by an undiagnosed debilitating mental illness.

Having been properly diagnosed with PTSD at age 35, I know that there is not one aspect of my life that has gone untouched by this mental illness. My PTSD was triggered by several traumas, most importantly a sexual attack at knifepoint that left me thinking I would die. I would never be the same after that attack. For me there was no safe place in the world, not even my home. I went to the police and filed a report. Rape counselors came to see me while I was in the hospital, but I declined their help, convinced that I didn't need it. This would be the most damaging decision of my life.

For months after the attack, I couldn't close my eyes without envisioning the face of my attacker. I suffered horrific flashbacks and nightmares. For four years after the attack I was unable to sleep alone in my house. I obsessively checked windows, doors, and locks. By age 17, I'd suffered my first panic attack. Soon I became unable to leave my apartment for weeks at a time, ending my modeling career abruptly. This just became a way of life. Years passed when I had few or no symptoms at all, and I led what I thought was a fairly normal life, just thinking I had a "panic problem."

Then another traumatic event retriggered the PTSD. It was as if the past had evaporated, and I was back in the place of my attack, only now I had uncontrollable thoughts of someone entering my house and harming my daughter. I saw violent images every time I closed my eyes. I lost all ability to concentrate or even complete simple tasks. Normally social, I stopped trying to make friends or get involved in my community. I often felt disoriented, forgetting where, or who, I was. I would panic on the freeway and became unable to drive, again ending a career. I felt as if I had completely lost my mind. For a time, I managed to keep it together on the outside, but then I became unable to leave my house again.

Around this time I was diagnosed with PTSD. I cannot express to you the enormous relief I felt when I discovered my condition was real and treatable. I felt safe for the first time in 32 years. Taking medication and undergoing behavioral therapy marked the turning point in my regaining control of my life. I'm rebuilding a satisfying career as an artist, and I am enjoying my life. The world is new to me and not limited by the restrictive vision of anxiety. It amazes me to think back to what my life was like only a year ago, and just how far I've come.

For me there is no cure, no final healing. But there are things I can do to ensure that I never have to suffer as I did before being diagnosed with PTSD. I'm no longer at the mercy of my disorder, and I would not be here today had I not had the proper diagnosis and treatment. The most important thing to know is that it's never too late to seek help. (Philips, 2010)[1]

The topic of this chapter is **learning**—*the relatively permanent change in knowledge or behavior that is the result of experience.* Although you might think of learning in terms of what you need to do before an upcoming exam, the knowledge that you take away from your classes, or new skills that you acquire through practice, these changes

learning

The relatively permanent change in knowledge or behavior due to experience.

represent only one component of learning. In fact, learning is a broad topic that is used to explain not only how we acquire new knowledge and behavior but also a wide variety of other psychological processes including the development of both appropriate and inappropriate social behaviors, and even how a person may acquire a debilitating psychological disorder such as PTSD.

FIGURE 7.1 Watson and Skinner
John B. Watson (right) and B. F. Skinner (left) were champions of the behaviorist school of learning.

Sources: Watson photo courtesy of Amaro Studios, http://www.flickr.com/photos/39584782@N08/4198517298. Skinner photo courtesy of pto0413, http://www.flickr.com/photos/pto0413/4776302017/in/photostream.

conditioning
The ability to connect stimuli (the changes that occur in our environment) with responses (behaviors or other actions).

Learning is perhaps the most important human capacity. Learning allows us to create effective lives by being able to respond to changes. We learn to avoid touching hot stoves, to find our way home from school, and to remember which people have helped us in the past and which people have been unkind. Without the ability to learn from our experiences, our lives would be remarkably dangerous and inefficient. The principles of learning can also be used to explain a wide variety of social interactions, including social dilemmas in which people make important, and often selfish, decisions about how to behave by calculating the costs and benefits of different outcomes.

The study of learning is closely associated with the behaviorist school of psychology, in which it was seen as an alternative scientific perspective to the failure of introspection. The behaviorists, including John B. Watson and B. F. Skinner, focused their research entirely on behavior, to the exclusion of any kinds of mental processes. For behaviorists, the fundamental aspect of learning is the process of **conditioning**—*the ability to connect* stimuli *(the changes that occur in the environment) with* responses *(behaviors or other actions).*

But conditioning is just one type of learning. We will also consider other types, including learning through *insight,* as well as *observational learning* (also known as *modeling*). In each case we will see not only what psychologists have learned about the topics but also the important influence that learning has on many aspects of our everyday lives. And we will see that in some cases learning can be maladaptive—for instance, when a person like P. K. Philips continually experiences disruptive memories and emotional responses to a negative event.

1.   LEARNING BY ASSOCIATION: CLASSICAL CONDITIONING

LEARNING OBJECTIVES

1. Describe how Pavlov's early work in classical conditioning influenced the understanding of learning.
2. Review the concepts of classical conditioning, including unconditioned stimulus (US), conditioned stimulus (CS), unconditioned response (UR), and conditioned response (CR).
3. Explain the roles that extinction, generalization, and discrimination play in conditioned learning.

1.1   Pavlov Demonstrates Conditioning in Dogs

In the early part of the 20th century, Russian physiologist Ivan Pavlov (1849–1936) was studying the digestive system of dogs when he noticed an interesting behavioral phenomenon: The dogs began to salivate when the lab technicians who normally fed them entered the room, even though the dogs had not yet received any food. Pavlov realized that the dogs were salivating because they knew that they were about to be fed; the dogs had begun to associate the arrival of the technicians with the food that soon followed their appearance in the room.

With his team of researchers, Pavlov began studying this process in more detail. He conducted a series of experiments in which, over a number of trials, dogs were exposed to a sound immediately before receiving food. He systematically controlled the onset of the sound and the timing of the delivery of the food, and recorded the amount of the dogs' salivation. Initially the dogs salivated only when they saw or smelled the food, but after several pairings of the sound and the food, the dogs began to salivate as soon as they heard the sound. The animals had learned to associate the sound with the food that followed.

Pavlov had identified a fundamental associative learning process called *classical conditioning.* **Classical conditioning** refers to *learning that occurs when a neutral stimulus (e.g., a tone) becomes associated with a stimulus (e.g., food) that naturally produces a behavior.* After the association is learned, the previously neutral stimulus is sufficient to produce the behavior.

As you can see in Figure 7.3, psychologists use specific terms to identify the stimuli and the responses in classical conditioning. The **unconditioned stimulus (US)** is *something (such as food) that triggers a natural occurring response,* and the **unconditioned response (UR)** is *the naturally occurring response (such as salivation) that follows the unconditioned stimulus.* The **conditioned stimulus (CS)** is *a neutral stimulus that, after being repeatedly presented prior to the unconditioned stimulus, evokes a similar response as the unconditioned stimulus.* In Pavlov's experiment, the sound of the tone served as the conditioned stimulus that, after learning, produced the **conditioned response (CR)**, which is *the acquired response to the formerly neutral stimulus.* Note that the UR and the CR are the same behavior—in this case salivation—but they are given different names because they are produced by different stimuli (the US and the CS, respectively).

FIGURE 7.3 4-Panel Image of Whistle and Dog

Top left: Before conditioning, the unconditioned stimulus (US) naturally produces the unconditioned response (UR). Top right: Before conditioning, the neutral stimulus (the whistle) does not produce the salivation response. Bottom left: The unconditioned stimulus (US), in this case the food, is repeatedly presented immediately after the neutral stimulus. Bottom right: After learning, the neutral stimulus (now known as the conditioned stimulus or CS), is sufficient to produce the conditioned responses (CR).

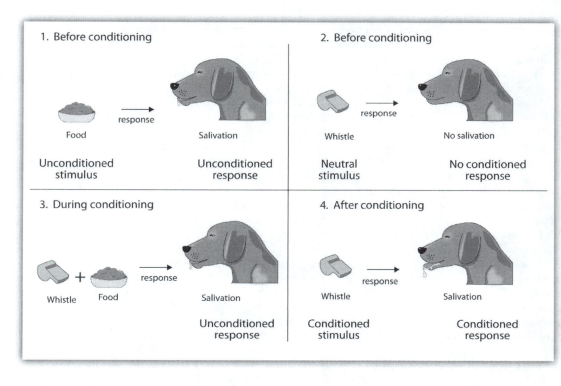

Conditioning is evolutionarily beneficial because it allows organisms to develop expectations that help them prepare for both good and bad events. Imagine, for instance, that an animal first smells a new food, eats it, and then gets sick. If the animal can learn to associate the smell (CS) with the food (US), then it will quickly learn that the food creates the negative outcome, and not eat it the next time.

FIGURE 7.2
Ivan Pavlov

Ivan Pavlov's research made substantial contributions to our understanding of learning.

Source: Photo courtesy of LIFE Photo Archive,

http://commons.wikimedia.org/wiki/File:Ivan_Pavlov_LIFE.jpg.

classical conditioning

Learning that occurs when a neutral stimulus (e.g., a tone) becomes associated with a stimulus (e.g., food) that naturally produces a behavior.

unconditioned stimulus (US)

Something (such as food) that naturally triggers a response.

unconditioned response (UR)

The naturally occuring response (such as salivation) that follows the unconditioned stimulus.

conditioned stimulus (CS)

A neutral stimulus that, after being repeatedly presented prior to the unconditioned stimulus, begins to evoke a similar response as the unconditioned stimulus.

conditioned response (CR)

An acquired response to the formerly neutral stimulus.

1.2   The Persistence and Extinction of Conditioning

extinction

The reduction in responding
that occurs when the
conditioned stimulus is
presented repeatedly without
the unconditioned stimulus.

After he had demonstrated that learning could occur through association, Pavlov moved on to study the variables that influenced the strength and the persistence of conditioning. In some studies, after the conditioning had taken place, Pavlov presented the sound repeatedly but without presenting the food afterward. Figure 7.4 shows what happened. As you can see, after the intial acquisition (learning) phase in which the conditioning occurred, when the CS was then presented alone, the behavior rapidly decreased—the dogs salivated less and less to the sound, and eventually the sound did not elicit salivation at all. **Extinction** refers to *the reduction in responding that occurs when the conditioned stimulus is presented repeatedly without the unconditioned stimulus.*

FIGURE 7.4 Acquisition, Extinction, and Spontaneous Recovery

Acquisition: The CS and the US are repeatedly paired together and behavior increases. Extinction: The CS is repeatedly presented alone, and the behavior slowly decreases. Spontaneous recovery: After a pause, when the CS is again presented alone, the behavior may again occur and then again show extinction.

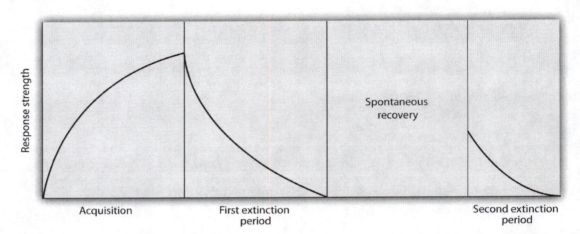

spontaneous recovery

The increase in responding to
the conditioned stimulus (CS)
after a pause that follows
extinction.

Although at the end of the first extinction period the CS was no longer producing salivation, the effects of conditioning had not entirely disappeared. Pavlov found that, after a pause, sounding the tone again elicited salivation, although to a lesser extent than before extinction took place. *The increase in responding to the CS following a pause after extinction* is known as **spontaneous recovery**. When Pavlov again presented the CS alone, the behavior again showed extinction until it disappeared again.

Although the behavior has disappeared, extinction is never complete. If conditioning is again attempted, the animal will learn the new associations much faster than it did the first time.

generalization

The tendency to respond to
stimuli that resemble the
original conditioned stimulus.

Pavlov also experimented with presenting new stimuli that were similar, but not identical to, the original conditioned stimulus. For instance, if the dog had been conditioned to being scratched before the food arrived, the stimulus would be changed to being rubbed rather than scratched. He found that the dogs also salivated upon experiencing the similar stimulus, a process known as *generalization*. **Generalization** refers to *the tendency to respond to stimuli that resemble the original conditioned stimulus.* The ability to generalize has important evolutionary significance. If we eat some red berries and they make us sick, it would be a good idea to think twice before we eat some purple berries. Although the berries are not exactly the same, they nevertheless are similar and may have the same negative properties.

Lewicki (1985)[2] conducted research that demonstrated the influence of stimulus generalization and how quickly and easily it can happen. In his experiment, high school students first had a brief interaction with a female experimenter who had short hair and glasses. The study was set up so that the students had to ask the experimenter a question, and (according to random assignment) the experimenter responded either in a negative way or a neutral way toward the students. Then the students were told to go into a second room in which two experimenters were present, and to approach either one of them. However, the researchers arranged it so that one of the two experimenters looked a lot like the original experimenter, while the other one did not (she had longer hair and no glasses). The students were significantly more likely to avoid the experimenter who looked like the earlier experimenter when that experimenter had been negative to them than when she had treated them more neutrally. The participants showed stimulus generalization such that the new, similar-looking experimenter created the same negative response in the participants as had the experimenter in the prior session.

The flip side of generalization is **discrimination**—*the tendency to respond differently to stimuli that are similar but not identical.* Pavlov's dogs quickly learned, for example, to salivate when they heard the specific tone that had preceded food, but not upon hearing similar tones that had never been associated with food. Discrimination is also useful—if we do try the purple berries, and if they do not make us sick, we will be able to make the distinction in the future. And we can learn that although the two people in our class, Courtney and Sarah, may look a lot alike, they are nevertheless different people with different personalities.

In some cases, *an existing conditioned stimulus can serve as an unconditioned stimulus for a pairing with a new conditioned stimulus*—a process known as **second-order conditioning**. In one of Pavlov's studies, for instance, he first conditioned the dogs to salivate to a sound, and then repeatedly paired a new CS, a black square, with the sound. Eventually he found that the dogs would salivate at the sight of the black square alone, even though it had never been directly associated with the food. Secondary conditioners in everyday life include our attractions to things that stand for or remind us of something else, such as when we feel good on a Friday because it has become associated with the paycheck that we receive on that day, which itself is a conditioned stimulus for the pleasures that the paycheck buys us.

1.3 The Role of Nature in Classical Conditioning

As we have seen in Chapter 1, scientists associated with the behavioralist school argued that all learning is driven by experience, and that nature plays no role. Classical conditioning, which is based on learning through experience, represents an example of the importance of the environment. But classical conditioning cannot be understood entirely in terms of experience. Nature also plays a part, as our evolutionary history has made us better able to learn some associations than others.

Clinical psychologists make use of classical conditioning to explain the learning of a **phobia**—*a strong and irrational fear of a specific object, activity, or situation.* For example, driving a car is a neutral event that would not normally elicit a fear response in most people. But if a person were to experience a panic attack in which he suddenly experienced strong negative emotions while driving, he may learn to associate driving with the panic response. The driving has become the CS that now creates the fear response.

Psychologists have also discovered that people do not develop phobias to just anything. Although people may in some cases develop a driving phobia, they are more likely to develop phobias toward objects (such as snakes, spiders, heights, and open spaces) that have been dangerous to people in the past. In modern life, it is rare for humans to be bitten by spiders or snakes, to fall from trees or buildings, or to be attacked by a predator in an open area. Being injured while riding in a car or being cut by a knife are much more likely. But in our evolutionary past, the potential of being bitten by snakes or spiders, falling out of a tree, or being trapped in an open space were important evolutionary concerns, and therefore humans are still evolutionarily prepared to learn these associations over others (Öhman & Mineka, 2001; LoBue & DeLoache, 2010).[3]

Another evolutionarily important type of conditioning is conditioning related to food. In his important research on food conditioning, John Garcia and his colleagues (Garcia, Kimeldorf, & Koelling, 1955; Garcia, Ervin, & Koelling, 1966)[4] attempted to condition rats by presenting either a taste, a sight, or a sound as a neutral stimulus before the rats were given drugs (the US) that made them nauseous. Garcia discovered that taste conditioning was extremely powerful—the rat learned to avoid the taste associated with illness, even if the illness occurred several hours later. But conditioning the behavioral response of nausea to a sight or a sound was much more difficult. These results contradicted the idea that conditioning occurs entirely as a result of environmental events, such that it would occur equally for any kind of unconditioned stimulus that followed any kind of conditioned stimulus. Rather, Garcia's research showed that genetics matters—organisms are evolutionarily prepared to learn some associations more easily than others. You can see that the ability to associate smells with illness is an important survival mechanism, allowing the organism to quickly learn to avoid foods that are poisonous.

Classical conditioning has also been used to help explain the experience of posttraumatic stress disorder (PTSD), as in the case of P. K. Philips described in the chapter opener. PTSD is a severe anxiety disorder that can develop after exposure to a fearful event, such as the threat of death (American Psychiatric Association, 1994).[5] PTSD occurs when the individual develops a strong association between the situational factors that surrounded the traumatic event (e.g., military uniforms or the sounds or smells of war) and the US (the fearful trauma itself). As a result of the conditioning, being exposed to, or even thinking about the situation in which the trauma occurred (the CS), becomes sufficient to produce the CR of severe anxiety (Keane, Zimering, & Caddell, 1985).[6]

discrimination

The tendency to respond differently to stimuli that are similar, but not identical.

second-order conditioning

Conditioning that occurs when an existing conditioned stimulus serves as an unconditioned stimulus for a new conditioned stimulus.

phobia

A strong and irrational fear of a specific object, activity, or situation.

FIGURE 7.5

Posttraumatic stress disorder (PTSD) represents a case of classical conditioning to a severe trauma that does not easily become extinct. In this case the original fear response, experienced during combat, has become conditioned to a loud noise. When the person with PTSD hears a loud noise, she experiences a fear response even though she is now far from the site of the original trauma.

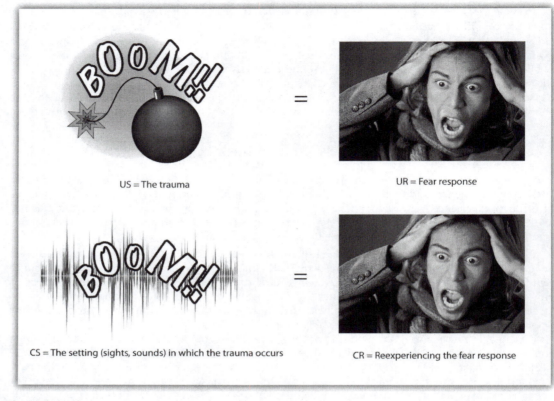

US = The trauma   UR = Fear response

CS = The setting (sights, sounds) in which the trauma occurs   CR = Reexperiencing the fear response

Photo © Thinkstock

PTSD develops because the emotions experienced during the event have produced neural activity in the amygdala and created strong conditioned learning. In addition to the strong conditioning that people with PTSD experience, they also show slower extinction in classical conditioning tasks (Milad et al., 2009).[7] In short, people with PTSD have developed very strong associations with the events surrounding the trauma and are also slow to show extinction to the conditioned stimulus.

KEY TAKEAWAYS

- In classical conditioning, a person or animal learns to associate a neutral stimulus (the conditioned stimulus, or CS) with a stimulus (the unconditioned stimulus, or US) that naturally produces a behavior (the unconditioned response, or UR). As a result of this association, the previously neutral stimulus comes to elicit the same response (the conditioned response, or CR).
- Extinction occurs when the CS is repeatedly presented without the US, and the CR eventually disappears, although it may reappear later in a process known as spontaneous recovery.
- Stimulus generalization occurs when a stimulus that is similar to an already-conditioned stimulus begins to produce the same response as the original stimulus does.
- Stimulus discrimination occurs when the organism learns to differentiate between the CS and other similar stimuli.
- In second-order conditioning, a neutral stimulus becomes a CS after being paired with a previously established CS.
- Some stimuli—response pairs, such as those between smell and food—are more easily conditioned than others because they have been particularly important in our evolutionary past.

E X E R C I S E S   A N D   C R I T I C A L   T H I N K I N G

1. A teacher places gold stars on the chalkboard when the students are quiet and attentive. Eventually, the students start becoming quiet and attentive whenever the teacher approaches the chalkboard. Can you explain the students' behavior in terms of classical conditioning?
2. Recall a time in your life, perhaps when you were a child, when your behaviors were influenced by classical conditioning. Describe in detail the nature of the unconditioned and conditioned stimuli and the response, using the appropriate psychological terms.
3. If posttraumatic stress disorder (PTSD) is a type of classical conditioning, how might psychologists use the principles of classical conditioning to treat the disorder?

2. CHANGING BEHAVIOR THROUGH REINFORCEMENT AND PUNISHMENT: OPERANT CONDITIONING

L E A R N I N G   O B J E C T I V E S

1. **Outline the principles of operant conditioning.**
2. **Explain how learning can be shaped through the use of reinforcement schedules and secondary reinforcers.**

In classical conditioning the organism learns to associate new stimuli with natural, biological responses such as salivation or fear. The organism does not learn something new but rather begins to perform in an existing behavior in the presence of a new signal. **Operant conditioning**, on the other hand, is *learning that occurs based on the consequences of behavior* and can involve the learning of new actions. Operant conditioning occurs when a dog rolls over on command because it has been praised for doing so in the past, when a schoolroom bully threatens his classmates because doing so allows him to get his way, and when a child gets good grades because her parents threaten to punish her if she doesn't. In operant conditioning the organism learns from the consequences of its own actions.

operant conditioning

Learning that occurs based on the consequences of behavior.

2.1 How Reinforcement and Punishment Influence Behavior: The Research of Thorndike and Skinner

Psychologist Edward L. Thorndike (1874–1949) was the first scientist to systematically study operant conditioning. In his research Thorndike (1898)[8] observed cats who had been placed in a "puzzle box" from which they tried to escape ("Video Clip: Thorndike's Puzzle Box"). At first the cats scratched, bit, and swatted haphazardly, without any idea of how to get out. But eventually, and accidentally, they pressed the lever that opened the door and exited to their prize, a scrap of fish. The next time the cat was constrained within the box it attempted fewer of the ineffective responses before carrying out the successful escape, and after several trials the cat learned to almost immediately make the correct response.

Observing these changes in the cats' behavior led Thorndike to develop his **law of effect**, *the principle that responses that create a typically pleasant outcome in a particular situation are more likely to occur again in a similar situation, whereas responses that produce a typically unpleasant outcome are less likely to occur again in the situation* (Thorndike, 1911).[9] The essence of the law of effect is that successful responses, because they are pleasurable, are "stamped in" by experience and thus occur more frequently. Unsuccessful responses, which produce unpleasant experiences, are "stamped out" and subsequently occur less frequently.

law of effect

The principle that responses that create a typically pleasant outcome in a particular situation are more likely to occur again in a similar situation, whereas responses that produce a typically unpleasant outcome are less likely to occur again in the situation.

Video Clip: Thorndike's Puzzle Box

When Thorndike placed his cats in a puzzle box, he found that they learned to engage in the important escape behavior faster after each trial. Thorndike described the learning that follows reinforcement in terms of the law of effect.

View the video online at: http://www.youtube.com/embed/BDujDOLre-8

Skinner box (operant chamber)

A structure used to study operant learning in small animals.

reinforcer

Any event that strengthens or increases the likelihood of a behavior.

punisher

Any event that weakens or decreases the likelihood of a behavior.

positive reinforcement

The strengthening of a response by presenting a typically pleasurable stimulus after the response.

negative reinforcement

The strengthening of a response by removing a typically unpleasant stimulus after the response.

The influential behavioral psychologist B. F. Skinner (1904–1990) expanded on Thorndike's ideas to develop a more complete set of principles to explain operant conditioning. Skinner created specially designed environments known as *operant chambers* (usually called *Skinner boxes*) to systemically study learning. A **Skinner box (operant chamber)** is *a structure that is big enough to fit a rodent or bird and that contains a bar or key that the organism can press or peck to release food or water. It also contains a device to record the animal's responses.*

The most basic of Skinner's experiments was quite similar to Thorndike's research with cats. A rat placed in the chamber reacted as one might expect, scurrying about the box and sniffing and clawing at the floor and walls. Eventually the rat chanced upon a lever, which it pressed to release pellets of food. The next time around, the rat took a little less time to press the lever, and on successive trials, the time it took to press the lever became shorter and shorter. Soon the rat was pressing the lever as fast as it could eat the food that appeared. As predicted by the law of effect, the rat had learned to repeat the action that brought about the food and cease the actions that did not.

Skinner studied, in detail, how animals changed their behavior through reinforcement and punishment, and he developed terms that explained the processes of operant learning (Table 7.1). Skinner used the term **reinforcer** to refer to *any event that strengthens or increases the likelihood of a behavior* and the term **punisher** to refer to *any event that weakens or decreases the likelihood of a behavior*. And he used the terms *positive* and *negative* to refer to whether a reinforcement was presented or removed, respectively. Thus **positive reinforcement** *strengthens a response by presenting something pleasant after the response* and **negative reinforcement** *strengthens a response by reducing or removing something unpleasant*. For example, giving a child praise for completing his homework represents positive reinforcement, whereas taking aspirin to reduced the pain of a headache represents negative reinforcement. In both cases, the reinforcement makes it more likely that behavior will occur again in the future.

TABLE 7.1 How Positive and Negative Reinforcement and Punishment Influence Behavior

Operant conditioning term	Description	Outcome	Example
Positive reinforcement	Add or increase a pleasant stimulus	Behavior is strengthened	Giving a student a prize after he gets an A on a test
Negative reinforcement	Reduce or remove an unpleasant stimulus	Behavior is strengthened	Taking painkillers that eliminate pain increases the likelihood that you will take painkillers again
Positive punishment	Present or add an unpleasant stimulus	Behavior is weakened	Giving a student extra homework after she misbehaves in class
Negative punishment	Reduce or remove a pleasant stimulus	Behavior is weakened	Taking away a teen's computer after he misses curfew

Reinforcement, either positive or negative, works by increasing the likelihood of a behavior. Punishment, on the other hand, refers to *any event that weakens or reduces the likelihood of a behavior*. *Positive punishment weakens a response by presenting something unpleasant after the response*, whereas *negative punishment weakens a response by reducing or removing something pleasant*. A child who is grounded after fighting with a sibling (positive punishment) or who loses out on the opportunity to go to recess after getting a poor grade (negative punishment) is less likely to repeat these behaviors.

Although the distinction between reinforcement (which increases behavior) and punishment (which decreases it) is usually clear, in some cases it is difficult to determine whether a reinforcer is positive or negative. On a hot day a cool breeze could be seen as a positive reinforcer (because it brings in cool air) or a negative reinforcer (because it removes hot air). In other cases, reinforcement can be both positive and negative. One may smoke a cigarette both because it brings pleasure (positive reinforcement) and because it eliminates the craving for nicotine (negative reinforcement).

It is also important to note that reinforcement and punishment are not simply opposites. The use of positive reinforcement in changing behavior is almost always more effective than using punishment. This is because positive reinforcement makes the person or animal feel better, helping create a positive relationship with the person providing the reinforcement. Types of positive reinforcement that are effective in everyday life include verbal praise or approval, the awarding of status or prestige, and direct financial payment. Punishment, on the other hand, is more likely to create only temporary changes in behavior because it is based on coercion and typically creates a negative and adversarial relationship with the person providing the reinforcement. When the person who provides the punishment leaves the situation, the unwanted behavior is likely to return.

2.2 Creating Complex Behaviors Through Operant Conditioning

Perhaps you remember watching a movie or being at a show in which an animal—maybe a dog, a horse, or a dolphin—did some pretty amazing things. The trainer gave a command and the dolphin swam to the bottom of the pool, picked up a ring on its nose, jumped out of the water through a hoop in the air, dived again to the bottom of the pool, picked up another ring, and then took both of the rings to the trainer at the edge of the pool. The animal was trained to do the trick, and the principles of operant conditioning were used to train it. But these complex behaviors are a far cry from the simple stimulus-response relationships that we have considered thus far. How can reinforcement be used to create complex behaviors such as these?

One way to expand the use of operant learning is to modify the schedule on which the reinforcement is applied. To this point we have only discussed a **continuous reinforcement schedule**, in which *the desired response is reinforced every time it occurs*; whenever the dog rolls over, for instance, it gets a biscuit. Continuous reinforcement results in relatively fast learning but also rapid extinction of the desired behavior once the reinforcer disappears. The problem is that because the organism is used to receiving the reinforcement after every behavior, the responder may give up quickly when it doesn't appear.

Most real-world reinforcers are not continuous; they occur on a **partial (or intermittent) reinforcement schedule**—*a schedule in which the responses are sometimes reinforced, and sometimes not*. In comparison to continuous reinforcement, partial reinforcement schedules lead to slower initial learning, but they also lead to greater resistance to extinction. Because the reinforcement does not appear after every behavior, it takes longer for the learner to determine that the reward is no longer coming, and thus extinction is slower. The four types of partial reinforcement schedules are summarized in Table 7.2.

FIGURE 7.6
Rat in a Skinner Box

B. F. Skinner used a Skinner box to study operant learning. The box contains a bar or key that the organism can press to receive food and water, and a device that records the organism's responses.

Source: Photo courtesy of YrVelouria, http://www.flickr.com/photos/yrvelouria/277353660/in/photostream.

positive punishment

The weakening of a response by presenting a typically unpleasant stimulus after the response.

negative punishment

The weakening of a response by removing a typically pleasant stimulus after the response.

continuous reinforcement schedule

A reinforcement schedule in which the desired response is reinforced every time it occurs.

partial (or intermittent) reinforcement schedule

A reinforcement schedule in which the desired reponse is sometimes reinforced, and sometimes not.

TABLE 7.2   Reinforcement Schedules

Reinforcement schedule	Explanation	Real-world example
Fixed-ratio	Behavior is reinforced after a specific number of responses	Factory workers who are paid according to the number of products they produce
Variable-ratio	Behavior is reinforced after an average, but unpredictable, number of responses	Payoffs from slot machines and other games of chance
Fixed-interval	Behavior is reinforced for the first response after a specific amount of time has passed	People who earn a monthly salary
Variable-interval	Behavior is reinforced for the first response after an average, but unpredictable, amount of time has passed	Person who checks voice mail for messages

fixed-interval schedule

A reinforcement schedule in which the reinforcement occurs for the first response made after a specific amount of time has passed.

variable-interval schedule

An interval reinforcement schedule in which the timing of the reinforcer is varied around the average interval, making the actual appearance of the reinforcer unpredictable.

Partial reinforcement schedules are determined by whether the reinforcement is presented on the basis of the time that elapses between reinforcement (interval) or on the basis of the number of responses that the organism engages in (ratio), and by whether the reinforcement occurs on a regular (fixed) or unpredictable (variable) schedule. In a **fixed-interval schedule**, *reinforcement occurs for the first response made after a specific amount of time has passed.* For instance, on a one-minute fixed-interval schedule the animal receives a reinforcement every minute, assuming it engages in the behavior at least once during the minute. As you can see in Figure 7.7, animals under fixed-interval schedules tend to slow down their responding immediately after the reinforcement but then increase the behavior again as the time of the next reinforcement gets closer. (Most students study for exams the same way.) In a **variable-interval schedule**, *the reinforcers appear on an interval schedule, but the timing is varied around the average interval, making the actual appearance of the reinforcer unpredictable.* An example might be checking your e-mail: You are reinforced by receiving messages that come, on average, say every 30 minutes, but the reinforcement occurs only at random times. Interval reinforcement schedules tend to produce slow and steady rates of responding.

FIGURE 7.7   Examples of Response Patterns by Animals Trained Under Different Partial Reinforcement Schedules

Schedules based on the number of responses (ratio types) induce greater response rate than do schedules based on elapsed time (interval types). Also, unpredictable schedules (variable types) produce stronger responses than do predictable schedules (fixed types).

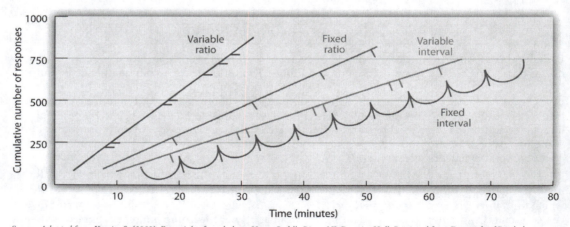

Source: Adapted from Kassin, S. (2003). Essentials of psychology. Upper Saddle River, NJ: Prentice Hall. Retrieved from Essentials of Psychology Prentice Hall Companion Website: http://wps.prenhall.com/hss_kassin_essentials_1/15/3933/1006917.cw/index.html.

In a **fixed-ratio schedule**, *a behavior is reinforced after a specific number of responses*. For instance, a rat's behavior may be reinforced after it has pressed a key 20 times, or a salesperson may receive a bonus after she has sold 10 products. As you can see in Figure 7.7, once the organism has learned to act in accordance with the fixed-reinforcement schedule, it will pause only briefly when reinforcement occurs before returning to a high level of responsiveness. A **variable-ratio schedule** *provides reinforcers after a specific but average number of responses*. Winning money from slot machines or on a lottery ticket are examples of reinforcement that occur on a variable-ratio schedule. For instance, a slot machine may be programmed to provide a win every 20 times the user pulls the handle, on average. As you can see in Figure 7.8, ratio schedules tend to produce high rates of responding because reinforcement increases as the number of responses increase.

Complex behaviors are also created through **shaping**, *the process of guiding an organism's behavior to the desired outcome through the use of successive approximation to a final desired behavior*. Skinner made extensive use of this procedure in his boxes. For instance, he could train a rat to press a bar two times to receive food, by first providing food when the animal moved near the bar. Then when that behavior had been learned he would begin to provide food only when the rat touched the bar. Further shaping limited the reinforcement to only when the rat pressed the bar, to when it pressed the bar and touched it a second time, and finally, to only when it pressed the bar twice. Although it can take a long time, in this way operant conditioning can create chains of behaviors that are reinforced only when they are completed.

Reinforcing animals if they correctly discriminate between similar stimuli allows scientists to test the animals' ability to learn, and the discriminations that they can make are sometimes quite remarkable. Pigeons have been trained to distinguish between images of Charlie Brown and the other Peanuts characters (Cerella, 1980),[10] and between different styles of music and art (Porter & Neuringer, 1984; Watanabe, Sakamoto & Wakita, 1995).[11]

Behaviors can also be trained through the use of *secondary reinforcers*. Whereas a **primary reinforcer** includes *stimuli that are naturally preferred or enjoyed by the organism, such as food, water, and relief from pain*, a **secondary reinforcer** (sometimes called *conditioned reinforcer*) is a *neutral event that has become associated with a primary reinforcer through classical conditioning*. An example of a secondary reinforcer would be the whistle given by an animal trainer, which has been associated over time with the primary reinforcer, food. An example of an everyday secondary reinforcer is money. We enjoy having money, not so much for the stimulus itself, but rather for the primary reinforcers (the things that money can buy) with which it is associated.

fixed-ratio schedule

A reinforcement schedule in which behavior is reinforced after a specific number of responses.

variable-ratio schedule

A ratio reinforcement schedule in which the reinforcer is provided after an average number of responses.

FIGURE 7.8 Slot Machine

Slot machines are examples of a variable-ratio reinforcement schedule.

© Thinkstock

shaping

The process of guiding an organism's behavior to the desired outcome through the use of successive approximation to a final desired behavior.

primary reinforcer

Stimuli that are naturally preferred or enjoyed by the organism, such as food, water, and relief from pain.

secondary reinforcer

Neutral events that have become associated with a primary reinforcer through classical conditioning.

KEY TAKEAWAYS

- Edward Thorndike developed the law of effect: the principle that responses that create a typically pleasant outcome in a particular situation are more likely to occur again in a similar situation, whereas responses that produce a typically unpleasant outcome are less likely to occur again in the situation.
- B. F. Skinner expanded on Thorndike's ideas to develop a set of principles to explain operant conditioning.
- Positive reinforcement strengthens a response by presenting something that is typically pleasant after the response, whereas negative reinforcement strengthens a response by reducing or removing something that is typically unpleasant.
- Positive punishment weakens a response by presenting something typically unpleasant after the response, whereas negative punishment weakens a response by reducing or removing something that is typically pleasant.
- Reinforcement may be either partial or continuous. Partial reinforcement schedules are determined by whether the reinforcement is presented on the basis of the time that elapses between reinforcements (interval) or on the basis of the number of responses that the organism engages in (ratio), and by whether the reinforcement occurs on a regular (fixed) or unpredictable (variable) schedule.
- Complex behaviors may be created through shaping, the process of guiding an organism's behavior to the desired outcome through the use of successive approximation to a final desired behavior.

EXERCISES AND CRITICAL THINKING

1. Give an example from daily life of each of the following: positive reinforcement, negative reinforcement, positive punishment, negative punishment.
2. Consider the reinforcement techniques that you might use to train a dog to catch and retrieve a Frisbee that you throw to it.
3. Watch the following two videos from current television shows. Can you determine which learning procedures are being demonstrated?
   a. *The Office*: http://www.break.com/usercontent/2009/11/the-office-altoid- experiment-1499823
   b. *The Big Bang Theory*: http://www.youtube.com/watch?v=JA96Fba-WHk

3. LEARNING BY INSIGHT AND OBSERVATION

LEARNING OBJECTIVE

1. **Understand the principles of learning by insight and observation.**

John B. Watson and B. F. Skinner were behaviorists who believed that all learning could be explained by the processes of conditioning—that is, that associations, and associations alone, influence learning. But some kinds of learning are very difficult to explain using only conditioning. Thus, although classical and operant conditioning play a key role in learning, they constitute only a part of the total picture.

One type of learning that is not determined only by conditioning occurs when we suddenly find the solution to a problem, as if the idea just popped into our head. This type of learning is known as **insight**, *the sudden understanding of a solution to a problem*. The German psychologist Wolfgang Köhler (1925)[12] carefully observed what happened when he presented chimpanzees with a problem that was not easy for them to solve, such as placing food in an area that was too high in the cage to be reached. He found that the chimps first engaged in trial-and-error attempts at solving the problem, but when these failed they seemed to stop and contemplate for a while. Then, after this period of contemplation, they would suddenly seem to know how to solve the problem, for instance by using a stick to knock the food down or by standing on a chair to reach it. Köhler argued that it was this flash of insight, not the prior trial-and-error approaches, which were so important for conditioning theories, that allowed the animals to solve the problem.

Edward Tolman (Tolman & Honzik, 1930)[13] studied the behavior of three groups of rats that were learning to navigate through mazes. The first group always received a reward of food at the end of the maze. The second group never received any reward, and the third group received a reward, but only beginning on the 11th day of the experimental period. As you might expect when considering the principles of conditioning, the rats in the first group quickly learned to negotiate the maze, while the rats of

insight

The sudden understanding of the solution to a problem.

the second group seemed to wander aimlessly through it. The rats in the third group, however, although they wandered aimlessly for the first 10 days, quickly learned to navigate to the end of the maze as soon as they received food on day 11. By the next day, the rats in the third group had caught up in their learning to the rats that had been rewarded from the beginning.

It was clear to Tolman that the rats that had been allowed to experience the maze, even without any reinforcement, had nevertheless learned something, and Tolman called this *latent learning*. **Latent learning** refers to *learning that is not reinforced and not demonstrated until there is motivation to do so*. Tolman argued that the rats had formed a "cognitive map" of the maze but did not demonstrate this knowledge until they received reinforcement.

latent learning

Learning that is not reinforced and not demonstrated until there is motivation to do so.

3.1 Observational Learning: Learning by Watching

The idea of latent learning suggests that animals, and people, may learn simply by experiencing or watching. **Observational learning (modeling)** is *learning by observing the behavior of others*. To demonstrate the importance of observational learning in children, Bandura, Ross, and Ross (1963)[14] showed children a live image of either a man or a woman interacting with a Bobo doll, a filmed version of the same events, or a cartoon version of the events. As you can see in "Video Clip: Bandura Discussing Clips From His Modeling Studies" the Bobo doll is an inflatable balloon with a weight in the bottom that makes it bob back up when you knock it down. In all three conditions, the model violently punched the clown, kicked the doll, sat on it, and hit it with a hammer.

observational learning (modeling)

Learning by observing the behavior of others.

Video Clip: Bandura Discussing Clips From His Modeling Studies

Take a moment to see how Albert Bandura explains his research into the modeling of aggression in children.

View the video online at: http://youtu.be/jWsxfoJEwQQ

The researchers first let the children view one of the three types of modeling, and then let them play in a room in which there were some really fun toys. To create some frustration in the children, Bandura let the children play with the fun toys for only a couple of minutes before taking them away. Then Bandura gave the children a chance to play with the Bobo doll.

If you guessed that most of the children imitated the model, you would be correct. Regardless of which type of modeling the children had seen, and regardless of the sex of the model or the child, the children who had seen the model behaved aggressively—just as the model had done. They also punched, kicked, sat on the doll, and hit it with the hammer. Bandura and his colleagues had demonstrated that these children had learned new behaviors, simply by observing and imitating others.

Observational learning is useful for animals and for people because it allows us to learn without having to actually engage in what might be a risky behavior. Monkeys that see other monkeys respond with fear to the sight of a snake learn to fear the snake themselves, even if they have been raised in a laboratory and have never actually seen a snake (Cook & Mineka, 1990).[15] As Bandura put it, *the prospects for [human] survival would be slim indeed if one could learn only by suffering the consequences of trial and error. For this reason, one does not teach children to swim, adolescents to drive automobiles, and novice medical students to perform surgery by having them discover the appropriate behavior through the consequences of their successes and failures. The more costly and hazardous the possible mistakes, the heavier is the reliance on observational learning from competent learners. (Bandura, 1977, p. 212)*[16]

Although modeling is normally adaptive, it can be problematic for children who grow up in violent families. These children are not only the victims of aggression, but they also see it happening to their parents and siblings. Because children learn how to be parents in large part by modeling the actions of their own parents, it is no surprise that there is a strong correlation between family violence in childhood and violence as an adult. Children who witness their parents being violent or who are themselves abused are more likely as adults to inflict abuse on intimate partners or their children, and to be victims of intimate violence (Heyman & Slep, 2002).[17] In turn, their children are more likely to interact violently with each other and to aggress against their parents (Patterson, Dishion, & Bank, 1984).[18]

Research Focus: The Effects of Violent Video Games on Aggression

The average American child watches more than 4 hours of television every day, and 2 out of 3 of the programs they watch contain aggression. It has been estimated that by the age of 12, the average American child has seen more than 8,000 murders and 100,000 acts of violence. At the same time, children are also exposed to violence in movies, video games, and virtual reality games, as well as in music videos that include violent lyrics and imagery (The Henry J. Kaiser Family Foundation, 2003; Schulenburg, 2007; Coyne & Archer, 2005).[19]

It might not surprise you to hear that these exposures to violence have an effect on aggressive behavior. The evidence is impressive and clear: The more media violence people, including children, view, the more aggressive they are likely to be (Anderson et al., 2003; Cantor et al., 2001).[20] The relation between viewing television violence and aggressive behavior is about as strong as the relation between smoking and cancer or between studying and academic grades. People who watch more violence become more aggressive than those who watch less violence.

It is clear that watching television violence can increase aggression, but what about violent video games? These games are more popular than ever, and also more graphically violent. Youths spend countless hours playing these games, many of which involve engaging in extremely violent behaviors. The games often require the player to take the role of a violent person, to identify with the character, to select victims, and of course to kill the victims. These behaviors are reinforced by winning points and moving on to higher levels, and are repeated over and over.

Again, the answer is clear—playing violent video games leads to aggression. A recent meta-analysis by Anderson and Bushman (2001)[21] reviewed 35 research studies that had tested the effects of playing violent video games on aggression. The studies included both experimental and correlational studies, with both male and female participants in both laboratory and field settings. They found that exposure to violent video games is significantly linked to increases in aggressive thoughts, aggressive feelings, psychological arousal (including blood pressure and heart rate), as well as aggressive behavior. Furthermore, playing more video games was found to relate to less altruistic behavior.

In one experiment, Bushman and Anderson (2002)[22] assessed the effects of viewing violent video games on aggressive thoughts and behavior. Participants were randomly assigned to play either a violent or a nonviolent video game for 20 minutes. Each participant played one of four violent video games (Carmageddon, Duke Nukem, Mortal Kombat, or Future Cop) or one of four nonviolent video games (Glider Pro, 3D Pinball, Austin Powers, or Tetra Madness).

Participants then read a story, for instance this one about Todd, and were asked to list 20 thoughts, feelings, and actions about how they would respond if they were Todd:

Todd was on his way home from work one evening when he had to brake quickly for a yellow light. The person in the car behind him must have thought Todd was going to run the light because he crashed into the back of Todd's car, causing a lot of damage to both vehicles. Fortunately, there were no injuries. Todd got out of his car and surveyed the damage. He then walked over to the other car.

As you can see in Figure 7.9, the students who had played one of the violent video games responded much more aggressively to the story than did those who played the nonviolent games. In fact, their responses were often extremely aggressive. They said things like "Call the guy an idiot," "Kick the other driver's car," "This guy's dead meat!" and "What a dumbass!"

Results From Bushman and Anderson, 2002

Anderson and Bushman (2002) found that college students who had just played a violent video game expressed significantly more violent responses to a story than did those who had just played a nonviolent video game.

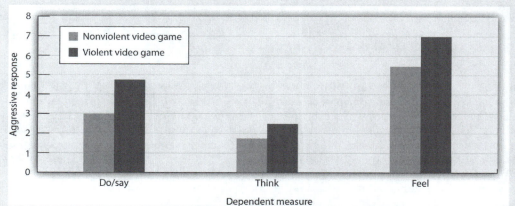

Source: *Adapted from Bushman, B. J., & Anderson, C. A. (2002). Violent video games and hostile expectations: A test of the general aggression model. Personality and Social Psychology Bulletin, 28(12), 1679–1686.*

However, although modeling can increase violence, it can also have positive effects. Research has found that, just as children learn to be aggressive through observational learning, they can also learn to be altruistic in the same way (Seymour, Yoshida, & Dolan, 2009).[23]

KEY TAKEAWAYS

- Not all learning can be explained through the principles of classical and operant conditioning.
- Insight is the sudden understanding of the components of a problem that makes the solution apparent.
- Latent learning refers to learning that is not reinforced and not demonstrated until there is motivation to do so.
- Observational learning occurs by viewing the behaviors of others.
- Both aggression and altruism can be learned through observation.

EXERCISES AND CRITICAL THINKING

1. Describe a time when you learned something by insight. What do you think led to your learning?
2. Imagine that you had a 12-year-old brother who spent many hours a day playing violent video games. Basing your answer on the material covered in this chapter, do you think that your parents should limit his exposure to the games? Why or why not?
3. How might we incorporate principles of observational learning to encourage acts of kindness and selflessness in our society?

4. USING THE PRINCIPLES OF LEARNING TO UNDERSTAND EVERYDAY BEHAVIOR

LEARNING OBJECTIVES

1. Review the ways that learning theories can be applied to understanding and modifying every-day behavior.
2. Describe the situations under which reinforcement may make people *less* likely to enjoy engaging in a behavior.
3. Explain how principles of reinforcement are used to understand social dilemmas such as the prisoner's dilemma and why people are likely to make competitive choices in them.

The principles of learning are some of the most general and most powerful in all of psychology. It would be fair to say that these principles account for more behavior using fewer principles than any other set of psychological theories. The principles of learning are applied in numerous ways in every-day settings. For example, operant conditioning has been used to motivate employees, to improve athletic performance, to increase the functioning of those suffering from developmental disabilities, and to help parents successfully toilet train their children (Simek & O'Brien, 1981; Pedalino & Gamboa, 1974; Azrin & Foxx, 1974; McGlynn, 1990).[24] In this section we will consider how learning theories are used in advertising, in education, and in understanding competitive relationships between individuals and groups.

4.1 Using Classical Conditioning in Advertising

Classical conditioning has long been, and continues to be, an effective tool in marketing and advertising (Hawkins, Best, & Coney, 1998).[25] The general idea is to create an advertisement that has positive features such that the ad creates enjoyment in the person exposed to it. The enjoyable ad serves as the unconditioned stimulus (US), and the enjoyment is the unconditioned response (UR). Because the product being advertised is mentioned in the ad, it becomes associated with the US, and then becomes the conditioned stimulus (CS). In the end, if everything has gone well, seeing the product online or in the store will then create a positive response in the buyer, leading him or her to be more likely to purchase the product.

Video Clip: Television Ads

Can you determine how classical conditioning is being used in these commercials?

View the video online at: http://www.youtube.com/embed/dsESVrArhbk

View the video online at: http://www.youtube.com/embed/870TqORDZSs

A similar strategy is used by corporations that sponsor teams or events. For instance, if people enjoy watching a college basketball team playing basketball, and if that team is sponsored by a product, such as Pepsi, then people may end up experiencing positive feelings when they view a can of Pepsi. Of course, the sponsor wants to sponsor only good teams and good athletes because these create more pleasurable responses.

Advertisers use a variety of techniques to create positive advertisements, including enjoyable music, cute babies, attractive models, and funny spokespeople. In one study, Gorn (1982)[26] showed research participants pictures of different writing pens of different colors, but paired one of the pens with pleasant music and the other with unpleasant music. When given a choice as a free gift, more people chose the pen color associated with the pleasant music. And Schemer, Matthes, Wirth, and Textor (2008)[27] found that people were more interested in products that had been embedded in music videos of artists that they liked and less likely to be interested when the products were in videos featuring artists that they did not like.

Another type of ad that is based on principles of classical conditioning is one that associates fear with the use of a product or behavior, such as those that show pictures of deadly automobile accidents to encourage seatbelt use or images of lung cancer surgery to discourage smoking. These ads have also been found to be effective (Das, de Wit, & Stroebe, 2003; Perloff, 2003; Witte & Allen, 2000),[28] due in large part to conditioning. When we see a cigarette and the fear of dying has been associated with it, we are hopefully less likely to light up.

Taken together then, there is ample evidence of the utility of classical conditioning, using both positive as well as negative stimuli, in advertising. This does not, however, mean that we are always influenced by these ads. The likelihood of conditioning being successful is greater for products that we do not know much about, where the differences between products are relatively minor, and when we do not think too carefully about the choices (Schemer et al., 2008).[29]

Psychology in Everyday Life: Operant Conditioning in the Classroom

John B. Watson and B. F. Skinner believed that all learning was the result of reinforcement, and thus that reinforcement could be used to educate children. For instance, Watson wrote in his book on behaviorism,

> *Give me a dozen healthy infants, well-formed, and my own specified world to bring them up in and I'll guarantee to take any one at random and train him to become any type of specialist I might select—doctor, lawyer, artist, merchant-chief and, yes, even beggar-man and thief, regardless of his talents, penchants, tendencies, abilities, vocations, and race of his ancestors. I am going beyond my facts and I admit it, but so have the advocates of the contrary and they have been doing it for many thousands of years (Watson, 1930, p. 82).[30]*

Skinner promoted the use of *programmed instruction*, an educational tool that consists of self-teaching with the aid of a specialized textbook or teaching machine that presents material in a logical sequence (Skinner, 1965).[31] Programmed instruction allows students to progress through a unit of study at their own rate, checking their own answers and advancing only after answering correctly. Programmed instruction is used today in many classes, for instance to teach computer programming (Emurian, 2009).[32]

Although reinforcement can be effective in education, and teachers make use of it by awarding gold stars, good grades, and praise, there are also substantial limitations to using reward to improve learning. To be most effective, rewards must be contingent on appropriate behavior. In some cases teachers may distribute rewards indiscriminately, for instance by giving praise or good grades to children whose work does not warrant it, in the hope that they will "feel good about themselves" and that this self-esteem will lead to better performance. Studies indicate, however, that high self-esteem alone does not improve academic performance (Baumeister, Campbell, Krueger, & Vohs, 2003).[33] When rewards are not earned, they become meaningless and no longer provide motivation for improvement.

Another potential limitation of rewards is that they may teach children that the activity should be performed for the reward, rather than for one's own interest in the task. If rewards are offered too often, the task itself becomes less appealing. Mark Lepper and his colleagues (Lepper, Greene, & Nisbett, 1973)[34] studied this possibility by leading some children to think that they engaged in an activity for a reward, rather than because they simply enjoyed it. First, they placed some fun felt-tipped markers in the classroom of the children they were studying. The children loved the markers and played with them right away. Then, the markers were taken out of the classroom, and the children were given a chance to play with the markers individually at an experimental session with the researcher. At the research session, the children were randomly assigned to one of three experimental groups. One group of children (the *expected reward* condition) was told that if they played with the markers they would receive a good drawing award. A second group (the *unexpected reward* condition) also played with the markers, and also got the award—but they were not told ahead of time that they would be receiving the award; it came as a surprise after the session. The third group (the *no reward* group) played with the markers too, but got no award.

Then, the researchers placed the markers back in the classroom and observed how much the children in each of the three groups played with them. As you can see in Figure 7.10, the children who had been led to expect a reward for playing with the markers during the experimental session played with the markers less at the second session than they had at the first session. The idea is that, when the children had to choose whether or not to play with the markers when the markers reappeared in the classroom, they based their decision on their own prior behavior. The children in the no reward groups and the children in the unexpected reward groups realized that they played with the markers because they liked them. Children in the expected award condition, however, remembered that they were promised a reward for the activity the last time they played with the markers. These children, then, were more likely to draw the inference that they play with the markers only for the external reward, and because they did not expect to get an award for playing with the markers in the classroom, they determined that they didn't like them. Expecting to receive the award at the session had undermined their initial interest in the markers.

Undermining Intrinsic Interest

Mark Lepper and his colleagues (1973) found that giving rewards for playing with markers, which the children naturally enjoyed, could reduce their interest in the activity.

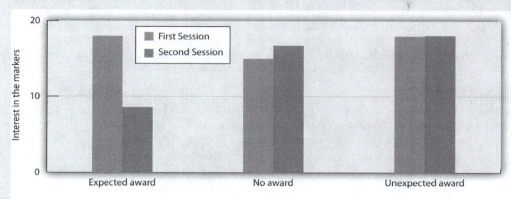

Source: Adapted from Lepper, M. R., Greene, D., & Nisbett, R. E. (1973). Undermining children's intrinsic interest with extrinsic reward: A test of the "overjustification" hypothesis. Journal of Personality & Social Psychology, 28(1), 129–137.

This research suggests that, although giving rewards may in many cases lead us to perform an activity more frequently or with more effort, reward may not always increase our liking for the activity. In some cases reward may actually make us like an activity less than we did before we were rewarded for it. This outcome is particularly likely when the reward is perceived as an obvious attempt on the part of others to get us to do something. When children are given money by their parents to get good grades in school, they may improve their school performance to gain the reward. But at the same time their liking for school may decrease. On the other hand, rewards that are seen as more internal to the activity, such as rewards that praise us, remind us of our achievements in the domain, and make us feel good about ourselves as a result of our accomplishments are more likely to be effective in increasing not only the performance of, but also the liking of, the activity (Hulleman, Durik, Schweigert, & Harackiewicz, 2008; Ryan & Deci, 2002).[35]

Other research findings also support the general principle that punishment is generally less effective than reinforcement in changing behavior. In a recent meta-analysis, Gershoff (2002)[36] found that although children who were spanked by their parents were more likely to immediately comply with the parents' demands, they were also more aggressive, showed less ability to control aggression, and had poorer mental health in the long term than children who were not spanked. The problem seems to be that children who are punished for bad behavior are likely to change their behavior only to avoid the punishment, rather than by internalizing the norms of being good for its own sake. Punishment also tends to generate anger, defiance, and a desire for revenge. Moreover, punishment models the use of aggression and ruptures the important relationship between the teacher and the learner (Kohn, 1993).[37]

4.2 Reinforcement in Social Dilemmas

The basic principles of reinforcement, reward, and punishment have been used to help understand a variety of human behaviors (Rotter, 1945; Bandura, 1977; Miller & Dollard, 1941).[38] The general idea is that, as predicted by principles of operant learning and the law of effect, people act in ways that maximize their *outcomes*, where outcomes are defined as the presence of reinforcers and the absence of punishers.

Consider, for example, a situation known as the *commons dilemma*, as proposed by the ecologist Garrett Hardin (1968).[39] Hardin noted that in many European towns there was at one time a centrally located pasture, known as the commons, which was shared by the inhabitants of the village to graze their livestock. But the commons was not always used wisely. The problem was that each individual who owned livestock wanted to be able to use the commons to graze his or her own animals. However, when each group member took advantage of the commons by grazing many animals, the commons became overgrazed, the pasture died, and the commons was destroyed.

Although Hardin focused on the particular example of the commons, the basic dilemma of individual desires versus the benefit of the group as whole can also be found in many contemporary public goods issues, including the use of limited natural resources, air pollution, and public land. In large cities most people may prefer the convenience of driving their own car to work each day rather than taking public transportation. Yet this behavior uses up public goods (the space on limited roadways, crude oil reserves, and clean air). People are lured into the dilemma by short-term rewards, seemingly without considering the potential long-term costs of the behavior, such as air pollution and the necessity of building even more highways.

social dilemma

A situation in which the behavior that creates the most rewards for the individual may in the long term lead to negative consequences for the group as a whole.

A **social dilemma** such as the commons dilemma is *a situation in which the behavior that creates the most positive outcomes for the individual may in the long term lead to negative consequences for the group as a whole*. The dilemmas are arranged in a way that it is easy to be selfish, because the personally beneficial choice (such as using water during a water shortage or driving to work alone in one's own car) produces reinforcements for the individual. Furthermore, social dilemmas tend to work on a type of "time delay." The problem is that, because the long-term negative outcome (the extinction of fish species or dramatic changes in the earth's climate) is far away in the future and the individual benefits are occurring right now, it is difficult for an individual to see how many costs there really are. The paradox, of course, is that if everyone takes the personally selfish choice in an attempt to maximize his or her own outcomes, the long-term result is poorer outcomes for every individual in the group. Each individual prefers to make use of the public goods for himself or herself, whereas the best outcome for the group as a whole is to use the resources more slowly and wisely.

One method of understanding how individuals and groups behave in social dilemmas is to create such situations in the laboratory and observe how people react to them. The best known of these laboratory simulations is called the **prisoner's dilemma game** (Poundstone, 1992).[40] This game *represents a social dilemma in which the goals of the individual compete with the goals of another individual (or sometimes with a group of other individuals)*. Like all social dilemmas, the prisoner's dilemma assumes that individuals will generally try to maximize their own outcomes in their interactions with others.

prisoner's dilemma game

A social dilemma in which the goals of the individual compete with the goals of another individual (or sometimes with a group of other individuals).

In the prisoner's dilemma game, the participants are shown a *payoff matrix* in which numbers are used to express the potential outcomes for each of the players in the game, given the decisions each player makes. The payoffs are chosen beforehand by the experimenter to create a situation that models some real-world outcome. Furthermore, in the prisoner's dilemma game, the payoffs are normally arranged as they would be in a typical social dilemma, such that each individual is better off acting in his or her immediate self-interest, and yet if all individuals act according to their self-interests, then everyone will be worse off.

In its original form, the prisoner's dilemma game involves a situation in which two prisoners (we'll call them Frank and Malik) have been accused of committing a crime. The police believe that the two worked together on the crime, but they have only been able to gather enough evidence to convict each of them of a more minor offense. In an attempt to gain more evidence, and thus to be able to convict the prisoners of the larger crime, each of the prisoners is interrogated individually, with the hope that he will confess to having been involved in the more major crime, in return for a promise of a reduced sentence if he confesses first. Each prisoner can make either the *cooperative choice* (which is to not confess) or the *competitive choice* (which is to confess).

The incentives for either confessing or not confessing are expressed in a payoff matrix such as the one shown in Figure 7.11. The top of the matrix represents the two choices that Malik might make (to either confess that he did the crime or not confess), and the side of the matrix represents the two choices that Frank might make (also to either confess or not confess). The payoffs that each prisoner receives, given the choices of each of the two prisoners, are shown in each of the four squares.

FIGURE 7.11 The Prisoner's Dilemma

In the prisoner's dilemma game, two suspected criminals are interrogated separately. The matrix indicates the outcomes for each prisoner, measured as the number of years each is sentenced to prison, as a result of each combination of cooperative (don't confess) and competitive (confess) decisions. Outcomes for Malik are in black and outcomes for Frank are in grey.

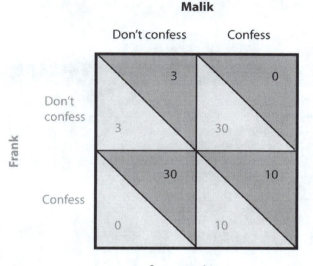

Sentence in years

If both prisoners take the cooperative choice by not confessing (the situation represented in the upper left square of the matrix), there will be a trial, the limited available information will be used to convict each prisoner, and they each will be sentenced to a relatively short prison term of three years. However, if either of the prisoners confesses, turning "state's evidence" against the other prisoner, then there will be enough information to convict the other prisoner of the larger crime, and that prisoner will receive a sentence of 30 years, whereas the prisoner who confesses will get off free. These outcomes are represented in the lower left and upper right squares of the matrix. Finally, it is possible that both players confess at the same time. In this case there is no need for a trial, and in return the prosecutors offer a somewhat reduced sentence (of 10 years) to each of the prisoners.

The prisoner's dilemma has two interesting characteristics that make it a useful model of a social dilemma. For one, the prisoner's dilemma is arranged such that a positive outcome for one player does not necessarily mean a negative outcome for the other player. If you consider again the matrix in Figure 7.11, you can see that if one player takes the cooperative choice (to not confess) and the other takes the competitive choice (to confess), then the prisoner who cooperates loses, whereas the other prisoner wins. However, if both prisoners make the cooperative choice, each remaining quiet, then neither gains more than the other, and both prisoners receive a relatively light sentence. In this sense both players can win at the same time.

Second, the prisoner's dilemma matrix is arranged such that each individual player is motivated to take the competitive choice, because this choice leads to a higher payoff regardless of what the other player does. Imagine for a moment that you are Malik, and you are trying to decide whether to cooperate (don't confess) or to compete (confess). And imagine that you are not really sure what Frank is going to do. Remember the goal of the individual is to maximize outcomes. The values in the matrix make it clear that if you think that Frank is going to confess, you should confess yourself (to get 10 rather than 30 years in prison). And, it is also clear that if you think Frank is not going to confess, you should still confess (to get 0 rather than 3 years in prison). So the matrix is arranged such that the "best" alternative for each player, at least in the sense of pure reward and self-interest, is to make the competitive choice, even though in the end both players would prefer the combination in which both players cooperate to the one in which they both compete.

Although initially specified in terms of the two prisoners, similar payoff matrices can be used to predict behavior in many different types of dilemmas involving two or more parties and including choices of helping and not helping, working and loafing, and paying and not paying debts. For instance, we can use the prisoner's dilemma to help us understand roommates living together in a house who might not want to contribute to the housework. Each of them would be better off if they relied on the other to clean the house. Yet if neither of them makes an effort to clean the house (the cooperative choice), the house becomes a mess and they will both be worse off.

KEY TAKEAWAYS

- Learning theories have been used to change behaviors in many areas of everyday life.
- Some advertising uses classical conditioning to associate a pleasant response with a product.
- Rewards are frequently and effectively used in education but must be carefully designed to be contingent on performance and to avoid undermining interest in the activity.
- Social dilemmas, such as the prisoner's dilemma, can be understood in terms of a desire to maximize one's outcomes in a competitive relationship.

EXERCISES AND CRITICAL THINKING

1. Find and share with your class some examples of advertisements that make use of classical conditioning to create positive attitudes toward products.
2. Should parents use both punishment as well as reinforcement to discipline their children? On what principles of learning do you base your opinion?
3. Think of a social dilemma other than one that has been discussed in this chapter, and explain people's behavior in it in terms of principles of learning.

5. CHAPTER SUMMARY

Classical conditioning was first studied by physiologist Ivan Pavlov. In classical conditioning a person or animal learns to associate a neutral stimulus (the conditioned stimulus, or CS) with a stimulus (the unconditioned stimulus, or US) that naturally produces a behavior (the unconditioned response, or UR). As a result of this association, the previously neutral stimulus comes to elicit the same or similar response (the conditioned response, or CR).

Classically conditioned responses show extinction if the CS is repeatedly presented without the US. The CR may reappear later in a process known as spontaneous recovery.

Organisms may show stimulus generalization, in which stimuli similar to the CS may produce similar behaviors, or stimulus discrimination, in which the organism learns to differentiate between the CS and other similar stimuli.

Second-order conditioning occurs when a second CS is conditioned to a previously established CS.

Psychologist Edward Thorndike developed the law of effect: the idea that responses that are reinforced are "stamped in" by experience and thus occur more frequently, whereas responses that are punishing are "stamped out" and subsequently occur less frequently.

B. F. Skinner (1904–1990) expanded on Thorndike's ideas to develop a set of principles to explain operant conditioning.

Positive reinforcement strengthens a response by presenting a something pleasant after the response, and negative reinforcement strengthens a response by reducing or removing something unpleasant. Positive punishment weakens a response by presenting something unpleasant after the response, whereas negative punishment weakens a response by reducing or removing something pleasant.

Shaping is the process of guiding an organism's behavior to the desired outcome through the use of reinforcers.

Reinforcement may be either partial or continuous. Partial-reinforcement schedules are determined by whether the reward is presented on the basis of the time that elapses between rewards (interval) or on the basis of the number of responses that the organism engages in (ratio), and by whether the reinforcement occurs on a regular (fixed) or unpredictable (variable) schedule.

Not all learning can be explained through the principles of classical and operant conditioning. Insight is the sudden understanding of the components of a problem that makes the solution apparent, and latent learning refers to learning that is not reinforced and not demonstrated until there is motivation to do so.

Learning by observing the behavior of others and the consequences of those behaviors is known as observational learning. Aggression, altruism, and many other behaviors are learned through observation.

Learning theories can and have been applied to change behaviors in many areas of everyday life. Some advertising uses classical conditioning to associate a pleasant response with a product.

Rewards are frequently and effectively used in education but must be carefully designed to be contingent on performance and to avoid undermining interest in the activity.

Social dilemmas, such as the prisoner's dilemma, can be understood in terms of a desire to maximize one's outcomes in a competitive relationship.

ENDNOTES

1. Philips, P. K. (2010). My story of survival: Battling PTSD. Anxiety Disorders Association of America. Retrieved from http://www.adaa.org/living-with-anxiety/personal-stories/my-story-survival-battling-ptsd

2. Lewicki, P. (1985). Nonconscious biasing effects of single instances on subsequent judgments. *Journal of Personality and Social Psychology, 48*, 563–574.

3. Öhman, A., & Mineka, S. (2001). Fears, phobias, and preparedness: Toward an evolved module of fear and fear learning. *Psychological Review, 108*(3), 483–522; LoBue, V., & DeLoache, J. S. (2010). Superior detection of threat-relevant stimuli in infancy. *Developmental Science, 13*(1), 221–228.

4. Garcia, J., Kimeldorf, D. J., & Koelling, R. A. (1955). Conditioned aversion to saccharin resulting from exposure to gamma radiation. *Science, 122*, 157–158; Garcia, J., Ervin, F. R., & Koelling, R. A. (1966). Learning with prolonged delay of reinforcement. *Psychonomic Science, 5*(3), 121–122.

5. American Psychiatric Association. (2000). *Diagnostic and statistical manual of mental disorders* (4th ed., text rev.). Washington, DC: Author.

6. Keane, T. M., Zimering, R. T., & Caddell, J. M. (1985). A behavioral formulation of posttraumatic stress disorder in Vietnam veterans. *The Behavior Therapist, 8*(1), 9–12.

7. Milad, M. R., Pitman, R. K., Ellis, C. B., Gold, A. L., Shin, L. M., Lasko, N. B.,…Rauch, S. L. (2009). Neurobiological basis of failure to recall extinction memory in posttraumatic stress disorder. *Biological Psychiatry, 66*(12), 1075–82.

8. Thorndike, E. L. (1898). *Animal intelligence: An experimental study of the associative processes in animals.* Washington, DC: American Psychological Association.

9. Thorndike, E. L. (1911). *Animal intelligence: Experimental studies.* New York, NY: Macmillan. Retrieved from http://www.archive.org/details/animalintelligen00thor

10. Cerella, J. (1980). The pigeon's analysis of pictures. *Pattern Recognition, 12*, 1–6.

11. Porter, D., & Neuringer, A. (1984). Music discriminations by pigeons. *Journal of Experimental Psychology: Animal Behavior Processes, 10*(2), 138–148; Watanabe, S., Sakamoto, J., & Wakita, M. (1995). Pigeons' discrimination of painting by Monet and Picasso. *Journal of the Experimental Analysis of Behavior, 63*(2), 165–174.

12. Köhler, W. (1925). *The mentality of apes* (E. Winter, Trans.). New York, NY: Harcourt Brace Jovanovich.

13. Tolman, E. C., & Honzik, C. H. (1930). Introduction and removal of reward, and maze performance in rats. *University of California Publications in Psychology, 4*, 257–275.

14. Bandura, A., Ross, D., & Ross, S. A. (1963). Imitation of film-mediated aggressive models. *The Journal of Abnormal and Social Psychology, 66*(1), 3–11.

15. Cook, M., & Mineka, S. (1990). Selective associations in the observational conditioning of fear in rhesus monkeys. *Journal of Experimental Psychology: Animal Behavior Processes, 16*(4), 372–389.

16. Bandura, A. (1977). Self-efficacy: Toward a unifying theory of behavior change. *Psychological Review, 84*, 191–215.

17. Heyman, R. E., & Slep, A. M. S. (2002). Do child abuse and interparental violence lead to adulthood family violence? *Journal of Marriage and Family, 64*(4), 864–870.

18. Patterson, G. R., Dishion, T. J., & Bank, L. (1984). Family interaction: A process model of deviancy training. *Aggressive Behavior, 10*(3), 253–267.

19. The Henry J. Kaiser Family Foundation. (2003, Spring). Key facts. Menlo Park, CA: Author. Retrieved from http://www.kff.org/entmedia/upload/Key-Facts-TV-Violence.pdf; Schulenburg, C. (2007, January). Dying to entertain: Violence on prime time broadcast television, 1998 to 2006. Los Angeles, CA: Parents Television Council. Retrieved from http://www.parentstv.org/PTC/publications/reports/violencestudy/exsummary.asp; Coyne, S. M., & Archer, J. (2005). The relationship between indirect and physical aggression on television and in real life. *Social Development, 14*(2), 324–337.

20. Anderson, C. A., Berkowitz, L., Donnerstein, E., Huesmann, L. R., Johnson, J. D., Linz, D.,…Wartella, E. (2003). The influence of media violence on youth. *Psychological Science in the Public Interest, 4*(3), 81–110; Cantor, J., Bushman, B. J., Huesmann, L. R., Groebel, J., Malamuth, N. M., Impett, E. A.,…Singer, J. L. (Eds.). (2001). *Some hazards of television viewing: Fears, aggression, and sexual attitudes.* Thousand Oaks, CA: Sage.

21. Anderson, C. A., & Bushman, B. J. (2001). Effects of violent video games on aggressive behavior, aggressive cognition, aggressive affect, physiological arousal, and prosocial behavior: A meta-analytic review of the scientific literature. *Psychological Science, 12*(5), 353–359.

22. Bushman, B. J., & Anderson, C. A. (2002). Violent video games and hostile expectations: A test of the general aggression model. *Personality and Social Psychology Bulletin, 28*(12), 1679–1686.

23. Seymour, B., Yoshida W., & Dolan, R. (2009) Altruistic learning. *Frontiers in Behavioral Neuroscience, 3*, 23. doi:10.3389/neuro.07.023.2009

24. Simek, T. C., & O'Brien, R. M. (1981). *Total golf: A behavioral approach to lowering your score and getting more out of your game.* New York, NY: Doubleday & Company; Pedalino, E., & Gamboa, V. U. (1974). Behavior modification and absenteeism: Intervention in one industrial setting. *Journal of Applied Psychology, 59*, 694–697; Azrin, N., & Foxx, R. M. (1974). *Toilet training in less than a day.* New York, NY: Simon & Schuster; McGlynn, S. M. (1990). Behavioral approaches to neuropsychological rehabilitation. *Psychological Bulletin, 108*, 420–441.

25. Hawkins, D., Best, R., & Coney, K. (1998.) *Consumer Behavior: Building Marketing Strategy* (7th ed.). Boston, MA: McGraw-Hill.

26. Gorn, G. J. (1982). The effects of music in advertising on choice behavior: A classical conditioning approach. *Journal of Marketing, 46*(1), 94–101.

27. Schemer, C., Matthes, J. R., Wirth, W., & Textor, S. (2008). Does "Passing the Courvoisier" always pay off? Positive and negative evaluative conditioning effects of brand placements in music videos. *Psychology & Marketing, 25*(10), 923–943.

28. Das, E. H. H. J., de Wit, J. B. F., & Stroebe, W. (2003). Fear appeals motivate acceptance of action recommendations: Evidence for a positive bias in the processing of persuasive messages. *Personality & Social Psychology Bulletin, 29*(5), 650–664; Perloff, R. M. (2003). *The dynamics of persuasion: Communication and attitudes in the 21st century* (2nd ed.). Mahwah, NJ: Lawrence Erlbaum Associates; Witte, K., & Allen, M. (2000). A meta-analysis of fear appeals: Implications for effective public health campaigns. *Health Education & Behavior, 27*(5), 591–615.

29. Schemer, C., Matthes, J. R., Wirth, W., & Textor, S. (2008). Does "Passing the Courvoisier" always pay off? Positive and negative evaluative conditioning effects of brand placements in music videos. *Psychology & Marketing, 25*(10), 923–943.

30. Watson, J. B. (1930). *Behaviorism* (Rev. ed.). New York, NY: Norton.

31. Skinner, B. F. (1965). The technology of teaching. *Proceedings of the Royal Society B Biological Sciences, 162*(989): 427–43. doi:10.1098/rspb.1965.0048

32. Emurian, H. H. (2009). Teaching Java: Managing instructional tactics to optimize student learning. *International Journal of Information & Communication Technology Education, 3*(4), 34–49.

33. Baumeister, R. F., Campbell, J. D., Krueger, J. I., & Vohs, K. D. (2003). Does high self-esteem cause better performance, interpersonal success, happiness, or healthier lifestyles? *Psychological Science in the Public Interest, 4*, 1–44.

34. Lepper, M. R., Greene, D., & Nisbett, R. E. (1973). Undermining children's intrinsic interest with extrinsic reward: A test of the "overjustification" hypothesis. *Journal of Personality & Social Psychology, 28*(1), 129–137.

35. Hulleman, C. S., Durik, A. M., Schweigert, S. B., & Harackiewicz, J. M. (2008). Task values, achievement goals, and interest: An integrative analysis. *Journal of Educational Psychology, 100*(2), 398–416; Ryan, R. M., & Deci, E. L. (2002). Overview of self-determination theory: An organismic-dialectical perspective. In E. L. Deci & R. M. Ryan (Eds.), *Handbook of self-determination research* (pp. 3–33). Rochester, NY: University of Rochester Press.

36. Gershoff, E. T. (2002). Corporal punishment by parents and associated child behaviors and experiences: A meta-analytic and theoretical review. *Psychological Bulletin, 128*(4), 539–579.

37. Kohn, A. (1993). *Punished by rewards: The trouble with gold stars, incentive plans, A's, praise, and other bribes.* Boston, MA: Houghton Mifflin and Company.

38. Rotter, J. B. (1945). *Social learning and clinical psychology.* Upper Saddle River, NJ: Prentice Hall; Bandura, A. (1977). *Social learning theory.* New York, NY: General Learning Press; Miller, N., & Dollard, J. (1941). *Social learning and imitation.* New Haven, CT: Yale University Press.

39. Hardin, G. (1968). The tragedy of the commons. *Science, 162*, 1243–1248.

40. Poundstone, W. (1992). *The prisoner's dilemma.* New York, NY: Doubleday.

CHAPTER 8
Remembering and Judging

She Was Certain, but She Was Wrong

In 1984 Jennifer Thompson was a 22-year-old college student in North Carolina. One night a man broke into her apartment, put a knife to her throat, and raped her. According to her own account, Ms. Thompson studied her rapist throughout the incident with great determination to memorize his face. She said:

> I studied every single detail on the rapist's face. I looked at his hairline; I looked for scars, for tattoos, for anything that would help me identify him. When and if I survived.

Ms. Thompson went to the police that same day to create a sketch of her attacker, relying on what she believed was her detailed memory. Several days later, the police constructed a photographic lineup. Thompson identified Ronald Cotton as the rapist, and she later testified against him at trial. She was positive it was him, with no doubt in her mind.

> I was sure. I knew it. I had picked the right guy, and he was going to go to jail. If there was the possibility of a death sentence, I wanted him to die. I wanted to flip the switch.

As positive as she was, it turned out that Jennifer Thompson was wrong. But it was not until after Mr. Cotton had served 11 years in prison for a crime he did not commit that conclusive DNA evidence indicated that Bobby Poole was the actual rapist, and Cotton was released from jail. Jennifer Thompson's memory had failed her, resulting in a substantial injustice. It took definitive DNA testing to shake her confidence, but she now knows that despite her confidence in her identification, it was wrong. Consumed by guilt, Thompson sought out Cotton when he was released from prison, and they have since become friends (Innocence Project, n.d.; Thompson, 2000).[1]

Picking Cotton: A Memoir of Injustice and Redemption

Although Jennifer Thompson was positive that it was Ronald Cotton who had raped her, her memory was inaccurate. Conclusive DNA testing later proved that he was not the attacker. Watch this book trailer about the story.

View the video online at: http://www.youtube.com/embed/nLGXrviy5lw

Jennifer Thompson is not the only person to have been fooled by her memory of events. Over the past 10 years, almost 400 people have been released from prison when DNA evidence confirmed that they could not have committed the crime for which they had been convicted. And in more than three-quarters of these cases, the cause of the innocent people being falsely convicted was erroneous eyewitness testimony (Wells, Memon, & Penrod, 2006).[2]

Eyewitness Testimony
Watch this video for Lesley Stahl's *60 Minutes* segment on this case.

View the video online at: http://www.youtube.com/embed/u-SBTRLoPuo

memory

The ability to store and retrieve information over time.

cognition

The processes of acquiring and using knowledge.

The two subjects of this chapter are **memory**, defined as *the ability to store and retrieve information over time*, and **cognition**, defined as *the processes of acquiring and using knowledge*. It is useful to consider memory and cognition in the same chapter because they work together to help us interpret and understand our environments.

Memory and cognition represent the two major interests of cognitive psychologists. The cognitive approach became the most important school of psychology during the 1960s, and the field of psychology has remained in large part cognitive since that time. The cognitive school was influenced in large part by the development of the electronic computer, and although the differences between computers and the human mind are vast, cognitive psychologists have used the computer as a model for understanding the workings of the mind.

Differences between Brains and Computers

- In computers, information can be accessed only if one knows the exact location of the memory. In the brain, information can be accessed through *spreading activation* from closely related concepts.

- The brain operates primarily in parallel, meaning that it is multitasking on many different actions at the same time. Although this is changing as new computers are developed, most computers are primarily serial—they finish one task before they start another.

- In computers, short-term (random-access) memory is a subset of long-term (read-only) memory. In the brain, the processes of short-term memory and long-term memory are distinct.

- In the brain, there is no difference between hardware (the mechanical aspects of the computer) and software (the programs that run on the hardware).

- In the brain, synapses, which operate using an electrochemical process, are much slower but also vastly more complex and useful than the transistors used by computers.

- Computers differentiate memory (e.g., the hard drive) from processing (the central processing unit), but in brains there is no such distinction. In the brain (but not in computers) existing memory is used to interpret and store incoming information, and retrieving information from memory changes the memory itself.

- The brain is self-organizing and self-repairing, but computers are not. If a person suffers a stroke, neural plasticity will help him or her recover. If we drop our laptop and it breaks, it cannot fix itself.

- The brain is significantly bigger than any current computer. The brain is estimated to have 25,000,000,000,000,000 (25 million billion) interactions among axons, dendrites, neurons, and neurotransmitters, and that doesn't include the approximately 1 trillion glial cells that may also be important for information processing and memory.

Although cognitive psychology began in earnest at about the same time that the electronic computer was first being developed, and although cognitive psychologists have frequently used the computer as a model for understanding how the brain operates, research in cognitive neuroscience has revealed many important differences between brains and computers. The neuroscientist Chris Chatham (2007)[3] provided the list of differences between brains and computers shown here. You might want to check out the website and the responses to it at http://scienceblogs.com/developingintelligence/2007/03/27/why-the-brain- is-not-like-a-co.

We will begin the chapter with the study of memory. Our memories allow us to do relatively simple things, such as remembering where we parked our car or the name of the current president of the United States, but also allow us to form complex memories, such as how to ride a bicycle or to write a computer program. Moreover, our memories define us as individuals—they are our experiences, our relationships, our successes, and our failures. Without our memories, we would not have a life.

At least for some things, our memory is very good (Bahrick, 2000).[4] Once we learn a face, we can recognize that face many years later. We know the lyrics of many songs by heart, and we can give definitions for tens of thousands of words. Mitchell (2006)[5] contacted participants 17 years after they had been briefly exposed to some line drawings in a lab and found that they still could identify the images significantly better than participants who had never seen them.

For some people, memory is truly amazing. Consider, for instance, the case of Kim Peek, who was the inspiration for the Academy Award–winning film *Rain Man* (Figure 8.1 and "Video Clip: Kim Peek"). Although Peek's IQ was only 87, significantly below the average of about 100, it is estimated that he memorized more than 10,000 books in his lifetime (Wisconsin Medical Society, n.d.; "Kim Peek," 2004).[6] The Russian psychologist A. R. Luria (2004)[7] has described the abilities of a man known as "S," who seems to have unlimited memory. S remembers strings of hundreds of random letters for years at a time, and seems in fact to never forget anything.

FIGURE 8.1
Kim Peek

Kim Peek, the subject of the movie *Rain Man*, was believed to have memorized the contents of more than 10,000 books. He could read a book in about an hour.

Source: Photo courtesy of Darold A. Treffert, MD, and the Wisconsin Medical Society, http://commons.wikimedia.org/wiki/File:Peek1.jpg.

Video Clip: Kim Peek

You can view an interview with Kim Peek and see some of his amazing memory abilities at this link.

View the video online at: http://www.youtube.com/embed/dhcQG_KltZM

In this chapter we will see how psychologists use behavioral responses (such as memory tests and reaction times) to draw inferences about what and how people remember. And we will see that although we have very good memory for some things, our memories are far from perfect (Schacter, 1996).[8] The errors that we make are due to the fact that our memories are not simply recording devices that input, store, and retrieve the world around us. Rather, we actively process and interpret information as we remember and recollect it, and these cognitive processes influence what we remember and how we remember it. Because memories are constructed, not recorded, when we remember events we don't reproduce exact replicas of those events (Bartlett, 1932).[9]

In the last section of the chapter we will focus primarily on cognition, with a particular consideration for cases in which cognitive processes lead us to distort our judgments or misremember information. We will see that our prior knowledge can influence our memory. People who read the words "*dream*, *sheets*, *rest*, *snore*, *blanket*, *tired*, and *bed*" and then are asked to remember the words often think that they saw the word *sleep* even though that word was not in the list (Roediger & McDermott, 1995).[10] And we will see that in other cases we are influenced by the ease with which we can retrieve information from memory or by the information that we are exposed to after we first learn something.

Although much research in the area of memory and cognition is basic in orientation, the work also has profound influence on our everyday experiences. Our cognitive processes influence the accuracy and inaccuracy of our memories and our judgments, and they lead us to be vulnerable to the types of errors that eyewitnesses such as Jennifer Thompson may make. Understanding these potential errors is the first step in learning to avoid them.

1. MEMORIES AS TYPES AND STAGES

LEARNING OBJECTIVES

1. **Compare and contrast explicit and implicit memory, identifying the features that define each.**
2. **Explain the function and duration of eidetic and echoic memories.**
3. **Summarize the capacities of short-term memory and explain how working memory is used to process information in it.**

As you can see in Table 8.1, psychologists conceptualize memory in terms of *types*, in terms of *stages*, and in terms of *processes*. In this section we will consider the two types of memory, *explicit memory* and *implicit memory*, and then the three major memory stages: *sensory*, *short-term*, and *long-term* (Atkinson & Shiffrin, 1968).[11] Then, in the next section, we will consider the nature of long-term memory, with a particular emphasis on the cognitive techniques we can use to improve our memories. Our discussion will focus on the three processes that are central to long-term memory: *encoding*, *storage*, and *retrieval*.

TABLE 8.1 Memory Conceptualized in Terms of Types, Stages, and Processes

As types	Explicit memory
	Implicit memory
As stages	Sensory memory
	Short-term memory
	Long-term memory
As processes	Encoding
	Storage
	Retrieval

1.1 Explicit Memory

When we assess memory by asking a person to consciously remember things, we are measuring *explicit memory*. **Explicit memory** refers to *knowledge or experiences that can be consciously remembered*. As you can see in Figure 8.2, there are two types of explicit memory: *episodic* and *semantic*. **Episodic memory** refers to *the firsthand experiences that we have had* (e.g., recollections of our high school graduation day or of the fantastic dinner we had in New York last year). **Semantic memory** refers to *our knowledge of facts and concepts about the world* (e.g., that the absolute value of −90 is greater than the absolute value of 9 and that one definition of the word "affect" is "the experience of feeling or emotion").

FIGURE 8.2 Types of Memory

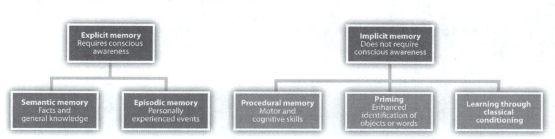

Explicit memory is assessed using measures in which the individual being tested must consciously attempt to remember the information. A **recall memory test** is *a measure of explicit memory that involves bringing from memory information that has previously been remembered*. We rely on our recall memory when we take an essay test, because the test requires us to generate previously remembered information. A multiple-choice test is an example of a **recognition memory test**, *a measure of explicit memory that involves determining whether information has been seen or learned before*.

Your own experiences taking tests will probably lead you to agree with the scientific research finding that recall is more difficult than recognition. Recall, such as required on essay tests, involves two steps: first generating an answer and then determining whether it seems to be the correct one. Recognition, as on multiple-choice test, only involves determining which item from a list seems most correct (Haist, Shimamura, & Squire, 1992).[12] Although they involve different processes, recall and recognition memory measures tend to be correlated. Students who do better on a multiple-choice exam will also, by and large, do better on an essay exam (Bridgeman & Morgan, 1996).[13]

A third way of measuring memory is known as *relearning* (Nelson, 1985).[14] Measures of **relearning (or savings)** *assess how much more quickly information is processed or learned when it is studied again after it has already been learned but then forgotten*. If you have taken some French courses in the past, for instance, you might have forgotten most of the vocabulary you learned. But if you were to work on your French again, you'd learn the vocabulary much faster the second time around. Relearning can be a more sensitive measure of memory than either recall or recognition because it allows assessing memory in terms of "how much" or "how fast" rather than simply "correct" versus "incorrect" responses. Relearning also allows us to measure memory for procedures like driving a car or playing a piano piece, as well as memory for facts and figures.

1.2 Implicit Memory

While explicit memory consists of the things that we can consciously report that we know, implicit memory refers to knowledge that we cannot consciously access. However, implicit memory is nevertheless exceedingly important to us because it has a direct effect on our behavior. **Implicit memory** refers to *the influence of experience on behavior, even if the individual is not aware of those influences*. As you can see in Figure 8.2, there are three general types of implicit memory: procedural memory, classical conditioning effects, and priming.

Procedural memory refers to *our often unexplainable knowledge of how to do things*. When we walk from one place to another, speak to another person in English, dial a cell phone, or play a video game, we are using procedural memory. Procedural memory allows us to perform complex tasks, even though we may not be able to explain to others how we do them. There is no way to tell someone how to ride a bicycle; a person has to learn by doing it. The idea of implicit memory helps explain how infants are able to learn. The ability to crawl, walk, and talk are procedures, and these skills are easily and

explicit memory

Knowledge or experiences that can be consciously remembered.

episodic memory

Explicit memory about the firsthand experiences that we have had.

semantic memory

Explicit memory of knowledge of facts and concepts about the world.

recall memory test

A measure of explicit memory that involves bringing from memory information that has previously been remembered.

recognition memory test

A measure of explicit memory that involves determining whether information has been seen or learned before.

relearning (or savings)

A measure of explicit memory that involves assessing how much more quickly information is processed or learned when it is studied again after it has already been learned but then forgotten.

implicit memory

The influence of experience on behavior, even if the individual is not aware of those influences.

procedural memory

Implicit memory about our often unexplainable knowledge of how to do things.

efficiently developed while we are children despite the fact that as adults we have no conscious memory of having learned them.

A second type of implicit memory is classical conditioning effects, in which we learn, often without effort or awareness, to associate neutral stimuli (such as a sound or a light) with another stimulus (such as food), which creates a naturally occurring response, such as enjoyment or salivation. The memory for the association is demonstrated when the conditioned stimulus (the sound) begins to create the same response as the unconditioned stimulus (the food) did before the learning.

The final type of implicit memory is known as **priming**, or *changes in behavior as a result of experiences that have happened frequently or recently*. Priming refers both to the activation of knowledge (e.g., we can prime the concept of "kindness" by presenting people with words related to kindness) and to the influence of that activation on behavior (people who are primed with the concept of kindness may act more kindly).

One measure of the influence of priming on implicit memory is the *word fragment test*, in which a person is asked to fill in missing letters to make words. You can try this yourself: First, try to complete the following word fragments, but work on each one for only three or four seconds. Do any words pop into mind quickly?

_ i b _ a _ y
_ h _ s _ _ i _ n
_ o _ k
_ h _ i s _

Now read the following sentence carefully:

> *"He got his materials from the shelves, checked them out, and then left the building."*

Then try again to make words out of the word fragments.

I think you might find that it is easier to complete fragments 1 and 3 as "library" and "book," respectively, after you read the sentence than it was before you read it. However, reading the sentence didn't really help you to complete fragments 2 and 4 as "physician" and "chaise." This difference in implicit memory probably occurred because as you read the sentence, the concept of "library" (and perhaps "book") was primed, even though they were never mentioned explicitly. Once a concept is primed it influences our behaviors, for instance, on word fragment tests.

Our everyday behaviors are influenced by priming in a wide variety of situations. Seeing an advertisement for cigarettes may make us start smoking, seeing the flag of our home country may arouse our patriotism, and seeing a student from a rival school may arouse our competitive spirit. And these influences on our behaviors may occur without our being aware of them.

priming

Changes in behavior as a result of experiences that have happened frequently or recently.

Research Focus: Priming Outside Awareness Influences Behavior

One of the most important characteristics of implicit memories is that they are frequently formed and used *automatically*, without much effort or awareness on our part. In one demonstration of the automaticity and influence of priming effects, John Bargh and his colleagues (Bargh, Chen, & Burrows, 1996)[15] conducted a study in which they showed college students lists of five scrambled words, each of which they were to make into a sentence. Furthermore, for half of the research participants, the words were related to stereotypes of the elderly. These participants saw words such as the following:

in Florida retired live people

bingo man the forgetful plays

The other half of the research participants also made sentences, but from words that had nothing to do with elderly stereotypes. The purpose of this task was to prime stereotypes of elderly people in memory for some of the participants but not for others.

The experimenters then assessed whether the priming of elderly stereotypes would have any effect on the students' behavior—and indeed it did. When the research participant had gathered all of his or her belongings, thinking that the experiment was over, the experimenter thanked him or her for participating and gave directions to the closest elevator. Then, without the participants knowing it, the experimenters recorded the amount of time that the participant spent walking from the doorway of the experimental room toward the elevator. As you can see in Figure 8.3, participants who had made sentences using words related to elderly stereotypes took on the behaviors of the elderly—they walked significantly more slowly as they left the experimental room.

Results From Bargh, Chen, and Burrows, 1996

Bargh, Chen, and Burrows (1996) found that priming words associated with the elderly made people walk more slowly.

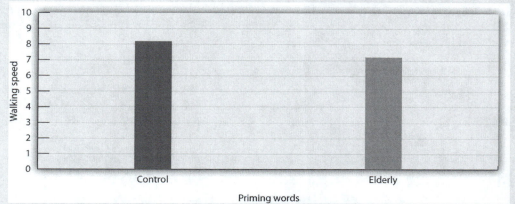

Source: Adapted from Bargh, J. A., Chen, M., & Burrows, L. (1996). Automaticity of social behavior: Direct effects of trait construct and stereotype activation on action. Journal of Personality & Social Psychology, 71, 230–244.

To determine if these priming effects occurred out of the awareness of the participants, Bargh and his colleagues asked still another group of students to complete the priming task and then to indicate whether they thought the words they had used to make the sentences had any relationship to each other, or could possibly have influenced their behavior in any way. These students had no awareness of the possibility that the words might have been related to the elderly or could have influenced their behavior.

1.3   Stages of Memory: Sensory, Short-Term, and Long-Term Memory

Another way of understanding memory is to think about it in terms of stages that describe the length of time that information remains available to us. According to this approach (see Figure 8.4), information begins in *sensory memory*, moves to *short-term memory*, and eventually moves to *long-term memory*. But not all information makes it through all three stages; most of it is forgotten. Whether the information moves from shorter-duration memory into longer-duration memory or whether it is lost from memory entirely depends on how the information is attended to and processed.

FIGURE 8.4 Memory Duration

Memory can characterized in terms of stages—the length of time that information remains available to us.

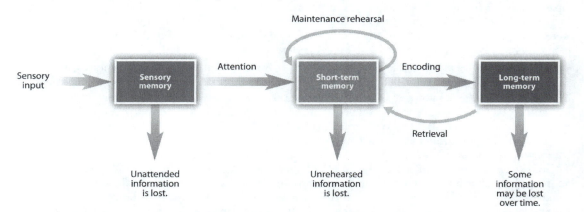

Source: Adapted from Atkinson, R. C., & Shiffrin, R. M. (1968). Human memory: A proposed system and its control processes. In K. Spence (Ed.), The psychology of learning and motivation (Vol. 2). Oxford, England: Academic Press.

Sensory Memory

sensory memory

The brief storage of sensory information.

iconic memory

The visual sensory memory.

Sensory memory refers to *the brief storage of sensory information*. Sensory memory is a memory buffer that lasts only very briefly and then, unless it is attended to and passed on for more processing, is forgotten. The purpose of sensory memory is to give the brain some time to process the incoming sensations, and to allow us to see the world as an unbroken stream of events rather than as individual pieces.

Visual sensory memory is known as **iconic memory**. Iconic memory was first studied by the psychologist George Sperling (1960).[16] In his research, Sperling showed participants a display of letters in rows, similar to that shown in Figure 8.5. However, the display lasted only about 50 milliseconds (1/20 of a second). Then, Sperling gave his participants a recall test in which they were asked to name all the letters that they could remember. On average, the participants could remember only about one-quarter of the letters that they had seen.

FIGURE 8.5 Measuring Iconic Memory

Sperling (1960) showed his participants displays such as this one for only 1/20th of a second. He found that when he cued the participants to report one of the three rows of letters, they could do it, even if the cue was given shortly after the display had been removed. The research demonstrated the existence of iconic memory.

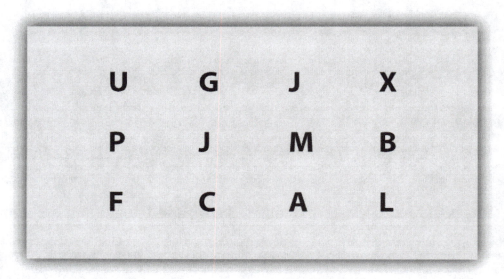

Source: Adapted from Sperling, G. (1960). The information available in brief visual presentation. Psychological Monographs, 74(11), 1–29.

Sperling reasoned that the participants had seen all the letters but could remember them only very briefly, making it impossible for them to report them all. To test this idea, in his next experiment he first showed the same letters, but then *after the display had been removed*, he signaled to the participants to report the letters from either the first, second, or third row. In this condition, the participants now reported almost all the letters in that row. This finding confirmed Sperling's hunch: Participants had access to all of the letters in their iconic memories, and if the task was short enough, they were able to report on the part of the display he asked them to. The "short enough" is the length of iconic memory, which turns out to be about 250 milliseconds (¼ of a second).

echoic memory

The auditory sensory memory.

Auditory sensory memory is known as **echoic memory**. In contrast to iconic memories, which decay very rapidly, echoic memories can last as long as 4 seconds (Cowan, Lichty, & Grove, 1990).[17] This is convenient as it allows you—among other things—to remember the words that you said at the beginning of a long sentence when you get to the end of it, and to take notes on your psychology professor's most recent statement even after he or she has finished saying it.

In some people iconic memory seems to last longer, a phenomenon known as *eidetic imagery* (or "photographic memory") in which people can report details of an image over long periods of time. These people, who often suffer from psychological disorders such as autism, claim that they can "see" an image long after it has been presented, and can often report accurately on that image. There is also some evidence for eidetic memories in hearing; some people report that their echoic memories persist for unusually long periods of time. The composer Wolfgang Amadeus Mozart may have possessed eidetic memory for music, because even when he was very young and had not yet had a great deal of musical training, he could listen to long compositions and then play them back almost perfectly (Solomon, 1995).[18]

Short-Term Memory

Most of the information that gets into sensory memory is forgotten, but information that we turn our attention to, with the goal of remembering it, may pass into *short-term memory*. **Short-term memory (STM)** is *the place where small amounts of information can be temporarily kept for more than a few seconds but usually for less than one minute* (Baddeley, Vallar, & Shallice, 1990).[19] Information in short-term memory is not stored permanently but rather becomes available for us to process, and *the processes that we use to make sense of, modify, interpret, and store information in STM* are known as **working memory**.

Although it is called "memory," working memory is not a store of memory like STM but rather a set of memory procedures or operations. Imagine, for instance, that you are asked to participate in a task such as this one, which is a measure of working memory (Unsworth & Engle, 2007).[20] Each of the following questions appears individually on a computer screen and then disappears after you answer the question:

> Is $10 \times 2 - 5 = 15$? (Answer YES OR NO) Then remember "S"
>
> Is $12 \div 6 - 2 = 1$? (Answer YES OR NO) Then remember "R"
>
> Is $10 \times 2 = 5$? (Answer YES OR NO) Then remember "P"
>
> Is $8 \div 2 - 1 = 1$? (Answer YES OR NO) Then remember "T"
>
> Is $6 \times 2 - 1 = 8$? (Answer YES OR NO) Then remember "U"
>
> Is $2 \times 3 - 3 = 0$? (Answer YES OR NO) Then remember "Q"

To successfully accomplish the task, you have to answer each of the math problems correctly and at the same time remember the letter that follows the task. Then, after the six questions, you must list the letters that appeared in each of the trials in the correct order (in this case S, R, P, T, U, Q).

To accomplish this difficult task you need to use a variety of skills. You clearly need to use STM, as you must keep the letters in storage until you are asked to list them. But you also need a way to make the best use of your available attention and processing. For instance, you might decide to use a strategy of "repeat the letters twice, then quickly solve the next problem, and then repeat the letters twice again including the new one." Keeping this strategy (or others like it) going is the role of working memory's *central executive*—the part of working memory that directs attention and processing. The central executive will make use of whatever strategies seem to be best for the given task. For instance, the central executive will direct the rehearsal process, and at the same time direct the visual cortex to form an image of the list of letters in memory. You can see that although STM is involved, the processes that we use to operate on the material in memory are also critical.

Short-term memory is limited in both the length and the amount of information it can hold. Peterson and Peterson (1959)[21] found that when people were asked to remember a list of three-letter strings and then were immediately asked to perform a distracting task (counting backward by threes), the material was quickly forgotten (see Figure 8.6), such that by 18 seconds it was virtually gone.

short-term memory (STM)

Memory where small amounts of information can be kept for more than a few seconds but less than one minute.

working memory

The processes that we use to make sense of, modify, interpret, and store information in STM.

FIGURE 8.6 STM Decay

Peterson and Peterson (1959) found that information that was not rehearsed decayed quickly from memory.

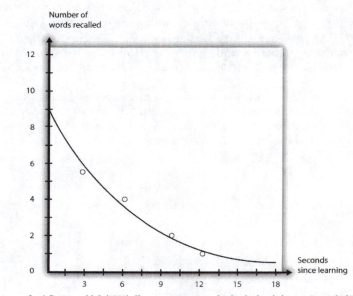

Source: Adapted from Peterson, L., & Peterson, M. J. (1959). Short-term retention of individual verbal items. Journal of Experimental Psychology, 58(3), 193–198.

maintenance rehearsal

The process of repeating information mentally or out loud with the goal of keeping it in short-term memory.

One way to prevent the decay of information from short-term memory is to use working memory to rehearse it. **Maintenance rehearsal** is *the process of repeating information mentally or out loud with the goal of keeping it in memory.* We engage in maintenance rehearsal to keep a something that we want to remember (e.g., a person's name, e-mail address, or phone number) in mind long enough to write it down, use it, or potentially transfer it to long-term memory.

If we continue to rehearse information it will stay in STM until we stop rehearsing it, but there is also a capacity limit to STM. Try reading each of the following rows of numbers, one row at a time, at a rate of about one number each second. Then when you have finished each row, close your eyes and write down as many of the numbers as you can remember.

019
3586
10295
861059
1029384
75674834
657874104
6550423897

If you are like the average person, you will have found that on this test of working memory, known as a *digit span test*, you did pretty well up to about the fourth line, and then you started having trouble. I bet you missed some of the numbers in the last three rows, and did pretty poorly on the last one.

The digit span of most adults is between five and nine digits, with an average of about seven. The cognitive psychologist George Miller (1956)[22] referred to "seven plus or minus two" pieces of information as the "magic number" in short-term memory. But if we can only hold a maximum of about nine digits in short-term memory, then how can we remember larger amounts of information than this? For instance, how can we ever remember a 10-digit phone number long enough to dial it?

One way we are able to expand our ability to remember things in STM is by using a memory technique called *chunking*. **Chunking** is *the process of organizing information into smaller groupings (chunks), thereby increasing the number of items that can be held in STM.* For instance, try to remember this string of 12 letters:

chunking

The process of organizing information into smaller groupings (chunks), thereby increasing the number of items that can be held in short-term memory.

XOFCBANNCVTM

You probably won't do that well because the number of letters is more than the magic number of seven.

Now try again with this one:

MTVCNNABCFOX

Would it help you if I pointed out that the material in this string could be chunked into four sets of three letters each? I think it would, because then rather than remembering 12 letters, you would only have to remember the names of four television stations. In this case, chunking changes the number of items you have to remember from 12 to only four.

Experts rely on chunking to help them process complex information. Herbert Simon and William Chase (1973)[23] showed chess masters and chess novices various positions of pieces on a chessboard for a few seconds each. The experts did a lot better than the novices in remembering the positions because they were able to see the "big picture." They didn't have to remember the position of each of the pieces individually, but chunked the pieces into several larger layouts. But when the researchers showed both groups random chess positions—positions that would be very unlikely to occur in real games—both groups did equally poorly, because in this situation the experts lost their ability to organize the layouts (see Figure 8.7). The same occurs for basketball. Basketball players recall actual basketball positions much better than do nonplayers, but only when the positions make sense in terms of what is happening on the court, or what is likely to happen in the near future, and thus can be chunked into bigger units (Didierjean & Marmèche, 2005).[24]

FIGURE 8.7   **Possible and Impossible Chess Positions**

Experience matters: Experienced chess players are able to recall the positions of the game on the right much better than are those who are chess novices. But the experts do no better than the novices in remembering the positions on the left, which cannot occur in a real game.

If information makes it past short term-memory it may enter **long-term memory (LTM)**, *memory storage that can hold information for days, months, and years.* The capacity of long-term memory is large, and there is no known limit to what we can remember (Wang, Liu, & Wang, 2003).[25] Although we may forget at least some information after we learn it, other things will stay with us forever. In the next section we will discuss the principles of long-term memory.

long-term memory (LTM)

Memory storage that can hold information for days, months, and years.

KEY TAKEAWAYS

- Memory refers to the ability to store and retrieve information over time.
- For some things our memory is very good, but our active cognitive processing of information assures that memory is never an exact replica of what we have experienced.
- Explicit memory refers to experiences that can be intentionally and consciously remembered, and it is measured using recall, recognition, and relearning. Explicit memory includes episodic and semantic memories.
- Measures of relearning (also known as savings) assess how much more quickly information is learned when it is studied again after it has already been learned but then forgotten.
- Implicit memory refers to the influence of experience on behavior, even if the individual is not aware of those influences. The three types of implicit memory are procedural memory, classical conditioning, and priming.
- Information processing begins in sensory memory, moves to short-term memory, and eventually moves to long-term memory.
- Maintenance rehearsal and chunking are used to keep information in short-term memory.
- The capacity of long-term memory is large, and there is no known limit to what we can remember.

EXERCISES AND CRITICAL THINKING

1. List some situations in which sensory memory is useful for you. What do you think your experience of the stimuli would be like if you had no sensory memory?
2. Describe a situation in which you need to use working memory to perform a task or solve a problem. How do your working memory skills help you?

2. HOW WE REMEMBER: CUES TO IMPROVING MEMORY

LEARNING OBJECTIVES

1. **Label and review the principles of encoding, storage, and retrieval.**
2. **Summarize the types of amnesia and their effects on memory.**
3. **Describe how the context in which we learn information can influence our memory of that information.**

Although it is useful to hold information in sensory and short-term memory, we also rely on our long-term memory (LTM). We want to remember the name of the new boy in the class, the name of the movie we saw last week, and the material for our upcoming psychology test. Psychological research has produced a great deal of knowledge about long-term memory, and this research can be useful as you try to learn and remember new material (see Table 8.2). In this section we will consider this question in terms of the types of processing that we do on the information we want to remember. To be successful, the information that we want to remember must be *encoded* and *stored*, and then *retrieved*.

TABLE 8.2 Helpful Memory Techniques Based on Psychological Research

Technique	Description	Useful example
Use elaborative encoding.	Material is better remembered if it is processed more fully.	Think, for instance, "Proactive interference is like retroactive interference but it occurs in a forward manner."
Make use of the self-reference effect.	Material is better remembered if it is linked to thoughts about the self.	Think, for instance, "I remember a time when I knew the answer to an exam question but couldn't quite get it to come to mind. This was an example of the tip-of-the-tongue phenomenon."
Be aware of the forgetting curve.	Information that we have learned drops off rapidly with time.	Review the material that you have already studied right before the exam to increase the likelihood it will remain in memory.
Make use of the spacing effect.	Information is learned better when it is studied in shorter periods spaced over time.	Study a little bit every day; do not cram at the last minute.
Rely on overlearning.	We can continue to learn even after we think we know the information perfectly.	Keep studying, even if you think you already have it down.
Use context-dependent retrieval.	We have better retrieval when it occurs in the same situation in which we learned the material.	If possible, study under conditions similar to the conditions in which you will take the exam.
Use state-dependent retrieval.	We have better retrieval when we are in the same psychological state as we were when we learned the material.	Many possibilities, but don't study under the influence of drugs or alcohol, unless you plan to use them on the day of the exam (which is not recommended).

2.1   Encoding and Storage: How Our Perceptions Become Memories

Encoding is *the process by which we place the things that we experience into memory*. Unless information is encoded, it cannot be remembered. I'm sure you've been to a party where you've been introduced to someone and then—maybe only seconds later—you realize that you do not remember the person's name. Of course it's not really surprising that you can't remember the name, because you probably were distracted and you never encoded the name to begin with.

Not everything we experience can or should be encoded. We tend to encode things that we need to remember and not bother to encode things that are irrelevant. Look at Figure 8.8, which shows different images of U.S. pennies. Can you tell which one is the real one? Nickerson and Adams (1979)[26] found that very few of the U.S. participants they tested could identify the right one. We see pennies a lot, but we don't bother to encode their features.

encoding

The process by which we place the things that we experience into memory.

FIGURE 8.8 Pennies in Different Styles

Can you identify the "real" penny? We tend to have poor memory for things that don't matter, even if we see them frequently.

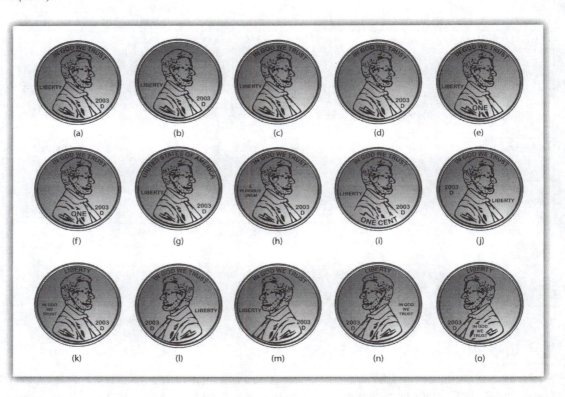

elaborative encoding

Learning by processing new information in ways that make it more relevant.

One way to improve our memory is to use better encoding strategies. Some ways of studying are more effective than others. Research has found that we are better able to remember information if we encode it in a meaningful way. When we engage in **elaborative encoding** we *process new information in ways that make it more relevant or meaningful* (Craik & Lockhart, 1972; Harris & Qualls, 2000).[27]

Imagine that you are trying to remember the characteristics of the different schools of psychology we discussed in Chapter 1. Rather than simply trying to remember the schools and their characteristics, you might try to relate the information to things you already know. For instance, you might try to remember the fundamentals of the cognitive school of psychology by linking the characteristics to the computer model. The cognitive school focuses on how information is input, processed, and retrieved, and you might think about how computers do pretty much the same thing. You might also try to organize the information into meaningful units. For instance, you might link the cognitive school to structuralism because both were concerned with mental processes. You also might try to use visual cues to help you remember the information. You might look at the image of Freud and imagine what he looked like as a child. That image might help you remember that childhood experiences were an important part of Freudian theory. Each person has his or her unique way of elaborating on information; the important thing is to try to develop unique and meaningful associations among the materials.

Research Focus: Elaboration and Memory

In an important study showing the effectiveness of elaborative encoding, Rogers, Kuiper, and Kirker (1977)[28] studied how people recalled information that they had learned under different processing conditions. All the participants were presented with the same list of 40 adjectives to learn, but through the use of random assignment, the participants were given one of four different sets of instructions about how to process the adjectives.

Participants assigned to the *structural task condition* were asked to judge whether the word was printed in uppercase or lowercase letters. Participants in the *phonemic task condition* were asked whether or not the word rhymed with another given word. In the *semantic task condition*, the participants were asked if the word was a synonym of another word. And in the *self-reference task condition*, participants were asked to indicate whether or not the given adjective was or was not true of themselves. After completing the specified task, each participant was asked to recall as many adjectives as he or she could remember.

Rogers and his colleagues hypothesized that different types of processing would have different effects on memory. As you can see in Figure 8.9, the students in the self-reference task condition recalled significantly more adjectives than did students in any other condition. This finding, known as the *self-reference effect*, is powerful evidence that the self-concept helps us organize and remember information. The next time you are studying for an exam, you might try relating the material to your own experiences. The self-reference effect suggests that doing so will help you better remember the information (Symons & Johnson, 1997).[29]

Self-Reference Effect Results

Participants recalled the same words significantly better when they were processed in relation to the self than when they were processed in other ways.

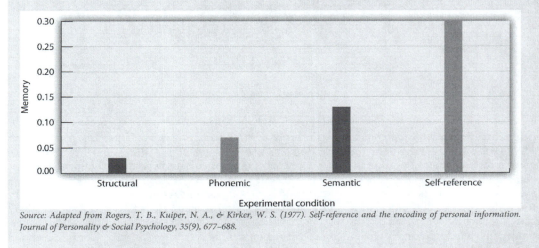

Source: Adapted from Rogers, T. B., Kuiper, N. A., & Kirker, W. S. (1977). Self-reference and the encoding of personal information. Journal of Personality & Social Psychology, 35(9), 677–688.

2.2   Using the Contributions of Hermann Ebbinghaus to Improve Your Memory

Hermann Ebbinghaus (1850–1909) was a pioneer of the study of memory. In this section we consider three of his most important findings, each of which can help you improve your memory. In his research, in which he was the only research participant, Ebbinghaus practiced memorizing lists of nonsense syllables, such as the following:

DIF, LAJ, LEQ, MUV, WYC, DAL, SEN, KEP, NUD

You can imagine that because the material that he was trying to learn was not at all meaningful, it was not easy to do. Ebbinghaus plotted how many of the syllables he could remember against the time that had elapsed since he had studied them. He discovered an important principle of memory: Memory decays rapidly at first, but the amount of decay levels off with time (Figure 8.10). Although Ebbinghaus looked at forgetting after days had elapsed, the same effect occurs on longer and shorter time scales. Bahrick (1984)[30] found that students who took a Spanish language course forgot about one half of the vocabulary that they had learned within three years, but that after that time their memory remained pretty much constant. Forgetting also drops off quickly on a shorter time frame. This suggests that you should try to review the material that you have already studied right before you take an exam; that way, you will be more likely to remember the material during the exam.

FIGURE 8.10 Ebbinghaus Forgetting Curve

Hermann Ebbinghaus found that memory for information drops off rapidly at first but then levels off after time.

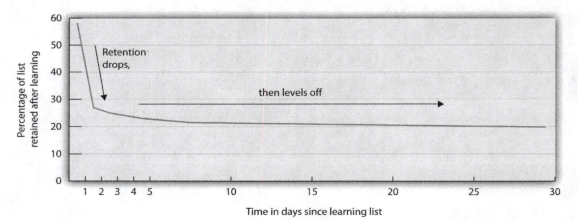

spacing effect

The fact that learning is better when the same amount of study is spread out over periods of time than it is when it occurs closer together or at the same time.

Ebbinghaus also discovered another important principle of learning, known as the *spacing effect*. The **spacing effect** refers to *the fact that learning is better when the same amount of study is spread out over periods of time than it is when it occurs closer together or at the same time.* This means that even if you have only a limited amount of time to study, you'll learn more if you study continually throughout the semester (a little bit every day is best) than if you wait to cram at the last minute before your exam (Figure 8.11). Another good strategy is to study and then wait as long as you can before you forget the material. Then review the information and again wait as long as you can before you forget it. (This probably will be a longer period of time than the first time.) Repeat and repeat again. The spacing effect is usually considered in terms of the difference between *distributed practice* (practice that is spread out over time) and *massed practice* (practice that comes in one block), with the former approach producing better memory.

FIGURE 8.11 Effects of Massed Versus Distributed Practice on Learning

The spacing effect refers to the fact that memory is better when it is *distributed* rather than *massed*. Leslie, Lee Ann, and Nora all studied for four hours total, but the students who spread out their learning into smaller study sessions did better on the exam.

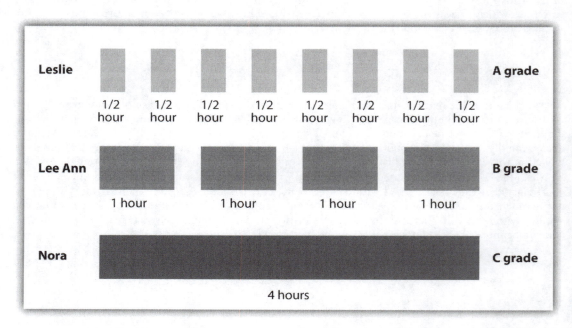

Ebbinghaus also considered the role of *overlearning*—that is, continuing to practice and study even when we think that we have mastered the material. Ebbinghaus and other researchers have found that overlearning helps encoding (Driskell, Willis, & Copper, 1992).[31] Students frequently think that they have already mastered the material but then discover when they get to the exam that they have not. The point is clear: Try to keep studying and reviewing, even if you think you already know all the material.

2.3 Retrieval

Even when information has been adequately encoded and stored, it does not do us any good if we cannot retrieve it. **Retrieval** refers to *the process of reactivating information that has been stored in memory.* You can get an idea of the difficulty posed by retrieval by simply reading each of the words (but not the categories) in the sidebar below to someone. Tell the person that after you have read all the words, you will ask her to recall the words.

After you read the list to your friend, give her enough time to write down all the words that she can recall. Make sure that she cannot recall any more and then, for the words that were not listed, prompt your friend with some of the category names: "Do you remember any words that were furniture? Do you remember any words that were tools?" I think you will find that the category names, which serve as retrieval cues, will help your friend remember information that she could not retrieve otherwise.

retrieval

The process of reactivating information that has been stored in memory.

Retrieval Demonstration

Try this test of the ability to retrieve information with a classmate. The instructions are in the text.

Apple	(Fruit)
Dresser	(Furniture)
Sander	(Tool)
Pomegranate	(Fruit)
Sunflower	(Flower)
Tangerine	(Fruit)
Chair	(Furniture)
Peony	(Flower)
Banana	(Fruit)
Sofa	(Furniture)
Bench	(Furniture)
Strawberry	(Fruit)
Television stand	(Furniture)
Magnolia	(Flower)
Rose	(Flower)
Wrench	(Tool)
Screwdriver	(Tool)
Dahlia	(Flower)
Drill press	(Tool)
Hammer	(Tool)

We've all experienced retrieval failure in the form of the frustrating **tip-of-the-tongue phenomenon**, in which *we are certain that we know something that we are trying to recall but cannot quite come up with it.* You can try this one on your friends as well. Read your friend the names of the 10 states listed in the sidebar below, and ask him to name the capital city of each state. Now, for the capital cities that your friend can't name, give him just the first letter of the capital city. You'll probably find that having the first letters of the cities helps with retrieval. The tip-of-the-tongue experience is a very good example of the inability to retrieve information that is actually stored in memory.

tip-of-the-tongue phenomenon

The experience of being certain that we know something that we are trying to recall, but yet we cannot quite come up with it.

States and Capital Cities

Try this demonstration of the tip-of-the-tongue phenomenon with a classmate. Instructions are in the text.

Georgia	(Atlanta)
Maryland	(Annapolis)
California	(Sacramento)
Louisiana	(Baton Rouge)
Florida	(Tallahassee)
Colorado	(Denver)
New Jersey	(Trenton)
Arizona	(Phoenix)
Nebraska	(Lincoln)
Kentucky	(Frankfort)

context-dependent learning

An increase in retrieval when the external situation in which information is learned matches the situation in which it is remembered.

We are more likely to be able to retrieve items from memory when conditions at retrieval are similar to the conditions under which we encoded them. **Context-dependent learning** refers to *an increase in retrieval when the external situation in which information is learned matches the situation in which it is remembered*. Godden and Baddeley (1975)[32] conducted a study to test this idea using scuba divers. They asked the divers to learn a list of words either when they were on land or when they were underwater. Then they tested the divers on their memory, either in the same or the opposite situation. As you can see in Figure 8.12, the divers' memory was better when they were tested in the same context in which they had learned the words than when they were tested in the other context.

FIGURE 8.12 Results From Godden and Baddeley, 1975

Godden and Baddeley (1975) tested the memory of scuba divers to learn and retrieve information in different contexts and found strong evidence for context-dependent learning.

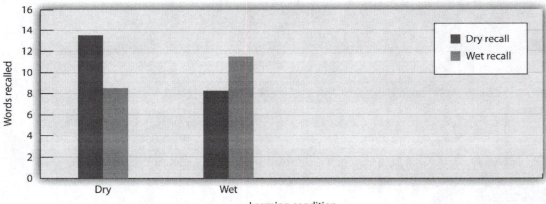

Source: Adapted from Godden, D. R., & Baddeley, A. D. (1975). Context-dependent memory in two natural environments: On land and underwater. British Journal of Psychology, 66(3), 325–331.

You can see that context-dependent learning might also be important in improving your memory. For instance, you might want to try to study for an exam in a situation that is similar to the one in which you are going to take the exam.

state-dependent learning

An increase in retrieval that occurs when the individual is tested in the same physiological or psychological state as during encoding.

Whereas context-dependent learning refers to a match in the external situation between learning and remembering, **state-dependent learning** refers to *superior retrieval of memories when the individual is in the same physiological or psychological state as during encoding*. Research has found, for instance, that animals that learn a maze while under the influence of one drug tend to remember their learning better when they are tested under the influence of the same drug than when they are tested without the drug (Jackson, Koek, & Colpaert, 1992).[33] And research with humans finds that bilinguals remember better when tested in the same language in which they learned the material (Marian & Kaushanskaya, 2007).[34] Mood states may also produce state-dependent learning. People who learn information when they are in a bad (rather than a good) mood find it easier to recall these memories when they are tested while they are in a bad mood, and vice versa. It is easier to recall unpleasant memories than pleasant ones when we're sad, and easier to recall pleasant memories than unpleasant ones when we're happy (Bower, 1981; Eich, 2008).[35]

Variations in the ability to retrieve information are also seen in the *serial position curve*. When we give people a list of words one at a time (e.g., on flashcards) and then ask them to recall them, the results look something like those in Figure 8.13. People are able to retrieve more words that were presented to them at the beginning and the end of the list than they are words that were presented in the middle of the list. This pattern, known as the serial position curve, is caused by two retrieval phenomenon: The **primacy effect** refers to *a tendency to better remember stimuli that are presented early in a list*. The **recency effect** refers to *the tendency to better remember stimuli that are presented later in a list*.

primacy effect
The tendency to better remember stimuli that are presented early in a list.

recency effect
The tendency to better remember stimuli that are presented later in a list.

FIGURE 8.13   The Serial Position Curve

The serial position curve is the result of both primacy effects and recency effects.

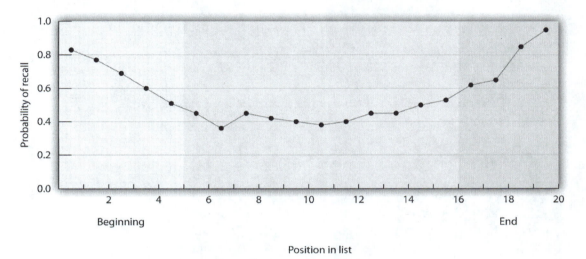

Position in list

There are a number of explanations for primacy and recency effects, but one of them is in terms of the effects of rehearsal on short-term and long-term memory (Baddeley, Eysenck, & Anderson, 2009).[36] Because we can keep the last words that we learned in the presented list in short-term memory by rehearsing them before the memory test begins, they are relatively easily remembered. So the recency effect can be explained in terms of maintenance rehearsal in short-term memory. And the primacy effect may also be due to rehearsal—when we hear the first word in the list we start to rehearse it, making it more likely that it will be moved from short-term to long-term memory. And the same is true for the other words that come early in the list. But for the words in the middle of the list, this rehearsal becomes much harder, making them less likely to be moved to LTM.

In some cases our existing memories influence our new learning. This may occur either in a backward way or a forward way. **Retroactive interference** occurs when *learning something new impairs our ability to retrieve information that was learned earlier*. For example, if you have learned to program in one computer language, and then you learn to program in another similar one, you may start to make mistakes programming the first language that you never would have made before you learned the new one. In this case the new memories work backward (retroactively) to influence retrieval from memory that is already in place.

In contrast to retroactive interference, *proactive interference* works in a forward direction. **Proactive interference** occurs when *earlier learning impairs our ability to encode information that we try to learn later*. For example, if we have learned French as a second language, this knowledge may make it more difficult, at least in some respects, to learn a third language (say Spanish), which involves similar but not identical vocabulary.

retroactive interference
Memory impairment that occurs when learning something new impairs memory for information that was learned earlier.

proactive interference
Memory impairment that occurs when earlier learning impairs our ability to encode information that we try to learn later.

FIGURE 8.14 Proactive and Retroactive Interference

Retroactive and proactive interference can both influence memory.

Retroactive interference works backward and interferes with retrieval:

Learn Spanish	Learn French	Remember Spanish
One = "uno"	One = "une"	One = ?
Man = "hombre"	Man = "homme"	Man = ?
Cherry = "cereza"	Cherry = "cerise"	Cherry = ?

Proactive interference works forward and interferes with encoding:

Learn Spanish	Learn French
One = "uno"	One = "une"? "uno"?
Man = "hombre"	Man = "homme"? "hombre"?
Cherry = "cereza"	Cherry = "cerise"? "cereza"?

2.4 The Structure of LTM: Categories, Prototypes, and Schemas

category

A network of associated memories that have features in common with each other.

Memories that are stored in LTM are not isolated but rather are linked together into **categories**—*networks of associated memories that have features in common with each other.* Forming categories, and using categories to guide behavior, is a fundamental part of human nature. Associated concepts within a category are connected through *spreading activation*, which occurs when activating one element of a category activates other associated elements. For instance, because tools are associated in a category, reminding people of the word "screwdriver" will help them remember the word "wrench." And, when people have learned lists of words that come from different categories (e.g., as in "Retrieval Demonstration"), they do not recall the information haphazardly. If they have just remembered the word "wrench," they are more likely to remember the word "screwdriver" next than they are to remember the word "dahlia," because the words are organized in memory by category and because "dahlia" is activated by spreading activation from "wrench" (Srull & Wyer, 1989).[37]

Some categories have *defining features* that must be true of all members of the category. For instance, all members of the category "triangles" have three sides, and all members of the category "birds" lay eggs. But most categories are not so well-defined; the members of the category share some common features, but it is impossible to define which are or are not members of the category. For instance, there is no clear definition of the category "tool." Some examples of the category, such as a hammer and a wrench, are clearly and easily identified as category members, whereas other members are not so obvious. Is an ironing board a tool? What about a car?

prototype

The member of the category that is most average or typical of the category.

Members of categories (even those with defining features) can be compared to the category **prototype**, which is *the member of the category that is most average or typical of the category.* Some category members are more prototypical of, or similar to, the category than others. For instance, some category members (robins and sparrows) are highly prototypical of the category "birds," whereas other category members (penguins and ostriches) are less prototypical. We retrieve information that is prototypical of a category faster than we retrieve information that is less prototypical (Rosch, 1975).[38]

FIGURE 8.15   Prototypicality

Category members vary in terms of their prototypicality. Some cats are "better" members of the category than are others.

© Thinkstock

Mental categories are sometimes referred to as **schemas**—*patterns of knowledge in long-term memory that help us organize information.* We have schemas about objects (that a triangle has three sides and may take on different angles), about people (that Sam is friendly, likes to golf, and always wears sandals), about events (the particular steps involved in ordering a meal at a restaurant), and about social groups (we call these group schemas *stereotypes*).

schema

A pattern of knowledge in long-term memory that helps us organize information.

FIGURE 8.16   Different Schemas

Our schemas about people, couples, and events help us organize and remember information.

© Thinkstock

Schemas are important in part because they help us remember new information by providing an organizational structure for it. Read the following paragraph (Bransford & Johnson, 1972)[39] and then try to write down everything you can remember.

The procedure is actually quite simple. First you arrange things into different groups. Of course, one pile may be sufficient depending on how much there is to do. If you have to go somewhere else due to lack of facilities, that is the next step; otherwise you are pretty well set. It is important not to overdo things. That is, it is better to do too few things at once than too many. In the short run this may not seem important, but complications can easily arise. A mistake can be expensive as well. At first the whole procedure will seem complicated. Soon, however, it will become just another facet of life. It is difficult to foresee any end to the necessity for this task in the immediate future, but then one never can tell. After the procedure is completed, one arranges the materials into different groups again. Then they can be put into their appropriate places. Eventually they will be used once more and the whole cycle will then have to be repeated. However, that is part of life.

It turns out that people's memory for this information is quite poor, unless they have been told ahead of time that the information describes "doing the laundry," in which case their memory for the material is much better. This demonstration of the role of schemas in memory shows how our existing knowledge can help us organize new information, and how this organization can improve encoding, storage, and retrieval.

2.5 The Biology of Memory

long-term potentiation (LTP)

The development of memory that occurs through strengthening of the synaptic connections between neurons.

Just as information is stored on digital media such as DVDs and flash drives, the information in LTM must be stored in the brain. The ability to maintain information in LTM involves a gradual strengthening of the connections among the neurons in the brain. When pathways in these neural networks are frequently and repeatedly fired, the synapses become more efficient in communicating with each other, and these changes create memory. This process, known as **long-term potentiation (LTP)**, refers to *the strengthening of the synaptic connections between neurons as result of frequent stimulation* (Lynch, 2002).[40] Drugs that block LTP reduce learning, whereas drugs that enhance LTP increase learning (Lynch et al., 1991).[41] Because the new patterns of activation in the synapses take time to develop, LTP happens gradually. The period of time in which LTP occurs and in which memories are stored is known as the period of *consolidation*.

Memory is not confined to the cortex; it occurs through sophisticated interactions between new and old brain structures (Figure 8.17). One of the most important brain regions in explicit memory is the hippocampus, which serves as a preprocessor and elaborator of information (Squire, 1992).[42] The hippocampus helps us encode information about spatial relationships, the context in which events were experienced, and the associations among memories (Eichenbaum, 1999).[43] The hippocampus also serves in part as a switching point that holds the memory for a short time and then directs the information to other parts of the brain, such as the cortex, to actually do the rehearsing, elaboration, and long-term storage (Jonides, Lacey, & Nee, 2005).[44] Without the hippocampus, which might be described as the brain's "librarian," our explicit memories would be inefficient and disorganized.

FIGURE 8.17   Schematic Image of Brain With Hippocampus, Amygdala, and Cerebellum Highlighted

Different brain structures help us remember different types of information. The hippocampus is particularly important in explicit memories, the cerebellum is particularly important in implicit memories, and the amygdala is particularly important in emotional memories.

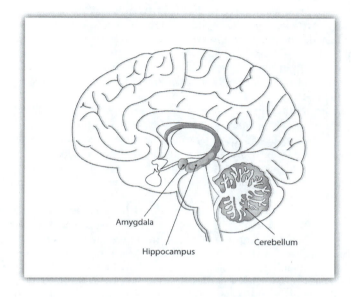

While the hippocampus is handling explicit memory, the *cerebellum* and the *amygdala* are concentrating on implicit and emotional memories, respectively. Research shows that the cerebellum is more active when we are learning associations and in priming tasks, and animals and humans with damage to the cerebellum have more difficulty in classical conditioning studies (Krupa, Thompson, & Thompson, 1993; Woodruff-Pak, Goldenberg, Downey-Lamb, Boyko, & Lemieux, 2000).[45] The storage of many of our most important emotional memories, and particularly those related to fear, is initiated and controlled by the amygdala (Sigurdsson, Doyère, Cain, & LeDoux, 2007).[46]

Evidence for the role of different brain structures in different types of memories comes in part from case studies of patients who suffer from **amnesia**, *a memory disorder that involves the inability to remember information*. As with memory interference effects, amnesia can work in either a forward or a backward direction, affecting retrieval or encoding. For people who suffer damage to the brain, for instance, as a result of a stroke or other trauma, the amnesia may work backward. The outcome is **retrograde amnesia**, *a memory disorder that produces an inability to retrieve events that occurred before a given time*. Demonstrating the fact that LTP takes time (the process of consolidation), retrograde amnesia is usually more severe for memories that occurred just prior to the trauma than it is for older memories, and events that occurred just before the event that caused memory loss may never be recovered because they were never completely encoded.

amnesia

A memory disorder that involves the inability to remember information.

retrograde amnesia

A memory disorder that involves the inability to retrieve events that occurred before a given time.

FIGURE 8.18 Scott Bolzan

Scott Bolzan is a motivational speaker, an entrepreneur, and a former NFL football player. In December 2008, he suffered a brain injury that has left him with profound retrograde amnesia. You can read more about him here: http://abcnews.go.com/Nightline/ amnesia-man-hits-head-loses-memories/ story?id=10396719.

Source: Photo courtesy of Scott Bolzan,
http://commons.wikimedia.org/wiki/File:Scott_Bolzan.jpeg.

anterograde amnesia

A memory disorder that involves the inability to transfer information from short-term to long-term memory.

Organisms with damage to the hippocampus develop a type of amnesia that works in a forward direction to affect encoding, known as *anterograde amnesia*. **Anterograde amnesia** is *the inability to transfer information from short-term into long-term memory*, making it impossible to form new memories. One well-known case study was a man named Henry Gustav Molaison (before he died in 2008, he was referred to only as H. M.) who had parts of his hippocampus removed to reduce severe seizures (Corkin, Amaral, González, Johnson, & Hyman, 1997).[47] Following the operation, Molaison developed virtually complete anterograde amnesia. Although he could remember most of what had happened before the operation, and particularly what had occurred early in his life, he could no longer create new memories. Molaison was said to have read the same magazines over and over again without any awareness of having seen them before.

Cases of anterograde amnesia also provide information about the brain structures involved in different types of memory (Bayley & Squire, 2005; Helmuth, 1999; Paller, 2004).[48] Although Molaison's explicit memory was compromised because his hippocampus was damaged, his implicit memory was not (because his cerebellum was intact). He could learn to trace shapes in a mirror, a task that requires procedural memory, but he never had any explicit recollection of having performed this task or of the people who administered the test to him.

Although some brain structures are particularly important in memory, this does not mean that all memories are stored in one place. The American psychologist Karl Lashley (1929)[49] attempted to determine where memories were stored in the brain by teaching rats how to run mazes, and then lesioning different brain structures to see if they were still able to complete the maze. This idea seemed straightforward, and Lashley expected to find that memory was stored in certain parts of the brain. But he discovered that no matter where he removed brain tissue, the rats retained at least some memory of the maze, leading him to conclude that memory isn't located in a single place in the brain, but rather is distributed around it.

Long-term potentiation occurs as a result of changes in the synapses, which suggests that chemicals, particularly neurotransmitters and hormones, must be involved in memory. There is quite a bit of evidence that this is true. *Glutamate*, a neurotransmitter and a form of the amino acid glutamic acid, is perhaps the most important neurotransmitter in memory (McEntee & Crook, 1993).[50] When animals, including people, are under stress, more glutamate is secreted, and this glutamate can help them remember (McGaugh, 2003).[51] The neurotransmitter *serotonin* is also secreted when animals learn, and *epinephrine* may also increase memory, particularly for stressful events (Maki & Resnick, 2000; Sherwin, 1998).[52] *Estrogen*, a female sex hormone, also seems critical, because women who are experiencing menopause, along with a reduction in estrogen, frequently report memory difficulties (Chester, 2001).[53]

Our knowledge of the role of biology in memory suggests that it might be possible to use drugs to improve our memories, and Americans spend several hundred million dollars per year on memory supplements with the hope of doing just that. Yet controlled studies comparing memory enhancers, including Ritalin, methylphenidate, ginkgo biloba, and amphetamines, with placebo drugs find very little evidence for their effectiveness (Gold, Cahill, & Wenk, 2002; McDaniel, Maier, & Einstein, 2002).[54] Memory supplements are usually no more effective than drinking a sugared soft drink, which also releases glucose and thus improves memory slightly. This is not to say that we cannot someday create drugs that will significantly improve our memory. It is likely that this will occur in the future, but the implications of these advances are as yet unknown (Farah et al., 2004; Turner & Sahakian, 2006).[55]

Although the most obvious potential use of drugs is to attempt to improve memory, drugs might also be used to help us forget. This might be desirable in some cases, such as for those suffering from *posttraumatic stress disorder (PTSD)* who are unable to forget disturbing memories. Although there are no existing therapies that involve using drugs to help people forget, it is possible that they will be available in the future. These possibilities will raise some important ethical issues: Is it ethical to erase memories, and if it is, is it desirable to do so? Perhaps the experience of emotional pain is a part of being a human being. And perhaps the experience of emotional pain may help us cope with the trauma.

KEY TAKEAWAYS

- Information is better remembered when it is meaningfully elaborated.
- Hermann Ebbinghaus made important contributions to the study of learning, including modeling the forgetting curve, and studying the spacing effect and the benefits of overlearning.
- Context- and state-dependent learning, as well as primacy and recency effects, influence long-term memory.
- Memories are stored in connected synapses through the process of long-term potentiation (LTP). In addition to the cortex, other parts of the brain, including the hippocampus, cerebellum, and the amygdala, are also important in memory.
- Damage to the brain may result in retrograde amnesia or anterograde amnesia. Case studies of patients with amnesia can provide information about the brain structures involved in different types of memory.
- Memory is influenced by chemicals including glutamate, serotonin, epinephrine, and estrogen.
- Studies comparing memory enhancers with placebo drugs find very little evidence for their effectiveness.

EXERCISES AND CRITICAL THINKING

1. Plan a course of action to help you study for your next exam, incorporating as many of the techniques mentioned in this section as possible. Try to implement the plan.
2. Make a list of some the schemas that you have stored in your memory. What are the contents of each schema, and how might you use the schema to help you remember new information?
3. In the film "Eternal Sunshine of the Spotless Mind," the characters undergo a medical procedure designed to erase their memories of a painful romantic relationship. Would you engage in such a procedure if it was safely offered to you?

3. ACCURACY AND INACCURACY IN MEMORY AND COGNITION

LEARNING OBJECTIVES

1. **Outline the variables that can influence the accuracy of our memory for events.**
2. **Explain how schemas can distort our memories.**
3. **Describe the representativeness heuristic and the availability heuristic and explain how they may lead to errors in judgment.**

As we have seen, our memories are not perfect. They fail in part due to our inadequate encoding and storage, and in part due to our inability to accurately retrieve stored information. But memory is also influenced by the setting in which it occurs, by the events that occur to us after we have experienced an event, and by the cognitive processes that we use to help us remember. Although our cognition allows us to attend to, rehearse, and organize information, cognition may also lead to distortions and errors in our judgments and our behaviors.

In this section we consider some of the *cognitive biases* that are known to influence humans. Cognitive biases are *errors in memory or judgment that are caused by the inappropriate use of cognitive processes* (Table 8.3). The study of cognitive biases is important both because it relates to the important psychological theme of accuracy versus inaccuracy in perception, and because being aware of the types of errors that we may make can help us avoid them and therefore improve our decision-making skills.

cognitive biases

Errors in memory or judgment that are caused by the inappropriate use of cognitive processes.

TABLE 8.3 Cognitive Processes That Pose Threats to Accuracy

Cognitive process	Description	Potential threat to accuracy
Source monitoring	The ability to accurately identify the source of a memory	Uncertainty about the source of a memory may lead to mistaken judgments.
Confirmation bias	The tendency to verify and confirm our existing memories rather than to challenge and disconfirm them	Once beliefs become established, they become self-perpetuating and difficult to change.
Functional fixedness	When schemas prevent us from seeing and using information in new and nontraditional ways	Creativity may be impaired by the overuse of traditional, expectancy-based thinking.
Misinformation effect	Errors in memory that occur when new but incorrect information influences existing accurate memories	Eyewitnesses who are questioned by the police may change their memories of what they observed at the crime scene.
Overconfidence	When we are more certain that our memories and judgments are accurate than we should be	Eyewitnesses may be very confident that they have accurately identified a suspect, even though their memories are incorrect.
Salience	When some stimuli, (e.g., those that are colorful, moving, or unexpected) grab our attention and make them more likely to be remembered	We may base our judgments on a single salient event while we ignore hundreds of other equally informative events that we do not see.
Representativeness heuristic	Tendency to make judgments according to how well the event matches our expectations	After a coin has come up "heads" many times in a row, we may erroneously think that the next flip is more likely to be "tails" (the gambler's fallacy).
Availability heuristic	Idea that things that come to mind easily are seen as more common	We may overestimate the crime statistics in our own area, because these crimes are so easy to recall.
Cognitive accessibility	Idea that some memories are more highly activated than others	We may think that we contributed more to a project than we really did because it is so easy to remember our own contributions.
Counterfactual thinking	When we "replay" events such that they turn out differently (especially when only minor changes in the events leading up to them make a difference)	We may feel particularly bad about events that might not have occurred if only a small change had occurred before them.

3.1 Source Monitoring: Did It Really Happen?

source monitoring

The ability to accurately identify the source of a memory.

One potential error in memory involves mistakes in differentiating the sources of information. **Source monitoring** refers to *the ability to accurately identify the source of a memory*. Perhaps you've had the experience of wondering whether you really experienced an event or only dreamed or imagined it. If so, you wouldn't be alone. Rassin, Merkelbach, and Spaan (2001)[56] reported that up to 25% of college students reported being confused about real versus dreamed events. Studies suggest that people who are fantasy-prone are more likely to experience source monitoring errors (Winograd, Peluso, & Glover, 1998),[57] and such errors also occur more often for both children and the elderly than for adolescents and younger adults (Jacoby & Rhodes, 2006).[58]

sleeper effect

Attitude change that occurs over time when we forget the source of information.

In other cases we may be sure that we remembered the information from real life but be uncertain about exactly where we heard it. Imagine that you read a news story in a tabloid magazine such as the *National Enquirer*. Probably you would have discounted the information because you know that its source is unreliable. But what if later you were to remember the story but forget the source of the information? If this happens, you might become convinced that the news story is true because you forget to discount it. The **sleeper effect** refers to *attitude change that occurs over time when we forget the source of information* (Pratkanis, Greenwald, Leippe, & Baumgardner, 1988).[59]

In still other cases we may forget where we learned information and mistakenly assume that we created the memory ourselves. Kaavya Viswanathan, the author of the book *How Opal Mehta Got Kissed, Got Wild, and Got a Life*, was accused of plagiarism when it was revealed that many parts of her book were very similar to passages from other material. Viswanathan argued that she had simply forgotten that she had read the other works, mistakenly assuming she had made up the material herself. And the musician George Harrison claimed that he was unaware that the melody of his song "My Sweet Lord" was almost identical to an earlier song by another composer. The judge in the copyright suit that followed ruled that Harrison didn't intentionally commit the plagiarism. (Please use this knowledge to become extra vigilant about source attributions in your written work, not to try to excuse yourself if you are accused of plagiarism.)

3.2 Schematic Processing: Distortions Based on Expectations

We have seen that schemas help us remember information by organizing material into coherent representations. However, although schemas can improve our memories, they may also lead to cognitive biases. Using schemas may lead us to falsely remember things that never happened to us and to distort or misremember things that did. For one, schemas lead to the **confirmation bias**, which is *the tendency to verify and confirm our existing memories rather than to challenge and disconfirm them*. The confirmation bias occurs because once we have schemas, they influence how we seek out and interpret new information. The confirmation bias leads us to remember information that fits our schemas better than we remember information that disconfirms them (Stangor & McMillan, 1992),[60] a process that makes our stereotypes very difficult to change. And we ask questions in ways that confirm our schemas (Trope & Thompson, 1997).[61] If we think that a person is an extrovert, we might ask her about ways that she likes to have fun, thereby making it more likely that we will confirm our beliefs. In short, once we begin to believe in something—for instance, a stereotype about a group of people—it becomes very difficult to later convince us that these beliefs are not true; the beliefs become self-confirming.

Darley and Gross (1983)[62] demonstrated how schemas about social class could influence memory. In their research they gave participants a picture and some information about a fourth-grade girl named Hannah. To activate a schema about her social class, Hannah was pictured sitting in front of a nice suburban house for one-half of the participants and pictured in front of an impoverished house in an urban area for the other half. Then the participants watched a video that showed Hannah taking an intelligence test. As the test went on, Hannah got some of the questions right and some of them wrong, but the number of correct and incorrect answers was the same in both conditions. Then the participants were asked to remember how many questions Hannah got right and wrong. Demonstrating that stereotypes had influenced memory, the participants who thought that Hannah had come from an upper-class background remembered that she had gotten more correct answers than those who thought she was from a lower-class background.

Our reliance on schemas can also make it more difficult for us to "think outside the box." Peter Wason (1960)[63] asked college students to determine the rule that was used to generate the numbers 2-4-6 by asking them to generate possible sequences and then telling them if those numbers followed the rule. The first guess that students made was usually "consecutive ascending even numbers," and they then asked questions designed to confirm their hypothesis ("Does 102-104-106 fit?" "What about 404-406-408?"). Upon receiving information that those guesses did fit the rule, the students stated that the rule was "consecutive ascending even numbers." But the students' use of the confirmation bias led them to ask only about instances that confirmed their hypothesis, and not about those that would disconfirm it. They never bothered to ask whether 1-2-3 or 3-11-200 would fit, and if they had they would have learned that the rule was not "consecutive ascending even numbers," but simply "any three ascending numbers." Again, you can see that once we have a schema (in this case a hypothesis), we continually retrieve that schema from memory rather than other relevant ones, leading us to act in ways that tend to confirm our beliefs.

Functional fixedness occurs when *people's schemas prevent them from using an object in new and nontraditional ways*. Duncker (1945)[64] gave participants a candle, a box of thumbtacks, and a book of matches, and asked them to attach the candle to the wall so that it did not drip onto the table below (Figure 8.19). Few of the participants realized that the box could be tacked to the wall and used as a platform to hold the candle. The problem again is that our existing memories are powerful, and they bias the way we think about new information. Because the participants were "fixated" on the box's normal function of holding thumbtacks, they could not see its alternative use.

confirmation bias

A cognitive bias that results in the tendency to verify and confirm our existing memories rather than to challenge and disconfirm them.

functional fixedness

A cognitive bias that occurs when people's schemas prevent them from using an object in new and nontraditional ways.

FIGURE 8.19 Functional Fixedness

In the candle-tack-box problem, functional fixedness may lead us to see the box only as a box and not as a potential candleholder.

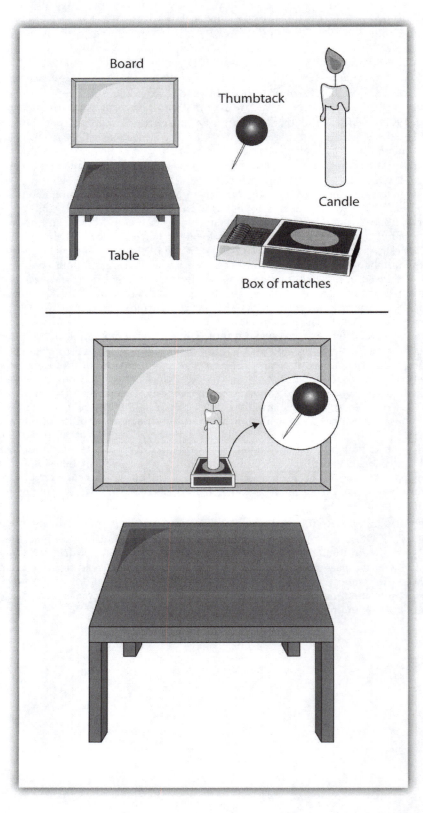

3.3 Misinformation Effects: How Information That Comes Later Can Distort Memory

A particular problem for eyewitnesses such as Jennifer Thompson is that our memories are often influenced by the things that occur to us after we have learned the information (Erdmann, Volbert, & Böhm, 2004; Loftus, 1979; Zaragoza, Belli, & Payment, 2007).[65] This new information can distort our original memories such that the we are no longer sure what is the real information and what was provided later. The **misinformation effect** refers to *errors in memory that occur when new information influences existing memories.*

In an experiment by Loftus and Palmer (1974),[66] participants viewed a film of a traffic accident and then, according to random assignment to experimental conditions, answered one of three questions:

> *"About how fast were the cars going when they hit each other?"*
>
> *"About how fast were the cars going when they smashed each other?"*
>
> *"About how fast were the cars going when they contacted each other?"*

As you can see in Figure 8.20, although all the participants saw the same accident, their estimates of the cars' speed varied by condition. Participants who had been asked about the cars "smashing" each other estimated the highest average speed, and those who had been asked the "contacted" question estimated the lowest average speed.

FIGURE 8.20 Misinformation Effect

Participants viewed a film of a traffic accident and then answered a question about the accident. According to random assignment, the verb in the question was filled by either "hit," "smashed," or "contacted" each other. The wording of the question influenced the participants' memory of the accident.

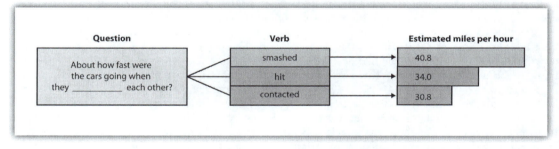

Source: Adapted from Loftus, E. F., & Palmer, J. C. (1974). Reconstruction of automobile destruction: An example of the interaction between language and memory. Journal of Verbal Learning & Verbal Behavior, *13(5), 585–589.*

In addition to distorting our memories for events that have actually occurred, misinformation may lead us to falsely remember information that never occurred. Loftus and her colleagues asked parents to provide them with descriptions of events that did (e.g., moving to a new house) and did not (e.g., being lost in a shopping mall) happen to their children. Then (without telling the children which events were real or made-up) the researchers asked the children to imagine both types of events. The children were instructed to "think real hard" about whether the events had occurred (Ceci, Huffman, Smith, & Loftus, 1994).[67] More than half of the children generated stories regarding at least one of the made-up events, and they remained insistent that the events did in fact occur even when told by the researcher that they could not possibly have occurred (Loftus & Pickrell, 1995).[68] Even college students are susceptible to manipulations that make events that did not actually occur seem as if they did (Mazzoni, Loftus, & Kirsch, 2001).[69]

The ease with which memories can be created or implanted is particularly problematic when the events to be recalled have important consequences. Therapists often argue that patients may repress memories of traumatic events they experienced as children, such as childhood sexual abuse, and then recover the events years later as the therapist leads them to recall the information—for instance, by using dream interpretation and hypnosis (Brown, Scheflin, & Hammond, 1998).[70]

misinformation effect

Errors in memory that occur when new information influences existing memories.

But other researchers argue that painful memories such as sexual abuse are usually very well remembered, that few memories are actually repressed, and that even if they are it is virtually impossible for patients to accurately retrieve them years later (McNally, Bryant, & Ehlers, 2003; Pope, Poliakoff, Parker, Boynes, & Hudson, 2007).[71] These researchers have argued that the procedures used by the therapists to "retrieve" the memories are more likely to actually implant false memories, leading the patients to erroneously recall events that did not actually occur. Because hundreds of people have been accused, and even imprisoned, on the basis of claims about "recovered memory" of child sexual abuse, the accuracy of these memories has important societal implications. Many psychologists now believe that most of these claims of recovered memories are due to implanted, rather than real, memories (Loftus & Ketcham, 1994).[72]

3.4 Overconfidence

overconfidence

A cognitive bias that involves the tendency for people to be too certain about their ability to accurately remember events and to make judgments.

One of the most remarkable aspects of Jennifer Thompson's mistaken identity of Ronald Cotton was her certainty. But research reveals a pervasive cognitive bias toward **overconfidence**, which is *the tendency for people to be too certain about their ability to accurately remember events and to make judgments.* David Dunning and his colleagues (Dunning, Griffin, Milojkovic, & Ross, 1990)[73] asked college students to predict how another student would react in various situations. Some participants made predictions about a fellow student whom they had just met and interviewed, and others made predictions about their roommates whom they knew very well. In both cases, participants reported their confidence in each prediction, and accuracy was determined by the responses of the people themselves. The results were clear: Regardless of whether they judged a stranger or a roommate, the participants consistently overestimated the accuracy of their own predictions.

Eyewitnesses to crimes are also frequently overconfident in their memories, and there is only a small correlation between how accurate and how confident an eyewitness is. The witness who claims to be absolutely certain about his or her identification (e.g., Jennifer Thompson) is not much more likely to be accurate than one who appears much less sure, making it almost impossible to determine whether a particular witness is accurate or not (Wells & Olson, 2003).[74]

flashbulb memory

A vivid and emotional memory of an unusual event that people believe they remember very well.

I am sure that you have a clear memory of when you first heard about the 9/11 attacks in 2001, and perhaps also when you heard that Princess Diana was killed in 1997 or when the verdict of the O. J. Simpson trial was announced in 1995. This type of memory, which we experience along with a great deal of emotion, is known as a **flashbulb memory**—*a vivid and emotional memory of an unusual event that people believe they remember very well.* (Brown & Kulik, 1977).[75]

People are very certain of their memories of these important events, and frequently overconfident. Talarico and Rubin (2003)[76] tested the accuracy of flashbulb memories by asking students to write down their memory of how they had heard the news about either the September 11, 2001, terrorist attacks or about an everyday event that had occurred to them during the same time frame. These recordings were made on September 12, 2001. Then the participants were asked again, either 1, 6, or 32 weeks later, to recall their memories. The participants became less accurate in their recollections of both the emotional event and the everyday events over time. But the participants' confidence in the accuracy of their memory of learning about the attacks did not decline over time. After 32 weeks the participants were overconfident; they were much more certain about the accuracy of their flashbulb memories than they should have been. Schmolck, Buffalo, and Squire (2000)[77] found similar distortions in memories of news about the verdict in the O. J. Simpson trial.

3.5 Heuristic Processing: Availability and Representativeness

heuristic

An information-processing strategy that is useful in many cases but may lead to errors when misapplied.

Another way that our information processing may be biased occurs when we use **heuristics**, which are *information-processing strategies that are useful in many cases but may lead to errors when misapplied.* Let's consider two of the most frequently applied (and misapplied) heuristics: the *representativeness heuristic* and the *availability heuristic.*

representativeness heuristic

A cognitive bias that may occur when we base our judgments on information that seems to represent, or match, what we expect will happen.

In many cases we *base our judgments on information that seems to represent, or match, what we expect will happen, while ignoring other potentially more relevant statistical information.* When we do so, we are using the **representativeness heuristic**. Consider, for instance, the puzzle presented in Table 8.4. Let's say that you went to a hospital, and you checked the records of the babies that were born today. Which pattern of births do you think you are most likely to find?

TABLE 8.4 The Representativeness Heuristic

List A		List B	
6:31 a.m.	Girl	6:31 a.m.	Boy
8:15 a.m.	Girl	8:15 a.m.	Girl
9:42 a.m.	Girl	9:42 a.m.	Boy
1:13 p.m.	Girl	1:13 p.m.	Girl
3:39 p.m.	Boy	3:39 p.m.	Girl
5:12 p.m.	Boy	5:12 p.m.	Boy
7:42 p.m.	Boy	7:42 p.m.	Girl
11:44 p.m.	Boy	11:44 p.m.	Boy
Using the representativeness heuristic may lead us to incorrectly believe that some patterns of observed events are more likely to have occurred than others. In this case, list B seems more random, and thus is judged as more likely to have occurred, but statistically both lists are equally likely.			

Most people think that list B is more likely, probably because list B looks more random, and thus matches (is "representative of") our ideas about randomness. But statisticians know that any pattern of four girls and four boys is mathematically equally likely. The problem is that we have a schema of what randomness should be like, which doesn't always match what is mathematically the case. Similarly, people who see a flipped coin come up "heads" five times in a row will frequently predict, and perhaps even wager money, that "tails" will be next. This behavior is known as the *gambler's fallacy*. But mathematically, the gambler's fallacy is an error: The likelihood of any single coin flip being "tails" is always 50%, regardless of how many times it has come up "heads" in the past.

Our judgments can also be influenced by how easy it is to retrieve a memory. *The tendency to make judgments of the frequency or likelihood that an event occurs on the basis of the ease with which it can be retrieved from memory* is known as the **availability heuristic** (MacLeod & Campbell, 1992; Tversky & Kahneman, 1973).[78] Imagine, for instance, that I asked you to indicate whether there are more words in the English language that begin with the letter "R" or that have the letter "R" as the third letter. You would probably answer this question by trying to think of words that have each of the characteristics, thinking of all the words you know that begin with "R" and all that have "R" in the third position. Because it is much easier to retrieve words by their first letter than by their third, we may incorrectly guess that there are more words that begin with "R," even though there are in fact more words that have "R" as the third letter.

The availability heuristic may also operate on episodic memory. We may think that our friends are nice people, because we see and remember them primarily when they are around us (their friends, who they are, of course, nice to). And the traffic might seem worse in our own neighborhood than we think it is in other places, in part because nearby traffic jams are more easily retrieved than are traffic jams that occur somewhere else.

3.6 Salience and Cognitive Accessibility

Still another potential for bias in memory occurs because we are more likely to attend to, and thus make use of and remember, some information more than other information. For one, we tend to attend to and remember things that are highly **salient**, meaning that *they attract our attention*. Things that are unique, colorful, bright, moving, and unexpected are more salient (McArthur & Post, 1977; Taylor & Fiske, 1978).[79] In one relevant study, Loftus, Loftus, and Messo (1987)[80] showed people images of a customer walking up to a bank teller and pulling out either a pistol or a checkbook. By tracking eye movements, the researchers determined that people were more likely to look at the gun than at the checkbook, and that this reduced their ability to accurately identify the criminal in a lineup that was given later. The salience of the gun drew people's attention away from the face of the criminal.

The salience of the stimuli in our social worlds has a big influence on our judgment, and in some cases may lead us to behave in ways that we might better not have. Imagine, for instance, that you wanted to buy a new music player for yourself. You've been trying to decide whether to get the iPod or the Zune. You checked *Consumer Reports* online and found that, although the players differed on many dimensions, including price, battery life, ability to share music, and so forth, the Zune was nevertheless rated significantly higher by owners than was the iPod. As a result, you decide to purchase the Zune the next day. That night, however, you go to a party, and a friend shows you her iPod. You check it out, and it seems really cool. You tell her that you were thinking of buying a Zune, and she tells you that you are crazy. She says she knows someone who had one and it had a lot of problems—it didn't

availability heuristic

A cognitive bias that involves the tendency to make judgments of the frequency or likelihood that an event occurs on the basis of the ease with which the event can be retrieved from memory.

salient

Attracting attention.

download music correctly, the battery died right after the warranty expired, and so forth—and that she would never buy one. Would you still buy the Zune, or would you switch your plans?

If you think about this question logically, the information that you just got from your friend isn't really all that important. You now know the opinion of one more person, but that can't change the overall rating of the two machines very much. On the other hand, the information your friend gives you, and the chance to use her iPod, are highly salient. The information is right there in front of you, in your hand, whereas the statistical information from *Consumer Reports* is only in the form of a table that you saw on your computer. The outcome in cases such as this is that people frequently ignore the less salient but more important information, such as the likelihood that events occur across a large population (these statistics are known as *base rates*), in favor of the less important but nevertheless more salient information.

People also vary in the schemas that they find important to use when judging others and when thinking about themselves. **Cognitive accessibility** refers to *the extent to which knowledge is activated in memory, and thus likely to be used in cognition and behavior.* For instance, you probably know a person who is a golf nut (or fanatic of another sport). All he can talk about is golf. For him, we would say that golf is a highly accessible construct. Because he loves golf, it is important to his self-concept, he sets many of his goals in terms of the sport, and he tends to think about things and people in terms of it ("if he plays golf, he must be a good person!"). Other people have highly accessible schemas about environmental issues, eating healthy food, or drinking really good coffee. When schemas are highly accessible, we are likely to use them to make judgments of ourselves and others, and this overuse may inappropriately color our judgments.

3.7 Counterfactual Thinking

In addition to influencing our judgments about ourselves and others, the ease with which we can retrieve potential experiences from memory can have an important effect on our own emotions. If we can easily imagine an outcome that is better than what actually happened, then we may experience sadness and disappointment; on the other hand, if we can easily imagine that a result might have been worse than what actually happened, we may be more likely to experience happiness and satisfaction. *The tendency to think about and experience events according to "what might have been"* is known as **counterfactual thinking** (Kahneman & Miller, 1986; Roese, 2005).[81]

Imagine, for instance, that you were participating in an important contest, and you won the silver (second-place) medal. How would you feel? Certainly you would be happy that you won the silver medal, but wouldn't you also be thinking about what might have happened if you had been just a little bit better—you might have won the gold medal! On the other hand, how might you feel if you won the bronze (third-place) medal? If you were thinking about the *counterfactuals* (the "what might have beens") perhaps the idea of not getting any medal at all would have been highly accessible; you'd be happy that you got the medal that you did get, rather than coming in fourth.

Tom Gilovich and his colleagues (Medvec, Madey, & Gilovich, 1995)[83] investigated this idea by videotaping the responses of athletes who won medals in the 1992 Summer Olympic Games. They videotaped the athletes both as they learned that they had won a silver or a bronze medal and again as they were awarded the medal. Then the researchers showed these videos, without any sound, to raters who did not know which medal which athlete had won. The raters were asked to indicate how they thought the athlete was feeling, using a range of feelings from "agony" to "ecstasy." The results showed that the bronze medalists were, on average, rated as happier than were the silver medalists. In a follow-up study, raters watched interviews with many of these same athletes as they talked about their performance. The raters indicated what we would expect on the basis of counterfactual thinking—the silver medalists talked about their disappointments in having finished second rather than first, whereas the bronze medalists focused on how happy they were to have finished third rather than fourth.

You might have experienced counterfactual thinking in other situations. Once I was driving across country, and my car was having some engine trouble. I really wanted to make it home when I got near the end of my journey; I would have been extremely disappointed if the car broke down only a few miles from my home. Perhaps you have noticed that once you get close to finishing something, you feel like you really need to get it done. Counterfactual thinking has even been observed in juries. Jurors who were asked to award monetary damages to others who had been in an accident offered them substantially more in compensation if they barely avoided injury than they offered if the accident seemed inevitable (Miller, Turnbull, & McFarland, 1988).[84]

cognitive accessibility

The extent to which knowledge is activated in memory, and thus likely to be used in cognition and behavior.

counterfactual thinking

A cognitive bias that involves the tendency to think about and experience events according to "what might have been."

FIGURE 8.21 Counterfactual Thinking

Does the bronze medalist look happier to you than the silver medalist? Medvec, Madey, and Gilovich (1995)[82] found that, on average, bronze medalists were happier.

Source: Photo courtesy of kinnigurl, http://commons.wikimedia.org/wiki/ File:2010_Winter_Olympic_Men%27s_Snowboard_ Cross_medalists.jpg.

Psychology in Everyday Life: Cognitive Biases in the Real World

Perhaps you are thinking that the kinds of errors that we have been talking about don't seem that important. After all, who really cares if we think there are more words that begin with the letter "R" than there actually are, or if bronze medal winners are happier than the silver medalists? These aren't big problems in the overall scheme of things. But it turns out that what seem to be relatively small cognitive biases on the surface can have profound consequences for people.

Why would so many people continue to purchase lottery tickets, buy risky investments in the stock market, or gamble their money in casinos when the likelihood of them ever winning is so low? One possibility is that they are victims of salience; they focus their attention on the salient likelihood of a big win, forgetting that the base rate of the event occurring is very low. The belief in astrology, which all scientific evidence suggests is not accurate, is probably driven in part by the salience of the occasions when the predictions are correct. When a horoscope comes true (which will, of course, happen sometimes), the correct prediction is highly salient and may allow people to maintain the overall false belief.

People may also take more care to prepare for unlikely events than for more likely ones, because the unlikely ones are more salient. For instance, people may think that they are more likely to die from a terrorist attack or a homicide than they are from diabetes, stroke, or tuberculosis. But the odds are much greater of dying from the latter than the former. And people are frequently more afraid of flying than driving, although the likelihood of dying in a car crash is hundreds of times greater than dying in a plane crash (more than 50,000 people are killed on U.S. highways every year). Because people don't accurately calibrate their behaviors to match the true potential risks (e.g., they drink and drive or don't wear their seatbelts), the individual and societal level costs are often quite large (Slovic, 2000).[85]

Salience and accessibility also color how we perceive our social worlds, which may have a big influence on our behavior. For instance, people who watch a lot of violent television shows also view the world as more dangerous (Doob & Macdonald, 1979),[86] probably because violence becomes more cognitively accessible for them. We also unfairly overestimate our contribution to joint projects (Ross & Sicoly, 1979),[87] perhaps in part because our own contributions are highly accessible, whereas the contributions of others are much less so.

Even people who should know better, and who *need* to know better, are subject to cognitive biases. Economists, stock traders, managers, lawyers, and even doctors make the same kinds of mistakes in their professional activities that people make in their everyday lives (Gilovich, Griffin, & Kahneman, 2002).[88] Just like us, these people are victims of overconfidence, heuristics, and other biases.

Furthermore, every year thousands of individuals, such as Ronald Cotton, are charged with and often convicted of crimes based largely on eyewitness evidence. When eyewitnesses testify in courtrooms regarding their memories of a crime, they often are completely sure that they are identifying the right person. But the most common cause of innocent people being falsely convicted is erroneous eyewitness testimony (Wells, Wright, & Bradfield, 1999).[89] The many people who were convicted by mistaken eyewitnesses prior to the advent of forensic DNA and who have now been exonerated by DNA tests have certainly paid for all-too-common memory errors (Wells, Memon, & Penrod, 2006).[90]

Although cognitive biases are common, they are not impossible to control, and psychologists and other scientists are working to help people make better decisions. One possibility is to provide people with better feedback about their judgments. Weather forecasters, for instance, learn to be quite accurate in their judgments because they have clear feedback about the accuracy of their predictions. Other research has found that accessibility biases can be reduced by leading people to consider multiple alternatives rather than focus only on the most obvious ones, and particularly by leading people to think about opposite possible outcomes than the ones they are expecting (Lilienfeld, Ammirtai, & Landfield, 2009).[91] Forensic psychologists are also working to reduce the incidence of false identification by helping police develop better procedures for interviewing both suspects and eyewitnesses (Steblay, Dysart, Fulero, & Lindsay, 2001).[92]

KEY TAKEAWAYS

- Our memories fail in part due to inadequate encoding and storage, and in part due to the inability to accurately retrieve stored information.
- The human brain is wired to develop and make use of social categories and schemas. Schemas help us remember new information but may also lead us to falsely remember things that never happened to us and to distort or misremember things that did.
- A variety of cognitive biases influence the accuracy of our judgments.

EXERCISES AND CRITICAL THINKING

1. Consider a time when you were uncertain if you really experienced an event or only imagined it. What impact did this have on you, and how did you resolve it?

2. Consider again some of the cognitive schemas that you hold in your memory. How do these knowledge structures bias your information processing and behavior, and how might you prevent them from doing so?

3. Imagine that you were involved in a legal case in which an eyewitness claimed that he had seen a person commit a crime. Based on your knowledge about memory and cognition, what techniques would you use to reduce the possibility that the eyewitness was making a mistaken identification?

4. CHAPTER SUMMARY

Memory and cognition are the two major interests of cognitive psychologists. The cognitive school was influenced in large part by the development of the electronic computer. Psychologists conceptualize memory in terms of types, stages, and processes.

Explicit memory is assessed using measures in which the individual being tested must consciously attempt to remember the information. Explicit memory includes semantic and episodic memory. Explicit memory tests include recall memory tests, recognition memory tests, and measures of relearning (also known as savings).

Implicit memory refers to the influence of experience on behavior, even if the individual is not aware of those influences. Implicit memory is made up of procedural memory, classical conditioning effects, and priming. Priming refers both to the activation of knowledge and to the influence of that activation on behavior. An important characteristic of implicit memories is that they are frequently formed and used automatically, without much effort or awareness on our part.

Sensory memory, including iconic and echoic memory, is a memory buffer that lasts only very briefly and then, unless it is attended to and passed on for more processing, is forgotten.

Information that we turn our attention to may move into short-term memory (STM). STM is limited in both the length and the amount of information it can hold. Working memory is a set of memory procedures or operations that operates on the information in STM. Working memory's central executive directs the strategies used to keep information in STM, such as maintenance rehearsal, visualization, and chunking.

Long-term memory (LTM) is memory storage that can hold information for days, months, and years. The information that we want to remember in LTM must be encoded and stored, and then retrieved. Some strategies for improving LTM include elaborative encoding, relating information to the self, making use of the forgetting curve and the spacing effect, overlearning, and being aware of context- and state-dependent retrieval effects.

Memories that are stored in LTM are not isolated but rather are linked together into categories and schemas. Schemas are important in part because they help us encode and retrieve information by providing an organizational structure for it.

The ability to maintain information in LTM involves a gradual strengthening of the connections among the neurons in the brain, known as long-term potentiation (LTP). The hippocampus is important in explicit memory, the cerebellum is important in implicit memory, and the amygdala is important in emotional memory. A number of neurotransmitters are important in consolidation and memory. Evidence for the role of different brain structures in different types of memories comes in part from case studies of patients who suffer from amnesia.

Cognitive biases are errors in memory or judgment that are caused by the inappropriate use of cognitive processes. These biases are caused by the overuse of schemas, the reliance on salient and cognitive accessible information, and the use of rule-of-thumb strategies known as heuristics. These biases include errors in source monitoring, the confirmation bias, functional fixedness, the misinformation effect, overconfidence, and counterfactual thinking. Understanding the potential cognitive errors we frequently make can help us make better decisions and engage in more appropriate behaviors.

ENDNOTES

1. Innocence Project. (n.d.). Ronald Cotton. Retrieved from http://www.innocenceproject.org/Content/72.php; Thompson, J. (2000, June 18). I was certain, but I was wrong. *New York Times*. Retrieved from http://faculty.washington.edu/gloftus/Other_Information/Legal_Stuff/Articles/News_Articles/Thompson_NYT_6_18_2000.html

2. Wells, G. L., Memon, A., & Penrod, S. D. (2006). Eyewitness evidence: Improving its probative value. *Psychological Science in the Public Interest, 7*(2), 45–75.

3. Chatham, C. (2007, March 27). 10 important differences between brains and computers. *Developing Intelligence*. Retrieved from http://scienceblogs.com/developingintelligence/2007/03/27/why-the-brain-is-not-like-a-co

4. Bahrick, H. P. (2000). Long-term maintenance of knowledge. In E. Tulving & F. I. M. Craik (Eds.), *The Oxford handbook of memory* (pp. 347–362). New York, NY: Oxford University Press.

5. Mitchell, D. B. (2006). Nonconscious priming after 17 years: Invulnerable implicit memory? *Psychological Science, 17*(11), 925–928.

6. Wisconsin Medical Society. (n.d.). Retrieved from http://www.wisconsinmedicalsociety.org/_SAVANT/_PROFILES/kim_peek/_media/video/expedition/video.html; Kim Peek: Savant who was the inspiration for the film *Rain Man*. (2009, December 23). *The Times*. Retrieved from http://www.timesonline.co.uk/tol/comment/obituaries/article6965115.ece

7. Luria, A. (2004). *The mind of a mnemonist: A little book about a vast memory.* Cambridge, MA: Harvard University Press.

8. Schacter, D. L. (1996). *Searching for memory: The brain, the mind, and the past* (1st ed.). New York, NY: Basic Books.

9. Bartlett, F. C. (1932). *Remembering.* Cambridge, MA: Cambridge University Press.

10. Roediger, H. L., & McDermott, K. B. (1995). Creating false memories: Remembering words not presented in lists. *Journal of Experimental Psychology: Learning, Memory, and Cognition, 21*(4), 803–814.

11. Atkinson, R. C., & Shiffrin, R. M. (1968). Human memory: A proposed system and its control processes. In K. Spence (Ed.), *The psychology of learning and motivation* (Vol. 2). Oxford, England: Academic Press.

12. Haist, F., Shimamura, A. P., & Squire, L. R. (1992). On the relationship between recall and recognition memory. *Journal of Experimental Psychology: Learning, Memory, and Cognition, 18*(4), 691–702.

13. Bridgeman, B., & Morgan, R. (1996). Success in college for students with discrepancies between performance on multiple-choice and essay tests. *Journal of Educational Psychology, 88*(2), 333–340.

14. Nelson, T. O. (1985). Ebbinghaus's contribution to the measurement of retention: Savings during relearning. *Journal of Experimental Psychology: Learning, Memory, and Cognition, 11*(3), 472–478.

15. Bargh, J. A., Chen, M., & Burrows, L. (1996). Automaticity of social behavior: Direct effects of trait construct and stereotype activation on action. *Journal of Personality & Social Psychology, 71*, 230–244.

16. Sperling, G. (1960). The information available in brief visual presentation. *Psychological Monographs, 74*(11), 1–29.

17. Cowan, N., Lichty, W., & Grove, T. R. (1990). Properties of memory for unattended spoken syllables. *Journal of Experimental Psychology: Learning, Memory, and Cognition, 16*(2), 258–268.

18. Solomon, M. (1995). *Mozart: A life.* New York, NY: Harper Perennial.

19. Baddeley, A. D., Vallar, G., & Shallice, T. (1990). The development of the concept of working memory: Implications and contributions of neuropsychology. In G. Vallar & T. Shallice (Eds.), *Neuropsychological impairments of short-term memory* (pp. 54–73). New York, NY: Cambridge University Press.

20. Unsworth, N., & Engle, R. W. (2007). On the division of short-term and working memory: An examination of simple and complex span and their relation to higher order abilities. *Psychological Bulletin, 133*(6), 1038–1066.

21. Peterson, L., & Peterson, M. J. (1959). Short-term retention of individual verbal items. *Journal of Experimental Psychology, 58*(3), 193–198.

22. Miller, G. A. (1956). The magical number seven, plus or minus two: Some limits on our capacity for processing information. *Psychological Review, 63*(2), 81–97.

23. Simon, H. A., & Chase, W. G. (1973). Skill in chess. *American Scientist, 61*(4), 394–403.

24. Didierjean, A., & Marmèche, E. (2005). Anticipatory representation of visual basketball scenes by novice and expert players. *Visual Cognition, 12*(2), 265–283.

25. Wang, Y., Liu, D., & Wang, Y. (2003). Discovering the capacity of human memory. *Brain & Mind, 4*(2), 189–198.

26. Nickerson, R. S., & Adams, M. J. (1979). Long-term memory for a common object. *Cognitive Psychology, 11*(3), 287–307.

27. Craik, F. I., & Lockhart, R. S. (1972). Levels of processing: A framework for memory research. *Journal of Verbal Learning & Verbal Behavior, 11*(6), 671–684; Harris, J. L., & Qualls, C. D. (2000). The association of elaborative or maintenance rehearsal with age, reading comprehension and verbal working memory performance. *Aphasiology, 14*(5–6), 515–526.

28. Rogers, T. B., Kuiper, N. A., & Kirker, W. S. (1977). Self-reference and the encoding of personal information. *Journal of Personality & Social Psychology, 35*(9), 677–688.

29. Symons, C. S., & Johnson, B. T. (1997). The self-reference effect in memory: A meta-analysis. *Psychological Bulletin, 121*(3), 371–394.

30. Bahrick, H. P. (1984). Semantic memory content in permastore: Fifty years of memory for Spanish learned in school. *Journal of Experimental Psychology: General, 113*(1), 1–29.

31. Driskell, J. E., Willis, R. P., & Copper, C. (1992). Effect of overlearning on retention. *Journal of Applied Psychology, 77*(5), 615–622.

32. Godden, D. R., & Baddeley, A. D. (1975). Context-dependent memory in two natural environments: On land and underwater. *British Journal of Psychology, 66*(3), 325–331.

33. Jackson, A., Koek, W., & Colpaert, F. (1992). NMDA antagonists make learning and recall state-dependent. *Behavioural Pharmacology, 3*(4), 415.

34. Marian, V. & Kaushanskaya, M. (2007). Language context guides memory content. *Psychonomic Bulletin and Review, 14*(5), 925–933.

35. Bower, G. H. (1981). Mood and memory. *American Psychologist, 36*, 129–148; Eich, E. (2008). Mood and memory at 26: Revisiting the idea of mood mediation in drug-dependent and place-dependent memory. In M. A. Gluck, J. R. Anderson, & S. M. Kosslyn (Eds.), *Memory and mind: A festschrift for Gordon H. Bower* (pp. 247–260). Mahwah, NJ: Lawrence Erlbaum Associates.

36. Baddeley, A., Eysenck, M. W., & Anderson, M. C. (2009). *Memory.* New York, NY: Psychology Press.

37. Srull, T., & Wyer, R. (1989). Person memory and judgment. *Psychological Review, 96*(1), 58–83.

38. Rosch, E. (1975). Cognitive representations of semantic categories. *Journal of Experimental Psychology: General, 104*(3), 192–233.

39. Bransford, J. D., & Johnson, M. K. (1972). Contextual prerequisites for understanding: Some investigations of comprehension and recall. *Journal of Verbal Learning & Verbal Behavior, 11*(6), 717–726.

40. Lynch, G. (2002). Memory enhancement: The search for mechanism-based drugs. *Nature Neuroscience, 5*(Suppl.), 1035–1038.

41. Lynch, G., Larson, J., Staubli, U., Ambros-Ingerson, J., Granger, R., Lister, R. G.,…Weingartner, H. J. (1991). Long-term potentiation and memory operations in cortical networks. In C. A. Wickliffe, M. Corballis, & G. White (Eds.), *Perspectives on cognitive neuroscience* (pp. 110–131). New York, NY: Oxford University Press.

42. Squire, L. R. (1992). Memory and the hippocampus: A synthesis from findings with rats, monkeys, and humans. *Psychological Review, 99*(2), 195–231.

43. Eichenbaum, H. (1999). Conscious awareness, memory, and the hippocampus. *Nature Neuroscience, 2*(9), 775–776.

44. Jonides, J., Lacey, S. C., & Nee, D. E. (2005). Processes of working memory in mind and brain. *Current Directions in Psychological Science, 14*(1), 2–5.

45. Krupa, D. J., Thompson, J. K., & Thompson, R. F. (1993). Localization of a memory trace in the mammalian brain. *Science, 260*(5110), 989–991; Woodruff-Pak, D. S., Goldenberg, G., Downey-Lamb, M. M., Boyko, O. B., & Lemieux, S. K. (2000). Cerebellar volume in humans related to magnitude of classical conditioning. *Neuroreport: For Rapid Communication of Neuroscience Research, 11*(3), 609–615.

46. Sigurdsson, T., Doyère, V., Cain, C. K., & LeDoux, J. E. (2007). Long-term potentiation in the amygdala: A cellular mechanism of fear learning and memory. *Neuropharmacology, 52*(1), 215–227.

47. Corkin, S., Amaral, D. G., González, R. G., Johnson, K. A., & Hyman, B. T. (1997). H. M.'s medial temporal lobe lesion: Findings from magnetic resonance imaging. *The Journal of Neuroscience, 17*(10), 3964–3979.

48. Bayley, P. J., & Squire, L. R. (2005). Failure to acquire new semantic knowledge in patients with large medial temporal lobe lesions. *Hippocampus, 15*(2), 273–280; Helmuth, Laura. (1999). New role found for the hippocampus. *Science, 285,* 1339–1341; Paller, K. A. (2004). Electrical signals of memory and of the awareness of remembering. *Current Directions in Psychological Science, 13*(2), 49–55.

49. Lashley, K. S. (1929). The effects of cerebral lesions subsequent to the formation of the maze habit: Localization of the habit. In *Brain mechanisms and intelligence: A quantitative study of injuries to the brain* (pp. 86–108). Chicago, IL: University of Chicago Press.

50. McEntee, W., & Crook, T. (1993). Glutamate: Its role in learning, memory, and the aging brain. *Psychopharmacology, 111*(4), 391–401.

51. McGaugh, J. L. (2003). *Memory and emotion: The making of lasting memories.* New York, NY: Columbia University Press.

52. Maki, P. M., & Resnick, S. M. (2000). Longitudinal effects of estrogen replacement therapy on PET cerebral blood flow and cognition. *Neurobiology of Aging, 21*, 373–383; Sherwin, B. B. (1998). Estrogen and cognitive functioning in women. *Proceedings of the Society for Experimental Biological Medicine, 217*, 17–22.

53. Chester, B. (2001). Restoring remembering: Hormones and memory. *McGill Reporter, 33*(10). Retrieved from http://www.mcgill.ca/reporter/33/10/sherwin

54. Gold, P. E., Cahill, L., & Wenk, G. L. (2002). Ginkgo biloba: A cognitive enhancer? *Psychological Science in the Public Interest, 3*(1), 2–11; McDaniel, M. A., Maier, S. F., & Einstein, G. O. (2002). "Brain-specific" nutrients: A memory cure? *Psychological Science in the Public Interest, 3*(1), 12–38.

55. Farah, M. J., Illes, J., Cook-Deegan, R., Gardner, H., Kandel, E., King, P.,…Wolpe, P. R. (2004). Neurocognitive enhancement: What can we do and what should we do? *Nature Reviews Neuroscience, 5*(5), 421–425; Turner, D. C., & Sahakian, B. J. (2006). Analysis of the cognitive enhancing effects of modafinil in schizophrenia. In J. L. Cummings (Ed.), *Progress in neurotherapeutics and neuropsychopharmacology* (pp. 133–147). New York, NY: Cambridge University Press.

56. Rassin, E., Merckelbach, H., & Spaan, V. (2001). When dreams become a royal road to confusion: Realistic dreams, dissociation, and fantasy proneness. *Journal of Nervous and Mental Disease, 189*(7), 478–481.

57. Winograd, E., Peluso, J. P., & Glover, T. A. (1998). Individual differences in susceptibility to memory illusions. *Applied Cognitive Psychology, 12*(Spec. Issue), S5–S27.

58. Jacoby, L. L., & Rhodes, M. G. (2006). False remembering in the aged. *Current Directions in Psychological Science, 15*(2), 49–53.

59. Pratkanis, A. R., Greenwald, A. G., Leippe, M. R., & Baumgardner, M. H. (1988). In search of reliable persuasion effects: III. The sleeper effect is dead: Long live the sleeper effect. *Journal of Personality and Social Psychology, 54*(2), 203–218.

60. Stangor, C., & McMillan, D. (1992). Memory for expectancy-congruent and expectancy-incongruent information: A review of the social and social developmental literatures. *Psychological Bulletin, 111*(1), 42–61.

61. Trope, Y., & Thompson, E. (1997). Looking for truth in all the wrong places? Asymmetric search of individuating information about stereotyped group members. *Journal of Personality and Social Psychology, 73*, 229–241.

62. Darley, J. M., & Gross, P. H. (1983). A hypothesis-confirming bias in labeling effects. *Journal of Personality and Social Psychology, 44*, 20–33.

63. Wason, P. (1960). On the failure to eliminate hypotheses in a conceptual task. *The Quarterly Journal of Experimental Psychology, 12*(3), 129–140.

64. Duncker, K. (1945). On problem-solving. *Psychological Monographs, 58*, 5.

65. Erdmann, K., Volbert, R., & Böhm, C. (2004). Children report suggested events even when interviewed in a non-suggestive manner: What are its implications for credibility assessment? *Applied Cognitive Psychology, 18*(5), 589–611; Loftus, E. F. (1979). The malleability of human memory. *American Scientist, 67*(3), 312–320; Zaragoza, M. S., Belli, R. F., & Payment, K. E. (2007). Misinformation effects and the suggestibility of eyewitness memory. In M. Garry & H. Hayne (Eds.), *Do justice and let the sky fall: Elizabeth Loftus and her contributions to science, law, and academic freedom* (pp. 35–63). Mahwah, NJ: Lawrence Erlbaum Associates.

66. Loftus, E. F., & Palmer, J. C. (1974). Reconstruction of automobile destruction: An example of the interaction between language and memory. *Journal of Verbal Learning & Verbal Behavior, 13*(5), 585–589.

67. Ceci, S. J., Huffman, M. L. C., Smith, E., & Loftus, E. F. (1994). Repeatedly thinking about a non-event: Source misattributions among preschoolers. *Consciousness and Cognition: An International Journal, 3*(3–4), 388–407.

68. Loftus, E. F., & Pickrell, J. E. (1995). The formation of false memories. *Psychiatric Annals, 25*(12), 720–725.

69. Mazzoni, G. A. L., Loftus, E. F., & Kirsch, I. (2001). Changing beliefs about implausible autobiographical events: A little plausibility goes a long way. *Journal of Experimental Psychology: Applied, 7*(1), 51–59.

70. Brown, D., Scheflin, A. W., & Hammond, D. C. (1998). *Memory, trauma treatment, and the law.* New York, NY: Norton.

71. McNally, R. J., Bryant, R. A., & Ehlers, A. (2003). Does early psychological intervention promote recovery from posttraumatic stress? *Psychological Science in the Public Interest, 4*(2), 45–79; Pope, H. G., Jr., Poliakoff, M. B., Parker, M. P., Boynes, M., & Hudson, J. I. (2007). Is dissociative amnesia a culture-bound syndrome? Findings from a survey of historical literature. *Psychological Medicine: A Journal of Research in Psychiatry and the Allied Sciences, 37*(2), 225–233.

72. Loftus, E. F., & Ketcham, K. (1994). *The myth of repressed memory: False memories and allegations of sexual abuse* (1st ed.). New York, NY: St. Martin's Press.

73. Dunning, D., Griffin, D. W., Milojkovic, J. D., & Ross, L. (1990). The overconfidence effect in social prediction. *Journal of Personality and Social Psychology, 58*(4), 568–581.

74. Wells, G. L., & Olson, E. A. (2003). Eyewitness testimony. *Annual Review of Psychology,* 277–295.

75. Brown, R., & Kulik, J. (1977). Flashbulb memories. *Cognition, 5*, 73–98.

76. Talarico, J. M., & Rubin, D. C. (2003). Confidence, not consistency, characterizes flashbulb memories. *Psychological Science, 14*(5), 455–461.

77. Schmolck, H., Buffalo, E. A., & Squire, L. R. (2000). Memory distortions develop over time: Recollections of the O. J. Simpson trial verdict after 15 and 32 months. *Psychological Science, 11*(1), 39–45.

78. MacLeod, C., & Campbell, L. (1992). Memory accessibility and probability judgments: An experimental evaluation of the availability heuristic. *Journal of Personality and Social Psychology, 63*(6), 890–902; Tversky, A., & Kahneman, D. (1973). Availability: A heuristic for judging frequency and probability. *Cognitive Psychology, 5*, 207–232.

79. McArthur, L. Z., & Post, D. L. (1977). Figural emphasis and person perception. *Journal of Experimental Social Psychology, 13*(6), 520–535; Taylor, S. E., & Fiske, S. T. (1978). Salience, attention and attribution: Top of the head phenomena. *Advances in Experimental Social Psychology, 11*, 249–288.

80. Loftus, E. F., Loftus, G. R., & Messo, J. (1987). Some facts about "weapon focus." *Law and Human Behavior, 11*(1), 55–62.

81. Kahneman, D., & Miller, D. T. (1986). Norm theory: Comparing reality to its alternatives. *Psychological Review, 93*, 136–153; Roese, N. (2005). *If only: How to turn regret into opportunity.* New York, NY: Broadway Books.

82. Medvec, V. H., Madey, S. F., & Gilovich, T. (1995). When less is more: Counterfactual thinking and satisfaction among Olympic medalists. *Journal of Personality & Social Psychology, 69*(4), 603–610.

83. Medvec, V. H., Madey, S. F., & Gilovich, T. (1995). When less is more: Counterfactual thinking and satisfaction among Olympic medalists. *Journal of Personality & Social Psychology, 69*(4), 603–610.

84. Miller, D. T., Turnbull, W., & McFarland, C. (1988). Particularistic and universalistic evaluation in the social comparison process. *Journal of Personality and Social Psychology, 55*, 908–917.

85. Slovic, P. (Ed.). (2000). *The perception of risk.* London, England: Earthscan Publications.

86. Doob, A. N., & Macdonald, G. E. (1979). Television viewing and fear of victimization: Is the relationship causal? *Journal of Personality and Social Psychology, 37*(2), 170–179.

87. Ross, M., & Sicoly, F. (1979). Egocentric biases in availability and attribution. *Journal of Personality and Social Psychology, 37*(3), 322–336.

88. Gilovich, T., Griffin, D., & Kahneman, D. (2002). *Heuristics and biases: The psychology of intuitive judgment.* New York, NY: Cambridge University Press.

89. Wells, G. L., Wright, E. F., & Bradfield, A. L. (1999). Witnesses to crime: Social and cognitive factors governing the validity of people's reports. In R. Roesch, S. D. Hart, & J. R. P. Ogloff (Eds.), *Psychology and law: The state of the discipline* (pp. 53–87). Dordrecht, Netherlands: Kluwer Academic Publishers.

90. Wells, G. L., Memon, A., & Penrod, S. D. (2006). Eyewitness evidence: Improving its probative value. *Psychological Science in the Public Interest, 7*(2), 45–75.

91. Lilienfeld, S. O., Ammirati, R., & Landfield, K. (2009). Giving debiasing away: Can psychological research on correcting cognitive errors promote human welfare? *Perspectives on Psychological Science, 4*(4), 390–398.

92. Steblay, N., Dysart, J., Fulero, S., & Lindsay, R. C. L. (2001). Eyewitness accuracy rates in sequential and simultaneous lineup presentations: A meta-analytic comparison. *Law and Human Behavior, 25*(5), 459–473.

CHAPTER 9
Intelligence and Language

How We Talk (or Do Not Talk) about Intelligence

In January 2005, the president of Harvard University, Lawrence H. Summers, sparked an uproar during a presentation at an economic conference on women and minorities in the science and engineering workforce. During his talk, Summers proposed three reasons why there are so few women who have careers in math, physics, chemistry, and biology. One explanation was that it might be due to discrimination against women in these fields, and a second was that it might be a result of women's preference for raising families rather than for competing in academia. But Summers also argued that women might be less genetically capable of performing science and mathematics—that they may have less "intrinsic aptitude" than do men.

Summers's comments on genetics set off a flurry of responses. One of the conference participants, a biologist at the Massachusetts Institute of Technology, walked out on the talk, and other participants said that they were deeply offended. Summers replied that he was only putting forward hypotheses based on the scholarly work assembled for the conference, and that research has shown that genetics have been found to be very important in many domains, compared with environmental factors. As an example, he mentioned the psychological disorder of autism, which was once believed to be a result of parenting but is now known to be primarily genetic in origin.

The controversy did not stop with the conference. Many Harvard faculty members were appalled that a prominent person could even consider the possibility that mathematical skills were determined by genetics, and the controversy and protests that followed the speech led to first ever faculty vote for a motion expressing a "lack of confidence" in a Harvard president. Summers resigned his position, in large part as a result of the controversy, in 2006 (Goldin, Goldin, & Foulkes, 2005).[1]

The characteristic that is most defining of human beings as a species is that our large cerebral cortexes make us very, very smart. In this chapter we consider how psychologists conceptualize and measure human **intelligence**—*the ability to think, to learn from experience, to solve problems, and to adapt to new situations*. We'll consider whether intelligence involves a single ability or many different abilities, how we measure intelligence, what intelligence predicts, and how cultures and societies think about it. We'll also consider intelligence in terms of nature versus nurture and in terms of similarities versus differences among people.

Intelligence is important because it has an impact on many human behaviors. Intelligence is more strongly related than any other individual difference variable to successful educational, occupational, economic, and social outcomes. Scores on intelligence tests predict academic and military performance, as well as success in a wide variety of jobs (Ones, Viswesvaran, & Dilchert, 2005; Schmidt & Hunter, 1998).[2] Intelligence is also negatively correlated with criminal behaviors—the average *intelligence quotient (IQ)* of delinquent adolescents is about 7 points lower than that of other adolescents (Wilson & Herrnstein, 1985)[3] —and positively correlated with health-related outcomes, including longevity (Gottfredson, 2004; Gottfredson & Deary, 2004).[4] At least some of this latter relationship may be due to the fact that people who are more intelligent are better able to predict and avoid accidents and to understand and follow instructions from doctors or on drug labels. Simonton (2006)[5] also found that among U.S. presidents, the ability to effectively lead was well predicted by ratings of the president's intelligence.

The advantages of having a higher IQ increase as life settings become more complex. The correlation between IQ and job performance is higher in more mentally demanding occupations, such as physician or lawyer, than in

intelligence

The ability to think, to learn from experience, to solve problems, and to adapt to new situations.

less mentally demanding occupations, like clerk or newspaper delivery person (Salgado et al., 2003).[6] Although some specific personality traits, talents, and physical abilities are important for success in some jobs, intelligence predicts performance across all types of jobs.

language

A system of communication that uses symbols in a regular way to create meaning.

Our vast intelligence also allows us to have **language**, *a system of communication that uses symbols in a regular way to create meaning*. Language gives us the ability communicate our intelligence to others by talking, reading, and writing. As the psychologist Steven Pinker put it, language is the "the jewel in the crown of cognition" (Pinker, 1994).[7] Although other species have at least some ability to communicate, none of them have language. In the last section of this chapter we will consider the structure and development of language, as well as its vital importance to human beings.

1. DEFINING AND MEASURING INTELLIGENCE

LEARNING OBJECTIVES

1. Define intelligence and list the different types of intelligences psychologists study.
2. Summarize the characteristics of a scientifically valid intelligence test.
3. Outline the biological and environmental determinants of intelligence.

Psychologists have long debated how to best conceptualize and measure intelligence (Sternberg, 2003).[8] These questions include how many types of intelligence there are, the role of nature versus nurture in intelligence, how intelligence is represented in the brain, and the meaning of group differences in intelligence.

1.1 General (g) Versus Specific (s) Intelligences

In the early 1900s, the French psychologist Alfred Binet (1857–1914) and his colleague Henri Simon (1872–1961) began working in Paris to develop a measure that would differentiate students who were expected to be better learners from students who were expected to be slower learners. The goal was to help teachers better educate these two groups of students. Binet and Simon developed what most psychologists today regard as the first intelligence test, which consisted of a wide variety of questions that included the ability to name objects, define words, draw pictures, complete sentences, compare items, and construct sentences.

Binet and Simon (Binet, Simon, & Town, 1915; Siegler, 1992)[9] believed that the questions they asked their students, even though they were on the surface dissimilar, all assessed the basic abilities to understand, reason, and make judgments. And it turned out that the correlations among these different types of measures were in fact all positive; students who got one item correct were more likely to also get other items correct, even though the questions themselves were very different.

On the basis of these results, the psychologist Charles Spearman (1863–1945) hypothesized that there must be a single underlying construct that all of these items measure. He called *the construct that the different abilities and skills measured on intelligence tests have in common* the **general intelligence factor (g)**. Virtually all psychologists now believe that there is a generalized intelligence factor, g, that relates to abstract thinking and that includes the abilities to acquire knowledge, to reason abstractly, to adapt to novel situations, and to benefit from instruction and experience (Gottfredson, 1997; Sternberg, 2003).[10] People with higher general intelligence learn faster.

Soon after Binet and Simon introduced their test, the American psychologist Lewis Terman (1877–1956) developed an American version of Binet's test that became known as the *Stanford-Binet Intelligence Test*. The Stanford-Binet is a measure of general intelligence made up of a wide variety of tasks including vocabulary, memory for pictures, naming of familiar objects, repeating sentences, and following commands.

Although there is general agreement among psychologists that g exists, there is also evidence for **specific intelligence (s)**, *a measure of specific skills in narrow domains*. One empirical result in support of the idea of s comes from intelligence tests themselves. Although the different types of questions do correlate with each other, some items correlate more highly with each other than do other items; they form clusters or clumps of intelligences.

One distinction is between *fluid intelligence*, which refers to the capacity to learn new ways of solving problems and performing activities, and *crystallized intelligence*, which refers to the accumulated knowledge of the world we have acquired throughout our lives (Salthouse, 2004).[11] These intelligences must be different because crystallized intelligence increases with age—older adults are as good as or better than young people in solving crossword puzzles—whereas fluid intelligence tends to decrease with age (Horn, Donaldson, & Engstrom, 1981; Salthouse, 2004).[12]

Other researchers have proposed even more types of intelligences. L. L. Thurstone (1938)[13] proposed that there were seven clusters of *primary mental abilities*, made up of word fluency, verbal comprehension, spatial ability, perceptual speed, numerical ability, inductive reasoning, and memory. But even these dimensions tend to be at least somewhat correlated, showing again the importance of g.

One advocate of the idea of multiple intelligences is the psychologist Robert Sternberg. Sternberg has proposed a **triarchic (three-part) theory of intelligence** that proposes that *people may display more or less analytical intelligence, creative intelligence, and practical intelligence*. Sternberg (1985, 2003)[14] argued that traditional intelligence tests assess analytical intelligence, the ability to answer problems with a single right answer, but that they do not well assess creativity (the ability to adapt to new situations and create new ideas) or practicality (e.g., the ability to write good memos or to effectively delegate responsibility).

As Sternberg proposed, research has found that creativity is not highly correlated with analytical intelligence (Furnham & Bachtiar, 2008),[15] and exceptionally creative scientists, artists, mathematicians, and engineers do not score higher on intelligence than do their less creative peers (Simonton, 2000).[16] Furthermore, the brain areas that are associated with *convergent thinking*, thinking that is directed toward finding the correct answer to a given problem, are different from those associated with *divergent thinking*, the ability to generate many different ideas for or solutions to a single problem (Tarasova, Volf, & Razoumnikova, 2010).[17] On the other hand, being creative often takes some of the basic abilities measured by g, including the abilities to learn from experience, to remember information, and to think abstractly (Bink & Marsh, 2000).[18]

FIGURE 9.1

This child is completing an intelligence test, in this case answering questions about pictures.

© *Thinkstock*

general intelligence factor (g)

The construct that the different abilities and skills measured on intelligence tests have in common.

specific intelligence (s)

A measure of a specific skill in a narrow domain.

triarchic (three-part) theory of intelligence

A theory proposed by Robert Sternberg that suggests that people may display more or less analytical intelligence, creative intelligence, and practical intelligence.

FIGURE 9.2

Test your divergent thinking. How many uses for a paper clip can you think of?

© Thinkstock

Studies of creative people suggest at least five components that are likely to be important for creativity:

1. *Expertise*. Creative people have carefully studied and know a lot about the topic that they are working in. Creativity comes with a lot of hard work (Ericsson, 1998; Weisberg, 2006).[19]

2. *Imaginative thinking*. Creative people often view a problem in a visual way, allowing them to see it from a new and different point of view.

3. *Risk taking*. Creative people are willing to take on new but potentially risky approaches.

4. *Intrinsic interest*. Creative people tend to work on projects because they love doing them, not because they are paid for them. In fact, research has found that people who are paid to be creative are often less creative than those who are not (Hennessey & Amabile, 2010).[20]

5. *Working in a creative environment*. Creativity is in part a social phenomenon. Simonton (1992)[21] found that the most creative people were supported, aided, and challenged by other people working on similar projects.

The last aspect of the triarchic model, practical intelligence, refers primarily to intelligence that cannot be gained from books or formal learning. Practical intelligence represents a type of "street smarts" or "common sense" that is learned from life experiences. Although a number of tests have been devised to measure practical intelligence (Sternberg, Wagner, & Okagaki, 1993; Wagner & Sternberg, 1985),[22] research has not found much evidence that practical intelligence is distinct from g or that it is predictive of success at any particular tasks (Gottfredson, 2003).[23] Practical intelligence may include, at least in part, certain abilities that help people perform well at specific jobs, and these abilities may not always be highly correlated with general intelligence (Sternberg, Wagner, & Okagaki, 1993).[24] On the other hand, these abilities or skills are very specific to particular occupations and thus do not seem to represent the broader idea of intelligence.

Another champion of the idea of multiple intelligences is the psychologist Howard Gardner (1983, 1999).[25] Gardner argued that it would be evolutionarily functional for different people to have different talents and skills, and proposed that there are eight intelligences that can be differentiated from each other (Table 9.1). Gardner noted that some evidence for multiple intelligences comes from the abilities of *autistic savants*, people who score low on intelligence tests overall but who nevertheless may have exceptional skills in a given domain, such as math, music, art, or in being able to recite statistics in a given sport (Treffert & Wallace, 2004).[26]

TABLE 9.1 Howard Gardner's Eight Specific Intelligences

Intelligence	Description
Linguistic	The ability to speak and write well
Logico-mathematical	The ability to use logic and mathematical skills to solve problems
Spatial	The ability to think and reason about objects in three dimensions
Musical	The ability to perform and enjoy music
Kinesthetic (body)	The ability to move the body in sports, dance, or other physical activities
Interpersonal	The ability to understand and interact effectively with others
Intrapersonal	The ability to have insight into the self
Naturalistic	The ability to recognize, identify, and understand animals, plants, and other living things

Source: Adapted from Gardner, H. (1999). Intelligence reframed: Multiple intelligences for the 21st century. New York, NY: Basic Books.

FIGURE 9.3

Although intelligence is often conceptualized in a general way (as the g factor), there is a variety of specific skills that can be useful for particular tasks.

© Thinkstock

The idea of multiple intelligences has been influential in the field of education, and teachers have used these ideas to try to teach differently to different students. For instance, to teach math problems to students who have particularly good kinesthetic intelligence, a teacher might encourage the students to move their bodies or hands according to the numbers. On the other hand, some have argued that these "intelligences" sometimes seem more like "abilities" or "talents" rather than real intelligence. And there is no clear conclusion about how many intelligences there are. Are sense of humor, artistic skills, dramatic skills, and so forth also separate intelligences? Furthermore, and again demonstrating the underlying power of a single intelligence, the many different intelligences are in fact correlated and thus represent, in part, g (Brody, 2003).[27]

1.2 Measuring Intelligence: Standardization and the Intelligence Quotient

The goal of most intelligence tests is to measure g, the general intelligence factor. Good intelligence tests are *reliable*, meaning that they are consistent over time, and also demonstrate *construct validity*, meaning that they actually measure intelligence rather than something else. Because intelligence is such an important individual difference dimension, psychologists have invested substantial effort in creating and improving measures of intelligence, and these tests are now the most accurate of all psychological tests. In fact, the ability to accurately assess intelligence is one of the most important contributions of psychology to everyday public life.

Intelligence changes with age. A 3-year-old who could accurately multiply 183 by 39 would certainly be intelligent, but a 25-year-old who could not do so would be seen as unintelligent. Thus understanding intelligence requires that we know the norms or standards in a given population of people at a given age. The **standardization** of a test involves *giving it to a large number of people at different ages and computing the average score on the test at each age level.*

standardization

Administering a test to a large number of people at different ages and computing the average score on the test at each age level.

Flynn effect

The observation that scores on intelligence tests worldwide have increased substantially over the past decades.

mental age

The age at which a person is performing intellectually.

intelligence quotient (IQ)

A measure of intelligence that is adjusted for age.

It is important that intelligence tests be standardized on a regular basis, because the overall level of intelligence in a population may change over time. The **Flynn effect** refers to the *observation that scores on intelligence tests worldwide have increased substantially over the past decades* (Flynn, 1999).[28] Although the increase varies somewhat from country to country, the average increase is about 3 IQ points every 10 years. There are many explanations for the Flynn effect, including better nutrition, increased access to information, and more familiarity with multiple-choice tests (Neisser, 1998).[29] But whether people are actually getting smarter is debatable (Neisser, 1997).[30]

Once the standardization has been accomplished, we have a picture of the average abilities of people at different ages and can calculate a person's **mental age**, which is *the age at which a person is performing intellectually*. If we compare the mental age of a person to the person's chronological age, the result is the **intelligence quotient (IQ)**, *a measure of intelligence that is adjusted for age*. A simple way to calculate IQ is by using the following formula:

$$IQ = \text{mental age} \div \text{chronological age} \times 100.$$

Thus a 10-year-old child who does as well as the average 10-year-old child has an IQ of 100 (10 ÷ 10 × 100), whereas an 8-year-old child who does as well as the average 10-year-old child would have an IQ of 125 (10 ÷ 8 × 100). Most modern intelligence tests are based the relative position of a person's score among people of the same age, rather than on the basis of this formula, but the idea of an intelligence "ratio" or "quotient" provides a good description of the score's meaning.

Wechsler Adult Intelligence Scale (WAIS)

The most widely used intelligence test for adults.

A number of scales are based on the IQ. The **Wechsler Adult Intelligence Scale (WAIS)** is *the most widely used intelligence test for adults* (Watkins, Campbell, Nieberding, & Hallmark, 1995).[31] The current version of the WAIS, the WAIS-IV, was standardized on 2,200 people ranging from 16 to 90 years of age. It consists of 15 different tasks, each designed to assess intelligence, including working memory, arithmetic ability, spatial ability, and general knowledge about the world (see Figure 9.4). The WAIS-IV yields scores on four domains: verbal, perceptual, working memory, and processing speed. The reliability of the test is high (more than 0.95), and it shows substantial construct validity. The WAIS-IV is correlated highly with other IQ tests such as the Stanford-Binet, as well as with criteria of academic and life success, including college grades, measures of work performance, and occupational level. It also shows significant correlations with measures of everyday functioning among the mentally retarded.

The Wechsler scale has also been adapted for preschool children in the form of the *Wechsler Primary and Preschool Scale of Intelligence (WPPSI-III)* and for older children and adolescents in the form of the *Wechsler Intelligence Scale for Children (WISC-IV)*.

FIGURE 9.4 Sample Items From the Wechsler Adult Intelligence Scale (WAIS)

VERBAL

General information

What day of the year is Independence Day?

Arithmetic reasoning

If eggs cost 60 cents a dozen, what does 1 egg cost?

Vocabulary

Tell me the meaning of corrupt.

Comprehension

Why do people buy fire insurance?

Digit span

Listen carefully, and when I am through, say the numbers right after me.

7	3	4	1	8	6

Now I am going to say some more numbers, but I want you to say them backward.

3	8	4	1	6

Block design

Using the four blocks, make one just like this.

Object assembly

If these pieces are put together correctly, they will make something. Go ahead and put them together as quickly as you can.

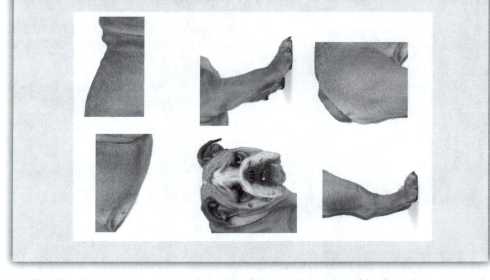

Source: Adapted from Thorndike, R. L., & Hagen, E. P. (1997). Cognitive Abilities Test (Form 5): Research handbook. Chicago, IL: Riverside Publishing.

The intelligence tests that you may be most familiar with are *aptitude tests*, which are designed to measure one's ability to perform a given task, for instance, to do well in college or in postgraduate training. Most U.S. colleges and universities require students to take the Scholastic Assessment Test

(SAT) or the American College Test (ACT), and postgraduate schools require the Graduate Record Examination (GRE), Medical College Admissions Test (MCAT), or the Law School Admission Test (LSAT). These tests are useful for selecting students because they predict success in the programs that they are designed for, particularly in the first year of the program (Kuncel, Hezlett, & Ones, 2010).[32] These aptitude tests also measure, in part, intelligence. Frey and Detterman (2004)[33] found that the SAT correlated highly (between about $r = .7$ and $r = .8$) with standard measures of intelligence.

Intelligence tests are also used by industrial and organizational psychologists in the process of *personnel selection*. **Personnel selection** is *the use of structured tests to select people who are likely to perform well at given jobs* (Schmidt & Hunter, 1998).[34] The psychologists begin by conducting a *job analysis* in which they determine what knowledge, skills, abilities, and personal characteristics (*KSAPs*) are required for a given job. This is normally accomplished by surveying and/or interviewing current workers and their supervisors. Based on the results of the job analysis, the psychologists choose selection methods that are most likely to be predictive of job performance. Measures include tests of cognitive and physical ability and job knowledge tests, as well as measures of IQ and personality.

1.3   The Biology of Intelligence

The brain processes underlying intelligence are not completely understood, but current research has focused on four potential factors: brain size, sensory ability, speed and efficiency of neural transmission, and working memory capacity.

There is at least some truth to the idea that smarter people have bigger brains. Studies that have measured brain volume using neuroimaging techniques find that larger brain size is correlated with intelligence (McDaniel, 2005),[35] and intelligence has also been found to be correlated with the number of neurons in the brain and with the thickness of the cortex (Haier, 2004; Shaw et al., 2006).[36] It is important to remember that these correlational findings do not mean that having more brain volume causes higher intelligence. It is possible that growing up in a stimulating environment that rewards thinking and learning may lead to greater brain growth (Garlick, 2003),[37] and it is also possible that a third variable, such as better nutrition, causes both brain volume and intelligence.

Another possibility is that the brains of more intelligent people operate faster or more efficiently than the brains of the less intelligent. Some evidence supporting this idea comes from data showing that people who are more intelligent frequently show less brain activity (suggesting that they need to use less capacity) than those with lower intelligence when they work on a task (Haier, Siegel, Tang, & Abel, 1992).[38] And the brains of more intelligent people also seem to run faster than the brains of the less intelligent. Research has found that the speed with which people can perform simple tasks—such as determining which of two lines is longer or pressing, as quickly as possible, one of eight buttons that is lighted—is predictive of intelligence (Deary, Der, & Ford, 2001).[39] Intelligence scores also correlate at about $r = .5$ with measures of working memory (Ackerman, Beier, & Boyle, 2005),[40] and working memory is now used as a measure of intelligence on many tests.

Although intelligence is not located in a specific part of the brain, it is more prevalent in some brain areas than others. Duncan et al. (2000)[41] administered a variety of intelligence tasks and observed the places in the cortex that were most active. Although different tests created different patterns of activation, as you can see in Figure 9.5, these activated areas were primarily in the outer parts of the cortex, the area of the brain most involved in planning, executive control, and short-term memory.

personnel selection

The use of structured tests to select people who are likely to perform well at given jobs.

FIGURE 9.5 Where Is Intelligence?

fMRI studies have found that the areas of the brain most related to intelligence are in the outer parts of the cortex.

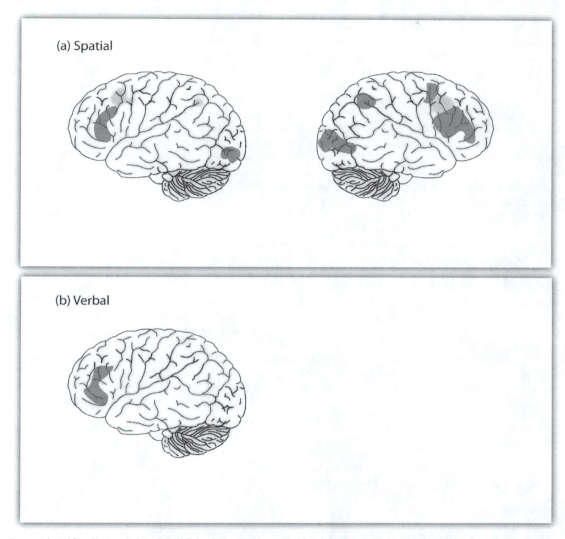

(a) Spatial

(b) Verbal

Source: Adapted from Duncan, J., Seitz, R. J., Kolodny, J., Bor, D., Herzog, H., Ahmed, A.,...Emslie, H. (2000). A neural basis for general intelligence. Science, 289(5478), 457–460.

1.4   Is Intelligence Nature or Nurture?

Intelligence has both genetic and environmental causes, and these have been systematically studied through a large number of twin and adoption studies (Neisser et al., 1996; Plomin, DeFries, Craig, & McGuffin, 2003).[42] These studies have found that between 40% and 80% of the variability in IQ is due to genetics, meaning that overall genetics plays a bigger role than does environment in creating IQ differences among individuals (Plomin & Spinath, 2004).[43] The IQs of identical twins correlate very highly (r = .86), much higher than do the scores of fraternal twins who are less genetically similar (r = .60). And the correlations between the IQs of parents and their biological children (r = .42) is significantly greater than the correlation between parents and adopted children (r = .19). The role of genetics gets stronger as children get older. The intelligence of very young children (less than 3 years old) does not predict adult intelligence, but by age 7 it does, and IQ scores remain very stable in adulthood (Deary, Whiteman, Starr, Whalley, & Fox, 2004).[44]

But there is also evidence for the role of nurture, indicating that individuals are not born with fixed, unchangeable levels of intelligence. Twins raised together in the same home have more similar IQs than do twins who are raised in different homes, and fraternal twins have more similar IQs than do nontwin siblings, which is likely due to the fact that they are treated more similarly than are siblings.

The fact that intelligence becomes more stable as we get older provides evidence that early environmental experiences matter more than later ones. Environmental factors also explain a greater proportion of the variance in intelligence for children from lower-class households than they do for children from upper-class households (Turkheimer, Haley, Waldron, D'Onofrio, & Gottesman, 2003).[45] This is because most upper-class households tend to provide a safe, nutritious, and supporting environment for children, whereas these factors are more variable in lower-class households.

Social and economic deprivation can adversely affect IQ. Children from households in poverty have lower IQs than do children from households with more resources even when other factors such as education, race, and parenting are controlled (Brooks-Gunn & Duncan, 1997).[46] Poverty may lead to diets that are undernourishing or lacking in appropriate vitamins, and poor children may also be more likely to be exposed to toxins such as lead in drinking water, dust, or paint chips (Bellinger & Needleman, 2003).[47] Both of these factors can slow brain development and reduce intelligence.

If impoverished environments can harm intelligence, we might wonder whether enriched environments can improve it. Government-funded after-school programs such as Head Start are designed to help children learn. Research has found that attending such programs may increase intelligence for a short time, but these increases rarely last after the programs end (McLoyd, 1998; Perkins & Grotzer, 1997).[48] But other studies suggest that Head Start and similar programs may improve emotional intelligence and reduce the likelihood that children will drop out of school or be held back a grade (Reynolds, Temple, Robertson, & Mann 2001).[49]

Intelligence is improved by education; the number of years a person has spent in school correlates at about $r = .6$ with IQ (Ceci, 1991).[50] In part this correlation may be due to the fact that people with higher IQ scores enjoy taking classes more than people with low IQ scores, and they thus are more likely to stay in school. But education also has a causal effect on IQ. Comparisons between children who are almost exactly the same age but who just do or just do not make a deadline for entering school in a given school year show that those who enter school a year earlier have higher IQ than those who have to wait until the next year to begin school (Baltes & Reinert, 1969; Ceci & Williams, 1997).[51] Children's IQs tend to drop significantly during summer vacations (Huttenlocher, Levine, & Vevea, 1998),[52] a finding that suggests that a longer school year, as is used in Europe and East Asia, is beneficial.

It is important to remember that the relative roles of nature and nurture can never be completely separated. A child who has higher than average intelligence will be treated differently than a child who has lower than average intelligence, and these differences in behaviors will likely amplify initial differences. This means that modest genetic differences can be multiplied into big differences over time.

emotional intelligence

The ability to identify, assess, manage, and control one's emotions.

Psychology in Everyday Life: Emotional Intelligence

Although most psychologists have considered intelligence a cognitive ability, people also use their emotions to help them solve problems and relate effectively to others. **Emotional intelligence** refers to *the ability to accurately identify, assess, and understand emotions, as well as to effectively control one's own emotions* (Feldman-Barrett & Salovey, 2002; Mayer, Salovey, & Caruso, 2000).[53]

The idea of emotional intelligence is seen in Howard Gardner's *interpersonal intelligence* (the capacity to understand the emotions, intentions, motivations, and desires of other people) and *intrapersonal intelligence* (the capacity to understand oneself, including one's emotions). Public interest in, and research on, emotional intelligence became widely prevalent following the publication of Daniel Goleman's best-selling book, *Emotional Intelligence: Why It Can Matter More Than IQ* (Goleman, 1998).[54]

There are a variety of measures of emotional intelligence (Mayer, Salovey, & Caruso, 2008; Petrides & Furnham, 2000).[55] One popular measure, the Mayer-Salovey-Caruso Emotional Intelligence Test (http://www.emotionaliq.org), includes items about the ability to understand, experience, and manage emotions, such as these:

- What mood(s) might be helpful to feel when meeting in-laws for the very first time?
- Tom felt anxious and became a bit stressed when he thought about all the work he needed to do. When his supervisor brought him an additional project, he felt _____ (fill in the blank).
- Contempt most closely combines which two emotions?

    1. anger and fear
    2. fear and surprise
    3. disgust and anger
    4. surprise and disgust

- Debbie just came back from vacation. She was feeling peaceful and content. How well would each of the following actions help her preserve her good mood?

    - Action 1: She started to make a list of things at home that she needed to do.

- Action 2: She began thinking about where and when she would go on her next vacation.
- Action 3: She decided it was best to ignore the feeling since it wouldn't last anyway.

One problem with emotional intelligence tests is that they often do not show a great deal of reliability or construct validity (Føllesdal & Hagtvet, 2009).[56] Although it has been found that people with higher emotional intelligence are also healthier (Martins, Ramalho, & Morin, 2010),[57] findings are mixed about whether emotional intelligence predicts life success—for instance, job performance (Harms & Credé, 2010).[58] Furthermore, other researchers have questioned the construct validity of the measures, arguing that emotional intelligence really measures knowledge about what emotions are, but not necessarily how to use those emotions (Brody, 2004),[59] and that emotional intelligence is actually a personality trait, a part of g, or a skill that can be applied in some specific work situations—for instance, academic and work situations (Landy, 2005).[60]

Although measures of the ability to understand, experience, and manage emotions may not predict effective behaviors, another important aspect of emotional intelligence—*emotion regulation*—does. Emotion regulation refers to the ability to control and productively use one's emotions. Research has found that people who are better able to override their impulses to seek immediate gratification and who are less impulsive also have higher cognitive and social intelligence. They have better SAT scores, are rated by their friends as more socially adept, and cope with frustration and stress better than those with less skill at emotion regulation (Ayduk et al., 2000; Eigsti et al., 2006; Mischel & Ayduk, 2004).[61]

Because emotional intelligence seems so important, many school systems have designed programs to teach it to their students. However, the effectiveness of these programs has not been rigorously tested, and we do not yet know whether emotional intelligence can be taught, or if learning it would improve the quality of people's lives (Mayer & Cobb, 2000).[62]

KEY TAKEAWAYS

- Intelligence is the ability to think, to learn from experience, to solve problems, and to adapt to new situations. Intelligence is important because it has an impact on many human behaviors.
- Psychologists believe that there is a construct that accounts for the overall differences in intelligence among people, known as general intelligence (g).
- There is also evidence for specific intelligences (s), measures of specific skills in narrow domains, including creativity and practical intelligence.
- The intelligence quotient (IQ) is a measure of intelligence that is adjusted for age. The Wechsler Adult Intelligence Scale (WAIS) is the most widely used IQ test for adults.
- Brain volume, speed of neural transmission, and working memory capacity are related to IQ.
- Between 40% and 80% of the variability in IQ is due to genetics, meaning that overall genetics plays a bigger role than does environment in creating IQ differences among individuals.
- Intelligence is improved by education and may be hindered by environmental factors such as poverty.
- Emotional intelligence refers to the ability to identify, assess, manage, and control one's emotions. People who are better able to regulate their behaviors and emotions are also more successful in their personal and social encounters.

EXERCISES AND CRITICAL THINKING

1. Consider your own IQ. Are you smarter than the average person? What specific intelligences do you think you excel in?
2. Did your parents try to improve your intelligence? Do you think their efforts were successful?
3. Consider the meaning of the Flynn effect. Do you think people are really getting smarter?
4. Give some examples of how emotional intelligence (or the lack of it) influences your everyday life and the lives of other people you know.

2.   THE SOCIAL, CULTURAL, AND POLITICAL ASPECTS OF INTELLIGENCE

L E A R N I N G   O B J E C T I V E S

1. Explain how very high and very low intelligence is defined and what it means to have them.
2. Consider and comment on the meaning of biological and environmental explanations for gender and racial differences in IQ.
3. Define stereotype threat and explain how it might influence scores on intelligence tests.

Intelligence is defined by the culture in which it exists. Most people in Western cultures tend to agree with the idea that intelligence is an important personality variable that should be admired in those who have it. But people from Eastern cultures tend to place less emphasis on individual intelligence and are more likely to view intelligence as reflecting wisdom and the desire to improve the society as a whole rather than only themselves (Baral & Das, 2004; Sternberg, 2007).[63] And in some cultures, such as the United States, it is seen as unfair and prejudicial to argue, even at a scholarly conference, that men and women might have different abilities in domains such as math and science and that these differences might be caused by genetics (even though, as we have seen, a great deal of intelligence *is* determined by genetics). In short, although psychological tests accurately measure intelligence, it is cultures that interpret the meanings of those tests and determine how people with differing levels of intelligence are treated.

2.1   Extremes of Intelligence: Retardation and Giftedness

normal distribution (or bell curve)

The pattern of scores usually observed in a variable that clusters around its average.

The results of studies assessing the measurement of intelligence show that IQ is distributed in the population in the form of a **normal distribution (or bell curve)**, which is *the pattern of scores usually observed in a variable that clusters around its average*. In a normal distribution, the bulk of the scores fall toward the middle, with many fewer scores falling at the extremes. The normal distribution of intelligence (Figure 9.6) shows that on IQ tests, as well as on most other measures, the majority of people cluster around the average (in this case, where IQ = 100), and fewer are either very smart or very dull. Because the standard deviation of an IQ test is about 15, this means that about 2% of people score above an IQ of 130 (often considered the threshold for *giftedness*), and about the same percentage score below an IQ of 70 (often being considered the threshold for *mental retardation*).

Although Figure 9.6 presents a single distribution, the actual IQ distribution varies by sex such that the distribution for men is more spread out than is the distribution for women. These sex differences mean that about 20% more men than women fall in the extreme (very smart or very dull) ends of the distribution (Johnson, Carothers, & Deary, 2009).[64] Boys are about five times more likely to be diagnosed with the reading disability dyslexia than are girls (Halpern, 1992),[65] and are also more likely to be classified as mentally retarded. But boys are also about 20% more highly represented in the upper end of the IQ distribution.

FIGURE 9.6 Distribution of IQ Scores in the General Population

The normal distribution of IQ scores in the general population shows that most people have about average intelligence, while very few have extremely high or extremely low intelligence.

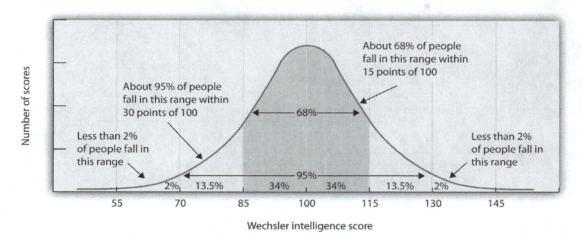

Extremely Low Intelligence

One end of the distribution of intelligence scores is defined by people with very low IQ. **Mental retardation** is *a generalized disorder ascribed to people who have an IQ below 70, who have experienced deficits since childhood, and who have trouble with basic life skills, such as dressing and feeding oneself and communicating with others* (Switzky & Greenspan, 2006).[66] About 1% of the United States population, most of them males, fulfill the criteria for mental retardation, but some children who are diagnosed as mentally retarded lose the classification as they get older and better learn to function in society. A particular vulnerability of people with low IQ is that they may be taken advantage of by others, and this is an important aspect of the definition of mental retardation (Greenspan, Loughlin, & Black, 2001).[67] Mental retardation is divided into four categories: mild, moderate, severe, and profound. Severe and profound mental retardation is usually caused by genetic mutations or accidents during birth, whereas mild forms have both genetic and environmental influences.

One cause of mental retardation is **Down syndrome**, *a chromosomal disorder leading to mental retardation caused by the presence of all or part of an extra 21st chromosome*. The incidence of Down syndrome is estimated at 1 per 800 to 1,000 births, although its prevalence rises sharply in those born to older mothers. People with Down syndrome typically exhibit a distinctive pattern of physical features, including a flat nose, upwardly slanted eyes, a protruding tongue, and a short neck.

Societal attitudes toward individuals with mental retardation have changed over the past decades. We no longer use terms such as "moron," "idiot," or "imbecile" to describe these people, although these were the official psychological terms used to describe degrees of retardation in the past. Laws such as the Americans with Disabilities Act (ADA) have made it illegal to discriminate on the basis of mental and physical disability, and there has been a trend to bring the mentally retarded out of institutions and into our workplaces and schools. In 2002 the U.S. Supreme Court ruled that the execution of people with mental retardation is "cruel and unusual punishment," thereby ending this practice (Atkins v. Virginia, 2002).[68]

Extremely High Intelligence

Having extremely high IQ is clearly less of a problem than having extremely low IQ, but there may also be challenges to being particularly smart. It is often assumed that schoolchildren who are labeled as "gifted" may have adjustment problems that make it more difficult for them to create social relationships. To study gifted children, Lewis Terman and his colleagues (Terman & Oden, 1959)[69] selected about 1,500 high school students who scored in the top 1% on the Stanford-Binet and similar IQ tests (i.e., who had IQs of about 135 or higher), and tracked them for more than seven decades (the children became known as the "termites" and are still being studied today). This study found, first, that these students were not unhealthy or poorly adjusted but rather were above average in physical health and were taller and heavier than individuals in the general population. The students also had above average social relationships—for instance, being less likely to divorce than the average person (Seagoe, 1975).[70]

mental retardation

A generalized disorder mostly found in males, ascribed to those who have an IQ below 70, who have experienced deficits since childhood, and who have trouble with basic life skills, such as dressing and feeding oneself and communicating with others.

Down syndrome

A chromosomal disorder leading to mental retardation and caused by the presence of all or part of an extra 21st chromosome.

FIGURE 9.7

About one in every 800 to 1,000 children has Down syndrome.

© Thinkstock

FIGURE 9.8

The popular stereotype of highly intelligent people as physically uncoordinated and unpopular is not true.

© Thinkstock

Terman's study also found that many of these students went on to achieve high levels of education and entered prestigious professions, including medicine, law, and science. Of the sample, 7% earned doctoral degrees, 4% earned medical degrees, and 6% earned law degrees. These numbers are all considerably higher than what would have been expected from a more general population. Another study of young adolescents who had even higher IQs found that these students ended up attending graduate school at a rate more than 50 times higher than that in the general population (Lubinski & Benbow, 2006).[71]

As you might expect based on our discussion of intelligence, kids who are gifted have higher scores on general intelligence (g). But there are also different types of giftedness. Some children are particularly good at math or science, some at automobile repair or carpentry, some at music or art, some at sports or leadership, and so on. There is a lively debate among scholars about whether it is appropriate or beneficial to label some children as "gifted and talented" in school and to provide them with accelerated special classes and other programs that are not available to everyone. Although doing so may help the gifted kids (Colangelo & Assouline, 2009),[72] it also may isolate them from their peers and make such provisions unavailable to those who are not classified as "gifted."

2.2 Sex Differences in Intelligence

As discussed in the introduction to Chapter 9, Lawrence Summers's claim about the reasons why women might be underrepresented in the hard sciences was based in part on the assumption that environment, such as the presence of gender discrimination or social norms, was important but also in part on the possibility that women may be less genetically capable of performing some tasks than are men. These claims, and the responses they provoked, provide another example of how cultural interpretations of the meanings of IQ can create disagreements and even guide public policy. The fact that women earn many fewer degrees in the hard sciences than do men is not debatable (as shown in Figure 9.9), but the reasons for these differences are.

FIGURE 9.9 Bachelor's Degrees Earned by Women in Selected Fields (2006)

Women tend to earn more degrees in the biological and social sciences, whereas men earn more in engineering, math, and the physical sciences.

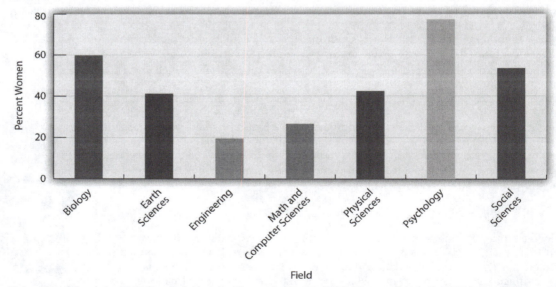

National Science Foundation (2010). Downloaded from: http://www.nsf.gov/statistics/nsf08321/content.cfm?pub_id=3785&id=2

Differences in degree choice are probably not due to overall intelligence because men and women have almost identical intelligence as measured by standard IQ and aptitude tests (Hyde, 2005).[73] On the other hand, it is possible that the differences are due to variability in intelligence, because more men than women have very high (as well as very low) intelligence. Perhaps success in the mathematical and physical sciences requires very high IQ, and this favors men.

There are also observed sex differences on some particular types of tasks. Women tend to do better than men on some verbal tasks, including spelling, writing, and pronouncing words (Halpern et al.,

2007),[74] and they have better emotional intelligence in the sense that they are better at detecting and recognizing the emotions of others (McClure, 2000).[75]

On average, men do better than women on tasks requiring spatial ability, such as the mental rotation tasks shown in Figure 9.10 (Voyer, Voyer, & Bryden, 1995).[76] Boys tend to do better than girls on both geography and geometry tasks (Vogel, 1996).[77] On the math part of the Scholastic Assessment Test (SAT), boys with scores of 700 or above outnumber girls by more than 10 to 1 (Benbow & Stanley, 1983),[78] but there are also more boys in the lowest end of the distribution as well.

FIGURE 9.10

Men outperform women on measures of spatial rotation, such as this task requires, but women are better at recognizing the emotions of others.

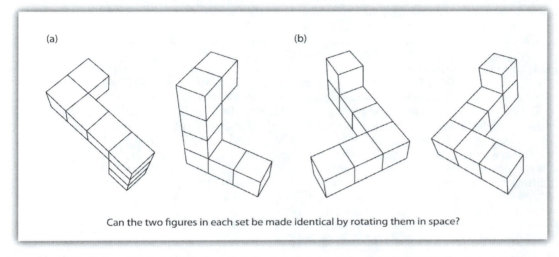

Can the two figures in each set be made identical by rotating them in space?

Source: Adapted from Halpern, D. F., Benbow, C. P., Geary, D. C., Gur, R. C., Hyde, J. S., & Gernsbache, M. A. (2007). The science of sex differences in science and mathematics. Psychological Science in the Public Interest, 8(1), 1–51.

Although these differences are real, and can be important, keep in mind that like virtually all sex group differences, the average difference between men and women is small compared to the average differences within each sex. There are many women who are better than the average man on spatial tasks, and many men who score higher than the average women in terms of emotional intelligence. Sex differences in intelligence allow us to make statements only about average differences and do not say much about any individual person.

Although society may not want to hear it, differences between men and women may be in part genetically determined, perhaps by differences in brain lateralization or by hormones (Kimura & Hampson, 1994; Voyer, Voyer, & Bryden, 1995).[79] But nurture is also likely important (Newcombe & Huttenlocker, 2006).[80] As infants, boys and girls show no or few differences in spatial or counting abilities, suggesting that the differences occur at least in part as a result of socialization (Spelke, 2005).[81] Furthermore, the number of women entering the hard sciences has been increasing steadily over the past years, again suggesting that some of the differences may have been due to gender discrimination and societal expectations about the appropriate roles and skills of women.

2.3   Racial Differences in Intelligence

Although their bell curves overlap considerably, there are also differences in which members of different racial and ethnic groups cluster along the IQ line. The bell curves for some groups (Jews and East Asians) are centered somewhat higher than for Whites in general (Lynn, 1996; Neisser et al., 1996).[82] Other groups, including Blacks and Hispanics, have averages somewhat lower than those of Whites. The center of the IQ distribution for African Americans is about 85, and that for Hispanics is about 93 (Hunt & Carlson, 2007).[83]

eugenics

The misguided proposal that one could improve the human species by encouraging or permitting reproduction of only those people with genetic characteristics judged desirable.

The observed average differences in intelligence between groups has at times led to malicious and misguided attempts to try to correct for them through discriminatory treatment of people from different races, ethnicities, and nationalities (Lewontin, Rose, & Kamin, 1984).[84] One of the most egregious was the spread of eugenics, *the proposal that one could improve the human species by encouraging or permitting reproduction of only those people with genetic characteristics judged desirable.*

Eugenics became immensely popular in the United States in the early 20th century and was supported by many prominent psychologists, including Sir Francis Galton. Dozens of universities, including those in the Ivy League, offered courses in eugenics, and the topic was presented in most high school and college biology texts (Selden, 1999).[85] Belief in the policies of eugenics led the U.S. Congress to pass laws designed to restrict immigration from other countries supposedly marked by low intelligence, particularly those in eastern and southern Europe. And because more than one-half of the U.S. states passed laws requiring the sterilization of low-IQ individuals, more than 60,000 Americans, mostly African Americans and other poor minorities, underwent forced sterilizations. Fortunately, the practice of sterilization was abandoned between the 1940s and the 1960s, although sterilization laws remained on the books in some states until the 1970s.

One explanation for race differences in IQ is that intelligence tests are biased against some groups and in favor of others. By bias, what psychologists mean is that a test predicts outcomes—such as grades or occupational success—better for one group than it does for another. If IQ is a better predictor of school grade point average for Whites than it is for Asian Americans, for instance, then the test would be biased against Asian Americans, even though the average IQ scores for Asians might be higher. But IQ tests do not seem to be racially biased because the observed correlations between IQ tests and both academic and occupational achievement are about equal across races (Brody, 1992).[86]

Another way that tests might be biased is if questions are framed such that they are easier for people from one culture to understand than for people from other cultures. For example, even a very smart person will not do well on a test if he or she is not fluent in the language in which the test is administered, or does not understand the meaning of the questions being asked. But modern intelligence tests are designed to be culturally neutral, and group differences are found even on tests that only ask about spatial intelligence. Although some researchers still are concerned about the possibility that intelligence tests are culturally biased, it is probably not the case that the tests are creating all of the observed group differences (Suzuki & Valencia, 1997).[87]

stereotype threat

Performance decrements that are caused by the knowledge of cultural stereotypes.

Research Focus: Stereotype Threat

Although intelligence tests may not be culturally biased, the situation in which one takes a test may be. One environmental factor that may affect how individuals perform and achieve is their expectations about their ability at a task. In some cases these beliefs may be positive, and they have the effect of making us feel more confident and thus better able to perform tasks. For instance, research has found that because Asian students are aware of the cultural stereotype that "Asians are good at math," reminding them of this fact before they take a difficult math test can improve their performance on the test (Walton & Cohen, 2003).[88] On the other hand, sometimes these beliefs are negative, and they create negative self-fulfilling prophecies such that we perform more poorly just because of our knowledge about the stereotypes.

In 1995 Claude Steele and Joshua Aronson tested the hypothesis that the differences in performance on IQ tests between Blacks and Whites might be due to the activation of negative stereotypes (Steele & Aronson, 1995).[89] Because Black students are aware of the stereotype that Blacks are intellectually inferior to Whites, this stereotype might create a negative expectation, which might interfere with their performance on intellectual tests through fear of confirming that stereotype.

In support of this hypothesis, the experiments revealed that Black college students performed worse (in comparison to their prior test scores) on standardized test questions when this task was described to them as being diagnostic of their verbal ability (and thus when the stereotype was relevant), but that their performance was not influenced when the same questions were described as an exercise in problem solving. And in another study, the researchers found that when Black students were asked to indicate their race before they took a math test (again activating the stereotype), they performed more poorly than they had on prior exams, whereas White students were not affected by first indicating their race.

Steele and Aronson argued that thinking about negative stereotypes that are relevant to a task that one is performing creates **stereotype threat**—*performance decrements that are caused by the knowledge of cultural stereotypes*. That is, they argued that the negative impact of race on standardized tests may be caused, at least in part, by the performance situation itself. Because the threat is "in the air," Black students may be negatively influenced by it.

Research has found that stereotype threat effects can help explain a wide variety of performance decrements among those who are targeted by negative stereotypes. For instance, when a math task is described as diagnostic of intelligence, Latinos and Latinas perform more poorly than do Whites (Gonzales, Blanton, & Williams, 2002).[90] Similarly, when stereotypes are activated, children with low socioeconomic status perform more poorly in math than do those with high socioeconomic status, and psychology students perform more poorly than do natural science students (Brown, Croizet, Bohner, Fournet, & Payne, 2003; Croizet & Claire, 1998).[91] Even groups who typically enjoy advantaged social status can be made to experience stereotype threat. White men perform more poorly on a math test when they are told that their performance will be compared with that of Asian men (Aronson, Lustina, Good, Keough, & Steele, 1999),[92] and Whites perform more poorly than Blacks on a sport-related task when it is described to them as measuring their natural athletic ability (Stone, 2002; Stone, Lynch, Sjomeling, & Darley, 1999).[93]

Research has found that stereotype threat is caused by both cognitive and emotional factors (Schmader, Johns, & Forbes, 2008).[94] On the cognitive side, individuals who are experiencing stereotype threat show an increased vigilance toward the environment as well as increased attempts to suppress stereotypic thoughts. Engaging in these behaviors takes cognitive capacity away from the task. On the affective side, stereotype threat occurs when there is a discrepancy between our positive concept of our own skills and abilities and the negative stereotypes that suggest poor performance. These discrepancies create stress and anxiety, and these emotions make it harder to perform well on the task.

Stereotype threat is not, however, absolute; we can get past it if we try. What is important is to reduce the self doubts that are activated when we consider the negative stereotypes. Manipulations that affirm positive characteristics about the self or one's social group are successful at reducing stereotype threat (Marx & Roman, 2002; McIntyre, Paulson, & Lord, 2003).[95] In fact, just knowing that stereotype threat exists and may influence our performance can help alleviate its negative impact (Johns, Schmader, & Martens, 2005).[96]

In summary, although there is no definitive answer to why IQ bell curves differ across racial and ethnic groups, and most experts believe that environment is important in pushing the bell curves apart, genetics can also be involved. It is important to realize that, although IQ is heritable, this does not mean that group differences are caused by genetics. Although some people are naturally taller than others (height is heritable), people who get plenty of nutritious food are taller than people who do not, and this difference is clearly due to environment. This is a reminder that group differences may be created by environmental variables but also able to be reduced through appropriate environmental actions such as educational and training programs.

KEY TAKEAWAYS

- IQ is distributed in the population in the form of a normal distribution (frequently known as a bell curve).
- Mental retardation is a generalized disorder ascribed to people who have an IQ below 70, who have experienced deficits since childhood, and who have trouble with basic life skills, such as dressing and feeding oneself and communicating with others. One cause of mental retardation is Down syndrome.
- Extremely intelligent individuals are not unhealthy or poorly adjusted, but rather are above average in physical health and taller and heavier than individuals in the general population.
- Men and women have almost identical intelligence, but men have more variability in their IQ scores than do women.
- On average, men do better than women on tasks requiring spatial ability, whereas women do better on verbal tasks and score higher on emotional intelligence.
- Although their bell curves overlap considerably, there are also average group differences for members of different racial and ethnic groups.
- The observed average differences in intelligence between racial and ethnic groups has at times led to malicious attempts to correct for them, such as the eugenics movement in the early part of the 20th century.
- The situation in which one takes a test may create stereotype threat—performance decrements that are caused by the knowledge of cultural stereotypes.

EXERCISES AND CRITICAL THINKING

1. Were Lawrence Summers's ideas about the potential causes of differences between men and women math and hard sciences careers offensive to you? Why or why not?

2. Do you think that we should give intelligence tests? Why or why not? Does it matter to you whether or not the tests have been standardized and shown to be reliable and valid?

3. Give your ideas about the practice of providing accelerated classes to children listed as "gifted" in high school. What are the potential positive and negative outcomes of doing so? What research evidence has helped you form your opinion?

4. Consider the observed sex and racial differences in intelligence. What implications do you think the differences have for education and career choices?

3. COMMUNICATING WITH OTHERS: THE DEVELOPMENT AND USE OF LANGUAGE

LEARNING OBJECTIVES

1. **Review the components and structure of language.**
2. **Explain the biological underpinnings of language.**
3. **Outline the theories of language development.**

Human language is the most complex behavior on the planet and, at least as far as we know, in the universe. Language involves both the ability to comprehend spoken and written words and to create communication in real time when we speak or write. Most languages are oral, generated through speaking. Speaking involves a variety of complex cognitive, social, and biological processes including operation of the vocal cords, and the coordination of breath with movements of the throat and mouth, and tongue. Other languages are sign languages, in which the communication is expressed by movements of the hands. The most common sign language is American Sign Language (ASL), currently spoken by more than 500,000 people in the United States alone.

Although language is often used for the transmission of information ("turn right at the next light and then go straight," "Place tab A into slot B"), this is only its most mundane function. Language also allows us to access existing knowledge, to draw conclusions, to set and accomplish goals, and to understand and communicate complex social relationships. Language is fundamental to our ability to think, and without it we would be nowhere near as intelligent as we are.

Language can be conceptualized in terms of sounds, meaning, and the environmental factors that help us understand it. *Phonemes* are the elementary sounds of our language, *morphemes* are the smallest units of meaning in a language, *syntax* is the set of grammatical rules that control how words are put together, and *contextual information* is the elements of communication that are not part of the content of language but that help us understand its meaning.

3.1 The Components of Language

phoneme

The smallest unit of sound that makes a meaningful difference in a language.

A **phoneme** is *the smallest unit of sound that makes a meaningful difference in a language*. The word "bit" has three phonemes, /b/, /i/, and /t/ (in transcription, phonemes are placed between slashes), and the word "pit" also has three: /p/, /i/, and /t/. In spoken languages, phonemes are produced by the positions and movements of the vocal tract, including our lips, teeth, tongue, vocal cords, and throat, whereas in sign languages phonemes are defined by the shapes and movement of the hands.

There are hundreds of unique phonemes that can be made by human speakers, but most languages only use a small subset of the possibilities. English contains about 45 phonemes, whereas other languages have as few as 15 and others more than 60. The Hawaiian language contains only about a dozen phonemes, including 5 vowels (a, e, i, o, and u) and 7 consonants (h, k, l, m, n, p, and w).

In addition to using a different set of phonemes, because the phoneme is actually a category of sounds that are treated alike within the language, speakers of different languages are able to hear the difference only between some phonemes but not others. This is known as the *categorical perception of speech sounds*. English speakers can differentiate the /r/ phoneme from the /l/ phoneme, and thus "rake" and "lake" are heard as different words. In Japanese, however, /r/ and /l/ are the same phoneme, and thus speakers of that language cannot tell the difference between the word "rake" and the word "lake." Try saying the words "cool" and "keep" out loud. Can you hear the difference between the two /k/ sounds? To English speakers they both sound the same, but to speakers of Arabic these represent two different phonemes.

Infants are born able to understand all phonemes, but they lose their ability to do so as they get older; by 10 months of age a child's ability to recognize phonemes becomes very similar to that of the adult speakers of the native language. Phonemes that were initially differentiated come to be treated as equivalent (Werker & Tees, 2002).[97]

FIGURE 9.11

When adults hear speech sounds that gradually change from one phoneme to another, they do not hear the continuous change; rather, they hear one sound until they suddenly begin hearing the other. In this case, the change is from /ba/ to /pa/.

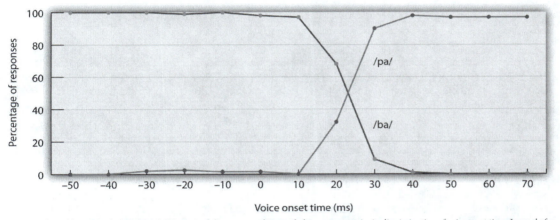

Source: Adapted from Wood, C. C. (1976). Discriminability, response bias, and phoneme categories in discrimination of voice onset time. Journal of the Acoustical Society of America, 60(6), 1381–1389.

Whereas phonemes are the smallest units of sound in language, a **morpheme** is *a string of one or more phonemes that makes up the smallest units of meaning in a language.* Some morphemes, such as one-letter words like "I" and "a," are also phonemes, but most morphemes are made up of combinations of phonemes. Some morphemes are prefixes and suffixes used to modify other words. For example, the syllable "re-" as in "rewrite" or "repay" means "to do again," and the suffix "-est" as in "happiest" or "coolest" means "to the maximum."

Syntax is *the set of rules of a language by which we construct sentences.* Each language has a different syntax. The syntax of the English language requires that each sentence have a noun and a verb, each of which may be modified by adjectives and adverbs. Some syntaxes make use of the order in which words appear, while others do not. In English, "The man bites the dog" is different from "The dog bites the man." In German, however, only the article endings before the noun matter. "Der Hund beisst den Mann" means "The dog bites the man" but so does "Den Mann beisst der Hund."

Words do not possess fixed meanings but change their interpretation as a function of the context in which they are spoken. We use **contextual information**—*the information surrounding language*—to help us interpret it. Examples of contextual information include the knowledge that we have and that we know that other people have, and nonverbal expressions such as facial expressions, postures, gestures, and tone of voice. Misunderstandings can easily arise if people aren't attentive to contextual information or if some of it is missing, such as it may be in newspaper headlines or in text messages.

morpheme

A string of one or more phonemes that makes up the smallest units of meaning in a language.

syntax

The set of rules of a language that is used to construct sentences.

contextual information

Information surrounding language that is used to help interpret it.

Examples in Which Syntax Is Correct but the Interpretation Can Be Ambiguous

- Grandmother of Eight Makes Hole in One
- Milk Drinkers Turn to Powder
- Farmer Bill Dies in House
- Old School Pillars Are Replaced by Alumni
- Two Convicts Evade Noose, Jury Hung
- Include Your Children When Baking Cookies

3.2 The Biology and Development of Language

Anyone who has tried to master a second language as an adult knows the difficulty of language learning. And yet children learn languages easily and naturally. Children who are not exposed to language early in their lives will likely never learn one. Case studies, including Victor the "Wild Child," who was abandoned as a baby in France and not discovered until he was 12, and Genie, a child whose parents kept her locked in a closet from 18 months until 13 years of age, are (fortunately) two of the only known examples of these deprived children. Both of these children made some progress in socialization after they were rescued, but neither of them ever developed language (Rymer, 1993).[98] This is also why it is important to determine quickly if a child is deaf and to begin immediately to communicate in sign language. Deaf children who are not exposed to sign language during their early years will likely never learn it (Mayberry, Lock, & Kazmi, 2002).[99]

critical period

A time in which learning can easily occur.

plasticity

The brain's ability to develop new neural connections.

Research Focus: When Can We Best Learn Language? Testing the Critical Period Hypothesis

For many years psychologists assumed that there was a **critical period** (*a time in which learning can easily occur*) for language learning, lasting between infancy and puberty, and after which language learning was more difficult or impossible (Lenneberg, 1967; Penfield & Roberts, 1959).[100] But more recent research has provided a different interpretation.

An important study by Jacqueline Johnson and Elissa Newport (1989)[101] using Chinese and Korean speakers who had learned English as a second language provided the first insight. The participants were all adults who had immigrated to the United States between 3 and 39 years of age and who were tested on their English skills by being asked to detect grammatical errors in sentences. Johnson and Newport found that the participants who had begun learning English before they were 7 years old learned it as well as native English speakers but that the ability to learn English dropped off gradually for the participants who had started later. Newport and Johnson also found a correlation between the age of acquisition and the variance in the ultimate learning of the language. While early learners were almost all successful in acquiring their language to a high degree of proficiency, later learners showed much greater individual variation.

Johnson and Newport's finding that children who immigrated before they were 7 years old learned English fluently seemed consistent with the idea of a "critical period" in language learning. But their finding of a gradual decrease in proficiency for those who immigrated between 8 and 39 years of age was not—rather, it suggested that there might not be a single critical period of language learning that ended at puberty, as early theorists had expected, but that language learning at later ages is simply better when it occurs earlier. This idea was reinforced in research by Hakuta, Bialystok, and Wiley (2003),[102] who examined U.S. census records of language learning in millions of Chinese and Spanish speakers living in the United States. The census form asks respondents to describe their own English ability using one of five categories: "not at all," "not well," "well," "very well," and "speak only English." The results of this research dealt another blow to the idea of the critical period, because it showed that regardless of what year was used as a cutoff point for the end of the critical period, there was no evidence for any discontinuity in language-learning potential. Rather, the results (Figure 9.12) showed that the degree of success in second-language acquisition declined steadily throughout the respondent's life span. The difficulty of learning language as one gets older is probably due to the fact that, with age, the brain loses its **plasticity**—that is, *its ability to develop new neural connections*.

English Proficiency in Native Chinese Speakers

Hakuta, Bialystok, and Wiley (2003) found no evidence for critical periods in language learning. Regardless of level of education, self-reported second-language skills decreased consistently across age of immigration.

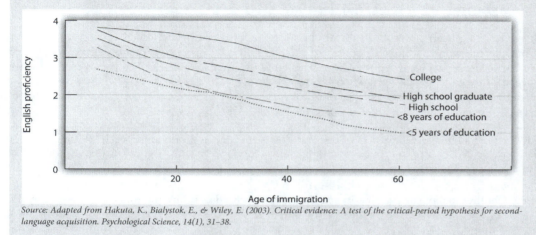

Source: Adapted from Hakuta, K., Bialystok, E., & Wiley, E. (2003). Critical evidence: A test of the critical-period hypothesis for second-language acquisition. Psychological Science, 14(1), 31–38.

For the 90% of people who are right-handed, language is stored and controlled by the left cerebral cortex, although for some left-handers this pattern is reversed. These differences can easily be seen in the results of neuroimaging studies that show that listening to and producing language creates greater activity in the left hemisphere than in the right. **Broca's area**, *an area in front of the left hemisphere near the motor cortex*, is responsible for language production (Figure 9.13). This area was first localized in the 1860s by the French physician Paul Broca, who studied patients with lesions to various parts of the brain. **Wernicke's area**, *an area of the brain next to the auditory cortex*, is responsible for language comprehension.

Broca's area

An area of the brain in front of the left hemisphere near the motor cortex that is responsible for language production.

Wernicke's area

An area of the brain next to the auditory cortex that is responsible for language comprehension.

FIGURE 9.13 Drawing of Brain Showing Broca's and Wernicke's Areas

For most people the left hemisphere is specialized for language. *Broca's area*, near the motor cortex, is involved in language production, whereas *Wernicke's area*, near the auditory cortex, is specialized for language comprehension.

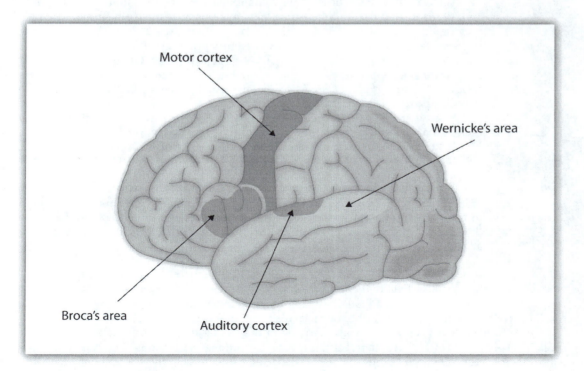

aphasia

A condition in which
language functions are
severely impaired.

Evidence for the importance of Broca's and Wernicke's areas in language is seen in patients who experience **aphasia**, *a condition in which language functions are severely impaired*. People with Broca's aphasia have difficulty producing speech, whereas people with damage to Wernicke's area can produce speech, but what they say makes no sense and they have trouble understanding language.

3.3 Learning Language

Language learning begins even before birth, because the fetus can hear muffled versions of speaking from outside the womb. Moon, Cooper, and Fifer (1993)[103] found that infants only two days old sucked harder on a pacifier when they heard their mothers' native language being spoken than when they heard a foreign language, even when strangers were speaking the languages. Babies are also aware of the patterns of their native language, showing surprise when they hear speech that has a different patterns of phonemes than those they are used to (Saffran, Aslin, & Newport, 2004).[104]

During the first year or so after birth, and long before they speak their first words, infants are already learning language. One aspect of this learning is practice in producing speech. By the time they are 6 to 8 weeks old, babies start making vowel sounds ("ooohh," "aaahh," "goo") as well as a variety of cries and squeals to help them practice.

At about 7 months, infants begin **babbling**, engaging in *intentional vocalizations that lack specific meaning*. Children babble as practice in creating specific sounds, and by the time they are 1 year old, the babbling uses primarily the sounds of the language that they are learning (de Boysson-Bardies, Sagart, & Durand, 1984).[105] These vocalizations have a conversational tone that sounds meaningful even though it isn't. Babbling also helps children understand the social, communicative function of language. Children who are exposed to sign language babble in sign by making hand movements that represent real language (Petitto & Marentette, 1991).[106]

babbling

Engaging in intentional
vocalizations that lack specific
meaning.

FIGURE 9.14

Babies often engage in vocal exchanges to help them practice language.

© *Thinkstock*

At the same time that infants are practicing their speaking skills by babbling, they are also learning to better understand sounds and eventually the words of language. One of the first words that children understand is their own name, usually by about 6 months, followed by commonly used words like "bottle," "mama," and "doggie" by 10 to 12 months (Mandel, Jusczyk, & Pisoni, 1995).[107]

The infant usually produces his or her first words at about 1 year of age. It is at this point that the child first understands that words are more than sounds—they refer to particular objects and ideas. By the time children are 2 years old, they have a vocabulary of several hundred words, and by kindergarten their vocabularies have increased to several thousand words. By fifth grade most children know about 50,000 words and by the time they are in college, about 200,000.

The early utterances of children contain many errors, for instance, confusing /b/ and /d/, or /c/ and /z/. And the words that children create are often simplified, in part because they are not yet able to make the more complex sounds of the real language (Dobrich & Scarborough, 1992).[108] Children may say "keekee" for kitty, "nana" for banana, and "vesketti" for spaghetti in part because it is easier. Often these early words are accompanied by gestures that may also be easier to produce than the words themselves. Children's pronunciations become increasingly accurate between 1 and 3 years, but some problems may persist until school age.

Most of a child's first words are nouns, and early sentences may include only the noun. "Ma" may mean "more milk please" and "da" may mean "look, there's Fido." Eventually the length of the utterances increases to two words ("mo ma" or "da bark"), and these primitive sentences begin to follow the appropriate syntax of the native language.

Because language involves the active categorization of sounds and words into higher level units, children make some mistakes in interpreting what words mean and how to use them. In particular, they often make *overextensions* of concepts, which means they use a given word in a broader context than appropriate. A child might at first call all adult men "daddy" or all animals "doggie."

Children also use contextual information, particularly the cues that parents provide, to help them learn language. Infants are frequently more attuned to the tone of voice of the person speaking than to the content of the words themselves, and are aware of the target of speech. Werker, Pegg, and McLeod (1994)[109] found that infants listened longer to a woman who was speaking to a baby than to a woman who was speaking to another adult.

Children learn that people are usually referring to things that they are looking at when they are speaking (Baldwin, 1993),[110] and that that the speaker's emotional expressions are related to the content of their speech. Children also use their knowledge of syntax to help them figure out what words mean. If a child hears an adult point to a strange object and say, "this is a dirb," they will infer that a "dirb" is a thing, but if they hear them say, "this is a one of those dirb things" they will infer that it refers to the color or other characteristic of the object. And if they hear the word "dirbing," they will infer that "dirbing" is something that we do (Waxman, 1990).[111]

3.4 How Children Learn Language: Theories of Language Acquisition

Psychological theories of language learning differ in terms of the importance they place on nature versus nurture. Yet it is clear that both matter. Children are not born knowing language; they learn to speak by hearing what happens around them. On the other hand, human brains, unlike those of any other animal, are prewired in a way that leads them, almost effortlessly, to learn language.

Perhaps the most straightforward explanation of language development is that it occurs through principles of learning, including association, reinforcement, and the observation of others (Skinner, 1965).[112] There must be at least some truth to the idea that language is learned, because children learn the language that they hear spoken around them rather than some other language. Also supporting this idea is the gradual improvement of language skills with time. It seems that children modify their language through imitation, reinforcement, and shaping, as would be predicted by learning theories.

But language cannot be entirely learned. For one, children learn words too fast for them to be learned through reinforcement. Between the ages of 18 months and 5 years, children learn up to 10 new words every day (Anglin, 1993).[113] More importantly, language is more *generative* than it is imitative. **Generativity** refers to *the fact that speakers of a language can compose sentences to represent new ideas that they have never before been exposed to*. Language is not a predefined set of ideas and sentences that we choose when we need them, but rather a system of rules and procedures that allows us to create an infinite number of statements, thoughts, and ideas, including those that have never previously occurred. When a child says that she "swimmed" in the pool, for instance, she is showing generativity. No adult speaker of English would ever say "swimmed," yet it is easily generated from the normal system of producing language.

Other evidence that refutes the idea that all language is learned through experience comes from the observation that children may learn languages better than they ever hear them. Deaf children whose parents do not speak ASL very well nevertheless are able to learn it perfectly on their own, and may even make up their own language if they need to (Goldin-Meadow & Mylander, 1998).[114] A group of deaf children in a school in Nicaragua, whose teachers could not sign, invented a way to communicate through made-up signs (Senghas, Senghas, & Pyers, 2005).[115] The development of this new Nicaraguan Sign Language has continued and changed as new generations of students have come to the school and started using the language. Although the original system was not a real language, it is becoming closer and closer every year, showing the development of a new language in modern times.

The linguist Noam Chomsky is a believer in the nature approach to language, arguing that human brains contain a *language acquisition device* that includes a *universal grammar* that underlies all human language (Chomsky, 1965, 1972).[116] According to this approach, each of the many languages spoken around the world (there are between 6,000 and 8,000) is an individual example of the same underlying set of procedures that are hardwired into human brains. Chomsky's account proposes that children are born with a knowledge of general rules of syntax that determine how sentences are constructed.

Chomsky differentiates between the **deep structure** of an idea—*how the idea is represented in the fundamental universal grammar that is common to all languages*, and the **surface structure** of the idea—*how it is expressed in any one language*. Once we hear or express a thought in surface structure, we generally forget exactly how it happened. At the end of a lecture, you will remember a lot of the deep structure (i.e., the ideas expressed by the instructor), but you cannot reproduce the surface structure (the exact words that the instructor used to communicate the ideas).

Although there is general agreement among psychologists that babies are genetically programmed to learn language, there is still debate about Chomsky's idea that there is a universal grammar that can account for all language learning. Evans and Levinson (2009)[117] surveyed the world's languages and found that none of the presumed underlying features of the language acquisition device were entirely universal. In their search they found languages that did not have noun or verb phrases, that did not have tenses (e.g., past, present, future), and even some that did not have nouns or verbs at all, even though a basic assumption of a universal grammar is that all languages should share these features.

3.5 Bilingualism and Cognitive Development

Although it is less common in the United States than in other countries, **bilingualism** (*the ability to speak two languages*) is becoming more and more frequent in the modern world. Nearly one-half of the world's population, including 18% of U.S. citizens, grows up bilingual.

generativity

The fact that speakers of a language can compose sentences to represent new ideas that they have never before been exposed to.

deep structure

How an idea is represented in the fundamental universal grammar that is common to all languages.

surface structure

How an idea is expressed in any one language.

bilingualism

The ability to speak two languages.

In recent years many U.S. states have passed laws outlawing bilingual education in schools. These laws are in part based on the idea that students will have a stronger identity with the school, the culture, and the government if they speak only English, and in part based on the idea that speaking two languages may interfere with cognitive development.

Some early psychological research showed that, when compared with monolingual children, bilingual children performed more slowly when processing language, and their verbal scores were lower. But these tests were frequently given in English, even when this was not the child's first language, and the children tested were often of lower socioeconomic status than the monolingual children (Andrews, 1982).[118]

More current research that has controlled for these factors has found that, although bilingual children may in some cases learn language somewhat slower than do monolingual children (Oller & Pearson, 2002),[119] bilingual and monolingual children do not significantly differ in the final depth of language learning, nor do they generally confuse the two languages (Nicoladis & Genesee, 1997).[120] In fact, participants who speak two languages have been found to have better cognitive functioning, cognitive flexibility, and analytic skills in comparison to monolinguals (Bialystok, 2009).[121] Research (Figure 9.15) has also found that learning a second language produces changes in the area of the brain in the left hemisphere that is involved in language, such that this area is denser and contains more neurons (Mechelli et al., 2004).[122] Furthermore, the increased density is stronger in those individuals who are most proficient in their second language and who learned the second language earlier. Thus, rather than slowing language development, learning a second language seems to increase cognitive abilities.

FIGURE 9.15 Gray Matter in Bilinguals

Andrea Mechelli and her colleagues (2004) found that children who were bilingual had increased gray matter density (i.e., more neurons) in cortical areas related to language in comparison to monolinguals (panel a), that gray matter density correlated positively with second language proficiency (panel b) and that gray matter density correlated negatively with the age at which the second language was learned (panel c).

(a)

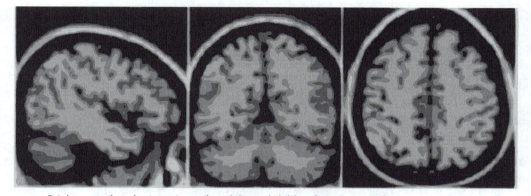

Bright areas show brain regions where bilingual children have increased gray matter density in comparison to monolinguals

(b)

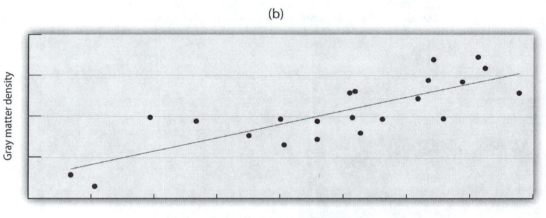

(c)

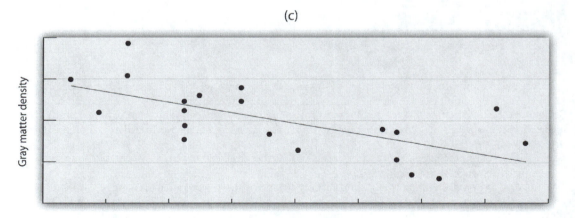

Source: Adapted from Mechelli, A., Crinion, J. T., Noppeney, U., O'Doherty, J., Ashburner, J., Frackowiak, R. S., & Price C. J. (2004). Structural plasticity in the bilingual brain: Proficiency in a second language and age at acquisition affect grey-matter density. Nature, 431, 757.

3.6 Can Animals Learn Language?

Nonhuman animals have a wide variety of systems of communication. Some species communicate using scents; others use visual displays, such as baring the teeth, puffing up the fur, or flapping the wings; and still others use vocal sounds. Male songbirds, such as canaries and finches, sing songs to attract mates and to protect territory, and chimpanzees use a combination of facial expressions, sounds, and actions, such as slapping the ground, to convey aggression (de Waal, 1989).[123] Honeybees use a "waggle dance" to direct other bees to the location of food sources (von Frisch, 1956).[124] The language of vervet monkeys is relatively advanced in the sense that they use specific sounds to communicate specific meanings. Vervets make different calls to signify that they have seen either a leopard, a snake, or a hawk (Seyfarth & Cheney, 1997).[125]

Despite their wide abilities to communicate, efforts to teach animals to use language have had only limited success. One of the early efforts was made by Catherine and Keith Hayes, who raised a chimpanzee named Viki in their home along with their own children. But Viki learned little and could never speak (Hayes & Hayes, 1952).[126] Researchers speculated that Viki's difficulties might have been in part because the she could not create the words in her vocal cords, and so subsequent attempts were made to teach primates to speak using sign language or by using boards on which they can point to symbols.

Allen and Beatrix Gardner worked for many years to teach a chimpanzee named Washoe to sign using ASL. Washoe, who lived to be 42 years old, could label up to 250 different objects and make simple requests and comments, such as "please tickle" and "me sorry" (Fouts, 1997).[127] Washoe's adopted daughter Loulis, who was never exposed to human signers, learned more than 70 signs simply by watching her mother sign.

The most proficient nonhuman language speaker is Kanzi, a bonobo who lives at the Language Learning Center at Georgia State University (Savage-Rumbaugh, & Lewin, 1994).[128] As you can see in "Video Clip: Language Recognition in Bonobos", Kanzi has a propensity for language that is in many ways similar to humans'. He learned faster when he was younger than when he got older, he learns by observation, and he can use symbols to comment on social interactions, rather than simply for food treats. Kanzi can also create elementary syntax and understand relatively complex commands. Kanzi can make tools and can even play Pac-Man.

 Video Clip: Language Recognition in Bonobos

The bonobo Kanzi is the most proficient known nonhuman language speaker.

View the video online at: http://www.youtube.com/embed/_opEeClIL1w

And yet even Kanzi does not have a true language in the same way that humans do. Human babies learn words faster and faster as they get older, but Kanzi does not. Each new word he learns is almost as difficult as the one before. Kanzi usually requires many trials to learn a new sign, whereas human babies can speak words after only one exposure. Kanzi's language is focused primarily on food and pleasure and only rarely on social relationships. Although he can combine words, he generates few new phrases and cannot master syntactic rules beyond the level of about a 2-year-old human child (Greenfield & Savage-Rumbaugh, 1991).[129]

In sum, although many animals communicate, none of them have a true language. With some exceptions, the information that can be communicated in nonhuman species is limited primarily to displays of liking or disliking, and related to basic motivations of aggression and mating. Humans also use this more primitive type of communication, in the form of *nonverbal behaviors* such as eye contact, touch, hand signs, and interpersonal distance, to communicate their like or dislike for others, but they (unlike animals) also supplant this more primitive communication with language. Although other animal brains share similarities to ours, only the human brain is complex enough to create language. What is perhaps most remarkable is that although language never appears in nonhumans, language is universal in humans. All humans, unless they have a profound brain abnormality or are completely isolated from other humans, learn language.

3.7 Language and Perception

To this point in the chapter we have considered intelligence and language as if they are separate concepts. But what if language influences our thinking? *The idea that language and its structures influence and limit human thought* is called **linguistic relativity**.

The most frequently cited example of this possibility was proposed by Benjamin Whorf (1897–1941), an American linguist who was particularly interested in Native American languages. Whorf argued that the Inuit people of Canada (sometimes known as Eskimos) had many words for snow, whereas English speakers have only one, and that this difference influenced how the different cultures perceived snow. Whorf argued that the Inuit perceived and categorized snow in finer details than English speakers possibly could, because the English language constrained perception.

Although the idea of linguistic relativism seemed reasonable, research has suggested that language has less influence on thinking than might be expected. For one, in terms of perceptions of snow, although it is true that the Inuit do make more distinctions among types of snow than do English speakers, the latter also make some distinctions (think "powder," "slush," "whiteout," and so forth). And it is also possible that thinking about snow may influence language, rather than the other way around.

In a more direct test of the possibility that language influences thinking, Eleanor Rosch (1973)[130] compared people from the Dani culture of New Guinea, who have only two terms for color ("dark" and "bright"), with English speakers who use many more terms. Rosch hypothesized that if language constrains perception and categorization, then the Dani should have a harder time distinguishing colors than would English speakers. But her research found that when the Dani were asked to categorize colors using new categories, they did so in almost the same way that English speakers did. Similar results were found by Frank, Everett, Fedorenko, and Gibson (2008),[131] who showed that the Amazonian tribe known as the Pirahã, who have no linguistic method for expressing exact quantities (not even the number "one"), were nevertheless able to perform matches with large numbers without problem.

Although these data led researchers to conclude that the language we use to describe color and number does not influence our underlying understanding of the underlying sensation, another more recent study has questioned this assumption. Roberson, Davies, and Davidoff (2000)[132] conducted another study with Dani participants and found that, at least for some colors, the names that they used to describe colors did influence their perceptions of the colors. Other researchers continue to test the possibility that our language influences our perceptions, and perhaps even our thoughts (Levinson, 1998),[133] and yet the evidence for this possibility is, as of now, mixed.

> **linguistic relativity**
>
> The idea that language and its structures influence and limit human thought.

KEY TAKEAWAYS

- Language involves both the ability to comprehend spoken and written words and to speak and write. Some languages are sign languages, in which the communication is expressed by movements of the hands.
- Phonemes are the elementary sounds of our language, morphemes are the smallest units of meaningful language, syntax is the grammatical rules that control how words are put together, and contextual information is the elements of communication that help us understand its meaning.
- Recent research suggests that there is not a single critical period of language learning, but that language learning is simply better when it occurs earlier.
- Broca's area is responsible for language production. Wernicke's area is responsible for language comprehension.
- Language learning begins even before birth. An infant usually produces his or her first words at about 1 year of age.
- One explanation of language development is that it occurs through principles of learning, including association, reinforcement, and the observation of others.
- Noam Chomsky argues that human brains contain a language acquisition module that includes a universal grammar that underlies all human language. Chomsky differentiates between the deep structure and the surface structure of an idea.
- Although other animals communicate and may be able to express ideas, only the human brain is complex enough to create real language.
- Our language may have some influence on our thinking, but it does not affect our underlying understanding of concepts.

EXERCISES AND CRITICAL THINKING

1. What languages do you speak? Did you ever try to learn a new one? What problems did you have when you did this? Would you consider trying to learn a new language?

2. Some animals, such as Kanzi, display at least some language. Do you think that this means that they are intelligent?

4. CHAPTER SUMMARY

Intelligence—the ability to think, to learn from experience, to solve problems, and to adapt to new situations—is more strongly related than any other individual difference variable to successful educational, occupational, economic, and social outcomes.

The French psychologist Alfred Binet and his colleague Henri Simon developed the first intelligence test in the early 1900s. Charles Spearman called the construct that the different abilities and skills measured on intelligence tests have in common the general intelligence factor, or simply "g."

There is also evidence for specific intelligences (s), measures of specific skills in narrow domains. Robert Sternberg has proposed a triarchic (three-part) theory of intelligence, and Howard Gardner has proposed that there are eight different specific intelligences.

Good intelligence tests both are reliable and have construct validity. Intelligence tests are the most accurate of all psychological tests. IQ tests are standardized, which allows calculation of mental age and the intelligence quotient (IQ),

The Wechsler Adult Intelligence Scale (WAIS) is the most widely used intelligence test for adults. Other intelligence tests include aptitude tests such as the Scholastic Assessment Test (SAT), American College Test (ACT), and Graduate Record Examination (GRE), and structured tests used for personnel selection.

Smarter people have somewhat larger brains, which operate more efficiently and faster than the brains of the less intelligent. Although intelligence is not located in a specific part of the brain, it is more prevalent in some brain areas than others.

Intelligence has both genetic and environmental causes, and between 40% and 80% of the variability in IQ is heritable. Social and economic deprivation, including poverty, can adversely affect IQ, and intelligence is improved by education.

Emotional intelligence refers to the ability to identify, assess, manage, and control one's emotions. However, tests of emotional intelligence are often unreliable, and emotional intelligence may be a part of g, or a skill that can be applied in some specific work situations.

About 3% of Americans score above an IQ of 130 (the threshold for giftedness), and about the same percentage score below an IQ of 70 (the threshold for mental retardation). Males are about 20% more common in these extremes than are women.

Women and men show overall equal intelligence, but there are sex differences on some types of tasks. There are also differences in which members of different racial and ethnic groups cluster along the IQ line. The causes of these differences are not completely known. These differences have at times led to malicious, misguided, and discriminatory attempts to try to correct for them, such as eugenics.

Language involves both the ability to comprehend spoken and written words and to create communication in real time when we speak or write. Language can be conceptualized in terms of sounds (phonemes), meaning (morphemes and syntax), and the environmental factors that help us understand it (contextual information).

Language is best learned during the critical period between 3 and 7 years of age.

Broca's area, an area of the brain in front of the left hemisphere near the motor cortex, is responsible for language production, and Wernicke's area, an area of the brain next to the auditory cortex, is responsible for language comprehension.

Children learn language quickly and naturally, progressing through stages of babbling, first words, first sentences, and then a rapid increase in vocabulary. Children often make overextensions of concepts.

Some theories of language learning are based on principles of learning. Noam Chomsky argues that human brains contain a language acquisition device that includes a universal grammar that underlies all human language and that allows generativity. Chomsky differentiates between the deep structure and the surface structure of an idea.

Bilingualism is becoming more and more frequent in the modern world. Bilingual children may show more cognitive function and flexibility than do monolingual children.

Nonhuman animals have a wide variety of systems of communication. But efforts to teach animals to use human language have had only limited success. Although many animals communicate, none of them have a true language.

ENDNOTES

1. Goldin, G., Goldin, R., & Foulkes, A. (2005, February 21). How Summers offended: Harvard president's comments underscored the gender bias we've experienced. *The Washington Post*, p. A27. Retrieved from http://www.washingtonpost.com/wp-dyn/articles/A40693-2005Feb20.html

2. Ones, D. S., Viswesvaran, C., & Dilchert, S. (2005). Cognitive ability in selection decisions. In O. Wilhelm & R. W. Engle (Eds.), *Handbook of understanding and measuring intelligence* (pp. 431–468). Thousand Oaks, CA: Sage; Schmidt, F., & Hunter, J. (1998). The validity and utility of selection methods in personnel psychology: Practical and theoretical implications of 85 years of research findings. *Psychological Bulletin, 124*(2), 262–274.

3. Wilson, J. Q., & Herrnstein, R. J. (1985). *Crime and human nature*. New York, NY: Simon & Schuster.

4. Gottfredson, L. S. (2004). Life, death, and intelligence. *Journal of Cognitive Education and Psychology, 4*(1), 23–46; Gottfredson, L. S., & Deary, I. J. (2004). Intelligence predicts health and longevity, but why? *Current Directions in Psychological Science, 13*(1), 1–4.

5. Simonton, D. K. (2006). Presidential IQ, openness, intellectual brilliance, and leadership: Estimates and correlations for 42 U.S. chief executives. *Political Psychology, 27*(4), 511–526.

6. Salgado, J. F., Anderson, N., Moscoso, S., Bertua, C., de Fruyt, F., & Rolland, J. P. (2003). A meta-analytic study of general mental ability validity for different occupations in the European Community. *Journal of Applied Psychology, 88*(6), 1068–1081.

7. Pinker, S. (1994). *The language instinct* (1st ed.). New York, NY: William Morrow.

8. Sternberg, R. J. (2003). Contemporary theories of intelligence. In W. M. Reynolds & G. E. Miller (Eds.), *Handbook of psychology: Educational psychology* (Vol. 7, pp. 23–45). Hoboken, NJ: John Wiley & Sons.

9. Binet, A., Simon, T., & Town, C. H. (1915). *A method of measuring the development of the intelligence of young children* (3rd ed.) Chicago, IL: Chicago Medical Book; Siegler, R. S. (1992). The other Alfred Binet. *Developmental Psychology, 28*(2), 179–190.

10. Gottfredson, L. S. (1997). Mainstream science on intelligence: An editorial with 52 signatories, history and bibliography. *Intelligence, 24*(1), 13–23; Sternberg, R. J. (2003). Contemporary theories of intelligence. In W. M. Reynolds & G. E. Miller (Eds.), *Handbook of psychology: Educational psychology* (Vol. 7, pp. 23–45). Hoboken, NJ: John Wiley & Sons.

11. Salthouse, T. A. (2004). What and when of cognitive aging. *Current Directions in Psychological Science, 13*(4), 140–144.

12. Horn, J. L., Donaldson, G., & Engstrom, R. (1981). Apprehension, memory, and fluid intelligence decline in adulthood. *Research on Aging, 3*(1), 33–84; Salthouse, T. A. (2004). What and when of cognitive aging. *Current Directions in Psychological Science, 13*(4), 140–144.

13. Thurstone, L. L. (1938). Primary mental abilities. *Psychometric Monographs, No. 1*. Chicago, IL: University of Chicago Press.

14. Sternberg, R. J. (1985). *Beyond IQ: A triarchic theory of human intelligence*. New York, NY: Cambridge University Press; Sternberg, R. J. (2003). Our research program validating the triarchic theory of successful intelligence: Reply to Gottfredson. *Intelligence, 31*(4), 399–413.

15. Furnham, A., & Bachtiar, V. (2008). Personality and intelligence as predictors of creativity. *Personality and Individual Differences, 45*(7), 613–617.

16. Simonton, D. K. (2000). Creativity: Cognitive, personal, developmental, and social aspects. *American Psychologist, 55*(1), 151–158.

17. Tarasova, I. V., Volf, N. V., & Razoumnikova, O. M. (2010). Parameters of cortical interactions in subjects with high and low levels of verbal creativity. *Human Physiology, 36*(1), 80–85.

18. Bink, M. L., & Marsh, R. L. (2000). Cognitive regularities in creative activity. *Review of General Psychology, 4*(1), 59–78.

19. Ericsson, K. (1998). The scientific study of expert levels of performance: General implications for optimal learning and creativity. *High Ability Studies, 9*(1), 75–100; Weisberg, R. (2006). *Creativity: Understanding innovation in problem solving, science, invention, and the arts*. Hoboken, NJ: John Wiley & Sons.

20. Hennessey, B. A., & Amabile, T. M. (2010). Creativity. *Annual Review of Psychology, 61*, 569–598.

21. Simonton, D. K. (1992). The social context of career success and course for 2,026 scientists and inventors. *Personality and Social Psychology Bulletin, 18*(4), 452–463.

22. Sternberg, R. J., Wagner, R. K., & Okagaki, L. (1993). Practical intelligence: The nature and role of tacit knowledge in work and at school. In J. M. Puckett & H. W. Reese (Eds.), *Mechanisms of everyday cognition* (pp. 205–227). Hillsdale, NJ: Lawrence Erlbaum Associates; Wagner, R., & Sternberg, R. (1985). Practical intelligence in real-world pursuits: The role of tacit knowledge. *Journal of Personality and Social Psychology, 49*(2), 436–458.

23. Gottfredson, L. S. (2003). Dissecting practical intelligence theory: Its claims and evidence. *Intelligence, 31*(4), 343–397.

24. Sternberg, R. J., Wagner, R. K., & Okagaki, L. (1993). Practical intelligence: The nature and role of tacit knowledge in work and at school. In J. M. Puckett & H. W. Reese (Eds.), *Mechanisms of everyday cognition* (pp. 205–227). Hillsdale, NJ: Lawrence Erlbaum Associates.

25. Gardner, H. (1983). *Frames of mind: The theory of multiple intelligences*. New York, NY: Basic Books; Gardner, H. (1999). *Intelligence reframed: Multiple intelligences for the 21st century*. New York, NY: Basic Books.

26. Treffert, D. A., & Wallace, G. L. (2004, January 1). Islands of genius. *Scientific American*, 14–23. Retrieved from http://gordonresearch.com/articles_autism/SciAm-Islands_of_Genius.pdf

27. Brody, N. (2003). Construct validation of the Sternberg Triarchic abilities test: Comment and reanalysis. *Intelligence, 31*(4), 319–329.

28. Flynn, J. R. (1999). Searching for justice: The discovery of IQ gains over time. *American Psychologist, 54*(1), 5–20.

29. Neisser, U. (Ed.). (1998). *The rising curve*. Washington, DC: American Psychological Association.

30. Neisser, U. (1997). Rising scores on intelligence tests. *American Scientist, 85*, 440–447.

31. Watkins, C. E., Campbell, V. L., Nieberding, R., & Hallmark, R. (1995). Contemporary practice of psychological assessment by clinical psychologists. *Professional Psychology: Research and Practice, 26*(1), 54–60.

32. Kuncel, N. R., Hezlett, S. A., & Ones, D. S. (2010). A comprehensive meta-analysis of the predictive validity of the graduate record examinations: Implications for graduate student selection and performance. *Psychological Bulletin, 127*(1), 162–181.

33. Frey, M. C., & Detterman, D. K. (2004). Scholastic assessment or g? The relationship between the scholastic assessment test and general cognitive ability. *Psychological Science, 15*(6), 373–378.

34. Schmidt, F. L., & Hunter, J. E. (1998). The validity and utility of selection methods in personnel psychology: Practical and theoretical implications of 85 years of research findings. *Psychological Bulletin, 124*, 262–274.

35. McDaniel, M. A. (2005). Big-brained people are smarter: A meta-analysis of the relationship between in vivo brain volume and intelligence. *Intelligence, 33*(4), 337–346.

36. Haier, R. J. (2004). Brain imaging studies of personality: The slow revolution. In R. M. Stelmack (Ed.), *On the psychobiology of personality: Essays in honor of Marvin Zuckerman* (pp. 329–340). New York, NY: Elsevier Science; Shaw, P., Greenstein, D., Lerch, J., Clasen, L., Lenroot, R., Gogtay, N.,…Giedd, J. (2006). Intellectual ability and cortical development in children and adolescents. *Nature, 440*(7084), 676–679.

37. Garlick, D. (2003). Integrating brain science research with intelligence research. *Current Directions in Psychological Science, 12*(5), 185–189.

38. Haier, R. J., Siegel, B. V., Tang, C., & Abel, L. (1992). Intelligence and changes in regional cerebral glucose metabolic rate following learning. *Intelligence, 16*(3–4), 415–426.

39. Deary, I. J., Der, G., & Ford, G. (2001). Reaction times and intelligence differences: A population-based cohort study. *Intelligence, 29*(5), 389–399.

40. Ackerman, P. L., Beier, M. E., & Boyle, M. O. (2005). Working memory and intelligence: The same or different constructs? *Psychological Bulletin, 131*(1), 30–60.

41. Duncan, J., Seitz, R. J., Kolodny, J., Bor, D., Herzog, H., Ahmed, A.,…Emslie, H. (2000). A neural basis for general intelligence. *Science, 289*(5478), 457–460.

42. Neisser, U., Boodoo, G., Bouchard, T. J., Jr., Boykin, A. W., Brody, N., Ceci, S. J.,…Urbina, S. (1996). Intelligence: Knowns and unknowns. *American Psychologist, 51*(2), 77–101; Plomin, R. (2003). General cognitive ability. In R. Plomin, J. C. DeFries, I. W. Craig, & P. McGuffin (Eds.), *Behavioral genetics in the postgenomic era* (pp. 183–201). Washington, DC: American Psychological Association.

43. Plomin, R., & Spinath, F. M. (2004). Intelligence: Genetics, genes, and genomics. *Journal of Personality and Social Psychology, 86*(1), 112–129.

44. Deary, I. J., Whiteman, M. C., Starr, J. M., Whalley, L. J., & Fox, H. C. (2004). The impact of childhood intelligence on later life: Following up the Scottish mental surveys of 1932 and 1947. *Journal of Personality and Social Psychology, 86*(1), 130–147.

45. Turkheimer, E., Haley, A., Waldron, M., D'Onofrio, B., & Gottesman, I. I. (2003). Socioeconomic status modifies heritability of IQ in young children. *Psychological Science, 14*(6), 623–628.

46. Brooks-Gunn, J., & Duncan, G. J. (1997). The effects of poverty on children. *The Future of Children, 7*(2), 55–71.

47. Bellinger, D. C., & Needleman, H. L. (2003). Intellectual impairment and blood lead levels [Letter to the editor]. *The New England Journal of Medicine, 349*(5), 500.

48. McLoyd, V. C. (1998). Children in poverty: Development, public policy and practice. In W. Damon, I. E. Sigel, & K. A. Renninger (Eds.), *Handbook of child psychology: Child psychology in practice* (5th ed., Vol. 4, pp. 135–208). Hoboken, NJ: John Wiley & Sons; Perkins, D. N., & Grotzer, T. A. (1997). Teaching intelligence. *American Psychologist, 52*(10), 1125–1133.

49. Reynolds, A. J., Temple, J. A., Robertson, D. L., & Mann, E. A. (2001). Long-term effects of an early childhood intervention on educational achievement and juvenile arrest: A 15-year follow-up of low-income children in public schools. *Journal of the American Medical Association, 285*(18), 2339–2346.

50. Ceci, S. J. (1991). How much does schooling influence general intelligence and its cognitive components? A reassessment of the evidence. *Developmental Psychology, 27*(5), 703–722.

51. Baltes, P. B., & Reinert, G. (1969). Cohort effects in cognitive development of children as revealed by cross-sectional sequences. *Developmental Psychology, 1*(2), 169–177; Ceci, S. J., & Williams, W. M. (1997). Schooling, intelligence, and income. *American Psychologist, 52*(10), 1051–1058.

52. Huttenlocher, J., Levine, S., & Vevea, J. (1998). Environmental input and cognitive growth: A study using time-period comparisons. *Child Development, 69*(4), 1012–1029.

53. Feldman-Barrett, L., & Salovey, P. (Eds.). (2002). *The wisdom in feeling: Psychological processes in emotional intelligence*. New York, NY: Guilford Press; Mayer, J. D., Salovey, P., & Caruso, D. (2000). Models of emotional intelligence. In R. J. Sternberg (Ed.), *Handbook of intelligence* (pp. 396–420). New York, NY: Cambridge University Press.

54. Goleman, D. (1998). *Working with emotional intelligence*. New York, NY: Bantam Books.

55. Mayer, J. D., Salovey, P., & Caruso, D. R. (2008). Emotional intelligence: New ability or eclectic traits. *American Psychologist, 63*(6), 503–517; Petrides, K. V., & Furnham, A. (2000). On the dimensional structure of emotional intelligence. *Personality and Individual Differences, 29*, 313–320.

56. Føllesdal, H., & Hagtvet, K. A. (2009). Emotional intelligence: The MSCEIT from the perspective of generalizability theory. *Intelligence, 37*(1), 94–105.

57. Martins, A., Ramalho, N., & Morin, E. (2010). A comprehensive meta-analysis of the relationship between emotional intelligence and health. *Personality and Individual Differences, 49*(6), 554–564.

58. Harms, P. D., & Credé, M. (2010). Emotional intelligence and transformational and transactional leadership: A meta-analysis. *Journal of Leadership & Organizational Studies, 17*(1), 5–17.

59. Brody, N. (2004). What cognitive intelligence is and what emotional intelligence is not. *Psychological Inquiry, 15*, 234–238.

60. Landy, F. J. (2005). Some historical and scientific issues related to research on emotional intelligence. *Journal of Organizational Behavior, 26*, 411–424.

61. Ayduk, O., Mendoza-Denton, R., Mischel, W., Downey, G., Peake, P. K., & Rodriguez, M. (2000). Regulating the interpersonal self: Strategic self-regulation for coping with rejection sensitivity. *Journal of Personality and Social Psychology, 79*(5), 776–792; Eigsti, I.-M., Zayas, V., Mischel, W., Shoda, Y., Ayduk, O., Dadlani, M. B.,…Casey, B. J. (2006). Predicting cognitive control from preschool to late adolescence and young adulthood. *Psychological Science, 17*(6), 478–484; Mischel, W., & Ayduk, O. (Eds.). (2004). *Willpower in a cognitive-affective processing system: The dynamics of delay of gratification.* New York, NY: Guilford Press.

62. Mayer, J. D., & Cobb, C. D. (2000). Educational policy on emotional intelligence: Does it make sense? *Educational Psychology Review, 12*(2), 163–183.

63. Baral, B. D., & Das, J. P. (2004). Intelligence: What is indigenous to India and what is shared? In R. J. Sternberg (Ed.), *International handbook of intelligence* (pp. 270–301). New York, NY: Cambridge University Press; Sternberg, R. J. (2007). Intelligence and culture. In S. Kitayama & D. Cohen (Eds.), *Handbook of cultural psychology* (pp. 547–568). New York, NY: Guilford Press.

64. Johnson, W., Carothers, A., & Deary, I. J. (2009). A role for the X chromosome in sex differences in variability in general intelligence? *Perspectives on Psychological Science, 4*(6), 598–611.

65. Halpern, D. F. (1992). *Sex differences in cognitive abilities* (2nd ed.). Hillsdale, NJ: Lawrence Erlbaum Associates.

66. Switzky, H. N., & Greenspan, S. (2006). *What is mental retardation? Ideas for an evolving disability in the 21st century.* Washington, DC: American Association on Mental Retardation.

67. Greenspan, S., Loughlin, G., & Black, R. S. (2001). Credulity and gullibility in people with developmental disorders: A framework for future research. In L. M. Glidden (Ed.), *International review of research in mental retardation* (Vol. 24, pp. 101–135). San Diego, CA: Academic Press.

68. Atkins v. Virginia, 536 U.S. 304 (2002).

69. Terman, L. M., & Oden, M. H. (1959). *Genetic studies of genius: The gifted group at mid-life* (Vol. 5). Stanford, CA: Stanford University Press.

70. Seagoe, M. V. (1975). *Terman and the gifted.* Los Altos, CA: William Kaufmann.

71. Lubinski, D., & Benbow, C. P. (2006). Study of mathematically precocious youth after 35 years: Uncovering antecedents for the development of math-science expertise. *Perspectives on Psychological Science, 1*(4), 316–345.

72. Colangelo, N., & Assouline, S. (2009). Acceleration: Meeting the academic and social needs of students. In T. Balchin, B. Hymer, & D. J. Matthews (Eds.), *The Routledge international companion to gifted education* (pp. 194–202). New York, NY: Routledge.

73. Hyde, J. S. (2005). The gender similarities hypothesis. *American Psychologist, 60*(6), 581–592.

74. Halpern, D. F., Benbow, C. P., Geary, D. C., Gur, R. C., Hyde, J. S., & Gernsbache, M. A. (2007). The science of sex differences in science and mathematics. *Psychological Science in the Public Interest, 8*(1), 1–51.

75. McClure, E. B. (2000). A meta-analytic review of sex differences in facial expression processing and their development in infants, children, and adolescents. *Psychological Bulletin, 126*(3), 424–453.

76. Voyer, D., Voyer, S., & Bryden, M. P. (1995). Magnitude of sex differences in spatial abilities: A meta-analysis and consideration of critical variables. *Psychological Bulletin, 117*(2), 250–270.

77. Vogel, G. (1996). School achievement: Asia and Europe top in world, but reasons are hard to find. *Science, 274*(5291), 1296.

78. Benbow, C. P., & Stanley, J. C. (1983). Sex differences in mathematical reasoning ability: More facts. *Science, 222*(4627), 1029–1031.

79. Kimura, D., & Hampson, E. (1994). Cognitive pattern in men and women is influenced by fluctuations in sex hormones. *Current Directions in Psychological Science, 3*(2), 57–61; Voyer, D., Voyer, S., & Bryden, M. P. (1995). Magnitude of sex differences in spatial abilities: A meta-analysis and consideration of critical variables. *Psychological Bulletin, 117*(2), 250–270.

80. Newcombe, N. S., & Huttenlocher, J. (2006). Development of spatial cognition. In D. Kuhn, R. S. Siegler, W. Damon, & R. M. Lerner (Eds.), *Handbook of child psychology: Cognition, perception, and language* (6th ed., Vol. 2, pp. 734–776). Hoboken, NJ: John Wiley & Sons.

81. Spelke, E. S. (2005). Sex differences in intrinsic aptitude for mathematics and science? A critical review. *American Psychologist, 60*(9), 950–958.

82. Lynn, R. (1996). Racial and ethnic differences in intelligence in the United States on the differential ability scale. *Personality and Individual Differences, 20*(2), 271–273;

Neisser, U., Boodoo, G., Bouchard, T. J., Jr., Boykin, A. W., Brody, N., Ceci, S. J.,…Urbina, S. (1996). Intelligence: Knowns and unknowns. *American Psychologist, 51*(2), 77–101.

83. Hunt, E., & Carlson, J. (2007). Considerations relating to the study of group differences in intelligence. *Perspectives on Psychological Science, 2*(2), 194–213.

84. Lewontin, R. C., Rose, S. P. R., & Kamin, L. J. (1984). *Not in our genes: Biology, ideology, and human nature* (1st ed.). New York, NY: Pantheon Books.

85. Selden, S. (1999). *Inheriting shame: The story of eugenics and racism in America.* New York, NY: Teachers College Press.

86. Brody, N. (1992). *Intelligence* (2nd ed.). San Diego, CA: Academic Press.

87. Suzuki, L. A., & Valencia, R. R. (1997). Race-ethnicity and measured intelligence: Educational implications. *American Psychologist, 52*(10), 1103–1114.

88. Walton, G. M., & Cohen, G. L. (2003). Stereotype lift. *Journal of Experimental Social Psychology, 39*(5), 456–467.

89. Steele, C. M., & Aronson, J. (1995). Stereotype threat and the intellectual performance of African Americans. *Journal of Personality and Social Psychology, 69*, 797–811.

90. Gonzales, P. M., Blanton, H., & Williams, K. J. (2002). The effects of stereotype threat and double-minority status on the test performance of Latino women. *Personality and Social Psychology Bulletin, 28*(5), 659–670.

91. Brown, R., Croizet, J.-C., Bohner, G., Fournet, M., & Payne, A. (2003). Automatic category activation and social behaviour: The moderating role of prejudiced beliefs. *Social Cognition, 21*(3), 167–193; Croizet, J.-C., & Claire, T. (1998). Extending the concept of stereotype and threat to social class: The intellectual underperformance of students from low socioeconomic backgrounds. *Personality and Social Psychology Bulletin, 24*(6), 588–594.

92. Aronson, J., Lustina, M. J., Good, C., Keough, K., & Steele, C. M. (1999). When white men can't do math: Necessary and sufficient factors in stereotype threat. *Journal of Experimental Social Psychology, 35*, 29–46.

93. Stone, J. (2002). Battling doubt by avoiding practice: The effects of stereotype threat on self-handicapping in White athletes. *Personality and Social Psychology Bulletin, 28*(12), 1667–1678; Stone, J., Lynch, C. I., Sjomeling, M., & Darley, J. M. (1999). Stereotype threat effects on Black and White athletic performance. *Journal of Personality and Social Psychology, 77*(6), 1213–1227.

94. Schmader, T., Johns, M., & Forbes, C. (2008). An integrated process model of stereotype threat effects on performance. *Psychological Review, 115*(2), 336–356.

95. Marx, D. M., & Roman, J. S. (2002). Female role models: Protecting women's math test performance. *Personality and Social Psychology Bulletin, 28*(9), 1183–1193; McIntyre, R. B., Paulson, R. M., & Lord, C. G. (2003). Alleviating women's mathematics stereotype threat through salience of group achievements. *Journal of Experimental Social Psychology, 39*(1), 83–90.

96. Johns, M., Schmader, T., & Martens, A. (2005). Knowing is half the battle: Teaching stereotype threat as a means of improving women's math performance. *Psychological Science, 16*(3), 175–179.

97. Werker, J. F., & Tees, R. C. (2002). Cross-language speech perception: Evidence for perceptual reorganization during the first year of life. *Infant Behavior & Development, 25*(1), 121–133.

98. Rymer, R. (1993). *Genie: An abused child's flight from silence.* New York, NY: HarperCollins.

99. Mayberry, R. I., Lock, E., & Kazmi, H. (2002). Development: Linguistic ability and early language exposure. *Nature, 417*(6884), 38.

100. Lenneberg, E. (1967). *Biological foundations of language.* New York, NY: John Wiley & Sons; Penfield, W., & Roberts, L. (1959). *Speech and brain mechanisms.* Princeton, NJ: Princeton University Press.

101. Johnson, J. S., & Newport, E. L. (1989). Critical period effects in second language learning: The influence of maturational state on the acquisition of English as a second language. *Cognitive Psychology, 21*(1), 60–99.

102. Hakuta, K., Bialystok, E., & Wiley, E. (2003). Critical evidence: A test of the critical-period hypothesis for second-language acquisition. *Psychological Science, 14*(1), 31–38.

103. Moon, C., Cooper, R. P., & Fifer, W. P. (1993). Two-day-olds prefer their native language. *Infant Behavior & Development, 16*(4), 495–500.

104. Saffran, J. R., Aslin, R. N., & Newport, E. L. (2004). *Statistical learning by 8-month-old infants.* New York, NY: Psychology Press.

105. de Boysson-Bardies, B., Sagart, L., & Durand, C. (1984). Discernible differences in the babbling of infants according to target language. *Journal of Child Language, 11*(1), 1–15.

106. Petitto, L. A., & Marentette, P. F. (1991). Babbling in the manual mode: Evidence for the ontogeny of language. *Science, 251*(5000), 1493–1496.

107. Mandel, D. R., Jusczyk, P. W., & Pisoni, D. B. (1995). Infants' recognition of the sound patterns of their own names. *Psychological Science, 6*(5), 314–317.

108. Dobrich, W., & Scarborough, H. S. (1992). Phonological characteristics of words young children try to say. *Journal of Child Language, 19*(3), 597–616.

109. Werker, J. F., Pegg, J. E., & McLeod, P. J. (1994). A cross-language investigation of infant preference for infant-directed communication. *Infant Behavior & Development, 17*(3), 323–333.

110. Baldwin, D. A. (1993). Early referential understanding: Infants' ability to recognize referential acts for what they are. *Developmental Psychology, 29*(5), 832–843.

111. Waxman, S. R. (1990). Linguistic biases and the establishment of conceptual hierarchies: Evidence from preschool children. *Cognitive Development, 5*(2), 123–150.

112. Skinner, B. F. (1965). *Science and human behavior.* New York, NY: Free Press.

113. Anglin, J. M. (1993). Vocabulary development: A morphological analysis. *Monographs of the Society for Research in Child Development, 58*(10), v–165.

114. Goldin-Meadow, S., & Mylander, C. (1998). Spontaneous sign systems created by deaf children in two cultures. *Nature, 391*(6664), 279–281.

115. Senghas, R. J., Senghas, A., & Pyers, J. E. (2005). The emergence of Nicaraguan Sign Language: Questions of development, acquisition, and evolution. In S. T. Parker, J. Langer, & C. Milbrath (Eds.), *Biology and knowledge revisited: From neurogenesis to psychogenesis* (pp. 287–306). Mahwah, NJ: Lawrence Erlbaum Associates.

116. Chomsky, N. (1965). *Aspects of the theory of syntax.* Cambridge, MA: MIT Press; Chomsky, N. (1972). *Language and mind* (Extended ed.). New York, NY: Harcourt, Brace & Jovanovich.

117. Evans, N., & Levinson, S. C. (2009). The myth of language universals: Language diversity and its importance for cognitive science. *Behavioral and Brain Sciences, 32*(5), 429–448.

118. Andrews, I. (1982). Bilinguals out of focus: A critical discussion. *International Review of Applied Linguistics in Language Teaching, 20*(4), 297–305.

119. Oller, D. K., & Pearson, B. Z. (2002). Assessing the effects of bilingualism: A background. In D. K. Oller & R. E. Eilers (Eds.), *Language and literacy in bilingual children* (pp. 3–21). Tonawanda, NY: Multilingual Matters.

120. Nicoladis, E., & Genesee, F. (1997). Language development in preschool bilingual children. *Journal of Speech-Language Pathology and Audiology, 21*(4), 258–270.

121. Bialystok, E. (2009). Bilingualism: The good, the bad, and the indifferent. *Bilingualism: Language and Cognition, 12*(1), 3–11.

122. Mechelli, A., Crinion, J. T., Noppeney, U., O'Doherty, J., Ashburner, J., Frackowiak, R. S., & Price C. J. (2004). Structural plasticity in the bilingual brain: Proficiency in a second language and age at acquisition affect grey-matter density. *Nature, 431*, 757.

123. De Waal, F. (1989). *Peacemaking among primates.* Cambridge, MA: Harvard University Press.

124. Von Frisch, K. (1956). *Bees: Their vision, chemical senses, and language.* Ithaca, NY: Cornell University Press.

125. Seyfarth, R. M., & Cheney, D. L. (1997). Behavioral mechanisms underlying vocal communication in nonhuman primates. *Animal Learning & Behavior, 25*(3), 249–267.

126. Hayes, K. J., and Hayes, C. (1952). Imitation in a home-raised chimpanzee. *Journal of Comparative and Physiological Psychology, 45*, 450–459.

127. Fouts, R. (1997). *Next of kin: What chimpanzees have taught me about who we are.* New York, NY: William Morrow.

128. Savage-Rumbaugh, S., & Lewin, R. (1994). *Kanzi: The ape at the brink of the human mind.* Hoboken, NJ: John Wiley & Sons.

129. Greenfield, P. M., & Savage-Rumbaugh, E. S. (1991). Imitation, grammatical development, and the invention of protogrammar by an ape. In N. A. Krasnegor, D. M. Rumbaugh, R. L. Schiefelbusch, & M. Studdert-Kennedy (Eds.), *Biological and behavioral determinants of language development* (pp. 235–258). Hillsdale, NJ: Lawrence Erlbaum Associates.

130. Rosch, E. H. (1973). Natural categories. *Cognitive Psychology, 4*(3), 328–350.

131. Frank, M. C., Everett, D. L., Fedorenko, E., & Gibson, E. (2008). Number as a cognitive technology: Evidence from Pirahã language and cognition. *Cognition, 108*(3), 819–824.

132. Roberson, D., Davies, I., & Davidoff, J. (2000). Color categories are not universal: Replications and new evidence from a stone-age culture. *Journal of Experimental Psychology: General, 129*(3), 369–398.

133. Levinson, S. C. (1998). Studying spatial conceptualization across cultures: Anthropology and cognitive science. *Ethos, 26*(1), 7–24.

CHAPTER 10

Emotions and Motivations

Captain Sullenberger Conquers His Emotions

He was 3,000 feet up in the air when the sudden loss of power in his airplane put his life, as well as the lives of 150 other passengers and crew members, in his hands. Both of the engines on flight 1539 had shut down, and his options for a safe landing were limited.

Sully kept flying the plane and alerted the control tower to the situation:

> This is Cactus 1539…hit birds. We lost thrust in both engines. We're turning back towards La Guardia.

When the tower gave him the compass setting and runway for a possible landing, Sullenberger's extensive experience allowed him to give a calm response:

> I'm not sure if we can make any runway…Anything in New Jersey?

Captain Sullenberger was not just any pilot in a crisis, but a former U.S. Air Force fighter pilot with 40 years of flight experience. He had served as a flight instructor and the Airline Pilots Association safety chairman. Training had quickened his mental processes in assessing the threat, allowing him to maintain what tower operators later called an "eerie calm." He knew the capabilities of his plane.

When the tower suggested a runway in New Jersey, Sullenberger calmly replied:

> We're unable. We may end up in the Hudson.

Captain Sullenberger and His Plane on the Hudson

Imagine that you are on a plane that you know is going to crash. What emotions would you experience, and how would you respond to them? Would the rush of fear cause you to panic, or could you control your emotions like Captain Sullenberger did, as he calmly calculated the heading, position, thrust, and elevation of the plane, and then landed it on the Hudson River?

Sources: Sullenberger photo courtesy of Ingrid Taylar, http://www.flickr.com/photos/taylar/4350610886. Plane photo courtesy of Greg L., http://commons.wikimedia.org/wiki/File:Plane_crash_into_Hudson_Rivercroped.jpg.

The last communication from Captain Sullenberger to the tower advised of the eventual outcome:

We're going to be in the Hudson.

He calmly set the plane down on the water. Passengers reported that the landing was like landing on a rough runway. The crew kept the passengers calm as women, children, and then the rest of the passengers were evacuated onto the boats of the rescue personnel that had quickly arrived. Captain Sullenberger then calmly walked the aisle of the plane to be sure that everyone was out before joining the 150 other rescued survivors (Levin, 2009; National Transportation Safety Board, 2009).[1]

Some called it "grace under pressure," and others the "miracle on the Hudson." But psychologists see it as the ultimate in *emotion regulation*—the ability to control and productively use one's emotions.

affect

The experience of feeling or emotion.

The topic of this chapter is **affect**, defined as *the experience of feeling or emotion*. Affect is an essential part of the study of psychology because it plays such an important role in everyday life. As we will see, affect guides behavior, helps us make decisions, and has a major impact on our mental and physical health.

arousal

Our experiences of the bodily responses created by the sympathetic division of the autonomic nervous system.

The two fundamental components of affect are *emotions* and *motivation*. Both of these words have the same underlying Latin root, meaning "to move." In contrast to cognitive processes that are calm, collected, and frequently rational, emotions and motivations involve **arousal**, or *our experiences of the bodily responses created by the sympathetic division of the autonomic nervous system (ANS)*. Because they involve arousal, emotions and motivations are "hot"—they "charge," "drive," or "move" our behavior.

When we experience emotions or strong motivations, we *feel* the experiences. When we become aroused, the sympathetic nervous system provides us with energy to respond to our environment. The liver puts extra sugar into the bloodstream, the heart pumps more blood, our pupils dilate to help us see better, respiration increases, and we begin to perspire to cool the body. The stress hormones *epinephrine* and *norepinephrine* are released. We experience these responses as arousal.

emotion

A mental and physiological feeling state that directs our attention and guides our behavior.

An **emotion** is *a mental and physiological feeling state that directs our attention and guides our behavior*. Whether it is the thrill of a roller-coaster ride that elicits an unexpected scream, the flush of embarrassment that follows a public mistake, or the horror of a potential plane crash that creates an exceptionally brilliant response in a pilot, emotions move our actions. Emotions normally serve an adaptive role: We care for infants because of the love we feel for them, we avoid making a left turn onto a crowded highway because we fear that a speeding truck may hit us, and we are particularly nice to Mandy because we are feeling guilty that we didn't go to her party. But emotions may also be destructive, such as when a frustrating experience leads us to lash out at others who do not deserve it.

motivation

A driving force that initiates and directs behavior.

Motivations are closely related to emotions. A **motivation** is *a driving force that initiates and directs behavior*. Some motivations are biological, such as the motivation for food, water, and sex. But there are a variety of other personal and social motivations that can influence behavior, including the motivations for social approval and acceptance, the motivation to achieve, and the motivation to take, or to avoid taking, risks (Morsella, Bargh, & Gollwitzer, 2009).[2] In each case we follow our motivations because they are rewarding. As predicted by basic theories of operant learning, motivations lead us to engage in particular behaviors because doing so makes us feel good.

Motivations are often considered in psychology in terms of *drives*, which are internal states that are activated when the physiological characteristics of the body are out of balance, and *goals*, which are desired end states that we strive to attain. Motivation can thus be conceptualized as a series of behavioral responses that lead us to attempt to reduce drives and to attain goals by comparing our current state with a desired end state (Lawrence, Carver, & Scheier, 2002).[3] Like a thermostat on an air conditioner, the body tries to maintain *homeostasis*, the natural state of the body's systems, with goals, drives, and arousal in balance. When a drive or goal is aroused—for instance, when we are hungry—the thermostat turns on and we start to behave in a way that attempts to reduce the drive or meet the goal (in this case to seek food). As the body works toward the desired end state, the thermostat continues to check whether or not the end state has been reached. Eventually, the need or goal is satisfied (we eat), and the relevant behaviors are turned off. The body's thermostat continues to check for homeostasis and is always ready to react to future needs.

In addition to more basic motivations such as hunger, a variety of other personal and social motivations can also be conceptualized in terms of drives or goals. When the goal of studying for an exam is hindered because we take a day off from our schoolwork, we may work harder on our studying on the next day to move us toward our goal. When we are dieting, we may be more likely to have a big binge on a day when the scale says that we have met our prior day's goals. And when we are lonely, the motivation to be around other people is aroused and we try to socialize. In many, if not most cases, our emotions and motivations operate out of our conscious awareness to guide our behavior (Freud, 1922; Hassin, Bargh, & Zimerman, 2009; Williams, Bargh, Nocera, & Gray, 2009).[4]

We begin this chapter by considering the role of affect on behavior, discussing the most important psychological theories of emotions. Then we will consider how emotions influence our mental and physical health. We will discuss how the experience of long-term *stress* causes illness, and then turn to research on *positive thinking* and what has been learned about the beneficial health effects of more positive emotions. Finally, we will review some of the most important human motivations, including the behaviors of eating and sex. The importance of this chapter is not only in helping you gain an understanding the principles of affect but also in helping you discover the important roles that affect plays in our everyday lives, and particularly in our mental and physical health. The study of the interface between affect and physical health—that principle that "everything that is physiological is also psychological"—is a key focus of the branch of psychology known as *health psychology*. The importance of this topic has made health psychology one of the fastest growing fields in psychology.

1. THE EXPERIENCE OF EMOTION

LEARNING OBJECTIVES

1. Explain the biological experience of emotion.
2. Summarize the psychological theories of emotion.
3. Give examples of the ways that emotion is communicated.

The most fundamental emotions, known as the **basic emotions**, are those of *anger, disgust, fear, happiness, sadness, and surprise.* The basic emotions have a long history in human evolution, and they have developed in large part to help us make rapid judgments about stimuli and to quickly guide appropriate behavior (LeDoux, 2000).[5] The basic emotions are determined in large part by one of the oldest parts of our brain, the limbic system, including the amygdala, the hypothalamus, and the thalamus.

basic emotions

The emotions of anger, disgust, fear, happiness, sadness, and surprise.

Because they are primarily evolutionarily determined, the basic emotions are experienced and displayed in much the same way across cultures (Ekman, 1992; Elfenbein & Ambady, 2002, 2003; Fridland, Ekman, & Oster, 1987),[6] and people are quite accurate at judging the facial expressions of people from different cultures. View "Video Clip: The Basic Emotions" to see a demonstration of the basic emotions.

Video Clip: The Basic Emotions

View the video online at: http://www.youtube.com/embed/haW6E7qsW2c

cognitive appraisal

The cognitive interpretations that accompany emotions.

Not all of our emotions come from the old parts of our brain; we also interpret our experiences to create a more complex array of emotional experiences. For instance, the amygdala may sense fear when it senses that the body is falling, but that fear may be interpreted completely differently (perhaps even as "excitement") when we are falling on a roller-coaster ride than when we are falling from the sky in an airplane that has lost power. The *cognitive interpretations that accompany emotions*—known as **cognitive appraisal**—allow us to experience a much larger and more complex set of *secondary emotions*, as shown in Figure 10.2. Although they are in large part cognitive, our experiences of the secondary emotions are determined in part by arousal (on the vertical axis of Figure 10.2) and in part by their *valence*—that is, whether they are pleasant or unpleasant feelings (on the horizontal axis of Figure 10.2)

FIGURE 10.2 The Secondary Emotions

The secondary emotions are those that have a major cognitive component. They are determined by both their level of arousal (low to high) and their valence (pleasant to unpleasant).

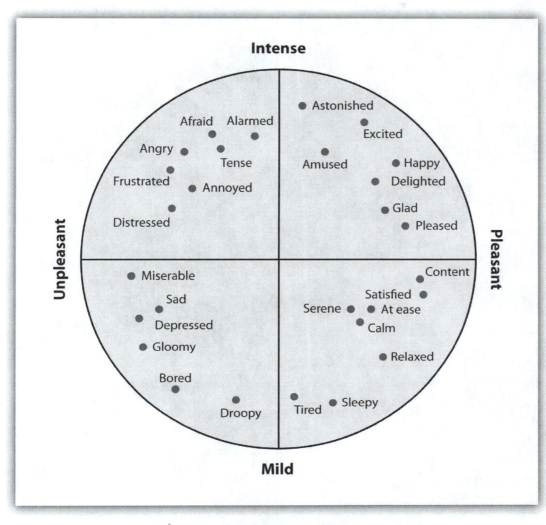

Source: Adapted from Russell, J. A. (1980). A circumplex model of affect. Journal of Personality and Social Psychology, 39, 1161–1178.

When you succeed in reaching an important goal, you might spend some time enjoying your secondary emotions, perhaps the experience of joy, satisfaction, and contentment. But when your close friend wins a prize that you thought you had deserved, you might also experience a variety of secondary emotions (in this case, the negative ones)—for instance, feeling angry, sad, resentful, and ashamed. You might mull over the event for weeks or even months, experiencing these negative emotions each time you think about it (Martin & Tesser, 2006).[7]

The distinction between the primary and the secondary emotions is paralleled by two brain pathways: a fast pathway and a slow pathway (Damasio, 2000; LeDoux, 2000; Ochsner, Bunge, Gross, & Gabrielli, 2002).[8] The thalamus acts as the major gatekeeper in this process (Figure 10.3). Our response to the basic emotion of fear, for instance, is primarily determined by the fast pathway through the limbic system. When a car pulls out in front of us on the highway, the thalamus activates and sends an immediate message to the amygdala. We quickly move our foot to the brake pedal. Secondary emotions are more determined by the slow pathway through the frontal lobes in the cortex. When we stew in jealousy over the loss of a partner to a rival or recollect on our win in the big tennis match, the process is more complex. Information moves from the thalamus to the frontal lobes for cognitive analysis and integration, and then from there to the amygdala. We experience the arousal of emotion, but it is accompanied by a more complex cognitive appraisal, producing more refined emotions and behavioral responses.

FIGURE 10.3 Slow and Fast Emotional Pathways

There are two emotional pathways in the brain (one slow and one fast), both of which are controlled by the thalamus.

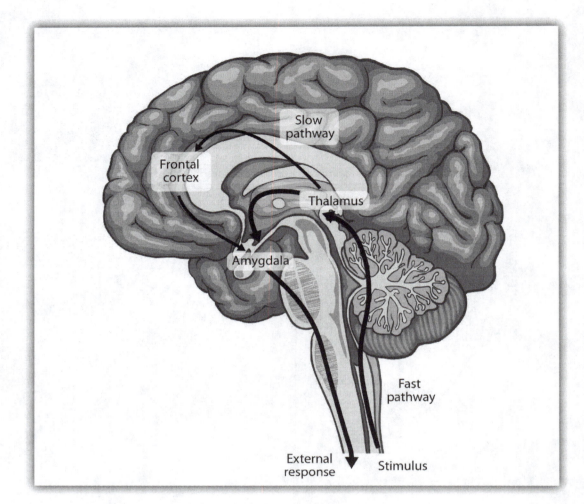

Although emotions might seem to you to be more frivolous or less important in comparison to our more rational cognitive processes, both emotions and cognitions can help us make effective decisions. In some cases we take action after rationally processing the costs and benefits of different choices, but in other cases we rely on our emotions. Emotions become particularly important in guiding decisions when the alternatives between many complex and conflicting alternatives present us with a high degree of uncertainty and ambiguity, making a complete cognitive analysis difficult. In these cases we often rely on our emotions to make decisions, and these decisions may in many cases be more accurate than those produced by cognitive processing (Damasio, 1994; Dijksterhuis, Bos, Nordgren, & van Baaren, 2006; Nordgren & Dijksterhuis, 2009; Wilson & Schooler, 1991).[9]

1.1   The Cannon-Bard and James-Lange Theories of Emotion

Recall for a moment a situation in which you have experienced an intense emotional response. Perhaps you woke up in the middle of the night in a panic because you heard a noise that made you think that someone had broken into your house or apartment. Or maybe you were calmly cruising down a street in your neighborhood when another car suddenly pulled out in front of you, forcing you to slam on your brakes to avoid an accident. I'm sure that you remember that your emotional reaction was in large part physical. Perhaps you remember being flushed, your heart pounding, feeling sick to your stomach, or having trouble breathing. You were experiencing the physiological part of emotion—arousal—and I'm sure you have had similar feelings in other situations, perhaps when you were in love, angry, embarrassed, frustrated, or very sad.

If you think back to a strong emotional experience, you might wonder about the order of the events that occurred. Certainly you experienced arousal, but did the arousal come before, after, or along with the experience of the emotion? Psychologists have proposed three different theories of emotion, which differ in terms of the hypothesized role of arousal in emotion (Figure 10.4).

FIGURE 10.4 Three Theories of Emotion

The Cannon-Bard theory proposes that emotions and arousal occur at the same time. The James-Lange theory proposes the emotion is the result of arousal. Schachter and Singer's two-factor model proposes that arousal and cognition combine to create emotion.

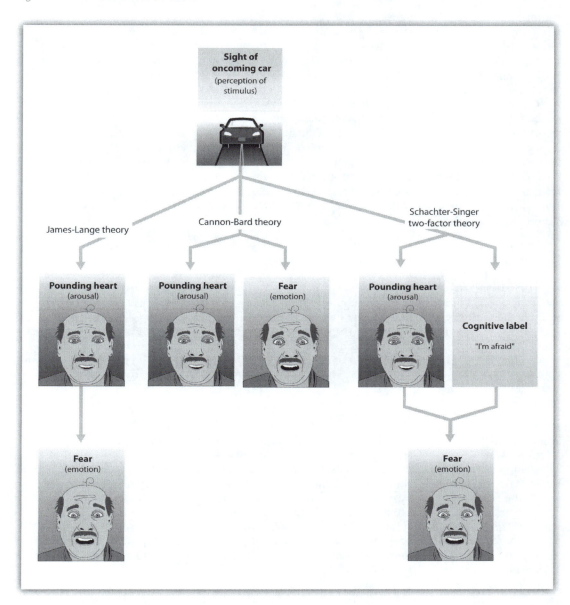

If your experiences are like mine, as you reflected on the arousal that you have experienced in strong emotional situations, you probably thought something like, "I was afraid and my heart started beating like crazy." At least some psychologists agree with this interpretation. According to the theory of emotion proposed by Walter Cannon and Philip Bard, the experience of the emotion (in this case, "I'm afraid") occurs alongside our experience of the arousal ("my heart is beating fast"). According to the **Cannon-Bard theory of emotion**, *the experience of an emotion is accompanied by physiological arousal.* Thus, according to this model of emotion, as we become aware of danger, our heart rate also increases.

Cannon-Bard theory of emotion

The idea that the experience of emotion is accompanied by physiological arousal.

James-Lange theory of emotion

The idea that the experience of emotion is the result of the arousal that we experience.

Although the idea that the experience of an emotion occurs alongside the accompanying arousal seems intuitive to our everyday experiences, the psychologists William James and Carl Lange had another idea about the role of arousal. According to the **James-Lange theory of emotion**, *our experience of an emotion is the result of the arousal that we experience*. This approach proposes that the arousal and the emotion are not independent, but rather that the emotion depends on the arousal. The fear does not occur along with the racing heart but occurs *because of* the racing heart. As William James put it, "We feel sorry because we cry, angry because we strike, afraid because we tremble" (James, 1884, p. 190).[10] A fundamental aspect of the James-Lange theory is that different patterns of arousal may create different emotional experiences.

There is research evidence to support each of these theories. The operation of the fast emotional pathway (Figure 10.3) supports the idea that arousal and emotions occur together. The emotional circuits in the limbic system are activated when an emotional stimulus is experienced, and these circuits quickly create corresponding physical reactions (LeDoux, 2000).[11] The process happens so quickly that it may feel to us as if emotion is simultaneous with our physical arousal.

On the other hand, and as predicted by the James-Lange theory, our experiences of emotion are weaker without arousal. Patients who have spinal injuries that reduce their experience of arousal also report decreases in emotional responses (Hohmann, 1966).[12] There is also at least some support for the idea that different emotions are produced by different patterns of arousal. People who view fearful faces show more amygdala activation than those who watch angry or joyful faces (Whalen et al., 2001; Witvliet & Vrana, 1995),[13] we experience a red face and flushing when we are embarrassed but not when we experience other emotions (Leary, Britt, Cutlip, & Templeton, 1992),[14] and different hormones are released when we experience compassion than when we experience other emotions (Oatley, Keltner, & Jenkins, 2006).[15]

1.2   The Two-Factor Theory of Emotion

two-factor theory of emotion

The idea that the strength of emotion is determined by the intensity of the arousal we are experiencing, but that the cognitive appraisal of the situation determines what the emotion will be.

Whereas the James-Lange theory proposes that each emotion has a different pattern of arousal, the *two-factor theory* of emotion takes the opposite approach, arguing that the arousal that we experience is basically the same in every emotion, and that all emotions (including the basic emotions) are differentiated only by our cognitive appraisal of the source of the arousal. The **two-factor theory of emotion** asserts that *the experience of emotion is determined by the intensity of the arousal we are experiencing, but that the cognitive appraisal of the situation determines what the emotion will be*. Because both arousal and appraisal are necessary, we can say that emotions have two factors: an arousal factor and a cognitive factor (Schachter & Singer, 1962):[16]

$$\text{emotion} = \text{arousal} + \text{cognition}$$

misattribution of arousal

When we incorrectly label the source of the arousal that we are experiencing.

In some cases it may be difficult for a person who is experiencing a high level of arousal to accurately determine which emotion she is experiencing. That is, she may be certain that she is feeling arousal, but the meaning of the arousal (the cognitive factor) may be less clear. Some romantic relationships, for instance, have a very high level of arousal, and the partners alternatively experience extreme highs and lows in the relationship. One day they are madly in love with each other and the next they are in a huge fight. In situations that are accompanied by high arousal, people may be unsure what emotion they are experiencing. In the high arousal relationship, for instance, the partners may be uncertain whether the emotion they are feeling is love, hate, or both at the same time (sound familiar?). *The tendency for people to incorrectly label the source of the arousal that they are experiencing* is known as the **misattribution of arousal**.

In one interesting field study by Dutton and Aron (1974),[17] an attractive young woman approached individual young men as they crossed a wobbly, long suspension walkway hanging more than 200 feet above a river in British Columbia, Canada. The woman asked each man to help her fill out a class questionnaire. When he had finished, she wrote her name and phone number on a piece of paper, and invited him to call if he wanted to hear more about the project. More than half of the men who had been interviewed on the bridge later called the woman. In contrast, men approached by the same woman on a low solid bridge, or who were interviewed on the suspension bridge by men, called significantly less frequently. The idea of misattribution of arousal can explain this result—the men were feeling arousal from the height of the bridge, but they misattributed it as romantic or sexual attraction to the woman, making them more likely to call her.

FIGURE 10.5
Capilano River Bridge

Arousal caused by the height of this bridge was misattributed as attraction by the men who were interviewed by an attractive woman as they crossed it.

Source: Photo courtesy of Goobiebilly, http://commons.wikimedia.org/wiki/File:Capilano_suspension_bridge_-g.jpg.

Research Focus: Misattributing Arousal

If you think a bit about your own experiences of different emotions, and if you consider the equation that suggests that emotions are represented by both arousal and cognition, you might start to wonder how much was determined by each. That is, do we know what emotion we are experiencing by monitoring our feelings (arousal) or by monitoring our thoughts (cognition)? The bridge study you just read about might begin to provide you an answer: The men seemed to be more influenced by their perceptions of how they should be feeling (their cognition) rather than by how they actually were feeling (their arousal).

Stanley Schachter and Jerome Singer (1962)[18] directly tested this prediction of the two-factor theory of emotion in a well-known experiment. Schachter and Singer believed that the cognitive part of the emotion was critical—in fact, they believed that the arousal that we are experiencing could be interpreted as any emotion, provided we had the right label for it. Thus they hypothesized that if an individual is experiencing arousal for which he has no immediate explanation, he will "label" this state in terms of the cognitions that are created in his environment. On the other hand, they argued that people who already have a clear label for their arousal would have no need to search for a relevant label, and therefore should not experience an emotion.

In the research, male participants were told that they would be participating in a study on the effects of a new drug, called "suproxin," on vision. On the basis of this cover story, the men were injected with a shot of the neurotransmitter epinephrine, a drug that normally creates feelings of tremors, flushing, and accelerated breathing in people. The idea was to give all the participants the experience of arousal.

Then, according to random assignment to conditions, the men were told that the drug would make them feel certain ways. The men in the *epinephrine informed* condition were told the truth about the effects of the drug—they were told that they would likely experience tremors, their hands would start to shake, their hearts would start to pound, and their faces might get warm and flushed. The participants in the *epinephrine-uninformed* condition, however, were told something untrue—that their feet would feel numb, that they would have an itching sensation over parts of their body, and that they might get a slight headache. The idea was to make some of the men think that the arousal they were experiencing was caused by the drug (the *informed condition*), whereas others would be unsure where the arousal came from (the *uninformed condition*).

Then the men were left alone with a confederate who they thought had received the same injection. While they were waiting for the experiment (which was supposedly about vision) to begin, the confederate behaved in a wild and crazy (Schachter and Singer called it "euphoric") manner. He wadded up spitballs, flew paper airplanes, and played with a hula-hoop. He kept trying to get the participant to join in with his games. Then right before the vision experiment was to begin, the participants were asked to indicate their current emotional states on a number of scales. One of the emotions they were asked about was euphoria.

If you are following the story, you will realize what was expected: The men who had a label for their arousal (the *informed* group) would not be experiencing much emotion because they already had a label available for their arousal. The men in the *misinformed* group, on the other hand, were expected to be unsure about the source of the arousal. They needed to find an explanation for their arousal, and the confederate provided one. As you can see in Figure 10.6 (left side), this is just what they found. The participants in the misinformed condition were more likely to be experiencing euphoria (as measured by their behavioral responses with the confederate) than were those in the informed condition.

Then Schachter and Singer conducted another part of the study, using new participants. Everything was exactly the same except for the behavior of the confederate. Rather than being euphoric, he acted angry. He complained about having to complete the questionnaire he had been asked to do, indicating that the questions were stupid and too personal. He ended up tearing up the questionnaire that he was working on, yelling "I don't have to tell them that!" Then he grabbed his books and stormed out of the room.

What do you think happened in this condition? The answer is the same thing: The misinformed participants experienced more anger (again as measured by the participant's behaviors during the waiting period) than did the informed participants. (Figure 10.6, right side) The idea is that because cognitions are such strong determinants of emotional states, the same state of physiological arousal could be labeled in many different ways, depending entirely on the label provided by the social situation. As Schachter and Singer put it: "Given a state of physiological arousal for which an individual has no immediate explanation, he will 'label' this state and describe his feelings in terms of the cognitions available to him" (Schachter & Singer, 1962, p. 381).[19]

Results From Schachter and Singer, 1962

Results of the study by Schachter and Singer (1962) support the two-factor theory of emotion. The participants who did not have a clear label for their arousal took on the emotion of the confederate.

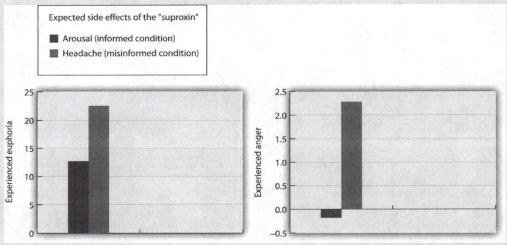

Source: Adapted from Schachter, S., & Singer, J. E. (1962). Cognitive, social and physiological determinants of emotional state. Psychological Review, 69, 379–399.

Because it assumes that arousal is constant across emotions, the two-factor theory also predicts that emotions may transfer or "spill over" from one highly arousing event to another. My university basketball team recently won the NCAA basketball championship, but after the final victory some students rioted in the streets near the campus, lighting fires and burning cars. This seems to be a very strange reaction to such a positive outcome for the university and the students, but it can be explained through the spillover of the arousal caused by happiness to destructive behaviors. The principle of *excitation transfer* refers to the phenomenon that occurs when people who are already experiencing arousal from one event tend to also experience unrelated emotions more strongly.

In sum, each of the three theories of emotion has something to support it. In terms of Cannon-Bard, emotions and arousal generally are subjectively experienced together, and the spread is very fast. In support of the James-Lange theory, there is at least some evidence that arousal is necessary for the experience of emotion, and that the patterns of arousal are different for different emotions. And in line with the two-factor model, there is also evidence that we may interpret the same patterns of arousal differently in different situations.

1.3 Communicating Emotion

nonverbal communication

Communication, primarily of liking or disliking, that does not involve words.

In addition to experiencing emotions internally, we also express our emotions to others, and we learn about the emotions of others by observing them. This communication process has evolved over time, and is highly adaptive. One way that we perceive the emotions of others is through their **nonverbal communication**, that is, *communication that does not involve words* (Ambady & Weisbuch, 2010; Anderson, 2007).[20] Nonverbal communication includes our tone of voice, gait, posture, touch, and facial expressions, and we can often accurately detect the emotions that other people are experiencing through these channels. Table 10.1 shows some of the important nonverbal behaviors that we use to express emotion and some other information (particularly liking or disliking, and dominance or submission).

TABLE 10.1 Some Common Nonverbal Communicators

Nonverbal cue	Description	Examples
Proxemics	Rules about the appropriate use of personal space	Standing nearer to someone can expressing liking or dominance.
Body appearance	Expressions based on alterations to our body	Body building, breast augmentation, weight loss, piercings, and tattoos are often used to appear more attractive to others.
Body positioning and movement	Expressions based on how our body appears	A more "open" body position can denote liking; a faster walking speed can communicate dominance.
Gestures	Behaviors and signs made with our hands or faces	The peace sign communicates liking; the "finger" communicates disrespect.
Facial expressions	The variety of emotions that we express, or attempt to hide, through our face	Smiling or frowning and staring or avoiding looking at the other can express liking or disliking, as well as dominance or submission.
Paralanguage	Clues to identity or emotions contained in our voices	Pronunciation, accents, and dialect can be used to communicate identity and liking.

Just as there is no "universal" spoken language, there is no universal nonverbal language. For instance, in the United States and many Western cultures we express disrespect by showing the middle finger (the "finger" or the "bird"). But in Britain, Ireland, Australia and New Zealand, the "V" sign (made with back of the hand facing the recipient) serves a similar purpose. In countries where Spanish, Portuguese, or French are spoken, a gesture in which a fist is raised and the arm is slapped on the bicep is equivalent to the finger, and in Russia, Indonesia, Turkey, and China a sign in which the hand and fingers are curled and the thumb is thrust between the middle and index fingers is used for the same purpose.

The most important communicator of emotion is the face. The face contains 43 different muscles that allow it to make more than 10,000 unique configurations and to express a wide variety of emotions. For example, happiness is expressed by smiles, which are created by two of the major muscles surrounding the mouth and the eyes, and anger is created by lowered brows and firmly pressed lips.

In addition to helping us express our emotions, the face also helps us feel emotion. The **facial feedback hypothesis** proposes that *the movement of our facial muscles can trigger corresponding emotions*. Fritz Strack and his colleagues (1988)[21] asked their research participants to hold a pen in their teeth (mimicking the facial action of a smile) or between their lips (similar to a frown), and then had them rate the funniness of a cartoon. They found that the cartoons were rated as more amusing when the pen was held in the "smiling" position—the subjective experience of emotion was intensified by the action of the facial muscles.

These results, and others like them, show that our behaviors, including our facial expressions, are influenced by, but also influence our affect. We may smile because we are happy, but we are also happy because we are smiling. And we may stand up straight because we are proud, but we are proud because we are standing up straight (Stepper & Strack, 1993).[22]

facial feedback hypothesis

The idea that the movement of our facial muscles can trigger corresponding emotions.

FIGURE 10.7

Stepper and Strack (1993) found that people rated cartoons more positively when they were led to smile, rather than frown, by holding pens in their mouths in different directions.

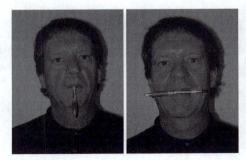

© Thinkstock

KEY TAKEAWAYS

- Emotions are the normally adaptive mental and physiological feeling states that direct our attention and guide our behavior.
- Emotional states are accompanied by arousal, our experiences of the bodily responses created by the sympathetic division of the autonomic nervous system.
- Motivations are forces that guide behavior. They can be biological, such as hunger and thirst; personal, such as the motivation for achievement; or social, such as the motivation for acceptance and belonging.
- The most fundamental emotions, known as the basic emotions, are those of anger, disgust, fear, happiness, sadness, and surprise.
- Cognitive appraisal allows us to also experience a variety of secondary emotions.
- According to the Cannon-Bard theory of emotion, the experience of an emotion is accompanied by physiological arousal.
- According to the James-Lange theory of emotion, our experience of an emotion is the result of the arousal that we experience.
- According to the two-factor theory of emotion, the experience of emotion is determined by the intensity of the arousal we are experiencing, and the cognitive appraisal of the situation determines what the emotion will be.
- When people incorrectly label the source of the arousal that they are experiencing, we say that they have misattributed their arousal.
- We express our emotions to others through nonverbal behaviors, and we learn about the emotions of others by observing them.

EXERCISES AND CRITICAL THINKING

1. Consider the three theories of emotion that we have discussed and provide an example of a situation in which a person might experience each of the three proposed patterns of arousal and emotion.
2. Describe a time when you used nonverbal behaviors to express your emotions or to detect the emotions of others. What specific nonverbal techniques did you use to communicate?

2. STRESS: THE UNSEEN KILLER

LEARNING OBJECTIVES

1. Define stress and review the body's physiological responses to it.
2. Summarize the negative health consequences of prolonged stress.
3. Explain the differences in how people respond to stress.
4. Review the methods that are successful in coping with stress.

stress

Physiological responses that occur when an organism fails to respond appropriately to emotional or physical threats.

posttraumatic stress disorder (PTSD)

A medical syndrome that includes symptoms of anxiety, sleeplessness, nightmares, and social withdrawal.

Emotions matter because they influence our behavior. And there is no emotional experience that has a more powerful influence on us than *stress*. Stress refers to the *physiological responses that occur when an organism fails to respond appropriately to emotional or physical threats* (Selye, 1956).[23] Extreme negative events, such as being the victim of a terrorist attack, a natural disaster, or a violent crime, may produce an extreme form of stress known as **posttraumatic stress disorder (PTSD)**, *a medical syndrome that includes symptoms of anxiety, sleeplessness, nightmares, and social withdrawal.* PTSD is frequently experienced by soldiers who return home from wars, with those who have experienced more extreme events during the war also experiencing more PTSD.

When it is extreme or prolonged, stress can create substantial health problems. Survivors of hurricane Katrina had three times the rate of heart attacks than the national average in the years following the disaster, and this is probably due to the stress that the hurricane created (American Medical Association, 2009).[24]   And people in New York City who lived nearer to the site of the 9/11 terrorist attacks reported experiencing more stress in the year following it than those who lived farther away (Pulcino et al., 2003).[25]   But stress is not unique to the experience of extremely traumatic events. It can also occur, and have a variety of negative outcomes, in our everyday lives.

2.1 The Negative Effects of Stress

The physiologist Hans Seyle (1907–1982) studied stress by examining how rats responded to being exposed to stressors such as extreme cold, infection, shock, or excessive exercise (Seyle, 1936, 1974, 1982).[26] Seyle found that regardless of the source of the stress, the rats experienced the same series of physiological changes as they suffered the prolonged stress. Seyle created the term **general adaptation syndrome** to refer to *the three distinct phases of physiological change that occur in response to long-term stress: alarm, resistance, and exhaustion* (Figure 10.8).

general adaptation syndrome

The distinct phases of physiological change that occur in response to long-term stress: alarm, resistance, and exhaustion.

FIGURE 10.8 General Adaptation Syndrome

Hans Seyle's research on the general adaptation syndrome documented the stages of prolonged exposure to stress.

Stage one:

General alarm reaction. The first reaction to stress.

The body releases stress hormones, including cortisol.

Stage two:

Resistance. After a period of chronic stress the body adapts to the ongoing threat and tries to return to its normal functions. Glucose levels increase to sustain energy, and blood pressure increases.

Stage three:

Exhaustion. In this stage, the body has run out of its reserves of energy and immunity. Blood sugar levels decrease, leading to decreased stress tolerance, progressive mental and physical exhaustion, illness, and collapse. The body's organs begin to fail, and eventually illness or death occurs.

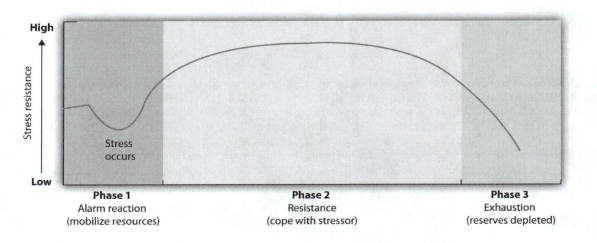

High

Stress resistance

Stress occurs

Low

Phase 1
Alarm reaction
(mobilize resources)

Phase 2
Resistance
(cope with stressor)

Phase 3
Exhaustion
(reserves depleted)

HPA axis

A physiological response to stress involving interactions among the hypothalamus, the pituitary, and the adrenal glands.

cortisol

A stress hormone that releases sugars into the blood, helping preparing the body to respond to threat.

The experience of stress creates both an increase in general arousal in the sympathetic division of the autonomic nervous system (ANS), as well as another, even more complex, system of physiological changes through the *HPA axis* ([Content Removed: #]). The HPA axis is *a physiological response to stress involving interactions among the hypothalamus, the pituitary, and the adrenal glands*. The HPA response begins when the hypothalamus secretes releasing hormones that direct the pituitary gland to release the hormone ACTH. ACTH then directs the adrenal glands to secrete more hormones, including epinephrine, norepinephrine, and cortisol, *a stress hormone that releases sugars into the blood, helping preparing the body to respond to threat* (Rodrigues, LeDoux, & Sapolsky, 2009).[27]

FIGURE 10.9 HPA Axis

Stress activates the HPA axis. The result is the secretion of epinephrine, norepinephrine, and cortisol.

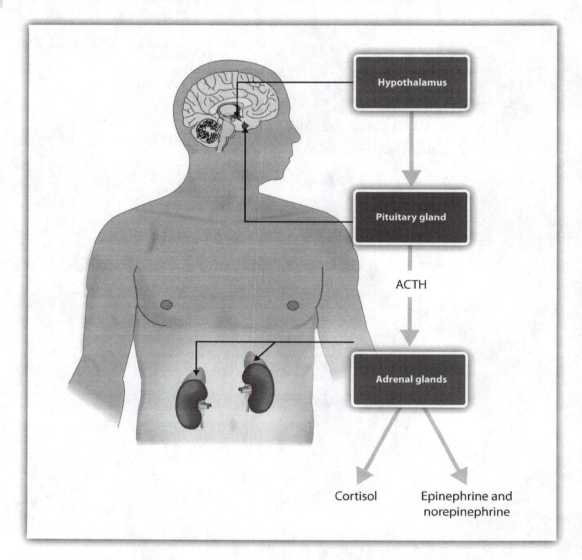

The initial arousal that accompanies stress is normally quite adaptive because it helps us respond to potentially dangerous events. The experience of prolonged stress, however, has a direct negative influence on our physical health, because at the same time that stress increases activity in the sympathetic division of the ANS, it also suppresses activity in the parasympathetic division of the ANS. When stress is long-term, the HPA axis remains active and the adrenals continue to produce cortisol. This increased cortisol production exhausts the stress mechanism, leading to fatigue and depression.

The HPA reactions to persistent stress lead to a weakening of the immune system, making us more susceptible to a variety of health problems including colds and other diseases (Cohen & Herbert, 1996; Faulkner & Smith, 2009; Miller, Chen, & Cole, 2009; Uchino, Smith, Holt-Lunstad, Campo, & Reblin, 2007).[28] Stress also damages our DNA, making us less likely to be able to repair wounds and respond to the genetic mutations that cause disease (Epel et al., 2006).[29] As a result, wounds heal more slowly when we are under stress, and we are more likely to get cancer (Kiecolt-Glaser, McGuire, Robles, & Glaser, 2002; Wells, 2006).[30]

Chronic stress is also a major contributor to heart disease. Although heart disease is caused in part by genetic factors, as well as high blood pressure, high cholesterol, and cigarette smoking, it is also caused by stress (Krantz & McCeney, 2002).[31] Long-term stress creates two opposite effects on the coronary system. Stress increases cardiac output (i.e., the heart pumps more blood) at the same time that it reduces the ability of the blood vessels to conduct blood through the arteries, as the increase in levels of cortisol leads to a buildup of plaque on artery walls (Dekker et al., 2008).[32] The combination of increased blood flow and arterial constriction leads to increased blood pressure (hypertension), which can damage the heart muscle, leading to heart attack and death.

2.2   Stressors in Our Everyday Lives

The stressors for Seyle's rats included electric shock and exposure to cold. Although these are probably not on your top-10 list of most common stressors, the stress that you experience in your everyday life can also be taxing. Thomas Holmes and Richard Rahe (1967)[33] developed a measure of some everyday life events that might lead to stress, and you can assess your own likely stress level by completing the measure in Table 10.2. You might want to pay particular attention to this score, because it can predict the likelihood that you will get sick. Rahe and colleagues (1970)[34] asked 2,500 members of the military to complete the rating scale and then assessed the health records of the soldiers over the following 6 months. The results were clear: The higher the scale score, the more likely the soldier was to end up in the hospital.

TABLE 10.2 The Holmes and Rahe Stress Scale

Life event	Score
Death of spouse	100
Divorce	73
Marital separation from mate	65
Detention in jail, other institution	63
Death of a close family member	63
Major personal injury or illness	53
Marriage	50
Fired from work	47
Marital reconciliation	45
Retirement	45
Major change in the health or behavior of a family member	44
Pregnancy	40
Sexual difficulties	39
Gaining a new family member (e.g., through birth, adoption, oldster moving, etc.)	39
Major business readjustment (e.g., merger, reorganization, bankruptcy)	39
Major change in financial status	38
Death of close friend	37
Change to different line of work	36
Major change in the number of arguments with spouse	35
Taking out a mortgage or loan for a major purchase	31
Foreclosure on a mortgage or loan	30
Major change in responsibilities at work	29
Son or daughter leaving home (e.g., marriage, attending college)	29
Trouble with in-laws	29
Outstanding personal achievement	28
Spouse beginning or ceasing to work outside the home	26
Beginning or ceasing formal schooling	26
Major change in living conditions	25
Revision of personal habits (dress, manners, associations, etc.)	24
Trouble with boss	23
Major change in working hours or conditions	20
Change in residence	20
Change to a new school	20
Major change in usual type and/or amount of recreation	19
Major change in church activities (a lot more or less than usual)	19
Major change in social activities (clubs, dancing, movies, visiting)	18
Taking out a mortgage or loan for a lesser purchase (e.g., for a car, television , freezer, etc.)	17
Major change in sleeping habits	16
Major change in the number of family get-togethers	15
Major change in eating habits	15
Vacation	13
Christmas season	12
Minor violations of the law (e.g., traffic tickets, etc.)	11
Total	_____

You can calculate your score on this scale by adding the total points across each of the events that you have experienced over the past year. Then use Table 10.3 to determine your likelihood of getting ill.

TABLE 10.3 Interpretation of Holmes and Rahe Stress Scale

Number of life-change units	Chance of developing a stress-related illness (%)
Less than 150	30
150–299	50
More than 300	80

Although some of the items on the Holmes and Rahe scale are more major, you can see that even minor stressors add to the total score. *Our everyday interactions with the environment that are essentially negative*, known as **daily hassles**, can also create stress as well as poorer health outcomes (Hutchinson & Williams, 2007).[35] Events that may seem rather trivial altogether, such as misplacing our keys, having to reboot our computer because it has frozen, being late for an assignment, or getting cut off by another car in rush-hour traffic, can produce stress (Fiksenbaum, Greenglass, & Eaton, 2006).[36] Glaser (1985)[37] found that medical students who were tested during, rather than several weeks before, their school examination periods showed lower immune system functioning. Other research has found that even more minor stressors, such as having to do math problems during an experimental session, can compromise the immune system (Cacioppo et al., 1998).[38]

daily hassles
Our everyday negative interactions with the environment.

2.3 Responses to Stress

Not all people experience and respond to stress in the same way, and these differences can be important. The cardiologists Meyer Friedman and R. H. Rosenman (1974)[39] were among the first to study the link between stress and heart disease. In their research they noticed that even though the partners in married couples often had similar lifestyles, diet, and exercise patterns, the husbands nevertheless generally had more heart disease than did the wives. As they tried to explain the difference, they focused on the personality characteristics of the partners, finding that the husbands were more likely than the wives to respond to stressors with negative emotions and hostility.

Recent research has shown that the strongest predictor of a physiological stress response from daily hassles is the amount of negative emotion that they evoke. People who experience strong negative emotions as a result of everyday hassles, and who respond to stress with hostility experience more negative health outcomes than do those who react in a less negative way (McIntyre, Korn, & Matsuo, 2008; Suls & Bunde, 2005).[40] Williams and his colleagues (2001)[41] found that people who scored high on measures of anger were three times more likely to suffer from heart attacks in comparison to those who scored lower on anger.

On average, men are more likely than are women to respond to stress by activating the **fight-or-flight response**, which is *an emotional and behavioral reaction to stress that increases the readiness for action*. The arousal that men experience when they are stressed leads them to either go on the attack, in an aggressive or revenging way, or else retreat as quickly as they can to safety from the stressor. The fight-or-flight response allows men to control the source of the stress if they think they can do so, or if that is not possible, it allows them to save face by leaving the situation. The fight-or-flight response is triggered in men by the activation of the HPA axis.

fight-or-flight response
An emotional and behavioral reaction to stress that increases the readiness for action.

Women, on the other hand, are less likely to take a fight-or-flight response to stress. Rather, they are more likely to take a *tend-and-befriend response* (Taylor et al., 2000).[42] The **tend-and-befriend response** is *a behavioral reaction to stress that involves activities designed to create social networks that provide protection from threats*. This approach is also self-protective because it allows the individual to talk to others about her concerns, as well as to exchange resources, such as child care. The tend-and-befriend response is triggered in women by the release of the hormone *ocytocin*, which promotes affiliation. Overall, the tend-and-befriend response is healthier than the flight-or-flight response because it does not produce the elevated levels of arousal related to the HPA, including the negative results that accompany increased levels of cortisol. This may help explain why women, on average, have less heart disease and live longer than men.

tend-and-befriend response
A behavioral reaction to stress that involves activities designed to create social networks that provide protection from threats.

2.4 Managing Stress

No matter how healthy and happy we are in our everyday lives, there are going to be times when we experience stress. But we do not need to throw up our hands in despair when things go wrong; rather, we can use our personal and social resources to help us.

Perhaps the most common approach to dealing with negative affect is to attempt to suppress, avoid, or deny it. You probably know people who seem to be stressed, depressed, or anxious, but they cannot or will not see it in themselves. Perhaps you tried to talk to them about it, to get them to open up to you, but were rebuffed. They seem to act as if there is no problem at all, simply moving on with life without admitting or even trying to deal with the negative feelings. Or perhaps you have even taken a similar approach yourself. Have you ever had an important test to study for or an important job interview coming up, and rather than planning and preparing for it, you simply tried put it out of your mind entirely?

Research has found that ignoring stress is not a good approach for coping with it. For one, ignoring our problems does not make them go away. If we experience so much stress that we get sick, these events will be detrimental to our life even if we do not or cannot admit that they are occurring. Suppressing our negative emotions is also not a very good option, at least in the long run, because it tends to fail (Gross & Levenson, 1997).[43] For one, if we know that we have that big exam coming up, we have to focus on the exam itself to suppress it. We can't really suppress or deny our thoughts, because we actually have to recall and face the event to make the attempt to not think about it. Doing so takes effort, and we get tired when we try to do it. Furthermore, we may continually worry that our attempts to suppress will fail. Suppressing our emotions might work out for a short while, but when we run out of energy the negative emotions may shoot back up into consciousness, causing us to reexperience the negative feelings that we had been trying to avoid.

Daniel Wegner and his colleagues (Wegner, Schneider, Carter, & White, 1987)[44] directly tested whether people would be able to effectively suppress a simple thought. He asked them to *not* think about a white bear for 5 minutes but to ring a bell in case they did. (Try it yourself; can you do it?) However, participants were unable to suppress the thought as instructed. The white bear kept popping into mind, even when the participants were instructed to avoid thinking about it. You might have had this experience when you were dieting or trying to study rather than party; the chocolate bar in the kitchen cabinet and the fun time you were missing at the party kept popping into mind, disrupting your work.

Suppressing our negative thoughts does not work, and there is evidence that the opposite is true: When we are faced with troubles, it is healthy to let out the negative thoughts and feelings by expressing them, either to ourselves or to others. James Pennebaker and his colleagues (Pennebaker, Colder, & Sharp, 1990; Watson & Pennebaker, 1989)[45] have conducted many correlational and experimental studies that demonstrate the advantages to our mental and physical health of opening up versus suppressing our feelings. This research team has found that simply talking about or writing about our emotions or our reactions to negative events provides substantial health benefits. For instance, Pennebaker and Beall (1986)[46] randomly assigned students to write about either the most traumatic and stressful event of their lives or trivial topics. Although the students who wrote about the traumas had higher blood pressure and more negative moods immediately after they wrote their essays, they were also less likely to visit the student health center for illnesses during the following six months. Other research studied individuals whose spouses had died in the previous year, finding that the more they talked about the death with others, the less likely they were to become ill during the subsequent year. Daily writing about one's emotional states has also been found to increase immune system functioning (Petrie, Fontanilla, Thomas, Booth, & Pennebaker, 2004).[47]

Opening up probably helps in various ways. For one, expressing our problems to others allows us to gain information, and possibly support, from them (remember the *tend-and-befriend response* that is so effectively used to reduce stress by women). Writing or thinking about one's experiences also seems to help people make sense of these events and may give them a feeling of control over their lives (Pennebaker & Stone, 2004).[48]

It is easier to respond to stress if we can interpret it in more positive ways. Kelsey et al. (1999)[49] found that some people interpret stress as a challenge (something that they feel that they can, with effort, deal with), whereas others see the same stress as a threat (something that is negative and fearful). People who viewed stress as a challenge had fewer physiological stress responses than those who viewed it as a threat—they were able to frame and react to stress in more positive ways.

2.5 Emotion Regulation

emotion regulation

The ability to successfully control our emotions.

Emotional responses such as the stress reaction are useful in warning us about potential danger and in mobilizing our response to it, so it is a good thing that we have them. However, we also need to learn how to control our emotions, to prevent them from letting our behavior get out of control. *The ability to successfully control our emotions* is known as **emotion regulation**.

Emotion regulation has some important positive outcomes. Consider, for instance, research by Walter Mischel and his colleagues. In their studies, they had 4- and 5-year-old children sit at a table in front of a yummy snack, such as a chocolate chip cookie or a marshmallow. The children were told that they could eat the snack right away if they wanted. However, they were also told that if they could wait for just a couple of minutes, they'd be able to have two snacks—both the one in front of them and another just like it. However, if they ate the one that was in front of them before the time was up, they would not get a second.

Mischel found that some children were able to override the impulse to seek immediate gratification to obtain a greater reward at a later time. Other children, of course, were not; they just ate the first snack right away. Furthermore, the inability to delay gratification seemed to occur in a spontaneous and emotional manner, without much thought. The children who could not resist simply grabbed the cookie because it looked so yummy, without being able to stop themselves (Metcalfe & Mischel, 1999; Strack & Deutsch, 2007).[50]

The ability to regulate our emotions has important consequences later in life. When Mischel followed up on the children in his original study, he found that those who had been able to self-regulate grew up to have some highly positive characteristics: They got better SAT scores, were rated by their friends as more socially adept, and were found to cope with frustration and stress better than those children who could not resist the tempting cookie at a young age. Thus effective self-regulation can be recognized as an important key to success in life (Ayduk et al., 2000; Eigsti et al., 2006; Mischel & Ayduk, 2004).[51]

Emotion regulation is influenced by body chemicals, particularly the neurotransmitter *serotonin*. Preferences for small, immediate rewards over large but later rewards have been linked to low levels of serotonin in animals (Bizot, Le Bihan, Peuch, Hamon, & Thiebot, 1999; Liu, Wilkinson, & Robbins, 2004),[52] and low levels of serotonin are tied to violence and impulsiveness in human suicides (Asberg, Traskman, & Thoren, 1976).[53]

Research Focus: Emotion Regulation Takes Effort

Emotion regulation is particularly difficult when we are tired, depressed, or anxious, and it is under these conditions that we more easily let our emotions get the best of us (Muraven & Baumeister, 2000).[54] If you are tired and worried about an upcoming exam, you may find yourself getting angry and taking it out on your roommate, even though she really hasn't done anything to deserve it and you don't really want to be angry at her. It is no secret that we are more likely fail at our diets when we are under a lot of stress, or at night when we are tired.

Muraven, Tice, and Baumeister (1998)[55] conducted a study to demonstrate that emotion regulation—that is, either increasing or decreasing our emotional responses—takes work. They speculated that self-control was like a muscle; it just gets tired when it is used too much. In their experiment they asked their participants to watch a short movie about environmental disasters involving radioactive waste and their negative effects on wildlife. The scenes included sick and dying animals and were very upsetting. According to random assignment to condition, one group (the *increase emotional response* condition) was told to really get into the movie and to express their emotions, one group was to hold back and decrease their emotional responses (the *decrease emotional response* condition), and the third (control) group received no emotional regulation instructions.

Both before and after the movie, the experimenter asked the participants to engage in a measure of physical strength by squeezing as hard as they could on a handgrip exerciser, a device used for strengthening hand muscles. The experimenter put a piece of paper in the grip and timed how long the participants could hold the grip together before the paper fell out. Figure 10.10 shows the results of this study. It seems that emotion regulation does indeed take effort, because the participants who had been asked to control their emotions showed significantly less ability to squeeze the handgrip after the movie than they had showed before it, whereas the control group showed virtually no decrease. The emotion regulation during the movie seems to have consumed resources, leaving the participants with less capacity to perform the handgrip task.

Results From Muraven, Tice, and Baumeister, 1998

Participants who were instructed to regulate their emotions, either by increasing or decreasing their emotional responses to a move, had less energy left over to squeeze a handgrip in comparison to those who did not regulate their emotions.

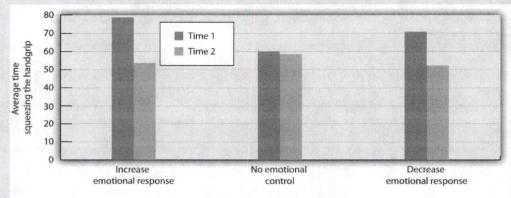

Source: Adapted from Muraven, M., Tice, D. M., & Baumeister, R. F. (1998). Self-control as a limited resource: Regulatory depletion patterns. Journal of Personality & Social Psychology, 74(3), 774–789.

In other studies, people who had to resist the temptation to eat chocolates and cookies, who made important decisions, or who were forced to conform to others all performed more poorly on subsequent tasks that took energy, including giving up on tasks earlier and failing to resist temptation (Vohs & Heatherton, 2000).[56]

Can we improve our emotion regulation? It turns out that training in self-regulation—just like physical training—can help. Students who practiced doing difficult tasks, such as exercising, avoiding swearing, or maintaining good posture, were later found to perform better in laboratory tests of emotion regulation such as maintaining a diet or completing a puzzle (Baumeister, Gailliot, DeWall, & Oaten, 2006; Baumeister, Schmeichel, & Vohs, 2007; Oaten & Cheng, 2006).[57]

KEY TAKEAWAYS

- Stress refers to the physiological responses that occur when an organism fails to respond appropriately to emotional or physical threats.
- The general adaptation syndrome refers to the three distinct phases of physiological change that occur in response to long-term stress: alarm, resistance, and exhaustion.
- Stress is normally adaptive because it helps us respond to potentially dangerous events by activating the sympathetic division of the autonomic nervous system. But the experience of prolonged stress has a direct negative influence on our physical health.
- Chronic stress is a major contributor to heart disease. It also decreases our ability to fight off colds and infections.
- Stressors can occur as a result of both major and minor everyday events.
- Men tend to respond to stress with the fight-or-flight response, whereas women are more likely to take a tend-and-befriend response.

EXERCISES AND CRITICAL THINKING

1. Consider a time when you experienced stress, and how you responded to it. Do you now have a better understanding of the dangers of stress? How will you change your coping mechanisms based on what you have learned?

2. Are you good at emotion regulation? Can you think of a time that your emotions got the better of you? How might you make better use of your emotions?

3.   POSITIVE EMOTIONS: THE POWER OF HAPPINESS

LEARNING OBJECTIVES

1. Understand the important role of positive emotions and happiness in responding to stress.
2. Understand the factors that increase, and do not increase, happiness.

Although stress is an emotional response that can kill us, our emotions can also help us cope with and protect ourselves from it. The stress of the Monday through Friday grind can be offset by the fun that we can have on the weekend, and the concerns that we have about our upcoming chemistry exam can be offset by a positive attitude toward school, life, and other people. Put simply, the best antidote for stress is a happy one: Think positively, have fun, and enjoy the company of others.

You have probably heard about the "power of positive thinking"—the idea that thinking positively helps people meet their goals and keeps them healthy, happy, and able to effectively cope with the negative events that occur to them. It turns out that positive thinking really works. People who think positively about their future, who believe that they can control their outcomes, and who are willing to open up and share with others are healthier people (Seligman, & Csikszentmihalyi, 2000).[58]

The power of positive thinking comes in different forms, but they are all helpful. Some researchers have focused on **optimism**, *a general tendency to expect positive outcomes*, finding that optimists are happier and have less stress (Carver & Scheier, 2009).[59] Others have focused on **self-efficacy**, *the belief in our ability to carry out actions that produce desired outcomes*. People with high self-efficacy respond to environmental and other threats in an active, constructive way—by getting information, talking to friends, and attempting to face and reduce the difficulties they are experiencing. These people too are better able to ward off their stresses in comparison to people with less self-efficacy (Thompson, 2009).[60]

Self-efficacy helps in part because it leads us to perceive that we can control the potential stressors that may affect us. Workers who have control over their work environment (e.g., by being able to move furniture and control distractions) experience less stress, as do patients in nursing homes who are able to choose their everyday activities (Rodin, 1986).[61] Glass, Reim, and Singer (1971)[62] found that participants who believed that they could stop a loud noise experienced less stress than those who did not think that they could, even though the people who had the option never actually used it. The ability to control our outcomes may help explain why animals and people who have higher status live longer (Sapolsky, 2005).[63]

Suzanne Kobasa and her colleagues (Kobasa, Maddi, & Kahn, 1982)[64] have argued that the tendency to be less affected by life's stressors can be characterized as an individual difference measure that has a relationship to both optimism and self-efficacy known as *hardiness*. Hardy individuals are those who are more positive overall about potentially stressful life events, who take more direct action to understand the causes of negative events, and who attempt to learn from them what may be of value for the future. Hardy individuals use effective coping strategies, and they take better care of themselves.

Taken together, these various coping skills, including optimism, self-efficacy, and hardiness, have been shown to have a wide variety of positive effects on our health. Optimists make faster recoveries from illnesses and surgeries (Carver et al., 2005).[65] People with high self-efficacy have been found to be better able to quit smoking and lose weight and are more likely to exercise regularly (Cohen & Pressman, 2006).[66] And hardy individuals seem to cope better with stress and other negative life events (Dolbier, Smith, & Steinhardt, 2007).[67] The positive effects of positive thinking are particularly important when stress is high. Baker (2007)[68] found that in periods of low stress, positive thinking made little difference in responses to stress, but that during stressful periods optimists were less likely to smoke on a day-to-day basis and to respond to stress in more productive ways, such as by exercising.

It is possible to learn to think more positively, and doing so can be beneficial. Antoni et al. (2001)[69] found that pessimistic cancer patients who were given training in optimism reported more optimistic outlooks after the training and were less fatigued after their treatments. And Maddi, Kahn, and Maddi (1998)[70] found that a "hardiness training" program that included focusing on ways to effectively cope with stress was effective in increasing satisfaction and decreasing self-reported stress.

The benefits of taking positive approaches to stress can last a lifetime. Christopher Peterson and his colleagues (Peterson, Seligman, Yurko, Martin, & Friedman, 1998)[71] found that the level of optimism reported by people who had first been interviewed when they were in college during the years between 1936 and 1940 predicted their health over the next 50 years. Students who had a more positive outlook on life in college were less likely to have died up to 50 years later of all causes, and they were

optimism

The general tendency to expect positive outcomes.

self-efficacy

The belief in our ability to carry out actions that produce desired outcomes.

particularly likely to have experienced fewer accidental and violent deaths, in comparison to students who were less optimistic. Similar findings were found for older adults. After controlling for loneliness, marital status, economic status, and other correlates of health, Levy and Myers found that older adults with positive attitudes and higher self-efficacy had better health and lived on average almost 8 years longer than their more negative peers (Levy & Myers, 2005; Levy, Slade, & Kasl, 2002).[72] And Diener, Nickerson, Lucas, and Sandvik (2002)[73] found that people who had cheerier dispositions earlier in life had higher income levels and less unemployment when they were assessed 19 years later.

3.1   Finding Happiness Through Our Connections With Others

social support

The experience of having positive and supportive social relationships with others.

Happiness is determined in part by genetic factors, such that some people are naturally happier than others (Braungart, Plomin, DeFries, & Fulker, 1992; Lykken, 2000),[74] but also in part by the situations that we create for ourselves. Psychologists have studied hundreds of variables that influence happiness, but there is one that is by far the most important. People who report that they *have positive social relationships with others*—the perception of **social support**—also report being happier than those who report having less social support (Diener, Suh, Lucas, & Smith, 1999; Diener, Tamir, & Scollon, 2006).[75] Married people report being happier than unmarried people (Pew, 2006),[76] and people who are connected with and accepted by others suffer less depression, higher self-esteem, and less social anxiety and jealousy than those who feel more isolated and rejected (Leary, 1990).[77]

Social support also helps us better cope with stressors. Koopman, Hermanson, Diamond, Angell, and Spiegel (1998)[78] found that women who reported higher social support experienced less depression when adjusting to a diagnosis of cancer, and Ashton et al. (2005)[79] found a similar buffering effect of social support for AIDS patients. People with social support are less depressed overall, recover faster from negative events, and are less likely to commit suicide (Au, Lau, & Lee, 2009; Bertera, 2007; Compton, Thompson, & Kaslow, 2005; Skärsäter, Langius, Ågren, Häagström, & Dencker, 2005).[80]

Social support buffers us against stress in several ways. For one, having people we can trust and rely on helps us directly by allowing us to share favors when we need them. These are the *direct effects* of social support. But having people around us also makes us feel good about ourselves. These are the *appreciation effects* of social support. Gençöz and Özlale (2004)[81] found that students with more friends felt less stress and reported that their friends helped them, but they also reported that having friends made them feel better about themselves. Again, you can see that the tend-and-befriend response, so often used by women, is an important and effective way to reduce stress.

3.2   What Makes Us Happy?

One difficulty that people face when trying to improve their happiness is that they may not always know what will make them happy. As one example, many of us think that if we just had more money we would be happier. While it is true that we do need money to afford food and adequate shelter for ourselves and our families, after this minimum level of wealth is reached, more money does not generally buy more happiness (Easterlin, 2005).[82] For instance, as you can see in Figure 10.11, even though income and material success has improved dramatically in many countries over the past decades, happiness has not. Despite tremendous economic growth in France, Japan, and the United States between 1946 to 1990, there was no increase in reports of well-being by the citizens of these countries. Americans today have about three times the buying power they had in the 1950s, and yet overall happiness has not increased. The problem seems to be that we never seem to have enough money to make us "really" happy. Csikszentmihalyi (1999)[83] reported that people who earned $30,000 per year felt that they would be happier if they made $50,000 per year, but that people who earned $100,000 per year said that they would need $250,000 per year to make them happy.

FIGURE 10.11 Income and Happiness

Although personal income keeps rising, happiness does not.

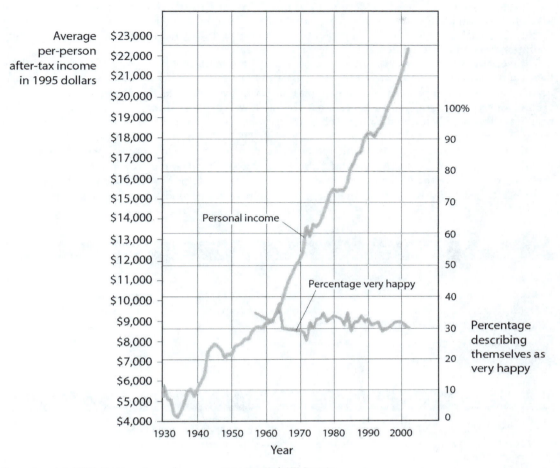

Source: Layard, R. (2005). Happiness: Lessons from a new science. New York, NY: Penguin.

These findings might lead us to conclude that we don't always know what does or what might make us happy, and this seems to be at least partially true. For instance, Jean Twenge and her colleagues (Twenge, Campbell & Foster, 2003)[84] have found in several studies that although people with children frequently claim that having children makes them happy, couples who do not have children actually report being happier than those who do.

Psychologists have found that people's ability to predict their future emotional states is not very accurate (Wilson & Gilbert, 2005).[85] For one, people overestimate their emotional reactions to events. Although people think that positive and negative events that might occur to them will make a huge difference in their lives, and although these changes do make at least some difference in life satisfaction, they tend to be less influential than we think they are going to be. Positive events tend to make us feel good, but their effects wear off pretty quickly, and the same is true for negative events. For instance, Brickman, Coates, and Janoff-Bulman (1978)[86] interviewed people who had won more than $50,000 in a lottery and found that they were not happier than they had been in the past, and were also not happier than a control group of similar people who had not won the lottery. On the other hand, the researchers found that individuals who were paralyzed as a result of accidents were not as unhappy as might be expected.

How can this possibly be? There are several reasons. For one, people are resilient; they bring their coping skills to play when negative events occur, and this makes them feel better. Secondly, most people do not continually experience very positive, or very negative, affect over a long period of time, but rather adapt to their current circumstances. Just as we enjoy the second chocolate bar we eat less than we enjoy the first, as we experience more and more positive outcomes in our daily lives we habituate to them and our life satisfaction returns to a more moderate level (Small, Zatorre, Dagher, Evans, & Jones-Gotman, 2001).[87]

Another reason that we may mispredict our happiness is that our social comparisons change when our own status changes as a result of new events. People who are wealthy compare themselves to other wealthy people, people who are poor tend to compare with other poor people, and people who are ill tend to compare with other ill people, When our comparisons change, our happiness levels are correspondingly influenced. And when people are asked to predict their future emotions, they may focus only on the positive or negative event they are asked about, and forget about all the other things that won't change. Wilson, Wheatley, Meyers, Gilbert, and Axsom (2000)[88] found that when people were asked to focus on all the more regular things that they will still be doing in the future (working, going to church, socializing with family and friends, and so forth), their predictions about how something really good or bad would influence them were less extreme.

If pleasure is fleeting, at least misery shares some of the same quality. We might think we can't be happy if something terrible, such as the loss of a partner or child, were to happen to us, but after a period of adjustment most people find that happiness levels return to prior levels (Bonnano et al., 2002).[89] Health concerns tend to put a damper on our feeling of well-being, and those with a serious disability or illness show slightly lowered mood levels. But even when health is compromised, levels of misery are lower than most people expect (Lucas, 2007; Riis et al., 2005).[90] For instance, although disabled individuals have more concern about health, safety, and acceptance in the community, they still experience overall positive happiness levels (Marinić & Brkljačić, 2008).[91] Taken together, it has been estimated that our wealth, health, and life circumstances account for only 15% to 20% of life satisfaction scores (Argyle, 1999).[92] Clearly the main ingredient in happiness lies beyond, or perhaps beneath, external factors.

KEY TAKEAWAYS

- Positive thinking can be beneficial to our health.
- Optimism, self-efficacy, and hardiness all relate to positive health outcomes.
- Happiness is determined in part by genetic factors, but also by the experience of social support.
- People may not always know what will make them happy.
- Material wealth plays only a small role in determining happiness.

EXERCISES AND CRITICAL THINKING

1. Are you a happy person? Can you think of ways to increase your positive emotions?
2. Do you know what will make you happy? Do you believe that material wealth is not as important as you might have thought it would be?

4. TWO FUNDAMENTAL HUMAN MOTIVATIONS: EATING AND MATING

LEARNING OBJECTIVES

1. **Understand the biological and social responses that underlie eating behavior.**
2. **Understand the psychological and physiological responses that underlie sexual behavior.**

4.1 Eating: Healthy Choices Make Healthy Lives

Along with the need to drink fresh water, which humans can normally attain in all except the most extreme situations, the need for food is the most fundamental and important human need. More than 1 in 10 U.S. households contain people who live without enough nourishing food, and this lack of proper nourishment has profound effects on their abilities to create effective lives (Hunger Notes, n.d.).[93] When people are extremely hungry, their motivation to attain food completely changes their behavior. Hungry people become listless and apathetic to save energy and then become completely obsessed with food. Ancel Keys and his colleagues (Keys, Brožek, Henschel, Mickelsen, & Taylor, 1950)[94] found that volunteers who were placed on severely reduced-calorie diets lost all interest in sex and social activities, becoming preoccupied with food.

Like most interesting psychological phenomena, the simple behavior of eating has both biological and social determinants (Figure 10.12). Biologically, hunger is controlled by the interactions among complex pathways in the nervous system and a variety of hormonal and chemical systems in the brain and body. The stomach is of course important. We feel more hungry when our stomach is empty than when it is full. But we can also feel hunger even without input from the stomach. Two areas of the hypothalamus are known to be particularly important in eating. The lateral part of the hypothalamus responds primarily to cues to start eating, whereas the ventromedial part of the hypothalamus primarily responds to cues to stop eating. If the lateral part of the hypothalamus is damaged, the animal will not eat even if food is present, whereas if the ventromedial part of the hypothalamus is damaged, the animal will eat until it is obese (Wolf & Miller, 1964).[95]

FIGURE 10.12 Biological, Psychological, and Social-Cultural Contributors to Eating

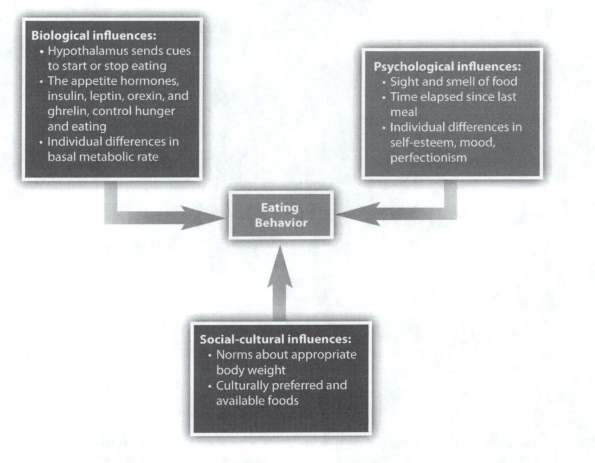

Hunger is also determined by hormone levels (Figure 10.13). *Glucose* is the main sugar that the body uses for energy, and the brain monitors blood glucose levels to determine hunger. Glucose levels in the bloodstream are regulated by *insulin*, a hormone secreted by the pancreas gland. When insulin is low, glucose is not taken up by body cells, and the body begins to use fat as an energy source. Eating and appetite are also influenced by other hormones, including *orexin*, *ghrelin*, and *leptin* (Brennan & Mantzoros, 2006; Nakazato et al., 2001).[96]

FIGURE 10.13 Eating Is Influenced by the Appetite Hormones

Insulin, secreted by the pancreas, controls blood glucose; leptin, secreted by fat cells, monitors energy levels; orexin, secreted by the hypothalamus, triggers hunger; ghrelin, secreted by an empty stomach, increases food intake.

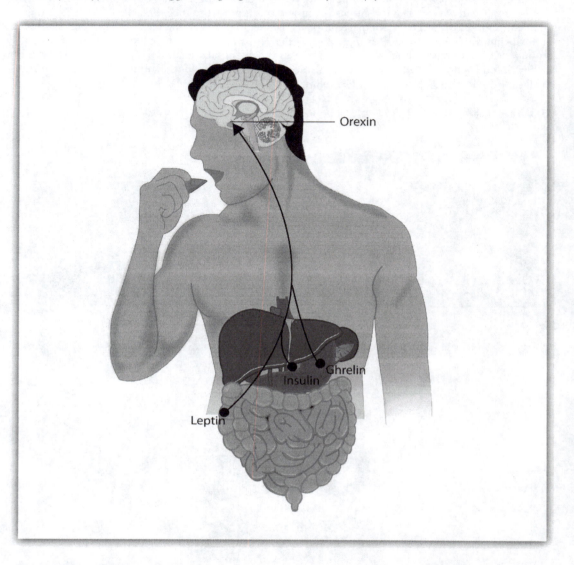

basal metabolic rate

The amount of energy expended while at rest, which influences one's weight.

Normally the interaction of the various systems that determine hunger creates a balance or *homeostasis* in which we eat when we are hungry and stop eating when we feel full. But homeostasis varies among people; some people simply weigh more than others, and there is little they can do to change their fundamental weight. Weight is determined in large part by the **basal metabolic rate**, *the amount of energy expended while at rest*. Each person's basal metabolic rate is different, due to his or her unique physical makeup and physical behavior. A naturally occurring low metabolic rate, which is determined entirely by genetics, makes weight management a very difficult undertaking for many people.

How we eat is also influenced by our environment. When researchers rigged clocks to move faster, people got hungrier and ate more, as if they thought they must be hungry again because so much time had passed since they last ate (Schachter, 1968).[97] And if we forget that we have already eaten, we are likely to eat again even if we are not actually hungry (Rozin, Dow, Moscovitch, & Rajaram, 1998).[98]

Cultural norms about appropriate weights also influence eating behaviors. Current norms for women in Western societies are based on a very thin body ideal, emphasized by television and movie actresses, models, and even children's dolls, such as the ever-popular Barbie. These norms for excessive thinness are very difficult for most women to attain: Barbie's measurements, if translated to human proportions, would be about 36 in.-18 in.-33 in. at bust-waist-hips, measurements that are attained by less than 1 in 100,000 women (Norton, Olds, Olive, & Dank, 1996).[99] Many women idealize being thin and yet are unable to reach the standard that they prefer.

Eating Disorders

In some cases, the desire to be thin can lead to eating disorders, which are estimated to affect about 1 million males and 10 million females the United States alone (Hoek & van Hoeken, 2003; Patrick, 2002).[100] **Anorexia nervosa** is *an eating disorder characterized by extremely low body weight, distorted body image, and an obsessive fear of gaining weight.* Nine out of 10 sufferers are women. Anorexia begins with a severe weight loss diet and develops into a preoccupation with food and dieting.

Bulimia nervosa is *an eating disorder characterized by binge eating followed by purging.* Bulimia nervosa begins after the dieter has broken a diet and gorged. Bulimia involves repeated episodes of overeating, followed by vomiting, laxative use, fasting, or excessive exercise. It is most common in women in their late teens or early 20s, and it is often accompanied by depression and anxiety, particularly around the time of the binging. The cycle in which the person eats to feel better, but then after eating becomes concerned about weight gain and purges, repeats itself over and over again, often with major psychological and physical results.

Eating disorders are in part heritable (Klump, Burt, McGue, & Iacono, 2007),[101] and it is not impossible that at least some have been selected through their evolutionary significance in coping with food shortages (Guisinger, 2008).[102] Eating disorders are also related psychological causes, including low self-esteem, perfectionism, and the perception that one's body weight is too high (Vohs et al., 2001),[103] as well as to cultural norms about body weight and eating (Crandall, 1988).[104] Because eating disorders can create profound negative health outcomes, including death, people who suffer from them should seek treatment. This treatment is often quite effective.

Obesity

Although some people eat too little, eating too much is also a major problem. **Obesity** is *a medical condition in which so much excess body fat has accumulated in the body that it begins to have an adverse impact on health.* In addition to causing people to be stereotyped and treated less positively by others (Crandall, Merman, & Hebl, 2009),[105] uncontrolled obesity leads to health problems including cardiovascular disease, diabetes, sleep apnea, arthritis, Alzheimer's disease, and some types of cancer (Gustafson, Rothenberg, Blennow, Steen, & Skoog, 2003).[106] Obesity also reduces life expectancy (Haslam & James, 2005).[107]

Obesity is determined by calculating the *body mass index (BMI)*, a measurement that compares one's weight and height. People are defined as overweight when their BMI is greater than 25 kg/m^2 and as obese when it is greater than 30 kg/m^2. If you know your height and weight, you can go to http://www.nhlbisupport.com/bmi to calculate your BMI.

Obesity is a leading cause of death worldwide. Its prevalence is rapidly increasing, and it is one of the most serious public health problems of the 21st century. Although obesity is caused in part by genetics, it is increased by overeating and a lack of physical activity (Nestle & Jacobson, 2000; James, 2008).[108]

There are really only two approaches to controlling weight: eat less and exercise more. Dieting is difficult for anyone, but it is particularly difficult for people with slow basal metabolic rates, who must cope with severe hunger to lose weight. Although most weight loss can be maintained for about a year, very few people are able to maintain substantial weight loss through dieting alone for more than three years (Miller, 1999).[109] Substantial weight loss of more than 50 pounds is typically seen only when weight loss surgery has been performed (Douketis, Macie, Thabane, & Williamson, 2005).[110] Weight loss surgery reduces stomach volume or bowel length, leading to earlier satiation and reduced ability to absorb nutrients from food.

Although dieting alone does not produce a great deal of weight loss over time, its effects are substantially improved when it is accompanied by more physical activity. People who exercise regularly, and particularly those who combine exercise with dieting, are less likely to be obese (Borer, 2008).[111] Exercise not only improves our waistline but also makes us healthier overall. Exercise increases cardiovascular capacity, lowers blood pressure, and helps improve diabetes, joint flexibility, and muscle strength (American Heart Association, 1998).[112] Exercise also slows the cognitive impairments that are associated with aging (Kramer, Erickson, & Colcombe, 2006).[113]

Because the costs of exercise are immediate but the benefits are long-term, it may be difficult for people who do not exercise to get started. It is important to make a regular schedule, to work exercise into one's daily activities, and to view exercise not as a cost but as an opportunity to improve oneself (Schomer & Drake, 2001).[114] Exercising is more fun when it is done in groups, so team exercise is recommended (Kirchhoff, Elliott, Schlichting, & Chin, 2008).[115]

A recent report found that only about one-half of Americans perform the 30 minutes of exercise 5 times a week that the Centers for Disease Control and Prevention suggests as the minimum healthy

anorexia nervosa

An eating disorder characterized by extremely low body weight, distorted body image, and an obsessive fear of gaining weight.

bulimia nervosa

An eating disorder characterized by binge eating followed by purging.

FIGURE 10.14

Eating disorders can lead people to be either too fat or too thin. Both are unhealthy.

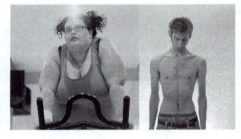

obesity

A medical condition in which so much excess body fat has accumulated in the body that it begins to have an adverse impact on health.

amount (Centers for Disease Control and Prevention, 2007).[116] As for the other half of Americans, they most likely are listening to the guidelines, but they are unable to stick to the regimen. Almost half of the people who start an exercise regimen give it up by the 6-month mark (American Heart Association, 1998).[117] This is a problem, given that exercise has long-term benefits only if it is continued.

4.2 Sex: The Most Important Human Behavior

Perhaps the most important aspect of human experience is the process of reproduction. Without it, none of us would be here. Successful reproduction in humans involves the coordination of a wide variety of behaviors, including courtship, sex, household arrangements, parenting, and child care.

The Experience of Sex

sexual response cycle

The biological sexual response in humans.

The sexual drive, with its reward of intense pleasure in orgasm, is highly motivating. The biology of the sexual response was studied in detail by Masters and Johnson (1966),[118] who monitored or filmed more than 700 men and women while they masturbated or had intercourse. Masters and Johnson found that the **sexual response cycle**—*the biological sexual response in humans*—was very similar in men and women, and consisted of four stages:

1. **Excitement**. The genital areas become engorged with blood. Women's breasts and nipples may enlarge and the vagina expands and secretes lubricant.

2. **Plateau**. Breathing, pulse, and blood pressure increase as orgasm feels imminent. The penis becomes fully enlarged. Vaginal secretions continue and the clitoris may retract.

3. **Orgasm**. Muscular contractions occur throughout the body, but particularly in the genitals. The spasmodic ejaculations of sperm are similar to the spasmodic contractions of vaginal walls, and the experience of orgasm is similar for men and women. The woman's orgasm helps position the uterus to draw sperm inward (Thornhill & Gangestad, 1995).[119]

4. **Resolution**. After orgasm the body gradually returns to its prearoused state. After one orgasm, men typically experience a *refractory period*, in which they are incapable of reaching another orgasm for several minutes, hours, or even longer. Women may achieve several orgasms before entering the resolution stage.

The sexual response cycle and sexual desire are regulated by the sex hormones *estrogen* in women and *testosterone* in both women and in men. Although the hormones are secreted by the ovaries and testes, it is the hypothalamus and the pituitary glands that control the process. Estrogen levels in women vary across the menstrual cycle, peaking during ovulation (Pillsworth, Haselton, & Buss, 2004).[120] Women are more interested in having sex during ovulation but can experience high levels of sexual arousal throughout the menstrual cycle.

In men, testosterone is essential to maintain sexual desire and to sustain an erection, and testosterone injections can increase sexual interest and performance (Aversa et al., 2000; Jockenhövel et al., 2009).[121] Testosterone is also important in the female sex cycle. Women who are experiencing menopause may develop a loss of interest in sex, but this interest may be rekindled through estrogen and testosterone replacement treatments (Meston & Frohlich, 2000).[122]

Although their biological determinants and experiences of sex are similar, men and women differ substantially in their overall interest in sex, the frequency of their sexual activities, and the mates they are most interested in. Men show a more consistent interest in sex, whereas the sexual desires of women are more likely to vary over time (Baumeister, 2000).[123] Men fantasize about sex more often than women, and their fantasies are more physical and less intimate (Leitenberg & Henning, 1995).[124] Men are also more willing to have casual sex than are women, and their standards for sex partners is lower (Petersen & Hyde, 2010; Saad, Eba, & Sejean, 2009).[125]

Gender differences in sexual interest probably occur in part as a result of the evolutionary predispositions of men and women, and this interpretation is bolstered by the finding that gender differences in sexual interest are observed cross-culturally (Buss, 1989).[126] Evolutionarily, women should be more selective than men in their choices of sex partners because they must invest more time in bearing and nurturing their children than do men (most men do help out, of course, but women simply do more [Buss & Kenrick, 1998]).[127] Because they do not need to invest a lot of time in child rearing, men may be evolutionarily predisposed to be more willing and desiring of having sex with many different partners and may be less selective in their choice of mates. Women, on the other hand, because they must invest substantial effort in raising each child, should be more selective.

The Many Varieties of Sexual Behavior

Sex researchers have found that sexual behavior varies widely, not only between men and women but within each sex (Kinsey, Pomeroy, & Martin, 1948/1998; Kinsey, 1953/1998).[128] About a quarter of women report having a low sexual desire, and about 1% of people report feeling no sexual attraction whatsoever (Bogaert, 2004; Feldhaus-Dahir, 2009; West et al., 2008).[129] There are also people who experience hyperactive sexual drives. For about 3% to 6% of the population (mainly men), the sex drive is so strong that it dominates life experience and may lead to *hyperactive sexual desire disorder* (Kingston & Firestone, 2008).[130]

There is also variety in **sexual orientation**, which is *the direction of our sexual desire toward people of the opposite sex, people of the same sex, or people of both sexes.* The vast majority of human beings have a heterosexual orientation—their sexual desire is focused toward members of the opposite sex. A smaller minority is primarily homosexual (i.e., they have sexual desire for members of their own sex). Between 3% and 4% of men are gay, and between 1% and 2% of women are lesbian. Another 1% of the population reports being bisexual (having desires for both sexes). The love and sexual lives of homosexuals are little different from those of heterosexuals, except where their behaviors are constrained by cultural norms and local laws. As with heterosexuals, some gays and lesbians are celibate, some are promiscuous, but most are in committed, long-term relationships (Laumann, Gagnon, Michael, & Michaels, 1994).[131]

Although homosexuality has been practiced as long as records of human behavior have been kept, and occurs in many animals at least as frequently as it does in humans, cultures nevertheless vary substantially in their attitudes toward it. In Western societies such as the United States and Europe, attitudes are becoming progressively more tolerant of homosexuality, but it remains unacceptable in many other parts of the world. The American Psychiatric Association no longer considers homosexuality to be a "mental illness," although it did so until 1973. Because prejudice against gays and lesbians can lead to experiences of ostracism, depression, and even suicide (Kulkin, Chauvin, & Percle, 2000),[132] these improved attitudes can benefit the everyday lives of gays, lesbians, and bisexuals.

Whether sexual orientation is driven more by nature or by nurture has received a great deal of research attention, and research has found that sexual orientation is primarily biological (Mustanski, Chivers, & Bailey, 2002).[133] Areas of the hypothalamus are different in homosexual men, as well as in animals with homosexual tendencies, than they are in heterosexual members of the species, and these differences are in directions such that gay men are more similar to women than are straight men (Gladue, 1994; Lasco, Jordan, Edgar, Petito, & Byrne, 2002; Rahman & Wilson, 2003).[134] Twin studies also support the idea that there is a genetic component to sexual orientation. Among male identical twins, 52% of those with a gay brother also reported homosexuality, whereas the rate in fraternal twins was just 22% (Bailey et al., 1999; Pillard & Bailey, 1998).[135] There is also evidence that sexual orientation is influenced by exposure and responses to sex hormones (Hershberger & Segal, 2004; Williams & Pepitone, 2000).[136]

sexual orientation

The direction of our sexual desire, toward people of the opposite sex, people of the same sex, or people of both sexes.

Psychology in Everyday Life: Regulating Emotions to Improve Our Health

Although smoking cigarettes, drinking alcohol, using recreational drugs, engaging in unsafe sex, and eating too much may produce enjoyable positive emotions in the short term, they are some of the leading causes of negative health outcomes and even death in the long term (Mokdad, Marks, Stroup, & Gerberding, 2004).[137] To avoid these negative outcomes, we must use our cognitive resources to plan, guide, and restrain our behaviors. And we (like Captain Sullenberger) can also use our emotion regulation skills to help us do better.

Even in an age where the addictive and detrimental health effects of cigarette smoking are well understood, more than 60% of children try smoking before they are 18 years old, and more than half who have smoked have tried and failed to quit (Fryar, Merino, Hirsch, & Porter, 2009).[138] Although smoking is depicted in movies as sexy and alluring, it is highly addictive and probably the most dangerous thing we can do to our body. Poor diet and physical inactivity combine to make up the second greatest threat to our health. But we can improve our diet by eating more natural and less processed food, and by monitoring our food intake. And we can start and maintain an exercise program. Exercise keeps us happier, improves fitness, and leads to better health and lower mortality (Fogelholm, 2010; Galper, Trivedi, Barlow, Dunn, & Kampert, 2006; Hassmén, Koivula, & Uutela, 2000).[139] And exercise also has a variety of positive influences on our cognitive processes, including academic performance (Hillman, Erickson, & Kramer, 2008).[140]

Alcohol abuse, and particularly binge drinking (i.e., having five or more drinks in one sitting), is often the norm among high school and college students, but it has severe negative health consequences. Bingeing leads to deaths from car crashes, drowning, falls, gunshots, and alcohol poisoning (Valencia-Martín, Galán, & Rodríguez-Artalejo, 2008).[141] Binge-drinking students are also more likely to be involved in other risky behaviors, such as smoking, drug use, dating violence, or attempted suicide (Miller, Naimi, Brewer, & Jones, 2007).[142] Binge drinking may also damage neural pathways in the brain (McQueeny et al., 2009)[143] and lead to lifelong alcohol abuse and dependency (Kim et al., 2008).[144] Illicit drug use has also been increasing and is linked to the spread of infectious diseases such as HIV, hepatitis B, and hepatitis C (Monteiro, 2001).[145]

Some teens abstain from sex entirely, particularly those who are very religious, but most experiment with it. About half of U.S. children under 18 report having had intercourse, a rate much higher than in other parts of the world. Although sex is fun, it can also kill us if we are not careful. Sexual activity can lead to guilt about having engaged in the act itself, and may also lead to unwanted pregnancies and sexually transmitted infections (STIs), including HIV infection. Alcohol consumption also leads to risky sexual behavior. Sex partners who have been drinking are less likely to practice safe sex and have an increased risk of STIs, including HIV infection (Hutton, McCaul, Santora, & Erbelding 2008; Raj et al., 2009).[146]

It takes some work to improve and maintain our health and happiness, and our desire for the positive emotional experiences that come from engaging in dangerous behaviors can get in the way of this work. But being aware of the dangers, working to control our emotions, and using our resources to engage in healthy behaviors and avoid unhealthy ones are the best things we can do for ourselves.

KEY TAKEAWAYS

- Biologically, hunger is controlled by the interactions among complex pathways in the nervous system and a variety of hormonal and chemical systems in the brain and body.
- How we eat is also influenced by our environment, including social norms about appropriate body size.
- Homeostasis varies among people and is determined by the basal metabolic rate. Low metabolic rates, which are determined entirely by genetics, make weight management a very difficult undertaking for many people.
- Eating disorders, including anorexia nervosa and bulimia nervosa, affect more than 10 million people (mostly women) in the United States alone.
- Obesity is a medical condition in which so much excess body fat has accumulated in the body that it begins to have an adverse impact on health. Uncontrolled obesity leads to health problems including cardiovascular disease, diabetes, sleep apnea, arthritis, and some types of cancer.
- The two approaches to controlling weight are to eat less and exercise more.
- Sex drive is regulated by the sex hormones estrogen in women and testosterone in both women and men.
- Although their biological determinants and experiences of sex are similar, men and women differ substantially in their overall interest in sex, the frequency of their sexual activities, and the mates they are most interested in.
- Sexual behavior varies widely, not only between men and women but also within each sex.
- There is also variety in sexual orientation: toward people of the opposite sex, people of the same sex, or people of both sexes. The determinants of sexual orientation are primarily biological.
- We can outwit stress, obesity, and other health risks through appropriate healthy action.

EXERCISE AND CRITICAL THINKING

1. Consider your own eating and sex patterns. Are they healthy or unhealthy? What can you do to improve them?

5. CHAPTER SUMMARY

Affect guides behavior, helps us make decisions, and has a major impact on our mental and physical health. Affect is guided by arousal—our experiences of the bodily responses created by the sympathetic division of the autonomic nervous system.

Emotions are the mental and physiological feeling states that direct our attention and guide our behavior. The most fundamental emotions, known as the basic emotions, are those of anger, disgust, fear, happiness, sadness, and surprise. A variety of secondary emotions are determined by the process of cognitive appraisal. The distinction between the primary and the secondary emotions is paralleled by two brain pathways: a fast pathway and a slow pathway.

There are three primary theories of emotion, each supported by research evidence. The Cannon-Bard theory of emotion proposed that the experience of an emotion is accompanied by physiological arousal. The James-Lange theory of emotion proposes that our experience of an emotion is the result of the arousal that we experience. The two-factor theory of emotion asserts that the experience of emotion is determined by the intensity of the arousal we are experiencing, but that the cognitive appraisal of the situation determines what the emotion will be. When people incorrectly label the source of the arousal that they are experiencing, we say that they have misattributed their arousal.

We communicate and perceive emotion in part through nonverbal communication and through facial expressions. The facial feedback hypothesis proposes that we also experience emotion in part through our own facial expressions.

Stress refers to the physiological responses that occur when an organism fails to respond appropriately to emotional or physical threats. When it is extreme or prolonged, stress can create substantial health problems.

The general adaptation syndrome describes the three phases of physiological change that occur in response to long-term stress: alarm, resistance, and exhaustion. Stress creates a long-term negative effect on the body by activating the HPA axis, which produces the stress hormone cortisol. The HPA reactions to persistent stress lead to a weakening of the immune system. Chronic stress is also a major contributor to heart disease.

The stress that we experience in our everyday lives, including daily hassles, can be taxing. People who experience strong negative emotions as a result of these hassles exhibit more negative stress responses those who react in a less negative way.

On average, men are more likely than are women to respond to stress by activating the fight-or-flight response, whereas women are more likely to respond using the tend-and-befriend response.

Attempting to ignore or suppress our stressors is not effective, in part because it is difficult to do. It is healthier to let out the negative thoughts and feelings by expressing them, either to ourselves or to others. It is easier to respond to stress if we can interpret it in more positive ways—for instance, as a challenge rather than a threat.

The ability to successfully control our emotions is known as emotion regulation. Regulating emotions takes effort, but the ability to do so can have important positive health outcomes.

The best antidote for stress is to think positively, have fun, and enjoy the company of others. People who express optimism, self-efficacy, and hardiness cope better with stress and experience better health overall. Happiness is determined in part by genetic factors such that some people are naturally happier than others, but it is also facilitated by social support—our positive social relationships with others.

People do not often know what will make them happy. After a minimum level of wealth is reached, more money does not generally buy more happiness. Although people think that positive and negative events will make a huge difference in their lives, and although these changes do make at least some difference in life satisfaction, they tend to be less influential than we think they are going to be.

A motivation is a driving force that initiates and directs behavior. Motivations are often considered in psychology in terms of drives and goals, with the goal of maintaining homeostasis.

Eating is a primary motivation determined by hormonal and social factors. Cultural norms about appropriate weights influence eating behaviors. The desire to be thin can lead to eating disorders including anorexia nervosa and bulimia nervosa.

Uncontrolled obesity leads to health problems including cardiovascular disease, diabetes, sleep apnea, arthritis, Alzheimer's disease, and some types of cancer. It is a leading preventable cause of death worldwide. The two approaches to controlling weight are eating less and exercising more.

Sex is a fundamental motivation that involves the coordination of a wide variety of behaviors, including courtship, sex, household arrangements, parenting, and child care. The sexual response cycle is similar in men and women. The sex hormone testosterone is particularly important for sex drive, in both men and women.

Sexual behavior varies widely, not only between men and women but within each sex.

The vast majority of human beings have a heterosexual orientation, but a smaller minority is primarily homosexual or bisexual. The love and sexual lives of homosexuals and bisexual are little different from those of heterosexuals, except where their behaviors are constrained by cultural norms and local laws.

ENDNOTES

1. Levin, A. (2009, June 9). Experience averts tragedy in Hudson landing. *USA Today*. Retrieved from http://www.usatoday.com/news/nation/2009-06-08-hudson_N.htm; National Transportation Safety Board. (2009, June 9). Excerpts of Flight 1549 cockpit communications. *USA Today*. Retrieved from http://www.usatoday.com/news/nation/2009-06-09-hudson-cockpit-transcript_N.htm

2. Morsella, E., Bargh, J. A., & Gollwitzer, P. M. (2009). *Oxford handbook of human action*. New York, NY: Oxford University Press.

3. Lawrence, J. W., Carver, C. S., & Scheier, M. F. (2002). Velocity toward goal attainment in immediate experience as a determinant of affect. *Journal of Applied Social Psychology, 32*(4), 788–802.

4. Freud, S. (1922). The unconscious. *The Journal of Nervous and Mental Disease, 56*(3), 291; Hassin, R. R., Bargh, J. A., & Zimerman, S. (2009). Automatic and flexible: The case of nonconscious goal pursuit. *Social Cognition, 27*(1), 20–36; Williams, L. E., Bargh, J. A., Nocera, C. C., & Gray, J. R. (2009). The unconscious regulation of emotion: Nonconscious reappraisal goals modulate emotional reactivity. *Emotion, 9*(6), 847–854.

5. LeDoux, J. E. (2000). Emotion circuits in the brain. *Annual Review of Neuroscience, 23*, 155–184.

6. Ekman, P. (1992). Are there basic emotions? *Psychological Review, 99*(3), 550–553; Elfenbein, H. A., & Ambady, N. (2002). On the universality and cultural specificity of emotion recognition: A meta-analysis. *Psychological Bulletin, 128*, 203–23; Fridlund, A. J., Ekman, P., & Oster, H. (1987). Facial expressions of emotion. In A. Siegman & S. Feldstein (Eds.), *Nonverbal behavior and communication* (2nd ed., pp. 143–223). Hillsdale, NJ: Lawrence Erlbaum Associates.

7. Martin, L. L., & Tesser, A. (2006). Extending the goal progress theory of rumination: Goal reevaluation and growth. In L. J. Sanna & E. C. Chang (Eds.), *Judgments over time: The interplay of thoughts, feelings, and behaviors* (pp. 145–162). New York, NY: Oxford University Press.

8. Damasio, A. (2000). *The feeling of what happens: Body and emotion in the making of consciousness*. New York, NY: Mariner Books; LeDoux, J. E. (2000). Emotion circuits in the brain. *Annual Review of Neuroscience, 23*, 155–184; Ochsner, K. N., Bunge, S. A., Gross, J. J., & Gabrieli, J. D. E. (2002). Rethinking feelings: An fMRI study of the cognitive regulation of emotion. *Journal of Cognitive Neuroscience, 14*(8), 1215–1229.

9. Damasio, A. R. (1994). *Descartes' error: Emotion, reason, and the human brain*. New York, NY: Grosset/Putnam; Dijksterhuis, A., Bos, M. W., Nordgren, L. F., & van Baaren, R. B. (2006). On making the right choice: The deliberation-without-attention effect. *Science, 311*(5763), 1005–1007; Nordgren, L. F., & Dijksterhuis, A. P. (2009). The devil is in the deliberation: Thinking too much reduces preference consistency. *Journal of Consumer Research, 36*(1), 39–46; Wilson, T. D., & Schooler, J. W. (1991). Thinking too much: Introspection can reduce the quality of preferences and decisions. *Journal of Personality and Social Psychology, 60*(2), 181–192.

10. James, W. (1884). What is an emotion? *Mind, 9*(34), 188–205.

11. LeDoux, J. E. (2000). Emotion circuits in the brain. *Annual Review of Neuroscience, 23*, 155–184.

12. Hohmann, G. W. (1966). Some effects of spinal cord lesions on experienced emotional feelings. *Psychophysiology, 3*(2), 143–156.

13. Whalen, P. J., Shin, L. M., McInerney, S. C., Fischer, H., Wright, C. I., & Rauch, S. L. (2001). A functional MRI study of human amygdala responses to facial expressions of fear versus anger. *Emotion, 1*(1), 70–83; Witvliet, C. V., & Vrana, S. R. (1995). Psychophysiological responses as indices of affective dimensions. *Psychophysiology, 32*(5), 436–443.

14. Leary, M. R., Britt, T. W., Cutlip, W. D., & Templeton, J. L. (1992). Social blushing. *Psychological Bulletin, 112*(3), 446–460.

15. Oatley, K., Keltner, D., & Jenkins, J. M. (2006). *Understanding emotions* (2nd ed.). Malden, MA: Blackwell.

16. Schachter, S., & Singer, J. (1962). Cognitive, social, and physiological determinants of emotional state. *Psychological Review, 69*, 379–399.

17. Dutton, D., & Aron, A. (1974). Some evidence for heightened sexual attraction under conditions of high anxiety. *Journal of Personality and Social Psychology, 30*, 510–517.

18. Schachter, S., & Singer, J. E. (1962). Cognitive, social and physiological determinants of emotional state. *Psychological Review, 69*, 379–399.

19. Schachter, S., & Singer, J. E. (1962). Cognitive, social and physiological determinants of emotional state. *Psychological Review, 69*, 379–399.

20. Ambady, N., & Weisbuch, M. (2010). Nonverbal behavior. In S. T. Fiske, D. T. Gilbert, & G. Lindzey (Eds.), *Handbook of social psychology* (5th ed., Vol. 1, pp. 464–497). Hoboken, NJ: John Wiley & Sons; Andersen, P. (2007). *Nonverbal communication: Forms and functions* (2nd ed.). Long Grove, IL: Waveland Press.

21. Strack, F., Martin, L., & Stepper, S. (1988). Inhibiting and facilitating conditions of the human smile: A nonobtrusive test of the facial feedback hypothesis. *Journal of Personality and Social Psychology, 54*(5), 768–777. doi:10.1037/0022-3514.54.5.768

22. Stepper, S., & Strack, F. (1993). Proprioceptive determinants of emotional and nonemotional feelings. *Journal of Personality and Social Psychology, 64*(2), 211–220.

23. Selye, H. (1956). *The stress of life*. New York, NY: McGraw-Hill.

24. American Medical Association. (2009). *Three-fold heart attack increase in Hurricane Katrina survivors*. Retrieved from http://www.ama-assn.org/ama/pub/news/news/heart-attack-katrina-survivors.shtml

25. Pulcino, T., Galea, S., Ahern, J., Resnick, H., Foley, M., & Vlahov, D. (2003). Posttraumatic stress in women after the September 11 terrorist attacks in New York City. *Journal of Women's Health, 12*(8), 809–820.

26. Seyle, Hans (1936). A syndrome produced by diverse nocuous agents. *Nature, 138*, 32. Retrieved from http://neuro.psychiatryonline.org/cgi/reprint/10/2/230a.pdf; Seyle, H. (1974). Forty years of stress research: Principal remaining problems and misconceptions. *Canadian Medical Association Journal, 115*(1), 53–56; Seyle, H. (1982). The nature of stress. Retrieved from http://www.icnr.com/articles/thenatureofstress.html

27. Rodrigues, S. M., LeDoux, J. E., & Sapolsky, R. M. (2009). The influence of stress hormones on fear circuitry. *Annual Review of Neuroscience, 32*, 289–313.

28. Cohen, S., & Herbert, T. B. (1996). Health psychology: Psychological factors and physical disease from the perspective of human psychoneuroimmunology. *Annual Review of Psychology, 47*, 113–142; Faulkner, S., & Smith, A. (2009). A prospective diary study of the role of psychological stress and negative mood in the recurrence of herpes simplex virus (HSV1). *Stress and Health: Journal of the International Society for the Investigation of Stress, 25*(2), 179–187; Miller, G., Chen, E., & Cole, S. W. (2009). Health psychology: Developing biologically plausible models linking the social world and physical health. *Annual Review of Psychology, 60*, 501–524; Uchino, B. N., Smith, T. W., Holt-Lunstad, J., Campo, R., & Reblin, M. (2007). Stress and illness. In J. T. Cacioppo, L. G. Tassinary, & G. G. Berntson (Eds.), *Handbook of psychophysiology* (3rd ed., pp. 608–632). New York, NY: Cambridge University Press.

29. Epel, E., Lin, J., Wilhelm, F., Wolkowitz, O., Cawthon, R., Adler, N.,…Blackburn, E. H. (2006). Cell aging in relation to stress arousal and cardiovascular disease risk factors. *Psychoneuroendocrinology, 31*(3), 277–287.

30. Kiecolt-Glaser, J. K., McGuire, L., Robles, T. F., & Glaser, R. (2002). Psychoneuroimmunology: Psychological influences on immune function and health. *Journal of Consulting & Clinical Psychology, 70*(3), 537–547; Wells, W. (2006). How chronic stress exacerbates cancer. *Journal of Cell Biology, 174*(4), 476.

31. Krantz, D. S., & McCeney, M. K. (2002). Effects of psychological and social factors on organic disease: A critical assessment of research on coronary heart disease. *Annual Review of Psychology, 53*, 341–369.

32. Dekker, M., Koper, J., van Aken, M., Pols, H., Hofman, A., de Jong, F.,…Tiemeier, H. (2008). Salivary cortisol is related to atherosclerosis of carotid arteries. *Journal of Clinical Endocrinology & Metabolism, 93*(10), 3741.

33. Holmes, T. H., & Rahe, R. H. (1967). The social readjustment rating scale. *Journal of Psychosomatic Research, 11*, 213–218.

34. Rahe, R. H., Mahan, J., Arthur, R. J., & Gunderson, E. K. E. (1970). The epidemiology of illness in naval environments: I. Illness types, distribution, severities and relationships to life change. *Military Medicine, 135*, 443–452.

35. Hutchinson, J. G., & Williams, P. G. (2007). Neuroticism, daily hassles, and depressive symptoms: An examination of moderating and mediating effects. *Personality and Individual Differences, 42*(7), 1367–1378.

36. Fiksenbaum, L. M., Greenglass, E. R., & Eaton, J. (2006). Perceived social support, hassles, and coping among the elderly. *Journal of Applied Gerontology, 25*(1), 17–30.

37. Glaser, R. (1985). Stress-related impairments in cellular immunity. *Psychiatry Research, 16*(3), 233–239.

38. Cacioppo, J. T., Berntson, G. G., Malarkey, W. B., Kiecolt-Glaser, J. K., Sheridan, J. F., Poehlmann, K. M.,…Glaser, R. (1998). Autonomic, neuroendocrine, and immune responses to psychological stress: The reactivity hypothesis. In *Annals of the New York Academy of Sciences: Neuroimmunomodulation: Molecular aspects, integrative systems, and clinical advances* (Vol. 840, pp. 664–673). New York, NY: New York Academy of Sciences.

39. Friedman, M., & Rosenman, R. H. (1974). *Type A behavior and your heart*. New York, NY: Knopf.

40. McIntyre, K., Korn, J., & Matsuo, H. (2008). Sweating the small stuff: How different types of hassles result in the experience of stress. *Stress & Health: Journal of the International Society for the Investigation of Stress, 24*(5), 383–392. doi:10.1002/smi.1190; Suls, J., & Bunde, J. (2005). Anger, anxiety, and depression as risk factors for cardiovascular disease: The problems and implications of overlapping affective dispositions. *Psychological Bulletin, 131*(2), 260–300.

41. Williams, R. B. (2001). Hostility: Effects on health and the potential for successful behavioral approaches to prevention and treatment. In A. Baum, T. A. Revenson, & J. E. Singer (Eds.), *Handbook of health psychology*. Mahwah, NJ: Lawrence Erlbaum Associates.

42. Taylor, S. E., Klein, L. C., Lewis, B. P., Gruenewald, T. L., Gurung, R. A. R., & Updegraff, J. A. (2000). Biobehavioral responses to stress in females: Tend-and-befriend, not fight-or-flight. *Psychological Review, 107*(3), 411–429.

43. Gross, J. J., & Levenson, R. W. (1997). Hiding feelings: The acute effects of inhibiting negative and positive emotion. *Journal of Abnormal Psychology, 106*(1), 95–103.

44. Wegner, D. M., Schneider, D. J., Carter, S. R., & White, T. L. (1987). Paradoxical effects of thought suppression. *Journal of Personality and Social Psychology, 53*(1), 5–13.

45. Pennebaker, J. W., Colder, M., & Sharp, L. K. (1990). Accelerating the coping process. *Journal of Personality and Social Psychology, 58*(3), 528–537; Watson, D., & Pennebaker, J. W. (1989). Health complaints, stress, and distress: Exploring the central role of negative affectivity. *Psychological Review, 96*(2), 234–254.

46. Pennebaker, J. W., & Beall, S. K. (1986). Confronting a traumatic event: Toward an understanding of inhibition and disease. *Journal of Abnormal Psychology, 95*(3), 274–281.

47. Petrie, K. J., Fontanilla, I., Thomas, M. G., Booth, R. J., & Pennebaker, J. W. (2004). Effect of written emotional expression on immune function in patients with human immunodeficiency virus infection: A randomized trial. *Psychosomatic Medicine, 66*(2), 272–275.

48. Pennebaker, J. W., & Stone, L. D. (Eds.). (2004). *Translating traumatic experiences into language: Implications for child abuse and long-term health*. Washington, DC: American Psychological Association.

49. Kelsey, R. M., Blascovich, J., Tomaka, J., Leitten, C. L., Schneider, T. R., & Wiens, S. (1999). Cardiovascular reactivity and adaptation to recurrent psychological stress: Effects of prior task exposure. *Psychophysiology, 36*(6), 818–831.

50. Metcalfe, J., & Mischel, W. (1999). A hot/cool-system analysis of delay of gratification: Dynamics of willpower. *Psychological Review, 106*(1), 3–19; Strack, F., & Deutsch, R. (2007). The role of impulse in social behavior. In A. W. Kruglanski & E. T. Higgins (Eds.), *Social Psychology: Handbook of Basic Principles* (Vol. 2). New York, NY: Guilford Press.

51. Ayduk, O., Mendoza-Denton, R., Mischel, W., Downey, G., Peake, P. K., & Rodriguez, M. (2000). Regulating the interpersonal self: Strategic self-regulation for coping with rejection sensitivity. *Journal of Personality and Social Psychology, 79*(5), 776–792; Eigsti, I.-M., Zayas, V., Mischel, W., Shoda, Y., Ayduk, O., Dadlani, M. B.,...Casey, B. J. (2006). Predicting cognitive control from preschool to late adolescence and young adulthood. *Psychological Science, 17*(6), 478–484; Mischel, W., & Ayduk, O. (Eds.). (2004). *Willpower in a cognitive-affective processing system: The dynamics of delay of gratification*. New York, NY: Guilford Press.

52. Bizot, J.-C., Le Bihan, C., Peuch, A. J., Hamon, M., & Thiebot, M.-H. (1999). Serotonin and tolerance to delay of reward in rats. *Psychopharmacology, 146*(4), 400–412; Liu, Y. P., Wilkinson, L. S., & Robbins, T. W. (2004). Effects of acute and chronic buspirone on impulsive choice and efflux of 5-HT and dopamine in hippocampus, nucleus accumbens and prefrontal cortex. *Psychopharmacology, 173*(1–2), 175–185.

53. Asberg, M., Traskman, L., & Thoren, P. (1976). 5-HIAA in the cerebrospinal fluid: A biochemical suicide predictor? *Archives of General Psychiatry, 33*(10), 1193–1197.

54. Muraven, M., & Baumeister, R. F. (2000). Self-regulation and depletion of limited resources: Does self-control resemble a muscle? *Psychological Bulletin, 126*(2), 247–259.

55. Muraven, M., Tice, D. M., & Baumeister, R. F. (1998). Self-control as a limited resource: Regulatory depletion patterns. *Journal of Personality & Social Psychology, 74*(3), 774–789.

56. Vohs, K. D., & Heatherton, T. F. (2000). Self-regulatory failure: A resource-depletion approach. *Psychological Science, 11*(3), 249–254.

57. Baumeister, R. F., Gailliot, M., DeWall, C. N., & Oaten, M. (2006). Self-regulation and personality: How interventions increase regulatory success, and how depletion moderates the effects of traits on behavior. *Journal of Personality, 74*(6), 1773–1801; Baumeister, R. F., Schmeichel, B., & Vohs, K. D. (2007). Self-regulation and the executive function: The self as controlling agent. In A. W. Kruglanski & E. T. Higgins (Eds.), *Social psychology: Handbook of basic principles* (Vol. 2). New York, NY: Guilford Press; Oaten, M., & Cheng, K. (2006). Longitudinal gains in self-regulation from regular physical exercise. *British Journal of Health Psychology, 11*(4), 717–733.

58. Seligman, M. E. P., & Csikszentmihalyi, M. (2000). Positive psychology: An introduction. *American Psychologist, 55*(1), 5–14.

59. Carver, C. S., & Scheier, M. F. (2009). Optimism. In M. R. Leary & R. H. Hoyle (Eds.), *Handbook of individual differences in social behavior* (pp. 330–342). New York, NY: Guilford Press.

60. Thompson, S. C. (2009). The role of personal control in adaptive functioning. In S. J. Lopez & C. R. Snyder (Eds.), *Oxford handbook of positive psychology* (2nd ed., pp. 271–278). New York, NY: Oxford University Press.

61. Rodin, J. (1986). Aging and health: Effects of the sense of control. *Science, 233*(4770), 1271–1276.

62. Glass, D. C., Reim, B., & Singer, J. E. (1971). Behavioral consequences of adaptation to controllable and uncontrollable noise. *Journal of Experimental Social Psychology, 7*(2), 244–257.

63. Sapolsky, R. M. (2005). The influence of social hierarchy on primate health. *Science, 308*(5722), 648–652.

64. Kobasa, S. C., Maddi, S. R., & Kahn, S. (1982). Hardiness and health: A prospective study. *Journal of Personality and Social Psychology, 42*(1), 168–177.

65. Carver, C. S., Smith, R. G., Antoni, M. H., Petronis, V. M., Weiss, S., & Derhagopian, R. P. (2005). Optimistic personality and psychosocial well-being during treatment predict psychosocial well-being among long-term survivors of breast cancer. *Health Psychology, 24*(5), 508–516.

66. Cohen, S., & Pressman, S. D. (2006). Positive affect and health. *Current Directions in Psychological Science, 15*(3), 122–125.

67. Dolbier, C. L., Smith, S. E., & Steinhardt, M. A. (2007). Relationships of protective factors to stress and symptoms of illness. *American Journal of Health Behavior, 31*(4), 423–433.

68. Baker, S. R. (2007). Dispositional optimism and health status, symptoms, and behaviors: Assessing ideothetic relationships using a prospective daily diary approach. *Psychology and Health, 22*(4), 431–455.

69. Antoni, M. H., Lehman, J. M., Klibourn, K. M., Boyers, A. E., Culver, J. L., Alferi, S. M.,...Kilbourn, K. (2001). Cognitive-behavioral stress management intervention decreases the prevalence of depression and enhances benefit finding among women under treatment for early-stage breast cancer. *Health Psychology, 20*(1), 20–32.

70. Maddi, S. R., Kahn, S., & Maddi, K. L. (1998). The effectiveness of hardiness training. *Consulting Psychology Journal: Practice and Research, 50*(2), 78–86.

71. Peterson, C., Seligman, M. E. P., Yurko, K. H., Martin, L. R., & Friedman, H. S. (1998). Catastrophizing and untimely death. *Psychological Science, 9*(2), 127–130.

72. Levy, B., & Myers, L. (2005). Relationship between respiratory mortality and self-perceptions of aging. *Psychology & Health, 20*(5), 553–564. doi:10.1080/14768320500066381; Levy, B., Slade, M., & Kasl, S. (2002). Longitudinal benefit of positive self-perceptions of aging on functional health. *Journals of Gerontology Series B: Psychological Sciences & Social Sciences, 57B*(5), P409. Retrieved from Academic Search Premier Database.

73. Diener, E., Nickerson, C., Lucas, R., & Sandvik, E. (2002). Dispositional affect and job outcomes. *Social Indicators Research, 59*(3), 229. Retrieved from Academic Search Premier Database.

74. Braungart, J. M., Plomin, R., DeFries, J. C., & Fulker, D. W. (1992). Genetic influence on tester-rated infant temperament as assessed by Bayley's Infant Behavior Record: Nonadoptive and adoptive siblings and twins. *Developmental Psychology, 28*(1), 40–47; Lykken, D. T. (2000). *Happiness: The nature and nurture of joy and contentment*. New York, NY: St. Martin's Press.

75. Diener, E., Suh, E. M., Lucas, R. E., & Smith, H. L. (1999). Subjective well-being: Three decades of progress. *Psychological Bulletin, 125*(2), 276–302; Diener, E., Tamir, M., & Scollon, C. N. (2006). Happiness, life satisfaction, and fulfillment: The social psychology of subjective well-being. In P. A. M. VanLange (Ed.), *Bridging social psychology: Benefits of transdisciplinary approaches*. Mahwah, NJ: Lawrence Erlbaum Associates.

76. Pew Research Center (2006, February 13). Are we happy yet? Retrieved from http://pewresearch.org/pubs/301/are-we-happy-yet

77. Leary, M. R. (1990). Responses to social exclusion: Social anxiety, jealousy, loneliness, depression, and low self-esteem. *Journal of Social and Clinical Psychology, 9*(2), 221–229.

78. Koopman, C., Hermanson, K., Diamond, S., Angell, K., & Spiegel, D. (1998). Social support, life stress, pain and emotional adjustment to advanced breast cancer. *Psycho-Oncology, 7*(2), 101–110.

79. Ashton, E., Vosvick, M., Chesney, M., Gore-Felton, C., Koopman, C., O'Shea, K.,...Spiegel, D. (2005). Social support and maladaptive coping as predictors of the change in physical health symptoms among persons living with HIV/AIDS. *AIDS Patient Care & STDs, 19*(9), 587–598. doi:10.1089/apc.2005.19.587

80. Au, A., Lau, S., & Lee, M. (2009). Suicide ideation and depression: The moderation effects of family cohesion and social self-concept. *Adolescence, 44*(176), 851–868. Retrieved from Academic Search Premier Database; Bertera, E. (2007). The role of positive and negative social exchanges between adolescents, their peers and family as predictors of suicide ideation. *Child & Adolescent Social Work Journal, 24*(6), 523–538. doi:10.1007/s10560-007-0104-y; Compton, M., Thompson, N., & Kaslow, N. (2005). Social environment factors associated with suicide attempt among low-income African Americans: The protective role of family relationships and social support. *Social Psychiatry & Psychiatric Epidemiology, 40*(3), 175–185. doi:10.1007/s00127-005-0865-6; Skärsäter, I., Langius, A., Ågren, H., Häggström, L., & Dencker, K. (2005). Sense of coherence and social support in relation to recovery in first-episode patients with major depression: A one-year prospective study. *International Journal of Mental Health Nursing, 14*(4), 258–264. doi:10.1111/j.1440-0979.2005.00390.x

81. Gençöz, T., & Özlale, Y. (2004). Direct and indirect effects of social support on psychological well-being. *Social Behavior & Personality: An International Journal, 32*(5), 449–458.

82. Easterlin, R. (2005). Feeding the illusion of growth and happiness: A reply to Hagerty and Veenhoven. *Social Indicators Research, 74*(3), 429–443. doi:10.1007/s11205-004-6170-z

83. Csikszentmihalyi, M. (1999). If we are so rich, why aren't we happy? *American Psychologist, 54*(10), 821–827.

84. Twenge, J. M., Campbell, W. K., & Foster, C. A. (2003). Parenthood and marital satisfaction: A meta-analytic review. *Journal of Marriage and Family, 65*(3), 574–583.

85. Wilson, T. D., & Gilbert, D. T. (2005). Affective forecasting: Knowing what to want. *Current Directions in Psychological Science, 14*(3), 131–134.

86. Brickman, P., Coates, D., & Janoff-Bulman, R. (1978). Lottery winners and accident victims: Is happiness relative? *Journal of Personality and Social Psychology, 36*(8), 917–927.

87. Small, D. M., Zatorre, R. J., Dagher, A., Evans, A. C., & Jones-Gotman, M. (2001). Changes in brain activity related to eating chocolate: From pleasure to aversion. *Brain, 124*(9), 1720–1733.

88. Wilson, T. D., Wheatley, T., Meyers, J. M., Gilbert, D. T., & Axsom, D. (2000). Focalism: A source of durability bias in affective forecasting. *Journal of Personality and Social Psychology, 78*(5), 821–836.

89. Bonanno, G. A., Wortman, C. B., Lehman, D. R., Tweed, R. G., Haring, M., Sonnega, J.,...Nesse, R. M. (2002). Resilience to loss and chronic grief: A prospective study from preloss to 18-months postloss. *Journal of Personality and Social Psychology, 83*(5), 1150–1164.

90. Lucas, R. (2007). Long-term disability is associated with lasting changes in subjective well-being: Evidence from two nationally representative longitudinal studies. *Journal of Personality & Social Psychology, 92*(4), 717–730. Retrieved from Academic Search Premier Database; Riis, J., Baron, J., Loewenstein, G., Jepson, C., Fagerlin, A., & Ubel, P. (2005). Ignorance of hedonic adaptation to hemodialysis: A study using ecological momentary assessment. *Journal of Experimental Psychology/General, 134*(1), 3–9. doi:10.1037/0096-3445.134.1.3

91. Marinić, M., & Brkljačić, T. (2008). Love over gold—The correlation of happiness level with some life satisfaction factors between persons with and without physical disability. *Journal of Developmental & Physical Disabilities, 20*(6), 527–540. doi:10.1007/s10882-008-9115-7

92. Argyle, M. (1999). Causes and correlates of happiness. In D. Kahneman, E. Diener, & N. Schwarz (Eds.), *Well being: The foundations of hedonic psychology*. New York, NY: Russell Sage Foundation.

93. Hunger Notes. (n.d.). How many children are hungry in the United States? Retrieved from http://www.worldhunger.org/articles/04/editorials/hungry_us_children.htm

94. Keys, A., Brožek, J., Henschel, A., Mickelsen, O., & Taylor, H. L. (1950). *The biology of human starvation* (Vols. 1–2). Oxford, England: University of Minnesota Press.

95. Wolf, G., & Miller, N. E. (1964). Lateral hypothalamic lesions: Effects on drinking elicited by carbachol in preoptic area and posterior hypothalamus. *Science, 143*(Whole No. 3606), 585–587.

96. Brennan, A. M., & Mantzoros, C. S. (2006). Drug insight: The role of leptin in human physiology and pathophysiology-emerging clinical applications. *Nature Clinical Practice Endocrinology Metabolism, 2*(6), 318–27. doi:10.1038/ncpendmet0196; Nakazato, M., Murakami, N., Date, Y., Kojima, M., Matsuo, H., Kangawa, K., & Matsukura S. (2001). A role for ghrelin in the central regulation of feeding. *Nature, 409*(6817), 194–198.

97. Schachter, S. (1968). Obesity and eating. *Science, 161*(3843), 751–756.

98. Rozin, P., Dow, S., Moscovitch, M., & Rajaram, S. (1998). What causes humans to begin and end a meal? A role for memory for what has been eaten, as evidenced by a

study of multiple meal eating in amnesic patients. *Psychological Science, 9*(5), 392–396.

99. Norton, K. I., Olds, T. S., Olive, S., & Dank, S. (1996). Ken and Barbie at life size. *Sex Roles, 34*(3–4), 287–294.

100. Hoek, H. W., & van Hoeken, D. (2003). Review of the prevalence and incidence of eating disorders. *International Journal of Eating Disorders, 34*(4), 383–396; Patrick, L. (2002). Eating disorders: A review of the literature with emphasis on medical complications and clinical nutrition. *Alternative Medicine Review, 7*(3), 184–202.

101. Klump, K. L., Burt, S. A., McGue, M., & Iacono, W. G. (2007). Changes in genetic and environmental influences on disordered eating across adolescence: A longitudinal twin study. *Archives of General Psychiatry, 64*(12), 1409–1415.

102. Guisinger, S. (2008). Competing paradigms for anorexia nervosa. *American Psychologist, 63*(3), 199–200.

103. Vohs, K. D., Voelz, Z. R., Pettit, J. W., Bardone, A. M., Katz, J., Abramson, L. Y.,…Joiner, T. E., Jr. (2001). Perfectionism, body dissatisfaction, and self-esteem: An interactive model of bulimic symptom development. *Journal of Social and Clinical Psychology, 20*(4), 476–497.

104. Crandall, C. S. (1988). Social contagion of binge eating. *Journal of Personality & Social Psychology, 55*(4), 588–598.

105. Crandall, C. S., Merman, A., & Hebl, M. (2009). Anti-fat prejudice. In T. D. Nelson (Ed.), *Handbook of prejudice, stereotyping, and discrimination* (pp. 469–487). New York, NY: Psychology Press.

106. Gustafson, D., Rothenberg, E., Blennow, K., Steen, B., & Skoog, I. (2003). An 18-year follow-up of overweight and risk of Alzheimer disease. *Archives of Internal Medicine, 163*(13), 1524.

107. Haslam, D. W., & James, W. P. (2005). Obesity. *Lancet, 366*(9492), 197–209. doi:10.1016/S0140-6736(05)67483-1

108. Nestle, M., & Jacobson, M. F. (2000). Halting the obesity epidemic: A public health policy approach. *Public Health Reports, 115*(1), 12–24. doi:10.1093/phr/115.1.12; James, W. P. (2008). The fundamental drivers of the obesity epidemic. *Obesity Review, 9*(Suppl. 1), 6–13.

109. Miller, W. C. (1999). How effective are traditional dietary and exercise interventions for weight loss? *Medicine & Science in Sports & Exercise, 31*(8), 1129–1134.

110. Douketis, J. D., Macie C., Thabane, L., & Williamson, D. F. (2005). Systematic review of long-term weight loss studies in obese adults: Clinical significance and applicability to clinical practice. *International Journal of Obesity, 29*, 1153–1167. doi:10.1038/sj.ijo.0802982

111. Borer, K. T. (2008). How effective is exercise in producing fat loss? *Kinesiology, 40*(2), 126–137.

112. American Heart Association. (1998). Statement on exercise, benefits and recommendations for physical activity programs for all Americans. *American Heart Association, 94*, 857–862. Retrieved from http://circ.ahajournals.org/cgi/content/full/94/4/857?ijkey=6e9ad2e53ba5b25f9002a707e5e4b5b8ee015481&keytype2=tf_ipsecsha

113. Kramer, A. F., Erickson, K. I., & Colcombe, S. J. (2006). Exercise, cognition, and the aging brain. *Journal of Applied Physiology, 101*(4), 1237–1242.

114. Schomer, H., & Drake, B. (2001). Physical activity and mental health. *International SportMed Journal, 2*(3), 1. Retrieved from Academic Search Premier Database.

115. Kirchhoff, A., Elliott, L., Schlichting, J., & Chin, M. (2008). Strategies for physical activity maintenance in African American women. *American Journal of Health Behavior, 32*(5), 517–524. Retrieved from Academic Search Premier Database.

116. Centers for Disease Control and Prevention. (2007). Prevalence of regular physical activity among adults—United States, 2001–2005. *Morbidity and Mortality Weekly Report, 56*(46), 1209–1212.

117. American Heart Association. (1998). Statement on exercise, benefits and recommendations for physical activity programs for all Americans. *American Heart Association, 94*, 857–862. Retrieved from http://circ.ahajournals.org/cgi/content/full/94/4/857?ijkey=6e9ad2e53ba5b25f9002a707e5e4b5b8ee015481&keytype2=tf_ipsecsha

118. Masters, W. H., & Johnson, V. E. (1966). *Human sexual response.* New York, NY: Bantam Books.

119. Thornhill, R., & Gangestad, S. (1995). Human female orgasm and mate fluctuating asymmetry. *Animal Behaviour, 50*(6), 1601. Retrieved from Academic Search Premier Database.

120. Pillsworth, E., Haselton, M., & Buss, D. (2004). Ovulatory shifts in female sexual desire. *Journal of Sex Research, 41*(1), 55–65. Retrieved from Academic Search Premier Database.

121. Aversa, A., Isidori, A., De Martino, M., Caprio, M., Fabbrini, E., Rocchietti-March, M.,…Fabri, A. (2000). Androgens and penile erection: evidence for a direct relationship between free testosterone and cavernous vasodilation in men with erectile dysfunction. *Clinical Endocrinology, 53*(4), 517–522. doi:10.1046/j.1365-2265.2000.01118.x; Jockenhövel, F., Minnemann, T., Schubert, M., Freude, S., Hübler, D., Schumann, C.,…Ernst, M. (2009). Timetable of effects of testosterone administration to hypogonadal men on variables of sex and mood. *Aging Male, 12*(4), 113–118. doi:10.3109/13685530903322858

122. Meston, C. M., & Frohlich, P. F. (2000). The neurobiology of sexual function. *Archives of General Psychiatry, 57*(11), 1012–1030.

123. Baumeister, R. F. (2000). Gender differences in erotic plasticity: The female sex drive as socially flexible and responsive. *Psychological Bulletin, 126*(3), 347–374.

124. Leitenberg, H., & Henning, K. (1995). Sexual fantasy. *Psychological Bulletin, 117*(3), 469–496.

125. Petersen, J. L., & Hyde, J. S. (2010). A meta-analytic review of research on gender differences in sexuality, 1993–2007. *Psychological Bulletin, 136*(1), 21–38; Saad, G., Eba,

A., & Sejean, R. (2009). Sex differences when searching for a mate: A process-tracing approach. *Journal of Behavioral Decision Making, 22*(2), 171–190.

126. Buss, D. M. (1989). Sex differences in human mate preferences: Evolutionary hypotheses tested in 37 cultures. *Behavioral and Brain Sciences, 12*(1), 1–49.

127. Buss, D., & Kenrick, D. (1998). Evolutionary social psychology. In D. T. Gilbert, S. T. Fiske, & G. Lindzey (Eds.), *Handbook of Social Psychology* (4th ed., Vol. 2, pp. 982–1026). Boston, MA: McGraw-Hill.

128. Kinsey, A. C., Pomeroy, W. B., & Martin, C. E. (1998). *Sexual behavior in the human male.* Bloomington: Indiana University Press. (Original work published 1948); Kinsey, A. C. (1998). *Sexual behavior in the human female.* Bloomington: Indiana University Press. (Original work published 1953)

129. Bogaert, A. (2004). Asexuality: Prevalence and associated factors in a national probability sample. *Journal of Sex Research, 41*(3), 279–287. Retrieved from Academic Search Premier Database; Feldhaus-Dahir, M. (2009). The causes and prevalence of hypoactive sexual desire disorder: Part I. *Urologic Nursing, 29*(4), 259–263. Retrieved from Academic Search Premier Database; West, S. L., D'Aloisio, A. A., Agans, R. P., Kalsbeek, W. D., Borisov, N. N., & Thorp, J. M. (2008). Prevalence of low sexual desire and hypoactive sexual desire disorder in a nationally representative sample of US women. *Archives of Internal Medicine, 168*(13), 1441–1449.

130. Kingston, D. A., & Firestone, P. (2008). Problematic hypersexuality: A review of conceptualization and diagnosis. *Sexual Addictions and Compulsivity, 15*, 284–310.

131. Laumann, E. O., Gagnon, J. H., Michael, R. T., & Michaels, S. (1994). *The social organization of sexuality in the United States.* Chicago, IL: University of Chicago Press.

132. Kulkin, H. S., Chauvin, E. A., & Percle, G. A. (2000). Suicide among gay and lesbian adolescents and young adults: A review of the literature. *Journal of Homosexuality, 40*(1), 1–29.

133. Mustanski, B. S., Chivers, M. L., & Bailey, J. M. (2002). A critical review of recent biological research on human sexual orientation. *Annual Review of Sex Research, 13*, 89–140.

134. Gladue, B. A. (1994). The biopsychology of sexual orientation. *Current Directions in Psychological Science, 3*(5), 150–154; Lasco, M., Jordan, T., Edgar, M., Petito, C., & Byne, W. (2002). A lack of dimorphism of sex or sexual orientation in the human anterior commissure. *Brain Research, 936*(1/2), 95; Rahman, Q., & Wilson, G. D. (2003). Born gay? The psychobiology of human sexual orientation. *Personality and Individual Differences, 34*(8), 1337–1382.

135. Bailey, J., Pillard, R., Dawood, K., Miller, M., Farrer, L., Shruti Trivedi, L.,…Murphy, R. L. (1999). A family history study of male sexual orientation using three independent samples. *Behavior Genetics, 29*(2), 79–86. Retrieved from Academic Search Premier Database; Pillard, R., & Bailey, J. (1998). Human sexual orientation has a heritable component. *Human Biology, 70*(2), 347. Retrieved from Academic Search Premier Database.

136. Hershberger, S., & Segal, N. (2004). The cognitive, behavioral, and personality profiles of a male monozygotic triplet set discordant for sexual orientation. *Archives of Sexual Behavior, 33*(5), 497–514. Retrieved from Academic Search Premier Database; Williams, T., & Pepitone, M. (2000.) Finger-length ratios and sexual orientation. *Nature, 404*, 455.

137. Mokdad, A. H., Marks, J. S., Stroup, D. F., & Gerberding, J. L. (2004). Actual causes of death in the United States, 2000. *Journal of the American Medical Association, 291*(10), 1238–1240.

138. Fryar, C. D., Merino, M. C., Hirsch, R., & Porter, K. S. (2009). Smoking, alcohol use, and illicit drug use reported by adolescents aged 12–17 years: United States, 1999–2004. *National Health Statistics Reports, 15*, 1–23.

139. Fogelholm, M. (2010). Physical activity, fitness and fatness: Relations to mortality, morbidity and disease risk factors. A systematic review. *Obesity Reviews, 11*(3), 202–221. doi:10.1111/j.1467-789X.2009.00653.x; Galper, D., Trivedi, M., Barlow, C., Dunn, A., & Kampert, J. (2006). Inverse association between physical inactivity and mental health in men and women. *Medicine & Science in Sports & Exercise, 38*(1), 173–178. doi:10.1249/01.mss.0000180883.32116.28; Hassmén, P., Koivula, N., & Uutela, A. (2000). Physical exercise and psychological well-being: A population study in Finland. *Preventive Medicine: An International Journal Devoted to Practice and Theory, 30*(1), 17–25.

140. Hillman, C. H., Erickson, K. I., & Kramer, A. F. (2008). Be smart, exercise your heart: Exercise effects on brain and cognition. *Nature Reviews Neuroscience, 9*(1), 58–65.

141. Valencia-Martín, J., Galán, I., & Rodríguez-Artalejo, F. (2008). The joint association of average volume of alcohol and binge drinking with hazardous driving behaviour and traffic crashes. *Addiction, 103*(5), 749–757. doi:10.1111/j.1360-0443.2008.02165.x

142. Miller, J., Naimi, T., Brewer, R., & Jones, S. (2007). Binge drinking and associated health risk behaviors among high school students. *Pediatrics, 119*(1), 76–85. doi:10.1542/peds.2006-1517

143. McQueeny, T., Schweinsburg, B., Schweinsburg, A., Jacobus, J., Bava, S., Frank, L.,…Tapert, S. F. (2009). Altered white matter integrity in adolescent binge drinkers. *Alcoholism: Clinical & Experimental Research, 33*(7), 1278–1285. doi:10.1111/j.1530-0277.2009.00953.x

144. Kim, J., Sing, L., Chow, J., Lau, J., Tsang, A., Choi, J.,…Griffiths, S. M. (2008). Prevalence and the factors associated with binge drinking, alcohol abuse, and alcohol dependence: A population-based study of Chinese adults in Hong Kong. *Alcohol & Alcoholism, 43*(3), 360–370. doi:10.1093/Alcalc/Agm181

145. Monteiro, M. (2001). A World Health Organization perspective on alcohol and illicit drug use and health. *European Addiction Research, 7*(3), 98–103. doi:10.1159/000050727

146. Hutton, H., McCaul, M., Santora, P., & Erbelding, E. (2008). The relationship between recent alcohol use and sexual behaviors: Gender differences among sexually transmitted disease clinic patients. *Alcoholism: Clinical & Experimental Research, 32*(11), 2008–2015; Raj, A., Reed, E., Santana, M., Walley, A., Welles, S., Horsburgh, C.,…Silverman, J. G. (2009). The associations of binge alcohol use with HIV/STI risk

and diagnosis among heterosexual African American men. *Drug & Alcohol Depend-ence, 101*(1/2), 101–106.

Personality

Identical Twins Reunited after 35 Years

Paula Bernstein and Elyse Schein were identical twins who were adopted into separate families immediately after their births in 1968. It was only at the age of 35 that the twins were reunited and discovered how similar they were to each other.

Paula Bernstein grew up in a happy home in suburban New York. She loved her adopted parents and older brother and even wrote an article titled "Why I Don't Want to Find My Birth Mother." Elyse's childhood, also a happy one, was followed by college and then film school abroad.

In 2003, 35 years after she was adopted, Elyse, acting on a whim, inquired about her biological family at the adoption agency. The response came back: "You were born on October 9, 1968, at 12:51 p.m., the younger of twin girls. You've got a twin sister Paula and she's looking for you."

"Oh my God, I'm a *twin*! Can you believe this? Is this really happening?" Elyse cried.

Elyse dialed Paula's phone number: "It's almost like I'm hearing my own voice in a recorder back at me," she said.

"It's funny because I feel like in a way I was talking to an old, close friend I never knew I had…we had an immediate intimacy, and yet, we didn't know each other at all," Paula said.

The two women met for the first time at a café for lunch and talked until the late evening.

"We had 35 years to catch up on," said Paula. "How do you start asking somebody, 'What have you been up to since we shared a womb together?' Where do you start?"

With each new detail revealed, the twins learned about their remarkable similarities. They'd both gone to graduate school in film. They both loved to write, and they had both edited their high school yearbooks. They have similar taste in music.

"I think, you know, when we met it was undeniable that we were twins. Looking at this person, you are able to gaze into your own eyes and see yourself from the outside. This identical individual has the exact same DNA and is essentially your clone. We don't have to imagine," Paula said.

Now they finally feel like sisters.

"But it's perhaps even closer than sisters," Elyse said, "Because we're also twins."

The twins, who both now live in Brooklyn, combined their writing skills to write a book called *Identical Strangers* about their childhoods and their experience of discovering an identical twin in their mid-30s (Spilius, 2007; Kuntzman, 2007).[1]

Elyse and Paula

You can learn more about the experiences of Paula Bernstein and Elyse Schein by viewing this video.

View the video online at: http://www.youtube.com/embed/gYvmcUt9mo0

One of the most fundamental tendencies of human beings is to size up other people. We say that Bill is fun, that

Marian is adventurous, or that Frank is dishonest. When we make these statements, we mean that we believe that

personality

An individual's consistent patterns of feeling, thinking, and behaving.

these people have stable individual characteristics—their *personalities*. **Personality** is defined as *an individual's consistent patterns of feeling, thinking, and behaving* (John, Robins, & Pervin, 2008).[2]

The tendency to perceive personality is a fundamental part of human nature, and a most adaptive one. If we can draw accurate generalizations about what other people are normally like, we can predict how they will behave in the future, and this can help us determine how they are likely to respond in different situations. Understanding personality can also help us better understand psychological disorders and the negative behavioral outcomes they may produce. In short, personality matters because it guides behavior.

In this chapter we will consider the wide variety of personality traits found in human beings. We'll consider how and when personality influences our behavior, and how well we perceive the personalities of others. We will also consider how psychologists measure personality, and the extent to which personality is caused by nature versus nurture. The fundamental goal of personality psychologists is to understand what makes people different from each other (the study of individual differences), but they also find that people who share genes (as do Paula Bernstein and Elyse Schein) have a remarkable similarity in personality.

1. PERSONALITY AND BEHAVIOR: APPROACHES AND MEASUREMENT

LEARNING OBJECTIVES

1. Outline and critique the early approaches to assessing personality.
2. Define and review the strengths and limitations of the trait approach to personality.
3. Summarize the measures that have been used to assess psychological disorders.

Early theories assumed that personality was expressed in people's physical appearance. One early approach, developed by the German physician Franz Joseph Gall (1758–1828) and known as *phrenology*, was based on the idea that we could measure personality by assessing the patterns of bumps on people's skulls (Figure 11.1). In the Victorian age, phrenology was taken seriously and many people promoted its use as a source of psychological insight and self-knowledge. Machines were even developed for helping people analyze skulls (Simpson, 2005).[3] However, because careful scientific research did not validate the predictions of the theory, phrenology has now been discredited in contemporary psychology.

FIGURE 11.1 Phrenology

This definition of phrenology with a chart of the skull appeared in Webster's Academic Dictionary, circa 1895.

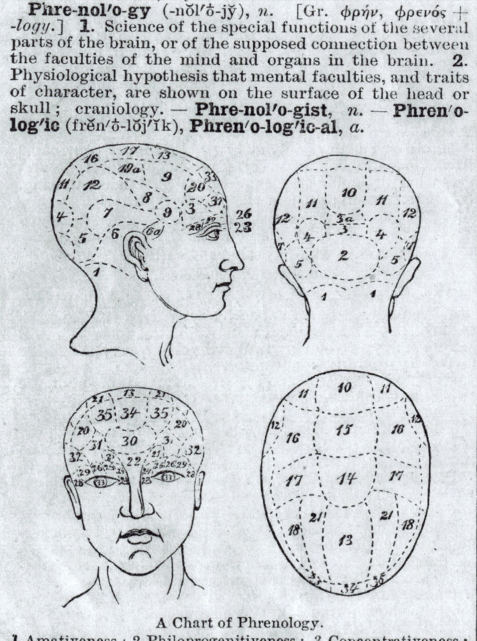

Phre-nol'o-gy (-nŏl'ō-jў), *n.* [Gr. φρήν, φρενός + *-logy.*] **1.** Science of the special functions of the several parts of the brain, or of the supposed connection between the faculties of the mind and organs in the brain. **2.** Physiological hypothesis that mental faculties, and traits of character, are shown on the surface of the head or skull; craniology. — **Phre-nol'o-gist**, *n.* — **Phren'o-log'ic** (frĕn'ō-lŏj'ĭk), **Phren'o-log'ic-al,** *a.*

A Chart of Phrenology.

1 Amativeness : 2 Philoprogenitiveness ; 3 Concentrativeness ; 3 *a* Inhabitiveness ; 4 Adhesiveness ; 5 Combativeness ; 6 Destructiveness ; 6 *a* Alimentiveness ; 7 Secretiveness ; 8 Acquisitiveness ; 9 Constructiveness ; 10 Self-esteem ; 11 Love of Approbation ; 12 Cautiousness ; 13 Benevolence ; 14 Veneration ; 15 Firmness ; 16 Conscientiousness ; 17 Hope ; 18 Wonder ; 19 Ideality ; 19 *a* (Not determined) ; 20 Wit : 21 Imitation ; 22 Individuality : 23 Form ; 24 Size ; 25 Weight ; 26 Coloring ; 27 Locality ; 28 Number ; 29 Order ; 30 Eventuality ; 31 Time ; 32 Tune ; 33 Language ; 34 Comparison ; 35 Causality. [Some raise the number of organs to forty-three.]

Source: Photo courtesy of Webster's Academic Dictionary, http://en.wikipedia.org/wiki/File:1895-Dictionary-Phrenolog.png.

Another approach, known as *somatology*, championed by the psychologist William Herbert Sheldon (1898–1977), was based on the idea that we could determine personality from people's body types (Figure 11.2). Sheldon (1940)[4] argued that people with more body fat and a rounder physique ("endomorphs") were more likely to be assertive and bold, whereas thinner people ("ectomorphs") were more likely to be introverted and intellectual. As with phrenology, scientific research did not validate the predictions of the theory, and somatology has now been discredited in contemporary psychology.

FIGURE 11.2 Sheldon's Body Types

William Sheldon erroneously believed that people with different body types had different personalities.

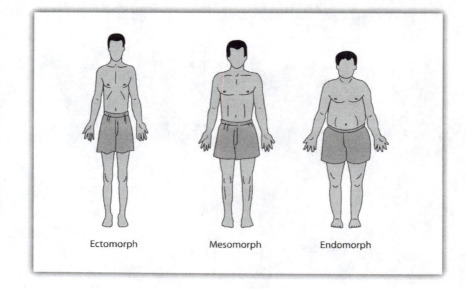

Another approach to detecting personality is known as *physiognomy*, or the idea that it is possible to assess personality from facial characteristics. In contrast to phrenology and somatology, for which no research support has been found, contemporary research has found that people are able to detect some aspects of a person's character—for instance, whether they are gay or straight and whether they are Democrats or Republicans—at above chance levels by looking only at his or her face (Rule & Ambady, 2010; Rule, Ambady, Adams, & Macrae, 2008; Rule, Ambady, & Hallett, 2009).[5]

Despite these results, the ability to detect personality from faces is not guaranteed. Olivola and Todorov (2010)[6] recently studied the ability of thousands of people to guess the personality characteristics of hundreds of thousands of faces on a public website. In contrast to the predictions of physiognomy, the researchers found that these people would have made more accurate judgments about the strangers if they had just guessed, using their expectations about what people in general are like, rather than trying to use the particular facial features of individuals to help them. It seems then that the predictions of physiognomy may also, in the end, find little empirical support.

1.1   Personality as Traits

traits

Relatively enduring characteristics that influence our behavior across many situations.

Personalities are characterized in terms of **traits**, which are *relatively enduring characteristics that influence our behavior across many situations*. Personality traits such as introversion, friendliness, conscientiousness, honesty, and helpfulness are important because they help explain consistencies in behavior.

The most popular way of measuring traits is by administering personality tests on which people self-report about their own characteristics. Psychologists have investigated hundreds of traits using the self-report approach, and this research has found many personality traits that have important implications for behavior. You can see some examples of the personality dimensions that have been studied by psychologists and their implications for behavior in Table 11.1, and you can try completing a trait measure at the website shown in "Example of a Trait Measure".

TABLE 11.1 Some Personality Traits That Predict Behavior

Trait	Description	Examples of behaviors exhibited by people who have the trait
Authoritarianism (Adorno, Frenkel-Brunswik, Levinson, & Sanford, 1950)	A cluster of traits including conventionalism, superstition, toughness, and exaggerated concerns with sexuality	Authoritarians are more likely to be prejudiced, to conform to leaders, and to display rigid behaviors.
Individualism-collectivism (Triandis, 1989)	Individualism is the tendency to focus on oneself and one's personal goals; collectivism is the tendency to focus on one's relations with others.	Individualists prefer to engage in behaviors that make them stand out from others, whereas collectivists prefer to engage in behaviors that emphasize their similarity to others.
Internal versus external locus of control (Rotter, 1966)	In comparison to those with an external locus of control, people with an internal locus of control are more likely to believe that life events are due largely to their own efforts and personal characteristics.	People with higher internal locus of control are happier, less depressed, and healthier in comparison to those with an external locus of control.
Need for achievement (McClelland, 1958)	The desire to make significant accomplishments by mastering skills or meeting high standards	Those high in need for achievement select tasks that are not too difficult to be sure they will succeed in them.
Need for cognition (Cacioppo & Petty, 1982)	The extent to which people engage in and enjoy effortful cognitive activities	People high in the need for cognition pay more attention to arguments in ads.
Regulatory focus (Shah, Higgins, & Friedman, 1998)	Refers to differences in the motivations that energize behavior, varying from a *promotion orientation* (seeking out new opportunities) to a *prevention orientation* (avoiding negative outcomes)	People with a promotion orientation are more motivated by goals of gaining money, whereas those with prevention orientation are more concerned about losing money.
Self-consciousness (Fenigstein, Sheier, & Buss, 1975)	The tendency to introspect and examine one's inner self and feelings	People high in self-consciousness spend more time preparing their hair and makeup before they leave the house.
Self-esteem (Rosenberg, 1965)	High self-esteem means having a positive attitude toward oneself and one's capabilities.	High self-esteem is associated with a variety of positive psychological and health outcomes.
Sensation seeking (Zuckerman, 2007)	The motivation to engage in extreme and risky behaviors	Sensation seekers are more likely to engage in risky behaviors such as extreme and risky sports, substance abuse, unsafe sex, and crime.

Sources: Adorno, T. W., Frenkel-Brunswik, E., Levinson, D. J., & Sanford, R. N. (1950). *The authoritarian personality.* New York, NY: Harper; Triandis, H. (1989). The self and social behavior in differing cultural contexts. *Psychological Review, 93,* 506–520; Rotter, J. (1966). Generalized expectancies of internal versus external locus of control of reinforcement. *Psychological Monographs, 80;* McClelland, D. C. (1958). Methods of measuring human motivation. In John W. Atkinson (Ed.), *Motives in fantasy, action and society.* Princeton, NJ: D. Van Nostrand; Cacioppo, J. T., & Petty, R. E. (1982). The need for cognition. *Journal of Personality and Social Psychology, 42,* 116–131; Shah, J., Higgins, T., & Friedman, R. S. (1998). Performance incentives and means: How regulatory focus influences goal attainment. *Journal of Personality and Social Psychology, 74(2),* 285–293; Fenigstein, A., Scheier, M. F., & Buss, A. H. (1975). Public and private self-consciousness: Assessment and theory. *Journal of Consulting and Clinical Psychology, 43,* 522–527; Rosenberg, M. (1965). *Society and the adolescent self-image.* Princeton, NJ: Princeton University Press; Zuckerman, M. (2007). *Sensation seeking and risky behavior.* Washington, DC: American Psychological Association.

Example of a Trait Measure

You can try completing a self-report measure of personality (a short form of the Five-Factor Personality Test) here. There are 120 questions and it should take you about 15–20 minutes to complete. You will receive feedback about your personality after you have finished the test.

http://www.personalitytest.net/ipip/ipipneo120.htm

As with intelligence tests, the utility of self-report measures of personality depends on their *reliability* and *construct validity*. Some popular measures of personality are not useful because they are unreliable or invalid. Perhaps you have heard of a personality test known as the Myers-Briggs Type Indicator

(MBTI). If so, you are not alone, because the MBTI is the most widely administered personality test in the world, given millions of times a year to employees in thousands of companies. The MBTI categorizes people into one of four categories on each of four dimensions: *introversion* versus *extraversion*, *sensing* versus *intuiting*, *thinking* versus *feeling*, and *judging* versus *perceiving*.

Although completing the MBTI can be useful for helping people think about individual differences in personality, and for "breaking the ice" at meetings, the measure itself is not psychologically useful because it is not reliable or valid. People's classifications change over time, and scores on the MBTI do not relate to other measures of personality or to behavior (Hunsley, Lee, & Wood, 2003).[7] Measures such as the MBTI remind us that it is important to scientifically and empirically test the effectiveness of personality tests by assessing their stability over time and their ability to predict behavior.

One of the challenges of the trait approach to personality is that there are so many of them; there are at least 18,000 English words that can be used to describe people (Allport & Odbert, 1936).[8] Thus a major goal of psychologists is to take this vast number of descriptors (many of which are very similar to each other) and to determine the underlying important or "core" traits among them (John, Angleitner, & Ostendorf, 1988).[9]

The trait approach to personality was pioneered by early psychologists, including Gordon Allport (1897–1967), Raymond Cattell (1905–1998), and Hans Eysenck (1916–1997). Each of these psychologists believed in the idea of the trait as the stable unit of personality, and each attempted to provide a list or taxonomy of the most important trait dimensions. Their approach was to provide people with a self-report measure and then to use statistical analyses to look for the underlying "factors" or "clusters" of traits, according to the frequency and the co-occurrence of traits in the respondents.

Allport (1937)[10] began his work by reducing the 18,000 traits to a set of about 4,500 traitlike words that he organized into three levels according to their importance. He called them "cardinal traits" (the most important traits), "central traits" (the basic and most useful traits), and "secondary traits" (the less obvious and less consistent ones). Cattell (1990)[11] used a statistical procedure known as *factor analysis* to analyze the correlations among traits and to identify the most important ones. On the basis of his research he identified what he referred to as "source" (more important) and "surface" (less important) traits, and he developed a measure that assessed 16 dimensions of traits based on personality adjectives taken from everyday language.

Hans Eysenck was particularly interested in the biological and genetic origins of personality and made an important contribution to understanding the nature of a fundamental personality trait: *extraversion* versus *introversion* (Eysenck, 1998).[12] Eysenck proposed that people who are extroverted (i.e., who enjoy socializing with others) have lower levels of naturally occurring arousal than do introverts (who are less likely to enjoy being with others). Eysenck argued that extroverts have a greater desire to socialize with others to increase their arousal level, which is naturally too low, whereas introverts, who have naturally high arousal, do not desire to engage in social activities because they are overly stimulating.

Five-Factor (Big Five) Model of Personality

The idea that there are five fundamental underlying trait dimensions that are stable across time, cross-culturally shared, and explain a substantial proportion of behavior.

The fundamental work on trait dimensions conducted by Allport, Cattell, Eysenck, and many others has led to contemporary trait models, the most important and well-validated of which is the **Five-Factor (Big Five) Model of Personality**. According to this model, *there are five fundamental underlying trait dimensions that are stable across time, cross-culturally shared, and explain a substantial proportion of behavior* (Costa & McCrae, 1992; Goldberg, 1982).[13] As you can see in Table 11.2, the five dimensions (sometimes known as the "Big Five") are *agreeableness, conscientiousness, extraversion, neuroticism, and openness to experience*. (You can remember them using the watery acronyms CANOE or OCEAN.)

TABLE 11.2 The Five Factors of the Five-Factor Model of Personality

Dimension	Sample items	Description	Examples of behaviors predicted by the trait
Openness to experience	"I have a vivid imagination"; "I have a rich vocabulary"; "I have excellent ideas."	A general appreciation for art, emotion, adventure, unusual ideas, imagination, curiosity, and variety of experience	Individuals who are highly open to experience tend to have distinctive and unconventional decorations in their home. They are also likely to have books on a wide variety of topics, a diverse music collection, and works of art on display.
Conscientiousness	"I am always prepared"; "I am exacting in my work"; "I follow a schedule."	A tendency to show self-discipline, act dutifully, and aim for achievement	Individuals who are conscientious have a preference for planned rather than spontaneous behavior.
Extraversion	"I am the life of the party"; "I feel comfortable around people"; "I talk to a lot of different people at parties."	The tendency to experience positive emotions and to seek out stimulation and the company of others	Extroverts enjoy being with people. In groups they like to talk, assert themselves, and draw attention to themselves.
Agreeableness	"I am interested in people"; "I feel others' emotions"; "I make people feel at ease."	A tendency to be compassionate and cooperative rather than suspicious and antagonistic toward others; reflects individual differences in general concern for social harmony	Agreeable individuals value getting along with others. They are generally considerate, friendly, generous, helpful, and willing to compromise their interests with those of others.
Neuroticism	"I am not usually relaxed"; "I get upset easily"; "I am easily disturbed"	The tendency to experience negative emotions, such as anger, anxiety, or depression; sometimes called "emotional instability"	Those who score high in neuroticism are more likely to interpret ordinary situations as threatening and minor frustrations as hopelessly difficult. They may have trouble thinking clearly, making decisions, and coping effectively with stress.

A large body of research evidence has supported the five-factor model. The Big Five dimensions seem to be cross-cultural, because the same five factors have been identified in participants in China, Japan, Italy, Hungary, Turkey, and many other countries (Triandis & Suh, 2002).[14] The Big Five dimensions also accurately predict behavior. For instance, a pattern of high conscientiousness, low neuroticism, and high agreeableness predicts successful job performance (Tett, Jackson, & Rothstein, 1991).[15] Scores on the Big Five dimensions also predict the performance of U.S. presidents; ratings of openness to experience are correlated positively with ratings of presidential success, whereas ratings of agreeableness are correlated negatively with success (Rubenzer, Faschingbauer, & Ones, 2000).[16] The Big Five factors are also increasingly being used in helping researchers understand the dimensions of psychological disorders such as anxiety and depression (Oldham, 2010; Saulsman & Page, 2004).[17]

An advantage of the five-factor approach is that it is parsimonious. Rather than studying hundreds of traits, researchers can focus on only five underlying dimensions. The Big Five may also capture other dimensions that have been of interest to psychologists. For instance, the trait dimension of *need for achievement* relates to the Big Five variable of conscientiousness, and *self-esteem* relates to low neuroticism. On the other hand, the Big Five factors do not seem to capture all the important dimensions of personality. For instance, the Big Five does not capture moral behavior, although this variable is important in many theories of personality. And there is evidence that the Big Five factors are not exactly the same across all cultures (Cheung & Leung, 1998).[18]

1.2 Situational Influences on Personality

One challenge to the trait approach to personality is that traits may not be as stable as we think they are. When we say that Malik is friendly, we mean that Malik is friendly today and will be friendly tomorrow and even next week. And we mean that Malik is friendlier than average in all situations. But what if Malik were found to behave in a friendly way with his family members but to be unfriendly with his fellow classmates? This would clash with the idea that traits are stable across time and situation.

The psychologist Walter Mischel (1968)[19] reviewed the existing literature on traits and found that there was only a relatively low correlation (about $r = .30$) between the traits that a person expressed in one situation and those that they expressed in other situations. In one relevant study, Hartshorne, May, Maller, & Shuttleworth (1928)[20] examined the correlations among various behavioral indicators of honesty in children. They also enticed children to behave either honestly or dishonestly in different situations, for instance, by making it easy or difficult for them to steal and cheat. The correlations among children's behavior was low, generally less than $r = .30$, showing that children who steal in one situation are not always the same children who steal in a different situation. And similar low correlations were found in adults on other measures, including dependency, friendliness, and conscientiousness (Bem & Allen, 1974).[21]

Psychologists have proposed two possibilities for these low correlations. One possibility is that the natural tendency for people to see traits in others leads us to believe that people have stable personalities when they really do not. In short, perhaps traits are more in the heads of the people who are doing the judging than they are in the behaviors of the people being observed. The fact that people tend to use human personality traits, such as the Big Five, to judge animals in the same way that they use these traits to judge humans is consistent with this idea (Gosling, 2001).[22] And this idea also fits with research showing that people use their knowledge representation (schemas) about people to help them interpret the world around them and that these schemas color their judgments of others' personalities (Fiske & Taylor, 2007).[23]

Research has also shown that people tend to see more traits in other people than they do in themselves. You might be able to get a feeling for this by taking the following short quiz. First, think about a person you know—your mom, your roommate, or a classmate—and choose which of the three responses on each of the four lines best describes him or her. Then answer the questions again, but this time about yourself.

1.   Energetic   Relaxed   Depends on the situation

2.   Skeptical   Trusting   Depends on the situation

3.   Quiet   Talkative   Depends on the situation

4.   Intense   Calm   Depends on the situation

Richard Nisbett and his colleagues (Nisbett, Caputo, Legant, & Marecek, 1973)[24] had college students complete this same task for themselves, for their best friend, for their father, and for the (at the time well-known) newscaster Walter Cronkite. As you can see in Figure 11.3, the participants chose one of the two trait terms more often for other people than they did for themselves, and chose "depends on the situation" more frequently for themselves than they did for the other people. These results also suggest that people may perceive more consistent traits in others than they should.

FIGURE 11.3 We Tend to Overestimate the Traits of Others.

Nisbett, Caputo, Legant, and Marecek (1973) found that participants checked off a trait term (such as "energetic" or "talkative") rather than "depends on the situation" less often when asked to describe themselves than when asked to describe others.

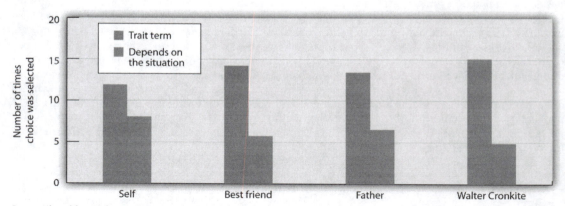

Source: Adapted from Nisbett, R. E., Caputo, C., Legant, P., & Marecek, J. (1973). Behavior as seen by the actor and as seen by the observer. Journal of Personality and Social Psychology, 27(2), 154–164.

The human tendency to perceive traits is so strong that it is very easy to convince people that trait descriptions of themselves are accurate. Imagine that you had completed a personality test and the psychologist administering the measure gave you this description of your personality:

You have a great need for other people to like and admire you. You have a tendency to be critical of yourself. You have a great deal of unused capacity, which you have not turned to your advantage. While you have some personality weaknesses, you are generally able to compensate for them. Disciplined and self-controlled outside, you tend to be worrisome and insecure inside. At times you have serious doubts as to whether you have made the right decision or done the right thing.

I would imagine that you might find that it described you. You probably do criticize yourself at least sometimes, and you probably do sometimes worry about things. The problem is that you would most likely have found some truth in a personality description that was the opposite. Could this description fit you too?

You frequently stand up for your own opinions even if it means that others may judge you negatively. You have a tendency to find the positives in your own behavior. You work to the fullest extent of your capabilities. You have few personality weaknesses, but some may show up under stress. You sometimes confide in others that you are concerned or worried, but inside you maintain discipline and self-control. You generally believe that you have made the right decision and done the right thing.

The **Barnum effect** refers to *the observation that people tend to believe in descriptions of their personality that supposedly are descriptive of them but could in fact describe almost anyone.* The Barnum effect helps us understand why many people believe in astrology, horoscopes, fortune-telling, palm reading, tarot card reading, and even some personality tests. People are likely to accept descriptions of their personality if they think that they have been written for them, even though they cannot distinguish their own tarot card or horoscope readings from those of others at better than chance levels (Hines, 2003).[25] Again, people seem to believe in traits more than they should.

A second way that psychologists responded to Mischel's findings was by searching even more carefully for the existence of traits. One insight was that the relationship between a trait and a behavior is less than perfect because people can express their traits in different ways (Mischel & Shoda, 2008).[26] People high in extraversion, for instance, may become teachers, salesmen, actors, or even criminals. Although the behaviors are very different, they nevertheless all fit with the meaning of the underlying trait.

Psychologists also found that, because people do behave differently in different situations, personality will only predict behavior when the behaviors are aggregated or averaged across different situations. We might not be able to use the personality trait of openness to experience to determine what Saul will do on Friday night, but we can use it to predict what he will do over the next year in a variety of situations. When many measurements of behavior are combined, there is much clearer evidence for the stability of traits and for the effects of traits on behavior (Roberts & DelVecchio, 2000; Srivastava, John, Gosling, & Potter, 2003).[27]

Taken together, these findings make a very important point about personality, which is that it not only comes from inside us but is also shaped by the situations that we are exposed to. Personality is derived from our interactions with and observations of others, from our interpretations of those interactions and observations, and from our choices of which social situations we prefer to enter or avoid (Bandura, 1986).[28] In fact, behaviorists such as B. F. Skinner explain personality entirely in terms of the environmental influences that the person has experienced. Because we are profoundly influenced by the situations that we are exposed to, our behavior does change from situation to situation, making personality less stable than we might expect. And yet personality does matter—we can, in many cases, use personality measures to predict behavior across situations.

Barnum effect

The observation that people tend to believe in descriptions of their personality that supposedly are descriptive of them but could in fact describe almost anyone.

FIGURE 11.4

The popularity of tarot card reading, crystal ball reading, horoscopes, palm reading, and other techniques shows the human propensity to believe in traits.

© Thinkstock

1.3   The MMPI and Projective Tests

Minnesota Multiphasic Personality Inventory (MMPI)

A test used around the world to identify personality and psychological disorders.

One of the most important measures of personality (which is used primarily to assess deviations from a "normal" or "average" personality) is the **Minnesota Multiphasic Personality Inventory (MMPI)**, *a test used around the world to identify personality and psychological disorders* (Tellegen et al., 2003).[29] The MMPI was developed by creating a list of more than 1,000 true-false questions and choosing those that best differentiated patients with different psychological disorders from other people. The current version (the MMPI-2) has more than 500 questions, and the items can be combined into a large number of different subscales. Some of the most important of these are shown in Table 11.3, but there are also scales that represent family problems, work attitudes, and many other dimensions. The MMPI also has questions that are designed to detect the tendency of the respondents to lie, fake, or simply not answer the questions.

TABLE 11.3   Some of the Major Subscales of the MMPI

Abbreviation	Description	What is measured	No. of items
Hs	Hypochondriasis	Concern with bodily symptoms	32
D	Depression	Depressive symptoms	57
Hy	Hysteria	Awareness of problems and vulnerabilities	60
Pd	Psychopathic deviate	Conflict, struggle, anger, respect for society's rules	50
MF	Masculinity/femininity	Stereotypical masculine or feminine interests/behaviors	56
Pa	Paranoia	Level of trust, suspiciousness, sensitivity	40
Pt	Psychasthenia	Worry, anxiety, tension, doubts, obsessiveness	48
Sc	Schizophrenia	Odd thinking and social alienation	78
Ma	Hypomania	Level of excitability	46
Si	Social introversion	People orientation	69

To interpret the results, the clinician looks at the pattern of responses across the different subscales and makes a diagnosis about the potential psychological problems facing the patient. Although clinicians prefer to interpret the patterns themselves, a variety of research has demonstrated that computers can often interpret the results as well as can clinicians (Garb, 1998; Karon, 2000).[30] Extensive research has found that the MMPI-2 can accurately predict which of many different psychological disorders a person suffers from (Graham, 2006).[31]

projective measure

A measure of personality in which unstructured stimuli, such as inkblots, drawings of social situations, or incomplete sentences, are shown to participants, who are asked to freely list what comes to mind as they think about the stimuli.

One potential problem with a measure like the MMPI is that it asks people to consciously report on their inner experiences. But much of our personality is determined by unconscious processes of which we are only vaguely or not at all aware. **Projective measures** are *measures of personality in which unstructured stimuli, such as inkblots, drawings of social situations, or incomplete sentences, are shown to participants, who are asked to freely list what comes to mind as they think about the stimuli.* Experts then score the responses for clues to personality. The proposed advantage of these tests is that they are more indirect—they allow the respondent to freely express whatever comes to mind, including perhaps the contents of their unconscious experiences.

Rorschach Inkblot Test

A projective measure of personality in which the respondent indicates his or her thoughts about a series of 10 symmetrical inkblots.

One commonly used projective test is the *Rorschach Inkblot Test*, developed by the Swiss psychiatrist Hermann Rorschach (1884–1922). The **Rorschach Inkblot Test** is *a projective measure of personality in which the respondent indicates his or her thoughts about a series of 10 symmetrical inkblots* (Figure 11.5). The Rorschach is administered millions of time every year. The participants are asked to respond to the inkblots, and their responses are systematically scored in terms of what, where, and why they saw what they saw. For example, people who focus on the details of the inkblots may have obsessive-compulsive tendencies, whereas those who talk about sex or aggression may have sexual or aggressive problems.

FIGURE 11.5 Rorschach Inkblots

The Rorschach Inkblot Test is a projective test designed to assess psychological disorders.

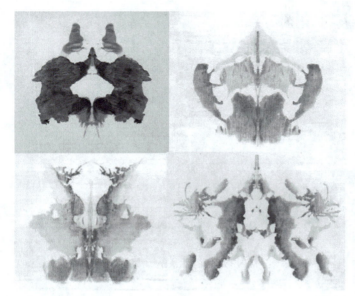

Another frequently administered projective test is the *Thematic Apperception Test (TAT)*, developed by the psychologist Henry Murray (1893–1988). The **Thematic Apperception Test (TAT)** is *a project-ive measure of personality in which the respondent is asked to create stories about sketches of ambiguous situations, most of them of people, either alone or with others* (Figure 11.6). The sketches are shown to individuals, who are asked to tell a story about what is happening in the picture. The TAT assumes that people may be unwilling or unable to admit their true feelings when asked directly but that these feel-ings will show up in the stories about the pictures. Trained coders read the stories and use them to de-velop a personality profile of the respondent.

Other popular projective tests include those that ask the respondent to draw pictures, such as the Draw-A-Person test (Machover, 1949),[32] and free association tests in which the respondent quickly responds with the first word that comes to mind when the examiner says a test word. Another ap-proach is the use of "anatomically correct" dolls that feature representations of the male and female genitals. Investigators allow children to play with the dolls and then try to determine on the basis of the play if the children may have been sexually abused.

The advantage of projective tests is that they are less direct, allowing people to avoid using their defense mechanisms and therefore show their "true" personality. The idea is that when people view ambiguous stimuli they will describe them according to the aspects of personality that are most import-ant to them, and therefore bypass some of the limitations of more conscious responding.

Despite their widespread use, however, the empirical evidence supporting the use of projective tests is mixed (Karon, 2000; Wood, Nezworski, Lilienfeld, & Garb, 2003).[33] The reliability of the meas-ures is low because people often produce very different responses on different occasions. The construct validity of the measures is also suspect because there are very few consistent associations between Rorschach scores or TAT scores and most personality traits. The projective tests often fail to distin-guish between people with psychological disorders and those without or to correlate with other meas-ures of personality or with behavior.

In sum, projective tests are more useful as icebreakers to get to know a person better, to make the person feel comfortable, and to get some ideas about topics that may be of importance to that person than for accurately diagnosing personality.

Thematic Apperception Test (TAT)

A projective measure of personality in which the respondent is asked to create stories about sketches of ambiguous situations, most of them of people, either alone or with others.

FIGURE 11.6
Sample Card From the TAT

This is one of the cards from the TAT. Note that the sex of the figure in the foreground is ambiguous as is the emotional expression of the woman in the background.

leadership

The ability to direct or inspire others to achieve goals.

charismatic leaders

Leaders who are enthusiastic, committed, and self-confident; who tend to talk about the importance of group goals at a broad level; and who make personal sacrifices for the group.

Psychology in Everyday Life: Leaders and Leadership

One trait that has been studied in thousands of studies is **leadership**, *the ability to direct or inspire others to achieve goals. Trait theories of leadership* are theories based on the idea that some people are simply "natural leaders" because they possess personality characteristics that make them effective (Zaccaro, 2007).[34] Consider Steve Jobs, the founder of the Apple, shown in Figure 11.7. What characteristics do you think he possessed that allowed him to create such a strong company, even though many similar companies failed?

Varieties of Leaders

Which personality traits do you think characterize these leaders?

Sources: Jackson portrait courtesy of Thomas Sully, http://commons.wikimedia.org/wiki/File:Andrew_Jackson.jpg. Roosevelt photo courtesy of the U.S. Library of Congress, http://commons.wikimedia.org/wiki/File:Franklin_Delano_Roosevelt_in_1933.jpg. Kennedy photo courtesy of the U.S. Navy, http://wikimediafoundation.org/wiki/File:John_F_Kennedy.jpg. Obama photo courtesy of James O'Malley, http://commons.wikimedia.org/wiki/File:Barack_Obama_Fold.jpg. Bloomberg photo courtesy of the U.S. Army, http://commons.wikimedia.org/wiki/File:Michael_Bloomberg_speech.jpg. Jobs photo courtesy of Matt Buchanan, http://commons.wikimedia.org/wiki/File:Steve_Jobs_with_the_Apple_iPad_no_logo.jpg.

Research has found that being intelligent is an important characteristic of leaders, as long as the leader communicates to others in a way that is easily understood by his or her followers (Simonton, 1994, 1995).[35] Other research has found that people with good social skills, such as the ability to accurately perceive the needs and goals of the group members and to communicate with others, also tend to make good leaders (Kenny & Zaccaro, 1983).[36]

Because so many characteristics seem to be related to leader skills, some researchers have attempted to account for leadership not in terms of individual traits, but rather in terms of a package of traits that successful leaders seem to have. Some have considered this in terms of charisma (Sternberg & Lubart, 1995; Sternberg, 2002).[37] **Charismatic leaders** are *leaders who are enthusiastic, committed, and self-confident; who tend to talk about the importance of group goals at a broad level; and who make personal sacrifices for the group.* Charismatic leaders express views that support and validate existing group norms but that also contain a vision of what the group could or should be. Charismatic leaders use their referent power to motivate, uplift, and inspire others. And research has found a positive relationship between a leader's charisma and effective leadership performance (Simonton, 1988).[38]

Another trait-based approach to leadership is based on the idea that leaders take either *transactional* or *transformational* leadership styles with their subordinates (Bass, 1999; Pieterse, Van Knippenberg, Schippers, & Stam, 2010).[39] *Transactional* leaders are the more regular leaders, who work with their subordinates to help them understand what is required of them and to get the job done. *Transformational* leaders, on the other hand, are more like charismatic leaders—they have a vision of where the group is going, and attempt to stimulate and inspire their workers to move beyond their present status and to create a new and better future.

Despite the fact that there appear to be at least some personality traits that relate to leadership ability, the most important approaches to understanding leadership take into consideration both the personality characteristics of the leader as well as the situation in which the leader is operating. In some cases the situation itself is important. For instance, you might remember that President George W. Bush's ratings as a leader increased dramatically after the September 11, 2001, terrorist attacks on the World Trade Center. This is a classic example of how a situation can influence the perceptions of a leader's skill.

In still other cases, different types of leaders may perform differently in different situations. Leaders whose personalities lead them to be more focused on fostering harmonious social relationships among the members of the group, for instance, are particularly effective in situations in which the group is already functioning well and yet it is important to keep the group members engaged in the task and committed to the group outcomes. Leaders who are more task-oriented and directive, on the other hand, are more effective when the group is not functioning well and needs a firm hand to guide it (Ayman, Chemers, & Fiedler, 1995).[40]

KEY TAKEAWAYS

- Personality is an individual's consistent patterns of feeling, thinking, and behaving.
- Personality is driven in large part by underlying individual motivations, where motivation refers to a need or desire that directs behavior.
- Early theories assumed that personality was expressed in people's physical appearance. One of these approaches, known as physiognomy, has been validated by current research.
- Personalities are characterized in terms of traits—relatively enduring characteristics that influence our behavior across many situations.
- The most important and well-validated theory about the traits of normal personality is the Five-Factor Model of Personality.
- There is often only a low correlation between the specific traits that a person expresses in one situation and those that he expresses in other situations. This is in part because people tend to see more traits in other people than they do in themselves. Personality predicts behavior better when the behaviors are aggregated or averaged across different situations.
- The Minnesota Multiphasic Personality Inventory (MMPI) is the most important measure of psychological disorders.
- Projective measures are measures of personality in which unstructured stimuli, such as inkblots, drawings of social situations, or incomplete sentences are shown to participants, who are asked to freely list what comes to mind as they think about the stimuli. Despite their widespread use, however, the empirical evidence supporting the use of projective tests is mixed.

EXERCISES AND CRITICAL THINKING

1. Consider your own personality and those of people you know. What traits do you enjoy in other people, and what traits do you dislike?
2. Consider some of the people who have had an important influence on you. What were the personality characteristics of these people that made them so influential?

2. THE ORIGINS OF PERSONALITY

LEARNING OBJECTIVES

1. **Describe the strengths and limitations of the psychodynamic approach to explaining personality.**
2. **Summarize the accomplishments of the neo-Freudians.**
3. **Identify the major contributions of the humanistic approach to understanding personality.**

Although measures such as the Big Five and the Minnesota Multiphasic Personality Inventory (MMPI) are able to effectively assess personality, they do not say much about where personality comes from. In this section we will consider two major theories of the origin of personality: *psychodynamic* and *humanistic* approaches.

2.1 Psychodynamic Theories of Personality: The Role of the Unconscious

psychodynamic psychology

An approach to understanding human behavior that focuses on the role of unconscious thoughts, feelings and memories.

One of the most important psychological approaches to understanding personality is based on the theorizing of the Austrian physician and psychologist Sigmund Freud (1856–1939), who founded what today is known as the **psychodynamic approach** to understanding personality. Many people know about Freud because his work has had a huge impact on our everyday thinking about psychology, and the psychodynamic approach is one of the most important approaches to psychological therapy (Roudinesco, 2003; Taylor, 2009).[41] Freud is probably the best known of all psychologists, in part because of his impressive observation and analyses of personality (there are 24 volumes of his writings). As is true of all theories, many of Freud's ingenious ideas have turned out to be at least partially incorrect, and yet other aspects of his theories are still influencing psychology.

Freud was influenced by the work of the French neurologist Jean-Martin Charcot (1825–1893), who had been interviewing patients (almost all women) who were experiencing what was at the time known as *hysteria*. Although it is no longer used to describe a psychological disorder, hysteria at the time referred to a set of personality and physical symptoms that included chronic pain, fainting, seizures, and paralysis.

Charcot could find no biological reason for the symptoms. For instance, some women experienced a loss of feeling in their hands and yet not in their arms, and this seemed impossible given that the nerves in the arms are the same that are in the hands. Charcot was experimenting with the use of hypnosis, and he and Freud found that under hypnosis many of the hysterical patients reported having experienced a traumatic sexual experience, such as sexual abuse, as children (Dolnick, 1998).[42]

Freud and Charcot also found that during hypnosis the remembering of the trauma was often accompanied by an outpouring of emotion, known as *catharsis*, and that following the catharsis the patient's symptoms were frequently reduced in severity. These observations led Freud and Charcot to conclude that these disorders were caused by psychological rather than physiological factors.

Freud used the observations that he and Charcot had made to develop his theory regarding the sources of personality and behavior, and his insights are central to the fundamental themes of psychology. In terms of free will, Freud did not believe that we were able to control our own behaviors. Rather, he believed that all behaviors are predetermined by motivations that lie outside our awareness, in the unconscious. These forces show themselves in our dreams, in neurotic symptoms such as obsessions, while we are under hypnosis, and in Freudian "slips of the tongue" in which people reveal their unconscious desires in language. Freud argued that we rarely understand why we do what we do, although we can make up explanations for our behaviors after the fact. For Freud the mind was like an iceberg, with the many motivations of the unconscious being much larger, but also out of sight, in comparison to the consciousness of which we are aware (Figure 11.8).

FIGURE 11.8 Mind as Iceberg

In Sigmund Freud's conceptualization of personality, the most important motivations are unconscious, just as the major part of an iceberg is under water.

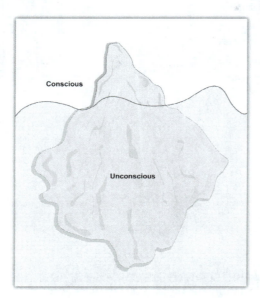

Id, Ego, and Superego

Freud proposed that the mind is divided into three components: *id*, *ego*, and *superego*, and that the interactions and conflicts among the components create personality (Freud, 1923/1943).[43] According to Freudian theory, the **id** is *the component of personality that forms the basis of our most primitive impulses*. The id is entirely unconscious, and it drives our most important motivations, including the sexual drive (*libido*) and the aggressive or destructive drive (*Thanatos*). According to Freud, the id is driven by the *pleasure principle*—the desire for immediate gratification of our sexual and aggressive urges. The id is why we smoke cigarettes, drink alcohol, view pornography, tell mean jokes about people, and engage in other fun or harmful behaviors, often at the cost of doing more productive activities.

In stark contrast to the id, the **superego** represents *our sense of morality and oughts*. The superego tell us all the things that we shouldn't do, or the duties and obligations of society. The superego strives for perfection, and when we fail to live up to its demands we feel guilty.

In contrast to the id, which is about the pleasure principle, the function of the *ego* is based on the *reality principle*—the idea that we must delay gratification of our basic motivations until the appropriate time with the appropriate outlet. The **ego** is *the largely conscious controller or decision-maker of personality*. The ego serves as the intermediary between the desires of the id and the constraints of society contained in the superego (Figure 11.9). We may wish to scream, yell, or hit, and yet our ego normally tells us to wait, reflect, and choose a more appropriate response.

id

In psychodynamic psychology, the component of personality that forms the basis of our most primitive impulses.

superego

In psychodynamic psychology, the component of personality that represents our sense of morality and oughts.

ego

In psychodynamic psychology, the component of personality that is the largely conscious controller or decision-maker of personality.

FIGURE 11.9 Ego, Id, and Superego in Interaction

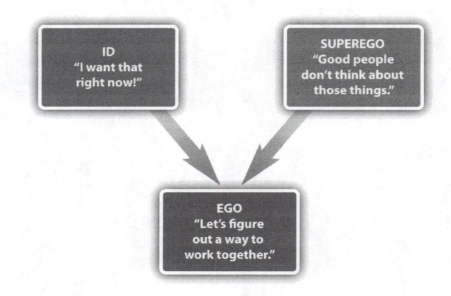

defense mechanisms

Unconscious psychological strategies used to cope with anxiety and to maintain a positive self-image.

Freud believed that psychological disorders, and particularly the experience of anxiety, occur when there is conflict or imbalance among the motivations of the id, ego, and superego. When the ego finds that the id is pressing too hard for immediate pleasure, it attempts to correct for this problem, often through the use of **defense mechanisms**—*unconscious psychological strategies used to cope with anxiety and to maintain a positive self-image.* Freud believed that the defense mechanisms were essential for effective coping with everyday life, but that any of them could be overused (Table 11.4).

TABLE 11.4 The Major Freudian Defense Mechanisms

Defense mechanism	Definition	Possible behavioral example
Displacement	Diverting threatening impulses away from the source of the anxiety and toward a more acceptable source	A student who is angry at her professor for a low grade lashes out at her roommate, who is a safer target of her anger.
Projection	Disguising threatening impulses by attributing them to others	A man with powerful unconscious sexual desires for women claims that women use him as a sex object.
Rationalization	Generating self-justifying explanations for our negative behaviors	A drama student convinces herself that getting the part in the play wasn't that important after all.
Reaction formation	Making unacceptable motivations appear as their exact opposite	Jane is sexually attracted to friend Jake, but she claims in public that she intensely dislikes him.
Regression	Retreating to an earlier, more childlike, and safer stage of development	A college student who is worried about an important test begins to suck on his finger.
Repression (or denial)	Pushing anxiety-arousing thoughts into the unconscious	A person who witnesses his parents having sex is later unable to remember anything about the event.
Sublimation	Channeling unacceptable sexual or aggressive desires into acceptable activities	A person participates in sports to sublimate aggressive drives. A person creates music or art to sublimate sexual drives.

The most controversial, and least scientifically valid, part of Freudian theory is its explanations of personality development. Freud argued that personality is developed through a series of *psychosexual stages*, each focusing on pleasure from a different part of the body (Table 11.5). Freud believed that sexuality begins in infancy, and that the appropriate resolution of each stage has implications for later personality development.

TABLE 11.5 Freud's Stages of Psychosexual Development

Stage	Approximate ages	Description
Oral	Birth to 18 months	Pleasure comes from the mouth in the form of sucking, biting, and chewing.
Anal	18 months to 3 years	Pleasure comes from bowel and bladder elimination and the constraints of toilet training.
Phallic	3 years to 6 years	Pleasure comes from the genitals, and the conflict is with sexual desires for the opposite-sex parent.
Latency	6 years to puberty	Sexual feelings are less important.
Genital	Puberty and older	If prior stages have been properly reached, mature sexual orientation develops.

In the first of Freud's proposed stages of psychosexual development, which begins at birth and lasts until about 18 months of age, the focus is on the mouth. During this *oral stage*, the infant obtains sexual pleasure by sucking and drinking. Infants who receive either too little or too much gratification become *fixated* or "locked" in the oral stage, and are likely to regress to these points of fixation under stress, even as adults. According to Freud, a child who receives too little oral gratification (e.g., who was underfed or neglected) will become *orally dependent* as an adult and be likely to manipulate others to fulfill his or her needs rather than becoming independent. On the other hand, the child who was overfed or overly gratified will resist growing up and try to return to the prior state of dependency by acting helpless, demanding satisfaction from others, and acting in a needy way.

The *anal stage*, lasting from about 18 months to 3 years of age is when children first experience psychological conflict. During this stage children desire to experience pleasure through bowel movements, but they are also being toilet trained to delay this gratification. Freud believed that if this toilet training was either too harsh or too lenient, children would become fixated in the anal stage and become likely to regress to this stage under stress as adults. If the child received too little anal gratification (i.e., if the parents had been very harsh about toilet training), the adult personality will be *anal retentive*—stingy, with a compulsive seeking of order and tidiness. On the other hand, if the parents had been too lenient, the *anal expulsive* personality results, characterized by a lack of self-control and a tendency toward messiness and carelessness.

The *phallic stage*, which lasts from age 3 to age 6 is when the penis (for boys) and clitoris (for girls) become the primary erogenous zone for sexual pleasure. During this stage, Freud believed that children develop a powerful but unconscious attraction for the opposite-sex parent, as well as a desire to eliminate the same-sex parent as a rival. Freud based his theory of sexual development in boys (the "Oedipus complex") on the Greek mythological character Oedipus, who unknowingly killed his father and married his mother, and then put his own eyes out when he learned what he had done. Freud argued that boys will normally eventually abandon their love of the mother, and instead identify with the father, also taking on the father's personality characteristics, but that boys who do not successfully resolve the Oedipus complex will experience psychological problems later in life. Although it was not as important in Freud's theorizing, in girls the phallic stage is often termed the "Electra complex," after the Greek character who avenged her father's murder by killing her mother. Freud believed that girls frequently experienced *penis envy*, the sense of deprivation supposedly experienced by girls because they do not have a penis.

The *latency stage* is a period of relative calm that lasts from about 6 years to 12 years. During this time, Freud believed that sexual impulses were repressed, leading boys and girls to have little or no interest in members of the opposite sex.

The fifth and last stage, the *genital stage*, begins about 12 years of age and lasts into adulthood. According to Freud, sexual impulses return during this time frame, and if development has proceeded normally to this point, the child is able to move into the development of mature romantic relationships. But if earlier problems have not been appropriately resolved, difficulties with establishing intimate love attachments are likely.

Freud's Followers: The Neo-Freudians

neo-Freudian theories

Theories based on Freudian principles that emphasize the role of the unconscious and early experience in shaping personality but place less evidence on sexuality as the primary motivating force in personality and are more optimistic concerning the prospects for personality growth and change in personality in adults.

Freudian theory was so popular that it led to a number of followers, including many of Freud's own students, who developed, modified, and expanded his theories. Taken together, these approaches are known as **neo-Freudian theories**. *The neo-Freudian theories are theories based on Freudian principles that emphasize the role of the unconscious and early experience in shaping personality but place less evidence on sexuality as the primary motivating force in personality and are more optimistic concerning the prospects for personality growth and change in personality in adults.*

Alfred Adler (1870–1937) was a follower of Freud who developed his own interpretation of Freudian theory. Adler proposed that the primary motivation in human personality was not sex or aggression, but rather the striving for superiority. According to Adler, we desire to be better than others and we accomplish this goal by creating a unique and valuable life. We may attempt to satisfy our need for superiority through our school or professional accomplishments, or by our enjoyment of music, athletics, or other activities that seem important to us.

Adler believed that psychological disorders begin in early childhood. He argued that children who are either overly nurtured or overly neglected by their parents are later likely to develop an *inferiority complex*—a psychological state in which people feel that they are not living up to expectations, leading them to have low self-esteem, with a tendency to try to overcompensate for the negative feelings. People with an inferiority complex often attempt to demonstrate their superiority to others at all costs, even if it means humiliating, dominating, or alienating them. According to Adler, most psychological disorders result from misguided attempts to compensate for the inferiority complex in order meet the goal of superiority.

collective unconscious

According to Carl Jung, a collection of shared ancestral memories.

Carl Jung (1875–1961) was another student of Freud who developed his own theories about personality. Jung agreed with Freud about the power of the unconscious but felt that Freud overemphasized the importance of sexuality. Jung argued that in addition to the personal unconscious, there was also a **collective unconscious**, or *a collection of shared ancestral memories*. Jung believed that the collective unconscious contains a variety of *archetypes*, or cross-culturally universal symbols, which explain the similarities among people in their emotional reactions to many stimuli. Important archetypes include the mother, the goddess, the hero, and the mandala or circle, which Jung believed symbolized a desire for wholeness or unity. For Jung, the underlying motivation that guides successful personality is *self-realization*, or learning about and developing the self to the fullest possible extent.

Karen Horney (the last syllable of her last name rhymes with "eye"; 1855–1952), was a German physician who applied Freudian theories to create a personality theory that she thought was more balanced between men and women. Horney believed that parts of Freudian theory, and particularly the ideas of the Oedipus complex and penis envy, were biased against women. Horney argued that women's sense of inferiority was not due to their lack of a penis but rather to their dependency on men, an approach that the culture made it difficult for them to break from. For Horney, the underlying motivation that guides personality development is the desire for *security*, the ability to develop appropriate and supportive relationships with others.

Another important neo-Freudian was Erich Fromm (1900–1980). Fromm's focus was on the negative impact of technology, arguing that the increases in its use have led people to feel increasingly isolated from others. Fromm believed that the independence that technology brings us also creates the need "escape from freedom," that is, to become closer to others.

Research Focus: How the Fear of Death Causes Aggressive Behavior

Fromm believed that the primary human motivation was to escape the fear of death, and contemporary research has shown how our concerns about dying can influence our behavior. In this research, people have been made to confront their death by writing about it or otherwise being reminded of it, and effects on their behavior are then observed. In one relevant study, McGregor et al. (1998)[44] demonstrated that people who are provoked may be particularly aggressive after they have been reminded of the possibility of their own death. The participants in the study had been selected, on the basis of prior reporting, to have either politically liberal or politically conservative views. When they arrived at the lab they were asked to write a short paragraph describing their opinion of politics in the United States. In addition, half of the participants (the *mortality salient condition*) were asked to "briefly describe the emotions that the thought of your own death arouses in you" and to "jot down as specifically as you can, what you think will happen to you as you physically die, and once you are physically dead." Participants in the *exam control condition* also thought about a negative event, but not one associated with a fear of death. They were instructed to "please briefly describe the emotions that the thought of your next important exam arouses in you" and to "jot down as specifically as you can, what you think will happen to you as you physically take your next exam, and once you are physically taking your next exam."

Then the participants read the essay that had supposedly just been written by another person. (The other person did not exist, but the participants didn't know this until the end of the experiment.) The essay that they read had been prepared by the experimenters to be very negative toward politically liberal views or to be very negative toward politically conservative views. Thus one-half of the participants were provoked by the other person by reading a statement that strongly conflicted with their own political beliefs, whereas the other half read an essay in which the other person's views supported their own (liberal or conservative) beliefs.

At this point the participants moved on to what they thought was a completely separate study in which they were to be tasting and giving their impression of some foods. Furthermore, they were told that it was necessary for the participants in the research to administer the food samples to each other. At this point, the participants found out that the food they were going to be sampling was spicy hot sauce and that they were going to be administering the sauce to the very person whose essay they had just read. In addition, the participants read some information about the other person that indicated that he very much disliked eating spicy food. Participants were given a taste of the hot sauce (it was really hot!) and then instructed to place a quantity of it into a cup for the other person to sample. Furthermore, they were told that the other person would have to eat all the sauce.

As you can see in Figure 11.10, McGregor et al. found that the participants who had not been reminded of their own death, even if they had been insulted by the partner, did not retaliate by giving him a lot of hot sauce to eat. On the other hand, the participants who were both provoked by the other person and who had also been reminded of their own death administered significantly more hot sauce than did the participants in the other three conditions. McGregor et al. (1998) argued that thinking about one's own death creates a strong concern with maintaining one's one cherished worldviews (in this case our political beliefs). When we are concerned about dying we become more motivated to defend these important beliefs from the challenges made by others, in this case by aggressing through the hot sauce.

Aggression as a Function of Mortality Salience and Provocation

Participants who had been provoked by a stranger who disagreed with them on important opinions, and who had also been reminded of their own death, administered significantly more unpleasant hot sauce to the partner than did the participants in the other three conditions.

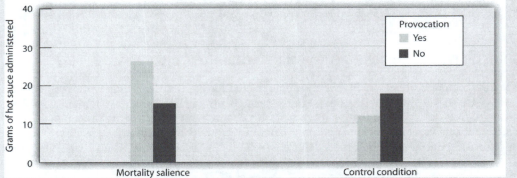

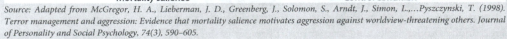

Source: Adapted from McGregor, H. A., Lieberman, J. D., Greenberg, J., Solomon, S., Arndt, J., Simon, L.,...Pyszczynski, T. (1998). Terror management and aggression: Evidence that mortality salience motivates aggression against worldview-threatening others. Journal of Personality and Social Psychology, 74(3), 590–605.

Strengths and Limitations of Freudian and Neo-Freudian Approaches

Freud has probably exerted a greater impact on the public's understanding of personality than any other thinker, and he has also in large part defined the field of psychology. Although Freudian psychologists no longer talk about oral, anal, or genital "fixations," they do continue to believe that our childhood experiences and unconscious motivations shape our personalities and our attachments with others, and they still make use of psychodynamic concepts when they conduct psychological therapy.

Nevertheless, Freud's theories, as well as those of the neo-Freudians, have in many cases failed to pass the test of empiricism, and as a result they are less influential now than they have been in the past (Crews, 1998).[45] The problems are first, that it has proved to be difficult to rigorously test Freudian theory because the predictions that it makes (particularly those regarding defense mechanisms) are often vague and unfalsifiable, and second, that the aspects of the theory that can be tested often have not received much empirical support.

As examples, although Freud claimed that children exposed to overly harsh toilet training would become fixated in the anal stage and thus be prone to excessive neatness, stinginess, and stubbornness in adulthood, research has found few reliable associations between toilet training practices and adult personality (Fisher & Greenberg, 1996).[46] And since the time of Freud, the need to repress sexual desires would seem to have become much less necessary as societies have tolerated a wider variety of sexual practices. And yet the psychological disorders that Freud thought we caused by this repression have not decreased.

There is also little scientific support for most of the Freudian defense mechanisms. For example, studies have failed to yield evidence for the existence of repression. People who are exposed to traumatic experiences in war have been found to remember their traumas only too well (Kihlstrom, 1997).[47] Although we may attempt to push information that is anxiety-arousing into our unconscious, this often has the ironic effect of making us think about the information even more strongly than if we hadn't tried to repress it (Newman, Duff, & Baumeister, 1997).[48] It is true that children remember little of their childhood experiences, but this seems to be true of both negative as well as positive experiences, is true for animals as well, and probably is better explained in terms of the brain's inability to form long-term memories than in terms of repression. On the other hand, Freud's important idea that expressing or talking through one's difficulties can be psychologically helpful has been supported in current research (Baddeley & Pennebaker, 2009)[49] and has become a mainstay of psychological therapy.

A particular problem for testing Freudian theories is that almost anything that conflicts with a prediction based in Freudian theory can be explained away in terms of the use of a defense mechanism. A man who expresses a lot of anger toward his father may be seen via Freudian theory to be experiencing the Oedipus complex, which includes conflict with the father. But a man who expresses no anger at all toward the father also may be seen as experiencing the Oedipus complex by repressing the anger. Because Freud hypothesized that either was possible, but did not specify when repression would or would not occur, the theory is difficult to falsify.

In terms of the important role of the unconscious, Freud seems to have been at least in part correct. More and more research demonstrates that a large part of everyday behavior is driven by processes that are outside our conscious awareness (Kihlstrom, 1987).[50] And yet, although our unconscious motivations influence every aspect of our learning and behavior Freud probably overestimated the extent to which these unconscious motivations are primarily sexual and aggressive.

Taken together, it is fair to say that Freudian theory, like most psychological theories, was not entirely correct and that it has had to be modified over time as the results of new studies have become available. But the fundamental ideas about personality that Freud proposed, as well as the use of talk therapy as an essential component of therapy, are nevertheless still a major part of psychology and are used by clinical psychologists every day.

2.2   Focusing on the Self: Humanism and Self-Actualization

humanistic psychology

An approach to psychology that embraces the notions of self-esteem, self-actualization, and free will.

self-concept

The set of beliefs about who we are.

self-esteem

Positive feelings about the self.

self-actualization

The motivation to develop our innate potential to the fullest possible extent.

Psychoanalytic models of personality were complemented during the 1950s and 1960s by the theories of **humanistic psychologists**. In contrast to the proponents of psychoanalysis, humanists embraced the notion of free will. Arguing that people are free to choose their own lives and make their own decisions, humanistic psychologists focused on the underlying motivations that they believed drove personality, focusing on the nature of the **self-concept**, *the set of beliefs about who we are*, and **self-esteem**, *our positive feelings about the self*.

One of the most important humanists, Abraham Maslow (1908–1970), conceptualized personality in terms of a pyramid-shaped *hierarchy of motives* (Figure 11.11). At the base of the pyramid are the lowest-level motivations, including hunger and thirst, and safety and belongingness. Maslow argued that only when people are able to meet the lower-level needs are they able to move on to achieve the higher-level needs of self-esteem, and eventually **self-actualization**, which is *the motivation to develop our innate potential to the fullest possible extent*.

Maslow studied how successful people, including Albert Einstein, Abraham Lincoln, Martin Luther King Jr., Helen Keller, and Mahatma Gandhi had been able to lead such successful and productive lives. Maslow (1970)[51] believed that self-actualized people are creative, spontaneous, and loving of themselves and others. They tend to have a few deep friendships rather than many superficial ones, and are generally private. He felt that these individuals do not need to conform to the opinions of others because they are very confident and thus free to express unpopular opinions. Self-actualized people are also likely to have *peak experiences*, or transcendent moments of tranquility accompanied by a strong sense of connection with others.

FIGURE 11.11 Maslow's Hierarchy of Needs

Abraham Maslow conceptualized personality in terms of a hierarchy of needs. The highest of these motivations is self-actualization.

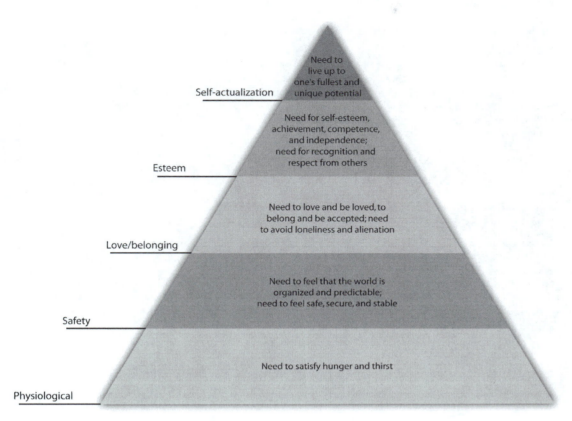

Perhaps the best-known humanistic theorist is Carl Rogers (1902–1987). Rogers was positive about human nature, viewing people as primarily moral and helpful to others, and believed that we can achieve our full potential for emotional fulfillment if the self-concept is characterized by **unconditional positive regard**—*a set of behaviors including being genuine, open to experience, transparent, able to listen to others, and self-disclosing and empathic.* When we treat ourselves or others with unconditional positive regard, we express understanding and support, even while we may acknowledge failings. Unconditional positive regard allows us to admit our fears and failures, to drop our pretenses, and yet at the same time to feel completely accepted for what we are. The principle of unconditional positive regard has become a foundation of psychological therapy; therapists who use it in their practice are more effective than those who do not (Prochaska & Norcross, 2007; Yalom, 1995).[52]

Although there are critiques of the humanistic psychologists (e.g., that Maslow focused on historically productive rather than destructive personalities in his research and thus drew overly optimistic conclusions about the capacity of people to do good), the ideas of humanism are so powerful and optimistic that they have continued to influence both everyday experiences as well as psychology. Today the *positive psychology movement* argues for many of these ideas, and research has documented the extent to which thinking positively and openly has important positive consequences for our relationships, our life satisfaction, and our psychological and physical health (Seligman & Csikszentmihalyi, 2000).[53]

unconditional positive regard

Behaviors including being genuine, open to experience, transparent, able to listen to others, and self-disclosing and empathic.

Research Focus: Self-Discrepancies, Anxiety, and Depression

Tory Higgins and his colleagues (Higgins, Bond, Klein, & Strauman, 1986; Strauman & Higgins, 1988)[54] have studied how different aspects of the self-concept relate to personality characteristics. These researchers focused on the types of emotional distress that we might experience as a result of how we are currently evaluating our self-concept. Higgins proposes that the emotions we experience are determined both by our perceptions of how well our own behaviors meet up to the standards and goals we have provided ourselves (our *internal standards*) and by our perceptions of how others think about us (our *external standards*). Furthermore, Higgins argues that different types of *self-discrepancies* lead to different types of negative emotions.

In one of Higgins's experiments (Higgins, Bond, Klein, & Strauman., 1986),[55] participants were first asked to describe themselves using a self-report measure. The participants listed 10 thoughts that they thought described the kind of person they actually are; this is the *actual self-concept*. Then, participants also listed 10 thoughts that they thought described the type of person they would "ideally like to be" (the *ideal self-concept*) as well as 10 thoughts describing the way that someone else—for instance, a parent—thinks they "ought to be" (the *ought self-concept*).

Higgins then divided his participants into two groups. Those with *low self-concept discrepancies* were those who listed similar traits on all three lists. Their ideal, ought, and actual self-concepts were all pretty similar and so they were not considered to be vulnerable to threats to their self-concept. The other half of the participants, those with *high self-concept discrepancies*, were those for whom the traits listed on the ideal and ought lists were very different from those listed on the actual self list. These participants were expected to be vulnerable to threats to the self-concept.

Then, at a later research session, Higgins first asked people to express their current emotions, including those related to sadness and anxiety. After obtaining this baseline measure Higgins activated either ideal or ought discrepancies for the participants. Participants in the *ideal self-discrepancy priming* condition were asked to think about and discuss their own and their parents' hopes and goals for them. Participants in the *ought self-priming condition* listed their own and their parents' beliefs concerning their duty and obligations. Then all participants again indicated their current emotions.

As you can see in Figure 11.12, for low self-concept discrepancy participants, thinking about their ideal or ought selves did not much change their emotions. For high self-concept discrepancy participants, however, priming the ideal self-concept increased their sadness and dejection, whereas priming the ought self-concept increased their anxiety and agitation. These results are consistent with the idea that discrepancies between the ideal and the actual self lead us to experience sadness, dissatisfaction, and other depression-related emotions, whereas discrepancies between the actual and ought self are more likely to lead to fear, worry, tension, and other anxiety-related emotions.

Results From Higgins, Bond, Klein, and Strauman, 1986

Higgins and his colleagues documented the impact of self-concept discrepancies on emotion. For participants with low self-concept discrepancies (right bars), seeing words that related to the self had little influence on emotions. For those with high self-concept discrepancies (left bars), priming the ideal self increased dejection whereas priming the ought self increased agitation.

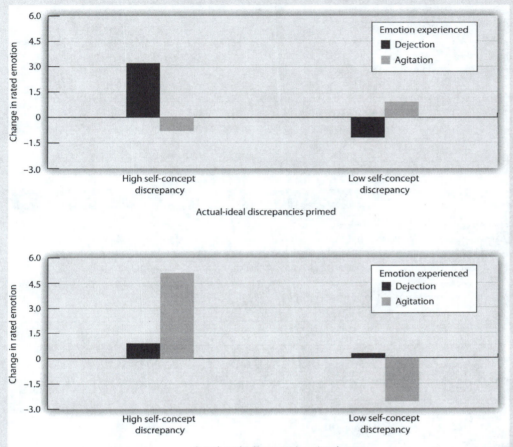

Source: Adapted from Higgins, E. T., Bond, R. N., Klein, R., & Strauman, T. (1986). Self-discrepancies and emotional vulnerability: How magnitude, accessibility, and type of discrepancy influence affect. Journal of Personality and Social Psychology, 51(1), 5–15.

One of the critical aspects of Higgins's approach is that, as is our personality, our feelings are also influenced both by our own behavior and by our expectations of how other people view us. This makes it clear that even though you might not care that much about achieving in school, your failure to do well may still produce negative emotions because you realize that your parents do think it is important.

KEY TAKEAWAYS

- One of the most important psychological approaches to understanding personality is based on the psychodynamic approach to personality developed by Sigmund Freud.
- For Freud the mind was like an iceberg, with the many motivations of the unconscious being much larger, but also out of sight, in comparison to the consciousness of which we are aware.
- Freud proposed that the mind is divided into three components: id, ego, and superego, and that the interactions and conflicts among the components create personality.
- Freud proposed that we use defense mechanisms to cope with anxiety and to maintain a positive self-image.
- Freud argued that personality is developed through a series of psychosexual stages, each focusing on pleasure from a different part of the body.
- The neo-Freudian theorists, including Adler, Jung, Horney, and Fromm, emphasized the role of the unconscious and early experience in shaping personality, but placed less evidence on sexuality as the primary motivating force in personality.
- Psychoanalytic and behavioral models of personality were complemented during the 1950s and 1960s by the theories of humanistic psychologists, including Maslow and Rogers.

EXERCISES AND CRITICAL THINKING

1. Based on your understanding of psychodynamic theories, how would you analyze your own personality? Are there aspects of the theory that might help you explain your own strengths and weaknesses?
2. Based on your understanding of humanistic theories, how would you try to change your behavior to better meet the underlying motivations of security, acceptance, and self-realization?
3. Consider your own self-concept discrepancies. Do you have an actual-ideal or actual-ought discrepancy? Which one is more important for you, and why?

3.   IS PERSONALITY MORE NATURE OR MORE NURTURE? BEHAVIORAL AND MOLECULAR GENETICS

LEARNING OBJECTIVES

1. **Explain how genes transmit personality from one generation to the next.**
2. **Outline the methods of behavioral genetics studies and the conclusions that we can draw from them about the determinants of personality.**
3. **Explain how molecular genetics research helps us understand the role of genetics in personality.**

One question that is exceedingly important for the study of personality concerns the extent to which it is the result of nature or nurture. If nature is more important, then our personalities will form early in our lives and will be difficult to change later. If nurture is more important, however, then our experiences are likely to be particularly important, and we may be able to flexibly alter our personalities over time. In this section we will see that the personality traits of humans and animals are determined in large part by their genetic makeup, and thus it is no surprise that identical twins Paula Bernstein and Elyse Schein turned out to be very similar even though they had been raised separately. But we will also see that genetics does not determine everything.

In the nucleus of each cell in your body are 23 pairs of *chromosomes*. One of each pair comes from your father, and the other comes from your mother. The chromosomes are made up of strands of the molecule *DNA* (deoxyribonucleic acid), and the DNA is grouped into segments known as *genes*. A **gene** is *the basic biological unit that transmits characteristics from one generation to the next.* Human cells have about 25,000 genes.

gene

The basic biological unit that transmits characteristics from one generation to the next.

The genes of different members of the same species are almost identical. The DNA in your genes, for instance, is about 99.9% the same as the DNA in my genes and in the DNA of every other human being. These common genetic structures lead members of the same species to be born with a variety of behaviors that come naturally to them and that define the characteristics of the species. These abilities and characteristics are known as **instincts**—*complex inborn patterns of behaviors that help ensure survival and reproduction* (Tinbergen, 1951).[56] Different animals have different instincts. Birds naturally build nests, dogs are naturally loyal to their human caretakers, and humans instinctively learn to walk and to speak and understand language.

But the strength of different traits and behaviors also varies within species. Rabbits are naturally fearful, but some are more fearful than others; some dogs are more loyal than others to their caretakers; and some humans learn to speak and write better than others do. These differences are determined in part by the small amount (in humans, the 0.1%) of the differences in genes among the members of the species.

Personality is not determined by any single gene, but rather by the actions of many genes working together. There is no "IQ gene" that determines intelligence and there is no "good marriage partner gene" that makes a person a particularly good marriage bet. Furthermore, even working together, genes are not so powerful that they can control or create our personality. Some genes tend to increase a given characteristic and others work to decrease that same characteristic—the complex relationship among the various genes, as well as a variety of random factors, produces the final outcome. Furthermore, genetic factors always work with environmental factors to create personality. Having a given pattern of genes doesn't necessarily mean that a particular trait will develop, because some traits might occur only in some environments. For example, a person may have a genetic variant that is known to increase his or her risk for developing emphysema from smoking. But if that person never smokes, then emphysema most likely will not develop.

3.1 Studying Personality Using Behavioral Genetics

Perhaps the most direct way to study the role of genetics in personality is to selectively breed animals for the trait of interest. In this approach the scientist chooses the animals that most strongly express the personality characteristics of interest and breeds these animals with each other. If the selective breeding creates offspring with even stronger traits, then we can assume that the trait has genetic origins. In this manner, scientists have studied the role of genetics in how worms respond to stimuli, how fish develop courtship rituals, how rats differ in play, and how pigs differ in their responses to stress.

Although selective breeding studies can be informative, they are clearly not useful for studying humans. For this psychologists rely on **behavioral genetics**—*a variety of research techniques that scientists use to learn about the genetic and environmental influences on human behavior by comparing the traits of biologically and nonbiologically related family members* (Baker, 2010).[57] Behavioral genetics is based on the results of *family studies, twin studies*, and *adoptive studies*.

A **family study** *starts with one person who has a trait of interest—for instance, a developmental disorder such as autism—and examines the individual's family tree to determine the extent to which other members of the family also have the trait*. The presence of the trait in first-degree relatives (parents, siblings, and children) is compared to the prevalence of the trait in second-degree relatives (aunts, uncles, grandchildren, grandparents, and nephews or nieces) and in more distant family members. The scientists then analyze the patterns of the trait in the family members to see the extent to which it is shared by closer and more distant relatives.

Although family studies can reveal whether a trait runs in a family, it cannot explain why. In a **twin study**, *researchers study the personality characteristics of twins*. Twin studies rely on the fact that identical (or monozygotic) twins have essentially the same set of genes, while fraternal (or dizygotic) twins have, on average, a half-identical set. The idea is that if the twins are raised in the same household, then the twins will be influenced by their environments to an equal degree, and this influence will be pretty much equal for identical and fraternal twins. In other words, if environmental factors are the same, then the only factor that can make identical twins more similar than fraternal twins is their greater genetic similarity.

In a twin study, *the data from many pairs of twins are collected and the rates of similarity for identical and fraternal pairs are compared*. A correlation coefficient is calculated that assesses the extent to which the trait for one twin is associated with the trait in the other twin. Twin studies divide the influence of nature and nurture into three parts:

- *Heritability (i.e., genetic influence)* is indicated when the correlation coefficient for identical twins exceeds that for fraternal twins, indicating that shared DNA is an important determinant of personality.

instinct

A complex inborn pattern of behaviors that help ensure survival and reproduction.

behavioral genetics

A variety of research techniques that scientists use to learn about the genetic and environmental influences on human behavior by comparing the traits of biologically and nonbiologically related family members.

family study

A behavioral genetics study that starts with one person who has a trait of interest and examines the individual's family tree to determine the extent to which other family members also have the trait.

twin study

A behavioral genetics study in which the data from many pairs of twins are collected and the rates of similarity for identical and fraternal pairs are compared.

■ *Shared environment* determinants are indicated when the correlation coefficients for identical and fraternal twins are greater than zero and also very similar. These correlations indicate that both twins are having experiences in the family that make them alike.

■ *Nonshared environment* is indicated when identical twins do not have similar traits. These influences refer to experiences that are not accounted for either by heritability or by shared environmental factors. Nonshared environmental factors are the experiences that make individuals within the same family *less* alike. If a parent treats one child more affectionately than another, and as a consequence this child ends up with higher self-esteem, the parenting in this case is a nonshared environmental factor.

In the typical twin study, all three sources of influence are operating simultaneously, and it is possible to determine the relative importance of each type.

adoption study

A behavioral genetics study that compares biologically related people, including twins, who have been reared either separately or apart.

An **adoption study** *compares biologically related people, including twins, who have been reared either separately or apart.* Evidence for genetic influence on a trait is found when children who have been adopted show traits that are more similar to those of their biological parents than to those of their adoptive parents. Evidence for environmental influence is found when the adoptee is more like his or her adoptive parents than the biological parents.

The results of family, twin, and adoption studies are combined to get a better idea of the influence of genetics and environment on traits of interest. Table 11.6 presents data on the correlations and heritability estimates for a variety of traits based on the results of behavioral genetics studies (Bouchard, Lykken, McGue, Segal, & Tellegen, 1990).[58]

TABLE 11.6 Data From Twin and Adoption Studies on the Heritability of Various Characteristics

	Correlation between children raised together		Correlation between children raised apart		Estimated percent of total due to		
	Identical twins	Fraternal twins	Identical twins	Fraternal twins	Heritability (%)	Shared environment (%)	Nonshared environment (%)
Age of puberty					45	5	50
Aggression	0.43	0.14	0.46	0.06			
Alzheimer disease	0.54	0.16					
Fingerprint patterns	0.96	0.47	0.96	0.47	100	0	0
General cognitive ability					56	0	44
Likelihood of divorce	0.52	0.22					
Sexual orientation	0.52	0.22			18–39	0–17	61–66
Big Five dimensions					40–50		

This table presents some of the observed correlations and heritability estimates for various characteristics.

Sources: Långström, N., Rahman, Q., Carlström, E., & Lichtenstein, P. (2008). Genetic and environmental effects on same-sex sexual behavior: A population study of twins in Sweden. Archives of Sexual Behavior, doi:10.1007/s10508-008-9386-1; Loehlin, J. C. (1992). Genes and environment in personality development. Thousand Oaks, CA: Sage Publications, Inc; McGue, M., & Lykken, D. T. (1992). Genetic influence on risk of divorce. Psychological Science, 3(6), 368–373; Plomin, R., Fulker, D. W., Corley, R., & DeFries, J. C. (1997). Nature, nurture, and cognitive development from 1 to 16 years: A parent-offspring adoption study. Psychological Science, 8(6), 442–447; Tellegen, A., Lykken, D. T., Bouchard, T. J., Wilcox, K. J., Segal, N. L., & Rich, S. (1988). Personality similarity in twins reared apart and together. Journal of Personality and Social Psychology, 54(6), 1031–1039.

If you look in the second column of Table 11.6, you will see the observed correlations for the traits between identical twins who have been raised together in the same house by the same parents. This column represents the pure effects of genetics, in the sense that environmental differences have been controlled to be a small as possible. You can see that these correlations are higher for some traits than for others. Fingerprint patterns are very highly determined by our genetics ($r = .96$), whereas the Big Five trait dimensions have a heritability of 40–50%.

You can also see from the table that, overall, there is more influence of nature than of parents. Identical twins, even when they are raised in separate households by different parents (column 4), turn out to be quite similar in personality, and are more similar than fraternal twins who are raised in separate households (column 5). These results show that genetics has a strong influence on personality, and helps explain why Elyse and Paula were so similar when they finally met.

Despite the overall role of genetics, you can see in Table 11.6 that the correlations between identical twins (column 2) and heritability estimates for most traits (column 6) are substantially less than 1.00, showing that the environment also plays an important role in personality (Turkheimer & Waldron, 2000).[59] For instance, for sexual orientation the estimates of heritability vary from 18% to 39% of the total across studies, suggesting that 61% to 82% of the total influence is due to environment.

You might at first think that parents would have a strong influence on the personalities of their children, but this would be incorrect. As you can see by looking in column 7 of Table 11.6, research finds that the influence of shared environment (i.e., the effects of parents or other caretakers) plays little or no role in adult personality (Harris, 2006).[60] Shared environment does influence the personality and behavior of young children, but this influence decreases rapidly as the child grows older. By the time we reach adulthood, the impact of shared environment on our personalities is weak at best (Roberts & DelVecchio, 2000).[61] What this means is that, although parents must provide a nourishing and stimulating environment for children, no matter how hard they try they are not likely to be able to turn their children into geniuses or into professional athletes, nor will they be able to turn them into criminals.

If parents are not providing the environmental influences on the child, then what is? The last column in Table 11.6, the influence of nonshared environment, represents whatever is "left over" after removing the effects of genetics and parents. You can see that these factors—the largely unknown things that happen to us that make us different from other people—often have the largest influence on personality.

3.2   Studying Personality Using Molecular Genetics

In addition to the use of behavioral genetics, our understanding of the role of biology in personality recently has been dramatically increased through the use of **molecular genetics**, which is *the study of which genes are associated with which personality traits* (Goldsmith et al., 2003 Strachan & Read, 1999).[62] These advances have occured as a result of new knowledge about the structure of human DNA made possible through the Human Genome Project and related work that has identified the genes in the human body (Human Genome Project, 2010).[63] Molecular genetics researchers have also developed new techniques that allow them to find the locations of genes within chromosomes and to identify the effects those genes have when activated or deactivated.

One approach that can be used in animals, usually in laboratory mice, is the *knockout study*. In this approach the researchers use specialized techniques to remove or modify the influence of a gene in a line of "knockout" mice (Crusio, Goldowitz, Holmes, & Wolfer, 2009).[64] The researchers harvest embryonic stem cells from mouse embryos and then modify the DNA of the cells. The DNA is created such that the action of certain genes will be eliminated or "knocked out." The cells are then injected into the embryos of other mice that are implanted into the uteruses of living female mice. When these animals are born, they are studied to see whether their behavior differs from a control group of normal animals. Research has found that removing or changing genes in mice can affect their anxiety, aggression, learning, and socialization patterns.

In humans, a molecular genetics study normally begins with the collection of a DNA sample from the participants in the study, usually by taking some cells from the inner surface of the cheek. In the lab, the DNA is extracted from the sampled cells and is combined with a solution containing a marker for the particular genes of interest as well as a fluorescent dye. If the gene is present in the DNA of the individual, then the solution will bind to that gene and activate the dye. The more the gene is expressed, the stronger the reaction.

molecular genetics

The study of which genes are associated with which personality traits.

FIGURE 11.13

These "knockout" mice are participating in studies in which some of their genes have been deactivated to determine the influence of the genes on behavior.

© *Thinkstock*

FIGURE 11.14

Researchers use dyes, such as these in a sample of stem cells, to determine the action of genes from DNA samples.

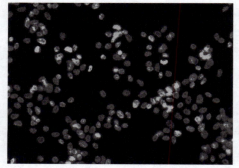

© Thinkstock

In one common approach, DNA is collected from people who have a particular personality characteristic and also from people who do not. The DNA of the two groups is compared to see which genes differ between them. These studies are now able to compare thousands of genes at the same time. Research using molecular genetics has found genes associated with a variety of personality traits including novelty-seeking (Ekelund, Lichtermann, Järvelin, & Peltonen, 1999),[65] attention-deficit/hyperactivity disorder (Waldman & Gizer, 2006),[66] and smoking behavior (Thorgeirsson et al., 2008).[67]

3.3   Reviewing the Literature: Is Our Genetics Our Destiny?

Over the past two decades scientists have made substantial progress in understanding the important role of genetics in behavior. Behavioral genetics studies have found that, for most traits, genetics is more important than parental influence. And molecular genetics studies have begun to pinpoint the particular genes that are causing these differences. The results of these studies might lead you to believe that your destiny is determined by your genes, but this would be a mistaken assumption.

For one, the results of all research must be interpreted carefully. Over time we will learn even more about the role of genetics, and our conclusions about its influence will likely change. Current research in the area of behavioral genetics is often criticized for making assumptions about how researchers categorize identical and fraternal twins, about whether twins are in fact treated in the same way by their parents, about whether twins are representative of children more generally, and about many other issues. Although these critiques may not change the overall conclusions, it must be kept in mind that these findings are relatively new and will certainly be updated with time (Plomin, 2000).[68]

Furthermore, it is important to reiterate that although genetics is important, and although we are learning more every day about its role in many personality variables, genetics does not determine everything. In fact, the major influence on personality is nonshared environmental influences, which include all the things that occur to us that make us unique individuals. These differences include variability in brain structure, nutrition, education, upbringing, and even interactions among the genes themselves.

The genetic differences that exist at birth may be either amplified or diminished over time through environmental factors. The brains and bodies of identical twins are not exactly the same, and they become even more different as they grow up. As a result, even genetically identical twins have distinct personalities, resulting in large part from environmental effects.

Because these nonshared environmental differences are nonsystematic and largely accidental or random, it will be difficult to ever determine exactly what will happen to a child as he or she grows up. Although we do inherit our genes, we do not inherit personality in any fixed sense. The effect of our genes on our behavior is entirely dependent upon the context of our life as it unfolds day to day. Based on your genes, no one can say what kind of human being you will turn out to be or what you will do in life.

KEY TAKEAWAYS

- Genes are the basic biological units that transmit characteristics from one generation to the next.
- Personality is not determined by any single gene, but rather by the actions of many genes working together.
- Behavioral genetics refers to a variety of research techniques that scientists use to learn about the genetic and environmental influences on human behavior.
- Behavioral genetics is based on the results of family studies, twin studies, and adoptive studies.
- Overall, genetics has more influence than do parents on shaping our personality.
- Molecular genetics is the study of which genes are associated with which personality traits.
- The largely unknown environmental influences, known as the nonshared environmental effects, have the largest impact on personality. Because these differences are nonsystematic and largely accidental or random, we do not inherit our personality in any fixed sense.

1. Think about the twins you know. Do they seem to be very similar to each other, or does it seem that their differences outweigh their similarities?

2. Describe the implications of the effects of genetics on personality, overall. What does it mean to say that genetics "determines" or "does not determine" our personality?

4. CHAPTER SUMMARY

Personality is defined as an individual's consistent patterns of feeling, thinking, and behaving. Early theories of personality, including phrenology and somatology, are now discredited, but there is at least some research evidence for physiognomy—the idea that it is possible to assess personality from facial characteristics.

Personalities are characterized in terms of traits, which are relatively enduring characteristics that influence our behavior across many situations. Psychologists have investigated hundreds of traits using the self-report approach.

The utility of self-report measures of personality depends on their reliability and construct validity. Some popular measures of personality, such as the Myers-Briggs Type Indicator (MBTI), do not have reliability or construct validity and therefore are not useful measures of personality.

The trait approach to personality was pioneered by early psychologists, including Allport, Cattell, and Eysenck, and their research helped produce the Five-Factor (Big Five) Model of Personality. The Big Five dimensions are cross-culturally valid and accurately predict behavior. The Big Five factors are also increasingly being used to help researchers understand the dimensions of psychological disorders.

A difficulty of the trait approach to personality is that there is often only a low correlation between the traits that a person expresses in one situation and those that he or she expresses in other situations. However, psychologists have also found that personality predicts behavior better when the behaviors are averaged across different situations.

People may believe in the existence of traits because they use their schemas to judge other people, leading them to believe that traits are more stable than they really are. An example is the Barnum effect—the observation that people tend to believe in descriptions of their personality that supposedly are descriptive of them but could in fact describe almost anyone.

An important personality test is the Minnesota Multiphasic Personality Inventory (MMPI) used to detect personality and psychological disorders. Another approach to measuring personality is to use projective measures, such as the Rorschach Inkblot Test and the Thematic Apperception Test (TAT). The advantage of projective tests is that they are less direct, but empirical evidence supporting their reliability and construct validity is mixed.

There are behaviorist, social-cognitive, psychodynamic, and humanist theories of personality.

The psychodynamic approach to understanding personality, begun by Sigmund Freud, is based on the idea that all behaviors are predetermined by motivations that lie outside our awareness, in the unconscious. Freud proposed that the mind is divided into three components: id, ego, and superego, and that the interactions and conflicts among the components create personality. Freud also believed that psychological disorders, and particularly the experience of anxiety, occur when there is conflict or imbalance among the motivations of the id, ego, and superego and that people use defense mechanisms to cope with this anxiety.

Freud argued that personality is developed through a series of psychosexual stages, each focusing on pleasure from a different part of the body, and that the appropriate resolution of each stage has implications for later personality development.

Freud has probably exerted a greater impact on the public's understanding of personality than any other thinker, but his theories have in many cases failed to pass the test of empiricism.

Freudian theory led to a number of followers known as the neo-Freudians, including Adler, Jung, Horney, and Fromm.

Humanistic theories of personality focus on the underlying motivations that they believed drive personality, focusing on the nature of the self-concept and the development of self-esteem. The idea of unconditional positive regard championed by Carl Rogers has led in part to the positive psychology movement, and it is a basis for almost all contemporary psychological therapy.

Personality traits of humans and animals are determined in large part by their genetic makeup. Personality is not determined by any single gene, but rather by the actions of many genes working together.

The role of nature and nurture in personality is studied by means of behavioral genetics studies including family studies, twin studies, and adoption studies. These studies partition variability in personality into the influence of genetics (known as heritability), shared environment, and nonshared environment. Although these studies find that many personality traits are highly heritable, genetics does not determine everything. The major influence on personality is nonshared environmental influences.

In addition to the use of behavioral genetics, our understanding of the role of biology in personality recently has been dramatically increased through the use of molecular genetics, the study of which genes are associated with which personality traits in animals and humans.

ENDNOTES

1. Spilius, A. (2007, October 27). Identical twins reunited after 35 years. *Telegraph.* Retrieved from http://www.telegraph.co.uk/news/worldnews/1567542/Identical-twins-reunited-after-35-years.html; Kuntzman, G. (2007, October 6). Separated twins Paula Bernstein and Elyse Schein. *The Brooklyn Paper.* Retrieved from http://www.brooklynpaper.com/stories/30/39/30_39twins.html

2. John, O. P., Robins, R. W., & Pervin, L. A. (2008). *Handbook of personality psychology: Theory and research* (3rd ed.). New York, NY: Guilford Press.

3. Simpson, D. (2005). Phrenology and the neurosciences: Contributions of F. J. Gall and J. G. Spurzheim. *ANZ Journal of Surgery, 75*(6), 475–482.

4. Sheldon, W. (1940). *The varieties of human physique: An introduction to constitutional psychology.* New York, NY: Harper.

5. Rule, N. O., & Ambady, N. (2010). Democrats and Republicans can be differentiated from their faces. *PLoS ONE, 5*(1), e8733; Rule, N. O., Ambady, N., Adams, R. B., Jr., & Macrae, C. N. (2008). Accuracy and awareness in the perception and categorization of male sexual orientation. *Journal of Personality and Social Psychology, 95*(5), 1019–1028; Rule, N. O., Ambady, N., & Hallett, K. C. (2009). Female sexual orientation is perceived accurately, rapidly, and automatically from the face and its features. *Journal of Experimental Social Psychology, 45*(6), 1245–1251.

6. Olivola, C. Y., & Todorov, A. (2010). Fooled by first impressions? Reexamining the diagnostic value of appearance-based inferences. *Journal of Experimental Social Psychology, 46*(2), 315–324.

7. Hunsley, J., Lee, C. M., & Wood, J. M. (2003). Controversial and questionable assessment techniques. In S. O. Lilienfeld, S. J. Lynn, & J. M. Lohr (Eds.), *Science and pseudoscience in clinical psychology* (pp. 39–76). New York, NY: Guilford Press.

8. Allport, G. W., & Odbert, H. (1936). *Trait-names: A psycho-lexical study. No. 211.* Princeton, NJ: Psychological Review Monographs.

9. John, O. P., Angleitner, A., & Ostendorf, F. (1988). The lexical approach to personality: A historical review of trait taxonomic research. *European Journal of Personality, 2*(3), 171–203.

10. Allport, G. W. (1937). *Personality: A psychological interpretation.* New York, NY: Holt, Rinehart, & Winston.

11. Cattell, R. B. (1990). Advances in Cattellian personality theory. In L. A. Pervin (Ed.), *Handbook of personality: Theory and research* (pp. 101–110). New York, NY: Guilford Press.

12. Eysenck, H. (1998). *Dimensions of personality.* Piscataway, NJ: Transaction.

13. Costa, P. T., Jr., & McCrae, R. R. (1992). *Revised NEO Personality Inventory (NEO-PI-R) and NEO Five-Factor Inventory (NEO-FFI) manual.* Odessa, FL: Psychological Assessment Resources; Goldberg, L. R. (1982). From ace to zombie: Some explorations in the language of personality. In C. D. Spielberger & J. N. Butcher (Eds.), *Advances in personality assessment* (Vol. 1). Hillsdale, NJ: Lawrence Erlbaum Associates.

14. Triandis, H. C., & Suh, E. M. (2002). Cultural influences on personality. *Annual Review of Psychology, 53*(1), 133–160.

15. Tett, R. P., Jackson, D. N., & Rothstein, M. (1991). Personality measures as predictors of job performance: A meta-analytic review. *Personnel Psychology, 44*(4), 703–742.

16. Rubenzer, S. J., Faschingbauer, T. R., & Ones, D. S. (2000). Assessing the U.S. presidents using the revised NEO Personality Inventory. *Assessment, 7*(4), 403–420.

17. Oldham, J. (2010). Borderline personality disorder and *DSM-5. Journal of Psychiatric Practice, 16*(3), 143–154; Saulsman, L. M., & Page, A. C. (2004). The five-factor model and personality disorder empirical literature: A meta-analytic review. *Clinical Psychology Review, 23*, 1055–1085.

18. Cheung, F. M., & Leung, K. (1998). Indigenous personality measures: Chinese examples. *Journal of Cross-Cultural Psychology, 29*(1), 233–248.

19. Mischel, W. (1968). *Personality and assessment.* New York, NY: John Wiley & Sons.

20. Hartshorne, H., May, M. A., Maller, J. B., Shuttleworth, F. K. (1928). *Studies in the nature of character.* New York, NY: Macmillan.

21. Bem, D. J., & Allen, A. (1974). On predicting some of the people some of the time: The search for cross-situational consistencies in behavior. *Psychological Review, 81*(6), 506–520.

22. Gosling, S. D. (2001). From mice to men: What can we learn about personality from animal research? *Psychological Bulletin, 127*(1), 45–86.

23. Fiske, S. T., & Taylor, S. E. (2007). *Social cognition, from brains to culture.* New York, NY: McGraw-Hill.

24. Nisbett, R. E., Caputo, C., Legant, P., & Marecek, J. (1973). Behavior as seen by the actor and as seen by the observer. *Journal of Personality and Social Psychology, 27*(2), 154–164.

25. Hines, T. (2003). *Pseudoscience and the paranormal* (2nd ed.). Amherst, NY: Prometheus Books.

26. Mischel, W., & Shoda, Y. (2008). Toward a unified theory of personality: Integrating dispositions and processing dynamics within the cognitive-affective processing system. In O. P. John, R. W. Robins, & L. A. Pervin (Eds.), *Handbook of personality psychology: Theory and research* (3rd ed., pp. 208–241). New York, NY: Guilford Press.

27. Roberts, B. W., & DelVecchio, W. F. (2000). The rank-order consistency of personality traits from childhood to old age: A quantitative review of longitudinal studies. *Psychological Bulletin, 126*(1), 3–25; Srivastava, S., John, O. P., Gosling, S. D., & Potter, J. (2003). Development of personality in early and middle adulthood: Set like plaster or persistent change? *Journal of Personality and Social Psychology, 84*(5), 1041–1053.

28. Bandura, A. (1986). *Social foundations of thought and action: A social cognitive theory.* Englewood Cliffs, NJ: Prentice Hall.

29. Tellegen, A., Ben-Porath, Y. S., McNulty, J. L., Arbisi, P. A., Graham, J. R., & Kaemmer, B. (2003). *The MMPI-2 Restructured Clinical Scales: Development, validation, and interpretation.* Minneapolis: University of Minnesota Press.

30. Garb, H. N. (1998). Computers and judgment. In H. N. Garb (Ed.), *Studying the clinician: Judgment research and psychological assessment* (pp. 207–229). Washington, DC: American Psychological Association; Karon, B. P. (2000). The clinical interpretation of the Thematic Apperception Test, Rorschach, and other clinical data: A reexamination of statistical versus clinical prediction. *Professional Psychology: Research and Practice, 31*(2), 230–233.

31. Graham, J. R. (2006). *MMPI-2: Assessing personality and psychopathology* (4th ed.). New York, NY: Oxford University Press.

32. Machover, K. (1949). Personality projection in the drawing of the human figure (A method of personality investigation). In K. Machover (Ed.), *Personality projection in the drawing of the human figure: A method of personality investigation* (pp. 3–32). Springfield, IL: Charles C. Thomas.

33. Karon, B. P. (2000). The clinical interpretation of the Thematic Apperception Test, Rorschach, and other clinical data: A reexamination of statistical versus clinical prediction. *Professional Psychology: Research and Practice, 31*(2), 230–233; Wood, J. M., Nezworski, M. T., Lilienfeld, S. O., & Garb, H. N. (2003). *What's wrong with the Rorschach? Science confronts the controversial inkblot test.* San Francisco, CA: Jossey-Bass.

34. Zaccaro, S. J. (2007). Trait-based perspectives of leadership. *American Psychologist, 62*(1), 6–16.

35. Simonton, D. K. (1994). *Greatness: Who makes history and why.* New York, NY: Guilford Press; Simonton, D. K. (1995). Personality and intellectual predictors of leadership. In D. H. Saklofske & M. Zeidner (Eds.), *International handbook of personality and intelligence. Perspectives on individual differences* (pp. 739–757). New York, NY: Plenum.

36. Kenny, D. A., & Zaccaro, S. J. (1983). An estimate of variance due to traits in leadership. *Journal of Applied Psychology, 68*(4), 678–685.

37. Sternberg, R., & Lubart, T. (1995). *Defying the crowd: Cultivating creativity in a culture of conformity.* New York, NY: Free Press; Sternberg, R. J. (2002). Successful intelligence: A new approach to leadership. In R. E. Riggio, S. E. Murphy, & F. J. Pirozzolo (Eds.), *Multiple intelligences and leadership* (pp. 9–28). Mahwah, NJ: Lawrence Erlbaum Associates.

38. Simonton, D. K. (1988). Presidential style: Personality, biography and performance. *Journal of Personality and Social Psychology, 55*, 928–936.

39. Bass, B. M. (1999). Current developments in transformational leadership: Research and applications. *Psychologist-Manager Journal, 3*(1), 5–21; Pieterse, A. N., Van Knippenberg, D., Schippers, M., & Stam, D. (2010). Transformational and transactional leadership and innovative behavior: The moderating role of psychological empowerment. *Journal of Organizational Behavior, 31*(4), 609–623.

40. Ayman, R., Chemers, M. M., & Fiedler, F. (1995). The contingency model of leadership effectiveness: Its level of analysis. *The Leadership Quarterly, 6*(2), 147–167.

41. Roudinesco, E. (2003). *Why psychoanalysis?* New York, NY: Columbia University Press; Taylor, E. (2009). *The mystery of personality: A history of psychodynamic theories.* New York, NY: Springer Science + Business Media.

42. Dolnick, E. (1998). *Madness on the couch: Blaming the victim in the heyday of psychoanalysis.* New York, NY: Simon & Schuster.

43. Freud, S. (1923/1949). *The ego and the id.* London, England: Hogarth Press. (Original work published 1923)

44. McGregor, H. A., Lieberman, J. D., Greenberg, J., Solomon, S., Arndt, J., Simon, L.,…Pyszczynski, T. (1998). Terror management and aggression: Evidence that mortality salience motivates aggression against worldview-threatening others. *Journal of Personality and Social Psychology, 74*(3), 590–605.

45. Crews, F. C. (1998). *Unauthorized Freud: Doubters confront a legend.* New York, NY: Viking Press.

46. Fisher, S., & Greenberg, R. P. (1996). *Freud scientifically reappraised: Testing the theories and therapy.* Oxford, England: John Wiley & Sons.

47. Kihlstrom, J. F. (1997). Memory, abuse, and science. *American Psychologist, 52*(9), 994–995.

48. Newman, L. S., Duff, K. J., & Baumeister, R. F. (1997). A new look at defensive projection: Thought suppression, accessibility, and biased person perception. *Journal of Personality and Social Psychology, 72*(5), 980–1001.

49. Baddeley, J. L., & Pennebaker, J. W. (2009). Expressive writing. In W. T. O'Donohue & J. E. Fisher (Eds.), *General principles and empirically supported techniques of cognitive behavior therapy* (pp. 295–299). Hoboken, NJ: John Wiley & Sons.

50. Kihlstrom, J. F. (1987). The cognitive unconscious. *Science, 237*(4821), 1445–1452.

51. Maslow, Abraham (1970). *Motivation and personality* (2nd ed.). New York, NY: Harper.

52. Prochaska, J. O., & Norcross, J. C. (2007). *Systems of psychotherapy: A transtheoretical analysis* (6th ed.). Pacific Grove, CA: Brooks/Cole; Yalom, I. (1995). Introduction. In C. Rogers, *A way of being.* (1980). New York, NY: Houghton Mifflin.

53. Seligman, M. E. P., & Csikszentmihalyi, M. (2000). Positive psychology: An introduction. *American Psychologist, 55*(1), 5–14.

54. Higgins, E. T., Bond, R. N., Klein, R., & Strauman, T. (1986). Self-discrepancies and emotional vulnerability: How magnitude, accessibility, and type of discrepancy influence affect. *Journal of Personality and Social Psychology, 51*(1), 5–15; Strauman, T. J., & Higgins, E. T. (1988). Self-discrepancies as predictors of vulnerability to distinct syndromes of chronic emotional distress. *Journal of Personality, 56*(4), 685–707.

55. Higgins, E. T., Bond, R. N., Klein, R., & Strauman, T. (1986). Self-discrepancies and emotional vulnerability: How magnitude, accessibility, and type of discrepancy influence affect. *Journal of Personality and Social Psychology, 51*(1), 5–15.

56. Tinbergen, N. (1951). *The study of instinct* (1st ed.). Oxford, England: Clarendon Press.

57. Baker, C. (2004). Behavioral genetics: An introduction to how genes and environments interact through development to shape differences in mood, personality, and intelligence. Retrieved from http://www.aaas.org/spp/bgenes/Intro.pdf

58. Bouchard, T. J., Lykken, D. T., McGue, M., Segal, N. L., & Tellegen, A. (1990). Sources of human psychological differences: The Minnesota study of twins reared apart. *Science, 250*(4978), 223–228. Retrieved from http://www.sciencemag.org/cgi/content/abstract/250/4978/223

59. Turkheimer, E., & Waldron, M. (2000). Nonshared environment: A theoretical, methodological, and quantitative review. *Psychological Bulletin, 126*(1), 78–108.

60. Harris, J. R. (2006). *No two alike: Human nature and human individuality.* New York, NY: Norton.

61. Roberts, B. W., & DelVecchio, W. F. (2000). The rank-order consistency of personality traits from childhood to old age: A quantitative review of longitudinal studies. *Psychological Bulletin, 126*(1), 3–25.

62. Goldsmith, H., Gernsbacher, M. A., Crabbe, J., Dawson, G., Gottesman, I. I., Hewitt, J.,…Swanson, J. (2003). Research psychologists' roles in the genetic revolution. *American Psychologist, 58*(4), 318–319; Strachan, T., & Read, A. P. (1999). *Human molecular genetics* (2nd ed.). Retrieved from http://www.ncbi.nlm.nih.gov/bookshelf/br.fcgi?book=hmg&part=A2858

63. Human Genome Project. (2010). Information. Retrieved from http://www.ornl.gov/sci/techresources/Human_Genome/home.shtml

64. Crusio, W. E., Goldowitz, D., Holmes, A., & Wolfer, D. (2009). Standards for the publication of mouse mutant studies. *Genes, Brain & Behavior, 8*(1), 1–4.

65. Ekelund, J., Lichtermann, D., Järvelin, M. R., & Peltonen, L. (1999). Association between novelty seeking and the type 4 dopamine receptor gene in a large Finnish cohort sample. *American Journal of Psychiatry, 156*, 1453–1455.

66. Waldman, I. D., & Gizer, I. R. (2006). The genetics of attention deficit hyperactivity disorder. *Clinical Psychology Review, 26*(4), 396–432.

67. Thorgeirsson, T. E., Geller, F., Sulem, P., Rafnar, T., Wiste, A., Magnusson, K. P.,…Stefansson, K. (2008). A variant associated with nicotine dependence, lung cancer and peripheral arterial disease. *Nature, 452*(7187), 638–641.

68. Plomin, R. (2000). Behavioural genetics in the 21st century. *International Journal of Behavioral Development, 24*(1), 30–34.

CHAPTER 12
Defining Psychological Disorders

When Minor Body Imperfections Lead to Suicide

"I think we probably noticed in his early teens that he became very conscious about aspects of his appearance…he began to brood over it quite a lot," said Maria as she called in to the talk radio program to describe her son Robert.

Maria described how Robert had begun to worry about his weight. A friend had commented that he had a "fat" stomach, and Robert began to cut down on eating. Then he began to worry that he wasn't growing enough and devised an elaborate series of stretching techniques to help him get taller.

Robert scrutinized his face and body in the mirror for hours, finding a variety of imagined defects. He believed that his nose was crooked, and he was particularly concerned about a lump that he saw on it: "A small lump," said his mother. "I should say it wasn't very significant, but it was significant to him."

Robert insisted that all his misery stemmed from this lump on his nose, that everybody noticed it. In his sophomore year of high school, he had cosmetic surgery to remove it.

Around this time, Robert had his first panic attack and began to worry that everybody could notice him sweating and blushing in public. He asked his parents for a $10,000 loan, which he said was for overseas study. He used the money for a procedure designed to reduce sweating and blushing. Then, dissatisfied with the results, he had the procedure reversed.

Robert was diagnosed with *body dysmorphic disorder*. His mother told the radio host,

> At the time we were really happy because we thought that finally we actually knew what we were trying to fight and to be quite honest, I must admit I thought well it sounds pretty trivial….
>
> …Things seemed to go quite well and he got a new girlfriend and he was getting excellent marks in his clinical work in hospital and he promised us that he wasn't going to have any more surgery.

However, a lighthearted comment from a friend about a noticeable vein in his forehead prompted a relapse. Robert had surgery to tie off the vein. When that didn't solve all his problems as he had hoped, he attempted to have the procedure reversed but learned that it would require complicated microsurgery. He then used injections on himself to try opening the vein again, but he could never completely reverse the first surgery.

Robert committed suicide shortly afterward, in 2001 (Mitchell, 2002).[1]

1. PSYCHOLOGICAL DISORDER: WHAT MAKES A BEHAVIOR "ABNORMAL"?

LEARNING OBJECTIVES

1. Define "psychological disorder" and summarize the general causes of disorder.
2. Explain why it is so difficult to define disorder, and how the *Diagnostic and Statistical Manual of Mental Disorders* (*DSM*) is used to make diagnoses.
3. Describe the stigma of psychological disorders and their impact on those who suffer from them.

abnormal psychology

The application of psychological science to understanding and treating mental disorders.

prevalence

The frequency of occurrence of a given condition in a population at a given time.

The focus of the next two chapters is to many people the heart of psychology. This emphasis on **abnormal psychology**—*the application of psychological science to understanding and treating mental disorders*—is appropriate, as more psychologists are involved in the diagnosis and treatment of psychological disorder than in any other endeavor, and these are probably the most important tasks psychologists face. About 1 in every 4 Americans (or over 78 million people) are affected by a psychological disorder during any one year (Kessler, Chiu, Demler, & Walters, 2005),[2] and at least a half billion people are affected worldwide. The impact of mental illness is particularly strong on people who are poorer, of lower socioeconomic class, and from disadvantaged ethnic groups.

People with psychological disorders are also stigmatized by the people around them, resulting in shame and embarrassment, as well as prejudice and discrimination against them. Thus the understanding and treatment of psychological disorder has broad implications for the everyday life of many people. Table 12.1 shows the **prevalence** (i.e., *the frequency of occurrence of a given condition in a population at a given time*) of some of the major psychological disorders in the United States.

TABLE 12.1 One-Year Prevalence Rates for Psychological Disorders in the United States, 2001–2003

Disease	Percentage affected	Number affected
Any mental disorder	26.2	81,744,000
Any anxiety disorder	18.1	56,472,000
Specific phobia	8.7	27,144,000
Social phobia	6.8	21,216,000
Agoraphobia	0.8	2,496,000
Generalized anxiety disorder	3.1	9,672,000
Panic disorder	2.7	8,424,000
Obsessive-compulsive disorder	1.0	3,120,000
Posttraumatic stress disorder	3.5	10,920,000
Any mood disorder	9.5	29,640,000
Major depressive disorder	6.7	20,904,000
Bipolar disorder	2.6	8,112,000
Schizophrenia	1.0	3,120,000
Personality disorders		
Antisocial personality disorder	1.5	4,680,000
Borderline personality disorder	1.5	4,680,000
Anorexia nervosa	0.1	312,000
Any substance abuse disorder	3.8	11,856,000
Alcohol use disorder	4.4	13,728,000
Drug use disorder	1.8	5,616,000
All cancers*	5.4	16,848,000
Diabetes*	10.7	33,348,000
* These nonpsychological conditions are included for comparison.		

Sources: Kessler, R. C., Chiu, W. T., Demler, O., & Walters, E. E. (2005). Prevalence, severity, and comorbidity of 12-month DSM-IV disorders in the National Comorbidity Survey Replication. Archives of General Psychiatry, 62(6), 617–627; Narrow, W. E., Rae, D. S., Robins, L. N., & Regier, D. A. (2002). Revised prevalence based estimates of mental disorders in the United States: Using a clinical significance criterion to reconcile 2 surveys' estimates. Archives of General Psychiatry, 59(2), 115–123.

In this chapter our focus is on the disorders themselves. We will review the major psychological disorders and consider their causes and their impact on the people who suffer from them. Then in Chapter 13, we will turn to consider the treatment of these disorders through psychotherapy and drug therapy.

1.1 Defining Disorder

A **psychological disorder** is *an ongoing dysfunctional pattern of thought, emotion, and behavior that causes significant distress, and that is considered deviant in that person's culture or society* (Butcher, Mineka, & Hooley, 2007).[3] Psychological disorders have much in common with other medical disorders. They are out of the patient's control, they may in some cases be treated by drugs, and their treatment is often covered by medical insurance. Like medical problems, psychological disorders have both biological (nature) as well as environmental (nurture) influences. These causal influences are reflected in the bio-psycho-social model of illness (Engel, 1977).[4]

The **bio-psycho-social model of illness** is *a way of understanding disorder that assumes that disorder is caused by biological, psychological, and social factors* (Figure 12.1). The *biological component* of the bio-psycho-social model refers to the influences on disorder that come from the functioning of the individual's body. Particularly important are genetic characteristics that make some people more vulnerable to a disorder than others and the influence of neurotransmitters. The *psychological component* of the bio-psycho-social model refers to the influences that come from the individual, such as patterns of negative thinking and stress responses. The *social component* of the bio-psycho-social model refers to the influences on disorder due to social and cultural factors such as socioeconomic status, homelessness, abuse, and discrimination.

psychological disorder

An ongoing dysfunctional pattern of thought, emotion, and behavior that causes significant distress, and that is considered deviant in that person's culture or society.

bio-psycho-social model of illness

A way of understanding disorder that assumes that disorder is caused by biological, psychological, and social factors.

FIGURE 12.1 The Bio-Psycho-Social Model

The bio-psycho-social model of disorder proposes that disorders are caused by biological, psychological, and social-cultural factors.

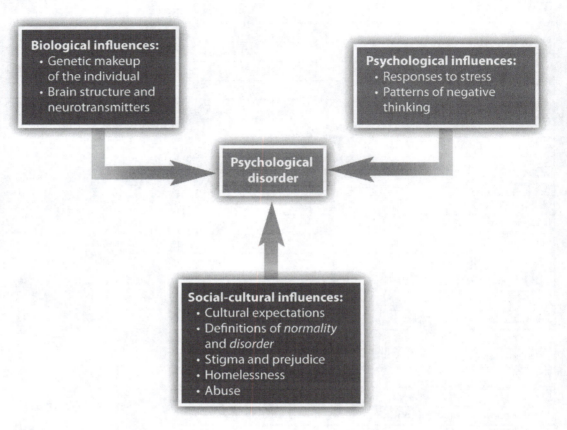

To consider one example, the psychological disorder of schizophrenia has a biological cause because it is known that there are patterns of genes that make a person vulnerable to the disorder (Gejman, Sanders, & Duan, 2010).[5] But whether or not the person with a biological vulnerability experiences the disorder depends in large part on psychological factors such as how the individual responds to the stress he experiences, as well as social factors such as whether or not he is exposed to stressful environments in adolescence and whether or not he has support from people who care about him (Sawa & Snyder, 2002; Walker, Kestler, Bollini, & Hochman, 2004).[6] Similarly, mood and anxiety disorders are caused in part by genetic factors such as hormones and neurotransmitters, in part by the individual's particular thought patterns, and in part by the ways that other people in the social environment treat the person with the disorder. We will use the bio-psycho-social model as a framework for considering the causes and treatments of disorder.

Although they share many characteristics with them, psychological disorders are nevertheless different from medical conditions in important ways. For one, diagnosis of psychological disorders can be more difficult. Although a medical doctor can see cancer in the lungs using an MRI scan or see blocked arteries in the heart using cardiac catheterization, there is no corresponding test for psychological disorder. Current research is beginning to provide more evidence about the role of brain structures in psychological disorder, but for now the brains of people with severe mental disturbances often look identical to those of people without such disturbances.

Because there are no clear biological diagnoses, psychological disorders are instead diagnosed on the basis of clinical observations of the behaviors that the individual engages in. These observations find that emotional states and behaviors operate on a continuum, ranging from more "normal" and "accepted" to more "deviant," "abnormal," and "unaccepted." The behaviors that are associated with disorder are in many cases the same behaviors we that engage in our "normal" everyday life. Washing one's hands is a normal healthy activity, but it can be overdone by those with an *obsessive-compulsive disorder (OCD)*. It is not unusual to worry about and try to improve one's body image, but Robert's struggle with his personal appearance, as discussed at the beginning of this chapter, was clearly unusual, unhealthy, and distressing to him.

Whether a given behavior is considered a psychological disorder is determined not only by whether a behavior is *unusual* (e.g., whether it is "mild" anxiety versus "extreme" anxiety) but also by whether a behavior is maladaptive—that is, the extent to which it causes *distress* (e.g., pain and suffering) and *dysfunction* (impairment in one or more important areas of functioning) to the individual (American Psychiatric Association, 2000).[7] An intense fear of spiders, for example, would not be considered a psychological disorder unless it has a significant negative impact on the sufferer's life, for instance by causing him or her to be unable to step outside the house. The focus on distress and dysfunction means that behaviors that are simply unusual (such as some political, religious, or sexual practices) are not classified as disorders.

Put your psychology hat on for a moment and consider the behaviors of the people listed in Table 12.2. For each, indicate whether you think the behavior is or is not a psychological disorder. If you're not sure, what other information would you need to know to be more certain of your diagnosis?

TABLE 12.2 Diagnosing Disorder

Yes	No	Need more information	Description
			Jackie frequently talks to herself while she is working out her math homework. Her roommate sometimes hears her and wonders if she is OK.
			Charlie believes that the noises made by cars and planes going by outside his house have secret meanings. He is convinced that he was involved in the start of a nuclear war and that the only way for him to survive is to find the answer to a difficult riddle.
			Harriet gets very depressed during the winter months when the light is low. She sometimes stays in her pajamas for the whole weekend, eating chocolate and watching TV.
			Frank seems to be afraid of a lot of things. He worries about driving on the highway and about severe weather that may come through his neighborhood. But mostly he fears mice, checking under his bed frequently to see if any are present.
			A worshipper speaking in "tongues" at an Evangelical church views himself as "filled" with the Holy Spirit and is considered blessed with the gift to speak the "language of angels."

A trained clinical psychologist would have checked off "need more information" for each of the examples in Table 12.2 because although the behaviors may seem unusual, there is no clear evidence that they are distressing or dysfunctional for the person. Talking to ourselves out loud is unusual and can be a symptom of schizophrenia, but just because we do it once in a while does not mean that there is anything wrong with us. It is natural to be depressed, particularly in the long winter nights, but how severe should this depression be, and how long should it last? If the negative feelings last for an extended time and begin to lead the person to miss work or classes, then they may become symptoms of a mood disorder. It is normal to worry about things, but when does worry turn into a debilitating anxiety disorder? And what about thoughts that seem to be irrational, such as being able to "speak the language of angels"? Are they indicators of a severe psychological disorder, or part of a normal religious experience? Again, the answer lies in the extent to which they are (or are not) interfering with the individual's functioning in society.

Another difficulty in diagnosing psychological disorders is that they frequently occur together. For instance, people diagnosed with anxiety disorders also often have mood disorders (Hunt, Slade, & Andrews, 2004),[8] and people diagnosed with one personality disorder frequently suffer from other personality disorders as well. **Comorbidity** *occurs when people who suffer from one disorder also suffer at the same time from other disorders.* Because many psychological disorders are comorbid, most severe mental disorders are concentrated in a small group of people (about 6% of the population) who have more than three of them (Kessler, Chiu, Demler, & Walters, 2005).[9]

FIGURE 12.2
How Thin Is Too Thin?

This dancer needs to be thin for her career, but when does her dieting turn into a psychological disorder? Psychologists believe this happens when the behavior becomes *distressing* and *dysfunctional* to the person.

© *Thinkstock*

comorbidity

A situation that occurs when people who suffer from one disorder also suffer at the same time from one or more other disorders.

stigma

A disgrace or defect that indicates that person belongs to a culturally devalued social group.

Psychology in Everyday Life: Combating the Stigma of Abnormal Behavior

Every culture and society has its own views on what constitutes abnormal behavior and what causes it (Brothwell, 1981).[10] The Old Testament Book of Samuel tells us that as a consequence of his sins, God sent King Saul an evil spirit to torment him (1 Samuel 16:14). Ancient Hindu tradition attributed psychological disorder to sorcery and witchcraft. During the Middle Ages it was believed that mental illness occurred when the body was infected by evil spirits, particularly the devil. Remedies included whipping, bloodletting, purges, and trepanation (cutting a hole in the skull) to release the demons.

Trepanation (drilling holes in the skull) has been used since prehistoric times in attempts to cure epilepsy, schizophrenia, and other psychological disorders.

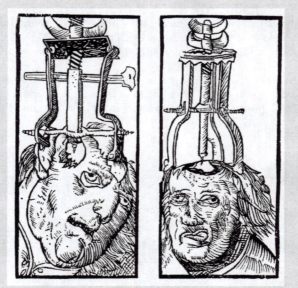

Source: Courtesy   of   Peter   Treveris,   http://commons.wikimedia.org/wiki/File:Peter_Treveris_-_engraving_of_Trepanation_for_Handywarke_of_surgeri_1525.png.

Until the 18th century, the most common treatment for the mentally ill was to incarcerate them in asylums or "madhouses." During the 18th century, however, some reformers began to oppose this brutal treatment of the mentally ill, arguing that mental illness was a medical problem that had nothing to do with evil spirits or demons. In France, one of the key reformers was Philippe Pinel (1745–1826), who believed that mental illness was caused by a combination of physical and psychological stressors, exacerbated by inhumane conditions. Pinel advocated the introduction of exercise, fresh air, and daylight for the inmates, as well as treating them gently and talking with them. In America, the reformers Benjamin Rush (1745–1813) and Dorothea Dix (1802–1887) were instrumental in creating mental hospitals that treated patients humanely and attempted to cure them if possible. These reformers saw mental illness as an underlying psychological disorder, which was diagnosed according to its symptoms and which could be cured through treatment.

Until the early 1900s people with mental disorders were often imprisoned in asylums such as these.

Source: Photo courtesy of the U.S. Library of Congress, http://commons.wikimedia.org/wiki/File:Sheriff_Hill_Lunatic_Asylum.jpg.

The reformers Philippe Pinel, Benjamin Rush, and Dorothea Dix fought the often brutal treatment of the mentally ill and were instrumental in changing perceptions and treatment of them.

Sources: Pinel portrait courtesy of Anna Mérimée, http://commons.wikimedia.org/wiki/File:Philippe_Pinel_%281745_-_1826%29.jpg. Rush portrait courtesy of Charles Wilson Peale, http://commons.wikimedia.org/wiki/File:Benjamin_Rush_Painting_by_Peale.jpg. Dix portrait courtesy of the U.S. Library of Congress, http://commons.wikimedia.org/wiki/File:Dix-Dorothea-LOC.jpg.

Despite the progress made since the 1800s in public attitudes about those who suffer from psychological disorders, people, including police, coworkers, and even friends and family members, still stigmatize people with psychological disorders. A **stigma** refers to *a disgrace or defect that indicates that person belongs to a culturally devalued social group.* In some cases the stigma of mental illness is accompanied by the use of disrespectful and dehumanizing labels, including names such as "crazy," "nuts," "mental," "schizo," and "retard."

The stigma of mental disorder affects people while they are ill, while they are healing, and even after they have healed (Schefer, 2003).[11] On a community level, stigma can affect the kinds of services social service agencies give to people with mental illness, and the treatment provided to them and their families by schools, workplaces, places of worship, and health-care providers. Stigma about mental illness also leads to employment discrimination, despite the fact that with appropriate support, even people with severe psychological disorders are able to hold a job (Boardman, Grove, Perkins, & Shepherd, 2003; Leff & Warner, 2006; Ozawa & Yaeda, 2007; Pulido, Diaz, & Ramirez, 2004).[12]

The mass media has a significant influence on society's attitude toward mental illness (Francis, Pirkis, Dunt, & Blood, 2001).[13] While media portrayal of mental illness is often sympathetic, negative stereotypes still remain in newspapers, magazines, film, and television. (See the following video for an example.)

Television advertisements may perpetuate negative stereotypes about the mentally ill. Burger King recently ran an ad called "The King's Gone Crazy," in which the company's mascot runs around an office complex carrying out acts of violence and wreaking havoc.

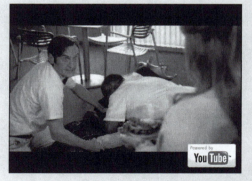

View the video online at: http://www.youtube.com/embed/xYA7AnVwejo

The most significant problem of the stigmatization of those with psychological disorder is that it slows their recovery. People with mental problems internalize societal attitudes about mental illness, often becoming so embarrassed or ashamed that they conceal their difficulties and fail to seek treatment. Stigma leads to lowered self-esteem, increased isolation, and hopelessness, and it may negatively influence the individual's family and professional life (Hayward & Bright, 1997).[14]

Despite all of these challenges, however, many people overcome psychological disorders and go on to lead productive lives. It is up to all of us who are informed about the causes of psychological disorder and the impact of these conditions on people to understand, first, that mental illness is not a "fault" any more than is cancer. People do not choose to have a mental illness. Second, we must all work to help overcome the stigma associated with disorder. Organizations such as the National Alliance on Mental Illness (NAMI; n.d.),[15] for example, work to reduce the negative impact of stigma through education, community action, individual support, and other techniques.

1.2 Diagnosing Disorder: The *DSM*

Diagnostic and Statistical Manual of Mental Disorders (DSM)

A document that provides a common language and standard criteria for the classification of mental disorders.

FIGURE 12.6

The *Diagnostic and Statistical Manual of Mental Disorders* (*DSM*) is used to classify psychological disorders in the United States.

Psychologists have developed criteria that help them determine whether behavior should be considered a psychological disorder and which of the many disorders particular behaviors indicate. These criteria are laid out in a 1,000-page manual known as the **Diagnostic and Statistical Manual of Mental Disorders (DSM)**, *a document that provides a common language and standard criteria for the classification of mental disorders* (American Psychiatric Association, 2000).[16] The *DSM* is used by therapists, researchers, drug companies, health insurance companies, and policymakers in the United States to determine what services are appropriately provided for treating patients with given symptoms.

The first edition of the *DSM* was published in 1952 on the basis of census data and psychiatric hospital statistics. Since then, the *DSM* has been revised five times. The last major revision was the fourth edition (*DSM-IV*), published in 1994, and an update of that document was produced in 2000 (*DSM-IV-TR*). The fifth edition (*DSM-V*) is currently undergoing review, planning, and preparation and is scheduled to be published in 2013. The *DSM-IV-TR* was designed in conjunction with the World Health Organization's 10th version of the *International Classification of Diseases* (*ICD-10*), which is used as a guide for mental disorders in Europe and other parts of the world.

As you can see in Figure 12.7, the *DSM* organizes the diagnosis of disorder according to five dimensions (or *axes*) relating to different aspects of disorder or disability. The axes are important to remember when we think about psychological disorder, because they make it clear not only that there are different types of disorder, but that those disorders have a variety of different causes. *Axis I* includes the most usual clinical disorders, including *mood disorders* and *anxiety disorders*; *Axis II* includes the less severe but long-lasting *personality disorders* as well as mental retardation; *Axis III* and *Axis IV* relate to physical symptoms and social-cultural factors, respectively. The axes remind us that when making a diagnosis we must look at the complete picture, including biological, personal, and social-cultural factors.

FIGURE 12.7

The *DSM* organizes psychological disorders into five dimensions (known as axes) that concern the different aspects of disorder.

Axis I: Is a clinical syndrome, such as a mood, anxiety, or learning disorder, present?
Axis II: Is a personality disorder or mental retardation present?
Axis III: Is a general medical condition, such as heart disease, diabetes, or cancer, present?
Axis IV: Are social or environmental problems, such as homelessness, divorce, school problems, or other stressors, present?
Axis V: What is the global assessment of this person's functioning (ranging from "persistent danger of hurting oneself or others" to "superior functioning in a wide range of activities")?

Source: Adapted from American Psychiatric Association. (2000). Diagnostic and statistical manual of mental disorders (4th ed., text rev.). Washington, DC: Author.

The *DSM* does not attempt to specify the exact symptoms that are required for a diagnosis. Rather, the *DSM* uses categories, and patients whose symptoms are similar to the description of the category are said to have that disorder. The *DSM* frequently uses qualifiers to indicate different levels of severity within a category. For instance, the disorder of mental retardation can be classified as mild, moderate, or severe.

Each revision of the *DSM* takes into consideration new knowledge as well as changes in cultural norms about disorder. Homosexuality, for example, was listed as a mental disorder in the *DSM* until 1973, when it was removed in response to advocacy by politically active gay rights groups and changing social norms. The current version of the *DSM* lists about 400 disorders. Some of the major categories are shown in Table 12.3, and you may go to http://en.wikipedia.org/wiki/DSM-IV_Codes_(alphabetical) and browse the complete list.

TABLE 12.3 Categories of Psychological Disorders Based on the *DSM*

Category and description	Examples
Disorders diagnosed in infancy and childhood	Mental retardation
	Communication, conduct, elimination, feeding, learning, and motor skills disorders
	Autism spectrum disorders
	Attention-deficit and disruptive behavior disorders including attention-deficit/hyperactivity disorder (ADHD)
	Separation anxiety disorder
Delirium, dementia, and amnesia (forgetting or memory distortions caused by physical factors)	Delirium
	Dementia and Alzheimer disease
Dissociative disorders (forgetting or memory distortions that do not involve physical factors)	Dissociative amnesia
	Dissociative fugue
	Dissociative identity disorder ("multiple personality")
Substance abuse disorders	Alcohol abuse
	Drug abuse
	Caffeine abuse
Schizophrenia and other psychotic disorders	
Mood disorders	Mood disorder
	Major depressive disorder
	Bipolar disorder
Anxiety disorders	Generalized anxiety disorder
	Panic disorder
	Specific phobia including agoraphobia
	Obsessive-compulsive disorder (OCD)
	Posttraumatic stress disorder (PTSD)
Somatoform disorders (physical symptoms that do not have a clear physical cause and thus must be psychological in origin)	Conversion disorder
	Pain disorder
	Hypochondriasis
	Body dysmorphic disorder (BDD)
Factitious disorders (conditions in which a person acts as if he or she has an illness by deliberately producing, feigning, or exaggerating symptoms)	
Sexual disorders	Sexual dysfunctions including erectile and orgasmic disorders
	Paraphilias
	Gender identity disorders
	Sexual abuse
Eating disorders	Anorexia nervosa
	Bulimia nervosa
Sleep disorders	Narcolepsy
	Sleep apnea
Impulse-control disorders	Kleptomania (stealing)
	Pyromania (fire lighting)
	Pathological gambling (addiction)
Personality disorders	
Cluster A (odd or eccentric behaviors)	Paranoid personality disorder
	Schizoid personality disorder
	Schizotypal personality disorder

Category and description	Examples
Cluster B (dramatic, emotional, or erratic behaviors)	Antisocial personality disorder
	Borderline personality disorder
	Histrionic personality disorder
	Narcissistic personality disorder
Cluster C (anxious or fearful behaviors)	Avoidant personality disorder
	Dependent personality disorder
	Obsessive-compulsive personality disorder
Other disorders	Includes academic problems, antisocial behavior, bereavement, child neglect, occupational problems, relational problems, physical abuse, and malingering

Although the *DSM* has been criticized regarding the nature of its categorization system (and it is frequently revised to attempt to address these criticisms), for the fact that it tends to classify more behaviors as disorders with every revision (even "academic problems" are now listed as a potential psychological disorder), and for the fact that it is primarily focused on Western illness, it is nevertheless a comprehensive, practical, and necessary tool that provides a common language to describe disorder. Most U.S. insurance companies will not pay for therapy unless the patient has a *DSM* diagnosis. The *DSM* approach allows a systematic assessment of the patient, taking into account the mental disorder in question, the patient's medical condition, psychological and cultural factors, and the way the patient functions in everyday life.

1.3 Diagnosis or Overdiagnosis? ADHD, Autistic Disorder, and Asperger's Disorder

Two common critiques of the *DSM* are that the categorization system leaves quite a bit of ambiguity in diagnosis and that it covers such a wide variety of behaviors. Let's take a closer look at three common disorders—*attention-deficit/hyperactivity disorder (ADHD)*, *autistic disorder*, and *Asperger's disorder*—that have recently raised controversy because they are being diagnosed significantly more frequently than they were in the past.

Attention-Deficit/Hyperactivity Disorder (ADHD)

> *Zack, aged 7 years, has always had trouble settling down. He is easily bored and distracted. In school, he cannot stay in his seat for very long and he frequently does not follow instructions. He is constantly fidgeting or staring into space. Zack has poor social skills and may overreact when someone accidentally bumps into him or uses one of his toys. At home, he chatters constantly and rarely settles down to do a quiet activity, such as reading a book.*

Symptoms such as Zack's are common among 7-year-olds, and particularly among boys. But what do the symptoms mean? Does Zack simply have a lot of energy and a short attention span? Boys mature more slowly than girls at this age, and perhaps Zack will catch up in the next few years. One possibility is for the parents and teachers to work with Zack to help him be more attentive, to put up with the behavior, and to wait it out.

But many parents, often on the advice of the child's teacher, take their children to a psychologist for diagnosis. If Zack were taken for testing today, it is very likely that he would be diagnosed with a psychological disorder known as **attention-deficit/hyperactivity disorder (ADHD)**. ADHD is *a developmental behavior disorder characterized by problems with focus, difficulty maintaining attention, and inability to concentrate, in which symptoms start before 7 years of age* (American Psychiatric Association, 2000; National Institute of Mental Health, 2010).[17] Although it is usually first diagnosed in childhood, ADHD can remain problematic in adults, and up to 7% of college students are diagnosed with it (Weyandt & DuPaul, 2006).[18] In adults the symptoms of ADHD include forgetfulness, difficulty paying attention to details, procrastination, disorganized work habits, and not listening to others. ADHD is about 70% more likely to occur in males than in females (Kessler, Chiu, Demler, & Walters, 2005),[19] and is often comorbid with other behavioral and conduct disorders.

The diagnosis of ADHD has quadrupled over the past 20 years such that it is now diagnosed in about 1 out of every 20 American children and is the most common psychological disorder among

attention-deficit/ hyperactivity disorder (ADHD)

A developmental behavior disorder characterized by problems with focus, difficulty maintaining attention, and inability to concentrate, in which symptoms start before 7 years of age.

children in the world (Olfson, Gameroff, Marcus, & Jensen, 2003).[20] ADHD is also being diagnosed much more frequently in adolescents and adults (Barkley, 1998).[21] You might wonder what this all means. Are the increases in the diagnosis of ADHD due to the fact that today's children and adolescents are actually more distracted and hyperactive than their parents were, due to a greater awareness of ADHD among teachers and parents, or due to psychologists and psychiatrists' tendency to overdiagnose the problem? Perhaps drug companies are also involved, because ADHD is often treated with prescription medications, including stimulants such as Ritalin.

Although skeptics argue that ADHD is overdiagnosed and is a handy excuse for behavioral problems, most psychologists believe that ADHD is a real disorder that is caused by a combination of genetic and environmental factors. Twin studies have found that ADHD is heritable (National Institute of Mental Health, 2008),[22] and neuroimaging studies have found that people with ADHD may have structural differences in areas of the brain that influence self-control and attention (Seidman, Valera, & Makris, 2005).[23] Other studies have also pointed to environmental factors, such as mothers' smoking and drinking alcohol during pregnancy and the consumption of lead and food additives by those who are affected (Braun, Kahn, Froehlich, Auinger, & Lanphear, 2006; Linnet et al., 2003; McCann et al., 2007).[24] Social factors, such as family stress and poverty, also contribute to ADHD (Burt, Krueger, McGue, & Iacono, 2001).[25]

Autistic Disorder and Asperger's Disorder

> Jared's kindergarten teacher has voiced her concern to Jared's parents about his difficulties with interacting with other children and his delay in developing normal language. Jared is able to maintain eye contact and enjoys mixing with other children, but he cannot communicate with them very well. He often responds to questions or comments with long-winded speeches about trucks or some other topic that interests him, and he seems to lack awareness of other children's wishes and needs.

Jared's concerned parents took him to a multidisciplinary child development center for consultation. Here he was tested by a pediatric neurologist, a psychologist, and a child psychiatrist.

The pediatric neurologist found that Jared's hearing was normal, and there were no signs of any neurological disorder. He diagnosed Jared with a *pervasive developmental disorder*, because while his comprehension and expressive language was poor, he was still able to carry out nonverbal tasks, such as drawing a picture or doing a puzzle.

autistic disorder (autism)

A disorder of neural development characterized by impaired social interaction and communication and by restricted and repetitive behavior and in which symptoms begin before 7 years of age.

Asperger's disorder

A developmental disorder that affects a child's ability to socialize and communicate effectively with others and in which symptoms begin before 7 years of age.

Based on her observation of Jared's difficulty interacting with his peers, and the fact that he did not respond warmly to his parents, the psychologist diagnosed Jared with **autistic disorder (autism)**, *a disorder of neural development characterized by impaired social interaction and communication and by restricted and repetitive behavior, and in which symptoms begin before 7 years of age*. The psychologist believed that the autism diagnosis was correct because, like other children with autism, Jared, has a poorly developed ability to see the world from the perspective of others; engages in unusual behaviors such as talking about trucks for hours; and responds to stimuli, such as the sound of a car or an airplane, in unusual ways.

The child psychiatrist believed that Jared's language problems and social skills were not severe enough to warrant a diagnosis of autistic disorder and instead proposed a diagnosis of **Asperger's disorder**, *a developmental disorder that affects a child's ability to socialize and communicate effectively with others and in which symptoms begin before 7 years of age*. The symptoms of Asperger's are almost identical to that of autism (with the exception of a delay in language development), and the child psychiatrist simply saw these problems as less extreme.

Imagine how Jared's parents must have felt at this point. Clearly there is something wrong with their child, but even the experts cannot agree on exactly what the problem is. Diagnosing problems such as Jared's is difficult, yet the number of children like him is increasing dramatically. Disorders related to autism and Asperger's disorder now affect almost 1% of American children (Kogan et al., 2007).[26] The milder forms of autism, and particularly Asperger's, have accounted for most of this increase in diagnosis.

Although for many years autism was thought to be primarily a socially determined disorder, in which parents who were cold, distant, and rejecting created the problem, current research suggests that biological factors are most important. The heritability of autism has been estimated to be as high as 90% (Freitag, 2007).[27] Scientists speculate that autism is caused by an unknown genetically determined brain abnormality that occurs early in development. It is likely that several different brain sites are affected (Moldin, 2003),[28] and the search for these areas is being conducted in many scientific laboratories.

But does Jared have autism or Asperger's? The problem is that diagnosis is not exact (remember the idea of "categories"), and the experts themselves are often unsure how to classify behavior. Furthermore, the appropriate classifications change with time and new knowledge. The American Psychiatric Association has recently posted on its website a proposal to eliminate the term *Asperger's syndrome* from the upcoming *DSM-V*. Whether or not Asperger's will remain a separate disorder will be made known when the next *DSM-V* is published in 2013.

KEY TAKEAWAYS

- More psychologists are involved in the diagnosis and treatment of psychological disorder than in any other endeavor, and those tasks are probably the most important psychologists face.
- The impact on people with a psychological disorder comes both from the disease itself and from the stigma associated with disorder.
- A psychological disorder is an ongoing dysfunctional pattern of thought, emotion, and behavior that causes significant distress and that is considered deviant in that person's culture or society.
- According to the bio-psycho-social model, psychological disorders have biological, psychological, and social causes.
- It is difficult to diagnose psychological disorders, although the *DSM* provides guidelines that are based on a category system. The *DSM* is frequently revised, taking into consideration new knowledge as well as changes in cultural norms about disorder.
- There is controversy about the diagnosis of disorders such as ADHD, autistic disorder, and Asperger's disorder.

EXERCISES AND CRITICAL THINKING

1. Do you or your friends hold stereotypes about the mentally ill? Can you think of or find clips from any films or other popular media that portray mental illness positively or negatively? Is it more or less acceptable to stereotype the mentally ill than to stereotype other social groups?
2. Consider the psychological disorders listed in Table 12.3. Do you know people who may suffer from any of them? Can you or have you talked to them about their experiences? If so, how do they experience the illness?
3. Consider the diagnosis of ADHD, autism, and Asperger's disorder from the biological, personal, and social-cultural perspectives. Do you think that these disorders are overdiagnosed? How might clinicians determine if ADHD is dysfunctional or distressing to the individual?

2. ANXIETY AND DISSOCIATIVE DISORDERS: FEARING THE WORLD AROUND US

LEARNING OBJECTIVES

1. Outline and describe the different types of anxiety disorders.
2. Outline and describe the different types of dissociative disorders.
3. Explain the biological and environmental causes of anxiety and dissociative disorders.

anxiety

The nervousness or agitation that we sometimes experience, often about something that is going to happen.

anxiety disorder

A psychological disturbance marked by irrational fears, often of everyday objects and situations.

Anxiety, *the nervousness or agitation that we sometimes experience, often about something that is going to happen,* is a natural part of life. We all feel anxious at times, maybe when we think about our upcoming visit to the dentist or the presentation we have to give to our class next week. Anxiety is an important and useful human emotion; it is associated with the activation of the sympathetic nervous system and the physiological and behavioral responses that help protect us from danger. But too much anxiety can be debilitating, and every year millions of people suffer from **anxiety disorders**, which are *psychological disturbances marked by irrational fears, often of everyday objects and situations* (Kessler, Chiu, Demler, & Walters, 2005).[29]

2.1 Generalized Anxiety Disorder

Consider the following, in which "Chase" describes her feelings of a persistent and exaggerated sense of anxiety, even when there is little or nothing in her life to provoke it:

> *For a few months now I've had a really bad feeling inside of me. The best way to describe it is like a really bad feeling of negative inevitability, like something really bad is impending, but I don't know what. It's like I'm on trial for murder or I'm just waiting to be sent down for something. I have it all of the time but it gets worse in waves that come from nowhere with no apparent triggers. I used to get it before going out for nights out with friends, and it kinda stopped me from doing it as I'd rather not go out and stress about the feeling, but now I have it all the time so it doesn't really make a difference anymore. (Chase, 2010)[30]*

generalized anxiety disorder (GAD)

A psychological disorder diagnosed in situations in which a person has been excessively worrying about money, health, work, family life, or relationships for at least 6 months, even though he or she knows that the concerns are exaggerated, and when the anxiety causes significant distress and dysfunction.

Chase is probably suffering from a **generalized anxiety disorder (GAD)**, *a psychological disorder diagnosed in situations in which a person has been excessively worrying about money, health, work, family life, or relationships for at least 6 months, even though he or she knows that the concerns are exaggerated, and when the anxiety causes significant distress and dysfunction.*

In addition to their feelings of anxiety, people who suffer from GAD may also experience a variety of physical symptoms, including irritability, sleep troubles, difficulty concentrating, muscle aches, trembling, perspiration, and hot flashes. The sufferer cannot deal with what is causing the anxiety, nor avoid it, because there is no clear cause for anxiety. In fact, the sufferer frequently knows, at least cognitively, that there is really nothing to worry about.

About 10 million Americans suffer from GAD, and about two thirds are women (Kessler, Chiu, Demler, & Walters, 2005; Robins & Regier, 1991).[31] Generalized anxiety disorder is most likely to develop between the ages of 7 and 40 years, but its influence may in some cases lessen with age (Rubio & Lopez-Ibor, 2007).[32]

2.2 Panic Disorder

> *When I was about 30 I had my first panic attack. I was driving home, my three little girls were in their car seats in the back, and all of a sudden I couldn't breathe, I broke out into a sweat, and my heart began racing and literally beating against my ribs! I thought I was going to die. I pulled off the road and put my head on the wheel. I remember songs playing on the CD for about 15 minutes and my kids' voices singing along. I was sure I'd never see them again. And then, it passed. I slowly got back on the road and drove home. I had no idea what it was. (Ceejay, 2006)[33]*

Ceejay is experiencing **panic disorder**, *a psychological disorder characterized by sudden attacks of anxiety and terror that have led to significant behavioral changes in the person's life*. Symptoms of a panic attack include shortness of breath, heart palpitations, trembling, dizziness, choking sensations, nausea, and an intense feeling of dread or impending doom. Panic attacks can often be mistaken for heart attacks or other serious physical illnesses, and they may lead the person experiencing them to go to a hospital emergency room. Panic attacks may last as little as one or as much as 20 minutes, but they often peak and subside within about 10 minutes.

Sufferers are often anxious because they fear that they will have another attack. They focus their attention on the thoughts and images of their fears, becoming excessively sensitive to cues that signal the possibility of threat (MacLeod, Rutherford, Campbell, Ebsworthy, & Holker, 2002).[34] They may also become unsure of the source of their arousal, misattributing it to situations that are not actually the cause. As a result, they may begin to avoid places where attacks have occurred in the past, such as driving, using an elevator, or being in public places. Panic disorder affects about 3% of the American population in a given year.

panic disorder

A psychological disorder characterized by sudden attacks of anxiety and terror that have led to significant behavioral changes in the person's life.

2.3 Phobias

A **phobia** (from the Greek word *phobos*, which means "fear") is *a specific fear of a certain object, situation, or activity*. The fear experience can range from a sense of unease to a full-blown panic attack. Most people learn to live with their phobias, but for others the fear can be so debilitating that they go to extremes to avoid the fearful situation. A sufferer of arachnophobia (fear of spiders), for example, may refuse to enter a room until it has been checked thoroughly for spiders, or may refuse to vacation in the countryside because spiders may be there. Phobias are characterized by their specificity and their irrationality. A person with acrophobia (a fear of height) could fearlessly sail around the world on a sailboat with no concerns yet refuse to go out onto the balcony on the fifth floor of a building.

A common phobia is **social phobia**, *extreme shyness around people or discomfort in social situations*. Social phobia may be specific to a certain event, such as speaking in public or using a public restroom, or it can be a more generalized anxiety toward almost all people outside of close family and friends. People with social phobia will often experience physical symptoms in public, such as sweating profusely, blushing, stuttering, nausea, and dizziness. They are convinced that everybody around them notices these symptoms as they are occurring. Women are somewhat more likely than men to suffer from social phobia.

The most incapacitating phobia is **agoraphobia**, defined as *anxiety about being in places or situations from which escape might be difficult or embarrassing, or in which help may not be available* (American Psychiatric Association, 2000).[35] Typical places that provoke the panic attacks are parking lots; crowded streets or shops; and bridges, tunnels, or expressways. People (mostly women) who suffer from agoraphobia may have great difficulty leaving their homes and interacting with other people.

Phobias affect about 9% of American adults, and they are about twice as prevalent in women as in men (Fredrikson, Annas, Fischer, & Wik, 1996; Kessler, Meron-Ruscio, Shear, & Wittchen, 2009).[36] In most cases phobias first appear in childhood and adolescence, and usually persist into adulthood. Table 12.4 presents a list of the common phobias that are diagnosed by psychologists.

phobia

A specific fear of a certain object, situation, or activity.

social phobia

Extreme shyness around people or discomfort in social situations.

agoraphobia

Anxiety about being in places or situations from which escape might be difficult or embarrassing or in which help may not be available.

TABLE 12.4 The Most Common Phobias

Name	Description
Acrophobia	Fear of heights
Agoraphobia	Fear of situations in which escape is difficult
Arachnophobia	Fear of spiders
Astraphobia	Fear of thunder and lightning
Claustrophobia	Fear of closed-in spaces
Cynophobia	Fear of dogs
Mysophobia	Fear of germs or dirt
Ophidiophobia	Fear of snakes
Pteromerhanophobia	Fear of flying
Social phobia	Fear of social situations
Trypanophobia	Fear of injections
Zoophobia	Fear of small animals

2.4 Obsessive-Compulsive Disorders

Although he is best known his perfect shots on the field, the soccer star David Beckham also suffers from Obsessive-Compulsive Disorder (OCD). As he describes it,

> I have got this obsessive-compulsive disorder where I have to have everything in a straight line or everything has to be in pairs. I'll put my Pepsi cans in the fridge and if there's one too many then I'll put it in another cupboard somewhere. I've got that problem. I'll go into a hotel room. Before I can relax, I have to move all the leaflets and all the books and put them in a drawer. Everything has to be perfect. (Dolan, 2006)[37]

David Beckham's experience with obsessive behavior is not unusual. We all get a little obsessive at times. We may continuously replay a favorite song in our heads, worry about getting the right outfit for an upcoming party, or find ourselves analyzing a series of numbers that seem to have a certain pattern. And our everyday compulsions can be useful. Going back inside the house once more to be sure that we really did turn off the sink faucet or checking the mirror a couple of times to be sure that our hair is combed are not necessarily bad ideas.

FIGURE 12.8

The soccer star David Beckham suffers from obsessive-compulsive disorder (OCD).

Source: Photo courtesy of Raj Patel, http://commons.wikimedia.org/wiki/File:Beckham_LA_Galaxy_cropped.jpg.

Obsessive-compulsive disorder (OCD) is *a psychological disorder that is diagnosed when an individual continuously experiences distressing or frightening thoughts, and engages in* obsessions *(repetitive thoughts) or* compulsions *(repetitive behaviors) in an attempt to calm these thoughts.* OCD is diagnosed when the obsessive thoughts are so disturbing and the compulsive behaviors are so time consuming that they cause distress and significant dysfunction in a person's everyday life. Washing your hands once or even twice to make sure that they are clean is normal; washing them 20 times is not. Keeping your fridge neat is a good idea; spending hours a day on it is not. The sufferers know that these rituals are senseless, but they cannot bring themselves to stop them, in part because the relief that they feel after they perform them acts as a reinforcer, making the behavior more likely to occur again.

Sufferers of OCD may avoid certain places that trigger the obsessive thoughts, or use alcohol or drugs to try to calm themselves down. OCD has a low prevalence rate (about 1% of the population in a given year) in relation to other anxiety disorders, and usually develops in adolescence or early adulthood (Horwath & Weissman, 2000; Samuels & Nestadt, 1997).[38] The course of OCD varies from person to person. Symptoms can come and go, decrease, or worsen over time.

> **obsessive-compulsive disorder (OCD)**
>
> A psychological disorder that is diagnosed when an individual continuously experiences distressing or frightening thoughts, and engages in obsessions (repetitive thoughts) or compulsions (repetitive behaviors) in an attempt to calm these thoughts.

2.5 Posttraumatic Stress Disorder (PTSD)

> *"If you imagine burnt pork and plastic; I can still taste it," says Chris Duggan, on his experiences as a soldier in the Falklands War in 1982. "These helicopters were coming in and we were asked to help get the boys off…when they opened the doors the stench was horrendous."*
>
> *When he left the army in 1986, he suffered from PTSD. "I was a bit psycho," he says. "I was verbally aggressive, very uncooperative. I was arguing with my wife, and eventually we divorced. I decided to change the kitchen around one day, get all new stuff, so I threw everything out of the window. I was 10 stories up in a flat. I poured brandy all over the video and it melted. I flooded the bathroom." (Gould, 2007)[39]*

People who have survived a terrible ordeal, such as combat, torture, sexual assault, imprisonment, abuse, natural disasters, or the death of someone close to them may develop *posttraumatic stress disorder (PTSD)*. The anxiety may begin months or even years after the event. People with PTSD experience *high levels of anxiety* along with *reexperiencing* the trauma (flashbacks), and a strong desire to *avoid any reminders of the event*. They may lose interest in things they used to enjoy; startle easily; have difficulty feeling affection; and may experience terror, rage, depression, or insomnia. The symptoms may be felt especially when approaching the area where the event took place or when the anniversary of that event is near.

PTSD affects about 5 million Americans, including victims of the 9/11 terrorist attacks, the wars in Afghanistan and Iraq, and Hurricane Katrina. Sixteen percent of Iraq war veterans, for example, reported experiencing symptoms of PTSD (Hoge & Castro, 2006).[40] PTSD is a frequent outcome of childhood or adult *sexual abuse*, a disorder that has its own *Diagnostic and Statistical Manual of Mental Disorders* (*DSM*) diagnosis. Women are more likely to develop PTSD than men (Davidson, 2000).[41]

Risk factors for PTSD include the degree of the trauma's severity, the lack of family and community support, and additional life stressors (Brewin, Andrews, & Valentine, 2000).[42] Many people with PTSD also suffer from another mental disorder, particularly depression, other anxiety disorders, and substance abuse (Brady, Back, & Coffey, 2004).[43]

2.6   Dissociative Disorders: Losing the Self to Avoid Anxiety

> On October 23, 2006, a man appeared on the television show Weekend Today and asked America to help him rediscover his identity. The man, who was later identified as Jeffrey Alan Ingram, had left his home in Seattle on September 9, 2006, and found himself in Denver a few days later, without being able to recall who he was or where he lived. He was reunited with family after being recognized on the show. According to a coworker of Ingram's fiancée, even after Ingram was reunited with his fiancée, his memory did not fully return. "He said that while her face wasn't familiar to him, her heart was familiar to him…He can't remember his home, but he said their home felt like home to him."

dissociative disorder

A condition that involves disruptions or breakdowns of memory, awareness, and identity.

People who experience anxiety are haunted by their memories and experiences, and although they desperately wish to get past them, they normally cannot. In some cases, however, such as with Jeffrey Ingram, people who become overwhelmed by stress experience an altered state of consciousness in which they become detached from the reality of what is happening to them. A **dissociative disorder** is *a condition that involves disruptions or breakdowns of memory, awareness, and identity*. The dissociation is used as a defense against the trauma.

Dissociative Amnesia and Fugue

dissociative amnesia

A psychological disorder that involves extensive, but selective, memory loss, but in which there is no physiological explanation for the forgetting.

Dissociative amnesia is *a psychological disorder that involves extensive, but selective, memory loss, but in which there is no physiological explanation for the forgetting* (van der Hart & Nijenhuis, 2009).[44] The amnesia is normally brought on by a trauma—a situation that causes such painful anxiety that the individual "forgets" in order to escape. These kinds of trauma include disasters, accidents, physical abuse, rape, and other forms of severe stress (Cloninger & Dokucu, 2008).[45] Although the personality of people who are experiencing dissociative amnesia remains fundamentally unchanged—and they recall how to carry out daily tasks such as reading, writing, and problem solving—they tend to forget things about their personal lives—for instance, their name, age, and occupation—and may fail to recognize family and friends (van der Hart & Nijenhuis, 2009).[46]

dissociative fugue

A psychological disorder in which an individual loses complete memory of his or her identity and may even assume a new one, often far from home.

A related disorder, **dissociative fugue**, is *a psychological disorder in which an individual loses complete memory of his or her identity and may even assume a new one, often far from home*. The individual with dissociative fugue experiences all the symptoms of dissociative amnesia but also leaves the situation entirely. The fugue state may last for just a matter of hours or may continue for months, as it did with Jeffrey Ingram. Recovery from the fugue state tends to be rapid, but when people recover they commonly have no memory of the stressful event that triggered the fugue or of events that occurred during their fugue state (Cardeña & Gleaves, 2007).[47]

Dissociative Identity Disorder

You may remember the story of *Sybil* (a pseudonym for Shirley Ardell Mason, who was born in 1923), a person who, over a period of 40 years, claimed to possess 16 distinct personalities. Mason was in therapy for many years trying to integrate these personalities into one complete self. A TV movie about Mason's life, starring Sally Field as Sybil, appeared in 1976.

Sybil suffered from the most severe of the dissociative disorders, *dissociative identity disorder*. **Dissociative identity disorder** is *a psychological disorder in which two or more distinct and individual personalities exist in the same person, and there is an extreme memory disruption regarding personal information about the other personalities* (van der Hart & Nijenhuis, 2009).[48] Dissociative identity disorder was once known as "multiple personality disorder," and this label is still sometimes used. This disorder is sometimes mistakenly referred to as schizophrenia.

In some cases of dissociative identity disorder, there can be more than 10 different personalities in one individual. Switches from one personality to another tend to occur suddenly, often triggered by a stressful situation (Gillig, 2009).[49] The *host personality* is the personality in control of the body most of the time, and the *alter personalities* tend to differ from each other in terms of age, race, gender, language, manners, and even sexual orientation (Kluft, 1996).[50] A shy, introverted individual may develop a boisterous, extroverted alter personality. Each personality has unique memories and social relationships (Dawson, 1990).[51] Women are more frequently diagnosed with dissociative identity disorder than are men, and when they are diagnosed also tend to have more "personalities" (American Psychiatric Association, 2000).[52]

The dissociative disorders are relatively rare conditions and are most frequently observed in adolescents and young adults. In part because they are so unusual and difficult to diagnose, clinicians and researchers disagree about the legitimacy of the disorders, and particularly about dissociative identity disorder. Some clinicians argue that the descriptions in the *DSM* accurately reflect the symptoms of these patients, whereas others believe that patients are faking, role-playing, or using the disorder as a way to justify behavior (Barry-Walsh, 2005; Kihlstrom, 2004; Lilienfeld & Lynn, 2003; Lipsanen et al., 2004).[53] Even the diagnosis of Shirley Ardell Mason (Sybil) is disputed. Some experts claim that Mason was highly hypnotizable and that her therapist unintentionally "suggested" the existence of her multiple personalities (Miller & Kantrowitz, 1999).[54]

FIGURE 12.9

Shirley Ardell Mason, also known as "Sybil," suffered from dissociative identity disorder.

Source: Photo courtesy of http://en.wikipedia.org/wiki/File:Shirley_Ardell_Mason.jpg.

dissociative identity disorder

A psychological disorder in which two or more distinct and individual personalities exist in the same person, and there is memory disruption regarding personal information about the other personalities.

2.7 Explaining Anxiety and Dissociation Disorders

Both nature and nurture contribute to the development of anxiety disorders. In terms of our evolutionary experiences, humans have evolved to fear dangerous situations. Those of us who had a healthy fear of the dark, of storms, of high places, of closed spaces, and of spiders and snakes were more likely to survive and have descendants. Our evolutionary experience can account for some modern fears as well. A fear of elevators may be a modern version of our fear of closed spaces, while a fear of flying may be related to a fear of heights.

Also supporting the role of biology, anxiety disorders, including PTSD, are heritable (Hettema, Neale, & Kendler, 2001),[55] and molecular genetics studies have found a variety of genes that are important in the expression of such disorders (Smoller et al., 2008; Thoeringer et al., 2009).[56] Neuroimaging studies have found that anxiety disorders are linked to areas of the brain that are associated with emotion, blood pressure and heart rate, decision making, and action monitoring (Brown & McNiff, 2009; Damsa, Kosel, & Moussally, 2009).[57] People who experience PTSD also have a somewhat smaller hippocampus in comparison with those who do not, and this difference leads them to have a very strong sensitivity to traumatic events (Gilbertson et al., 2002).[58]

Whether the genetic predisposition to anxiety becomes expressed as a disorder depends on environmental factors. People who were abused in childhood are more likely to be anxious than those who had normal childhoods, even with the same genetic disposition to anxiety sensitivity (Stein, Schork, & Gelernter, 2008).[59] And the most severe anxiety and dissociative disorders, such as PTSD, are usually triggered by the experience of a major stressful event. One problem is that modern life creates a lot of anxiety. Although our life expectancy and quality of life have improved over the past 50 years, the same period has also created a sharp increase in anxiety levels (Twenge, 2006).[60] These changes suggest that most anxiety disorders stem from perceived, rather than actual, threats to our well-being.

Anxieties are also learned through classical and operant conditioning. Just as rats that are shocked in their cages develop a chronic anxiety toward their laboratory environment (which has become a conditioned stimulus for fear), rape victims may feel anxiety when passing by the scene of the crime, and victims of PTSD may react to memories or reminders of the stressful event. Classical conditioning may also be accompanied by *stimulus generalization*. A single dog bite can lead to generalized fear of all dogs; a panic attack that follows an embarrassing moment in one place may be generalized to a fear of all public places. People's responses to their anxieties are often reinforced. Behaviors become compulsive because they provide relief from the torment of anxious thoughts. Similarly, leaving or avoiding fear-inducing stimuli leads to feelings of calmness or relief, which reinforces phobic behavior.

In contrast to the anxiety disorders, the causes of the dissociative orders are less clear, which is part of the reason that there is disagreement about their existence. Unlike most psychological orders, there is little evidence of a genetic predisposition; they seem to be almost entirely environmentally determined. Severe emotional trauma during childhood, such as physical or sexual abuse, coupled with a strong stressor, is typically cited as the underlying cause (Alpher, 1992; Cardeña & Gleaves, 2007).[61] Kihlstrom, Glisky, and Angiulo (1994)[62] suggest that people with personalities that lead them to fantasize and become intensely absorbed in their own personal experiences are more susceptible to developing dissociative disorders under stress. Dissociative disorders can in many cases be successfully treated, usually by psychotherapy (Lilienfeld & Lynn, 2003).[63]

KEY TAKEAWAYS

- Anxiety is a natural part of life, but too much anxiety can be debilitating. Every year millions of people suffer from anxiety disorders.
- People who suffer from generalized anxiety disorder experience anxiety, as well as a variety of physical symptoms.
- Panic disorder involves the experience of panic attacks, including shortness of breath, heart palpitations, trembling, and dizziness.
- Phobias are specific fears of a certain object, situation, or activity. Phobias are characterized by their specificity and their irrationality.
- A common phobia is social phobia, extreme shyness around people or discomfort in social situations.
- Obsessive-compulsive disorder is diagnosed when a person's repetitive thoughts are so disturbing and their compulsive behaviors so time consuming that they cause distress and significant disruption in a person's everyday life.
- People who have survived a terrible ordeal, such as combat, torture, rape, imprisonment, abuse, natural disasters, or the death of someone close to them, may develop PTSD.
- Dissociative disorders, including dissociative amnesia and dissociative fugue, are conditions that involve disruptions or breakdowns of memory, awareness, and identity. The dissociation is used as a defense against the trauma.
- Dissociative identity disorder, in which two or more distinct and individual personalities exist in the same person, is relatively rare and difficult to diagnose.
- Both nature and nurture contribute to the development of anxiety disorders.

EXERCISES AND CRITICAL THINKING

1. Under what situations do you experience anxiety? Are these experiences rational or irrational? Does the anxiety keep you from doing some things that you would like to be able to do?
2. Do you or people you know suffer from phobias? If so, what are the phobias and how do you think the phobias began? Do they seem more genetic or more environmental in origin?

3.   MOOD DISORDERS: EMOTIONS AS ILLNESS

LEARNING OBJECTIVES

1. **Summarize and differentiate the various forms of mood disorders, in particular dysthymia, major depressive disorder, and bipolar disorder.**
2. **Explain the genetic and environmental factors that increase the likelihood that a person will develop a mood disorder.**

mood

The positive or negative feelings that are in the background of our everyday experiences.

The everyday variations in our feelings of happiness and sadness reflect our **mood**, which can be defined as *the positive or negative feelings that are in the background of our everyday experiences*. In most cases we are in a relatively good mood, and this positive mood has some positive consequences—it encourages us to do what needs to be done and to make the most of the situations we are in (Isen, 2003).[64] When we are in a good mood our thought processes open up, and we are more likely to approach others. We are more friendly and helpful to others when we are in a good mood than we are when we are in a bad mood, and we may think more creatively (De Dreu, Baas, & Nijstad, 2008).[65]

On the other hand, when we are in a bad mood we are more likely to prefer to be alone rather than interact with others, we focus on the negative things around us, and our creativity suffers.

It is not unusual to feel "down" or "low" at times, particularly after a painful event such as the death of someone close to us, a disappointment at work, or an argument with a partner. We often get depressed when we are tired, and many people report being particularly sad during the winter when the days are shorter. **Mood (or affective) disorders** are *psychological disorders in which the person's mood negatively influences his or her physical, perceptual, social, and cognitive processes*. People who suffer from *mood disorders* tend to experience more intense—and particularly more intense negative—moods. About 10% of the U.S. population suffers from a mood disorder in a given year.

The most common symptom of mood disorders is negative mood, also known as sadness or *depression*. Consider the feelings of this person, who was struggling with depression and was diagnosed with *major depressive disorder*:

> *I didn't want to face anyone; I didn't want to talk to anyone. I didn't really want to do anything for myself…I couldn't sit down for a minute really to do anything that took deep concentration…It was like I had big huge weights on my legs and I was trying to swim and just kept sinking. And I'd get a little bit of air, just enough to survive and then I'd go back down again. It was just constantly, constantly just fighting, fighting, fighting, fighting, fighting. (National Institute of Mental Health, 2010)[66]*

Mood disorders can occur at any age, and the median age of onset is 32 years (Kessler, Berglund, Demler, Jin, & Walters, 2005).[67] Recurrence of depressive episodes is fairly common and is greatest for those who first experience depression before the age of 15 years. About twice as many women suffer from depression than do men (Culbertson, 1997).[68] This gender difference is consistent across many countries and cannot be explained entirely by the fact that women are more likely to seek treatment for their depression. Rates of depression have been increasing over the past years, although the reasons for this increase are not known (Kessler et al., 2003).[69]

As you can see below, the experience of depression has a variety of negative effects on our behaviors. In addition to the loss of interest, productivity, and social contact that accompanies depression, the person's sense of hopelessness and sadness may become so severe that he or she considers or even succeeds in committing suicide. Suicide is the 11th leading cause of death in the United States, and a suicide occurs approximately every 16 minutes. Almost all the people who commit suicide have a diagnosable psychiatric disorder at the time of their death (American Association of Suicidology, 2010; American Foundation for Suicide Prevention, 2007; Sudak, 2005).[70]

mood (or affective) disorders

Psychological conditions in which the person's mood influences his or her physical, perceptual, social, and cognitive processes.

FIGURE 12.10

It is not unusual to feel "down" or "low" at times, but about 10% of the population suffers from dysfunctional and distressing mood disorders.

© Thinkstock

Behaviors Associated with Depression

- Changes in appetite; weight loss or gain
- Difficulty concentrating, remembering details, and making decisions
- Fatigue and decreased energy
- Feelings of hopelessness, helplessness, and pessimism
- Increased use of alcohol or drugs
- Irritability, restlessness
- Loss of interest in activities or hobbies once pleasurable, including sex
- Loss of interest in personal appearance
- Persistent aches or pains, headaches, cramps, or digestive problems that do not improve with treatment
- Sleep disorders, either trouble sleeping or excessive sleeping
- Thoughts of suicide or attempts at suicide

3.1   Dysthymia and Major Depressive Disorder

dysthymia

A psychological disorder characterized by mild, but chronic, depressive symptoms that last for at least 2 years.

The level of depression observed in people with mood disorders varies widely. People who experience depression for many years, such that it becomes to seem normal and part of their everyday life, and who feel that they are rarely or never happy, will likely be diagnosed with a mood disorder. If the depression is mild but long-lasting, they will be diagnosed with **dysthymia**, *a condition characterized by mild, but chronic, depressive symptoms that last for at least 2 years.*

major depressive disorder (clinical depression)

A psychological disorder characterized by an all-encompassing low mood accompanied by low self-esteem and by loss of interest or pleasure in normally enjoyable activities.

If the depression continues and becomes even more severe, the diagnosis may become that of *major depressive disorder.* **Major depressive disorder (clinical depression)** is *a mental disorder characterized by an all-encompassing low mood accompanied by low self-esteem and by loss of interest or pleasure in normally enjoyable activities.* Those who suffer from major depressive disorder feel an intense sadness, despair, and loss of interest in pursuits that once gave them pleasure. These negative feelings profoundly limit the individual's day-to-day functioning and ability to maintain and develop interests in life (Fairchild & Scogin, 2008).[71]

About 21 million American adults suffer from a major depressive disorder in any given year; this is approximately 7% of the American population. Major depressive disorder occurs about twice as often in women as it does in men (Kessler, Chiu, Demler, & Walters, 2005; Kessler et al., 2003).[72] In some cases clinically depressed people lose contact with reality and may receive a diagnosis of *major depressive episode with psychotic features.* In these cases the depression includes delusions and hallucinations.

3.2   Bipolar Disorder

Juliana is a 21-year-old single woman. Over the past several years she had been treated by a psychologist for depression, but for the past few months she had been feeling a lot better. Juliana had landed a good job in a law office and found a steady boyfriend. She told her friends and parents that she had been feeling particularly good—her energy level was high and she was confident in herself and her life.

One day Juliana was feeling so good that she impulsively quit her new job and left town with her boyfriend on a road trip. But the trip didn't turn out well because Juliana became impulsive, impatient, and easily angered. Her euphoria continued, and in one of the towns that they visited she left her boyfriend and went to a party with some strangers that she had met. She danced into the early morning and ended up having sex with several of the men.

Eventually Juliana returned home to ask for money, but when her parents found out about her recent behavior, and when she acted aggressively and abusively to them when they confronted her about it, they referred her to a social worker. Juliana was hospitalized, where she was diagnosed with bipolar disorder.

bipolar disorder

A psychological disorder characterized by swings in mood from overly "high" to sad and hopeless, and back again, with periods of near-normal mood in between.

While dysthymia and major depressive disorder are characterized by overwhelming negative moods, **bipolar disorder** is *a psychological disorder characterized by swings in mood from overly "high" to sad and hopeless, and back again, with periods of near-normal mood in between.* Bipolar disorder is diagnosed in cases such as Juliana's, where experiences with depression are followed by a more normal period and then a period of mania or euphoria in which the person feels particularly awake, alive, excited, and involved in everyday activities but is also impulsive, agitated, and distracted. Without treatment, it is likely that Juliana would cycle back into depression and then eventually into mania again, with the likelihood that she would harm herself or others in the process.

Bipolar disorder is an often chronic and lifelong condition that may begin in childhood. Although the normal pattern involves swings from high to low, in some cases the person may experience both highs and lows at the same time. Determining whether a person has bipolar disorder is difficult due to the frequent presence of comorbidity with both depression and anxiety disorders. Bipolar disorder is more likely to be diagnosed when it is initially observed at an early age, when the frequency of depressive episodes is high, and when there is a sudden onset of the symptoms (Bowden, 2001).[74]

3.3 Explaining Mood Disorders

Mood disorders are known to be at least in part genetic, because they are heritable. (Berrettini, 2006; Merikangas et al., 2002).[75] Neurotransmitters also play an important role in mood disorders. Serotonin, dopamine, and norepinephrine are all known to influence mood (Sher & Mann, 2003),[76] and drugs that influence the actions of these chemicals are often used to treat mood disorders.

The brains of those with mood disorders may in some cases show structural differences from those without them. Videbech and Ravnkilde (2004)[77] found that the hippocampus was smaller in depressed subjects than in normal subjects, and this may be the result of reduced *neurogenesis* (the process of generating new neurons) in depressed people (Warner-Schmidt & Duman, 2006).[78] Antidepressant drugs may alleviate depression in part by increasing neurogenesis (Duman & Monteggia, 2006).[79]

FIGURE 12.11 *Starry Night* **by Vincent van Gogh**

Based on his intense bursts of artistic productivity (in one 2-month period in 1889 he produced 60 paintings), personal writings, and behavior (including cutting off his own ear), it is commonly thought that van Gogh suffered from bipolar disorder. He committed suicide at age 37 (Thomas & Bracken, 2001).[73]

Research Focus: Using Molecular Genetics to Unravel the Causes of Depression

Avshalom Caspi and his colleagues (Caspi et al., 2003)[80] used a longitudinal study to test whether genetic predispositions might lead some people, but not others, to suffer from depression as a result of environmental stress. Their research focused on a particular gene, the 5-HTT gene, which is known to be important in the production and use of the neurotransmitter *serotonin*. The researchers focused on this gene because serotonin is known to be important in depression, and because selective serotonin reuptake inhibitors (SSRIs) have been shown to be effective in treating depression.

People who experience stressful life events, for instance involving threat, loss, humiliation, or defeat, are likely to experience depression. But biological-situational models suggest that a person's sensitivity to stressful events depends on his or her genetic makeup. The researchers therefore expected that people with one type of genetic pattern would show depression following stress to a greater extent than people with a different type of genetic pattern.

The research included a sample of 1,037 adults from Dunedin, New Zealand. Genetic analysis on the basis of DNA samples allowed the researchers to divide the sample into two groups on the basis of the characteristics of their 5-HTT gene. One group had a short version (or *allele*) of the gene, whereas the other group did not have the short allele of the gene.

The participants also completed a measure where they indicated the number and severity of stressful life events that they had experienced over the past 5 years. The events included employment, financial, housing, health, and relationship stressors. The dependent measure in the study was the level of depression reported by the participant, as assessed using a structured interview test (Robins, Cottler, Bucholtz, & Compton, 1995).[81]

As you can see in Figure 12.12, as the number of stressful experiences the participants reported increased from 0 to 4, depression also significantly increased for the participants with the short version of the gene (top panel). But for the participants who did not have a short allele, increasing stress did not increase depression (bottom panel). Furthermore, for the participants who experienced 4 stressors over the past 5 years, 33% of the participants who carried the short version of the gene became depressed, whereas only 17% of participants who did not have the short version did.

Results From Caspi et al., 2003

Caspi et al. (2003) found that the number of stressful life experiences was associated with increased depression for people with the short allele of the 5-HTT gene (top panel) but not for people who did not have the short allele (bottom panel).

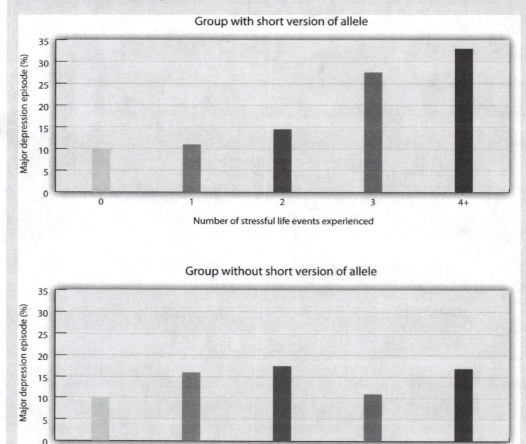

Source: Adapted from Caspi, A., Sugden, K., Moffitt, T. E., Taylor, A., Craig, I. W., Harrington, H.,…Poulton, R. (2003). Influence of life stress on depression: Moderation by a polymorphism in the 5-HTT gene. Science, 301(5631), 386–389.

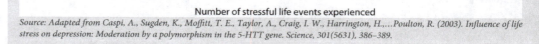

This important study provides an excellent example of how genes and environment work together: An individual's response to environmental stress was influenced by his or her genetic makeup.

But psychological and social determinants are also important in creating mood disorders and depression. In terms of psychological characteristics, mood states are influenced in large part by our cognitions. Negative thoughts about ourselves and our relationships to others create negative moods, and a goal of cognitive therapy for mood disorders is to attempt to change people's cognitions to be more positive. Negative moods also create negative behaviors toward others, such as acting sad, slouching, and avoiding others, which may lead those others to respond negatively to the person, for instance by isolating that person, which then creates even more depression (Figure 12.13). You can see how it might become difficult for people to break out of this "cycle of depression."

FIGURE 12.13 Cycle of Depression

Negative emotions create negative behaviors, which lead people to respond negatively to the individual, creating even more depression.

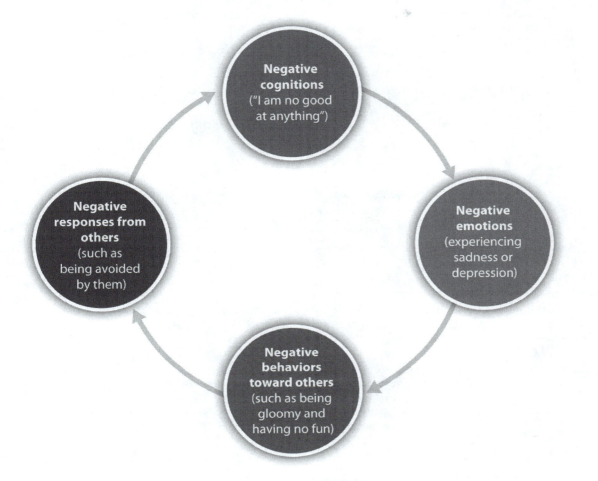

Weissman et al. (1996)[82] found that rates of depression varied greatly among countries, with the highest rates in European and American countries and the lowest rates in Asian countries. These differences seem to be due to discrepancies between individual feelings and cultural expectations about what one *should* feel. People from European and American cultures report that it is important to experience emotions such as happiness and excitement, whereas the Chinese report that it is more important to be stable and calm. Because Americans may feel that they are not happy or excited but that they are supposed to be, this may increase their depression (Tsai, Knutson, & Fung, 2006).[83]

KEY TAKEAWAYS

- Mood is the positive or negative feelings that are in the background of our everyday experiences.
- We all may get depressed in our daily lives, but people who suffer from mood disorders tend to experience more intense—and particularly more intense negative—moods.
- The most common symptom of mood disorders is negative mood.
- If a person experiences mild but long-lasting depression, she will be diagnosed with dysthymia. If the depression continues and becomes even more severe, the diagnosis may become that of major depressive disorder.
- Bipolar disorder is characterized by swings in mood from overly "high" to sad and hopeless, and back again, with periods of near-normal mood in between.
- Mood disorders are caused by the interplay among biological, psychological, and social variables.

EXERCISES AND CRITICAL THINKING

1. Give a specific example of the negative cognitions, behaviors, and responses of others that might contribute to a cycle of depression like that shown in Figure 12.13.

2. Given the discussion about the causes of negative moods and depression, what might people do to try to feel better on days that they are experiencing negative moods?

4. SCHIZOPHRENIA: THE EDGE OF REALITY AND CONSCIOUSNESS

LEARNING OBJECTIVES

1. Categorize and describe the three major symptoms of schizophrenia.
2. Differentiate the five types of schizophrenia and their characteristics.
3. Identify the biological and social factors that increase the likelihood that a person will develop schizophrenia.

schizophrenia

A serious psychological disorder marked by delusions, hallucinations, loss of contact with reality, inappropriate affect, disorganized speech, social withdrawal, and deterioration of adaptive behavior.

The term *schizophrenia*, which in Greek means "split mind," was first used to describe a psychological disorder by Eugen Bleuler (1857–1939), a Swiss psychiatrist who was studying patients who had very severe thought disorders. **Schizophrenia** is *a serious psychological disorder marked by delusions, hallucinations, loss of contact with reality, inappropriate affect, disorganized speech, social withdrawal, and deterioration of adaptive behavior.*

Schizophrenia is the most chronic and debilitating of all psychological disorders. It affects men and women equally, occurs in similar rates across ethnicities and across cultures, and affects at any one time approximately 3 million people in the United States (National Institute of Mental Health, 2010).[84] Onset of schizophrenia is usually between the ages of 16 and 30 and rarely after the age of 45 or in children (Mueser & McGurk, 2004; Nicholson, Lenane, Hamburger, Fernandez, Bedwell, & Rapoport, 2000).[85]

FIGURE 12.14

People with schizophrenia may exhibit disorganized behavior, as this person does.

Source: Photo courtesy of Max Avdeev,
http://www.flickr.com/photos/avdeev/4203380988.

psychosis

A psychological condition characterized by a loss of contact with reality.

4.1 Symptoms of Schizophrenia

Schizophrenia is accompanied by a variety of symptoms, but not all patients have all of them (Lindenmayer & Khan, 2006).[86] As you can see in Table 12.5, the symptoms are divided into *positive symptoms*, *negative symptoms*, and *cognitive symptoms* (American Psychiatric Association, 2008; National Institute of Mental Health, 2010).[87] Positive symptoms refer to the presence of abnormal behaviors or experiences (such as hallucinations) that are not observed in normal people, whereas negative symptoms (such as lack of affect and an inability to socialize with others) refer to the loss or deterioration of thoughts and behaviors that are typical of normal functioning. Finally, cognitive symptoms are the changes in cognitive processes that accompany schizophrenia (Skrabalo, 2000).[88] Because the patient has lost contact with reality, we say that he or she is experiencing **psychosis**, which is *a psychological condition characterized by a loss of contact with reality.*

TABLE 12.5   Positive, Negative, and Cognitive Symptoms of Schizophrenia

Positive symptoms	Negative symptoms	Cognitive symptoms
Hallucinations	Social withdrawal	Poor executive control
Delusions (of grandeur or persecution)	Flat affect and lack of pleasure in everyday life	Trouble focusing
Derailment	Apathy and loss of motivation	Working memory problems
Grossly disorganized behavior	Distorted sense of time	Poor problem-solving abilities
Inappropriate affect	Lack of goal-oriented activity	
Movement disorders	Limited speech	
	Poor hygiene and grooming	

People with schizophrenia almost always suffer from **hallucinations**—*imaginary sensations that occur in the absence of a real stimulus or which are gross distortions of a real stimulus.* Auditory hallucinations are the most common and are reported by approximately three quarters of patients (Nicolson, Mayberg, Pennell, & Nemeroff, 2006).[89] Schizophrenic patients frequently report hearing imaginary voices that curse them, comment on their behavior, order them to do things, or warn them of danger (National Institute of Mental Health, 2009).[90] Visual hallucinations are less common and frequently involve seeing God or the devil (De Sousa, 2007).[91]

Schizophrenic people also commonly experience **delusions**, which are *false beliefs not commonly shared by others within one's culture, and maintained even though they are obviously out of touch with reality.* People with *delusions of grandeur* believe that they are important, famous, or powerful. They often become convinced that they are someone else, such as the president or God, or that they have some special talent or ability. Some claim to have been assigned to a special covert mission (Buchanan & Carpenter, 2005).[92] People with *delusions of persecution* believe that a person or group seeks to harm them. They may think that people are able to read their minds and control their thoughts (Maher, 2001).[93] If a person suffers from delusions of persecution, there is a good chance that he or she will become violent, and this violence is typically directed at family members (Buchanan & Carpenter, 2005).[94]

People suffering from schizophrenia also often suffer from the positive symptom of *derailment*—the shifting from one subject to another, without following any one line of thought to conclusion—and may exhibit *grossly disorganized behavior* including inappropriate sexual behavior, peculiar appearance and dress, unusual agitation (e.g., shouting and swearing), strange body movements, and awkward facial expressions. It is also common for schizophrenia sufferers to experience *inappropriate affect*. For example, a patient may laugh uncontrollably when hearing sad news. Movement disorders typically appear as agitated movements, such as repeating a certain motion again and again, but can in some cases include *catatonia*, a state in which a person does not move and is unresponsive to others (Janno, Holi, Tuisku, & Wahlbeck, 2004; Rosebush & Mazurek, 2010).[95]

Negative symptoms of schizophrenia include social withdrawal, poor hygiene and grooming, poor problem-solving abilities, and a distorted sense of time (Skrabalo, 2000).[96] Patients often suffer from flat affect, which means that they express almost no emotional response (e.g., they speak in a monotone and have a blank facial expression) even though they may report feeling emotions (Kring, 1999).[97] Another negative symptom is the tendency toward incoherent language, for instance, to repeat the speech of others ("echo speech"). Some schizophrenics experience motor disturbances, ranging from complete catatonia and apparent obliviousness to their environment to random and frenzied motor activity during which they become hyperactive and incoherent (Kirkpatrick & Tek, 2005).[98]

Not all schizophrenic patients exhibit negative symptoms, but those who do also tend to have the poorest outcomes (Fenton & McGlashan, 1994).[99] Negative symptoms are predictors of deteriorated functioning in everyday life and often make it impossible for sufferers to work or to care for themselves.

Cognitive symptoms of schizophrenia are typically difficult for outsiders to recognize but make it extremely difficult for the sufferer to lead a normal life. These symptoms include difficulty comprehending information and using it to make decisions (the lack of *executive control*), difficulty maintaining focus and attention, and problems with working memory (the ability to use information immediately after it is learned).

hallucination

An imaginary sensation that occurs in the absence of a real stimulus or that is a gross distortion of a real stimulus.

delusion

A false belief not commonly shared by others within one's culture, and maintained even though it is obviously out of touch with reality.

4.2 Explaining Schizophrenia

There is no single cause of schizophrenia. Rather, a variety of biological and environmental risk factors interact in a complex way to increase the likelihood that someone might develop schizophrenia (Walker, Kestler, Bollini, & Hochman, 2004).[100]

Studies in molecular genetics have not yet identified the particular genes responsible for schizophrenia, but it is evident from research using family, twin, and adoption studies that genetics are important (Walker & Tessner, 2008).[101] As you can see in Figure 12.15, the likelihood of developing schizophrenia increases dramatically if a close relative also has the disease.

FIGURE 12.15 Genetic Disposition to Develop Schizophrenia

The risk of developing schizophrenia increases substantially if a person has a relative with the disease.

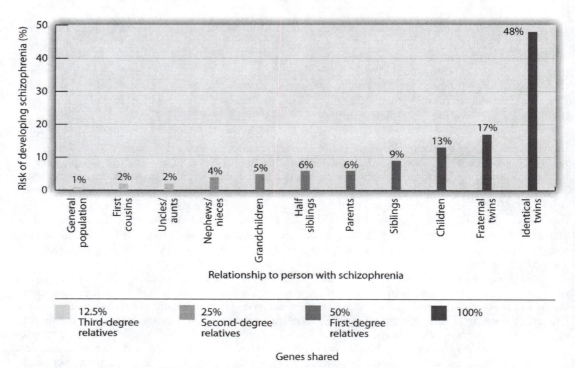

Source: Adapted from Gottesman, I. I. (1991). Schizophrenia genesis: The origins of madness. New York, NY: W. H. Freeman.

Neuroimaging studies have found some differences in brain structure between schizophrenic and normal patients. In some people with schizophrenia, the cerebral ventricles (fluid-filled spaces in the brain) are enlarged (Suddath, Christison, Torrey, Casanova, & Weinberger, 1990).[102] People with schizophrenia also frequently show an overall loss of neurons in the cerebral cortex, and some show less activity in the frontal and temporal lobes, which are the areas of the brain involved in language, attention, and memory. This would explain the deterioration of functioning in language and thought processing that is commonly experienced by schizophrenic patients (Galderisi et al., 2008).[103]

Many researchers believe that schizophrenia is caused in part by excess dopamine, and this theory is supported by the fact that most of the drugs useful in treating schizophrenia inhibit dopamine activity in the brain (Javitt & Laruelle, 2006).[104] Levels of serotonin may also play a part (Inayama et al., 1996).[105] But recent evidence suggests that the role of neurotransmitters in schizophrenia is more complicated than was once believed. It also remains unclear whether observed differences in the neurotransmitter systems of people with schizophrenia cause the disease, or if they are the result of the disease itself or its treatment (Csernansky & Grace, 1998).[106]

A genetic predisposition to developing schizophrenia does not always develop into the actual disorder. Even if a person has an identical twin with schizophrenia, he still has less than a 50% chance of getting it himself, and over 60% of all schizophrenic people have no first- or second-degree relatives with schizophrenia (Gottesman & Erlenmeyer-Kimling, 2001; Riley & Kendler, 2005).[107] This suggests that there are important environmental causes as well.

One hypothesis is that schizophrenia is caused in part by disruptions to normal brain development in infancy that may be caused by poverty, malnutrition, and disease (Brown et al., 2004; Murray & Bramon, 2005; Susser et al., 1996; Waddington, Lane, Larkin, O'Callaghan, 1999).[108] Stress also increases the likelihood that a person will develop schizophrenic symptoms; onset and relapse of schizophrenia typically occur during periods of increased stress (Walker, Mittal, & Tessner, 2008).[109] However, it may be that people who develop schizophrenia are more vulnerable to stress than others and not necessarily that they experience more stress than others (Walker, Mittal, & Tessner, 2008).[110] Many homeless people are likely to be suffering from undiagnosed schizophrenia.

Another social factor that has been found to be important in schizophrenia is the degree to which one or more of the patient's relatives is highly critical or highly emotional in their attitude toward the patient. Hooley and Hiller (1998)[111] found that schizophrenic patients who ended a stay in a hospital and returned to a family with high expressed emotion were three times more likely to relapse than patients who returned to a family with low expressed emotion. It may be that the families with high expressed emotion are a source of stress to the patient.

KEY TAKEAWAYS

- Schizophrenia is a serious psychological disorder marked by delusions, hallucinations, and loss of contact with reality.
- Schizophrenia is accompanied by a variety of symptoms, but not all patients have all of them.
- Because the schizophrenic patient has lost contact with reality, we say that he or she is experiencing psychosis.
- Positive symptoms of schizophrenia include hallucinations, delusions, derailment, disorganized behavior, inappropriate affect, and catatonia.
- Negative symptoms of schizophrenia include social withdrawal, poor hygiene and grooming, poor problem-solving abilities, and a distorted sense of time.
- Cognitive symptoms of schizophrenia include difficulty comprehending and using information and problems maintaining focus.
- There is no single cause of schizophrenia. Rather, there are a variety of biological and environmental risk factors that interact in a complex way to increase the likelihood that someone might develop schizophrenia.

EXERCISE AND CRITICAL THINKING

1. How should society deal with people with schizophrenia? Is it better to keep patients in psychiatric facilities against their will, but where they can be observed and supported, or to allow them to live in the community, where they may commit violent crimes against themselves or others? What factors influence your opinion?

5.   PERSONALITY DISORDERS

LEARNING OBJECTIVES

1. Categorize the different types of personality disorders and differentiate antisocial personality disorder from borderline personality disorder.
2. Outline the biological and environmental factors that may contribute to a person developing a personality disorder.

To this point in the chapter we have considered the psychological disorders that fall on Axis I of the *Diagnostic and Statistical Manual of Mental Disorders* (*DSM*) categorization system. In comparison to the Axis I disorders, which may frequently be severe and dysfunctional and are often brought on by stress, the disorders that fall on Axis II are longer-term disorders that are less likely to be severely incapacitating. Axis II consists primarily of *personality disorders*. A **personality disorder** is *a disorder characterized by inflexible patterns of thinking, feeling, or relating to others that cause problems in personal, social, and work situations.* Personality disorders tend to emerge during late childhood or adolescence and usually continue throughout adulthood (Widiger, 2006).[112] The disorders can be problematic for the people who have them, but they are less likely to bring people to a therapist for treatment than are Axis I disorders.

personality disorder

A condition characterized by inflexible patterns of thinking, feeling, or relating to others that causes problems in personal, social, and work situations.

The personality disorders are summarized in Table 12.6. They are categorized into three types: those characterized by *odd or eccentric behavior*, those characterized by *dramatic or erratic behavior*, and those characterized by *anxious or inhibited* behavior. As you consider the personality types described in Table 12.6, I'm sure you'll think of people that you know who have each of these traits, at least to some degree. Probably you know someone who seems a bit suspicious and paranoid, who feels that other people are always "ganging up on him," and who really doesn't trust other people very much. Perhaps you know someone who fits the bill of being overly dramatic—the "drama queen" who is always raising a stir and whose emotions seem to turn everything into a big deal. Or you might have a friend who is overly dependent on others and can't seem to get a life of her own.

The personality traits that make up the personality disorders are common—we see them in the people whom we interact with every day—yet they may become problematic when they are rigid, overused, or interfere with everyday behavior (Lynam & Widiger, 2001).[113] What is perhaps common to all the disorders is the person's inability to accurately understand and be sensitive to the motives and needs of the people around them.

TABLE 12.6 Descriptions of the Personality Disorders (Axis II)

Cluster	Personality disorder	Characteristics
A. Odd/ eccentric	Schizotypal	Peculiar or eccentric manners of speaking or dressing. Strange beliefs. "Magical thinking" such as belief in ESP or telepathy. Difficulty forming relationships. May react oddly in conversation, not respond, or talk to self. Speech elaborate or difficult to follow. (Possibly a mild form of schizophrenia.)
	Paranoid	Distrust in others, suspicion that people have sinister motives. Apt to challenge the loyalties of friends and read hostile intentions into others' actions. Prone to anger and aggressive outbursts but otherwise emotionally cold. Often jealous, guarded, secretive, overly serious.
	Schizoid	Extreme introversion and withdrawal from relationships. Prefers to be alone, little interest in others. Humorless, distant, often absorbed with own thoughts and feelings, a daydreamer. Fearful of closeness, with poor social skills, often seen as a "loner."
B. Dramatic/ erratic	Antisocial	Impoverished moral sense or "conscience." History of deception, crime, legal problems, impulsive and aggressive or violent behavior. Little emotional empathy or remorse for hurting others. Manipulative, careless, callous. At high risk for substance abuse and alcoholism.
	Borderline	Unstable moods and intense, stormy personal relationships. Frequent mood changes and anger, unpredictable impulses. Self-mutilation or suicidal threats or gestures to get attention or manipulate others. Self-image fluctuation and a tendency to see others as "all good" or "all bad."
	Histrionic	Constant attention seeking. Grandiose language, provocative dress, exaggerated illnesses, all to gain attention. Believes that everyone loves him. Emotional, lively, overly dramatic, enthusiastic, and excessively flirtatious.
	Narcissistic	Inflated sense of self-importance, absorbed by fantasies of self and success. Exaggerates own achievement, assumes others will recognize they are superior. Good first impressions but poor longer-term relationships. Exploitative of others.
C. Anxious/ inhibited	Avoidant	Socially anxious and uncomfortable unless he or she is confident of being liked. In contrast with schizoid person, yearns for social contact. Fears criticism and worries about being embarrassed in front of others. Avoids social situations due to fear of rejection.
	Dependent	Submissive, dependent, requiring excessive approval, reassurance, and advice. Clings to people and fears losing them. Lacking self-confidence. Uncomfortable when alone. May be devastated by end of close relationship or suicidal if breakup is threatened.
	Obsessive-compulsive	Conscientious, orderly, perfectionist. Excessive need to do everything "right." Inflexibly high standards and caution can interfere with his or her productivity. Fear of errors can make this person strict and controlling. Poor expression of emotions. (Not the same as obsessive-compulsive disorder.)

Source: American Psychiatric Association. (2000). Diagnostic and statistical manual of mental disorders (4th ed., text rev.). Washington, DC: Author.

The personality disorders create a bit of a problem for diagnosis. For one, it is frequently difficult for the clinician to accurately diagnose which of the many personality disorders a person has, although the friends and colleagues of the person can generally do a good job of it (Oltmanns & Turkheimer, 2006).[114] And the personality disorders are highly comorbid; if a person has one, it's likely that he or she has others as well. Also, the number of people with personality disorders is estimated to be as high as 15% of the population (Grant et al., 2004),[115] which might make us wonder if these are really "disorders" in any real sense of the word.

Although they are considered as separate disorders, the personality disorders are essentially milder versions of more severe Axis I disorders (Huang et al., 2009).[116] For example, *obsessive-compulsive personality disorder* is a milder version of obsessive-compulsive disorder (OCD), and *schizoid and schizotypal personality disorders* are characterized by symptoms similar to those of schizophrenia. This overlap in classification causes some confusion, and some theorists have argued that the personality disorders should be eliminated from the *DSM*. But clinicians normally differentiate Axis I and Axis II disorders, and thus the distinction is useful for them (Krueger, 2005; Phillips, Yen, & Gunderson, 2003; Verheul, 2005).[117]

Although it is not possible to consider the characteristics of each of the personality disorders in this book, let's focus on two that have important implications for behavior. The first, *borderline personality disorder (BPD)*, is important because it is so often associated with suicide, and the second, *antisocial personality disorder (APD)*, because it is the foundation of criminal behavior. Borderline and antisocial personality disorders are also good examples to consider because they are so clearly differentiated in terms of their focus. BPD (more frequently found in women than men) is known as an *internalizing disorder* because the behaviors that it entails (e.g., suicide and self-mutilation) are mostly directed toward the self. APD (mostly found in men), on the other hand, is a type of *externalizing disorder* in which the problem behaviors (e.g., lying, fighting, vandalism, and other criminal activity) focus primarily on harm to others.

5.1   Borderline Personality Disorder

Borderline personality disorder (BPD) is *a psychological disorder characterized by a prolonged disturbance of personality accompanied by mood swings, unstable personal relationships, identity problems, threats of self-destructive behavior, fears of abandonment, and impulsivity.* BPD is widely diagnosed—up to 20% of psychiatric patients are given the diagnosis, and it may occur in up to 2% of the general population (Hyman, 2002).[118] About three quarters of diagnosed cases of BDP are women.

> **borderline personality disorder (BPD)**
>
> A condition characterized by a prolonged disturbance of personality accompanied by mood swings, unstable personal relationships, identity problems, threats of self-destructive behavior, fears of abandonment, and impulsivity.

People with BPD fear being abandoned by others. They often show a clinging dependency on the other person and engage in manipulation to try to maintain the relationship. They become angry if the other person limits the relationship, but also deny that they care about the person. As a defense against fear of abandonment, borderline people are compulsively social. But their behaviors, including their intense anger, demands, and suspiciousness, repel people.

People with BPD often deal with stress by engaging in self-destructive behaviors, for instance by being sexually promiscuous, getting into fights, binge eating and purging, engaging in self-mutilation or drug abuse, and threatening suicide. These behaviors are designed to call forth a "saving" response from the other person. People with BPD are a continuing burden for police, hospitals, and therapists. Borderline individuals also show disturbance in their concepts of identity: They are uncertain about self-image, gender identity, values, loyalties, and goals. They may have chronic feelings of emptiness or boredom and be unable to tolerate being alone.

BPD has both genetic as well as environmental roots. In terms of genetics, research has found that those with BPD frequently have neurotransmitter imbalances (Zweig-Frank et al., 2006),[119] and the disorder is heritable (Minzenberg, Poole, & Vinogradov, 2008).[120] In terms of environment, many theories about the causes of BPD focus on a disturbed early relationship between the child and his or her parents. Some theories focus on the development of attachment in early childhood, while others point to parents who fail to provide adequate attention to the child's feelings. Others focus on parental abuse (both sexual and physical) in adolescence, as well as on divorce, alcoholism, and other stressors (Lobbestael & Arntz, 2009).[121] The dangers of BPD are greater when they are associated with childhood sexual abuse, early age of onset, substance abuse, and aggressive behaviors. The problems are amplified when the diagnosis is comorbid (as it often is) with other disorders, such as substance abuse disorder, major depressive disorder, and posttraumatic stress disorder (PTSD; Skodol et al., 2002).[122]

Research Focus: Affective and Cognitive Deficits in BPD

Posner et al. (2003)[123] hypothesized that the difficulty that individuals with BPD have in regulating their lives (e.g., in developing meaningful relationships with other people) may be due to imbalances in the fast and slow emotional pathways in the brain. Specifically, they hypothesized that the fast emotional pathway through the amygdala is too active, and the slow cognitive-emotional pathway through the prefrontal cortex is not active enough in those with BPD.

The participants in their research were 16 patients with BPD and 14 healthy comparison participants. All participants were tested in a functional magnetic resonance imaging (fMRI) machine while they performed a task that required them to read emotional and nonemotional words, and then press a button as quickly as possible whenever a word appeared in a normal font and not press the button whenever the word appeared in an italicized font.

The researchers found that while all participants performed the task well, the patients with BPD had more errors than the controls (both in terms of pressing the button when they should not have and not pressing it when they should have). These errors primarily occurred on the negative emotional words.

Figure 12.16 shows the comparison of the level of brain activity in the emotional centers in the amygdala (left panel) and the prefrontal cortex (right panel). In comparison to the controls, the borderline patients showed relatively larger affective responses when they were attempting to quickly respond to the negative emotions, and showed less cognitive activity in the prefrontal cortex in the same conditions. This research suggests that excessive affective reactions and lessened cognitive reactions to emotional stimuli may contribute to the emotional and behavioral volatility of borderline patients.

Results From Posner et al., 2003

Individuals with BPD showed less cognitive and greater emotional brain activity in response to negative emotional words.

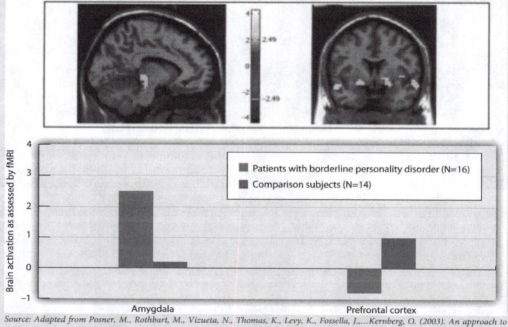

Source: Adapted from Posner, M., Rothbart, M., Vizueta, N., Thomas, K., Levy, K., Fossella, J.,...Kernberg, O. (2003). An approach to the psychobiology of personality disorders. Development and Psychopathology, 15(4), 1093–1106. doi:10.1017/S0954579403000506.

5.2 Antisocial Personality Disorder (APD)

antisocial personality disorder (APD)

A condition characterized by a pervasive pattern of violation of the rights of others that begins in childhood or early adolescence and continues into adulthood.

In contrast to borderline personality disorder, which involves primarily feelings of inadequacy and a fear of abandonment, **antisocial personality disorder (APD)** is characterized by a disregard of the rights of others, and a tendency to violate those rights without being concerned about doing so. APD is *a pervasive pattern of violation of the rights of others that begins in childhood or early adolescence and continues into adulthood*. APD is about three times more likely to be diagnosed in men than in women. To be diagnosed with APD the person must be 18 years of age or older and have a documented history of conduct disorder before the age of 15. People having antisocial personality disorder are sometimes referred to as "sociopaths" or "psychopaths."

People with APD feel little distress for the pain they cause others. They lie, engage in violence against animals and people, and frequently have drug and alcohol abuse problems. They are egocentric and frequently impulsive, for instance suddenly changing jobs or relationships. People with APD soon end up with a criminal record and often spend time incarcerated. The intensity of antisocial symptoms tends to peak during the 20s and then may decrease over time.

Biological and environmental factors are both implicated in the development of antisocial personality disorder (Rhee & Waldman, 2002).[124] Twin and adoption studies suggest a genetic predisposition (Rhee & Waldman, 2002),[125] and biological abnormalities include low autonomic activity during stress, biochemical imbalances, right hemisphere abnormalities, and reduced gray matter in the frontal lobes (Lyons-Ruth et al., 2007; Raine, Lencz, Bihrle, LaCasse, & Colletti, 2000).[126] Environmental factors include neglectful and abusive parenting styles, such as the use of harsh and inconsistent discipline and inappropriate modeling (Huesmann & Kirwil, 2007).[127]

KEY TAKEAWAYS

- A personality disorder is a disorder characterized by inflexible patterns of thinking, feeling, or relating to others that causes problems in personal, social, and work situations.
- Personality disorders are categorized into three clusters: those characterized by odd or eccentric behavior, dramatic or erratic behavior, and anxious or inhibited behavior.
- Although they are considered as separate disorders, the personality disorders are essentially milder versions of more severe Axis I disorders.
- *Borderline personality disorder* is a prolonged disturbance of personality accompanied by mood swings, unstable personal relationships, and identity problems, and it is often associated with suicide.
- *Antisocial personality disorder* is characterized by a disregard of others' rights and a tendency to violate those rights without being concerned about doing so.

EXERCISES AND CRITICAL THINKING

1. What characteristics of men and women do you think make them more likely to have APD and BDP, respectively? Do these differences seem to you to be more genetic or more environmental?
2. Do you know people who suffer from antisocial personality disorder? What behaviors do they engage in, and why are these behaviors so harmful to them and others?

6. SOMATOFORM, FACTITIOUS, AND SEXUAL DISORDERS

LEARNING OBJECTIVES

1. **Differentiate the symptoms of somatoform and factitious disorders.**
2. **Summarize the sexual disorders and paraphilias.**

Although mood, anxiety, and personality disorders represent the most prevalent psychological disorders, as you saw in Table 12.3 there are a variety of other disorders that affect people. This complexity of symptoms and classifications helps make it clear how difficult it is to accurately and consistently diagnose and treat psychological disorders. In this section we will review three other disorders that are of interest to psychologists and that affect millions of people: *somatoform disorder*, *factitious disorder*, and *sexual disorder*.

6.1 Somatoform and Factitious Disorders

Somatoform and factitious disorders both occur in cases where psychological disorders are related to the experience or expression of physical symptoms. The important difference between them is that in somatoform disorders the physical symptoms are real, whereas in factitious disorders they are not.

One case in which psychological problems create real physical impairments is in the somatoform disorder known as **somatization disorder (also called Briquet's syndrome or Brissaud-Marie syndrome)**. Somatization disorder is *a psychological disorder in which a person experiences numerous long-lasting but seemingly unrelated physical ailments that have no identifiable physical cause*. A person with somatization disorder might complain of joint aches, vomiting, nausea, muscle weakness, as well as sexual dysfunction. The symptoms that result from a somatoform disorder are real and cause distress to the individual, but they are due entirely to psychological factors. The somatoform disorder is more likely to occur when the person is under stress, and it may disappear naturally over time. Somatoform disorder is more common in women than in men, and usually first appears in adolescents or those in their early 20s.

somatization disorder (Briquet's syndrome or Brissaud-Marie syndrome)

A psychological disorder in which a person experiences numerous long-lasting but seemingly unrelated physical ailments that have no identifiable physical cause.

conversion disorder

A psychological disorder in which patients experience specific neurological symptoms such as numbness, blindness, or paralysis, but where no neurological explanation exists.

hypochondriasis (hypochondria)

A psychological disorder accompanied by excessive worry about having a serious illness.

factitious disorder

A psychological disorder in which participants fake physical symptoms in large part because they enjoy the attention and treatment that they receive in the hospital.

sexual dysfunction

A psychological disorder that occurs when the physical sexual response cycle is inadequate for reproduction or for sexual enjoyment.

Another type of somatoform disorder is **conversion disorder**, *a psychological disorder in which patients experience specific neurological symptoms such as numbness, blindness, or paralysis, but where no neurological explanation is observed or possible* (Agaki & House, 2001).[128] The difference between conversion and somatoform disorders is in terms of the location of the physical complaint. In somatoform disorder the malaise is general, whereas in conversion disorder there are one or several specific neurological symptoms.

Conversion disorder gets its name from the idea that the existing psychological disorder is "converted" into the physical symptoms. It was the observation of conversion disorder (then known as "hysteria") that first led Sigmund Freud to become interested in the psychological aspects of illness in his work with Jean-Martin Charcot. Conversion disorder is not common (a prevalence of less than 1%), but it may in many cases be undiagnosed. Conversion disorder occurs twice or more frequently in women than in men.

There are two somatoform disorders that involve preoccupations. We have seen an example of one of them, *body dysmorphic disorder*, in the Chapter 12 opener. Body dysmorphic disorder (BDD) is a psychological disorder accompanied by an imagined or exaggerated defect in body parts or body odor. There are no sex differences in prevalence, but men are most often obsessed with their body build, their genitals, and hair loss, whereas women are more often obsessed with their breasts and body shape. BDD usually begins in adolescence.

Hypochondriasis (hypochondria) is another *psychological disorder that is focused on preoccupation, accompanied by excessive worry about having a serious illness.* The patient often misinterprets normal body symptoms such as coughing, perspiring, headaches, or a rapid heartbeat as signs of serious illness, and the patient's concerns remain even after he or she has been medically evaluated and assured that the health concerns are unfounded. Many people with hypochondriasis focus on a particular symptom such as stomach problems or heart palpitations.

Two other psychological disorders relate to the experience of physical problems that are not real. Patients with **factitious disorder** fake physical symptoms in large part because they enjoy the attention and treatment that they receive in the hospital. They may lie about symptoms, alter diagnostic tests such as urine samples to mimic disease, or even injure themselves to bring on more symptoms. In the more severe form of factitious disorder known as *Münchausen syndrome*, the patient has a lifelong pattern of a series of successive hospitalizations for faked symptoms.

Factitious disorder is distinguished from another related disorder known as *malingering*, which also involves fabricating the symptoms of mental or physical disorders, but where the motivation for doing so is to gain financial reward; to avoid school, work, or military service; to obtain drugs; or to avoid prosecution.

The somatoform disorders are almost always comorbid with other psychological disorders, including anxiety and depression and dissociative states (Smith et al., 2005).[129] People with BDD, for instance, are often unable to leave their house, are severely depressed or anxious, and may also suffer from other personality disorders.

Somatoform and factitious disorders are problematic not only for the patient, but they also have societal costs. People with these disorders frequently follow through with potentially dangerous medical tests and are at risk for drug addiction from the drugs they are given and for injury from the complications of the operations they submit to (Bass, Peveler, & House, 2001; Looper & Kirmayer, 2002).[130] In addition, people with these disorders may take up hospital space that is needed for people who are really ill. To help combat these costs, emergency room and hospital workers use a variety of tests for detecting these disorders.

6.2 Sexual Disorders

Sexual disorders refer to a variety of problems revolving around performing or enjoying sex. These include disorders related to *sexual function*, *gender identity*, and *sexual preference*.

Disorders of Sexual Function

Sexual dysfunction is a *psychological disorder that occurs when the physical sexual response cycle is inadequate for reproduction or for sexual enjoyment.* There are a variety of potential problems (Table 12.7), and their nature varies for men and women (Figure 12.17). Sexual disorders affect up to 43% of women and 31% of men (Laumann, Paik, & Rosen, 1999).[131] Sexual disorders are often difficult to diagnose because in many cases the dysfunction occurs at the partner level (one or both of the partners are disappointed with the sexual experience) rather than at the individual level.

TABLE 12.7 Sexual Dysfunctions as Described in the *DSM*

Disorder	Description
Hypoactive sexual desire disorder	Persistently or recurrently deficient (or absent) sexual fantasies and desire for sexual activity
Sexual aversion disorder	Persistent or recurrent extreme aversion to, and avoidance of, all (or almost all) genital sexual contact with a sexual partner
Female sexual arousal disorder	Persistent or recurrent inability to attain, or to maintain until completion of the sexual activity, an adequate lubrication-swelling response of sexual excitement
Male erectile disorder	Persistent or recurrent inability to attain or maintain an adequate erection until completion of the sexual activity
Female orgasmic disorder	Persistent or recurrent delay in, or absence of, orgasm following a normal sexual excitement phase
Male orgasmic disorder	Persistent or recurrent delay in, or absence of, orgasm following a normal sexual excitement phase during sexual activity
Premature ejaculation	Persistent or recurrent ejaculation with minimal sexual stimulation before, on, or shortly after penetration and before the person wishes it
Dyspareunia	Recurrent or persistent genital pain associated with sexual intercourse in either a male or a female
Vaginismus	Recurrent or persistent involuntary spasm of the musculature of the outer third of the vagina that interferes with sexual intercourse

Source: American Psychiatric Association. (2000). Diagnostic and statistical manual of mental disorders (4th ed., text rev.). Washington, DC: Author.

FIGURE 12.17 Prevalence of Sexual Dysfunction in Men and Women

This chart shows the percentage of respondents who reported each type of sexual difficulty over the previous 12 months.

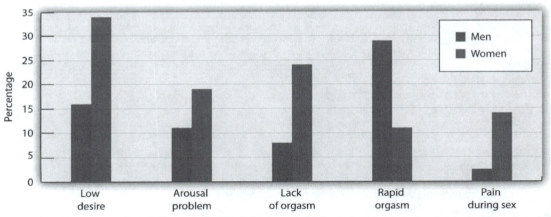

Source: Adapted from Laumann, E. O., Paik, A., & Rosen, R. C. (1999). Sexual dysfunction in the United States: Prevalence and predictors. Journal of the American Medical Association, 281(6), 537–544.

Hypoactive sexual desire disorder, one of the most common sexual dysfunctions, refers to a persistently low or nonexistent sexual desire. How "low sexual desire" is defined, however, is problematic because it depends on the person's sex and age, on cultural norms, as well as on the relative desires of the individual and the partner. Again, the importance of dysfunction and distress is critical. If neither partner is much interested in sex, for instance, the lack of interest may not cause a problem. Hypoactive sexual desire disorder is often comorbid with other psychological disorders, including mood disorders and problems with sexual arousal or sexual pain (Donahey & Carroll, 1993).[132]

Sexual aversion disorder refers to an avoidance of sexual behavior caused by disgust or aversion to genital contact. The aversion may be a phobic reaction to an early sexual experience or sexual abuse, a misattribution of negative emotions to sex that are actually caused by something else, or a reaction to a sexual problem such as erectile dysfunction (Kingsberg & Janata, 2003).[133]

Female sexual arousal disorder refers to persistent difficulties becoming sexually aroused or sufficiently lubricated in response to sexual stimulation in women. The disorder may be comorbid with hypoactive sexual desire or orgasmic disorder, or mood or anxiety disorders.

Male erectile disorder (sometimes referred to as "impotence") refers to persistent and dysfunctional difficulty in achieving or maintaining an erection sufficient to complete sexual activity. Prevalence rates vary by age, from about 6% of college-aged males to 35% of men in their 70s. About half the men aged 40 to 70 report having problems getting or maintaining an erection "now and then."

Most erectile dysfunction occurs as a result of physiological factors, including illness, and the use of medications, alcohol, or other recreational drugs. Erectile dysfunction is also related to anxiety, low self-esteem, and general problems in the particular relationship. Assessment for physiological causes of erectile dysfunction is made using a test in which a device is attached to the man's penis before he goes to sleep. During the night the man may have an erection, and if he does the device records its occurrence. If the man has erections while sleeping, this provides assurance that the problem is not physiological.

One of the most common sexual dysfunctions in men is *premature ejaculation*. It is not possible to exactly specify what defines "premature," but if the man ejaculates before or immediately upon insertion of the penis into the vagina, most clinicians will identify the response as premature. Most men diagnosed with premature ejaculation ejaculate within one minute after insertion (Waldinger, 2003).[134] Premature ejaculation is one of the most prevalent sexual disorders and causes much anxiety in many men.

Female orgasmic disorder refers to the inability to obtain orgasm in women. The woman enjoys sex and foreplay and shows normal signs of sexual arousal but cannot reach the peak experience of orgasm. *Male orgasmic disorder* includes a delayed or retarded ejaculation (very rare) or (more commonly) premature ejaculation.

Finally, *dyspareunia* and *vaginismus* refer to sexual pain disorders that create pain and involuntary spasms, respectively, in women, and thus make it painful to have sex. In most cases these problems are biological and can be treated with hormones, creams, or surgery.

Sexual dysfunctions have a variety of causes. In some cases the primary problem is biological, and the disorder may be treated with medication. Other causes include a repressive upbringing in which the parents have taught the person that sex is dirty or sinful, or the experience of sexual abuse (Beitchman, Zucker, Hood, & DaCosta, 1992).[135] In some cases the sex problem may be due to the fact that the person has a different sexual orientation than he or she is engaging in. Other problems include poor communication between the partners, a lack of sexual skills, and (particularly for men) performance anxiety.

It is important to remember that most sexual disorders are temporary—they are experienced for a period of time, in certain situations or with certain partners, and then (without, or if necessary with, the help of therapy) go away. It is also important to remember that there are a wide variety of sex acts that are enjoyable. Couples with happy sex lives work together to find ways that work best for their own styles. Sexual problems often develop when the partners do not communicate well with each other, and are reduced when they do.

Gender Identity Disorder

gender identity

Identification with a sex.

gender identity disorder (GID, or transsexualism)

A psychological disorder in which the individual displays a repeated and strong desire to be the other sex, a persistent discomfort with one's sex, and a belief that one was born the wrong sex, accompanied by significant dysfunction and distress.

Gender identity refers to the *identification with a sex*. Most children develop an appropriate attachment to their own sex. In some cases, however, children or adolescents—sometimes even those as young as 3 or 4 years old—believe that they have been trapped in a body of the wrong sex. **Gender identity disorder (GID, or transsexualism)** is diagnosed *when the individual displays a repeated and strong desire to be the other sex, a persistent discomfort with one's sex, and a belief that one was born the wrong sex, accompanied by significant dysfunction and distress.* GID usually appears in adolescence or adulthood and may intensify over time (Bower, 2001).[136] Since many cultures strongly disapprove of cross-gender behavior, it often results in significant problems for affected persons and those in close relationships with them.

Gender identity disorder is rare, occurring only in about 1 in every 12,000 males and 1 in every 30,000 females (Olsson & Möller, 2003).[137] The causes of GID are as of yet unknown, although they seem to be related in part to the amount of testosterone and other hormones in the uterus (Kraemer, Noll, Delsignore, Milos, Schnyder, & Hepp, 2009).[138]

The classification of GID as a mental disorder has been challenged because people who suffer from GID do not regard their own cross-gender feelings and behaviors as a disorder and do not feel that they are distressed or dysfunctional. People suffering from GID often argue that a "normal" gender identity may not necessarily involve an identification with one's own biological sex. GID represents another example, then, of how culture defines disorder, and the next edition of the *DSM* may change the categorizations used in this domain accordingly.

Paraphilias

A third class of sexual disorders relates to sexual practices and interest. In some cases sexual interest is so unusual that it is known as a **paraphilia**—*a sexual deviation where sexual arousal is obtained from a consistent pattern of inappropriate responses to objects or people, and in which the behaviors associated with the feelings are distressing and dysfunctional*. Paraphilias may sometimes be only fantasies, and in other cases may result in actual sexual behavior (Table 12.8).

TABLE 12.8 Some Paraphilias

Paraphilia	Behavior or fantasy that creates arousal
Bestiality	Sex with animals
Exhibitionism	Exposing genitals to an unsuspecting person
Fetishism	Nonliving or unusual objects or clothing of the opposite sex
Frotteurism	Rubbing up against unsuspecting persons
Masochism	Being beaten, humiliated, bound, or otherwise made to suffer
Pedophilia	Sexual activity with a prepubescent child
Sadism	Witnessing suffering of another person
Voyeurism	Observing an unsuspecting person who is naked, disrobing, or engaged in intimate behavior

People with paraphilias are usually rejected by society but for two different reasons. In some cases, such as *voyeurism* and *pedophilia*, the behavior is unacceptable (and illegal) because it involves a lack of consent on the part of the recipient of the sexual advance. But other paraphilias are rejected simply because they are unusual, even though they are consensual and do not cause distress or dysfunction to the partners. *Sexual sadism* and *sexual masochism*, for instance, are usually practiced consensually, and thus may not be harmful to the partners or to society. A recent survey found that individuals who engage in sadism and masochism are as psychologically healthy as those who do not (Connolly, 2006).[139] Again, as cultural norms about the appropriateness of behaviors change, the new revision of the *DSM*, due in 2013, will likely change its classification system of these behaviors.

FIGURE 12.18

Cultural norms about the categorization of transsexuality as a psychological disorder are changing, and the upcoming revision of the *DSM* may take this into consideration.

© Thinkstock

paraphilia

A psychological disorder in which sexual arousal is obtained from a consistent pattern of inappropriate responses to objects or people, and in which the behaviors associated with the feelings are distressing and dysfunctional.

KEY TAKEAWAYS

- Somatoform disorders, including body dysmorphic disorder and hypochondriasis, occur when people become excessively and inaccurately preoccupied with the potential that they have an illness or stigma.

- Patients with factitious disorder fake physical symptoms in large part because they enjoy the attention and treatment that they receive in the hospital. In the more severe form of factitious disorder known as Münchhausen syndrome, the patient has a lifelong pattern with a series of successive hospitalizations for faked symptoms.

- Sexual dysfunction is a psychological disorder that occurs when the physical sexual response cycle is inadequate for reproduction or for sexual enjoyment. The types of problems experienced are different for men and women. Many sexual dysfunctions are only temporary or can be treated with therapy or medication.

- Gender identity disorder (GID, also called transsexualism) is a rare disorder that is diagnosed when the individual displays a repeated and strong desire to be the other sex, a persistent discomfort with one's sex, and a belief that one was born the wrong sex, accompanied by significant dysfunction and distress.

- The classification of GID as a mental disorder has been challenged because people who suffer from it do not regard their own cross-gender feelings and behaviors as a disorder and do not feel that they are distressed or dysfunctional.

- A paraphilia is a sexual deviation where sexual arousal is obtained from a consistent pattern of inappropriate responses to objects or people, and in which the behaviors associated with the feelings are distressing and dysfunctional. Some paraphilias are illegal because they involve a lack of consent on the part of the recipient of the sexual advance, but other paraphilias are simply unusual, even though they may not cause distress or dysfunction.

EXERCISES AND CRITICAL THINKING

1. Consider the biological, personal, and social-cultural aspects of gender identity disorder. Do you think that this disorder is really a "disorder," or is it simply defined by social-cultural norms and beliefs?

2. Consider the paraphilias in Table 12.8. Do they seem like disorders to you, and how would one determine if they were or were not?

3. View one of the following films and consider the diagnosis that might be given to the characters in it: *Antwone Fisher, Ordinary People, Girl Interrupted, Grosse Pointe Blank, A Beautiful Mind, What About Bob?, Sybil, One Flew Over the Cuckoo's Nest.*

7. CHAPTER SUMMARY

More psychologists are involved in the diagnosis and treatment of psychological disorder than in any other aspect of psychology.

About 1 in every 4 Americans (over 78 million people) are estimated to be affected by a psychological disorder during any one year. The impact of mental illness is particularly strong on people who are poorer, of lower socioeconomic class, and from disadvantaged ethnic groups.

A psychological disorder is an unusual, distressing, and dysfunctional pattern of thought, emotion, or behavior. Psychological disorders are often comorbid, meaning that a given person suffers from more than one disorder.

The stigma of mental disorder affects people while they are ill, while they are healing, and even after they have healed. But mental illness is not a "fault," and it is important to work to help overcome the stigma associated with disorder.

All psychological disorders are multiply determined by biological, psychological, and social factors.

Psychologists diagnose disorder using the *Diagnostic and Statistical Manual of Mental Disorders* (*DSM*). The *DSM* organizes the diagnosis of disorder according to five dimensions (or axes) relating to different aspects of disorder or disability. The *DSM* uses categories, and patients with close approximations to the prototype are said to have that disorder.

One critique of the *DSM* is that many disorders—for instance, attention-deficit/hyperactivity disorder (ADHD), autistic disorder, and Asperger's disorder—are being diagnosed significantly more frequently than they were in the past.

Anxiety disorders are psychological disturbances marked by irrational fears, often of everyday objects and situations. They include generalized anxiety disorder (GAD), panic disorder, phobia, obsessive-compulsive disorder (OCD), and posttraumatic stress disorder (PTSD). Anxiety disorders affect about 57 million Americans every year.

Dissociative disorders are conditions that involve disruptions or breakdowns of memory, awareness, and identity. They include dissociative amnesia, dissociative fugue, and dissociative identity disorder.

Mood disorders are psychological disorders in which the person's mood negatively influences his or her physical, perceptual, social, and cognitive processes. They include dysthymia, major depressive disorder, and bipolar disorder. Mood disorders affect about 30 million Americans every year.

Schizophrenia is a serious psychological disorder marked by delusions, hallucinations, loss of contact with reality, inappropriate affect, disorganized speech, social withdrawal, and deterioration of adaptive behavior. About 3 million Americans have schizophrenia.

A personality disorder is a long-lasting but frequently less severe disorder characterized by inflexible patterns of thinking, feeling, or relating to others that causes problems in personal, social, and work situations. They are characterized by odd or eccentric behavior, by dramatic or erratic behavior, or by anxious or inhibited behavior. Two of the most important personality disorders are borderline personality disorder (BPD) and antisocial personality disorder (APD).

Somatization disorder is a psychological disorder in which a person experiences numerous long-lasting but seemingly unrelated physical ailments that have no identifiable physical cause. Somatization disorders include conversion disorder, body dysmorphic disorder (BDD), and hypochondriasis.

Patients with factitious disorder fake physical symptoms in large part because they enjoy the attention and treatment that they receive in the hospital.

Sexual disorders refer to a variety of problems revolving around performing or enjoying sex. Sexual dysfunctions include problems relating to loss of sexual desire, sexual response or orgasm, and pain during sex.

Gender identity disorder (GID, also called transsexualism) is diagnosed when the individual displays a repeated and strong desire to be the other sex, a persistent discomfort with one's sex, and a belief that one was born the wrong sex, accompanied by significant dysfunction and distress. The classification of GID as a mental disorder has been challenged because people who suffer from GID do not regard their own cross-gender feelings and behaviors as a disorder and do not feel that they are distressed or dysfunctional.

A paraphilia is a sexual deviation where sexual arousal is obtained from a consistent pattern of inappropriate responses to objects or people, and in which the behaviors associated with the feelings are distressing and dysfunctional.

ENDNOTES

1. Mitchell, N. (Producer). (2002, April 28). *Body dysmorphic disorder and cosmetic "surgery of the psyche."* All in the mind. ABC Radio National. Retrieved from http://www.abc.net.au/rn/allinthemind/stories/2003/746058.htm

2. Kessler, R. C., Chiu, W. T., Demler, O., & Walters, E. E. (2005). Prevalence, severity, and comorbidity of 12-month *DSM-IV* disorders in the National Comorbidity Survey Replication. *Archives of General Psychiatry, 62*(6), 617–627.

3. Butcher, J., Mineka, S., & Hooley, J. (2007). *Abnormal psychology and modern life* (13th ed.). Boston, MA: Allyn & Bacon.

4. Engel, G. (1977). The need for a new medical model: A challenge for biomedicine. *Science, 196*(4286), 129. doi:10.1126/science.847460

5. Gejman, P., Sanders, A., & Duan, J. (2010). The role of genetics in the etiology of schizophrenia. *Psychiatric Clinics of North America, 33*(1), 35–66. doi:10.1016/j.psc.2009.12.003

6. Sawa, A., & Snyder, S. (2002). Schizophrenia: Diverse approaches to a complex disease. *Science, 296*(5568), 692–695. doi:10.1126/science.1070532; Walker, E., Kestler, L., Bollini, A., & Hochman, K. (2004). Schizophrenia: Etiology and course. *Annual Review of Psychology, 55*, 401–430. doi:10.1146/annurev.psych.55.090902.141950

7. American Psychiatric Association. (2000). *Diagnostic and statistical manual of mental disorders* (4th ed., text rev.). Washington, DC: Author.

8. Hunt, C., Slade, T., & Andrews, G. (2004). Generalized anxiety disorder and major depressive disorder comorbidity in the National Survey of Mental Health and Well Being. *Depression and Anxiety, 20*, 23–31.

9. Kessler, R. C., Chiu, W. T., Demler, O., & Walters, E. E. (2005). Prevalence, severity, and comorbidity of 12-month *DSM-IV* disorders in the National Comorbidity Survey Replication. *Archives of General Psychiatry, 62*(6), 617–627.

10. Brothwell, D. (1981). *Digging up bones: The excavation, treatment, and study of human skeletal remains.* Ithaca, NY: Cornell University Press.

11. Schefer, R. (2003, May 28). *Addressing stigma: Increasing public understanding of mental illness.* Presented to the Standing Senate Committee on Social Affairs, Science and Technology. Retrieved from http://www.camh.net/education/Resources_communities_organizations/addressing_stigma_senatepres03.pdf

12. Boardman, J., Grove, B., Perkins, R., & Shepherd, G. (2003). Work and employment for people with psychiatric disabilities. *British Journal of Psychiatry, 182*(6), 467–468. doi:10.1192/bjp.182.6.467; Leff, J., & Warner, R. (2006). *Social inclusion of people with mental illness.* New York, NY: Cambridge University Press; Ozawa, A., & Yaeda, J. (2007). Employer attitudes toward employing persons with psychiatric disability in Japan. *Journal of Vocational Rehabilitation, 26*(2), 105–113; Pulido, F., Diaz, M., & Ramírez, M. (2004). Work integration of people with severe mental disorder: A pending question. *Revista Psiquis, 25*(6), 26–43.

13. Francis, C., Pirkis, J., Dunt, D., & Blood, R. (2001). *Mental health and illness in the media: A review of the literature.* Canberra, Australia: Commonwealth Department of Health & Aged Care.

14. Hayward, P., & Bright, J. (1997). Stigma and mental illness: A review and critique. *Journal of Mental Health, 6*(4), 345–354.

15. National Alliance on Mental Illness. (n.d.). Fight stigma. Retrieved from http://www.nami.org/template.cfm?section=fight_stigma

16. American Psychiatric Association. (2000). *Diagnostic and statistical manual of mental disorders* (4th ed., text rev.). Washington, DC: Author.

17. American Psychiatric Association. (2000). *Diagnostic and statistical manual of mental disorders* (4th ed., text rev.). Washington, DC: Author; National Institute of Mental Health. (2010). *Attention-deficit hyperactivity disorder (ADHD).* Retrieved from http://www.nimh.nih.gov/health/topics/attention-deficit-hyperactivity-disorder-adhd/index.shtml

18. Weyandt, L. L., & DuPaul, G. (2006). ADHD in college students. *Journal of Attention Disorders, 10*(1), 9–19.

19. Kessler, R. C., Chiu, W. T., Demler, O., & Walters, E. E. (2005). Prevalence, severity, and comorbidity of 12-month *DSM-IV* disorders in the National Comorbidity Survey Replication. *Archives of General Psychiatry, 62*(6), 617–627.

20. Olfson, M., Gameroff, M., Marcus, S., & Jensen, P. (2003). National trends in the treatment of attention deficit hyperactivity disorder. *American Journal of Psychiatry, 160*, 1071–1077.

21. Barkley, R. A. (1998). *Attention-deficit hyperactivity disorder: A handbook for diagnosis and treatment* (2nd ed.). New York, NY: Guilford Press.

22. National Institute of Mental Health. (2010). *Attention-deficit hyperactivity disorder (ADHD).* Retrieved from http://www.nimh.nih.gov/health/topics/attention-deficit-hyperactivity-disorder-adhd/index.shtml

23. Seidman, L., Valera, E., & Makris, N. (2005). Structural brain imaging of attention deficit/hyperactivity disorder. *Biological Psychiatry, 57*, 1263–1272.

24. Braun, J., Kahn, R., Froehlich, T., Auinger, P., & Lanphear, B. (2006). Exposures to environmental toxicants and attention-deficit/hyperactivity disorder in U.S. children. *Environmental Health Perspectives, 114*(12), 1904–1909; Linnet K., Dalsgaard, S., Obel, C., Wisborg, K., Henriksen T., Rodriguez, A.,...Jarvelin, M. (2003). Maternal lifestyle factors in pregnancy risk of attention-deficit/hyperactivity disorder and associated behaviors: Review of the current evidence. *American Journal of Psychiatry, 160*(6), 1028–1040; McCann, D., Barrett, A., Cooper, A., Crumpler, D., Dalen, L., Grimshaw, K.,...Stevenson, J. (2007). Food additives and hyperactive behaviour in 3-year-old and 8/9-year-old children in the community: A randomised, double-blinded, placebo-controlled trial. *Lancet, 370*(9598), 1560–1567.

25. Burt, S. A., Krueger, R. F., McGue, M., & Iacono, W. G. (2001). Sources of covariation among attention-deficit/hyperactivity disorder, oppositional defiant disorder, and conduct disorder: The importance of shared environment. *Journal of Abnormal Psychology, 110*(4), 516–525.

26. Kogan, M., Blumberg, S., Schieve, L., Boyle, C., Perrin, J., Ghandour, R.,...van Dyck, P. (2009). Prevalence of parent-reported diagnosis of autism spectrum disorder among children in the US, 2007. *Pediatrics, 124*(5), 1395–1403. doi:10.1542/peds.2009-1522

27. Freitag C. M. (2007). The genetics of autistic disorders and its clinical relevance: A review of the literature. *Molecular Psychiatry, 12*(1), 2–22.

28. Moldin, S. O. (2003). Editorial: Neurobiology of autism: The new frontier. *Genes, Brain & Behavior, 2*(5), 253–254.

29. Kessler, R., Chiu, W., Demler, O., & Walters, E. (2005). Prevalence, severity, and comorbidity of 12-month *DSM-IV* disorders in the National Comorbidity Survey Replication. *Archives of General Psychiatry, 62*(6), 617–627.

30. Chase. (2010, February 28). Re: "anxiety?" [Online forum comment]. Mental Health Forum. Retrieved from http://www.mentalhealthforum.net/forum/showthread.php?t=9359

31. Kessler, R., Chiu, W., Demler, O., & Walters, E. (2005). Prevalence, severity, and comorbidity of 12-month *DSM-IV* disorders in the National Comorbidity Survey Replication. *Archives of General Psychiatry, 62*(6), 617–27; Robins, L., & Regier, D. A. (1991). *Psychiatric disorders in America: The Epidemiologic Catchment Area Study.* New York, NY: Free Press.

32. Rubio, G., & Lopez-Ibor, J. (2007). Generalized anxiety disorder: A 40-year follow up study. *Acta Psychiatric Scandinavica, 115*, 372–379.

33. Ceejay. (2006, September). My dance with panic [Web log post]. Panic Survivor. Retrieved from http://www.panicsurvivor.com/index.php/2007102366/Survivor-Stories/My-Dance-With-Panic.html

34. MacLeod, C., Rutherford, E., Campbell, L., Ebsworthy, G., & Holker, L. (2002). Selective attention and emotional vulnerability: Assessing the causal basis of their association through the experimental manipulation of attentional bias. *Journal of Abnormal Psychology, 111*(1), 107–123.

35. American Psychiatric Association. (2000). *Diagnostic and statistical manual of mental disorders* (4th ed., text rev.). Washington, DC: Author.

36. Fredrikson, M., Annas, P., Fischer, H., & Wik, G. (1996). Gender and age differences in the prevalence of specific fears and phobias. *Behaviour Research and Therapy, 34*(1), 33–39. doi:10.1016/0005-7967(95)00048-3; Kessler, R., Meron-Ruscio, A., Shear, K., & Wittchen, H. (2009). Epidemiology of anxiety disorders. In M. Anthony, & M. Stein (Eds.) *Oxford handbook of anxiety and related disorders.* New York, NY: Oxford University Press.

37. Dolan, A. (2006, April 3). The obsessive disorder that haunts my life. *Daily Mail.* Retrieved from http://www.dailymail.co.uk/tvshowbiz/article-381802/The-obsessive-disorder-haunts-life.html

38. Horwath, E., & Weissman, M. (2000). The epidemiology and cross-national presentation of obsessive-compulsive disorder. *Psychiatric Clinics of North America, 23*(3), 493–507. doi:10.1016/S0193-953X(05)70176-3; Samuels, J., & Nestadt, G. (1997). Epidemiology and genetics of obsessive-compulsive disorder. *International Review of Psychiatry, 9*, 61–71.

39. Gould, M. (2007, October 10). You can teach a man to kill but not to see dying. *The Guardian.* Retrieved from http://www.guardian.co.uk/society/2007/oct/10/guardiansocietysupplement.socialcare2

40. Hoge, C., & Castro, C. (2006). Post traumatic stress disorder in UK and U.S. forces deployed to Iraq. *Lancet, 368*, 867.

41. Davidson, J. (2000). Trauma: The impact of post-traumatic stress disorder. *Journal of Psychopharmacology, 14*(2 Suppl 1), S5–S12.

42. Brewin, C., Andrews, B., & Valentine, J. (2000). Meta-analysis of risk factors for posttraumatic stress disorder in trauma-exposed adults. *Journal of Consulting and Clinical Psychology, 68*(5), 748–766. doi:10.1037//0022-006X.68.5.748

43. Brady, K. T., Back, S. E., & Coffey, S. F. (2004). Substance abuse and posttraumatic stress disorder. *Current Directions in Psychological Science, 13*(5), 206–209.

44. van der Hart, O., & Nijenhuis, E. R. S. (2009). Dissociative disorders. In P. H. Blaney & T. M. Millon (Eds.), *Oxford textbook of psychological disorder* (2nd ed., pp. 452–481). New York, NY: Oxford University Press.

45. Cloninger, C., & Dokucu, M. (2008). Somatoform and dissociative disorders. In S. H. Fatemi & P. J. Clayton (Eds.), *The medical basis of psychiatry* (3rd ed., pp. 181–194). Totowa, NJ: Humana Press. doi:10.1007/978-1-59745-252-6_11

46. van der Hart, O., & Nijenhuis, E. R. S. (2009). Dissociative disorders. In P. H. Blaney & T. M. Millon (Eds.), *Oxford textbook of psychological disorder* (2nd ed., pp. 452–481). New York, NY: Oxford University Press.

47. Cardeña, E., & Gleaves, D. (2007). Dissociative disorders. In M. M. Hersen, S. M. Turner, & D. C. Beidel (Eds.), *Adult psychological disorder and diagnosis* (5th ed., pp. 473–503). Hoboken, NJ: John Wiley & Sons.

48. van der Hart, O., & Nijenhuis, E. R. S. (2009). Dissociative disorders. In P. H. Blaney, & T. M. Millon (Eds.), *Oxford textbook of psychological disorder* (2nd ed., pp. 452–481). New York, NY: Oxford University Press.

49. Gillig, P. M. (2009). Dissociative identity disorder: A controversial diagnosis. *Psychiatry, 6*(3), 24–29.

50. Kluft, R. P. (1996). The diagnosis and treatment of dissociative identity disorder. In *The Hatherleigh guide to psychiatric disorders* (1st ed., Vol. 1, pp. 49–96). New York, NY: Hatherleigh Press.

51. Dawson, P. L. (1990). Understanding and cooperation among alter and host personalities. *American Journal of Occupational Therapy, 44*(11), 994–997.

52. American Psychiatric Association. (2000). *Diagnostic and statistical manual of mental disorders* (4th ed., text rev.). Washington, DC: Author.

53. Barry-Walsh, J. (2005). Dissociative identity disorder. *Australian and New Zealand Journal of Psychiatry, 39,* 109–110; Kihlstrom, J. F. (2004). An unbalanced balancing act: Blocked, recovered, and false memories in the laboratory and clinic. *Clinical Psychology: Science and Practice, 11*(1), 34–41; Lilienfeld, S. O., & Lynn, S. J. (2003). Dissociative identity disorder: Multiple personalities, multiple controversies. In S. O. Lilienfeld, S. J. Lynn, & J. M. Lohr (Eds.), *Science and pseudoscience in clinical psychology* (pp. 109–142). New York, NY: Guilford Press; Lipsanen, T., Korkeila, J., Peltola, P., Jarvinen, J., Langen, K., & Lauerma, H. (2004). Dissociative disorders among psychiatric patients: Comparison with a nonclinical sample. *European Psychiatry, 19*(1), 53–55.

54. Miller, M., & Kantrowitz, B. (1999, January 25). Unmasking Sybil: A reexamination of the most famous psychiatric patient in history. *Newsweek,* pp. 11–16.

55. Hettema, J. M., Neale, M. C., & Kendler, K. S. (2001). A review and meta-analysis of the genetic epidemiology of anxiety disorders. *The American Journal of Psychiatry, 158*(10), 1568–1578.

56. Smoller, J., Paulus, M., Fagerness, J., Purcell, S., Yamaki, L., Hirshfeld-Becker, D.,…Stein, M. (2008). Influence of RGS2 on anxiety-related temperament, personality, and brain function. *Archives of General Psychiatry, 65*(3), 298–308. doi:10.1001/archgenpsychiatry.2007.48; Thoeringer, C., Ripke, S., Unschuld, P., Lucae, S., Ising, M., Bettecken, T.,…Erhardt, A. (2009). The GABA transporter 1 (SLC6A1): A novel candidate gene for anxiety disorders. *Journal of Neural Transmission, 116*(6), 649–657. doi:10.1007/s00702-008-0075-y

57. Brown, T., & McNiff, J. (2009). Specificity of autonomic arousal to *DSM-IV* panic disorder and posttraumatic stress disorder. *Behaviour Research and Therapy, 47*(6), 487–493. doi:10.1016/j.brat.2009.02.016; Damsa, C., Kosel, M., & Moussally, J. (2009). Current status of brain imaging in anxiety disorders. *Current Opinion in Psychiatry, 22*(1), 96–110. doi:10.1097/YCO.0b013e328319bd10

58. Gilbertson, M. W., Shenton, M. E., Ciszewski, A., Kasai, K., Lasko, N. B., Orr, S. P.,…Pitman, R. K. (2002). Smaller hippocampal volume predicts pathologic vulnerability to psychological trauma. *Nature Neuroscience, 5*(11), 1242.

59. Stein, M., Schork, N., & Gelernter, J. (2008). Gene-by-environment (serotonin transporter and childhood maltreatment) interaction for anxiety sensitivity, an intermediate phenotype for anxiety disorders. *Neuropsychopharmacology, 33*(2), 312–319. doi:10.1038/sj.npp.1301422

60. Twenge, J. (2006). *Generation me.* New York, NY: Free Press.

61. Alpher, V. S. (1992). Introject and identity: Structural-interpersonal analysis and psychological assessment of multiple personality disorder. *Journal of Personality Assessment. 58*(2), 347–367. doi:10.1207/s15327752jpa5802_12; Cardeña, E., & Gleaves, D. (2007). Dissociative disorders. In M. M. Hersen, S. M. Turner, & D. C. Beidel (Eds.), *Adult psychological disorder and diagnosis* (5th ed., pp. 473–503). Hoboken, NJ: John Wiley & Sons.

62. Kihlstrom, J. F., Glisky, M. L., & Angiulo, M. J. (1994). Dissociative tendencies and dissociative disorders. *Journal of Abnormal Psychology, 103,* 117–124.

63. Lilienfeld, S. O., & Lynn, S. J. (2003). Dissociative identity disorder: Multiple personalities, multiple controversies. In S. O. Lilienfeld, S. J. Lynn, & J. M. Lohr (Eds.), *Science and pseudoscience in clinical psychology* (pp. 109–142). New York, NY: Guilford Press.

64. Isen, A. M. (2003). Positive affect as a source of human strength. In J. Aspinall, *A psychology of human strengths: Fundamental questions and future directions for a positive psychology* (pp. 179–195). Washington, DC: American Psychological Association.

65. De Dreu, C. K. W., Baas, M., & Nijstad, B. A. (2008). Hedonic tone and activation level in the mood-creativity link: Toward a dual pathway to creativity model. *Journal of Personality and Social Psychology, 94*(5), 739–756.

66. National Institute of Mental Health. (2010, April 8). People with depression discuss their illness. Retrieved from http://www.nimh.nih.gov/media/video/health/depression.shtml

67. Kessler, R. C., Berglund, P. A., Demler, O., Jin, R., & Walters, E. E. (2005). Lifetime prevalence and age-of-onset distributions of *DSM-IV* disorders in the National Comorbidity Survey Replication (NCS-R). *Archives of General Psychiatry, 62*(6), 593–602.

68. Culbertson, F. M. (1997). Depression and gender: An international review. *American Psychologist, 52,* 25–31.

69. Kessler, R. C., Berglund, P., Demler, O, Jin, R., Koretz, D., Merikangas, K. R.,…Wang, P. S. (2003). The epidemiology of major depressive disorder: Results from the National Comorbidity Survey Replication (NCS-R). *Journal of the American Medical Association, 289*(23), 3095–3105.

70. American Association of Suicidology. (2010, June 29). *Some facts about suicide and depression.* Retrieved from http://www.suicidology.org/c/document_library/get_file?folderId=232&name=DLFE-246.pdf; American Foundation for Suicide Prevention. (2007). *About suicide: Facts and figures. National statistics.* Retrieved from http://www.afsp.org/index.cfm?fuseaction=home.viewpage&page_id=050FEA9F-B064-4092-B1135C3A70DE1FDA; Sudak, H. S. (2005). Suicide. In B. J. Sadock & V. A. Sadock (Eds.), *Kaplan & Sadock's comprehensive textbook of psychiatry.* Philadelphia, PA: Lippincott Williams & Wilkins.

71. Fairchild, K., & Scogin, F. (2008). Assessment and treatment of depression. In K. Laidlow & B. Knight (Eds.), *Handbook of emotional disorders in later life: Assessment and treatment.* New York, NY: Oxford University Press.

72. Kessler, R. C., Chiu, W. T., Demler, O., & Walters, E. E. (2005). Prevalence, severity, and comorbidity of 12-month *DSM-IV* disorders in the National Comorbidity Survey Replication. *Archives of General Psychiatry, 62*(6), 617–27; Kessler, R. C., Berglund, P., Demler, O, Jin, R., Koretz, D., Merikangas, K. R.,…Wang, P. S. (2003). The epidemiology of major depressive disorder: Results from the National Comorbidity Survey Replication (NCS-R). *Journal of the American Medical Association, 289*(23), 3095–3105.

73. Thomas, P., & Bracken, P. (2001). Vincent's bandage: The art of selling a drug for bipolar disorder. *British Medical Journal, 323,* 1434.

74. Bowden, C. L. (2001). Strategies to reduce misdiagnosis of bipolar depression. *Psychiatric Services, 52*(1), 51–55.

75. Berrettini, W. (2006). Genetics of bipolar and unipolar disorders. In D. J. Stein, D. J. Kupfer, & A. F. Schatzberg (Eds.), *Textbook of mood disorders.* Washington, DC: American Psychiatric Publishing; Merikangas, K., Chakravarti, A., Moldin, S., Araj, H., Blangero, J., Burmeister, M,…Takahashi, A. S. (2002). Future of genetics of mood disorders research. *Biological Psychiatry, 52*(6), 457–477.

76. Sher, L., & Mann, J. J. (2003). Psychiatric pathophysiology: Mood disorders. In A. Tasman, J. Kay, & J. A. Lieberman (Eds.), *Psychiatry.* New York, NY: John Wiley & Sons.

77. Videbech, P., & Ravnkilde, B. (2004). Hippocampal volume and depression: A meta-analysis of MRI studies. *American Journal of Psychiatry, 161,* 1957–1966.

78. Warner-Schmidt, J. L., & Duman, R. S. (2006). Hippocampal neurogenesis: Opposing effects of stress and antidepressant treatment. *Hippocampus, 16,* 239–249.

79. Duman, R. S., & Monteggia, L. M. (2006). A neurotrophic model for stress-related mood disorders. *Biological Psychiatry, 59,* 1116–1127.

80. Caspi, A., Sugden, K., Moffitt, T. E., Taylor, A., Craig, I. W., Harrington, H.,…Poulton, R. (2003). Influence of life stress on depression: Moderation by a polymorphism in the 5-HTT gene. *Science, 301*(5631), 386–389.

81. Robins, L. N., Cottler, L., Bucholtz, K., & Compton, W. (1995). *Diagnostic interview schedule for DSM-1V.* St. Louis, MO: Washington University.

82. Weissman, M. M., Bland, R. C., Canino, G. J., Greenwald, S., Hwu, H-G., Joyce, P. R.,…Yeh, E-K. (1996). Cross-national epidemiology of major depression and bipolar disorder. *Journal of the American Medical Association, 276,* 293–299.

83. Tsai, J. L., Knutson, B., & Fung, H. H. (2006). Cultural variation in affect valuation. *Journal of Personality and Social Psychology, 90,* 288–307.

84. National Institute of Mental Health. (2010, April 26). What is schizophrenia? Retrieved from http://www.nimh.nih.gov/health/topics/schizophrenia/index.shtml

85. Mueser, K. T., & McGurk, S. R. (2004). Schizophrenia. *Lancet, 363*(9426), 2063–2072; Nicolson, R., Lenane, M., Hamburger, S. D., Fernandez, T., Bedwell, J., & Rapoport, J. L. (2000). Lessons from childhood-onset schizophrenia. *Brain Research Review, 31*(2–3), 147–156.

86. Lindenmayer, J. P., & Khan, A. (2006). Psychological disorder. In J. A. Lieberman, T. S. Stroup, & D. O. Perkins (Eds.), *Textbook of schizophrenia* (pp. 187–222). Washington, DC: American Psychiatric Publishing.

87. American Psychiatric Association. (2000). *Diagnostic and statistical manual of mental disorders* (4th ed., text rev.). Washington, DC: Author; National Institute of Mental Health. (2010, April 26). What is schizophrenia? Retrieved from http://www.nimh.nih.gov/health/topics/schizophrenia/index.shtml

88. Skrabalo, A. (2000). Negative symptoms in schizophrenia(s): The conceptual basis. *Harvard Brain, 7,* 7–10.

89. Nicolson, S. E., Mayberg, H. S., Pennell, P. B., & Nemeroff, C. B. (2006). Persistent auditory hallucinations that are unresponsive to antipsychotic drugs. *The American Journal of Psychiatry, 163,* 1153–1159. doi:10.1176/appi.ajp.163.7.1153

90. National Institute of Mental Health. (2009, September 8). What are the symptoms of schizophrenia? Retrieved from http://www.nimh.nih.gov/health/publications/schizophrenia/what-are-the-symptoms-of-schizophrenia.shtml

91. De Sousa, A. (2007). Types and contents of hallucinations in schizophrenia. *Journal of Pakistan Psychiatric Society, 4*(1), 29.

92. Buchanan, R. W., & Carpenter, W. T. (2005). Concept of schizophrenia. In B. J. Sadock & V. A. Sadock (Eds.), *Kaplan & Sadock's comprehensive textbook of psychiatry.* Philadelphia, PA: Lippincott Williams & Wilkins.

93. Maher, B. A. (2001). Delusions. In P. B. Sutker & H. E. Adams (Eds.), *Comprehensive handbook of psychological disorder* (3rd ed., pp. 309–370). New York, NY: Kluwer Academic/Plenum.

94. Buchanan, R. W., & Carpenter, W. T. (2005). Concept of schizophrenia. In B. J. Sadock & V. A. Sadock (Eds.), *Kaplan & Sadock's comprehensive textbook of psychiatry.* Philadelphia, PA: Lippincott Williams & Wilkins.

95. Janno, S., Holi, M., Tuisku, K., & Wahlbeck, K. (2004). Prevalence of neuroleptic-induced movement disorders in chronic schizophrenia patients. *American Journal of Psychiatry, 161,* 160–163; Rosebush, P. I., & Mazurek, M. F. (2010). Catatonia and its treatment. *Schizophrenia Bulleting, 36*(2), 239–242. doi:10.1093/schbul/sbp141

96. Skrabalo, A. (2000). Negative symptoms in schizophrenia(s): The conceptual basis. *Harvard Brain, 7,* 7–10.

97. Kring, A. M. (1999). Emotion in schizophrenia: Old mystery, new understanding. *Current Directions in Psychological Science, 8,* 160–163.

98. Kirkpatrick, B., & Tek, C. (2005). Schizophrenia: Clinical features and psychological disorder concepts. In B. J. Sadock & S. V. Sadock (Eds.), *Kaplan & Sadock's comprehensive textbook of psychiatry* (pp. 1416–1435). Philadelphia, PA: Lippincott Williams & Wilkins.

99. Fenton, W. S., & McGlashan, T. H. (1994). Antecedents, symptom progression, and long-term outcome of the deficit syndrome in schizophrenia. *American Journal of Psychiatry, 151,* 351–356.

100. Walker, E., Kesler, L., Bollini, A., & Hochman, K. (2004). Schizophrenia: Etiology and course. *Annual Review of Psychology, 55,* 401–430.

101. Walker, E., & Tessner, K. (2008). Schizophrenia. *Perspectives on Psychological Science, 3*(1), 30–37.

102. Suddath, R. L., Christison, G. W., Torrey, E. F., Casanova, M. F., & Weinberger, D. R. (1990). Anatomical abnormalities in the brains of monozygotic twins discordant for schizophrenia. *New England Journal of Medicine, 322*(12), 789–794.

103. Galderisi, S., Quarantelli, M., Volper, U., Mucci, A., Cassano, G. B., Invernizzi, G.,…Maj, M. (2008). Patterns of structural MRI abnormalities in deficit and nondeficit schizophrenia. *Schizophrenia Bulletin, 34*, 393–401.

104. Javitt, D. C., & Laruelle, M. (2006). Neurochemical theories. In J. A. Lieberman, T. S. Stroup, & D. O. Perkins (Eds.), *Textbook of schizophrenia* (pp. 85–116). Washington, DC: American Psychiatric Publishing.

105. Inayama, Y., Yoneda, H., Sakai, T., Ishida, T., Nonomura, Y., Kono, Y.,…Asaba, H. (1996). Positive association between a DNA sequence variant in the serotonin 2A receptor gene and schizophrenia. *American Journal of Medical Genetics, 67*(1), 103–105.

106. Csernansky, J. G., & Grace, A. A. (1998). New models of the pathophysiology of schizophrenia: Editors' introduction. *Schizophrenia Bulletin, 24*(2), 185–187.

107. Gottesman, I. I., & Erlenmeyer-Kimling, L. (2001). Family and twin studies as a head start in defining prodomes and endophenotypes for hypothetical early interventions in schizophrenia. *Schizophrenia Research, 5*(1), 93–102; Riley, B. P., & Kendler, K. S. (2005). Schizophrenia: Genetics. In B. J. Sadock & V. A. Sadock (Eds.), *Kaplan & Sadock's comprehensive textbook of psychiatry* (pp.1354–1370). Philadelphia, PA: Lippincott Williams & Wilkins.

108. Brown, A. S., Begg, M. D., Gravenstein, S., Schaefer, C. S., Wyatt, R. J., Bresnahan, M.,…Susser, E. S. (2004). Serologic evidence of prenatal influenza in the etiology of schizophrenia. *Archives of General Psychiatry, 61*, 774–780; Murray, R. M., & Bramon, E. (2005). Developmental model of schizophrenia. In B. J. Sadock & V. A. Sadock (Eds.), *Kaplan & Sadock's comprehensive textbook of psychiatry* (pp. 1381–1395). Philadelphia, PA: Lippincott Williams & Wilkins; Susser, E. B., Neugebauer, R., Hock, H.W., Brown, A. S., Lin, S., Labowitz, D., & Gorman, J. M. (1996). Schizophrenia after prenatal famine: Further evidence. *Archives of general psychiatry, 53*, 25–31; Waddington J. L., Lane, A., Larkin, C., & O'Callaghan, E. (1999). The neurodevelopmental basis of schizophrenia: Clinical clues from cerebro-craniofacial dysmorphogenesis, and the roots of a life-time trajectory of disease. *Biological Psychiatry, 46*(1), 31–9.

109. Walker, E., Mittal, V., & Tessner, K. (2008). Stress and the hypothalamic pituitary adrenal axis in the developmental course of schizophrenia. *Annual Review of Clinical Psychology, 4*, 189–216.

110. Walker, E., Mittal, V., & Tessner, K. (2008). Stress and the hypothalamic pituitary adrenal axis in the developmental course of schizophrenia. *Annual Review of Clinical Psychology, 4*, 189–216.

111. Hooley, J. M., & Hiller, J. B. (1998). Expressed emotion and the pathogenesis of relapse in schizophrenia. In M. F. Lenzenweger & R. H. Dworkin (Eds.), *Origins and development of schizophrenia: Advances in experimental psychopathology* (pp. 447–468). Washington, DC: American Psychological Association.

112. Widiger, T.A. (2006). Understanding personality disorders. In S. K. Huprich (Ed.), *Rorschach assessment to the personality disorders. The LEA series in personality and clinical psychology* (pp. 3–25). Mahwah, NJ: Lawrence Erlbaum Associates.

113. Lynam, D., & Widiger, T. (2001). Using the five-factor model to represent the *DSM-IV* personality disorders: An expert consensus approach. *Journal of Abnormal Psychology, 110*(3), 401–412.

114. Oltmanns, T. F., & Turkheimer, E. (2006). Perceptions of self and others regarding pathological personality traits. In R. F. Krueger & J. L. Tackett (Eds.), *Personality and psychopathology* (pp. 71–111). New York, NY: Guilford Press.

115. Grant, B., Hasin, D., Stinson, F., Dawson, D., Chou, S., Ruan, W., & Pickering, R. P. (2004). Prevalence, correlates, and disability of personality disorders in the United States: Results from the national epidemiologic survey on alcohol and related conditions. *Journal of Clinical Psychiatry, 65*(7), 948–958.

116. Huang, Y., Kotov, R., de Girolamo, G., Preti, A., Angermeyer, M., Benjet, C.,…Kessler, R. C. (2009). DSM-IV personality disorders in the WHO World Mental Health Surveys. *British Journal of Psychiatry, 195*(1), 46–53. doi:10.1192/bjp.bp.108.058552

117. Krueger, R. F. (2005). Continuity of Axes I and II: Towards a unified model of personality, personality disorders, and clinical disorders. *Journal of Personality Disorders, 19*, 233–261; Phillips, K. A., Yen, S., & Gunderson, J. G. (2003). Personality disorders. In R. E. Hales & S. C. Yudofsky (Eds.), *Textbook of clinical psychiatry*. Washington, DC: American Psychiatric Publishing; Verheul, R. (2005). Clinical utility for dimensional models of personality pathology. *Journal of Personality Disorders, 19*, 283–302.

118. Hyman, S. E. (2002). A new beginning for research on borderline personality disorder. *Biological Psychiatry, 51*(12), 933–935.

119. Zweig-Frank, H., Paris, J., Kin, N. M. N. Y., Schwartz, G., Steiger, H., & Nair, N. P. V. (2006). Childhood sexual abuse in relation to neurobiological challenge tests in patients with borderline personality disorder and normal controls. *Psychiatry Research, 141*(3), 337–341.

120. Minzenberg, M. J., Poole, J. H., & Vinogradov, S. (2008). A neurocognitive model of borderline personality disorder: Effects of childhood sexual abuse and relationship to adult social attachment disturbance. *Development and Psychological disorder. 20*(1), 341–368. doi:10.1017/S0954579408000163

121. Lobbestael, J., & Arntz, A. (2009). Emotional, cognitive and physiological correlates of abuse-related stress in borderline and antisocial personality disorder. *Behaviour Research and Therapy, 48*(2), 116–124. doi:10.1016/j.brat.2009.09.015

122. Skodol, A. E., Gunderson, J. G., Pfohl, B., Widiger, T. A., Livesley, W. J., & Siever, L. J. (2002). The borderline diagnosis I: Psychopathology, comorbidity, and personality structure. *Biological Psychiatry, 51*(12), 936–950.

123. Posner, M., Rothbart, M., Vizueta, N., Thomas, K., Levy, K., Fossella, J.,…Kernberg, O. (2003). An approach to the psychobiology of personality disorders. *Development and Psychopathology, 15*(4), 1093–1106. doi:10.1017/S0954579403000506

124. Rhee, S. H., & Waldman, I. D. (2002). Genetic and environmental influences on anti-social behavior: A meta-analysis of twin and adoptions studies. *Psychological Bulletin, 128*(3), 490–529.

125. Rhee, S. H., & Waldman, I. D. (2002). Genetic and environmental influences on anti-social behavior: A meta-analysis of twin and adoptions studies. *Psychological Bulletin, 128*(3), 490–529.

126. Lyons-Ruth, K., Holmes, B. M., Sasvari-Szekely, M., Ronai, Z., Nemoda, Z., & Pauls, D. (2007). Serotonin transporter polymorphism and borderline or antisocial traits among low-income young adults. *Psychiatric Genetics, 17*, 339–343; Raine, A., Lencz, T., Bihrle, S., LaCasse, L., & Colletti, P. (2000). Reduced prefrontal gray matter volume and reduced autonomic activity in antisocial personality disorder. *Archive of General Psychiatry, 57*, 119–127.

127. Huesmann, L. R., & Kirwil, L. (2007). Why observing violence increases the risk of violent behavior by the observer. In D. J. Flannery, A. T. Vazsonyi, & I. D. Waldman (Eds.), *The Cambridge handbook of violent behavior and aggression* (pp. 545–570). New York, NY: Cambridge University Press.

128. Akagi, H., & House, A. O. (2001). The epidemiology of hysterical conversion. In P. Halligan, C. Bass, & J. Marshall (Eds.), *Hysterical conversion: Clinical and theoretical perspectives* (pp. 73–87). Oxford, England: Oxford University Press.

129. Smith, R. C., Gardiner, J. C., Lyles, J. S., Sirbu, C., Dwamena, F. C., Hodges, A.,…Goddeeris, J. (2005). Exploration of *DSM-IV* criteria in primary care patients with medically unexplained symptoms. *Psychosomatic Medicine, 67*(1), 123–129.

130. Bass, C., Peveler, R., & House, A. (2001). Somatoform disorders: Severe psychiatric illnesses neglected by psychiatrists. *British Journal of Psychiatry, 179*, 11–14; Looper, K. J., & Kirmayer, L. J. (2002). Behavioral medicine approaches to somatoform disorders. *Journal of Consulting and Clinical Psychology, 70*(3), 810–827.

131. Laumann, E. O., Paik, A., Rosen, R. (1999). Sexual dysfunction in the United States. *Journal of the American Medical Association, 281*(6), 537–544.

132. Donahey, K. M., & Carroll, R. A. (1993). Gender differences in factors associated with hypoactive sexual desire. *Journal of Sex & Marital Therapy, 19*(1), 25–40.

133. Kingsberg, S. A., & Janata, J. W. (2003). The sexual aversions. In S. B. Levine, C. B. Risen, & S. E. Althof (Eds.), *Handbook of clinical sexuality for mental health professionals* (pp. 153–165). New York, NY: Brunner-Routledge.

134. Waldinger, M. D. (2003). Rapid ejaculation. In S. B. Levine, C. B. Risen, & S. E. Althof (Eds.), *Handbook of clinical sexuality for mental health professionals* (pp. 257–274). New York, NY: Brunner-Routledge.

135. Beitchman, J. H., Zucker, K. J., Hood, J. E., & DaCosta, G. A. (1992). A review of the long-term effects of child sexual abuse. *Child Abuse & Neglect, 16*(1), 101–118.

136. Bower, H. (2001). The gender identity disorder in the *DSM-IV* classification: A critical evaluation. *Australian and New Zealand Journal of Psychiatry, 35*(1), 1–8.

137. Olsson, S.-E., & Möller, A. R. (2003). On the incidence and sex ratio of transsexualism in Sweden, 1972–2002. *Archives of Sexual Behavior, 32*(4), 381–386.

138. Kraemer, B., Noll, T., Delsignore, A., Milos, G., Schnyder, U., & Hepp, U. (2009). Finger length ratio (2D:4D) in adults with gender identity disorder. *Archives of Sexual Behavior, 38*(3), 359–363.

139. Connolly, P. (2006). Psychological functioning of bondage/domination/sado-masochism (BDSM) practitioners. *Journal of Psychology & Human Sexuality, 18*(1), 79–120. doi:10.1300/j056v18n01_05

Treating Psychological Disorders

Therapy on Four Legs

Lucien Masson, a 60-year-old Vietnam veteran from Arizona, put it simply: "Sascha is the best medicine I've ever had."

Lucien is speaking about his friend, companion, and perhaps even his therapist, a Russian wolfhound named Sascha. Lucien suffers from posttraumatic stress disorder (PTSD), a disorder that has had a profoundly negative impact on his life for many years. His symptoms include panic attacks, nightmares, and road rage. Lucien has tried many solutions, consulting with doctors, psychiatrists, and psychologists, and using a combination of drugs, group therapy, and anger-management classes.

But Sascha seems to be the best therapist of all. He helps out in many ways. If a stranger gets too close to Lucien in public, Sascha will block the stranger with his body. Sascha is trained to sense when Lucien is about to have a nightmare, waking him before it starts. Before road rage can set in, Sascha gently whimpers, reminding his owner that it doesn't pay to get upset about nutty drivers.

In the same way, former Army medic Jo Hanna Schaffer speaks of her Chihuahua, Cody: "I never took a pill for PTSD that did as much for me as Cody has done." Persian Gulf War veteran Karen Alexander feels the same way about her Bernese mountain dog, Cindy:

> *She'll come up and touch me, and that is enough of a stimulus to break the loop, bring me back to reality. Sometimes I'll scratch my hand until it's raw and won't realize until she comes up to me and brings me out. She's such a grounding influence for me.*

Can psychiatric therapy dogs help people who suffer from PTSD?

© Thinkstock

These dramatic stories of improvement from debilitating disorders can be attributed to an alternative psychological therapy, based on established behavioral principles, provided by "psychiatric service dogs." The dogs are trained to help people with a variety of mental disorders, including panic attacks, anxiety disorder, obsessive-compulsive disorder, and bipolar disorder. They help veterans of Iraq and Afghanistan cope with their traumatic brain injuries as well as with PTSD.

The dogs are trained to perform specific behaviors that are helpful to their owners. If the dog's owner is depressed, the dog will snuggle up and offer physical comfort; if the owner is having a panic attack, the owner can calm himself by massaging the dog's body. The serenity shown by the dogs in all situations seems to reassure the PTSD sufferer that all must be well. Service dogs are constant, loving companions who provide emotional support and companionship to their embattled, often isolated owners (Shim, 2008; Lorber, 2010; Alaimo, 2010; Schwartz, 2008).[1]

Despite the reports of success from many users, it is important to keep in mind that the utility of psychiatric service dogs has not yet been tested, and thus would never be offered as a therapy by a trained clinician or paid for by an insurance company. Although interaction between humans and dogs can create positive physiological responses (Odendaal, 2000),[2] whether the dogs actually help people recover from PTSD is not yet known.

Psychological disorders create a tremendous individual, social, and economic drain on society. Disorders make it difficult for people to engage in productive lives and effectively contribute to their family and to society. Disorders lead to disability and absenteeism in the workplace, as well as physical problems, premature death, and suicide. At a societal level the costs are staggering. It has been estimated that the annual financial burden of each case of anxiety disorder is over $3,000 per year, meaning that the annual cost of anxiety disorders alone in the United States runs into the trillions of dollars (Konnopka, Leichsenring, Leibing, & König, 2009; Smit et al., 2006).[3]

The goal of this chapter is to review the techniques that are used to treat psychological disorder. Just as psychologists consider the causes of disorder in terms of the bio-psycho-social model of illness, treatment is also based on psychological, biological, and social approaches.

- The *psychological approach* to reducing disorder involves providing help to individuals or families through psychological therapy, including psychoanalysis, humanistic-oriented therapy, cognitive-behavioral therapy (CBT), and other approaches.

- The *biomedical approach to reducing disorder* is based on the use of medications to treat mental disorders such as schizophrenia, depression, and anxiety, as well as the employment of brain intervention techniques, including *electroconvulsive therapy (ECT)*, *transcranial magnetic stimulation (TMS)*, and *psychosurgery*.

- The *social approach to reducing disorder* focuses on changing the social environment in which individuals live to reduce the underlying causes of disorder. These approaches include *group, couples, and family therapy*, as well as *community outreach programs*. The community approach is likely to be the most effective of the three approaches because it focuses not only on treatment, but also on prevention of disorders (World Health Organization, 2004).[4]

A clinician may focus on any or all of the three approaches to treatment, but in making a decision about which to use, he or she will always rely on his or her knowledge about existing empirical tests of the effectiveness of different treatments. These tests, known as *outcome studies*, carefully compare people who receive a given treatment with people who do not receive a treatment, or with people who receive a different type of treatment. Taken together, these studies have confirmed that many types of therapies are effective in treating disorder.

1. REDUCING DISORDER BY CONFRONTING IT: PSYCHOTHERAPY

LEARNING OBJECTIVES

1. Outline and differentiate the psychodynamic, humanistic, behavioral, and cognitive approaches to psychotherapy.
2. Explain the behavioral and cognitive aspects of cognitive-behavioral therapy and how CBT is used to reduce psychological disorders.

Treatment for psychological disorder begins when the individual who is experiencing distress visits a counselor or therapist, perhaps in a church, a community center, a hospital, or a private practice. The therapist will begin by systematically learning about the patient's needs through a formal **psychological assessment**, which is *an evaluation of the patient's psychological and mental health*. During the assessment the psychologist may give personality tests such as the Minnesota Multiphasic Personal Inventory (MMPI-2) or projective tests, and will conduct a thorough interview with the patient. The therapist may get more information from family members or school personnel.

In addition to the psychological assessment, the patient is usually seen by a physician to gain information about potential Axis III (physical) problems. In some cases of psychological disorder—and particularly for sexual problems—medical treatment is the preferred course of action. For instance, men who are experiencing erectile dysfunction disorder may need surgery to increase blood flow or local injections of muscle relaxants. Or they may be prescribed medications (Viagra, Cialis, or Levitra) that provide an increased blood supply to the penis, which are successful in increasing performance in about 70% of men who take them.

After the medical and psychological assessments are completed, the therapist will make a formal diagnosis using the detailed descriptions of the disorder provided in the *Diagnostic and Statistical Manual of Mental Disorders* (*DSM*; see below). The therapist will summarize the information about the patient on each of the five *DSM* axes, and the diagnosis will likely be sent to an insurance company to justify payment for the treatment.

psychological assessment

An evaluation of the patient's psychological and mental health.

DSM-IV-TR Criteria for Diagnosing Attention-Deficit/Hyperactivity Disorder (ADHD)

To be diagnosed with ADHD the individual must display either A or B below (American Psychiatric Association, 2000):[5]

A. *Six or more of the following symptoms of inattention have been present for at least 6 months to a point that is disruptive and inappropriate for developmental level:*

- Often does not give close attention to details or makes careless mistakes in schoolwork, work, or other activities
- Often has trouble keeping attention on tasks or play activities
- Often does not seem to listen when spoken to directly
- Often does not follow instructions and fails to finish schoolwork, chores, or duties in the workplace (not due to oppositional behavior or failure to understand instructions)
- Often has trouble organizing activities
- Often avoids, dislikes, or doesn't want to do things that take a lot of mental effort for a long period of time (such as schoolwork or homework)
- Often loses things needed for tasks and activities (e.g., toys, school assignments, pencils, books, or tools)
- Is often easily distracted
- Is often forgetful in daily activities

B. *Six or more of the following symptoms of hyperactivity-impulsivity have been present for at least 6 months to an extent that is disruptive and inappropriate for developmental level:*

- Often fidgets with hands or feet or squirms in seat
- Often gets up from seat when remaining in seat is expected
- Often runs about or climbs when and where it is not appropriate (adolescents or adults may feel very restless)

- Often has trouble playing or enjoying leisure activities quietly
- Is often "on the go" or often acts as if "driven by a motor"
- Often talks excessively
- Often blurts out answers before questions have been finished
- Often has trouble waiting one's turn
- Often interrupts or intrudes on others (e.g., butts into conversations or games)

psychotherapy

Professional treatment for psychological disorder through techniques designed to encourage communication of conflicts and insight.

If a diagnosis is made, the therapist will select a course of therapy that he or she feels will be most effective. One approach to treatment is **psychotherapy**, *the professional treatment for psychological disorder through techniques designed to encourage communication of conflicts and insight*. The fundamental aspect of psychotherapy is that the patient directly confronts the disorder and works with the therapist to help reduce it. Therapy includes assessing the patient's issues and problems, planning a course of treatment, setting goals for change, the treatment itself, and an evaluation of the patient's progress. Therapy is practiced by thousands of psychologists and other trained practitioners in the United States and around the world, and is responsible for billions of dollars of the health budget.

To many people therapy involves a patient lying on a couch with a therapist sitting behind and nodding sagely as the patient speaks. Though this approach to therapy (known as *psychoanalysis*) is still practiced, it is in the minority. It is estimated that there are over 400 different kinds of therapy practiced by people in many fields, and the most important of these are shown in Figure 13.2. The therapists who provide these treatments include psychiatrists (who have a medical degree and can prescribe drugs) and clinical psychologists, as well as social workers, psychiatric nurses, and couples, marriage, and family therapists.

FIGURE 13.2 The Many Types of Therapy Practiced in the United States

These data show the proportion of psychotherapists who reported practicing each type of therapy.

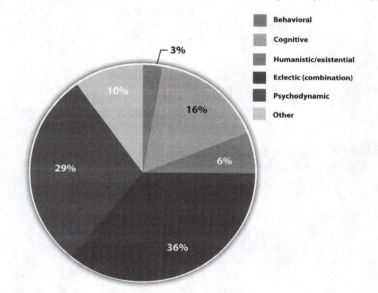

Source: Adapted from Norcross, J. C., Hedges, M., & Castle, P. H. (2002). Psychologists conducting psychotherapy in 2001: A study of the Division 29 membership. Psychotherapy: Theory, Research, Practice, Training, 39(1), 97–102.

Psychology in Everyday Life: Seeking Treatment for Psychological Difficulties

Many people who would benefit from psychotherapy do not get it, either because they do not know how to find it or because they feel that they will be stigmatized and embarrassed if they seek help. The decision to not seek help is a very poor choice because the effectiveness of mental health treatments is well documented and, no matter where a person lives, there are treatments available (U.S. Department of Health and Human Services, 1999).[6]

The first step in seeking help for psychological problems is to accept the stigma. It is possible that some of your colleagues, friends, and family members will know that you are seeking help and some may at first think more negatively of you for it. But you must get past these unfair and close-minded responses. Feeling good about yourself is the most important thing you can do, and seeking help may be the first step in doing so.

One question is how to determine if someone needs help. This question is not always easy to answer because there is no clear demarcation between "normal" and "abnormal" behavior. Most generally, you will know that you or others need help when the person's psychological state is negatively influencing his or her everyday behavior, when the behavior is adversely affecting those around the person, and when the problems continue over a period of time. Often people seek therapy as a result of a life-changing event such as diagnosis of a fatal illness, an upcoming marriage or divorce, or the death of a loved one. But therapy is also effective for general depression and anxiety, as well as for specific everyday problems.

There are a wide variety of therapy choices, many of which are free. Begin in your school, community, or church, asking about community health or counseling centers and pastoral counseling. You may want to *ask friends and family members for recommendations*. You'll probably be surprised at how many people have been to counseling, and how many recommend it.

There are many therapists who offer a variety of treatment options. Be sure to ask about the degrees that the therapist has earned, and about the reputation of the center in which the therapy occurs. If you have choices, try to find a person or location that you like, respect, and trust. This will allow you to be more open, and you will get more out of the experience. Your sessions with the help provider will require discussing your family history, personality, and relationships, and you should feel comfortable sharing this information.

Remember also that confronting issues requires time to reflect, energy to get to the appointments and deal with consequential feelings, and discipline to explore your issues on your own. Success at therapy is difficult, and it takes effort.

The bottom line is that going for therapy should not be a difficult decision for you. All people have the right to appropriate mental health care just as they have a right to general health care. Just as you go to a dentist for a toothache, you may go to therapy for psychological difficulties. Furthermore, you can be confident that you will be treated with respect and that your privacy will be protected, because therapists follow ethical principles in their practices. The following provides a summary of these principles as developed by the American Psychological Association (2010).[7]

- Psychologists inform their clients/patients as early as possible in the therapeutic relationship about the nature and anticipated course of therapy, fees, involvement of third parties, and limits of confidentiality, and provide sufficient opportunity for the client/patient to ask questions and receive answers.

- Psychologists inform their clients/patients of the developing nature of the treatment, the potential risks involved, alternative treatments that may be available, and about the voluntary nature of their participation.

- When the therapist is a trainee, the client/patient is informed that the therapist is in training and is being supervised, and is given the name of the supervisor.

- When psychologists agree to provide services to several persons who have a relationship (such as spouses, significant others, or parents and children), they take reasonable steps to clarify at the outset which of the individuals are clients/patients and the relationship the psychologist will have with each person.

- If it becomes apparent that a psychologist may be called on to perform potentially conflicting roles (such as family therapist and then witness for one party in divorce proceedings), the psychologist takes reasonable steps to clarify and modify, or withdraw from, roles appropriately.

- When psychologists provide services to several persons in a group setting, they describe at the outset the roles and responsibilities of all parties and the limits of confidentiality.

- Psychologists do not engage in sexual intimacies with current therapy clients/patients, or with individuals they know to be close relatives, guardians, or significant others of current clients/patients. Psychologists do not terminate therapy to circumvent this standard. Psychologists do not accept as therapy clients/patients persons with whom they have engaged in sexual intimacies, nor do they have sexual intimacies with former clients/patients for at least 2 years after cessation or termination of therapy.

- Psychologists terminate therapy when it becomes reasonably clear that the client/patient no longer needs the service, is not likely to benefit, or is being harmed by continued service.

1.1 Psychodynamic Therapy

psychodynamic therapy (psychoanalysis)

A psychological treatment based on Freudian and neo-Freudian personality theories in which the therapist helps the patient explore the unconscious dynamics of personality.

interpretation

A technique of psychotherapy in which the therapist uses the patient's expressed thoughts to understand the underlying unconscious problems.

free association

A technique of psychotherapy in which the therapist listens while the client talks about whatever comes to mind, without any censorship or filtering.

dream analysis

A technique of psychotherapy in which the therapist listens while the client describes his or her dreams and then analyzes the symbolism of the dreams.

insight

An understanding in psychotherapy of the unconscious causes of the disorder.

resistance

An occurrence in psychotherapy in which the patient uses defense mechanisms to avoid the painful feelings in his or her unconscious.

transference

An occurrence in psychotherapy in which the patient redirects feelings experienced in an important personal relationship toward the therapist.

Psychodynamic therapy (psychoanalysis) is *a psychological treatment based on Freudian and neo-Freudian personality theories in which the therapist helps the patient explore the unconscious dynamics of personality.* The analyst engages with the patient, usually in one-on-one sessions, often with the patient lying on a couch and facing away. The goal of the psychotherapy is for the patient to talk about his or her personal concerns and anxieties, *allowing the therapist to try to understand the underlying unconscious problems that are causing the symptoms* (the process of **interpretation**). The analyst may try out some interpretations on the patient and observe how he or she responds to them.

The patient may be asked to verbalize his or her thoughts through **free association**, in which the *therapist listens while the client talks about whatever comes to mind, without any censorship or filtering.* The client may also be asked to report on his or her dreams, and the therapist will use **dream analysis** to *analyze the symbolism of the dreams in an effort to probe the unconscious thoughts of the client and interpret their significance.* On the basis of the thoughts expressed by the patient, the analyst discovers the unconscious conflicts causing the patient's symptoms and interprets them for the patient.

The goal of psychotherapy is to help the patient develop **insight**—that is, *an understanding of the unconscious causes of the disorder* (Epstein, Stern, & Silbersweig, 2001; Lubarsky & Barrett, 2006),[8] but the patient often shows **resistance** to these new understandings, *using defense mechanisms to avoid the painful feelings in his or her unconscious.* The patient might forget or miss appointments, or act out with hostile feelings toward the therapist. The therapist attempts to help the patient develop insight into the causes of the resistance. The sessions may also lead to **transference**, in which *the patient unconsciously redirects feelings experienced in an important personal relationship toward the therapist.* For instance, the patient may transfer feelings of guilt that come from the father or mother to the therapist. Some therapists believe that transference should be encouraged, as it allows the client to resolve hidden conflicts and work through feelings that are present in the relationships.

Important Characteristics and Experiences in Psychoanalysis

- *Free association.* The therapist listens while the client talks about whatever comes to mind, without any censorship or filtering. The therapist then tries to interpret these free associations, looking for unconscious causes of symptoms.
- *Dream analysis.* The therapist listens while the client describes his or her dreams and then analyzes the symbolism of the dreams in an effort to probe the unconscious thoughts of the client and interpret their significance.
- *Insight.* An understanding by the patient of the unconscious causes of his or her symptoms.
- *Interpretation.* The therapist uses the patient's expressed thoughts to try to understand the underlying unconscious problems. The analyst may try out some interpretations on the patient and observe how he or she responds to them.
- *Resistance.* The patient's use of defense mechanisms to avoid the painful feelings in his or her unconscious. The patient might forget or miss appointments, or act out with hostile feelings toward the therapist. The therapist attempts to help the patient develop insight into the causes of the resistance.
- *Transference.* The unconscious redirection of the feelings experienced in an important personal relationship toward the therapist. For instance, the patient may transfer feelings of guilt that come from the father or mother to the therapist.

One problem with traditional psychoanalysis is that the sessions may take place several times a week, go on for many years, and cost thousands of dollars. To help more people benefit, modern psychodynamic approaches frequently use shorter-term, focused, and goal-oriented approaches. In these "brief psychodynamic therapies," the therapist helps the client determine the important issues to be discussed at the beginning of treatment and usually takes a more active role than in classic psychoanalysis (Levenson, 2010).[9]

1.2 Humanistic Therapies

Just as psychoanalysis is based on the personality theories of Freud and the neo-Freudians, **humanistic therapy** is *a psychological treatment based on the personality theories of Carl Rogers and other humanistic psychologists.* Humanistic therapy is based on the idea that people develop psychological problems when they are burdened by limits and expectations placed on them by themselves and others, and the treatment emphasizes the person's capacity for self-realization and fulfillment. Humanistic therapies attempt to promote growth and responsibility by helping clients consider their own situations and the world around them and how they can work to achieve their life goals.

Carl Rogers developed **person-centered therapy (or client-centered therapy)**, *an approach to treatment in which the client is helped to grow and develop as the therapist provides a comfortable, nonjudgmental environment.* In his book, *A Way of Being* (1980),[10] Rogers argued that therapy was most productive when the therapist created a positive relationship with the client—a *therapeutic alliance.* The **therapeutic alliance** is *a relationship between the client and the therapist that is facilitated when the therapist is* genuine *(i.e., he or she creates no barriers to free-flowing thoughts and feelings), when the therapist treats the client with* unconditional positive regard *(i.e., values the client without any qualifications, displaying an accepting attitude toward whatever the client is feeling at the moment), and when the therapist develops* empathy *with the client (i.e., that he or she actively listens to and accurately perceives the personal feelings that the client experiences).*

The development of a positive therapeutic alliance has been found to be exceedingly important to successful therapy. The ideas of genuineness, empathy, and unconditional positive regard in a nurturing relationship in which the therapist actively listens to and reflects the feelings of the client is probably the most fundamental part of contemporary psychotherapy (Prochaska & Norcross, 2007).[11]

1.3

Psychodynamic and humanistic therapies are recommended primarily for people suffering from generalized anxiety or mood disorders, and who desire to feel better about themselves overall. But the goals of people with other psychological disorders, such as phobias, sexual problems, and obsessive-compulsive disorder (OCD), are more specific. A person with a social phobia may want to be able to leave his or her house, a person with a sexual dysfunction may want to improve his or her sex life, and a person with OCD may want to learn to stop letting his obsessions or compulsions interfere with everyday activities. In these cases it is not necessary to revisit childhood experiences or consider our capacities for self-realization—we simply want to deal with what is happening in the present.

Cognitive-behavior therapy (CBT) is *a structured approach to treatment that attempts to reduce psychological disorders through systematic procedures based on cognitive and behavioral principles.* As you can see in Figure 13.4, CBT is based on the idea that there is a recursive link among our thoughts, our feelings, and our behavior. For instance, if we are feeling depressed, our negative thoughts ("I am doing poorly in my chemistry class") lead to negative feelings ("I feel hopeless and sad"), which then contribute to negative behaviors (lethargy, disinterest, lack of studying). When we or other people look at the negative behavior, the negative thoughts are reinforced and the cycle repeats itself (Beck, 1976).[12] Similarly, in panic disorder a patient may misinterpret his or her feelings of anxiety as a sign of an impending physical or mental catastrophe (such as a heart attack), leading to an avoidance of a particular place or social situation. The fact that the patient is avoiding the situation reinforces the negative thoughts. Again, the thoughts, feelings, and behavior amplify and distort each other.

humanistic therapy

A psychological treatment based on the personality theories of Carl Rogers and other humanistic psychologists.

person-centered therapy (or client-centered therapy)

An approach to treatment in which the client is helped to grow and develop as the therapist provides a comfortable, nonjudgmental environment.

therapeutic alliance

A relationship between patient and client that occurs when the therapist is genuine, treats the client with unconditional positive regard, and develops empathy with the client.

FIGURE 13.3

Carl Rogers was among the founders of the humanistic approach to therapy and developed the fundamentals of person-centered therapy.

Source: Courtesy of http://commons.wikimedia.org/wiki/File:Carl_Ransom_Rogers.jpg.

cognitive-behavior therapy (CBT)

A structured approach to treatment that attempts to reduce psychological disorders through systematic procedures based on *cognitive* and *behavioral* principles.

FIGURE 13.4 Cognitive-Behavior Therapy

Cognitive-behavior therapy (CBT) is based on the idea that our thoughts, feelings, and behavior reinforce each other and that changing our thoughts or behavior can make us feel better.

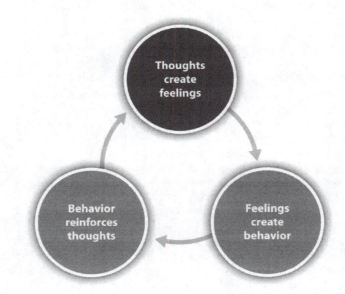

CBT is a very broad approach that is used for the treatment of a variety of problems, including mood, anxiety, personality, eating, substance abuse, attention-deficit, and psychotic disorders. CBT treats the symptoms of the disorder (the behaviors or the cognitions) and does not attempt to address the underlying issues that cause the problem. The goal is simply to stop the negative cycle by intervening to change cognition or behavior. The client and the therapist work together to develop the goals of the therapy, the particular ways that the goals will be reached, and the timeline for reaching them. The procedures are problem-solving and action-oriented, and the client is forced to take responsibility for his or her own treatment. The client is assigned tasks to complete that will help improve the disorder and takes an active part in the therapy. The treatment usually lasts between 10 and 20 sessions.

Depending on the particular disorder, some CBT treatments may be primarily behavioral in orientation, focusing on the principles of classical, operant, and observational learning, whereas other treatments are more cognitive, focused on changing negative thoughts related to the disorder. But almost all CBT treatments use a combination of behavioral and cognitive approaches.

Behavioral Aspects of CBT

behavioral therapy

Psychological treatment that is based on principles of learning.

In some cases the primary changes that need to be made are behavioral. **Behavioral therapy** is *psychological treatment that is based on principles of learning.* The most direct approach is through operant conditioning using reward or punishment. Reinforcement may be used to teach new skills to people, for instance, those with autism or schizophrenia (Granholm et al., 2008; Herbert et al., 2005; Scattone, 2007).[13] If the patient has trouble dressing or grooming, then reinforcement techniques, such as providing tokens that can be exchanged for snacks, are used to reinforce appropriate behaviors such as putting on one's clothes in the morning or taking a shower at night. If the patient has trouble interacting with others, reinforcement will be used to teach the client how to more appropriately respond in public, for instance, by maintaining eye contact, smiling when appropriate, and modulating tone of voice.

As the patient practices the different techniques, the appropriate behaviors are shaped through reinforcement to allow the client to manage more complex social situations. In some cases observational learning may also be used; the client may be asked to observe the behavior of others who are more socially skilled to acquire appropriate behaviors. People who learn to improve their interpersonal skills through skills training may be more accepted by others and this social support may have substantial positive effects on their emotions.

When the disorder is anxiety or phobia, then the goal of the CBT is to reduce the negative affective responses to the feared stimulus. **Exposure therapy** is *a behavioral therapy based on the classical conditioning principle of extinction, in which people are confronted with a feared stimulus with the goal of decreasing their negative emotional responses to it* (Wolpe, 1973).[14] Exposure treatment can be carried out in real situations or through imagination, and it is used in the treatment of panic disorder, agoraphobia, social phobia, OCD, and posttraumatic stress disorder (PTSD).

In *flooding,* a client is exposed to the source of his fear all at once. An agoraphobic might be taken to a crowded shopping mall or someone with an extreme fear of heights to the top of a tall building. The assumption is that the fear will subside as the client habituates to the situation while receiving emotional support from the therapist during the stressful experience. An advantage of the flooding technique is that it is quick and often effective, but a disadvantage is that the patient may relapse after a short period of time.

More frequently, the exposure is done more gradually. **Systematic desensitization** is *a behavioral treatment that combines imagining or experiencing the feared object or situation with relaxation exercises* (Wolpe, 1973).[15] The client and the therapist work together to prepare a *hierarchy of fears,* starting with the least frightening, and moving to the most frightening scenario surrounding the object (Table 13.1). The patient then confronts her fears in a systematic manner, sometimes using her imagination but usually, when possible, in real life.

exposure therapy

A behavioral therapy based on the classical conditioning principle of extinction in which people are confronted with a feared stimulus with the goal of decreasing their negative emotional responses to it.

systematic desensitization

A behavioral treatment that combines imagining or experiencing the feared object or situation with relaxation exercises.

TABLE 13.1 Hierarchy of Fears Used in Systematic Desensitization

Behavior	Fear rating
Think about a spider.	10
Look at a photo of a spider.	25
Look at a real spider in a closed box.	50
Hold the box with the spider.	60
Let a spider crawl on your desk.	70
Let a spider crawl on your shoe.	80
Let a spider crawl on your pants leg.	90
Let a spider crawl on your sleeve.	95
Let a spider crawl on your bare arm.	100

Desensitization techniques use the principle of *counterconditioning,* in which a second incompatible response (relaxation, e.g., through deep breathing) is conditioned to an already conditioned response (the fear response). The continued pairing of the relaxation responses with the feared stimulus as the patient works up the hierarchy gradually leads the fear response to be extinguished and the relaxation response to take its place.

Behavioral therapy works best when people directly experience the feared object. Fears of spiders are more directly habituated when the patient interacts with a real spider, and fears of flying are best extinguished when the patient gets on a real plane. But it is often difficult and expensive to create these experiences for the patient. Recent advances in virtual reality have allowed clinicians to provide CBT in what seem like real situations to the patient. In *virtual reality CBT,* the therapist uses computer-generated, three-dimensional, lifelike images of the feared stimulus in a systematic desensitization program. Specially designed computer equipment, often with a head-mount display, is used to create a simulated environment. A common use is in helping soldiers who are experiencing PTSD return to the scene of the trauma and learn how to cope with the stress it invokes.

Some of the advantages of the virtual reality treatment approach are that it is economical, the treatment session can be held in the therapist's office with no loss of time or confidentiality, the session can easily be terminated as soon as a patient feels uncomfortable, and many patients who have resisted live exposure to the object of their fears are willing to try the new virtual reality option first.

FIGURE 13.5

Trained clinicians use computer-generated, three-dimensional, lifelike images of spiders instead of the real thing in systematic desensitization programs to help combat client fears. Specially designed computer equipment with a head-mount display is used to create a simulated environment.

Source: Courtesy of Hunter Hoffman and Firsthand Technology, http://www.firsthand.com/creations/images/SpiderHand02_800.png.

aversion therapy

A behavioral therapy in which positive punishment is used to reduce the frequency of an undesirable behavior.

cognitive therapy

A psychological treatment that helps clients identify incorrect or distorted beliefs that are contributing to disorder.

FIGURE 13.6

Aaron Beck and Albert Ellis were pioneers in cognitive therapy.

Sources: Beck photo courtesy of Michael Britt, http://www.flickr.com/photos/psychfiles/2282352636. Ellis photo courtesy of the Albert Ellis Institute, http://rebtinstitute.org/public/about-albert-ellis4.html.

Aversion therapy is *a type of behavior therapy in which positive punishment is used to reduce the frequency of an undesirable behavior.* An unpleasant stimulus is intentionally paired with a harmful or socially unacceptable behavior until the behavior becomes associated with unpleasant sensations and is hopefully reduced. A child who wets his bed may be required to sleep on a pad that sounds an alarm when it senses moisture. Over time, the positive punishment produced by the alarm reduces the bedwetting behavior (Houts, Berman, & Abramson, 1994).[16] Aversion therapy is also used to stop other specific behaviors such as nail biting (Allen, 1996).[17]

Alcoholism has long been treated with aversion therapy (Baker & Cannon, 1988).[18] In a standard approach, patients are treated at a hospital where they are administered a drug, *antabuse*, that makes them nauseous if they consume any alcohol. The technique works very well if the user keeps taking the drug (Krampe et al., 2006),[19] but unless it is combined with other approaches the patients are likely to relapse after they stop the drug.

Cognitive Aspects of CBT

While behavioral approaches focus on the actions of the patient, **cognitive therapy** is *a psychological treatment that helps clients identify incorrect or distorted beliefs that are contributing to disorder.* In cognitive therapy the therapist helps the patient develop new, healthier ways of thinking about themselves and about the others around them. The idea of cognitive therapy is that changing thoughts will change emotions, and that the new emotions will then influence behavior (see Figure 13.4).

The goal of cognitive therapy is not necessarily to get people to think more positively but rather to think more accurately. For instance, a person who thinks "no one cares about me" is likely to feel rejected, isolated, and lonely. If the therapist can remind the person that she has a mother or daughter who does care about her, more positive feelings will likely follow. Similarly, changing beliefs from "I have to be perfect" to "No one is always perfect—I'm doing pretty good," from "I am a terrible student" to "I am doing well in some of my courses," or from "She did that on purpose to hurt me" to "Maybe she didn't realize how important it was to me" may all be helpful.

The psychiatrist Aaron T. Beck and the psychologist Albert Ellis (1913–2007) together provided the basic principles of cognitive therapy. Ellis (2004)[20] called his approach *rational emotive behavior therapy (REBT)* or *rational emotive therapy (RET)*, and he focused on pointing out the flaws in the patient's thinking. Ellis noticed that people experiencing strong negative emotions tend to personalize and overgeneralize their beliefs, leading to an inability to see situations accurately (Leahy, 2003).[21] In REBT, the therapist's goal is to challenge these irrational thought patterns, helping the patient replace the irrational thoughts with more rational ones, leading to the development of more appropriate emotional reactions and behaviors.

Beck's (Beck, 1995; Beck, Freeman, & Davis, 2004))[22] cognitive therapy was based on his observation that people who were depressed generally had a large number of highly accessible negative thoughts that influenced their thinking. His goal was to develop a short-term therapy for depression that would modify these unproductive thoughts. Beck's approach challenges the client to test his beliefs against concrete evidence. If a client claims that "everybody at work is out to get me," the therapist might ask him to provide instances to corroborate the claim. At the same time the therapist might point out contrary evidence, such as the fact that a certain coworker is actually a loyal friend or that the patient's boss had recently praised him.

1.4 Combination (Eclectic) Approaches to Therapy

To this point we have considered the different approaches to psychotherapy under the assumption that a therapist will use only one approach with a given patient. But this is not the case; as you saw in Figure 13.2, the most commonly practiced approach to therapy is an **eclectic therapy**, *an approach to treatment in which the therapist uses whichever techniques seem most useful and relevant for a given patient.* For bipolar disorder, for instance, the therapist may use both psychological skills training to help the patient cope with the severe highs and lows, but may also suggest that the patient consider biomedical drug therapies (Newman, Leahy, Beck, Reilly-Harrington, & Gyulai, 2002).[23] Treatment for major depressive disorder usually involves antidepressant drugs as well as CBT to help the patient deal with particular problems (McBride, Farvolden, & Swallow, 2007).[24]

As we have seen in Chapter 12, one of the most commonly diagnosed disorders is borderline personality disorder (BPD). Consider this description, typical of the type of borderline patient who arrives at a therapist's office:

> *Even as an infant, it seemed that there was something different about Bethany. She was an intense baby, easily upset and difficult to comfort. She had very severe separation anxiety—if her mother left the room, Bethany would scream until she returned. In her early teens, Bethany became increasingly sullen and angry. She started acting out more and more—yelling at her parents and teachers and engaging in impulsive behavior such as promiscuity and running away from home. At times Bethany would have a close friend at school, but some conflict always developed and the friendship would end.*
>
> *By the time Bethany turned 17, her mood changes were totally unpredictable. She was fighting with her parents almost daily, and the fights often included violent behavior on Bethany's part. At times she seemed terrified to be without her mother, but at other times she would leave the house in a fit of rage and not return for a few days. One day, Bethany's mother noticed scars on Bethany's arms. When confronted about them, Bethany said that one night she just got more and more lonely and nervous about a recent breakup until she finally stuck a lit cigarette into her arm. She said "I didn't really care for him that much, but I had to do something dramatic."*
>
> *When she was 18 Bethany rented a motel room where she took an overdose of sleeping pills. Her suicide attempt was not successful, but the authorities required that she seek psychological help.*

Most therapists will deal with a case such as Bethany's using an eclectic approach. First, because her negative mood states are so severe, they will likely recommend that she start taking antidepressant medications. These drugs are likely to help her feel better and will reduce the possibility of another suicide attempt, but they will not change the underlying psychological problems. Therefore, the therapist will also provide psychotherapy.

The first sessions of the therapy will likely be based primarily on creating trust. Person-centered approaches will be used in which the therapist attempts to create a therapeutic alliance conducive to a frank and open exchange of information.

If the therapist is trained in a psychodynamic approach, he or she will probably begin intensive face-to-face psychotherapy sessions at least three times a week. The therapist may focus on childhood experiences related to Bethany's attachment difficulties but will also focus in large part on the causes of the present behavior. The therapist will understand that because Bethany does not have good relationships with other people, she will likely seek a close bond with the therapist, but the therapist will probably not allow the transference relationship to develop fully. The therapist will also realize that Bethany will probably try to resist the work of the therapist.

Most likely the therapist will also use principles of CBT. For one, cognitive therapy will likely be used in an attempt to change Bethany's distortions of reality. She feels that people are rejecting her, but she is probably bringing these rejections on herself. If she can learn to better understand the meaning of other people's actions, she may feel better. And the therapist will likely begin using some techniques of behavior therapy, for instance, by rewarding Bethany for successful social interactions and progress toward meeting her important goals.

The eclectic therapist will continue to monitor Bethany's behavior as the therapy continues, bringing into play whatever therapeutic tools seem most beneficial. Hopefully, Bethany will stay in treatment long enough to make some real progress in repairing her broken life.

eclectic therapy

An approach to treatment in which the therapist uses whichever techniques seem most useful and relevant for a given patient.

One example of an eclectic treatment approach that has been shown to be successful in treating BPD is *dialectical behavioral therapy* (DBT; Linehan & Dimeff, 2001).[25] DBT is essentially a cognitive therapy, but it includes a particular emphasis on attempting to enlist the help of the patient in his or her own treatment. A dialectical behavioral therapist begins by attempting to develop a positive therapeutic alliance with the client, and then tries to encourage the patient to become part of the treatment process. In DBT the therapist aims to accept and validate the client's feelings at any given time while nonetheless informing the client that some feelings and behaviors are maladaptive, and showing the client better alternatives. The therapist will use both individual and group therapy, helping the patient work toward improving interpersonal effectiveness, emotion regulation, and distress tolerance skills.

KEY TAKEAWAYS

- Psychoanalysis is based on the principles of Freudian and neo-Freudian personality theories. The goal is to explore the unconscious dynamics of personality.
- Humanist therapy, derived from the personality theory of Carl Rogers, is based on the idea that people experience psychological problems when they are burdened by limits and expectations placed on them by themselves and others. Its focus is on helping people reach their life goals.
- Behavior therapy applies the principles of classical and operant conditioning, as well as observational learning, to the elimination of maladaptive behaviors and their replacement with more adaptive responses.
- Albert Ellis and Aaron Beck developed cognitive-based therapies to help clients stop negative thoughts and replace them with more objective thoughts.
- Eclectic therapy is the most common approach to treatment. In eclectic therapy, the therapist uses whatever treatment approaches seem most likely to be effective for the client.

EXERCISES AND CRITICAL THINKING

1. Imagine that your friend has been feeling depressed for several months but refuses to consider therapy as an option. What might you tell her that might help her feel more comfortable about seeking treatment?
2. Imagine that you have developed a debilitating fear of bees after recently being attacked by a swarm of them. What type of therapy do you think would be best for your disorder?
3. Imagine that your friend has a serious drug abuse problem. Based on what you've learned in this section, what treatment options would you explore in your attempt to provide him with the best help available? Which combination of therapies might work best?

2. REDUCING DISORDER BIOLOGICALLY: DRUG AND BRAIN THERAPY

LEARNING OBJECTIVES

1. **Classify the different types of drugs used in the treatment of mental disorders and explain how they each work to reduce disorder.**
2. **Critically evaluate direct brain intervention methods that may be used by doctors to treat patients who do not respond to drug or other therapy.**

biomedical therapies

Treatments designed to reduce psychological disorder by influencing the action of the central nervous system.

Like other medical problems, psychological disorders may in some cases be treated biologically. **Biomedical therapies** are *treatments designed to reduce psychological disorder by influencing the action of the central nervous system.* These therapies primarily involve the use of medications but also include direct methods of brain intervention, including *electroconvulsive therapy (ECT)*, *transcranial magnetic stimulation (TMS)*, and *psychosurgery*.

2.1 Drug Therapies

Psychologists understand that an appropriate balance of neurotransmitters in the brain is necessary for mental health. If there is a proper balance of chemicals, then the person's mental health will be acceptable, but psychological disorder will result if there is a chemical imbalance. The most frequently used biological treatments provide the patient with medication that influences the production and reuptake of neurotransmitters in the central nervous system (CNS). The use of these drugs is rapidly increasing, and drug therapy is now the most common approach to treatment of most psychological disorders.

Unlike some medical therapies that can be targeted toward specific symptoms, current psychological drug therapies are not so specific; they don't change particular behaviors or thought processes, and they don't really solve psychological disorders. However, although they cannot "cure" disorder, drug therapies are nevertheless useful therapeutic approaches, particularly when combined with psychological therapy, in treating a variety of psychological disorders. The best drug combination for the individual patient is usually found through trial and error (Biedermann & Fleischhacker, 2009).[26]

The major classes and brand names of drugs used to treat psychological disorders are shown in Table 13.2.

TABLE 13.2 Common Medications Used to Treat Psychological Disorders

Class	Type	Brand names	Disorder	Notes
Psychostimulants		Ritalin, Adderall, Dexedrine	Attention-deficit/hyperactivity disorder (ADHD)	Very effective in most cases, at least in the short term, at reducing hyperactivity and inattention
Antidepressants	Tricyclics	Elavil, Tofranil	Depression and anxiety disorders	Less frequently prescribed today than are the serotonin reuptake inhibitors (SSRIs)
	Monamine oxidase inhibitors (MAOIs)	Ensam, Nardil, Parnate, Marpaln	Depression and anxiety disorders	Less frequently prescribed today than are the SSRIs
	SSRIs	Prozac, Paxil, Zoloft	Depression and anxiety disorders	The most frequently prescribed antidepressant medications; work by blocking the reuptake of serotonin
	Other reuptake inhibitors	Effexor, Celexa, Wellbutrin	Depression and anxiety disorders	Prescribed in some cases; work by blocking the reuptake of serotonin, norepinephrine, and dopamine
Mood stabilizers		Eskalith, Lithobid, Depakene	Bipolar disorder	Effective in reducing the mood swings associated with bipolar disorder
Antianxiety drugs	Tranquilizers (benzodiazepines)	Valium, Xanax	Anxiety, panic, and mood disorders	Work by increasing the action of the neurotransmitter GABA (gamma-aminobutyric acid)
Antipsychotics (Neuroleptics)		Thorazine, Haldol, Clozaril, Risperdal, Zyprexa	Schizophrenia	Treat the positive and, to some extent, the negative symptoms of schizophrenia by reducing the transmission of dopamine and increasing the transmission of serotonin

Using Stimulants to Treat ADHD

Attention-deficit/hyperactivity disorder (ADHD) is frequently treated with biomedical therapy, usually along with cognitive-behavior therapy (CBT). The most commonly prescribed drugs for ADHD are psychostimulants, including Ritalin, Adderall, and Dexedrine. Short-acting forms of the drugs are taken as pills and last between 4 and 12 hours, but some of the drugs are also available in long-acting forms (skin patches) that can be worn on the hip and last up to 12 hours. The patch is placed on the child early in the morning and worn all day.

Stimulants improve the major symptoms of ADHD, including inattention, impulsivity, and hyperactivity, often dramatically, in about 75% of the children who take them (Greenhill, Halperin, & Abikof, 1999).[27] But the effects of the drugs wear off quickly. Additionally, the best drug and best dosage varies from child to child, so it may take some time to find the correct combination.

It may seem surprising to you that a disorder that involves hyperactivity is treated with a psychostimulant, a drug that normally increases activity. The answer lies in the dosage. When large doses of stimulants are taken, they increase activity, but in smaller doses the same stimulants improve attention and decrease motor activity (Zahn, Rapoport, & Thompson, 1980).[28]

The most common side effects of psychostimulants in children include decreased appetite, weight loss, sleeping problems, and irritability as the effect of the medication tapers off. Stimulant medications may also be associated with a slightly reduced growth rate in children, although in most cases growth isn't permanently affected (Spencer, Biederman, Harding, & O'Donnell, 1996).[29]

Antidepressant Medications

antidepressant medications

Drugs designed to improve moods.

Antidepressant medications are *drugs designed to improve moods*. Although they are used primarily in the treatment of depression, they are also effective for patients who suffer from anxiety, phobias, and obsessive-compulsive disorders. Antidepressants work by influencing the production and reuptake of neurotransmitters that relate to emotion, including serotonin, norepinephrine, and dopamine. Although exactly why they work is not yet known, as the amount of the neurotransmitters in the CNS is increased through the action of the drugs, the person often experiences less depression.

The original antidepressants were the *tricyclic antidepressants*, with the brand names of Tofranil and Elavil, and the *monamine oxidase inhibitors (MAOIs)*. These medications work by increasing the amount of serotonin, norepinephrine, and dopamine at the synapses, but they also have severe side effects including potential increases in blood pressure and the need to follow particular diets.

The antidepressants most prescribed today are the *selective serotonin reuptake inhibitors* (*SSRIs*), including Prozac, Paxil, and Zoloft, which are designed to selectively block the reuptake of serotonin at the synapse, thereby leaving more serotonin available in the CNS. SSRIs are safer and have fewer side effects than the tricyclics or the MAOIs (Fraser, 2000; Hollon, Thase, & Markowitz, 2002).[30] SSRIs are effective, but patients taking them often suffer a variety of sometimes unpleasant side effects, including dry mouth, constipation, blurred vision, headache, agitation, drowsiness, as well as a reduction in sexual enjoyment.

Recently, there has been concern that SSRIs may increase the risk of suicide among teens and young adults, probably because when the medications begin working they give patients more energy, which may lead them to commit the suicide that they had been planning but lacked the energy to go through with. This concern has led the FDA to put a warning label on SSRI medications and has led doctors to be more selective about prescribing antidepressants to this age group (Healy & Whitaker, 2003; Simon, 2006; Simon, Savarino, Operskalski, & Wang, 2006).[31]

Because the effects of antidepressants may take weeks or even months to develop, doctors usually work with each patient to determine which medications are most effective, and may frequently change medications over the course of therapy. In some cases other types of antidepressants may be used instead of or in addition to the SSRIs. These medications also work by blocking the reuptake of neurotransmitters, including serotonin, norepinephrine, and dopamine. Brand names of these medications include Effexor and Wellbutrin.

Patients who are suffering from bipolar disorder are not helped by the SSRIs or other antidepressants because their disorder also involves the experience of overly positive moods. Treatment is more complicated for these patients, often involving a combination of antipsychotics and antidepressants along with *mood stabilizing medications* (McElroy & Keck, 2000).[32] The most well-known mood stabilizer, lithium carbonate (or "lithium"), was approved by the FDA in the 1970s for treating both manic and depressive episodes, and it has proven very effective. Anticonvulsant medications can also be used as mood stabilizers. Another drug, Depakote, has also proven very effective, and some bipolar patients may do better with it than with lithium (Kowatch et al., 2000).[33]

People who take lithium must have regular blood tests to be sure that the levels of the drug are in the appropriate range. Potential negative side effects of lithium are loss of coordination, slurred speech, frequent urination, and excessive thirst. Though side effects often cause patients to stop taking their medication, it is important that treatment be continuous, rather than intermittent. There is no cure for bipolar disorder, but drug therapy does help many people.

Antianxiety Medications

antianxiety medications

Drugs designed to help relieve fear or anxiety.

Antianxiety medications are *drugs that help relieve fear or anxiety*. They work by increasing the action of the neurotransmitter GABA. The increased level of GABA helps inhibit the action of the sympathetic division of the autonomic nervous system, creating a calming experience.

The most common class of antianxiety medications is the *tranquilizers*, known as *benzodiazepines*. These drugs, which are prescribed millions of times a year, include Ativan, Valium, and Xanax. The benzodiazepines act within a few minutes to treat mild anxiety disorders but also have major side effects. They are addictive, frequently leading to tolerance, and they can cause drowsiness, dizziness, and unpleasant withdrawal symptoms including relapses into increased anxiety (Otto et al., 1993).[34] Furthermore, because the effects of the benzodiazepines are very similar to those of alcohol, they are very dangerous when combined with it.

Antipsychotic Medications

Until the middle of the 20th century, schizophrenia was inevitably accompanied by the presence of positive symptoms, including bizarre, disruptive, and potentially dangerous behavior. As a result, schizophrenics were locked in asylums to protect them from themselves and to protect society from them. In the 1950s, a drug called chlorpromazine (Thorazine) was discovered that could reduce many of the positive symptoms of schizophrenia. Chlorpromazine was the first of many *antipsychotic drugs*.

Antipsychotic drugs (neuroleptics) are *drugs that treat the symptoms of schizophrenia and related psychotic disorders*. Today there are many antipsychotics, including Thorazine, Haldol, Clozaril, Risperdal, and Zyprexa. Some of these drugs treat the positive symptoms of schizophrenia, and some treat both the positive, negative, and cognitive symptoms.

The discovery of chlorpromazine and its use in clinics has been described as the single greatest advance in psychiatric care, because it has dramatically improved the prognosis of patients in psychiatric hospitals worldwide. Using antipsychotic medications has allowed hundreds of thousands of people to move out of asylums into individual households or community mental health centers, and in many cases to live near-normal lives.

Antipsychotics reduce the positive symptoms of schizophrenia by reducing the transmission of dopamine at the synapses in the limbic system, and they improve negative symptoms by influencing levels of serotonin (Marangell, Silver, Goff, & Yudofsky, 2003).[35] Despite their effectiveness, antipsychotics have some negative side effects, including restlessness, muscle spasms, dizziness, and blurred vision. In addition, their long-term use can cause permanent neurological damage, a condition called *tardive dyskinesia* that causes uncontrollable muscle movements, usually in the mouth area (National Institute of Mental Health, 2008).[36] Newer antipsychotics treat more symptoms with fewer side effects than older medications do (Casey, 1996).[37]

> **antipsychotic drugs (neuroleptics)**
>
> Drugs that treat the symptoms of schizophrenia and related disorders.

2.2 Direct Brain Intervention Therapies

In cases of severe disorder it may be desirable to directly influence brain activity through electrical activation of the brain or through brain surgery. **Electroconvulsive therapy (ECT)** is *a medical procedure designed to alleviate psychological disorder in which electric currents are passed through the brain, deliberately triggering a brief seizure* (Figure 13.7). ECT has been used since the 1930s to treat severe depression.

When it was first developed, the procedure involved strapping the patient to a table before the electricity was administered. The patient was knocked out by the shock, went into severe convulsions, and awoke later, usually without any memory of what had happened. Today ECT is used only in the most severe cases when all other treatments have failed, and the practice is more humane. The patient is first given muscle relaxants and a general anesthesia, and precisely calculated electrical currents are used to achieve the most benefit with the fewest possible risks.

ECT is very effective; about 80% of people who undergo three sessions of ECT report dramatic relief from their depression. ECT reduces suicidal thoughts and is assumed to have prevented many suicides (Kellner et al., 2005).[38] On the other hand, the positive effects of ECT do not always last; over one-half of patients who undergo ECT experience relapse within one year, although antidepressant medication can help reduce this outcome (Sackheim et al., 2001).[39] ECT may also cause short-term memory loss or cognitive impairment (Abrams, 1997; Sackheim et al., 2007).[40]

> **electroconvulsive therapy (ECT)**
>
> A medical procedure designed to alleviate psychological disorder in which electric currents are passed through the brain, deliberately triggering a brief seizure.

FIGURE 13.7 Electroconvulsive Therapy (ECT)

Today's ECT uses precisely calculated electrical currents to achieve the most benefit with the fewest possible risks.

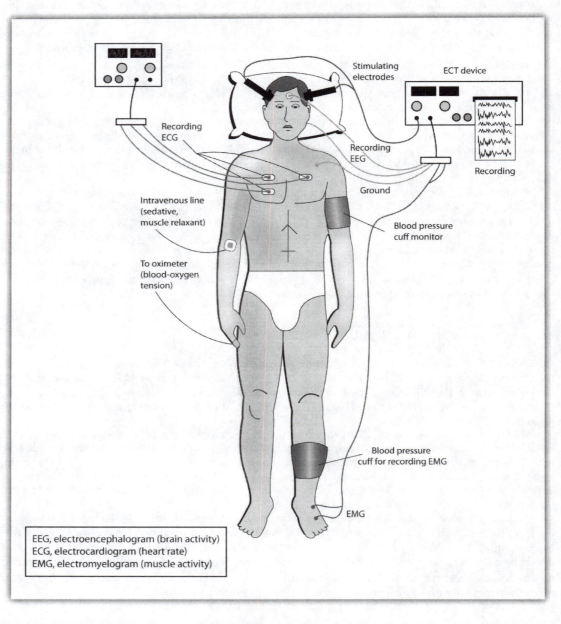

EEG, electroencephalogram (brain activity)
ECG, electrocardiogram (heart rate)
EMG, electromyelogram (muscle activity)

transcranial magnetic stimulation (TMS)

A medical procedure designed to reduce psychological disorder that uses a pulsing magnetic coil to electrically stimulate the brain.

Although ECT continues to be used, newer approaches to treating chronic depression are also being developed. A newer and gentler method of brain stimulation is **transcranial magnetic stimulation (TMS)**, *a medical procedure designed to reduce psychological disorder that uses a pulsing magnetic coil to electrically stimulate the brain* (Figure 13.8). TMS seems to work by activating neural circuits in the prefrontal cortex, which is less active in people with depression, causing an elevation of mood. TMS can be performed without sedation, does not cause seizures or memory loss, and may be as effective as ECT (Loo, Schweitzer, & Pratt, 2006; Rado, Dowd, & Janicak, 2008).[41] TMS has also been used in the treatment of Parkinson's disease and schizophrenia.

FIGURE 13.8   Transcranial Magnetic Stimulation (TMS)

TMS is a noninvasive procedure that uses a pulsing magnetic coil to electrically stimulate the brain. Recently, TMS has been used in the treatment of Parkinson's disease.

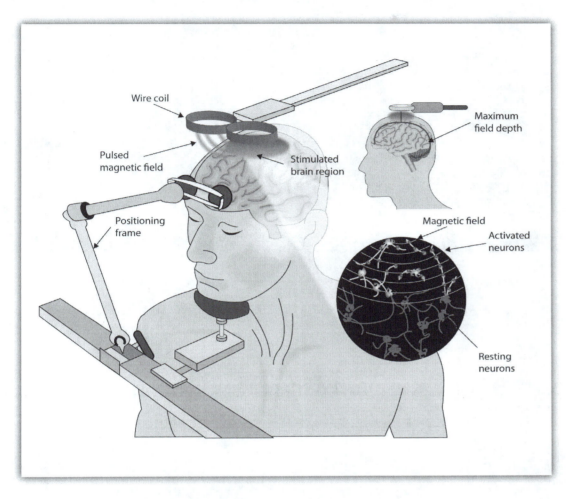

Still other biomedical therapies are being developed for people with severe depression that persists over years. One approach involves implanting a device in the chest that stimulates the vagus nerve, a major nerve that descends from the brain stem toward the heart (Corcoran, Thomas, Phillips, & O'Keane, 2006; Nemeroff et al., 2006).[42] When the vagus nerve is stimulated by the device, it activates brain structures that are less active in severely depressed people.

Psychosurgery, that is, *surgery that removes or destroys brain tissue in the hope of improving disorder,* is reserved for the most severe cases. The most well-known psychosurgery is the *prefrontal lobotomy.* Developed in 1935 by Nobel Prize winner Egas Moniz to treat severe phobias and anxiety, the procedure destroys the connections between the prefrontal cortex and the rest of the brain. Lobotomies were performed on thousands of patients. The procedure—which was never validated scientifically—left many patients in worse condition than before, subjecting the already suffering patients and their families to further heartbreak (Valenstein, 1986).[43] Perhaps the most notable failure was the lobotomy performed on Rosemary Kennedy, the sister of President John F. Kennedy, which left her severely incapacitated.

There are very few centers that still conduct psychosurgery today, and when such surgeries are performed they are much more limited in nature and called *cingulotomy* (Dougherty et al., 2002).[44] The ability to more accurately image and localize brain structures using modern neuroimaging techniques suggests that new, more accurate, and more beneficial developments in psychosurgery may soon be available (Sachdev & Chen, 2009).[45]

psychosurgery

Surgery that removes or destroys brain tissue in the hope of improving disorder.

KEY TAKEAWAYS

- Psychostimulants are commonly prescribed to reduce the symptoms of ADHD.
- Antipsychotic drugs play a crucial role in the treatment of schizophrenia. They do not cure schizophrenia, but they help reduce the positive, negative, and cognitive symptoms, making it easier to live with the disease.
- Antidepressant drugs are used in the treatment of depression, anxiety, phobias, and obsessive-compulsive disorder. They gradually elevate mood by working to balance neurotransmitters in the CNS. The most commonly prescribed antidepressants are the SSRIs.
- Antianxiety drugs (tranquilizers) relieve apprehension, tension, and nervousness and are prescribed for people with diagnoses of generalized anxiety disorder (GAD), obsessive-compulsive disorder (OCD), posttraumatic stress disorder (PTSD), and panic disorder. The drugs are effective but have severe side effects including dependence and withdrawal symptoms.
- Electroconvulsive therapy (ECT) is a controversial procedure used to treat severe depression, in which electric currents are passed through the brain, deliberately triggering a brief seizure.
- A newer method of brain stimulation is transcranial magnetic stimulation (TMS), a noninvasive procedure that employs a pulsing magnetic coil to electrically stimulate the brain.

EXERCISES AND CRITICAL THINKING

1. What are your opinions about taking drugs to improve psychological disorders? Would you take an antidepressant or antianxiety medication if you were feeling depressed or anxious? Do you think children with ADHD should be given stimulants? Why or why not?
2. Based on what you have just read, would you be willing to undergo ECT or TMS if you were chronically depressed and drug therapy had failed? Why or why not?

3. REDUCING DISORDER BY CHANGING THE SOCIAL SITUATION

LEARNING OBJECTIVES

1. Explain the advantages of group therapy and self-help groups for treating disorder.
2. Evaluate the procedures and goals of community mental health services.

Although the individual therapies that we have discussed so far in this chapter focus primarily on the psychological and biological aspects of the bio-psycho-social model of disorder, the social dimension is never out of the picture. Therapists understand that disorder is caused, and potentially prevented, in large part by the people with whom we interact. A person with schizophrenia does not live in a vacuum. He interacts with his family members and with the other members of the community, and the behavior of those people may influence his disease. And depression and anxiety are created primarily by the affected individual's perceptions (and misperceptions) of the important people around them. Thus prevention and treatment are influenced in large part by the social context in which the person is living.

3.1 Group, Couples, and Family Therapy

group therapy

Psychotherapy in which clients receive psychological treatment together with others.

Practitioners sometimes incorporate the social setting in which disorder occurs by conducting therapy in groups. **Group therapy** is *psychotherapy in which clients receive psychological treatment together with others*. A professionally trained therapist guides the group, usually between 6 and 10 participants, to create an atmosphere of support and emotional safety for the participants (Yalom & Leszcz, 2005).[46]

Group therapy provides a safe place where people come together to share problems or concerns, to better understand their own situations, and to learn from and with each other. Group therapy is often cheaper than individual therapy, as the therapist can treat more people at the same time, but economy is only one part of its attraction. Group therapy allows people to help each other, by sharing ideas, problems, and solutions. It provides social support, offers the knowledge that other people are facing and successfully coping with similar situations, and allows group members to model the successful behaviors of other group members. Group therapy makes explicit the idea that our interactions with others may create, intensify, and potentially alleviate disorders.

Group therapy has met with much success in the more than 50 years it has been in use, and it has generally been found to be as or more effective than individual therapy (McDermut, Miller, & Brown, 2001).[47] Group therapy is particularly effective for people who have life-altering illness, as it helps them cope better with their disease, enhances the quality of their lives, and in some cases has even been shown to help them live longer (American Group Psychotherapy Association, 2000).[48]

Sometimes group therapy is conducted with people who are in close relationships. *Couples therapy* is treatment in which two people who are cohabitating, married, or dating meet together with the practitioner to discuss their concerns and issues about their relationship. These therapies are in some cases educational, providing the couple with information about what is to be expected in a relationship. The therapy may focus on such topics as sexual enjoyment, communication, or the symptoms of one of the partners (e.g., depression).

Family therapy involves families meeting together with a therapist. In some cases the meeting is precipitated by a particular problem with one family member, such as a diagnosis of bipolar disorder in a child. Family therapy is based on the assumption that the problem, even if it is primarily affecting one person, is the result of an interaction among the people in the family.

3.2 Self-Help Groups

Group therapy is based on the idea that people can be helped by the positive social relationships that others provide. One way for people to gain this social support is by joining a **self-help group**, which is *a voluntary association of people who share a common desire to overcome psychological disorder or improve their well-being* (Humphreys & Rappaport, 1994).[49] Self-help groups have been used to help individuals cope with many types of addictive behaviors. Three of the best-known self-help groups are Alcoholics Anonymous, of which there are more than two million members in the United States, Gamblers Anonymous, and Overeaters Anonymous.

The idea behind self-groups is very similar to that of group therapy, but the groups are open to a broader spectrum of people. As in group therapy, the benefits include social support, education, and observational learning. Religion and spirituality are often emphasized, and self-blame is discouraged. Regular group meetings are held with the supervision of a trained leader.

3.3 Community Mental Health: Service and Prevention

The social aspect of disorder is also understood and treated at the community level. **Community mental health services** are *psychological treatments and interventions that are distributed at the community level*. Community mental health services are provided by nurses, psychologists, social workers, and other professionals in sites such as schools, hospitals, police stations, drug treatment clinics, and residential homes. The goal is to establish programs that will help people get the mental health services that they need (Gonzales, Kelly, Mowbray, Hays, & Snowden, 1991).[50]

Unlike traditional therapy, the primary goal of community mental health services is prevention. Just as widespread vaccination of children has eliminated diseases such as polio and smallpox, mental health services are designed to prevent psychological disorder (Institute of Medicine, 1994).[51] Community prevention can be focused on one more of three levels: primary prevention, secondary prevention, and tertiary prevention.

Primary prevention is prevention in which all members of the community receive the treatment. Examples of primary prevention are programs designed to encourage all pregnant women to avoid cigarettes and alcohol because of the risk of health problems for the fetus, and programs designed to remove dangerous lead paint from homes.

Secondary prevention is more limited and focuses on people who are most likely to need it—those who display *risk factors* for a given disorder. **Risk factors** are *the social, environmental, and economic vulnerabilities that make it more likely than average that a given individual will develop a disorder* (Werner & Smith, 1992).[52] The following presents a list of potential risk factors for psychological disorders.

FIGURE 13.9

Group therapy provides a therapeutic setting where people meet with others to share problems or concerns, to better understand their own situation, and to learn from and with each other.

© Thinkstock

self-help group

A voluntary association of people who share a common desire to overcome psychological disorder or improve their well-being.

community mental health services

Psychological treatments and interventions that are distributed at the community level. The focus of community mental health services is prevention.

risk factors

The social, environmental, and economic vulnerabilities that make it more likely than average that a given individual will develop a disorder.

Some Risk Factors for Psychological Disorders

Community mental health workers practicing secondary prevention will focus on youths with these markers of future problems.

- Academic difficulties
- Attention-deficit/hyperactivity disorder (ADHD)
- Child abuse and neglect
- Developmental disorders
- Drug and alcohol abuse
- Dysfunctional family
- Early pregnancy
- Emotional immaturity
- Homelessness
- Learning disorder
- Low birth weight
- Parental mental illness
- Poor nutrition
- Poverty

Finally, *tertiary prevention* is treatment, such as psychotherapy or biomedical therapy, that focuses on people who are already diagnosed with disorder.

Community prevention programs are designed to provide support during childhood or early adolescence with the hope that the interventions will prevent disorders from appearing or will keep existing disorders from expanding. Interventions include such things as help with housing, counseling, group therapy, emotional regulation, job and skills training, literacy training, social responsibility training, exercise, stress management, rehabilitation, family therapy, or removing a child from a stressful or dangerous home situation.

The goal of community interventions is to make it easier for individuals to continue to live a normal life in the face of their problems. Community mental health services are designed to make it less likely that vulnerable populations will end up in institutions or on the streets. In summary, their goal is to allow at-risk individuals to continue to participate in community life by assisting them within their own communities.

Research Focus: The Implicit Association Test as a Behavioral Marker for Suicide

Secondary prevention focuses on people who are at risk for disorder or for harmful behaviors. Suicide is a leading cause of death worldwide, and prevention efforts can help people consider other alternatives, particularly if it can be determined who is most at risk. Determining whether a person is at risk of suicide is difficult, however, because people are motivated to deny or conceal such thoughts to avoid intervention or hospitalization. One recent study found that 78% of patients who die by suicide explicitly deny suicidal thoughts in their last verbal communications before killing themselves (Busch, Fawcett, & Jacobs, 2003).[53]

Nock et al. (2010)[54] tested the possibility that implicit measures of the association between the self-concept and death might provide a more direct behavioral marker of suicide risk that would allow professionals to more accurately determine whether a person is likely to commit suicide in comparison to existing self-report measures. They measured implicit associations about death and suicide in 157 people seeking treatment at a psychiatric emergency department.

The participants all completed a version of the Implicit Association Test (IAT), which was designed to assess the strength of a person's mental associations between death and the self (Greenwald, McGhee, & Schwartz, 1998).[55] Using a notebook computer, participants classified stimuli representing the constructs of "death" (i.e., die, dead, deceased, lifeless, and suicide) and "life" (i.e., alive, survive, live, thrive, and breathing) and the attributes of "me" (i.e., I, myself, my, mine, and self) and "not me" (i.e., they, them, their, theirs, and other). Response latencies for all trials were recorded and analyzed, and the strength of each participant's association between "death" and "me" was calculated.

The researchers then followed participants over the next 6 months to test whether the measured implicit association of death with self could be used to predict future suicide attempts. The authors also tested whether scores on the IAT would add to prediction of risk above and beyond other measures of risk, including questionnaire and interview measures of suicide risk. Scores on the IAT predicted suicide attempts in the next 6 months above all the other risk factors that were collected by the hospital staff, including past history of suicide attempts. These results suggest that measures of implicit cognition may be useful for determining risk factors for clinical behaviors such as suicide.

KEY TAKEAWAYS

- Group therapy is psychotherapy in which clients receive psychological treatment together with others. A professionally trained therapist guides the group. Types of group therapy include couples therapy and family therapy.
- Self-help groups have been used to help individuals cope with many types of disorder.
- The goal of community health service programs is to act during childhood or early adolescence with the hope that interventions might prevent disorders from appearing or keep existing disorders from expanding. The prevention provided can be primary, secondary, or tertiary.

EXERCISE AND CRITICAL THINKING

1. Imagine the impact of a natural disaster like Hurricane Katrina on the population of the city of New Orleans. How would you expect such an event to affect the prevalence of psychological disorders in the community? What recommendations would you make in terms of setting up community support centers to help the people in the city?

4. EVALUATING TREATMENT AND PREVENTION: WHAT WORKS?

LEARNING OBJECTIVES

1. Summarize the ways that scientists evaluate the effectiveness of psychological, behavioral, and community service approaches to preventing and reducing disorders.
2. Summarize which types of therapy are most effective for which disorders.

We have seen that psychologists and other practitioners employ a variety of treatments in their attempts to reduce the negative outcomes of psychological disorders. But we have not yet considered the important question of whether these treatments are effective, and if they are, which approaches are most effective for which people and for which disorders. Accurate empirical answers to these questions are important as they help practitioners focus their efforts on the techniques that have been proven to be most promising, and will guide societies as they make decisions about how to spend public money to improve the quality of life of their citizens (Hunsley & Di Giulio, 2002).[56]

Psychologists use **outcome research**, that is, *studies that assess the effectiveness of medical treatments*, to determine the effectiveness of different therapies. As you can see in Figure 13.10, in these studies the independent variable is the type of the treatment—for instance, whether it was psychological or biological in orientation or how long it lasted. In most cases characteristics of the client (e.g., his or her gender, age, disease severity, and prior psychological histories) are also collected as control variables. The dependent measure is an assessment of the benefit received by the client. In some cases we might simply ask the client if she feels better, and in other cases we may directly measure behavior: Can the client now get in the airplane and take a flight? Has the client remained out of juvenile detention?

outcome research

Studies that assess the effectiveness of medical treatments.

FIGURE 13.10 Outcome Research

The design of an outcome study includes a dependent measure of benefit received by the client, as predicted by independent variables including type of treatment and characteristics of the individual.

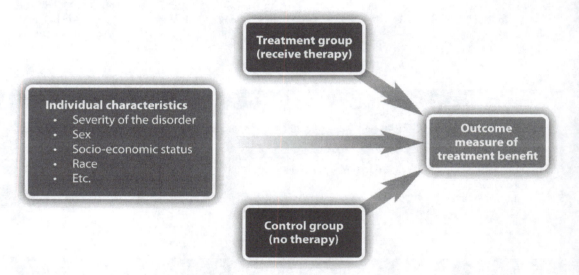

In every case the scientists evaluating the therapy must keep in mind the potential that other effects rather than the treatment itself might be important, that some treatments that seem effective might not be, and that some treatments might actually be harmful, at least in the sense that money and time are spent on programs or drugs that do not work.

One threat to the validity of outcome research studies is *natural improvement*—the possibility that people might get better over time, even without treatment. People who begin therapy or join a self-help group do so because they are feeling bad or engaging in unhealthy behaviors. After being in a program over a period of time, people frequently feel that they are getting better. But it is possible that they would have improved even if they had not attended the program, and that the program is not actually making a difference. To demonstrate that the treatment is effective, the people who participate in it must be compared with another group of people who do not get treatment.

Another possibility is that therapy works, but that it doesn't really matter which type of therapy it is. *Nonspecific treatment effects* occur when the patient gets better over time simply by coming to therapy, even though it doesn't matter what actually happens at the therapy sessions. The idea is that therapy works, in the sense that it is better than doing nothing, but that all therapies are pretty much equal in what they are able to accomplish. Finally, *placebo effects* are improvements that occur as a result of the expectation that one will get better rather than from the actual effects of a treatment.

4.1   Effectiveness of Psychological Therapy

Thousands of studies have been conducted to test the effectiveness of psychotherapy, and by and large they find evidence that it works. Some outcome studies compare a group that gets treatment with another (control) group that gets no treatment. For instance, Ruwaard, Broeksteeg, Schrieken, Emmelkamp, and Lange (2010)[57] found that patients who interacted with a therapist over a website showed more reduction in symptoms of panic disorder than did a similar group of patients who were on a waiting list but did not get therapy. Although studies such as this one control for the possibility of natural improvement (the treatment group improved more than the control group, which would not have happened if both groups had only been improving naturally over time), they do not control for either nonspecific treatment effects or for placebo effects. The people in the treatment group might have improved simply by being in the therapy (nonspecific effects), or they may have improved because they expected the treatment to help them (placebo effects).

An alternative is to compare a group that gets "real" therapy with a group that gets only a placebo. For instance, Keller et al. (2001)[58] had adolescents who were experiencing anxiety disorders take pills that they thought would reduce anxiety for 8 weeks. However, one-half of the patients were randomly assigned to actually receive the antianxiety drug Paxil, while the other half received a placebo drug that did not have any medical properties. The researchers ruled out the possibility that only placebo effects were occurring because they found that both groups improved over the 8 weeks, but the group that received Paxil improved significantly more than the placebo group did.

Studies that use a control group that gets no treatment or a group that gets only a placebo are informative, but they also raise ethical questions. If the researchers believe that their treatment is going to work, why would they deprive some of their participants, who are in need of help, of the possibility for improvement by putting them in a control group?

Another type of outcome study compares different approaches with each other. For instance, Herbert et al. (2005)[59] tested whether social skills training could boost the results received for the treatment of social anxiety disorder with cognitive-behavioral therapy (CBT) alone. As you can see in Figure 13.11, they found that people in both groups improved, but CBT coupled with social skills training showed significantly greater gains than CBT alone.

FIGURE 13.11

Herbert et al. (2005) compared the effectiveness of CBT alone with CBT along with social skills training. Both groups improved, but the group that received both therapies had significantly greater gains than the group that received CBT alone.

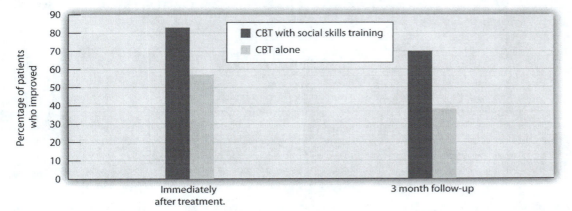

Source: Adapted from Herbert, J. D., Gaudiano, B. A., Rheingold, A. A., Myers, V. H., Dalrymple, K., & Nolan, E. M. (2005). Social skills training augments the effectiveness of cognitive behavioral group therapy for social anxiety disorder. Behavior Therapy, 36(2), 125–138.

Other studies (Crits-Christoph, 1992; Crits-Christoph et al., 2004)[60] have compared brief sessions of psychoanalysis with longer-term psychoanalysis in the treatment of anxiety disorder, humanistic therapy with psychodynamic therapy in treating depression, and cognitive therapy with drug therapy in treating anxiety (Dalgleish, 2004; Hollon, Thase, & Markowitz, 2002).[61] These studies are advantageous because they compare the specific effects of one type of treatment with another, while allowing all patients to get treatment.

meta-analysis

A statistical technique that uses the results of existing studies to integrate and draw conclusions about those studies.

Research Focus: Meta-Analyzing Clinical Outcomes

Because there are thousands of studies testing the effectiveness of psychotherapy, and the independent and dependent variables in the studies vary widely, the results are often combined using a *meta-analysis*. A **meta-analysis** is *a statistical technique that uses the results of existing studies to integrate and draw conclusions about those studies.* In one important meta-analysis analyzing the effect of psychotherapy, Smith, Glass, and Miller (1980)[62] summarized studies that compared different types of therapy or that compared the effectiveness of therapy against a control group. To find the studies, the researchers systematically searched computer databases and the reference sections of previous research reports to locate every study that met the inclusion criteria. Over 475 studies were located, and these studies used over 10,000 research participants.

The results of each of these studies were systematically coded, and a measure of the effectiveness of treatment known as the *effect size* was created for each study. Smith and her colleagues found that the average effect size for the influence of therapy was 0.85, indicating that psychotherapy had a relatively large positive effect on recovery. What this means is that, overall, receiving psychotherapy for behavioral problems is substantially better for the individual than not receiving therapy (Figure 13.12). Although they did not measure it, psychotherapy presumably has large societal benefits as well—the cost of the therapy is likely more than made up for by the increased productivity of those who receive it.

Normal Curves of Those Who Do and Do Not Get Treatment

Meta-analyses of the outcomes of psychotherapy have found that, on average, the distribution for people who get treatment is higher than for those who do not get treatment.

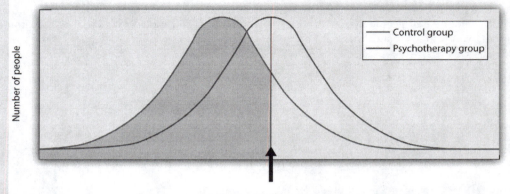

Other meta-analyses have also found substantial support for the effectiveness of specific therapies, including cognitive therapy, CBT (Butler, Chapman, Forman, & Beck, 2006; Deacon & Abramowitz, 2004),[63] couples and family therapy (Shadish & Baldwin, 2002),[64] and psychoanalysis (Shedler, 2010).[65] On the basis of these and other meta-analyses, a list of *empirically supported therapies*—that is, therapies that are known to be effective—has been developed (Chambless & Hollon, 1998; Hollon, Stewart, & Strunk (2006).[66] These therapies include cognitive therapy and behavioral therapy for depression; cognitive therapy, exposure therapy, and stress inoculation training for anxiety; CBT for bulimia; and behavior modification for bed-wetting.

Smith, Glass, and Miller (1980)[67] did not find much evidence that any one type of therapy was more effective than any other type, and more recent meta-analyses have not tended to find many differences either (Cuijpers, van Straten, Andersson, & van Oppen, 2008).[68] What this means is that a good part of the effect of therapy is nonspecific, in the sense that simply coming to any type of therapy is helpful in comparison to not coming. This is true partly because there are fewer distinctions among the ways that different therapies are practiced than the theoretical differences among them would suggest. What a good therapist practicing psychodynamic approaches does in therapy is often not much different from what a humanist or a cognitive-behavioral therapist does, and so no one approach is really likely to be better than the other.

What all good therapies have in common is that they give people hope; help them think more carefully about themselves and about their relationships with others; and provide a positive, empathic, and trusting relationship with the therapist—the therapeutic alliance (Ahn & Wampold, 2001).[69] This is why many self-help groups are also likely to be effective and perhaps why having a psychiatric service dog may also make us feel better.

4.2   Effectiveness of Biomedical Therapies

Although there are fewer of them because fewer studies have been conducted, meta-analyses also support the effectiveness of drug therapies for psychological disorder. For instance, the use of psychostimulants to reduce the symptoms of attention-deficit/hyperactivity disorder (ADHD) is well known to be successful, and many studies find that the positive and negative symptoms of schizophrenia are substantially reduced by the use of antipsychotic medications (Lieberman et al., 2005).[70]

People who take antidepressants for mood disorders or antianxiety medications for anxiety disorders almost always report feeling better, although drugs are less helpful for phobic disorder and obsessive-compulsive disorder. Some of these improvements are almost certainly the result of placebo effects (Cardeña & Kirsch, 2000),[71] but the medications do work, at least in the short term. An analysis of U.S. Food and Drug Administration databases found effect sizes of 0.26 for Prozac, 0.26 for Zoloft, 0.24 for Celexa, 0.31 for Lexapro, and 0.30 for Cymbalta. The overall average effect size for antidepressant medications approved by the FDA between 1987 and 2004 was 0.31 (Deshauer et al., 2008; Turner, Matthews, Linardatos, Tell, & Rosenthal, 2008).[72]

One problem with drug therapies is that although they provide temporary relief, they don't treat the underlying cause of the disorder. Once the patient stops taking the drug, the symptoms often return in full force. In addition many drugs have negative side effects, and some also have the potential for addiction and abuse. Different people have different reactions, and all drugs carry warning labels. As a result, although these drugs are frequently prescribed, doctors attempt to prescribe the lowest doses possible for the shortest possible periods of time.

Older patients face special difficulties when they take medications for mental illness. Older people are more sensitive to drugs, and drug interactions are more likely because older patients tend to take a variety of different drugs every day. They are more likely to forget to take their pills, to take too many or too few, or to mix them up due to poor eyesight or faulty memory.

Like all types of drugs, medications used in the treatment of mental illnesses can carry risks to an unborn infant. Tranquilizers should not be taken by women who are pregnant or expecting to become pregnant, because they may cause birth defects or other infant problems, especially if taken during the first trimester. Some selective serotonin reuptake inhibitors (SSRIs) may also increase risks to the fetus (Louik, Lin, Werler, Hernandez, & Mitchell, 2007; U.S. Food and Drug Administration, 2004),[73] as do antipsychotics (Diav-Citrin et al., 2005).[74]

Decisions on medication should be carefully weighed and based on each person's needs and circumstances. Medications should be selected based on available scientific research, and they should be prescribed at the lowest possible dose. All people must be monitored closely while they are on medications.

4.3   Effectiveness of Social-Community Approaches

Measuring the effectiveness of community action approaches to mental health is difficult because they occur in community settings and impact a wide variety of people, and it is difficult to find and assess valid outcome measures. Nevertheless, research has found that a variety of community interventions can be effective in preventing a variety of psychological disorders (Price, Cowen, Lorion, & Ramos-McKay,1988).[75]

Data suggest that federally funded prevention programs such as the *Special Supplemental Program for Women, Infants, and Children (WIC)*, which provides federal grants to states for supplemental foods, health-care referral, and nutrition education for low-income women and their children, are successful. WIC mothers have higher birth weight babies and lower infant mortality than other low-income mothers (Ripple & Zigler, 2003).[76] And the average blood-lead levels among children have fallen approximately 80% since the late 1970s as a result of federal legislation designed to remove lead paint from housing (Centers for Disease Control and Prevention, 2000).[77]

Although some of the many community-based programs designed to reduce alcohol, tobacco, and drug abuse; violence and delinquency; and mental illness have been successful, the changes brought about by even the best of these programs are, on average, modest (Wandersman & Florin, 2003; Wilson, Gottfredson, & Najaka, 2001).[78] This does not necessarily mean that the programs are not useful. What is important is that community members continue to work with researchers to help determine which aspects of which programs are most effective, and to concentrate efforts on the most productive approaches (Weissberg, Kumpfer, & Seligman, 2003).[79] The most beneficial preventive interventions for young people involve coordinated, systemic efforts to enhance their social and emotional competence and health. Many psychologists continue to work to promote policies that support community prevention as a model of preventing disorder.

KEY TAKEAWAYS

- Outcome research is designed to differentiate the effects of a treatment from natural improvement, nonspecific treatment effects, and placebo effects.
- Meta-analysis is used to integrate and draw conclusions about studies.
- Research shows that getting psychological therapy is better at reducing disorder than not getting it, but many of the results are due to nonspecific effects. All good therapies give people hope and help them think more carefully about themselves and about their relationships with others.
- Biomedical treatments are effective, at least in the short term, but overall they are less effective than psychotherapy.
- One problem with drug therapies is that although they provide temporary relief, they do not treat the underlying cause of the disorder.
- Federally funded community mental health service programs are effective, but their preventive effects may in many cases be minor.

EXERCISES AND CRITICAL THINKING

1. Revisit the chapter opener that focuses on the use of "psychiatric service dogs." What factors might lead you to believe that such "therapy" would or would not be effective? How would you propose to empirically test the effectiveness of the therapy?

2. Given your knowledge about the effectiveness of therapies, what approaches would you take if you were making recommendations for a person who is seeking treatment for severe depression?

5. CHAPTER SUMMARY

Psychological disorders create a tremendous individual, social, and economic drain on society. Psychologists work to reduce this burden by preventing and treating disorder. Psychologists base this treatment and prevention of disorder on the bio-psycho-social model, which proposes that disorder has biological, psychological, and social causes, and that each of these aspects can be the focus of reducing disorder.

Treatment for psychological disorder begins with a formal psychological assessment. In addition to the psychological assessment, the patient is usually seen by a physician to gain information about potential Axis III (physical) problems.

One approach to treatment is psychotherapy. The fundamental aspect of psychotherapy is that the patient directly confronts the disorder and works with the therapist to help reduce it.

Psychodynamic therapy (also known as psychoanalysis) is a psychological treatment based on Freudian and neo-Freudian personality theories. The analyst engages with the patient in one-on-one sessions during which the patient verbalizes his or her thoughts through free associations and by reporting on his or her dreams. The goal of the therapy is to help the patient develop insight—that is, an understanding of the unconscious causes of the disorder.

Humanistic therapy is a psychological treatment based on the personality theories of Carl Rogers and other humanistic psychologists. Humanistic therapies attempt to promote growth and responsibility by helping clients consider their own situations and the world around them and how they can work to achieve their life goals.

The humanistic therapy promotes the ideas of genuineness, empathy, and unconditional positive regard in a nurturing relationship in which the therapist actively listens to and reflects the feelings of the client; this relationship is probably the most fundamental part of contemporary psychotherapy

Cognitive-behavior therapy (CBT) is a structured approach to treatment that attempts to reduce psychological disorders through systematic procedures based on cognitive and behavioral principles. CBT is a very broad approach used for the treatment of a variety of problems.

Behavioral aspects of CBT may include operant conditioning using reward or punishment. When the disorder is anxiety or phobia, then the goal of the CBT is to reduce the negative affective responses to the feared stimulus through exposure therapy, flooding, or systematic desensitization. Aversion therapy is a type of behavior therapy in which positive punishment is used to reduce the frequency of an undesirable behavior.

Cognitive aspects of CBT include treatment that helps clients identify incorrect or distorted beliefs that are contributing to disorder.

The most commonly used approaches to therapy are eclectic, such that the therapist uses whichever techniques seem most useful and relevant for a given patient.

Biomedical therapies are treatments designed to reduce psychological disorder by influencing the action of the central nervous system. These therapies primarily involve the use of medications but also include direct methods of brain intervention, including electroconvulsive therapy (ECT), transcranial magnetic stimulation (TMS), and psychosurgery.

Attention-deficit/hyperactivity disorder (ADHD) is treated using low doses of psychostimulants, including Ritalin, Adderall, and Dexedrine.

Mood disorders are most commonly treated with the antidepressant medications known as selective serotonin reuptake inhibitors (SSRIs), including Prozac, Paxil, and Zoloft. The SSRIs selectively block the reuptake of serotonin at the synapse. Bipolar disorder is treated with mood stabilizing medications.

Antianxiety medications, including the tranquilizers Ativan, Valium, and Xanax, are used to treat anxiety disorders.

Schizophrenia is treated with antipsychotic drugs, including Thorazine, Haldol, Clozaril, Risperdal, and Zyprexa. Some of these drugs treat the positive symptoms of schizophrenia, and some treat both the positive, negative, and cognitive symptoms.

Practitioners frequently incorporate the social setting in which disorder occurs by conducting therapy in groups, with couples, or with families. One way for people to gain this social support is by joining a self-help group.

Community mental health services refer to psychological treatments and interventions that are distributed at the community level. These centers provide primary, secondary, and tertiary prevention.

Psychologists use outcome research to determine the effectiveness of different therapies. These studies help determine if improvement is due to natural improvement, nonspecific treatment effects, or placebo effects. Research finds that psychotherapy and biomedical therapies are both effective in treating disorder, but there is not much evidence that any one type of therapy is more effective than any other type. What all good therapies have in common is that they give people hope; help them think more carefully about themselves and about their relationships with others; and provide a positive, empathic, and trusting relationship with the therapist—the therapeutic alliance.

One problem with drug therapies is that although they provide temporary relief, they don't treat the underlying cause of the disorder. Once the patient stops taking the drug, the symptoms often return in full force.

Data suggest that although some community prevention programs are successful, the changes brought about by even the best of these programs are, on average, modest.

ENDNOTES

1. Shim, J. (2008, January 29). Dogs chase nightmares of war away. *CNN*. Retrieved from http://edition.cnn.com/2008/LIVING/personal/01/29/dogs.veterans; Lorber, J. (2010, April 3). For the battle-scarred, comfort at leash's end. *The New York Times*. Retrieved from http://www.nytimes.com/2010/04/04/us/04dogs.html; Alaimo, C. A. (2010, April 11). Psychiatric service dogs use senses to aid owners. *Arizona Daily Star*. Retrieved from http://azstarnet.com/news/local/article_d24b5799-9b31-548c-afec-c0160e45f49c.html; Schwartz, A. N. (2008, March 16). Psychiatric service dogs, very special dogs, indeed. *Dr. Schwartz's Weblog*. Retrieved from http://www.mentalhelp.net/poc/view_doc.php?type=doc&id=14844

2. Odendaal, J. S. J. (2000). Animal-assisted therapy—Magic or medicine? *Journal of Psychosomatic Research, 49*(4), 275–280.

3. Konnopka, A., Leichsenring, F., Leibing, E., & König, H.-H. (2009). Cost-of-illness studies and cost-effectiveness analyses in anxiety disorders: A systematic review. *Journal of Affective Disorders, 114*(1–3), 14–31; Smit, F., Cuijpers, P., Oostenbrink, J., Batelaan, N., de Graaf, R., & Beekman, A. (2006). Costs of nine common mental disorders: Implications for curative and preventive psychiatry. *Journal of Mental Health Policy and Economics, 9*(4), 193–200.

4. World Health Organization. (2004). *Prevention of mental disorders: Effective interventions and policy options: Summary report*. Retrieved from http://www.who.int/mental_health/evidence/en/Prevention_of_Mental_Disorders.pdf

5. American Psychiatric Association. (2000). *Diagnostic and statistical manual of mental disorders* (4th ed., text rev.). Washington, DC: Author.

6. U.S. Department of Health and Human Services. (1999). *Mental health: A report of the surgeon general*. Washington, DC: U.S. Government Printing Office.

7. American Psychological Association. (2010). Ethical principles of psychologists and code of conduct. Retrieved from http://www.apa.org/ethics/code/index.aspx?item=7#402

8. Epstein J., Stern E., & Silbersweig, D. (2001). Neuropsychiatry at the millennium: The potential for mind/brain integration through emerging interdisciplinary research strategies. *Clinical Neuroscience Research, 1*, 10–18; Lubarsky, L., & Barrett, M. S. (2006). The history and empirical status of key psychoanalytic concepts. *Annual Review of Clinical Psychology, 2*, 1–19.

9. Levenson, H. (2010). *Brief dynamic therapy*. Washington, DC: American Psychological Association.

10. Rogers, C. (1980). *A way of being*. New York, NY: Houghton Mifflin.

11. Prochaska, J. O., & Norcross, J. C. (2007). *Systems of psychotherapy: A transtheoretical analysis* (6th ed.). Pacific Grove, CA: Brooks/Cole.

12. Beck, A. T. (1976). *Cognitive therapy and the emotional disorders*. New York, NY: New American Library.

13. Granholm, E., McQuaid, J. R., Link, P. C., Fish, S., Patterson, T., & Jeste, D. V. (2008). Neuropsychological predictors of functional outcome in cognitive behavioral social skills training for older people with schizophrenia. *Schizophrenia Research, 100*, 133–143. doi:10.1016/j.schres.2007.11.032; Herbert, J. D., Gaudini, B. A., Rheingold, A. A., Myers, V. H., Dalrymple, K., & Nolan, E. M. (2005). Social skills training augments the effectiveness of cognitive behavioral group therapy for social anxiety disorder. *Behavior Therapy, 36*, 125–138; Scattone, D. (2007). Social skills interventions for children with autism. *Psychology in the schools, 44*, 717–726.

14. Wolpe J. (1973). *The practice of behavior therapy*. New York, NY: Pergamon.

15. Wolpe J. (1973). *The practice of behavior therapy*. New York, NY: Pergamon.

16. Houts, A. C., Berman, J. S., & Abramson, H. (1994). Effectiveness of psychological and pharmacological treatments for nocturnal enuresis. *Journal of Consulting and Clinical Psychology, 62*(4), 737–745.

17. Allen K. W. (1996). Chronic nailbiting: A controlled comparison of competing response and mild aversion treatments. *Behaviour Research and Therapy, 34*, 269–272. doi:10.1016/0005-7967(95)00078-X

18. Baker, T. B., & Cannon, D. S. (1988). *Assessment and treatment of addictive disorders*. New York, NY: Praeger.

19. Krampe, H., Stawicki, S., Wagner, T., Bartels, C., Aust, C., Rüther, E.,…Ehrenreich, H. (2006). Follow-up of 180 alcoholic patients for up to 7 years after outpatient treatment: Impact of alcohol deterrents on outcome. *Alcoholism: Clinical and Experimental Research, 30*(1), 86–95.

20. Ellis, A. (2004). Why rational emotive behavior therapy is the most comprehensive and effective form of behavior therapy. *Journal of Rational-Emotive & Cognitive-Behavior Therapy, 22*, 85–92.

21. Leahy, R. L. (2003). *Cognitive therapy techniques: A practitioner's guide*. New York, NY: Guilford Press.

22. Beck, J. S. (1995). *Cognitive therapy: Basics and beyond*. New York, NY: Guilford Press; Beck, A. T., Freeman, A., & Davis, D. D. (2004). *Cognitive therapy of personality disorders* (2nd ed.). New York, NY: Guilford Press.

23. Newman, C. F., Leahy, R. L., Beck, A. T., Reilly-Harrington, N. A., & Gyulai, L. (2002). Clinical management of depression, hopelessness, and suicidality in patients with bipolar disorder. In C. F. Newman, R. L. Leahy, A. T. Beck, N. A. Reilly-Harrington, & L. Gyulai (Eds.), *Bipolar disorder: A cognitive therapy approach* (pp. 79–100). Washington, DC: American Psychological Association. doi:10.1037/10442-004

24. McBride, C., Farvolden, P., & Swallow, S. R. (2007). Major depressive disorder and cognitive schemas. In L. P. Riso, P. L. du Toit, D. J. Stein, & J. E. Young (Eds.), *Cognitive schemas and core beliefs in psychological problems: A scientist-practitioner guide* (pp. 11–39). Washington, DC: American Psychological Association.

25. Linehan, M. M., & Dimeff, L. (2001). Dialectical behavior therapy in a nutshell. *The California Psychologist, 34*, 10–13.

26. Biedermann, F., & Fleischhacker, W. W. (2009). Antipsychotics in the early stage of development. *Current Opinion Psychiatry, 22*, 326–330.

27. Greenhill, L. L., Halperin, J. M., & Abikof, H. (1999). Stimulant medications. *Journal of the American Academy of Child & Adolescent Psychiatry, 38*(5), 503–512.

28. Zahn, T. P., Rapoport, J. L., & Thompson, C. L. (1980). Autonomic and behavioral effects of dextroamphetamine and placebo in normal and hyperactive prepubertal boys. *Journal of Abnormal Child Psychology, 8*(2), 145–160.

29. Spencer, T. J., Biederman, J., Harding, M., & O'Donnell, D. (1996). Growth deficits in ADHD children revisited: Evidence for disorder-associated growth delays? *Journal of the American Academy of Child & Adolescent Psychiatry, 35*(11), 1460–1469.

30. Fraser, A. R. (2000). Antidepressant choice to minimize treatment resistance. *The British Journal of Psychiatry, 176*, 493; Hollon, S. D., Thase, M. E., & Markowitz, J. C. (2002). Treatment and prevention of depression. *Psychological Science in the Public Interest, 3*, 39–77.

31. Healy, D., & Whitaker, C. J. (2003). Antidepressants and suicide: Risk-benefit conundrums. *Journal of Psychiatry & Neuroscience, 28*, 331–339; Simon, G. E. (2006). The antidepressant quandary—Considering suicide risk when treating adolescent depression. *The New England Journal of Medicine, 355*, 2722–2723; Simon, G. E., Savarino, J., Operskalski, B., & Wang, P. S. (2006). Suicide risk during antidepressant treatment. *American Journal of Psychiatry, 163*, 41–47. doi:10.1176/appi.ajp.163.1.41

32. McElroy, S. L., & Keck, P. E. (2000). Pharmacologic agents for the treatment of acute bipolar mania. *Biological Psychiatry, 48*, 539–557.

33. Kowatch, R. A., Suppes, T., Carmody, T. J., Bucci, J. P., Hume, J. H., Kromelis, M.,…Rush, A. J. (2000). Effect size of lithium, divalproex sodium, and carbamazepine in children and adolescents with bipolar disorder. *Journal of the American Academy of Child & Adolescent Psychiatry, 39*, 713–20.

34. Otto, M. W., Pollack, M. H., Sachs, G. S., Reiter, S. R., Meltzer-Brody, S., & Rosenbaum, J. F. (1993). Discontinuation of benzodiazepine treatment: Efficacy of cognitive-behavioral therapy for patients with panic disorder. *American Journal of Psychiatry, 150*, 1485–1490.

35. Marangell, L. B., Silver, J. M., Goff, D. C., & Yudofsky, S. C. (2003). Psychopharmacology and electroconvulsive therapy. In R. E. Hales & S. C. Yudofsky (Eds.), *The American Psychiatric Publishing textbook of clinical psychiatry* (4th ed., pp. 1047–1149). Arlington, VA: American Psychiatric Publishing.

36. National Institute of Mental Health. (2008). *Mental health medications* (NIH Publication No. 08-3929). Retrieved from http://www.nimh.nih.gov/health/publications/mental-health-medications/complete-index.shtml#pub4

37. Casey, D. E. (1996). Side effect profiles of new antipsychotic agents. *Journal of Clinical Psychiatry, 57*(Suppl. 11), 40–45.

38. Kellner, C. H., Fink, M., Knapp, R., Petrides, G., Husain, M., Rummans, T.,…Malur, C. (2005). Relief of expressed suicidal intent by ECT: A consortium for research in ECT study. *The American Journal of Psychiatry, 162*(5), 977–982.

39. Sackheim, H. A., Haskett, R. F., Mulsant, B. H., Thase, M. E., Mann, J. J., Pettinati, H.,…Prudic, J. (2001). Continuation pharmacotherapy in the prevention of relapse following electroconvulsive therapy: A randomized controlled trial. *Journal of the American Medical Association, 285*, 1299–1307.

40. Abrams, R. (1997). *Electroconvulsive therapy* (3rd ed.). Oxford, England: Oxford University Press; Sackeim, H. A., Prudic, J., Fuller, R., Keilp, J., Philip, W., Lavori, P. W., & Olfson, M. (2007). The cognitive effects of electroconvulsive therapy in community settings. *Neuropsychopharmacology, 32*, 244–254. doi:10.1038/sj.npp.1301180

41. Loo, C. K., Schweitzer, I., & Pratt, C. (2006). Recent advances in optimizing electroconvulsive therapy. *Australian and New Zealand Journal of Psychiatry, 40*, 632–638; Rado, J., Dowd, S. M., & Janicak, P. G. (2008). The emerging role of transcranial magnetic stimulation (TMS) for treatment of psychiatric disorders. *Directions in Psychiatry, 28*(4), 315–332.

42. Corcoran, C. D., Thomas, P., Phillips, J., & O'Keane, V. (2006). Vagus nerve stimulation in chronic treatment-resistant depression: Preliminary findings of an open-label study. *The British Journal of Psychiatry, 189*, 282–283; Nemeroff, C., Mayberg, H., Krahl, S., McNamara, J., Frazer, A., Henry, T.,…Brannan, S. (2006). VNS therapy in treatment-resistant depression: Clinical evidence and putative neurobiological mechanisms. *Neuropsychopharmacology, 31*(7), 1345–1355.

43. Valenstein, E. (1986). *Great and desperate cures: The rise and decline of psychosurgery and other radical treatments for mental illness*. New York, NY: Basic Books.

44. Dougherty, D., Baer, L., Cosgrove, G., Cassem, E., Price, B., Nierenberg, A.,…Rauch, S. L. (2002). Prospective long-term follow-up of 44 patients who received cingulotomy for treatment-refractory obsessive-compulsive disorder. *American Journal of Psychiatry, 159*(2), 269.

45. Sachdev, P. S., & Chen, X. (2009). Neurosurgical treatment of mood disorders: Traditional psychosurgery and the advent of deep brain stimulation. *Current Opinion in Psychiatry, 22*(1), 25–31.

46. Yalom, I., & Leszcz, M. (2005). *The theory and practice of group psychotherapy* (5th ed.). New York, NY: Basic Books.

47. McDermut, W., Miller, I. W., & Brown, R. A. (2001). The efficacy of group psychotherapy for depression: A meta-analysis and review of the empirical research. *Clinical Psychology: Science and Practice, 8*(1), 98–116.

48. American Group Psychotherapy Association. (2000). *About group psychotherapy*. Retrieved from http://www.groupsinc.org/group/consumersguide2000.html

49. Humphreys, K., & Rappaport, J. (1994). Researching self-help/mutual aid groups and organizations: Many roads, one journey. *Applied and Preventative Psychology, 3*(4), 217–231.

50. Gonzales, L. R., Kelly, J. G., Mowbray, C. T., Hays, R. B., & Snowden, L. R. (1991). Community mental health. In M. Hersen, A. E. Kazdin, & A. S. Bellack (Eds.), *The clinical psychology handbook* (2nd ed., pp. 762–779). Elmsford, NY: Pergamon Press.

51. Institute of Medicine. (1994). *Reducing risks for mental disorders: Frontiers for preventive intervention research.* Washington, DC: National Academy Press.

52. Werner, E. E., & Smith, R. S. (1992). *Overcoming the odds: High risk children from birth to adulthood.* New York, NY: Cornell University Press.

53. Busch, K. A., Fawcett, J., & Jacobs, D. G. (2003). Clinical correlates of inpatient suicide. *Journal of Clinical Psychiatry, 64*(1), 14–19.

54. Nock, M. K., Park, J. M., Finn, C. T., Deliberto, T. L., Dour, H. J., & Banaji, M. R. (2010). Measuring the suicidal mind: Implicit cognition predicts suicidal behavior. *Psychological Science, 21*(4), 511–517.

55. Greenwald, A. G., McGhee, D. E., & Schwartz, J. L. K. (1998). Measuring individual differences in implicit cognition: The Implicit Association Test. *Journal of Personality and Social Psychology, 74,* 1464–1480.

56. Hunsley, J., & Di Giulio, G. (2002). Dodo bird, phoenix, or urban legend? The question of psychotherapy equivalence. *The Scientific Review of Mental Health Practice: Objective Investigations of Controversial and Unorthodox Claims in Clinical Psychology, Psychiatry, and Social Work, 1*(1), 11–22.

57. Ruwaard, J., Broeksteeg, J., Schrieken, B., Emmelkamp, P., & Lange, A. (2010). Web-based therapist-assisted cognitive behavioral treatment of panic symptoms: A randomized controlled trial with a three-year follow-up. *Journal of Anxiety Disorders, 24*(4), 387–396.

58. Keller, M. B., Ryan, N. D., Strober, M., Klein, R. G., Kutcher, S. P., Birmaher, B.,…McCafferty, J. P. (2001). Efficacy of paroxetine in the treatment of adolescent major depression: A randomized, controlled trial. *Journal of the American Academy of Child & Adolescent Psychiatry, 40*(7), 762–772.

59. Herbert, J. D., Gaudiano, B. A., Rheingold, A. A., Myers, V. H., Dalrymple, K., & Nolan, E. M. (2005). Social skills training augments the effectiveness of cognitive behavioral group therapy for social anxiety disorder. *Behavior Therapy, 36*(2), 125–138.

60. Crits-Christoph, P. (1992). The efficacy of brief dynamic psychotherapy: A meta-analysis. *American Journal of Psychiatry, 149,* 151–158; Crits-Christoph, P., Gibbons, M. B., Losardo, D., Narducci, J., Schamberger, M., & Gallop, R. (2004). Who benefits from brief psychodynamic therapy for generalized anxiety disorder? *Canadian Journal of Psychoanalysis, 12,* 301–324.

61. Dalgleish, T. (2004). Cognitive approaches to posttraumatic stress disorder: The evolution of multirepresentational theorizing. *Psychological Bulletin, 130,* 228–260; Hollon, S. D., Thase, M. E., & Markowitz, J. C. (2002). Treatment and prevention of depression. *Psychological Science in the Public Interest, 3,* 39–77.

62. Smith, M. L., Glass, G. V., & Miller, R. L. (1980). The benefits of psychotherapy. Baltimore, MD: Johns Hopkins University Press.

63. Butler A. C., Chapman, J. E., Forman, E. M., & Beck, A. T. (2006). The empirical status of cognitive-behavioral therapy: A review of meta-analyses. *Clinical Psychology Review, 26*(1), 17–31. doi:10.1016/j.cpr.2005.07.003; Deacon, B. J., & Abramowitz, J. S. (2004). Cognitive and behavioral treatments for anxiety disorders: A review of meta-analytic findings. *Journal of Clinical Psychology, 60*(4), 429–441.

64. Shadish, W. R., & Baldwin, S. A. (2002). Meta-analysis of MFT interventions. In D. H. Sprenkle (Ed.), *Effectiveness research in marriage and family therapy* (pp. 339–370). Alexandria, VA: American Association for Marriage and Family Therapy.

65. Shedler, J. (2010). The efficacy of psychodynamic psychotherapy. *American Psychologist, 65*(2), 98–109.

66. Chambless, D. L., & Hollon, S. D. (1998). Defining empirically supported therapies. *Journal of Consulting and Clinical Psychology, 66*(1), 7–18; Hollon, S., Stewart, M., & Strunk, D. (2006). Enduring effects for cognitive therapy in the treatment of depression and anxiety. *Annual Review of Psychology, 57,* 285–316.

67. Smith, M. L., Glass, G. V., & Miller, R. L. (1980). *The benefits of psychotherapy.* Baltimore, MD: Johns Hopkins University Press.

68. Cuijpers, P., van Straten, A., Andersson, G., & van Oppen, P. (2008). Psychotherapy for depression in adults: A meta-analysis of comparative outcome studies. *Journal of Consulting and Clinical Psychology, 76*(6), 909–922.

69. Ahn, H.-N., & Wampold, B. E. (2001). Where oh where are the specific ingredients? A meta-analysis of component studies in counseling and psychotherapy. *Journal of Counseling Psychology, 48*(3), 251–257.

70. Lieberman, J., Stroup, T., McEvoy, J., Swartz, M., Rosenheck, R., Perkins, D.,…Lebowitz, B. D. (2005). Effectiveness of antipsychotic drugs in patients with chronic schizophrenia. *New England Journal of Medicine, 353*(12), 1209.

71. Cardeña, E., & Kirsch, I. (2000). True or false: The placebo effect as seen in drug studies is definitive proof that the mind can bring about clinically relevant changes in the body: What is so special about the placebo effect? *Advances in Mind-Body Medicine, 16*(1), 16–18.

72. Deshauer, D., Moher, D., Fergusson, D., Moher, E., Sampson, M., & Grimshaw, J. (2008). Selective serotonin reuptake inhibitors for unipolar depression: A systematic review of classic long-term randomized controlled trials. *Canadian Medical Association Journal, 178*(10), 1293–301. doi:10.1503/cmaj.071068; Turner, E. H., Matthews, A. M., Linardatos, E., Tell, R. A., & Rosenthal, R. (2008). Selective publication of antidepressant trials and its influence on apparent efficacy. *New England Journal of Medicine, 358*(3), 252–60.

73. Louik, C., Lin, A. E., Werler M. M., Hernandez, S., & Mitchell, A. A. (2007). First-trimester use of selective serotonin-reuptake inhibitors and the risk of birth defects. *New England Journal of Medicine, 356,* 2675–2683; U.S. Food and Drug Administration. (2004). FDA Medwatch drug alert on Effexor and SSRIs. Retrieved from http://www.fda.gov/medwatch/safety/2004/safety04.htm#effexor

74. Diav-Citrin, O., Shechtman, S., Ornoy, S., Arnon, J., Schaefer, C., Garbis, H.,…Ornoy, A. (2005). Safety of haloperidol and penfluridol in pregnancy: A multicenter, prospective, controlled study. *Journal of Clinical Psychiatry, 66,* 317–322.

75. Price, R. H., Cowen, E. L., Lorion, R. P., & Ramos-McKay, J. (Eds.). (1988). *Fourteen ounces of prevention: A casebook for practitioners.* Washington, DC: American Psychological Association.

76. Ripple, C. H., & Zigler, E. (2003). Research, policy, and the federal role in prevention initiatives for children. *American Psychologist, 58*(6–7), 482–490.

77. Centers for Disease Control and Prevention. (2000). Blood lead levels in young children: United States and selected states, 1996–1999. *Morbidity and Mortality Weekly Report, 49,* 1133–1137.

78. Wandersman, A., & Florin, P. (2003). Community interventions and effective prevention. *American Psychologist, 58*(6–7), 441–448; Wilson, D. B., Gottfredson, D. C., & Najaka, S. S. (2001). School-based prevention of problem behaviors: A meta-analysis. *Journal of Quantitative Criminology, 17*(3), 247–272.

79. Weissberg, R. P., Kumpfer, K. L., & Seligman, M. E. P. (2003). Prevention that works for children and youth: An introduction. *American Psychologist, 58*(6–7), 425–432.

CHAPTER 14
Psychology in Our Social Lives

Binge Drinking and the Death of a Homecoming Queen

Sam Spady, a 19-year-old student at Colorado State University, had been a homecoming queen, a class president, a captain of the cheerleading team, and an honor student in high school. But despite her outstanding credentials and her hopes and plans for the future, Sam Spady died on September 5, 2004, after a night of binge drinking with her friends.

Sam had attended a number of different parties on the Saturday night that she died, celebrating the CSU football game against the University of Colorado–Boulder. When she passed out, after consuming 30 to 40 beers and shots over the evening, her friends left her alone in an empty room in a fraternity house to sleep it off. The next morning a member of the fraternity found her dead (Sidman, 2006).[1]

Sam is one of an estimated 1,700 college students between the ages of 18 and 24 who die from alcohol-related injuries each year. These deaths come from motor vehicle crashes, assaults, and overdosing as a result of binge drinking (National Institute on Alcohol Abuse and Alcoholism, 2010).[2]

"Nobody is immune," said Sam's father. "She was a smart kid, and she was a good kid. And if it could happen to her, it could happen to anybody."

Despite efforts at alcohol education, Pastor Reza Zadeh, a former CSU student, says little has changed in the drinking culture since Sam's death: "People still feel invincible. The bars still have 25-cent shot night and two-for-ones and no cover for girls"(Sidman, 2006).[3]

Sam's parents have created a foundation in her memory, dedicated to informing people, particularly college students, about the dangers of binge drinking, and to helping them resist the peer pressure that brings it on. You can learn more at http://samspadyfoundation.org about the foundation.

We have now reached the last chapter of our journey through the field of psychology. The subdiscipline of psychology discussed in this chapter reflects the highest level of explanation that we will consider. This topic, known as **social psychology**, is defined as *the scientific study of how we feel about, think about, and behave toward the other people around us, and how those people influence our thoughts, feelings, and behavior.*

The subject matter of social psychology is our everyday interactions with people, including the social groups to which we belong. Questions these psychologists ask include why we are often helpful to other people but at other times are unfriendly or aggressive; why we sometimes conform to the behaviors of others but at other times are able to assert our independence; and what factors help groups work together in effective and productive, rather than in ineffective and unproductive, ways. A fundamental principle of social psychology is that, although we may not always be aware of it, our cognitions, emotions, and behaviors are substantially influenced by the **social situation**, or *the people with whom we are interacting.*

In this chapter we will introduce the principles of **social cognition**—*the part of human thinking that helps us understand and predict the behavior of ourselves and others*—and consider the ways that our judgments about other people guide our behaviors toward them. We'll explore how we form impressions of other people, and what makes us like or dislike them. We'll also see how our **attitudes**—*our enduring evaluations of people or things*—influence, and are influenced by, our behavior.

social psychology

The scientific study of how we feel about, think about, and behave toward the other people around us, and how those people influence our thoughts, feelings, and behavior.

social situation

The people with whom we are interacting.

social cognition

The part of human thinking that helps us understand and predict the behavior of ourselves and others.

attitudes

Our enduring evaluations of people or things.

social norms

The accepted beliefs about what we do or what we should do in particular social situations.

Then we will consider the social psychology of interpersonal relationships, including the behaviors of *altruism, aggression,* and *conformity.* We will see that humans have a natural tendency to help each other, but that we may also become aggressive if we feel that we are being threatened. And we will see how **social norms**, *the accepted beliefs about what we do or what we should do in particular social situations* (such as the norm of binge drinking common on many college campuses), influence our behavior. Finally, we will consider the social psychology of social groups, with a particular focus on the conditions that limit and potentially increase productive group performance and decision-making.

The principles of social psychology can help us understand tragic events such as the death of Sam Spady. Many people might blame the tragedy on Sam herself, asking, for instance, "Why did she drink so much?" or "Why didn't she say no?" As we will see in this chapter, research conducted by social psychologists shows that the poor decisions Sam made on the night she died may have been due less to her own personal weaknesses or deficits than to her desires to fit in with and be accepted by the others around her—desires that in her case led to a disastrous outcome.

1. SOCIAL COGNITION: MAKING SENSE OF OURSELVES AND OTHERS

> **LEARNING OBJECTIVES**
>
> 1. Review the principles of social cognition, including the fundamentals of how we form judgments about other people.
> 2. Define the concept of attitude and review the ways that attitudes are developed and changed, and how attitudes relate to behavior.

One important aspect of social cognition involves forming impressions of other people. Making these judgments quickly and accurately helps us guide our behavior to interact appropriately with the people we know. If we can figure out why our roommate is angry at us, we can react to resolve the problem; if we can determine how to motivate the people in our group to work harder on a project, then the project might be better.

1.1 Perceiving Others

Our initial judgments of others are based in large part on what we see. The physical features of other people, particularly their sex, race, age, and physical attractiveness, are very salient, and we often focus our attention on these dimensions (Schneider, 2003; Zebrowitz & Montepare, 2006).[4]

Although it may seem inappropriate or shallow to admit it, we are strongly influenced by the physical attractiveness of others, and many cases physical attractiveness is the most important determinant of our initial liking for other people (Walster, Aronson, Abrahams, & Rottmann, 1966).[5] Infants who are only a year old prefer to look at faces that adults consider to be attractive than at unattractive faces (Langlois, Ritter, Roggman, & Vaughn, 1991).[6] Evolutionary psychologists have argued that our belief that "what is beautiful is also good" may be because we use attractiveness as a cue for health; people whom we find more attractive may also, evolutionarily, have been healthier (Zebrowitz, Fellous, Mignault, & Andreoletti, 2003).[7]

FIGURE 14.1

Can you read a book by its cover? Which of these people do you think is more fun and friendly? Who is smarter or more competent? Do you think your judgments are accurate?

© Thinkstock

One indicator of health is youth. Leslie Zebrowitz and her colleagues (Zebrowitz, 1996; Zebrowitz, Luevano, Bronstad, & Aharon, 2009)[8] have extensively studied the tendency for both men and women to prefer people whose faces have characteristics similar to those of babies. These features include large, round, and widely spaced eyes, a small nose and chin, prominent cheekbones, and a large forehead. People who have baby faces (both men and women) are seen as more attractive than people who are not baby-faced.

FIGURE 14.2

People with baby faces are perceived as attractive.

Source: Efron photo courtesy of Johan Ferreira, http://www.flickr.com/photos/23664669@N08/2874031622. Bilson photo courtesy of Stephen Lovekin / Getty Images, http://www.flickr.com/photos/34128229@N06/3182841715.

Another indicator of health is symmetry. People are more attracted to faces that are more symmetrical than they are to those that are less symmetrical, and this may be due in part to the perception that symmetrical faces are perceived as healthier (Rhodes et al., 2001).[9]

Although you might think that we would prefer faces that are unusual or unique, in fact the opposite is true. Langlois and Roggman (1990)[10] showed college students the faces of men and women. The faces were composites made up of the average of 2, 4, 8, 16, or 32 faces. The researchers found that the more faces that were averaged into the stimulus, the more attractive it was judged. Again, our liking for average faces may be because they appear healthier.

Although preferences for youthful, symmetrical, and average faces have been observed cross-culturally, and thus appear to be common human preferences, different cultures may also have unique beliefs about what is attractive. In modern Western cultures, "thin is in," and people prefer those who have little excess fat (Crandall, Merman, & Hebl, 2009).[11] The need to be thin to be attractive is particularly strong for women in contemporary society, and the desire to maintain a low body weight can lead to low self-esteem, eating disorders, and other unhealthy behaviors. However, the norm of thinness has not always been in place; the preference for women with slender, masculine, and athletic looks has become stronger over the past 50 years. In contrast to the relatively universal preferences for youth, symmetry, and averageness, other cultures do not show such a strong propensity for thinness (Sugiyama, 2005).[12]

1.2 Forming Judgments on the Basis of Appearance: Stereotyping, Prejudice, and Discrimination

stereotyping

The tendency to attribute personality characteristics to people on the basis of their external appearance or their social group memberships.

We frequently use people's appearances to form our judgments about them and to determine our responses to them. The *tendency to attribute personality characteristics to people on the basis of their external appearance or their social group memberships* is known as **stereotyping**. Our stereotypes about physically attractive people lead us to see them as more dominant, sexually warm, mentally healthy, intelligent, and socially skilled than we perceive physically unattractive people (Langlois et al., 2000).[13] And our stereotypes lead us to treat people differently—the physically attractive are given better grades on essay exams, are more successful on job interviews, and receive lighter sentences in court judgments than their less attractive counterparts (Hosoda, Stone-Romero, & Coats, 2003; Zebrowitz & McDonald, 1991).[14]

prejudice

The tendency to dislike people because of their appearance or group memberships.

discrimination

Negative behaviors toward others based on prejudice.

In addition to stereotypes about physical attractiveness, we also regularly stereotype people on the basis of their sex, race, age, religion, and many other characteristics, and these stereotypes are frequently negative (Schneider, 2004).[15] Stereotyping is unfair to the people we judge because stereotypes are based on our preconceptions and negative emotions about the members of the group. Stereotyping is closely related to **prejudice**, *the tendency to dislike people because of their appearance or group memberships*, and **discrimination**, *negative behaviors toward others based on prejudice*. Stereotyping, prejudice, and discrimination work together. We may not vote for a gay person for public office because of our negative stereotypes about gays, and we may avoid people from other religions or those with mental illness because of our prejudices.

self-fulfilling prophecy

A situation that occurs when our expectations about the personality characteristics of others lead us to behave toward those others in ways that make those beliefs come true.

Some stereotypes may be accurate in part. Research has found, for instance, that attractive people are actually more sociable, more popular, and less lonely than less attractive individuals (Langlois et al., 2000).[16] And, consistent with the stereotype that women are "emotional," women are, on average, more empathic and attuned to the emotions of others than are men (Hall & Schmid Mast, 2008).[17] Group differences in personality traits may occur in part because people act toward others on the basis of their stereotypes, creating a *self-fulfilling prophecy*. A **self-fulfilling prophecy** occurs *when our expectations about the personality characteristics of others lead us to behave toward those others in ways that make those beliefs come true*. If I have a stereotype that attractive people are friendly, then I may act in a friendly way toward people who are attractive. This friendly behavior may be reciprocated by the attractive person, and if many other people also engage in the same positive behaviors with the person, in the long run he or she may actually become friendlier.

But even if attractive people are on average friendlier than unattractive people, not all attractive people are friendlier than all unattractive people. And even if women are, on average, more emotional than men, not all men are less emotional than all women. Social psychologists believe that it is better to treat people as individuals rather than rely on our stereotypes and prejudices, because stereotyping and prejudice are always unfair and often inaccurate (Fiske, 1989; Stangor, 1995).[18] Furthermore, many of our stereotypes and prejudices occur out of our awareness, such that we do not even know that we are using them.

Implicit Association Test

You might want to test your own stereotypes and prejudices by completing the Implicit Association Test, a measure of unconscious stereotyping.

https://implicit.harvard.edu/implicit/demo

social identity

The positive emotions that we experience as a result of our group memberships.

We use our stereotypes and prejudices in part because they are easy; if we can quickly size up people on the basis of their physical appearance, that can save us a lot of time and effort. We may be evolutionarily disposed to stereotyping. Because our primitive ancestors needed to accurately separate members of their own kin group from those of others, categorizing people into "us" (the *ingroup*) and "them" (the *outgroup*) was useful and even necessary (Neuberg, Kenrick, & Schaller, 2010).[19] And *the positive emotions that we experience as a result of our group memberships*—known as **social identity**—can be an important and positive part of our everyday experiences (Hogg, 2003).[20] We may gain social identity as members of our university, our sports teams, our religious and racial groups, and many other groups.

But the fact that we *may* use our stereotypes does not mean that we *should* use them. Stereotypes, prejudice, and discrimination, whether they are consciously or unconsciously applied, make it difficult for some people to effectively contribute to society and may create both mental and physical health problems for them (Swim & Stangor, 1998).[21] In some cases getting beyond our prejudices is required by law, as detailed in the U.S. Civil Rights Act of 1964, the Equal Opportunity Employment Act of 1972, and the Fair Housing Act of 1978.

There are individual differences in prejudice, such that some people are more likely to try to control and confront their stereotypes and prejudices whereas others apply them more freely (Czopp, Monteith, & Mark, 2006; Plant & Devine, 1998).[22] For instance, some people believe in group hierarchies—that some groups are naturally better than others—whereas other people are more egalitarian and hold fewer prejudices (Sidanius & Pratto, 1999; Stangor & Leary, 2006).[23]

Social psychologists believe that we should work to get past our prejudices. The tendency to hold stereotypes and prejudices and to act on them can be reduced, for instance, through positive interactions and friendships with members of other groups, through practice in avoiding using them, and through education (Hewstone, 1996).[24]

FIGURE 14.3

Social identity is the positive emotions that we experience as a member of an important social group.

Source: Photo courtesy of Caitlin Regan,
http://www.flickr.com/photos/caitlinator/4006197725.

Research Focus: Forming Judgments of People in Seconds

Research has demonstrated that people can draw very accurate conclusions about others on the basis of very limited data. Ambady and Rosenthal (1993)[25] made videotapes of six female and seven male graduate students while they were teaching an undergraduate course. The courses covered diverse areas of the college curriculum, including humanities, social sciences, and natural sciences. For each teacher, three 10-second video clips were taken: 10 seconds from the first 10 minutes of the class, 10 seconds from the middle of the class, and 10 seconds from the last 10 minutes of the class.

The researchers then asked nine female undergraduates to rate the clips of the teachers on 15 dimensions including *optimistic, confident, active, enthusiastic, dominant, likable, warm, competent,* and *supportive.* Ambady and her colleagues then compared the ratings of the participants who had seen the teacher for only 30 seconds with the ratings of the same instructors that had been made by students who had spent a whole semester with the teacher, and who had rated her at the end of the semester on scales such as "Rate the quality of the section overall" and "Rate section leader's performance overall." As you can see in Table 14.1, the ratings of the participants and the ratings of the students were highly positively correlated.

Accurate Perceptions in 30 Seconds

Variable	Pearson Correlation Coefficient (r)
Accepting	0.50
Active	0.77
Attentive	0.48
Competent	0.56
Confident	0.82
Dominant	0.79
Empathic	0.45
Enthusiastic	0.76
Honest	0.32
Likable	0.73
(Not) anxious	0.26
Optimistic	0.84
Professional	0.53
Supportive	0.55
Warm	0.67
Overall, across all traits	0.76

This table shows the Pearson correlation coefficients between the impressions that a group of students made after they had seen a video of instructors teaching for only 30 seconds and the teaching ratings of the same instructors made by students who had spent a whole semester in the class. You can see that the correlations are all positive, and that many of them are quite large. The conclusion is that people are sometimes able to draw accurate impressions about other people very quickly.

Source: Ambady, N., & Rosenthal, R. (1993). Half a minute: Predicting teacher evaluations from thin slices of nonverbal behavior and physical attractiveness. Journal of Personality & Social Psychology, 64(3), 431–441.

If the finding that judgments made about people in 30 seconds correlate highly with judgments made about the same people after a whole semester surprises you, then perhaps you may be even more surprised to hear that we do not even need that much time. Indeed, Willis and Todorov (2006)[26] found that even a tenth of a second was enough to make judgments that correlated highly with those same judgments made by other people who were given several minutes to make the judgments. Other research has found that we can make accurate judgments, for instance, about our perceptions of salespersons (Ambady, Krabbenhoft, & Hogan, 2006)[27] and about the sexual orientation of other people (Ambady, Hallahan, & Conner, 1999),[28] in just a few seconds. Todorov, Mandisodza, Goren, and Hall (2005)[29] found that people voted for political candidates in large part on the basis of whether or not their faces, seen only for one second, looked like faces of competent people. Taken together, this research shows that we are well able to form initial impressions of others quickly and often quite accurately.

1.3 Close Relationships

close relationships

Long-term intimate and romantic relationships—for instance, a marriage.

One of the most important tasks faced by humans is to develop successful relationships with others. These relationships include acquaintanceships and friendships but also the more important **close relationships**, which are *the long-term intimate and romantic relationships that we develop with another person—for instance, in a marriage* (Hendrick & Hendrick, 2000).[30] Because most of us will want to enter into a close relationship at some point, and because close relationships are evolutionarily important as they form the basis for effective child rearing, it is useful to know what psychologists have learned about the principles of liking and loving within them.

A major interest of social psychologists is the study of *interpersonal attraction*, or what makes people like, and even love, each other. One important factor is a perceived similarity in values and beliefs between the partners (Davis & Rusbult, 2001).[31] Similarity is important for relationships both because it is more convenient (it's easier if both partners like to ski or go to the movies than if only one does), but also because similarity supports our values—I can feel better about myself and my choice of activities if I see that you also enjoy doing the same things that I do.

FIGURE 14.4

Close relationships are characterized by responsiveness, disclosure, intimacy, equity, and passion.

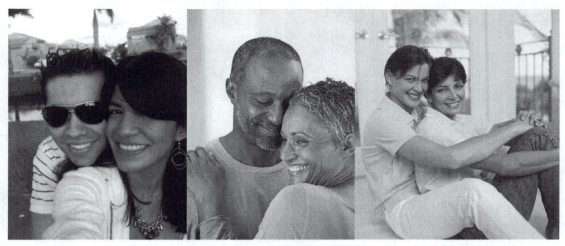

Source: Top left photo courtesy of Scarleth White, http://www.flickr.com/photos/iloveblue/2528773058. Other photos © Thinkstock.

Liking is also enhanced by *self-disclosure*, the tendency to communicate frequently, without fear of reprisal, and in an accepting and empathetic manner. Friends are friends because we can talk to them openly about our needs and goals, and because they listen to and respond to our needs (Reis & Aron, 2008).[32] But self-disclosure must be balanced. If I open up to you about the concerns that are important to me, I expect you to do the same in return. If the self-disclosure is not reciprocal, the relationship may not last.

Another important determinant of liking is *proximity*, or the extent to which people are physically near us. Research has found that we are more likely to develop friendships with people who are nearby, for instance, those who live in the same dorm that we do, and even with people who just happen to sit nearer to us in our classes (Back, Schmukle, & Egloff, 2008).[33]

Proximity has its effect on liking through the principle of **mere exposure**, which is *the tendency to prefer stimuli (including but not limited to people) that we have seen more frequently*. Moreland and Beach (1992)[34] studied mere exposure by having female confederates attend a large lecture class of over 100 students 0, 5, 10, or 15 times during a semester. At the end of the term, the other students in the class were shown pictures of the confederates and asked to indicate both if they recognized them and also how much they liked them. The number of times the confederates had attended class didn't influence the other students' ability to recognize them, but it did influence their liking for them. As predicted by the mere exposure hypothesis, students who had attended class more often were liked more (Figure 14.5).

mere exposure

The tendency to prefer stimuli (including but not limited to people) that we have seen more frequently.

FIGURE 14.5 Mere Exposure in the Classroom

Richard Moreland and Scott Beach (1992) had female confederates visit classrooms 0, 5, 10, or 15 times over the course of a semester. Then the students rated their liking of the confederates. As predicted by the principles of mere exposure, confederates who had attended class more often were also liked more.

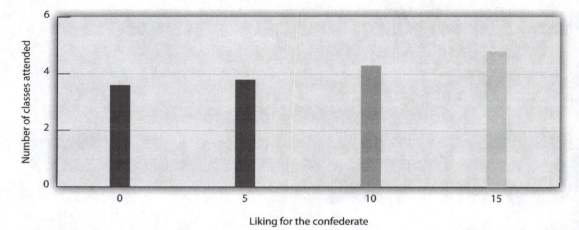

Source: Adapted from Moreland, R. L., & Beach, S. R. (1992). Exposure effects in the classroom: The development of affinity among students. Journal of Experimental Social Psychology, 28(3), 255–276.

The effect of mere exposure is powerful and occurs in a wide variety of situations. Infants tend to smile at a photograph of someone they have seen before more than they smile at a photograph of someone they are seeing for the first time (Brooks-Gunn & Lewis, 1981),[35] and people prefer side-to-side reversed images of their own faces over their normal (nonreversed) face, whereas their friends prefer their normal face over the reversed one (Mita, Dermer, & Knight, 1977).[36] This is expected on the basis of mere exposure, since people see their own faces primarily in mirrors and thus are exposed to the reversed face more often.

Mere exposure may well have an evolutionary basis. We have an initial fear of the unknown, but as things become more familiar they seem more similar and safe, and thus produce more positive affect and seem less threatening and dangerous (Freitas, Azizian, Travers, & Berry, 2005).[37] In fact, research has found that stimuli tend to produce more positive affect as they become more familiar (Harmon-Jones & Allen, 2001).[38] When the stimuli are people, there may well be an added effect. Familiar people become more likely to be seen as part of the ingroup rather than the outgroup, and this may lead us to like them more. Leslie Zebrowitz and her colleagues found that we like people of our own race in part because they are perceived as similar to us (Zebrowitz, Bornstad, & Lee, 2007).[39]

In the most successful relationships the two people begin to see themselves as a single unit. Arthur Aron and his colleagues (Aron, Aron, & Smollan, 1992)[40] assessed the role of closeness in relationships using the *Inclusion of Other in the Self Scale* as shown in Figure 14.6. You might try completing the measure yourself for some different people that you know—for instance, your family members, friends, spouse, or girlfriend or boyfriend. The measure is simple to use and to interpret; if people see the circles representing the self and the other as more overlapping, this means that the relationship is close. But if they choose the circles that are less overlapping, then the relationship is less so.

FIGURE 14.6   The Inclusion of Other in the Self Scale

This scale is used to determine how close two partners feel to each other. The respondent simply circles which of the seven figures he or she feels best characterizes the relationship.

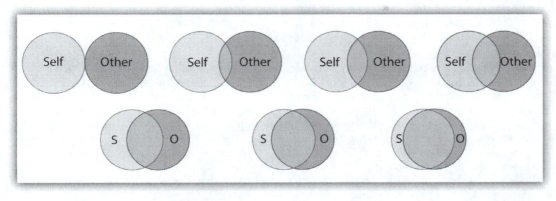

Source: Adapted from Aron, A., Aron, E. N., & Smollan, D. (1992). Inclusion of other in the self scale and the structure of interpersonal closeness. Journal of Personality & Social Psychology, 63(4), 596–612.

Although the closeness measure is very simple, it has been found to be predictive of people's satisfaction with their close relationships, and of the tendency for couples to stay together (Aron, Aron, Tudor, & Nelson, 1991; Aron, Paris, & Aron, 1995).[41] When the partners in a relationship feel that they are close, and when they indicate that the relationship is based on caring, warmth, acceptance and social support, we can say that the relationship is *intimate* (Reis & Aron, 2008).[42]

When a couple begins to take care of a household together, has children, and perhaps has to care for elderly parents, the requirements of the relationship become correspondingly bigger. As a result of this complexity, the partners in close relationships increasingly turn to each other for help in coordinating activities, remembering dates and appointments, and accomplishing tasks. Relationships are close in part because the couple becomes highly *interdependent*, relying on each other to meet important goals (Berscheid & Reis, 1998).[43]

In relationships in which a positive rapport between the partners is developed and maintained over a period of time, the partners are naturally happy with the relationship and they become committed to it. *Commitment* refers to the feelings and actions that keep partners working together to maintain the relationship (Rusbult, Olsen, Davis, Hannon, 2001)[44] and is characterized by mutual expectations that the self and the partner will be responsive to each other's needs (Clark & Mills, 2004).[45] Partners who are committed to the relationship see their mates as more attractive, are less able to imagine themselves with another partner, express less interest in other potential mates, and are less likely to break up (Simpson & Harris, 1994).[46]

People also find relationships more satisfactory, and stay in them longer, when they feel that they are being rewarded by them. When the needs of either or both of the partners are not being met, the relationship is in trouble. This is not to say that people only think about the benefits they are getting; they will also consider the needs of the other. But over the long term, both partners must benefit from the relationship.

Although sexual arousal and excitement are more important early on in relationships, intimacy is also determined by sexual and romantic attraction. Indeed, intimacy is also dependent on *passion*—the partners must display positive affect toward each other. Happy couples are in positive moods when they are around each other; they laugh with each other, express approval rather than criticism of each other's behaviors, and enjoy physical contact. People are happier in their relationships when they view the other person in a positive or even an "idealized" sense, rather than a more realistic and perhaps more negative one (Murray, Holmes, & Griffin, 1996).[47]

Margaret Clark and Edward Lemay (2010)[48] recently reviewed the literature on close relationships and argued that their most important characteristic is a sense of *responsiveness*. People are happy, healthy, and likely to stay in relationships in which they are sure that they can trust the other person to understand, validate, and care for them. It is this unconditional giving and receiving of love that promotes the welfare of both partners and provides the *secure base* that allows both partners to thrive.

1.4   Causal Attribution: Forming Judgments by Observing Behavior

causal attribution

The process of trying to determine the causes of people's behavior, with the goal of learning about their personalities.

When we observe people's behavior we may attempt to determine if the behavior really reflects their underlying personality. If Frank hits Joe, we might wonder if Frank is naturally aggressive or if perhaps Joe had provoked him. If Leslie leaves a big tip for the waitress, we might wonder if she is a generous person or if the service was particularly excellent. *The process of trying to determine the causes of people's behavior, with the goal of learning about their personalities*, is known as **causal attribution** (Jones et al., 1987).[49]

Making causal attributions is a bit like conducting an experiment. We carefully observe the people we are interested in and note how they behave in different social situations. After we have made our observations, we draw our conclusions. Sometimes we may decide that the behavior was caused primarily by the person; this is called making a *person attribution*. At other times, we may determine that the behavior was caused primarily by the situation; this is called making a *situation attribution*. And at other times we may decide that the behavior was caused by both the person and the situation.

It is easier to make personal attributions when behavior is more unusual or unexpected. Imagine that you go to a party and you are introduced to Tess. Tess shakes your hand and says "Nice to meet you!" Can you readily conclude, on the basis of this behavior, that Tess is a friendly person? Probably not. Because the social situation demands that people act in a friendly way (shaking your hand and saying "nice to meet you"), it is difficult to know whether Tess acted friendly because of the situation or because she is really friendly. Imagine, however, that instead of shaking your hand, Tess sticks out her tongue at you and walks away. I think you would agree that it is easier in this case to infer that Tess is unfriendly because her behavior is so contrary to what one would expect (Jones, Davis, & Gergen, 1961).[50]

Although people are reasonably accurate in their attributions (we could say, perhaps, that they are "good enough"; Fiske, 2003),[51] they are far from perfect. One error that we frequently make when making judgments about ourselves is to make *self-serving attributions* by judging the causes of our own behaviors in overly positive ways. If you did well on a test, you will probably attribute that success to person causes ("I'm smart," "I studied really hard"), but if you do poorly on the test you are more likely to make situation attributions ("The test was hard," "I had bad luck"). Although making causal attributions is expected to be logical and scientific, our emotions are not irrelevant.

fundamental attribution error (or correspondence bias)

The common tendency to overestimate the role of person factors and overlook the impact of social situations in judging others.

Another way that our attributions are often inaccurate is that we are, by and large, too quick to attribute the behavior of other people to something personal about them rather than to something about their situation. We are more likely to say, "Leslie left a big tip, so she must be generous" than "Leslie left a big tip, but perhaps that was because the service was really excellent." *The common tendency to overestimate the role of person factors and overlook the impact of situations in judging others* is known as the **fundamental attribution error (or correspondence bias)**.

The fundamental attribution error occurs in part because other people are so salient in our social environments. When I look at you, I see you as my focus, and so I am likely to make personal attributions about you. If the situation is reversed such that people see situations from the perspectives of others, the fundamental attribution error is reduced (Storms, 1973).[52] And when we judge people, we often see them in only one situation. It's easy for you to think that your math professor is "picky and detail-oriented" because that describes her behavior in class, but you don't know how she acts with her friends and family, which might be completely different. And we also tend to make person attributions because they are easy. We are more likely to commit the fundamental attribution error—quickly jumping to the conclusion that behavior is caused by underlying personality—when we are tired, distracted, or busy doing other things (Trope & Alfieri, 1997).[53]

An important moral about perceiving others applies here: *We should not be too quick to judge other people.* It is easy to think that poor people are lazy, that people who say something harsh are rude or unfriendly, and that all terrorists are insane madmen. But these attributions may frequently overemphasize the role of the person, resulting in an inappropriate and inaccurate tendency to *blame the victim* (Lerner, 1980; Tennen & Affleck, 1990).[54] Sometimes people are lazy and rude, and some terrorists are probably insane, but these people may also be influenced by the situation in which they find themselves. Poor people may find it more difficult to get work and education because of the environment they grow up in, people may say rude things because they are feeling threatened or are in pain, and terrorists may have learned in their family and school that committing violence in the service of their beliefs is justified. When you find yourself making strong person attributions for the behaviors of others, I hope you will stop and think more carefully. Would you want other people to make person attributions for your behavior in the same situation, or would you prefer that they more fully consider the situation surrounding your behavior? Are you perhaps making the fundamental attribution error?

1.5 Attitudes and Behavior

Attitude refer to *our relatively enduring evaluations of people and things* (Albarracín, Johnson, & Zanna, 2005).[55] We each hold many thousands of attitudes, including those about family and friends, political parties and political figures, abortion rights, preferences for music, and much more. Some of our attitudes, including those about sports, roller coaster rides, and capital punishment, are heritable, which explains in part why we are similar to our parents on many dimensions (Olson, Vernon, Harris, & Jang, 2001).[56] Other attitudes are learned through direct and indirect experiences with the attitude objects (De Houwer, Thomas, & Baeyens, 2001).[57]

Attitudes are important because they frequently (but not always) predict behavior. If we know that a person has a more positive attitude toward Frosted Flakes than toward Cheerios, then we will naturally predict that she will buy more of the former when she gets to the market. If we know that Charlie is madly in love with Charlene, then we will not be surprised when he proposes marriage. Because attitudes often predict behavior, people who wish to change behavior frequently try to change attitudes through the use of *persuasive communications*. Table 14.2 presents some of the many techniques that can be used to change people's attitudes (Cialdini, 2001).[58]

FIGURE 14.7

The tendency to make person attributions (such as poor people are lazy) for the behaviors of others, even where situational factors such as poor education and growing up in poverty might be better explanations, is caused by the fundamental attribution error.

© *Thinkstock*

attitude

Our relatively enduring evaluations of people and things.

TABLE 14.2 Techniques That Can Be Effective in Persuading Others

Technique	Examples
Choose effective communicators.	Communicators who are attractive, expert, trustworthy, and similar to the listener are most persuasive.
Consider the goals of the listener.	If the listener wants to be entertained, then it is better to use a humorous ad; if the listener is processing the ad more carefully, use a more thoughtful one.
Use humor.	People are more easily persuaded when they are in a good mood.
Use classical conditioning.	Try to associate your product with positive stimuli such as funny jokes or attractive models.
Make use of the listener's emotions.	Humorous and fear-arousing ads can be effective because they arouse the listener's emotions.
Use the listener's behavior to modify his or her attitude.	One approach is the *foot-in-the-door technique*. First ask for a minor request, and then ask for a larger request after the smaller request has been accepted.

Attitudes predict behavior better for some people than for others. People who are high in **self-monitoring**—*the tendency to regulate behavior to meet the demands of social situations*—tend to change their behaviors to match the social situation and thus do not always act on their attitudes (Gangestad & Snyder, 2000).[59] High self-monitors agree with statements such as, "In different situations and with different people, I often act like very different persons" and "I guess I put on a show to impress or entertain people." Attitudes are more likely to predict behavior for low self-monitors, who are more likely to act on their own attitudes even when the social situation suggests that they should behave otherwise. Low self-monitors are more likely to agree with statements such as "At parties and social gatherings, I do not attempt to do or say things that others will like" and "I can only argue for ideas that I already believe."

The match between the social situations in which the attitudes are expressed and the behaviors are engaged in also matters, such that there is a greater attitude-behavior correlation when the social situations match. Imagine for a minute the case of Magritte, a 16-year-old high school student. Magritte

self-monitoring

The tendency to regulate behavior to meet the demands of social situations.

tells her parents that she hates the idea of smoking cigarettes. But how sure are you that Magritte's attitude will predict her behavior? Would you be willing to bet that she'd never try smoking when she's out with her friends?

The problem here is that Magritte's attitude is being expressed in one social situation (when she is with her parents) whereas the behavior (trying a cigarette) is going to occur in a very different social situation (when she is out with her friends). The relevant social norms are, of course, much different in the two situations. Magritte's friends might be able to convince her to try smoking, despite her initial negative attitude, by enticing her with peer pressure. Behaviors are more likely to be consistent with attitudes when the social situation in which the behavior occurs is similar to the situation in which the attitude is expressed (Ajzen, 1991).[60]

Although it might not have surprised you to hear that our attitudes predict our behaviors, you might be more surprised to learn that our behaviors also have an influence on our attitudes. It makes sense that if I like Frosted Flakes I'll buy them, because my positive attitude toward the product influences my behavior. But my attitudes toward Frosted Flakes may also become more positive if I decide—for whatever reason—to buy some. It makes sense that Charlie's love for Charlene will lead him to propose marriage, but it is also the case that he will likely love Charlene even more after he does so.

self-perception

Using our behavior to help us determine our own thoughts and feelings.

Behaviors influence attitudes in part through the process of *self-perception*. **Self-perception** occurs *when we use our own behavior as a guide to help us determine our own thoughts and feelings* (Bem, 1972; Olson & Stone, 2005).[61] In one demonstration of the power of self-perception, Wells and Petty (1980)[62] assigned their research participants to shake their heads either up and down or side to side as they read newspaper editorials. The participants who had shaken their heads up and down later agreed with the content of the editorials more than the people who had shaken them side to side. Wells and Petty argued that this occurred because the participants used their own head-shaking behaviors to determine their attitudes about the editorials.

Persuaders may use the principles of self-perception to change attitudes. The *foot-in-the-door technique* is a method of persuasion in which the person is first persuaded to accept a rather minor request and then asked for a larger one after that. In one demonstration, Guéguen and Jacob (2002)[63] found that students in a computer discussion group were more likely to volunteer to complete a 40-question survey on their food habits (which required 15 to 20 minutes of their time) if they had already, a few minutes earlier, agreed to help the same requestor with a simple computer-related question (about how to convert a file type) than if they had not first been given the smaller opportunity to help. The idea is that when asked the second time, the people looked at their past behavior (having agreed to the small request) and inferred that they are helpful people.

cognitive dissonance

The discomfort we experience when we choose to behave in ways that we see as inappropriate, and which leads our behavior to change our attitudes.

Behavior also influences our attitudes through a more emotional process known as *cognitive dissonance*. **Cognitive dissonance** refers to *the discomfort we experience when we choose to behave in ways that we see as inappropriate* (Festinger, 1957; Harmon-Jones & Mills, 1999).[64] If we feel that we have wasted our time or acted against our own moral principles, we experience negative emotions (dissonance) and may change our attitudes about the behavior to reduce the negative feelings.

Elliot Aronson and Judson Mills (1959)[65] studied whether the cognitive dissonance created by an initiation process could explain how much commitment students felt to a group that they were part of. In their experiment, female college students volunteered to join a group that would be meeting regularly to discuss various aspects of the psychology of sex. According to random assignment, some of the women were told that they would be required to perform an embarrassing procedure (they were asked to read some obscene words and some sexually oriented passages from a novel in public) before they could join the group, whereas other women did not have to go through this initiation. Then all the women got a chance to listen to the group's conversation, which turned out to be very boring.

Aronson and Mills found that the women who had gone through the embarrassing experience subsequently reported more liking for the group than those who had not. They argued that the more effort an individual expends to become a member of the group (e.g., a severe initiation), the more they will become committed to the group, to justify the effort they have put in during the initiation. The idea is that the effort creates dissonant cognitions ("I did all this work to join the group"), which are then justified by creating more consonant ones ("OK, this group is really pretty fun"). Thus the women who spent little effort to get into the group were able to see the group as the dull and boring conversation that it was. The women who went through the more severe initiation, however, succeeded in convincing themselves that the same discussion was a worthwhile experience.

When we put in effort for something—an initiation, a big purchase price, or even some of our precious time—we will likely end up liking the activity more than we would have if the effort had been less; not doing so would lead us to experience the unpleasant feelings of dissonance. After we buy a product, we convince ourselves that we made the right choice because the product is excellent. If we fail to lose the weight we wanted to, we decide that we look good anyway. If we hurt someone else's feelings, we may even decide that he or she is a bad person who deserves our negative behavior. To escape from feeling poorly about themselves, people will engage in quite extraordinary rationalizing. No wonder that most of us believe that "If I had it all to do over again, I would not change anything important."

KEY TAKEAWAYS

- Social psychology is the scientific study of how we influence, and are influenced by, the people around us.
- Social cognition involves forming impressions of ourselves and other people. Doing so quickly and accurately is functional for social life.
- Our initial judgments of others are based in large part on what we see. The physical features of other people—and particularly their sex, race, age, and physical attractiveness—are very salient, and we often focus our attention on these dimensions.
- We are attracted to people who appear to be healthy. Indicators of health include youth, symmetry, and averageness.
- We frequently use people's appearances to form our judgments about them, and to determine our responses to them. These responses include stereotyping, prejudice, and discrimination. Social psychologists believe that people should get past their prejudices and judge people as individuals.
- Close relationships are based on intimacy. Intimacy is determined by similarity, self-disclosure, interdependence, commitment, rewards, and passion.
- Causal attribution is the process of trying to determine the causes of people's behavior with the goal of learning about their personalities. Although people are reasonably accurate in their attributions, they also succumb to biases such as the fundamental attribution error.
- Attitudes refer to our relatively enduring evaluations of people and things. Attitudes are determined in part by genetic transmission from our parents and in part through direct and indirect experiences.
- Although attitudes predict behaviors, behaviors also predict attitudes. This occurs through the processes of self-perception and cognitive dissonance.

EXERCISES AND CRITICAL THINKING

1. What kinds of people are you attracted to? Do your preferences match the factors that we have just discussed?
2. What stereotypes and prejudices do you hold? Are you able to get past them and judge people as individuals? Do you think that your stereotypes influence your behavior without your being aware of them?
3. Consider a time when your behavior influenced your attitudes. Did this occur as a result of self-perception or cognitive dissonance?

2. INTERACTING WITH OTHERS: HELPING, HURTING, AND CONFORMING

LEARNING OBJECTIVES

1. **Summarize the genetic and environmental factors that contribute to human altruism.**
2. **Provide an overview of the causes of human aggression.**
3. **Explain the situations under which people conform to others and their motivations for doing so.**

Humans have developed a variety of social skills that enhance our ability to successfully interact with others. We are often helpful, even when that helping comes at some cost to ourselves, and we often change our opinions and beliefs to fit in with the opinions of those whom we care about. Yet we also are able to be aggressive if we feel the situation warrants it.

2.1 Helping Others: Altruism Helps Create Harmonious Relationships

altruism

Any behavior that is designed to increase another person's welfare, and particularly those actions that do not seem to provide a direct reward to the person who performs them.

Altruism refers to *any behavior that is designed to increase another person's welfare, and particularly those actions that do not seem to provide a direct reward to the person who performs them* (Dovidio, Piliavin, Schroeder, & Penner, 2006).[66] Altruism occurs when we stop to help a stranger who has been stranded on the highway, when we volunteer at a homeless shelter, or when we donate to a charity. According to a survey given by an established coalition that studies and encourages volunteering (http://www.independentsector.org), in 2001 over 83 million American adults reported that they helped others by volunteering, and did so an average of 3.6 hours per week. The survey estimated that the value of the volunteer time that was given was over 239 billion dollars.

Why Are We Altruistic?

Because altruism is costly, you might wonder why we engage in it at all. There are a variety of explanations for the occurrence of altruism, and Table 14.3 summarizes some of the variables that are known to increase helping.

TABLE 14.3 Some of the Variables Known to Increase Helping

Positive moods	We help more when we are in a good mood (Guéguen & De Gail, 2003).
Similarity	We help people who we see as similar to us, for instance, those who mimic our behaviors (van Baaren, Holland, Kawakami, & van Knippenberg, 2004).
Guilt	If we are experiencing guilt, we may help relieve those negative feelings.
Empathy	We help more when we feel empathy for the other person (Batson, O'Quin, Fultz, Varnderplas, & Isen, 1983).
Benefits	We are more likely to help if we can feel good about ourselves by doing so (Snyder, Omoto, & Lindsay, 2004).
Personal responsibility	We are more likely to help if it is clear that others are not helping.
Self-presentation	We may help in order to show others that we are good people (Hardy & Van Vugt, 2006).

Sources: Guéguen, N., & De Gail, M.-A. (2003). The effect of smiling on helping behavior: Smiling and Good Samaritan behavior. Communication Reports, 16(2), 133–140; van Baaren, R. B., Holland, R. W., Kawakami, K., & van Knippenberg, A. (2004). Mimicry and prosocial behavior. Psychological Science, 15(1), 71–74; Batson, C. D., O'Quin, K., Fultz, J., Varnderplas, M., & Isen, A. M. (1983). Influence of self-reported distress and empathy on egoistic versus altruistic motivation to help. Journal of Personality and Social Psychology, 45(3), 706–718; Snyder, M., Omoto, A. M., & Lindsay, J. J. (Eds.). (2004). Sacrificing time and effort for the good of others: The benefits and costs of volunteerism. New York, NY: Guilford Press; Hardy, C. L., & Van Vugt, M. (2006). Nice guys finish first: The competitive altruism hypothesis. Personality and Social Psychology Bulletin, 32(10), 1402–1413.

The tendency to help others in need is in part a functional evolutionary adaptation. Although helping others can be costly to us as individuals, helping people who are related to us can perpetuate our own genes (Madsen et al., 2007; McAndrew, 2002; Stewart-Williams, 2007).[67] Burnstein, Crandall, and Kitayama (1994)[68] found that students indicated they would be more likely to help a person who was closely related to them (e.g., a sibling, parent, or child) than they would be to help a person who was more distantly related (e.g., a niece, nephew, uncle, or grandmother). People are more likely to donate kidneys to relatives than to strangers (Borgida, Conner, & Manteufel, 1992),[69] and even children indicate that they are more likely to help their siblings than they are to help a friend (Tisak & Tisak, 1996).[70]

Although it makes evolutionary sense that we would help people who we are related to, why would we help people to whom we not related? One explanation for such behavior is based on the principle of *reciprocal altruism* (Krebs & Davies, 1987; Trivers, 1971).[71] **Reciprocal altruism** is *the principle that, if we help other people now, those others will return the favor should we need their help in the future.* By helping others, we both increase our chances of survival and reproductive success and help others increase their survival too. Over the course of evolution, those who engage in reciprocal altruism should be able to reproduce more often than those who do not, thus enabling this kind of altruism to continue.

We also learn to help by modeling the helpful behavior of others. Although people frequently worry about the negative impact of the violence that is seen on TV, there is also a great deal of helping behavior shown on television. Smith et al. (2006)[72] found that 73% of TV shows had some altruism, and that about three altruistic behaviors were shown every hour. Furthermore, the prevalence of altruism was particularly high in children's shows. But just as viewing altruism can increase helping, modeling of behavior that is not altruistic can decrease altruism. For instance, Anderson and Bushman (2001)[73] found that playing violent video games led to a decrease in helping.

We are more likely to help when we receive rewards for doing so and less likely to help when helping is costly. Parents praise their children who share their toys with others, and may reprimand children who are selfish. We are more likely to help when we have plenty of time than when we are in a hurry (Darley and Batson 1973).[74] Another potential reward is the status we gain as a result of helping. When we act altruistically, we gain a reputation as a person with high status who is able and willing to help others, and this status makes us more desirable in the eyes of others (Hardy & Van Vugt, 2006).[75]

The outcome of the reinforcement and modeling of altruism is the development of social norms about helping—standards of behavior that we see as appropriate and desirable regarding helping. The *reciprocity norm* reminds us that we should follow the principles of reciprocal altruism. If someone helps us, then we should help them in the future, and we should help people now with the expectation that they will help us later if we need it. The reciprocity norm is found in everyday adages such as "Scratch my back and I'll scratch yours" and in religious and philosophical teachings such as the "Golden Rule": "Do unto other as you would have them do unto you."

Because helping based on the reciprocity norm is based on the return of earlier help and the expectation of a future return from others, it might not seem like true altruism. We might hope that our children internalize another relevant social norm that seems more altruistic: the *social responsibility norm*. The social responsibility norm tells us that we should try to help others who need assistance, even without any expectation of future paybacks. The teachings of many religions are based on the social responsibility norm; that we should, as good human beings, reach out and help other people whenever we can.

How the Presence of Others Can Reduce Helping

Late at night on March 13, 1964, 28-year-old Kitty Genovese was murdered within a few yards of her apartment building in New York City after a violent fight with her killer in which she struggled and screamed. When the police interviewed Kitty's neighbors about the crime, they discovered that 38 of the neighbors indicated that they had seen or heard the fight occurring but not one of them had bothered to intervene, and only one person had called the police.

FIGURE 14.8

We help in part to make ourselves feel good, but also because we care about the welfare of others.

© Thinkstock

reciprocal altruism

The principle that, if we help other people now, those others will return the favor should we need their help in the future.

Video Clip: The Case of Kitty Genovese

Was Kitty Genovese murdered because there were too many people who heard her cries? Watch this video for an analysis.

View the video online at: http://www.youtube.com/embed/JozmWS6xYEw

Two social psychologists, Bibb Latané and John Darley, were interested in the factors that influenced people to help (or to not help) in such situations (Latané & Darley, 1968).[76] They developed a model (see Figure 14.9) that took into consideration the important role of the social situation in determining helping. The model has been extensively tested in many studies, and there is substantial support for it. Social psychologists have discovered that it was the 38 people themselves that contributed to the tragedy, because people are less likely to notice, interpret, and respond to the needs of others when they are with others than they are when they are alone.

FIGURE 14.9

The Latané and Darley model of helping is based on the idea that a variety of situational factors can influence whether or not we help.

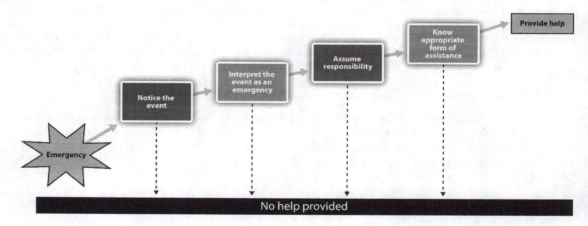

The first step in the model is noticing the event. Latané and Darley (1968)[77] demonstrated the important role of the social situation in noticing by asking research participants to complete a questionnaire in a small room. Some of the participants completed the questionnaire alone, whereas others completed the questionnaire in small groups in which two other participants were also working on questionnaires. A few minutes after the participants had begun the questionnaires, the experimenters started to let some white smoke come into the room through a vent in the wall. The experimenters timed how long it took before the first person in the room looked up and noticed the smoke.

The people who were working alone noticed the smoke in about 5 seconds, and within 4 minutes most of the participants who were working alone had taken some action. On the other hand, on average, the first person in the group conditions did not notice the smoke until over 20 seconds had elapsed. And, although 75% of the participants who were working alone reported the smoke within 4 minutes, the smoke was reported in only 12% of the groups by that time. In fact, in only 3 of the 8 groups did anyone report the smoke, even after it had filled the room. You can see that the social situation has a powerful influence on noticing; we simply don't see emergencies when other people are with us.

Even if we notice an emergency, we might not interpret it as one. Were the cries of Kitty Genovese really calls for help, or were they simply an argument with a boyfriend? The problem is compounded when others are present, because when we are unsure how to interpret events we normally look to others to help us understand them, and at the same time they are looking to us for information. The problem is that each bystander thinks that other people aren't acting because they don't see an emergency. Believing that the others know something that they don't, each observer concludes that help is not required.

Even if we have noticed the emergency and interpret it as being one, this does not necessarily mean that we will come to the rescue of the other person. We still need to decide that it is our responsibility to do something. The problem is that when we see others around, it is easy to assume that they are going to do something, and that we don't need to do anything ourselves. **Diffusion of responsibility** occurs *when we assume that others will take action and therefore we do not take action ourselves.* The irony again, of course, is that people are more likely to help when they are the only ones in the situation than when there are others around.

Perhaps you have noticed diffusion of responsibility if you participated in an Internet users group where people asked questions of the other users. Did you find that it was easier to get help if you directed your request to a smaller set of users than when you directed it to a larger number of people? Markey (2000)[78] found that people received help more quickly (in about 37 seconds) when they asked for help by specifying a participant's name than when no name was specified (51 seconds).

The final step in the helping model is knowing how to help. Of course, for many of us the ways to best help another person in an emergency are not that clear; we are not professionals and we have little training in how to help in emergencies. People who do have training in how to act in emergencies are more likely to help, whereas the rest of us just don't know what to do, and therefore we may simply walk by. On the other hand, today many people have cell phones, and we can do a lot with a quick call; in fact, a phone call made in time might have saved Kitty Genovese's life.

diffusion of responsibility

The assumption that others will take action and therefore we do not take action ourselves.

2.2 Human Aggression: An Adaptive yet Potentially Damaging Behavior

Aggression is *behavior that is intended to harm another individual.* Aggression may occur in the heat of the moment, for instance, when a jealous lover strikes out in rage or the sports fans at a university light fires and destroy cars after an important basketball game. Or it may occur in a more cognitive, deliberate, and planned way, such as the aggression of a bully who steals another child's toys, a terrorist who kills civilians to gain political exposure, or a hired assassin who kills for money.

Not all aggression is physical. Aggression also occurs in nonphysical ways, as when children exclude others from activities, call them names, or spread rumors about them. Paquette and Underwood (1999)[79] found that both boys and girls rated nonphysical aggression such as name-calling as making them feel more "sad and bad" than did physical aggression.

aggression

Behavior intended to harm another individual.

The Ability to Aggress Is Part of Human Nature

We may aggress against others in part because it allows us to gain access to valuable resources such as food, territory, and desirable mates, or to protect ourselves from direct attack by others. If aggression helps in the survival of our genes, then the process of natural selection may well have caused humans, as it would any other animal, to be aggressive (Buss & Duntley, 2006).[80]

There is evidence for the genetics of aggression. Aggression is controlled in large part by the amygdala. One of the primary functions of the amygdala is to help us learn to associate stimuli with the rewards and the punishment that they may provide. The amygdala is particularly activated in our responses to stimuli that we see as threatening and fear-arousing. When the amygdala is stimulated, in either humans or in animals, the organism becomes more aggressive.

But just because we *can* aggress does not mean that we *will* aggress. It is not necessarily evolutionarily adaptive to aggress in all situations. Neither people nor animals are always aggressive; they rely on aggression only when they feel that they absolutely need to (Berkowitz, 1993).[81] The prefrontal cortex serves as a control center on aggression; when it is more highly activated, we are more able to control our aggressive impulses. Research has found that the cerebral cortex is less active in murderers and death row inmates, suggesting that violent crime may be caused at least in part by a failure or reduced ability to regulate aggression (Davidson, Putnam, & Larson, 2000).[82]

Hormones are also important in regulating aggression. Most important in this regard is the male sex hormone *testosterone*, which is associated with increased aggression in both males and females. Research conducted on a variety of animals has found a positive correlation between levels of testosterone and aggression. This relationship seems to be weaker among humans than among animals, yet it is still significant (Dabbs, Hargrove, & Heusel, 1996).[83]

Consuming alcohol increases the likelihood that people will respond aggressively to provocations, and even people who are not normally aggressive may react with aggression when they are intoxicated

(Graham, Osgood, Wells, & Stockwell, 2006).[84] Alcohol reduces the ability of people who have consumed it to inhibit their aggression because when people are intoxicated, they become more self-focused and less aware of the social constraints that normally prevent them from engaging aggressively (Bushman & Cooper, 1990; Steele & Southwick, 1985).[85]

Negative Experiences Increase Aggression

If I were to ask you about the times that you have been aggressive, I bet that you would tell me that many of them occurred when you were angry, in a bad mood, tired, in pain, sick, or frustrated. And you would be right—we are much more likely to aggress when we are experiencing negative emotions. One important determinant of aggression is frustration. When we are frustrated we may lash out at others, even at people who did not cause the frustration. In some cases the aggression is *displaced aggression*, which is aggression that is directed at an object or person other than the person who caused the frustration.

Other negative emotions also increase aggression. Griffit and Veitch (1971)[86] had students complete questionnaires in rooms in which the heat was at a normal temperature or in which the temperature was over 90 degrees Fahrenheit. The students in the latter conditions expressed significantly more hostility. Aggression is greater on hot days than it is on cooler days and during hot years than during cooler years, and most violent riots occur during the hottest days of the year (Bushman, Wang, & Anderson, 2005).[87] Pain also increases aggression (Berkowitz, 1993).[88]

catharsis

The idea that observing or engaging in less harmful aggressive actions will reduce the tendency to aggress later in a more harmful way.

If we are aware that we are feeling negative emotions, we might think that we could release those emotions in a relatively harmless way, such as by punching a pillow or kicking something, with the hopes that doing so will release our aggressive tendencies. Catharsis—*the idea that observing or engaging in less harmful aggressive actions will reduce the tendency to aggress later in a more harmful way*—has been considered by many as a way of decreasing violence, and it was an important part of the theories of Sigmund Freud.

As far as social psychologists have been able to determine, however, catharsis simply does not work. Rather than decreasing aggression, engaging in aggressive behaviors of any type increases the likelihood of later aggression. Bushman, Baumeister, and Stack (1999)[89] first angered their research participants by having another student insult them. Then half of the participants were allowed to engage in a cathartic behavior: They were given boxing gloves and then got a chance to hit a punching bag for 2 minutes. Then all the participants played a game with the person who had insulted them earlier in which they had a chance to blast the other person with a painful blast of white noise. Contrary to the catharsis hypothesis, the students who had punched the punching bag set a higher noise level and delivered longer bursts of noise than the participants who did not get a chance to hit the punching bag. It seems that if we hit a punching bag, punch a pillow, or scream as loud as we can to release our frustration, the opposite may occur—rather than decreasing aggression, these behaviors in fact increase it.

Viewing Violent Media Increases Aggression

The average American watches over 4 hours of television every day, and these programs contain a substantial amount of aggression. At the same time, children are also exposed to violence in movies and video games, as well as in popular music and music videos that include violent lyrics and imagery. Research evidence makes it very clear that, on average, people who watch violent behavior become more aggressive. The evidence supporting this relationship comes from many studies conducted over many years using both correlational designs as well as laboratory studies in which people have been randomly assigned to view either violent or nonviolent material (Anderson et al., 2003).[90] Viewing violent behavior also increases aggression in part through observational learning. Children who witness violence are more likely to be aggressive. One example is in the studies of Albert Bandura, as shown in below.

Video Clip

This video shows Professor Albert Bandura describing his studies on the observational learning of aggression in children.

View the video online at: http://www.youtube.com/embed/jWsxfoJEwQQ

Another outcome of viewing large amounts of violent material is **desensitization**, which is *the tendency over time to show weaker emotional responses to emotional stimuli*. When we first see violence, we are likely to be shocked, aroused, and even repulsed by it. However, over time, as we see more and more violence, we become habituated to it, such that the subsequent exposures produce fewer and fewer negative emotional responses. Continually viewing violence also makes us more distrustful and more likely to behave aggressively (Bartholow, Bushman, & Sestir, 2006; Nabi & Sullivan, 2001).[91]

Of course, not everyone who views violent material becomes aggressive; individual differences also matter. People who experience a lot of negative affect and who feel that they are frequently rejected by others whom they care about are more aggressive (Downey, Irwin, Ramsay, & Ayduk, 2004).[92] People with inflated or unstable self-esteem are more prone to anger and are highly aggressive when their high self-image is threatened (Baumeister, Smart, & Boden, 1996).[93] For instance, classroom bullies are those children who always want to be the center of attention, who think a lot of themselves, and who cannot take criticism (Salmivalli & Nieminen, 2002).[94] Bullies are highly motivated to protect their inflated self-concepts, and they react with anger and aggression when it is threatened.

There is a culturally universal tendency for men to be more physically violent than women (Archer & Coyne, 2005; Crick & Nelson, 2002).[95] Worldwide, about 99% of rapes and about 90% of robberies, assaults, and murders are committed by men (Graham & Wells, 2001).[96] These sex differences do not imply that women are never aggressive. Both men and women respond to insults and provocation with aggression; the differences between men and women are smaller after they have been frustrated, insulted, or threatened (Bettencourt & Miller, 1996).[97]

Research Focus: The Culture of Honor

In addition to differences across cultures, there are also regional differences in the incidence of violence in different parts of the United States. As one example, the homicide rate is significantly higher in the southern and the western states but lower in the eastern and northern states. One explanation for these differences is variation in cultural norms about the appropriate reactions to threats against one's social status. These cultural differences apply primarily to men. In short, some men react more violently than others when they believe that others are threatening them.

The social norm that condones and even encourages responding to insults with aggression is known as the **culture of honor**. The culture of honor leads people to view even relatively minor conflicts or disputes as challenges to one's social status and reputation and can therefore trigger aggressive responses. Beliefs in culture of honor norms are stronger among men who live or who were raised in the South and West than among men who are from or living in the North and East.

In one series of experiments, Cohen, Nisbett, Bosdle, and Schwarz (1996)[98] investigated how white male students who had grown up either in the northern or in the southern regions of the United States responded to insults. The experiments, which were conducted at the University of Michigan, involved an encounter in which the research participant was walking down a narrow hallway. The experimenters enlisted the help of a confederate who did not give way to the participant but rather bumped into him and insulted him. Compared with

desensitization

The tendency over time to show weaker emotional responses to emotional stimuli.

culture of honor

A social norm that condones and even encourages responding to insults with aggression.

Northerners, students from the South who had been bumped were more likely to think that their masculine reputations had been threatened, exhibited greater physiological signs of being upset, had higher testosterone levels, engaged in more aggressive and dominant behavior (gave firmer handshakes), and were less willing to yield to a subsequent confederate (Figure 14.10).

Results From Cohen, Nisbett, Bosdle, and Schwarz, 1996

Students from southern U.S. states expressed more anger and had greater levels of testosterone after being insulted than did students from northern states.

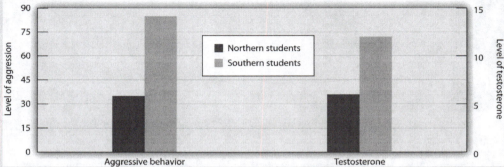

Source: Adapted from Cohen, D., Nisbett, R. E., Bosdle, B., & Schwarz, N. (1996). Insult, aggression, and the southern culture of honor: An "experimental ethnography." Journal of Personality and Social Psychology, 70, 945–960.

In another test of the impact of culture of honor, Cohen and Nisbett (1997)[99] sent letters to employers across the United States from a fictitious job applicant who admitted having been convicted of a felony. To half the employers, the applicant reported that he had impulsively killed a man who had been having an affair with his fiancée and then taunted him about it in a crowded bar. To the other half, the applicant reported that he had stolen a car because he needed the money to pay off debts. Employers from the South and the West, places in which the culture of honor is strong, were more likely than employers in the North and East to respond in an understanding and cooperative way to the letter from the convicted killer, but there were no cultural differences for the letter from the auto thief.

One possible explanation for regional differences in the culture of honor involves the kind of activities typically engaged in by men in the different regions. While people in the northern parts of the United States were usually farmers who grew crops, people from southern climates were more likely to raise livestock. Unlike the crops grown by the northerners, the herds were mobile and vulnerable to theft, and it was difficult for law enforcement officials to protect them. To be successful in an environment where theft was common, a man had to build a reputation for strength and toughness, and this was accomplished by a willingness to use swift, and sometimes violent, punishment against thieves.

2.3 Conformity and Obedience: How Social Influence Creates Social Norms

conformity

A change in beliefs or behavior that occurs as the result of the presence of the other people around us.

When we decide on what courses to enroll in by asking for advice from our friends, change our beliefs or behaviors as a result of the ideas that we hear from others, or binge drink because our friends are doing it, we are engaging in **conformity**, *a change in beliefs or behavior that occurs as the result of the presence of the other people around us.* We conform not only because we believe that other people have accurate information and we want to have knowledge (*informational conformity*) but also because we want to be liked by others (*normative conformity*).

The typical outcome of conformity is that our beliefs and behaviors become more similar to those of others around us. But some situations create more conformity than others, and some of the factors that contribute to conformity are shown in Table 14.4.

TABLE 14.4 Variables That Increase Conformity

Variable	Description	Example
Number in majority	As the number of people who are engaging in a behavior increases, the tendency to conform to those people also increases.	People are more likely to stop and look up in the air when many, rather than few, people are also looking up (Milgram, Bickman, & Berkowitz, 1969).
Unanimity	Conformity reduces sharply when any one person deviates from the norm.	In Solomon Asch's line-matching research, when any one person gave a different answer, conformity was eliminated.
Status and authority	People who have higher status, such as those in authority, create more conformity.	Milgram (1974) found that conformity in his obedience studies was greatly reduced when the person giving the command to shock was described as an "ordinary man" rather than a scientist at Yale University.

Sources: Milgram, S., Bickman, L., & Berkowitz, L. (1969). Note on the drawing power of crowds of different size. Journal of Personality and Social Psychology, 13, 79–82; Milgram, S. (1974). Obedience to authority: An experimental view. New York, NY: Harper and Row.

At times conformity occurs in a relatively spontaneous and unconscious way, without any obvious intent of one person to change the other, or an awareness that the conformity is occurring. Robert Cialdini and his colleagues (Cialdini, Reno, & Kallgren, 1990)[100] found that college students were more likely to throw litter on the ground themselves when they had just seen another person throw some paper on the ground, and Cheng and Chartrand (2003)[101] found that people unconsciously mimicked the behaviors of others, such as by rubbing their face or shaking their foot, and that that mimicry was greater when the other person was of high versus low social status.

Muzafer Sherif (1936)[102] studied how norms develop in ambiguous situations. In his studies, college students were placed in a dark room with a single point of light and were asked to indicate, each time the light was turned on, how much it appeared to move. (The movement, which is not actually real, occurs because of the saccadic movement of the eyes.) Each group member gave his or her response on each trial aloud and each time in a different random order. As you can see in Figure 14.11, Sherif found a conformity effect: Over time, the responses of the group members became more and more similar to each other such that after four days they converged on a common norm. When the participants were interviewed after the study, they indicated that they had not realized that they were conforming.

FIGURE 14.11 Sherif's (1936) Studies on Conformity

The participants in the studies by Muzafer Sherif initially had different beliefs about the degree to which a point of light appeared to be moving. (You can see these differences as expressed on Day 1.) However, as they shared their beliefs with other group members over several days, a common group norm developed. Shown here are the estimates made by a group of three participants who met together on four different days.

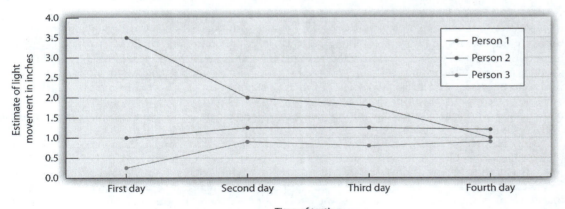

Source: Adapted from Sherif, M. (1936). The psychology of social norms. New York, NY: Harper and Row.

Not all conformity is passive. In the research of Solomon Asch (1955)[103] the judgments that group members were asked to make were entirely unambiguous, and the influence of the other people on judgments was apparent. The research participants were male college students who were told that they were to be participating in a test of visual abilities. The men were seated in front of a board that displayed the visual stimuli that they were going to judge. The men were told that there would be 18 trials during the experiment, and on each trial they would see two cards. The standard card had a single line that was to be judged, and the test card had three lines that varied in length between about 2 and 10 inches.

FIGURE 14.12

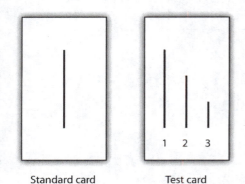

Standard card   Test card

On each trial, each person in the group answered out loud, beginning with one end of the group and moving toward the other end. Although the real research participant did not know it, the other group members were actually not participants but experimental confederates who gave predetermined answers on each trial. Because the real participant was seated next to last in the row, he always made his judgment following most of the other group members. Although on the first two trials the confederates each gave the correct answer, on the third trial, and on 11 of the subsequent trials, they all had been instructed to give the same wrong choice. For instance, even though the correct answer was Line 1, they would all say it was Line 2. Thus when it became the participant's turn to answer, he could either give the clearly correct answer or conform to the incorrect responses of the confederates.

Remarkably, in this study about 76% of the 123 men who were tested gave at least one incorrect response when it was their turn, and 37% of the responses, overall, were conforming. This is indeed evidence for the power of conformity because the participants were making clearly incorrect responses in public. However, conformity was not absolute; in addition to the 24% of the men who never conformed, only 5% of the men conformed on all 12 of the critical trials.

Video Clip

Asch's Line Matching Studies
Watch this video to see a demonstration of Asch's line studies.

View the video online at: http://www.youtube.com/embed/TYlh4MkcfJA

obedience

Conformity toward those with authority.

The tendency to conform to those in authority, known as **obedience**, was demonstrated in a remarkable set of studies performed by Stanley Milgram (1974).[104] Milgram designed a study in which he could observe the extent to which a person who presented himself as an authority would be able to produce obedience, even to the extent of leading people to cause harm to others. Like many other researchers who were interested in conformity, Milgram's interest stemmed in part from his desire to understand how the presence of a powerful social situation—in this case the directives of Adolph Hitler, the German dictator who ordered the killing of millions of Jews and other "undesirable" people during World War II—could produce obedience.

Milgram used newspaper ads to recruit men (and in one study, women) from a wide variety of backgrounds to participate in his research. When the research participant arrived at the lab, he or she was introduced to a man who was ostensibly another research participant but who actually was a confederate working with the experimenter as part of the experimental team. The experimenter explained that the goal of the research was to study the effects of punishment on learning. After the participant and the confederate both consented to be in the study, the researcher explained that one of them would be the teacher, and the other the learner. They were each given a slip of paper and asked to open it and indicate what it said. In fact both papers read "teacher," which allowed the confederate to pretend that he had been assigned to be the learner and thus to assure that the actual participant was always the teacher.

While the research participant (now the teacher) looked on, the learner was taken into the adjoining shock room and strapped to an electrode that was to deliver the punishment. The experimenter explained that the teacher's job would be to sit in the control room and read a list of word pairs to the learner. After the teacher read the list once, it would be the learner's job to remember which words went together. For instance, if the word pair was "blue sofa," the teacher would say the word "blue" on the testing trials, and the learner would have to indicate which of four possible words ("house," "sofa," "cat," or "carpet") was the correct answer by pressing one of four buttons in front of him.

After the experimenter gave the "teacher" a mild shock to demonstrate that the shocks really were painful, the experiment began. The research participant first read the list of words to the learner and then began testing him on his learning. The shock apparatus (Figure 14.13) was in front of the teacher, and the learner was not visible in the shock room. The experimenter sat behind the teacher and explained to him that each time the learner made a mistake he was to press one of the shock switches to administer the shock. Moreover, the switch that was to be pressed increased by one level with each mistake, so that each mistake required a stronger shock.

FIGURE 14.13 Materials Used in Milgram's Experiments on Obedience

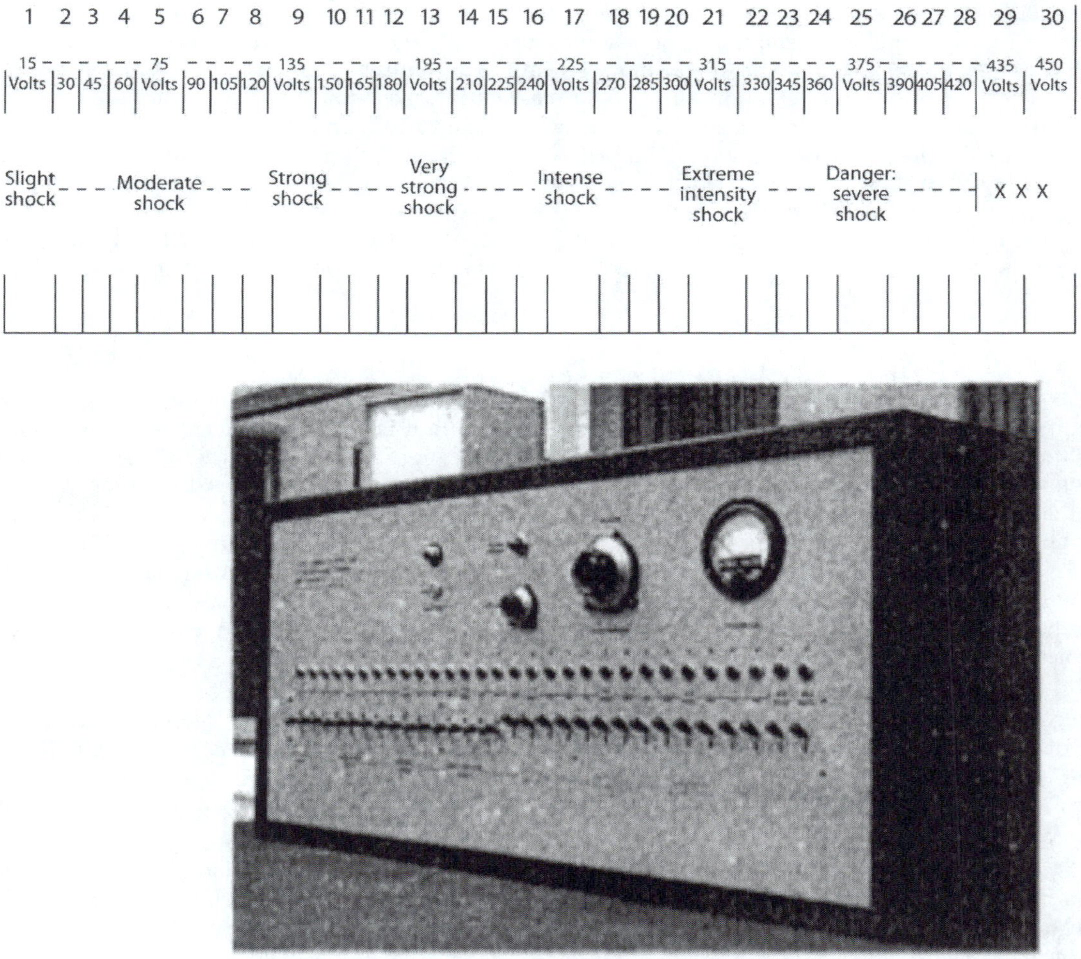

Source: Adapted from Milgram, S. (1974). Obedience to authority: An experimental view. New York, NY: Harper and Row.

Once the learner (who was, of course, actually the experimental confederate) was alone in the shock room, he unstrapped himself from the shock machine and brought out a tape recorder that he used to play a prerecorded series of responses that the teacher could hear through the wall of the room.

The teacher heard the learner say "ugh!" after the first few shocks. After the next few mistakes, when the shock level reached 150 V, the learner was heard to exclaim, "Let me out of here. I have heart trouble!" As the shock reached about 270 V, the protests of the learner became more vehement, and after 300 V the learner proclaimed that he was not going to answer any more questions. From 330 V and up, the learner was silent. At this point the experimenter responded to participants' questions, if any, with a scripted response indicating that they should continue reading the questions and applying increasing shock when the learner did not respond.

The results of Milgram's research were themselves quite shocking. Although all the participants gave the initial mild levels of shock, responses varied after that. Some refused to continue after about

150 V, despite the insistence of the experimenter to continue to increase the shock level. Still others, however, continued to present the questions and to administer the shocks, under the pressure of the experimenter, who demanded that they continue. In the end, 65% of the participants continued giving the shock to the learner all the way up to the 450 V maximum, even though that shock was marked as "danger: severe shock" and no response had been heard from the participant for several trials. In other words, well over half of the men who participated had, as far as they knew, shocked another person to death, all as part of a supposed experiment on learning.

In case you are thinking that such high levels of obedience would not be observed in today's modern culture, there is fact evidence that they would. Milgram's findings were almost exactly replicated, using men and women from a wide variety of ethnic groups, in a study conducted this decade at Santa Clara University (Burger, 2009).[105] In this replication of the Milgram experiment, 67% of the men and 73% of the women agreed to administer increasingly painful electric shocks when an authority figure ordered them to. The participants in this study were not, however, allowed to go beyond the 150 V shock switch.

Although it might be tempting to conclude that Burger's and Milgram's experiments demonstrate that people are innately bad creatures who are ready to shock others to death, this is not in fact the case. Rather it is the social situation, and not the people themselves, that is responsible for the behavior. When Milgram created variations on his original procedure, he found that changes in the situation dramatically influenced the amount of conformity. Conformity was significantly reduced when people were allowed to choose their own shock level rather than being ordered to use the level required by the experimenter, when the experimenter communicated by phone rather than from within the experimental room, and when other research participants refused to give the shock. These findings are consistent with a basic principle of social psychology: The situation in which people find themselves has a major influence on their behavior.

Do We Always Conform?

The research that we have discussed to this point suggests that most people conform to the opinions and desires of others. But it is not always the case that we blindly conform. For one, there are individual differences in conformity. People with lower self-esteem are more likely to conform than are those with higher self-esteem, and people who are dependent on and who have a strong need for approval from others are also more conforming (Bornstein, 1993).[106] People who highly identify with or who have a high degree of commitment to a group are also more likely to conform to group norms than those who care less about the group (Jetten, Spears, & Manstead, 1997).[107] Despite these individual differences among people in terms of their tendency to conform, however, research has generally found that the impact of individual difference variables on conformity is smaller than the influence of situational variables, such as the number and unanimity of the majority.

We have seen that conformity usually occurs such that the opinions and behaviors of individuals become more similar to the opinions and behaviors of the majority of the people in the group. However, and although it is much more unusual, there are cases *in which a smaller number of individuals is able to influence the opinions or behaviors of the larger group*—a phenomenon known as **minority influence**. Minorities who are consistent and confident in their opinions may in some cases be able to be persuasive (Moscovici, Mugny, & Van Avermaet, 1985).[108]

Persuasion that comes from minorities has another, and potentially even more important, effect on the opinions of majority group members: It can lead majorities to engage in fuller, as well as more divergent, innovative, and creative thinking about the topics being discussed (Martin, Hewstone, Martin, & Gardikiotis, 2008).[109] Nemeth and Kwan (1987)[110] found that participants working together in groups solved problems more creatively when only one person gave a different and unusual response than the other members did (minority influence) in comparison to when three people gave the same unusual response.

It is a good thing that minorities can be influential; otherwise, the world would be pretty boring indeed. When we look back on history, we find that it is the unusual, divergent, innovative minority groups or individuals, who—although frequently ridiculed at the time for their unusual ideas—end up being respected for producing positive changes.

Another case where conformity does not occur is when people feel that their freedom is being threatened by influence attempts, yet they also have the ability to resist that persuasion. In these cases they may develop *a strong emotional reaction that leads people to resist pressures to conform* known as **psychological reactance** (Miron & Brehm, 2006).[111] Reactance is aroused when our ability to choose which behaviors to engage in is eliminated or threatened with elimination. The outcome of the experience of reactance is that people may not conform at all, in fact moving their opinions or behaviors away from the desires of the influencer. Consider an experiment conducted by Pennebaker and Sanders (1976),[112] who attempted to get people to stop writing graffiti on the walls of campus restrooms. In the first group of restrooms they put a sign that read "Do not write on these walls under

minority influence

Conformity in which a smaller number of individuals is able to influence the opinions or behaviors of the larger group.

psychological reactance

A strong emotional reaction that leads people to resist pressures to conform.

any circumstances!" whereas in the second group they placed a sign that simply said "Please don't write on these walls." Two weeks later, the researchers returned to the restrooms to see if the signs had made a difference. They found that there was significantly less graffiti in the second group of restrooms than in the first one. It seems as if people who were given strong pressures to not engage in the behavior were more likely to react against those directives than were people who were given a weaker message.

Reactance represents a desire to restore freedom that is being threatened. A child who feels that his or her parents are forcing him to eat his asparagus may react quite vehemently with a strong refusal to touch the plate. And an adult who feels that she is being pressured by a car salesman might feel the same way and leave the showroom entirely, resulting in the opposite of the salesman's intended outcome.

KEY TAKEAWAYS

- Altruism is behavior that is designed to increase another person's welfare, and particularly those actions that do not seem to provide a direct reward to the person who performs them. The tendency to help others in need is in part a functional evolutionary adaptation and in part determined by environmental factors.
- Although helping others can be costly to us as individuals, helping people who are related to us can perpetuate our own genes. Some helping is based on reciprocal altruism, the principle that if we help other people now, those others will return the favor should we need their help in the future.
- We also learn to help through modeling and reinforcement. The result of this learning is norms about helping, including the reciprocity norm and the social responsibility norm.
- Research testing the Latané and Darley model of helping has shown the importance of the social situation in noticing, interpreting, and acting in emergency situations.
- Aggression is physical or nonphysical behavior that is intended to harm another individual. Aggression has both genetic and environmental causes. The experience of negative emotions tends to increase aggression.
- Viewing violence tends to increase aggression.
- The social norm that condones and even encourages responding to insults with aggression is known as the culture of honor.
- Conformity, the change in beliefs or behavior that occurs as the result of the presence of the other people around us, can occur in both active and passive ways. The typical outcome of conformity is that our beliefs and behaviors become more similar to those of others around us.
- The situation is the most powerful determinant of conformity, but individual differences may also matter. The important influence of the social situation on conformity was demonstrated in the research by Sherif, Asch, Milgram, and others.
- Minority influence can change attitudes and change how majorities process information.

EXERCISES AND CRITICAL THINKING

1. Consider a time when you were helpful. Was the behavior truly altruistic, or did you help for selfish reasons?
2. Consider a time when you or someone you know was aggressive. What do you think caused the aggression?
3. Should parents limit the amount of violent TV shows and video games that their children are exposed to? Why or why not?
4. Is conformity a "good thing" or a "bad thing" for society? What determines whether it is good or bad? What role do you think conformity played in Sam Spady's death?

3. WORKING WITH OTHERS: THE COSTS AND BENEFITS OF SOCIAL GROUPS

LEARNING OBJECTIVES

1. Summarize the advantages and disadvantages of working together in groups to perform tasks and make decisions.
2. Review the factors that can increase group productivity.

Just as our primitive ancestors lived together in small social groups, including families, tribes, and clans, people today still spend a great deal of time in groups. We study together in study groups, we work together on production lines, and we decide the fates of others in courtroom juries. We work in groups because groups can be beneficial. A rock band that is writing a new song or a surgical team in the middle of a complex operation may coordinate their efforts so well that it is clear that the same outcome could never have occurred if the individuals had worked alone. But group performance will only be better than individual performance to the extent that the group members are motivated to meet the group goals, effectively share information, and efficiently coordinate their efforts. Because these things do not always happen, group performance is almost never as good as we would expect, given the number of individuals in the group, and may even in some cases be inferior to that which could have been made by one or more members of the group working alone.

FIGURE 14.14

Working groups are used to perform tasks and make decisions, but are they effective?

© Thinkstock

social facilitation

The tendency to perform tasks better or faster in the presence of others.

social inhibition

The tendency to perform tasks more poorly or more slowly in the presence of others.

3.1 Working in Front of Others: Social Facilitation and Social Inhibition

In an early social psychological study, Norman Triplett (1898)[113] found that bicycle racers who were competing with other bicyclers on the same track rode significantly faster than bicyclers who were racing alone, against the clock. This led Triplett to hypothesize that people perform tasks better when there are other people present than they do when they are alone. Subsequent findings validated Triplett's results, and experiments have shown that the presence of others can increase performance on many types of tasks, including jogging, shooting pool, lifting weights, and solving problems (Bond & Titus, 1983).[114] *The tendency to perform tasks better or faster in the presence of others* is known as **social facilitation**.

However, although people sometimes perform better when they are in groups than they do alone, the situation is not that simple. Perhaps you remember an experience when you performed a task (playing the piano, shooting basketball free throws, giving a public presentation) very well alone but poorly with, or in front of, others. Thus it seems that the conclusion that being with others increases performance cannot be entirely true. *The tendency to perform tasks more poorly or more slowly in the presence of others* is known as **social inhibition**.

Robert Zajonc (1965)[115] explained the observed influence of others on task performance using the concept of physiological arousal. According to Zajonc, when we are with others we experience more arousal than we do when we are alone, and this arousal increases the likelihood that we will perform the *dominant response*, the action that we are most likely to emit in any given situation (Figure 14.15).

FIGURE 14.15 Drive-Arousal Model of Social Facilitation

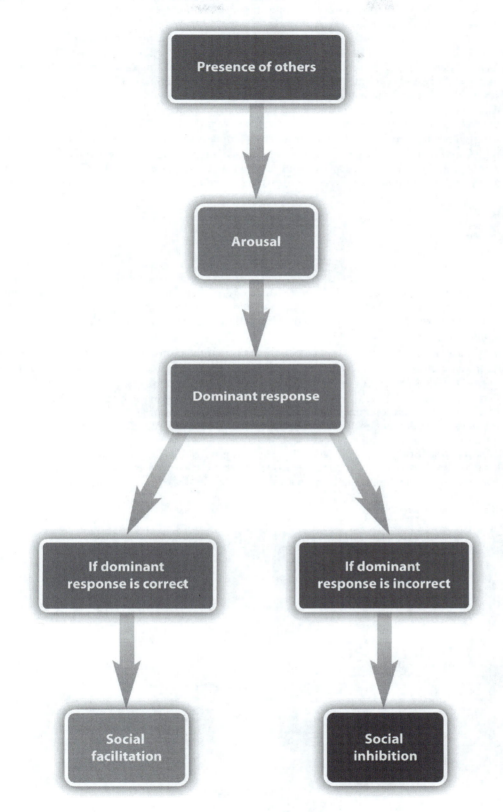

The most important aspect of Zajonc's theory was that the experience of arousal and the resulting increase in the occurrence of the dominant response could be used to predict whether the presence of
others would produce social facilitation or social inhibition. Zajonc argued that when the task to be
performed was relatively easy, or if the individual had learned to perform the task very well (a task such
as pedaling a bicycle), the dominant response was likely to be the correct response, and the increase in
arousal caused by the presence of others would create social facilitation. On the other hand, when the

task was difficult or not well learned (a task such as giving a speech in front of others), the dominant response is likely to be the incorrect one, and thus, because the increase in arousal increases the occurrence of the (incorrect) dominant response, performance is hindered.

A great deal of experimental research has now confirmed these predictions. A meta-analysis by Bond and Titus (1983),[116] which looked at the results of over 200 studies using over 20,000 research participants, found that the presence of others significantly increased the rate of performing on simple tasks, and also decreased both rate and quality of performance on complex tasks.

Although the arousal model proposed by Zajonc is perhaps the most elegant, other explanations have also been proposed to account for social facilitation and social inhibition. One modification argues that we are particularly influenced by others when we perceive that the others are evaluating us or competing with us (Baron, 1986).[117] In one study supporting this idea, Strube, Miles, and Finch (1981)[118] found that the presence of spectators increased joggers' speed only when the spectators were facing the joggers, so that the spectators could see the joggers and assess their performance. The presence of others did not influence joggers' performance when the joggers were facing in the other direction and thus could not see them.

3.2 Working Together in Groups

The ability of a group to perform well is determined by the characteristics of the group members (e.g., are they knowledgeable and skilled?) as well as by the *group process*—that is, the events that occur while the group is working on the task. When the outcome of group performance is better than we would expect given the individuals who form the group, we call the outcome a *group process gain,* and when the group outcome is worse than we would have expected given the individuals who form the group, we call the outcome a *group process loss.*

One group process loss that may occur in groups is that the group members may engage in **social loafing**, *a group process loss that occurs when people do not work as hard in a group as they do when they are working alone.* In one of the earliest social psychology experiments, Ringelmann (1913; reported in Kravitz & Martin, 1986)[119] had individual men, as well as groups of various numbers of men, pull as hard as they could on ropes while he measured the maximum amount that they were able to pull. As you can see in Figure 14.16, although larger groups pulled harder than any one individual, Ringelmann also found a substantial process loss. In fact, the loss was so large that groups of three men pulled at only 85% of their expected capability, whereas groups of eight pulled at only 37% of their expected capability. This type of process loss, in which group productivity decreases as the size of the group increases, has been found to occur on a wide variety of tasks.

> **social loafing**
>
> A group process loss that occurs when people do not work as hard in a group as they do when they are working alone.

FIGURE 14.16 Group Process Loss

Ringlemann found that although more men pulled harder on a rope than fewer men did, there was a substantial process loss in comparison to what would have been expected on the basis of their individual performances.

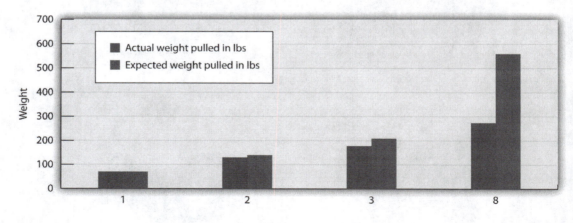

Group process losses can also occur when group members conform to each other rather than expressing their own divergent ideas. **Groupthink** is *a phenomenon that occurs when a group made up of members who may be very competent and thus quite capable of making excellent decisions nevertheless ends up, as a result of a flawed group process and strong conformity pressures, making a poor decision* (Baron, 2005; Janis, 2007).[120] Groupthink is more likely to occur in groups whose members feel a strong group identity, when there is a strong and directive leader, and when the group needs to make an important decision quickly. The problem is that groups suffering from groupthink become unwilling to seek out or discuss discrepant or unsettling information about the topic at hand, and the group members do not express contradictory opinions. Because the group members are afraid to express opinions that contradict those of the leader, or to bring in outsiders who have other information, the group is prevented from making a fully informed decision. Figure 14.17 summarizes the basic causes and outcomes of groupthink.

groupthink

An outcome that occurs when a group, as a result of a flawed group process and strong conformity pressures, makes a very poor decision.

FIGURE 14.17 Causes and Outcomes of Groupthink

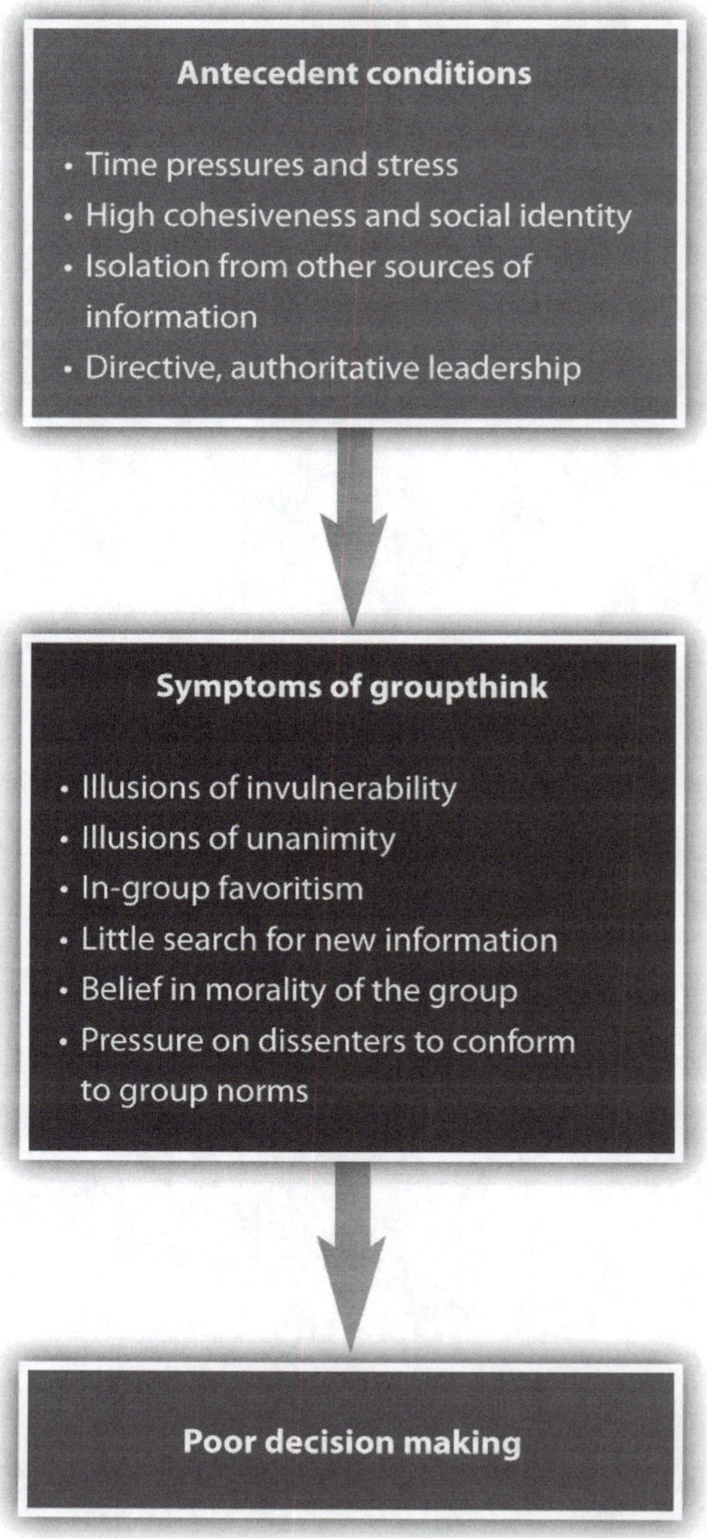

Antecedent conditions

- Time pressures and stress
- High cohesiveness and social identity
- Isolation from other sources of information
- Directive, authoritative leadership

Symptoms of groupthink

- Illusions of invulnerability
- Illusions of unanimity
- In-group favoritism
- Little search for new information
- Belief in morality of the group
- Pressure on dissenters to conform to group norms

Poor decision making

It has been suggested that groupthink was involved in a number of well-known and important, but very poor, decisions made by government and business groups, including the decision to invade Iraq made by President Bush and his advisors in 2002, the crashes of two Space Shuttle missions in 1986 and 2003, and the decision of President John Kennedy and his advisors to commit U.S. forces to help invade Cuba and overthrow Fidel Castro in 1962. Analyses of the decision-making processes in these cases have documented the role of conformity pressures.

As a result of the high levels of conformity in these groups, the group begins to see itself as extremely valuable and important, highly capable of making high-quality decisions, and invulnerable. The group members begin to feel that they are superior and do not need to seek outside information. Such a situation is conducive to terrible decision-making and resulting fiascoes.

Psychology in Everyday Life: Do Juries Make Good Decisions?

Although many other countries rely on judges to make judgments in civil and criminal trials, the jury is the foundation of the legal system in the United States. The notion of a "trial by one's peers" is based on the assumption that average individuals can make informed and fair decisions when they work together in groups. But given the potential for group process losses, are juries really the best way to approach these important decisions?

As a small working group, juries have the potential to produce either good or poor decisions, depending on the outcome of the characteristics of the individual members as well as the group process. In terms of individual group characteristics, people who have already served on juries are more likely to be seen as experts, are more likely to be chosen to be the jury foreman, and give more input during the deliberation. It has also been found that status matters; jury members with higher status occupations and education, males rather than females, and those who talk first are more likely be chosen as the foreman, and these individuals also contribute more to the jury discussion (Stasser, Kerr, & Bray, 1982).[121]

However, although at least some member characteristics have an influence on jury decision making, group process plays a more important role in the outcome of jury decisions than do member characteristics. Like any group, juries develop their own individual norms, and these norms can have a profound impact on how they reach their decision. Analysis of group process within juries shows that different juries take very different approaches to reaching a verdict. Some spend a lot of time in initial planning, whereas others immediately jump into the deliberation. Some juries base their discussion around a review and reorganization of the evidence, waiting to make a vote until it has all been considered, whereas other juries first determine which decision is preferred in the group by taking a poll and then (if the first vote does not lead to a final verdict) organize their discussion around these opinions. These two approaches are used quite equally but may in some cases lead to different decisions (Davis, Stasson, Ono, & Zimmerman, 1988).[122]

Perhaps most importantly, conformity pressures have a strong impact on jury decision making. As you can see in Figure 14.18, when there are a greater number of jury members who hold the majority position, it becomes more and more certain that their opinion will prevail during the discussion. This does not mean that minorities can never be persuasive, but it is very difficult for them to do so. The strong influence of the majority is probably due to both informational conformity (i.e., that there are more arguments supporting the favored position) and normative conformity (the people on the majority side have greater social influence).

Results From Stasser, Kerr, and Bray, 1982

This figure shows the decisions of 6-member mock juries that made "majority rules" decisions. When the majority of the 6 initially favored voting guilty, the jury almost always voted guilty; when the majority of the 6 initially favored voting innocent, the jury almost always voted innocent. The juries were frequently hung (could not make a decision) when the initial split was 3–3.

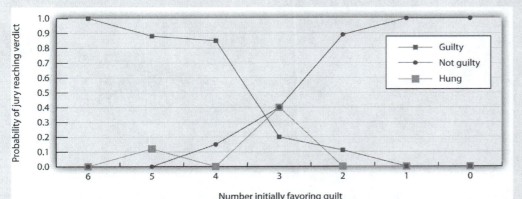

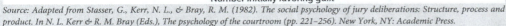
Source: Adapted from Stasser, G., Kerr, N. L., & Bray, R. M. (1982). The social psychology of jury deliberations: Structure, process and product. In N. L. Kerr & R. M. Bray (Eds.), The psychology of the courtroom (pp. 221–256). New York, NY: Academic Press.

Given the potential difficulties that groups face in making good decisions, you might be worried that the verdicts rendered by juries may not be particularly effective, accurate, or fair. However, despite these concerns, the evidence suggests that juries may not do as badly as we would expect. The deliberation process seems to cancel out many individual juror biases, and the importance of the decision leads the jury members to carefully consider the evidence itself.

3.3 Using Groups Effectively

Taken together, working in groups has both positive and negative outcomes. On the positive side, it makes sense to use groups to make decisions because people can create outcomes working together that any one individual could not hope to accomplish alone. In addition, once a group makes a decision, the group will normally find it easier to get other people to implement it, because many people feel that decisions made by groups are fairer than are those made by individuals.

illusion of group productivity

The tendency to overvalue the productivity of group in comparison to individual performance.

Yet groups frequently succumb to process losses, leading them to be less effective than they should be. Furthermore, group members often don't realize that the process losses are occurring around them. For instance, people who participate in brainstorming groups report that they have been more productive than those who work alone, even if the group has actually not done that well (Nijstad, Stroebe, Lodewijkx, 2006; Stroebe, Diehl, & Abakoumkin, 1992).[123] *The tendency for group members to overvalue the productivity of the groups they work in* is known as the **illusion of group productivity**, and it seems to occur for several reasons. For one, the productivity of the group as a whole is highly accessible, and this productivity generally seems quite good, at least in comparison to the contributions of single individuals. The group members hear many ideas expressed by themselves and the other group members, and this gives the impression that the group is doing very well, even if objectively it is not. And, on the affective side, group members receive a lot of positive social identity from their group memberships. These positive feelings naturally lead them to believe that the group is strong and performing well.

What we need to do, then, is to recognize both the strengths and limitations of group performance and use whatever techniques we can to increase process gains and reduce process losses. Table 14.5 presents some of the techniques that are known to help groups achieve their goals.

TABLE 14.5 Techniques That Can Be Used to Improve Group Performance

Technique	Example
Provide rewards for performance.	Rewarding employees and team members with bonuses will increase their effort toward the group goal. People will also work harder in groups when they feel that they are contributing to the group goal than when they feel that their contributions are not important.
Keep group member contributions identifiable.	Group members will work harder if they feel that their contributions to the group are known and potentially seen positively by the other group members than they will if their contributions are summed into the group total and thus unknown (Szymanski & Harkins, 1987).
Maintain distributive justice (equity).	Workers who feel that their rewards are proportional to their efforts in the group will be happier and work harder than will workers who feel that they are underpaid (Geurts, Buunk, & Schaufeli, 1994).
Keep groups small.	Larger groups are more likely to suffer from coordination problems and social loafing. The most effective working groups are of relatively small size—about four or five members.
Create positive group norms.	Group performance is increased when the group members care about the ability of the group to do a good job (e.g., a cohesive sports or military team). On the other hand, some groups develop norms that prohibit members from working to their full potential and thus encourage loafing.
Improve information sharing.	Leaders must work to be sure that each member of the group is encouraged to present the information that he or she has in group discussions. One approach to increasing full discussion of the issues is to have the group break up into smaller subgroups for discussion.
Allow plenty of time.	Groups take longer to reach consensus, and allowing plenty of time will help keep the group from coming to premature consensus and making an unwise choice. Time to consider the issues fully also allows the group to gain new knowledge by seeking information and analysis from outside experts.
Set specific and attainable goals.	Groups that set specific, difficult, yet attainable goals (e.g., "improve sales by 10% over the next 6 months") are more effective than groups that are given goals that are not very clear (e.g., "let's sell as much as we can!"; Locke & Latham, 2006).

Sources: Szymanski, K., & Harkins, S. G. (1987). Social loafing and self-evaluation with a social standard. Journal of Personality & Social Psychology, 53(5), 891–897; Geurts, S. A., Buunk, B. P., & Schaufeli, W. B. (1994). Social comparisons and absenteeism: A structural modeling approach. Journal of Applied Social Psychology, 24(21), 1871–1890; Locke, E. A., & Latham, G. P. (2006). New directions in goal-setting theory. Current Directions in Psychological Science, 15(5), 265–268.

KEY TAKEAWAYS

- The performance of working groups is almost never as good as we would expect, given the number of individuals in the group, and in some cases may even be inferior to the performance of one or more members of the group working alone.

- The tendency to perform tasks better or faster in the presence of others is known as social facilitation. The tendency to perform tasks more poorly or more slowly in the presence of others is known as social inhibition.

- The ability of a group to perform well is determined by the characteristics of the group members as well as by the events that occur in the group itself—the group process.

- One group process loss that may occur in groups is that the group members may engage in social loafing. Group process losses can also occur as a result of groupthink, when group members conform to each other rather than expressing their own divergent ideas.

- Taken together, working in groups has both positive and negative outcomes. It is important to recognize both the strengths and limitations of group performance and use whatever techniques we can to increase process gains and reduce process losses.

EXERCISE AND CRITICAL THINKING

1. Consider a time when you worked together with others in a group. Do you think the group experienced group process gains or group process losses? If the latter, what might you do now in a group to encourage effective group performance?

4.   CHAPTER SUMMARY

Social psychology is the scientific study of how we feel about, think about, and behave toward the other people around us, and how those people influence our thoughts, feelings, and behavior. A fundamental principle of social psychology is that although we may not always be aware of it, our cognitions, emotions, and behaviors are substantially influenced by the people with whom we are interacting.

Our initial judgments of others are based in large part on what we see. The physical features of other people—particularly their sex, race, age, and physical attractiveness—are very salient, and we often focus our attention on these dimensions. At least in some cases, people can draw accurate conclusions about others on the basis of physical appearance.

Youth, symmetry, and averageness have been found to be cross-culturally consistent determinants of perceived attractiveness, although different cultures may also have unique beliefs about what is attractive.

We frequently use people's appearances to form our judgments about them, and these judgments may lead to stereotyping, prejudice, and discrimination. We use our stereotypes and prejudices in part because they are easy and we may be evolutionarily disposed to stereotyping. We can change and learn to avoid using them through positive interaction with members of other groups, practice, and education.

Liking and loving in friendships and close relationships are determined by variables including similarity, disclosure, proximity, intimacy, interdependence, commitment, passion, and responsiveness.

Causal attribution is the process of trying to determine the causes of people's behavior. Attributions may be made to the person, to the situation, or to a combination of both. Although people are reasonably accurate in their attributions, they may make self-serving attributions and fall victim to the fundamental attribution error.

Attitudes refer to our relatively enduring evaluations of people and things. Attitudes are important because they frequently (but not always) predict behavior. Attitudes can be changed through persuasive communications. Attitudes predict behavior better for some people than for others, and in some situations more than others.

Our behaviors also influence our attitudes through the cognitive processes of self-perception and the more emotional process of cognitive dissonance.

The tendency to help others in need is in part a functional evolutionary adaptation. We help others to benefit ourselves and to benefit the others. Reciprocal altruism leads us to help others now with the expectation those others will return the favor should we need their help in the future. The outcome of the reinforcement and modeling of altruism is the development of social norms about helping, including the reciprocity norm and the social responsibility norm. Latané and Darley's model of helping proposes that the presence of others can reduce noticing, interpreting, and responding to emergencies.

Aggression may be physical or nonphysical. Aggression is activated in large part by the amygdala and regulated by the prefrontal cortex. Testosterone is associated with increased aggression in both males and females. Aggression is also caused by negative experiences and emotions, including frustration, pain, and heat. As predicted by principles of observational learning, research evidence makes it very clear that, on average, people who watch violent behavior become more aggressive.

The social norm that condones and even encourages responding to insults with aggression, known as the culture of honor, is stronger among men who live or were raised in the South and West than among men who are from or living in the North and East.

We conform not only because we believe that other people have accurate information and we want to have knowledge (informational conformity) but also because we want to be liked by others (normative conformity). The typical outcome of conformity is that our beliefs and behaviors become more similar to those of others around us. Studies demonstrating the power of conformity include those by Sherif and Asch, and Milgram's work on obedience.

Although majorities are most persuasive, numerical minorities that are consistent and confident in their opinions may in some cases be able to be persuasive.

The tendency to perform tasks better or faster in the presence of others is known as social facilitation, whereas the tendency to perform tasks more poorly or more slowly in the presence of others is known as social inhibition. Zajonc explained the influence of others on task performance using the concept of physiological arousal.

Working in groups involves both costs and benefits. When the outcome of group performance is better than we would expect given the individuals who form the group, we call the outcome a group process gain, and when the group outcome is worse that we would have expected given the individuals who form the group, we call the outcome a group process loss.

Process losses are observed in phenomena such as social loafing, groupthink. Process losses can be reduced by better motivation and coordination among the group members, by keeping contributions identifiable, and by providing difficult but attainable goals.

ENDNOTES

1. Sidman, J. (2006, June 26). A college student's death may help save lives. *USA Today.* Retrieved from http://www.usatoday.com/news/health/2006-06-26-spady-binge-drinking_x.htm

2. National Institute on Alcohol Abuse and Alcoholism. (2010). Statistical snapshot of college drinking. Retrieved from http://www.niaaa.nih.gov/AboutNIAAA/NIAAASponsoredPrograms/StatisticalSnapshotCollegeDrinking.htm

3. Sidman, J. (2006, June 26). A college student's death may help save lives. *USA Today.* Retrieved from http://www.usatoday.com/news/health/2006-06-26-spady-binge-drinking_x.htm

4. Schneider, D. J. (2004). *The psychology of stereotyping.* New York, NY: Guilford Press; Zebrowitz, L. A., & Montepare, J. (2006). The ecological approach to person perception: Evolutionary roots and contemporary offshoots. In M. Schaller, J. A. Simpson, & D. T. Kenrick (Eds.), *Evolution and social psychology* (pp. 81–113). Madison, CT: Psychosocial Press.

5. Walster, E., Aronson, V., Abrahams, D., & Rottmann, L. (1966). Importance of physical attractiveness in dating behavior. *Journal of Personality and Social Psychology, 4*(5), 508–516.

6. Langlois, J. H., Ritter, J. M., Roggman, L. A., & Vaughn, L. S. (1991). Facial diversity and infant preferences for attractive faces. *Developmental Psychology, 27*(1), 79–84.

7. Zebrowitz, L. A., Fellous, J.-M., Mignault, A., & Andreoletti, C. (2003). Trait impressions as overgeneralized responses to adaptively significant facial qualities: Evidence from connectionist modeling. *Personality and Social Psychology Review, 7*(3), 194–215.

8. Zebrowitz, L. A. (1996). Physical appearance as a basis of stereotyping. In C. N. Macrae, C. Stangor, & M. Hewstone (Eds.), *Stereotypes and stereotyping* (pp. 79–120). New York, NY: Guilford Press; Zebrowitz, L. A., Luevano, V. X., Bronstad, P. M., & Aharon, I. (2009). Neural activation to babyfaced men matches activation to babies. *Social Neuroscience, 4*(1), 1–10.

9. Rhodes, G., Zebrowitz, L. A., Clark, A., Kalick, S. M., Hightower, A., & McKay, R. (2001). Do facial averageness and symmetry signal health? *Evolution and Human Behavior, 22*(1), 31–46.

10. Langlois, J. H., & Roggman, L. A. (1990). Attractive faces are only average. *Psychological Science, 1*(2), 115–121.

11. Crandall, C. S., Merman, A., & Hebl, M. (2009). Anti-fat prejudice. In T. D. Nelson (Ed.), *Handbook of prejudice, stereotyping, and discrimination* (pp. 469–487). New York, NY: Psychology Press.

12. Sugiyama, L. S. (2005). Physical attractiveness in adaptationist perspective. In D. M. Buss (Ed.), *The handbook of evolutionary psychology* (pp. 292–343). Hoboken, NJ: John Wiley & Sons.

13. Langlois, J. H., Kalakanis, L., Rubenstein, A. J., Larson, A., Hallam, M., & Smoot, M. (2000). Maxims or myths of beauty? A meta-analytic and theoretical review. *Psychological Bulletin, 126*(3), 390–423.

14. Hosoda, M., Stone-Romero, E. F., & Coats, G. (2003). The effects of physical attractiveness on job-related outcomes: A meta-analysis of experimental studies. *Personnel Psychology, 56*(2), 431–462; Zebrowitz, L. A., & McDonald, S. M. (1991). The impact of litigants' baby-facedness and attractiveness on adjudications in small claims courts. *Law & Human Behavior, 15*(6), 603–623.

15. Schneider, D. J. (2004). *The psychology of stereotyping.* New York, NY: Guilford Press.

16. Langlois, J. H., Kalakanis, L., Rubenstein, A. J., Larson, A., Hallam, M., & Smoot, M. (2000). Maxims or myths of beauty? A meta-analytic and theoretical review. *Psychological Bulletin, 126*(3), 390–423.

17. Hall, J. A., & Schmid Mast, M. (2008). Are women always more interpersonally sensitive than men? Impact of goals and content domain. *Personality and Social Psychology Bulletin, 34*(1), 144–155.

18. Fiske, S. T. (1989). Examining the role of intent: Toward understanding its role in stereotyping and prejudice. In J. S. Uleman & J. A. Bargh (Eds.), *Unintended thought* (pp. 253–286). New York, NY: Guilford Press; Stangor, C. (1995). Content and application inaccuracy in social stereotyping. In Y. T. Lee, L. J. Jussim, & C. R. McCauley (Eds.), *Stereotype accuracy: Toward appreciating group differences* (pp. 275–292). Washington, DC: American Psychological Association.

19. Neuberg, S. L., Kenrick, D. T., & Schaller, M. (2010). Evolutionary social psychology. In S. T. Fiske, D. T. Gilbert, & G. Lindzey (Eds.), *Handbook of social psychology* (5th ed., Vol. 2, pp. 761–796). Hoboken, NJ: John Wiley & Sons.

20. Hogg, M. A. (2003). Social identity. In M. R. Leary & J. P. Tangney (Eds.), *Handbook of self and identity* (pp. 462–479). New York, NY: Guilford Press.

21. Swim, J. T., & Stangor, C. (1998). *Prejudice: The target's perspective.* Santa Barbara, CA: Academic Press.

22. Czopp, A. M., Monteith, M. J., & Mark, A. Y. (2006). Standing up for a change: Reducing bias through interpersonal confrontation. *Journal of Personality and Social Psychology, 90*(5), 784–803; Plant, E. A., & Devine, P. G. (1998). Internal and external motivation to respond without prejudice. *Journal of Personality and Social Psychology, 75*(3), 811–832.

23. Sidanius, J., & Pratto, F. (1999). *Social dominance: An intergroup theory of social hierarchy and oppression.* New York, NY: Cambridge University Press; Stangor, C., & Leary, S. (2006). Intergroup beliefs: Investigations from the social side. *Advances in Experimental Social Psychology, 38,* 243–283.

24. Hewstone, M. (1996). Contact and categorization: Social psychological interventions to change intergroup relations. In C. N. Macrae, C. Stangor, & M. Hewstone (Eds.), *Stereotypes and stereotyping* (pp. 323–368). New York, NY: Guilford Press.

25. Ambady, N., & Rosenthal, R. (1993). Half a minute: Predicting teacher evaluations from thin slices of nonverbal behavior and physical attractiveness. *Journal of Personality & Social Psychology, 64*(3), 431–441.

26. Willis, J., & Todorov, A. (2006). First impressions: Making up your mind after a 100-ms exposure to a face. *Psychological Science, 17*(7), 592–598.

27. Ambady, N., Krabbenhoft, M. A., & Hogan, D. (2006). The 30-sec sale: Using thin-slice judgments to evaluate sales effectiveness. *Journal of Consumer Psychology, 16*(1), 4–13.

28. Ambady, N., Hallahan, M., & Conner, B. (1999). Accuracy of judgments of sexual orientation from thin slices of behavior. *Journal of Personality and Social Psychology, 77*(3), 538–547.

29. Todorov, A., Mandisodza, A. N., Goren, A., & Hall, C. C. (2005). Inferences of competence from faces predict election outcomes. *Science, 308*(5728), 1623–1626.

30. Hendrick, C., & Hendrick, S. S. (Eds.). (2000). *Close relationships: A sourcebook.* Thousand Oaks, CA: Sage.

31. Davis, J. L., & Rusbult, C. E. (2001). Attitude alignment in close relationships. *Journal of Personality & Social Psychology, 81*(1), 65–84.

32. Reis, H. T., & Aron, A. (2008). Love: What is it, why does it matter, and how does it operate? *Perspectives on Psychological Science, 3*(1), 80–86.

33. Back, M. D., Schmukle, S. C., & Egloff, B. (2008). Becoming friends by chance. *Psychological Science, 19*(5), 439–440.

34. Moreland, R. L., & Beach, S. R. (1992). Exposure effects in the classroom: The development of affinity among students. *Journal of Experimental Social Psychology, 28*(3), 255–276.

35. Brooks-Gunn, J., & Lewis, M. (1981). Infant social perception: Responses to pictures of parents and strangers. *Developmental Psychology, 17*(5), 647–649.

36. Mita, T. H., Dermer, M., & Knight, J. (1977). Reversed facial images and the mere-exposure hypothesis. *Journal of Personality & Social Psychology, 35*(8), 597–601.

37. Freitas, A. L., Azizian, A., Travers, S., & Berry, S. A. (2005). The evaluative connotation of processing fluency: Inherently positive or moderated by motivational context? *Journal of Experimental Social Psychology, 41*(6), 636–644.

38. Harmon-Jones, E., & Allen, J. J. B. (2001). The role of affect in the mere exposure effect: Evidence from psychophysiological and individual differences approaches. *Personality & Social Psychology Bulletin, 27*(7), 889–898.

39. Zebrowitz, L. A., Bronstad, P. M., & Lee, H. K. (2007). The contribution of face familiarity to ingroup favoritism and stereotyping. *Social Cognition, 25*(2), 306–338.

40. Aron, A., Aron, E. N., & Smollan, D. (1992). Inclusion of other in the self scale and the structure of interpersonal closeness. *Journal of Personality & Social Psychology, 63*(4), 596–612.

41. Aron, A., Aron, E. N., Tudor, M., & Nelson, G. (1991). Close relationships as including other in the self. *Journal of Personality & Social Psychology, 60,* 241–253; Aron, A., Paris, M., & Aron, E. N. (1995). Falling in love: Prospective studies of self-concept change. *Journal of Personality & Social Psychology, 69*(6), 1102–1112.

42. Reis, H. T., & Aron, A. (2008). Love: What is it, why does it matter, and how does it operate? *Perspectives on Psychological Science, 3*(1), 80–86.

43. Berscheid, E., & Reis, H. T. (1998). Attraction and close relationships. In D. T. Gilbert, S. T. Fiske, & G. Lindzey (Eds.), *The handbook of social psychology* (4th ed., Vols. 1–2, pp. 193–281). New York, NY: McGraw-Hill.

44. Rusbult, C. E., Olsen, N., Davis, J. L., & Hannon, P. A. (2001). Commitment and relationship maintenance mechanisms. In J. Harvey & A. Wenzel (Eds.), *Close romantic relationships: Maintenance and enhancement* (pp. 87–113). Mahwah, NJ: Lawrence Erlbaum Associates.

45. Clark, M. S., & Mills, J. (2004). Interpersonal attraction in exchange and communal relationships. In H. T. Reis & C. E. Rusbult (Eds.), *Close relationships: Key readings* (pp. 245–256). Philadelphia, PA: Taylor & Francis.

46. Simpson, J. A., & Harris, B. A. (1994). Interpersonal attraction. In A. L. Weber & J. H. Harvey (Eds.), *Perspectives on close relationships* (pp. 45–66). Boston, MA: Allyn & Bacon.

47. Murray, S. L., Holmes, J. G., & Griffin, D. W. (1996). The benefits of positive illusions: Idealization and the construction of satisfaction in close relationships. *Journal of Personality & Social Psychology, 70*(1), 79–98.

48. Clark, M. S., & Lemay, E. P., Jr. (2010). Close relationships. In S. T. Fiske, D. T. Gilbert, & G. Lindzey (Eds.), *Handbook of social psychology* (5th ed., Vol. 2, pp. 898–940). Hoboken, NJ: John Wiley & Sons.

49. Jones, E. E., Kanouse, D. E., Kelley, H. H., Nisbett, R. E., Valins, S., & Weiner, B. (Eds.). (1987). *Attribution: Perceiving the causes of behavior.* Hillsdale, NJ: Lawrence Erlbaum Associates.

50. Jones, E. E., Davis, K. E., & Gergen, K. J. (1961). Role playing variations and their informational value for person perception. *Journal of Abnormal & Social Psychology, 63*(2), 302–310.

51. Fiske, S. T. (2003). *Social beings.* Hoboken, NJ: John Wiley & Sons.

52. Storms, M. D. (1973). Videotape and the attribution process: Reversing actors' and observers' points of view. *Journal of Personality and Social Psychology, 27*(2), 165–175.

53. Trope, Y., & Alfieri, T. (1997). Effortfulness and flexibility of dispositional judgment processes. *Journal of Personality and Social Psychology, 73*(4), 662–674.

54. Lerner, M. (1980). *The belief in a just world: A fundamental delusion.* New York, NY: Plenum; Tennen, H., & Affleck, G. (1990). Blaming others for threatening events. *Psychological Bulletin, 108*(2), 209–232.

55. Albarracín, D., Johnson, B. T., & Zanna, M. P. (Eds.). (2005). *The handbook of attitudes.* Mahwah, NJ: Lawrence Erlbaum Associates.

56. Olson, J. M., Vernon, P. A., Harris, J. A., & Jang, K. L. (2001). The heritability of attitudes: A study of twins. *Journal of Personality & Social Psychology, 80*(6), 845–860.

57. De Houwer, J., Thomas, S., & Baeyens, F. (2001). Association learning of likes and dislikes: A review of 25 years of research on human evaluative conditioning. *Psychological Bulletin, 127*(6), 853–869.

58. Cialdini, R. B. (2001). *Influence: Science and practice* (4th ed.). Boston, MA: Allyn & Bacon.

59. Gangestad, S. W., & Snyder, M. (2000). Self-monitoring: Appraisal and reappraisal. *Psychological Bulletin, 126*(4), 530–555.

60. Ajzen, I. (1991). The theory of planned behavior. *Organizational Behavior & Human Decision Processes, 50*(2), 179–211.

61. Bem, D. J. (1972). Self perception theory. In L. Berkowitz (Ed.), *Advances in Experimental Social Psychology* (Vol. 6). New York, NY: Academic Press; Olson, J. M., & Stone, J. (2005). The influence of behavior on attitudes. In D. Albarracín, B. T. Johnson, & M. P. Zanna (Eds.), *The handbook of attitudes* (pp. 223–271). Mahwah, NJ: Lawrence Erlbaum Associates.

62. Wells, G. L., & Petty, R. E. (1980). The effects of overt head movements on persuasion: Compatibility and incompatibility of responses. *Basic and Applied Social Psychology, 1*(3), 219–230.

63. Guéguen, N., & Jacob, C. (2002). Solicitation by e-mail and solicitor's status: A field study of social influence on the web. *CyberPsychology & Behavior, 5*(4), 377–383.

64. Festinger, L. (1957). *A theory of cognitive dissonance.* Evanston, IL: Row, Peterson; Harmon-Jones, E., & Mills, J. (1999). *Cognitive dissonance: Progress on a pivotal theory in social psychology.* Washington, DC: American Psychological Association.

65. Aronson, E., & Mills, J. (1959). The effect of severity of initiation on liking for a group. *Journal of Abnormal and Social Psychology, 59,* 171–181.

66. Dovidio, J. F., Piliavin, J. A., Schroeder, D. A., & Penner, L. (2006). *The social psychology of prosocial behavior.* Mahwah, NJ: Lawrence Erlbaum Associates.

67. Madsen, E. A., Tunney, R. J., Fieldman, G., Plotkin, H. C., Dunbar, R. I. M., Richardson, J.-M.,…McFarland, D. (2007). Kinship and altruism: A cross-cultural experimental study. *British Journal of Psychology, 98*(2), 339–359; McAndrew, F. T. (2002). New evolutionary perspectives on altruism: Multilevel-selection and costly-signaling theories. *Current Directions in Psychological Science, 11*(2), 79–82; Stewart-Williams, S. (2007). Altruism among kin vs. nonkin: Effects of cost of help and reciprocal exchange. *Evolution and Human Behavior, 28*(3), 193–198.

68. Burnstein, E., Crandall, C., & Kitayama, S. (1994). Some neo-Darwinian decision rules for altruism: Weighing cues for inclusive fitness as a function of the biological importance of the decision. *Journal of Personality and Social Psychology, 67*(5), 773–789.

69. Borgida, E., Conner, C., & Manteufel, L. (Eds.). (1992). *Understanding living kidney donation: A behavioral decision-making perspective.* Thousand Oaks, CA: Sage.

70. Tisak, M. S., & Tisak, J. (1996). My sibling's but not my friend's keeper: Reasoning about responses to aggressive acts. *Journal of Early Adolescence, 16*(3), 324–339.

71. Krebs, J. R., & Davies, N. B. (1987). *An introduction to behavioural ecology* (2nd ed.). Sunderland, MA: Sinauer Associates; Trivers, R. L. (1971). The evolution of reciprocal altruism. *Quarterly Review of Biology, 46,* 35–57.

72. Smith, S. W., Smith, S. L., Pieper, K. M., Yoo, J. H., Ferris, A. L., Downs, E.,…Bowden, B. (2006). Altruism on American television: Examining the amount of, and context surrounding, acts of helping and sharing. *Journal of Communication, 56*(4), 707–727.

73. Anderson, C. A., & Bushman, B. J. (2001). Effects of violent video games on aggressive behavior, aggressive cognition, aggressive affect, physiological arousal, and prosocial behavior: A meta-analytic review of the scientific literature. *Psychological Science, 12*(5), 353–359.

74. Darley, J. M., & Batson, C. D. (1973). "From Jerusalem to Jericho": A study of situational and dispositional variables in helping behavior. *Journal of Personality and Social Psychology, 27*(1), 100–108.

75. Hardy, C. L., & Van Vugt, M. (2006). Nice guys finish first: The competitive altruism hypothesis. *Personality and Social Psychology Bulletin, 32*(10), 1402–1413.

76. Latané, B., & Darley, J. M. (1968). Group inhibition of bystander intervention in emergencies. *Journal of Personality and Social Psychology, 10*(3), 215–221.

77. Latané, B., & Darley, J. M. (1968). Group inhibition of bystander intervention in emergencies. *Journal of Personality and Social Psychology, 10*(3), 215–221.

78. Markey, P. M. (2000). Bystander intervention in computer-mediated communication. *Computers in Human Behavior, 16*(2), 183–188.

79. Paquette, J. A., & Underwood, M. K. (1999). Gender differences in young adolescents' experiences of peer victimization: Social and physical aggression. *Merrill-Palmer Quarterly, 45*(2), 242–266.

80. Buss, D. M., & Duntley, J. D. (Eds.). (2006). *The Evolution of Aggression.* Madison, CT: Psychosocial Press.

81. Berkowitz, L. (1993). *Aggression: Its causes, consequences and control.* New York, NY: McGraw-Hill.

82. Davidson, R. J., Putnam, K. M., & Larson, C. L. (2000). Dysfunction in the neural circuitry of emotion regulation—A possible prelude to violence. *Science, 289*(5479), 591–594.

83. Dabbs, J. M. Jr., Hargrove, M. F., & Heusel, C. (1996). Testosterone differences among college fraternities: Well-behaved vs. rambunctious. *Personality and Individual Differences, 20*(2), 157–161.

84. Graham, K., Osgood, D. W., Wells, S., & Stockwell, T. (2006). To what extent is intoxication associated with aggression in bars? A multilevel analysis. *Journal of Studies on Alcohol, 67*(3), 382–390.

85. Bushman, B. J., & Cooper, H. M. (1990). Effects of alcohol on human aggression: An integrative research review. *Psychological Bulletin, 107*(3), 341–354; Steele, C. M., &

Southwick, L. (1985). Alcohol and social behavior: I. The psychology of drunken excess. *Journal of Personality and Social Psychology, 48*(1), 18–34.

86. Griffit, W., & Veitch, R. (1971). Hot and crowded: Influence of population density and temperature on interpersonal affective behavior. *Journal of Personality and Social Psychology, 17*(1), 92–98.

87. Bushman, B. J., Wang, M. C., & Anderson, C. A. (2005). Is the curve relating temperature to aggression linear or curvilinear? Assaults and temperature in Minneapolis reexamined. *Journal of Personality and Social Psychology, 89*(1), 62–66.

88. Berkowitz, L. (1993). Pain and aggression: Some findings and implications. *Motivation and Emotion, 17*(3), 277–293.

89. Bushman, B. J., Baumeister, R. F., & Stack, A. D. (1999). Catharsis, aggression, and persuasive influence: Self-fulfilling or self-defeating prophecies? *Journal of Personality and Social Psychology, 76*(3), 367–376.

90. Anderson, C. A., Berkowitz, L., Donnerstein, E., Huesmann, L. R., Johnson, J. D., Linz, D.,…Wartella, E. (2003). The influence of media violence on youth. *Psychological Science in the Public Interest, 4*(3), 81–110.

91. Bartholow, B. D., Bushman, B. J., & Sestir, M. A. (2006). Chronic violent video game exposure and desensitization to violence: Behavioral and event-related brain potential data. *Journal of Experimental Social Psychology, 42*(4), 532–539; Nabi, R. L., & Sullivan, J. L. (2001). Does television viewing relate to engagement in protective action against crime? A cultivation analysis from a theory of reasoned action perspective. *Communication Research, 28*(6), 802–825.

92. Downey, G., Irwin, L., Ramsay, M., & Ayduk, O. (Eds.). (2004). *Rejection sensitivity and girls' aggression.* New York, NY: Kluwer Academic/Plenum Publishers.

93. Baumeister, R. F., Smart, L., & Boden, J. M. (1996). Relation of threatened egotism to violence and aggression: The dark side of high self-esteem. *Psychological Review, 103*(1), 5–33.

94. Salmivalli, C., & Nieminen, E. (2002). Proactive and reactive aggression among school bullies, victims, and bully-victims. *Aggressive Behavior, 28*(1), 30–44.

95. Archer, J., & Coyne, S. M. (2005). An integrated review of indirect, relational, and social aggression. *Personality and Social Psychology Review, 9*(3), 212–230; Crick, N. R., & Nelson, D. A. (2002). Relational and physical victimization within friendships: Nobody told me there'd be friends like these. *Journal of Abnormal Child Psychology, 30*(6), 599–607.

96. Graham, K., & Wells, S. (2001). The two worlds of aggression for men and women. *Sex Roles, 45*(9–10), 595–622.

97. Bettencourt, B., & Miller, N. (1996). Gender differences in aggression as a function of provocation: A meta-analysis. *Psychological Bulletin, 119,* 422–447.

98. Cohen, D., Nisbett, R. E., Bosdle, B., & Schwarz, N. (1996). Insult, aggression, and the southern culture of honor: An "experimental ethnography." *Journal of Personality and Social Psychology, 70,* 945–960.

99. Cohen, D., & Nisbett, R. E. (1997). Field experiments examining the culture of honor: The role of institutions in perpetuating norms about violence. *Personality and Social Psychology Bulletin, 23*(11), 1188–1199.

100. Cialdini, R. B., Reno, R. R., & Kallgren, C. A. (1990). A focus theory of normative conduct: Recycling the concept of norms to reduce littering in public places. *Journal of Personality and Social Psychology, 58,* 1015–1026.

101. Cheng, C. M., & Chartrand, T. L. (2003). Self-monitoring without awareness: Using mimicry as a nonconscious affiliation strategy. *Journal of Personality and Social Psychology, 85*(6), 1170–1179.

102. Sherif, M. (1936). *The psychology of social norms.* New York, NY: Harper and Row.

103. Asch, S. (1955). Opinions and social pressure. *Scientific American, 11,* 32.

104. Milgram, S. (1974). *Obedience to authority: An experimental view.* New York, NY: Harper and Row.

105. Burger, J. M. (2009). Replicating Milgram: Would people still obey today? *American Psychologist, 64*(1), 1–11.

106. Bornstein, R. F. (1993). *The dependent personality.* New York, NY: Guilford Press.

107. Jetten, J., Spears, R., & Manstead, A. S. R. (1997). Strength of identification and intergroup differentiation: The influence of group norms. *European Journal of Social Psychology, 27*(5), 603–609.

108. Moscovici, S., Mugny, G., & Van Avermaet, E. (1985). *Perspectives on minority influence.* New York, NY: Cambridge University Press.

109. Martin, R., Hewstone, M., Martin, P. Y., & Gardikiotis, A. (2008). Persuasion from majority and minority groups. In W. D. Crano & R. Prislin (Eds.), *Attitudes and attitude change* (pp. 361–384). New York, NY: Psychology Press.

110. Nemeth, C., & Kwan, J. L. (1987). Minority influence, divergent thinking and the detection of correct solutions. *Journal of Applied Social Psychology, 17,* 788–799.

111. Miron, A. M., & Brehm, J. W. (2006). Reaktanz theorie—40 Jahre sparer. *Zeitschrift fur Sozialpsychologie, 37*(1), 9–18.

112. Pennebaker, J. W., & Sanders, D. Y. (1976). American graffiti: Effects of authority and reactance arousal. *Personality & Social Psychology Bulletin, 2*(3), 264–267.

113. Triplett, N. (1898). The dynamogenic factors in pacemaking and competition. *American Journal of Psychology, 9*(4), 507–533.

114. Bond, C. F., & Titus, L. J. (1983). Social facilitation: A meta-analysis of 241 studies. *Psychological Bulletin, 94*(2), 265–292.

115. Zajonc, R. B. (1965). Social facilitation. *Science, 149,* 269–274.

116. Bond, C. F., & Titus, L. J. (1983). Social facilitation: A meta-analysis of 241 studies. *Psychological Bulletin, 94*(2), 265–292.

117. Baron, R. (1986). Distraction/conflict theory: Progress and problems. In L. Berkowitz (Ed.), *Advances in experimental social psychology* (Vol. 19). New York, NY: Academic Press.

118. Strube, M. J., Miles, M. E., & Finch, W. H. (1981). The social facilitation of a simple task: Field tests of alternative explanations. *Personality & Social Psychology Bulletin, 7*(4), 701–707.

119. Kravitz, D. A., & Martin, B. (1986). Ringelmann rediscovered: The original article. *Journal of Personality and Social Psychology, 50,* 936–941.

120. Baron, R. S. (2005). So right it's wrong: Groupthink and the ubiquitous nature of polarized group decision making. In M. P. Zanna (Ed.), *Advances in experimental social psychology* (Vol. 37, pp. 219–253). San Diego, CA: Elsevier Academic Press; Janis, I. L. (2007). Groupthink. In R. P. Vecchio (Ed.), *Leadership: Understanding the dynamics of power and influence in organizations* (2nd ed., pp. 157–169). Notre Dame, IN: University of Notre Dame Press.

121. Stasser, G., Kerr, N. L., & Bray, R. M. (1982). The social psychology of jury deliberations: Structure, process and product. In N. L. Kerr & R. M. Bray (Eds.), *The psychology of the courtroom* (pp. 221–256). New York, NY: Academic Press.

122. Davis, J. H., Stasson, M. F., Ono, K., & Zimmerman, S. (1988). Effects of straw polls on group decision making: Sequential voting pattern, timing, and local majorities. *Journal of Personality & Social Psychology, 55*(6), 918–926.

123. Nijstad, B. A., Stroebe, W., & Lodewijkx, H. F. M. (2006). The illusion of group productivity: A reduction of failures explanation. *European Journal of Social Psychology, 36*(1), 31–48; Stroebe, W., Diehl, M., & Abakoumkin, G. (1992). The illusion of group effectivity. *Personality & Social Psychology Bulletin, 18*(5), 643–650.

Index

This book is fully searchable online at www.flatworldknowledge.com

This book is fully searchable online at www.flatworldknowledge.com